Huntington Library Publications

FREDERICK JACKSON TURNER ABOUT 1905

Frederick Jackson Turner's
Legacy

Unpublished Writings in American History

Edited with an Introduction

By Wilbur R. Jacobs

Mcmlxv

The Huntington Library

San Marino, California

Copyright 1965

Henry E. Huntington Library and Art Gallery

The publication of this volume has been assisted by the James Irvine Foundation Publication Fund of the Huntington Library.

LIBRARY OF CONGRESS CATALOG CARD NUMBER 65-15371

FOR BETSY AND CATHY

Preface

FREDERICK JACKSON TURNER, recognized as one of our greatest and most influential historians, was a pioneer whose brilliant and persuasive writings and teachings have helped American historians to create a new image of our past. Turner's interpretive essays, vivid syntheses of United States history growing out of a highly original use of interdisciplinary research, provide a panoramic view of American history which emphasizes, at the same time, the significance of detail.

For those who wish to observe the cast of Frederick Jackson Turner's mind, who wish to study that dexterous mind in action, this volume of selected essays, speeches, lectures, and memorandums from the Huntington Library collection of his papers should be of vital interest. The pieces published for the first time in this volume give us an expanded view of the seminal character of his research and writings and show how Turner's fascination with the present was linked with his study of the past. Incomplete though some of these essays are, they are valuable because of their inherent merit and because they illustrate the development of Turner's ideas.

In a period of over a decade of studying Turner and his writings I have taken on intellectual debts which are indeed difficult to pay or even acknowledge. For friendly counsel and advice I am deeply indebted to Ray A. Billington, Merle Curti, Frederick Merk, and Fulmer Mood. Edgar Eugene Robinson, Edward E. Dale, and the late Herbert Eugene Bolton have also assisted me, and Homer C. Hockett before his death suggested materials and interpretations concerning Turner which I should otherwise have overlooked.

A number of interested individuals, colleagues, and officials of libraries and document repositories have made special efforts to assist me with this book and a biographical study on Turner which is now in progress. I am particularly indebted to members of the staff of the Huntington Library, especially Norma B. Cuthbert, who catalogued and classified the large Turner collection. Herbert C. Schulz, Helen Mangold, Mary Isabel Fry, Edwin H. Carpenter, and John E. Pomfret have all put their expert knowledge of the library's rich collections and reference works at my disposal.

Officers and librarians at the Harvard College Library have likewise extended every courtesy to me. For assistance in using the Turner materials in the Houghton Library I wish to thank Carolyn E. Jakeman and William A. Jackson. For obtaining copies of Turner materials in the Woodrow Wilson collection at the Library of Congress I am indebted to David C. Mearns, and for help in using Turner's papers at the Wisconsin State Historical Society I am grateful to Josephine L. Harper. At Johns Hopkins University my former teachers, Charles A. Barker and the late Sidney Painter, were kind enough to make available the records of the Herbert Baxter Adams seminary. At the Bancroft Library in Berkeley, California, George P. Hammond permitted me to use Turner materials in the papers of Herbert Eugene Bolton. I also appreciate the aid given me by library staff members at Princeton University, the University of Illinois, the University of Minnesota, and the University of California, Santa Barbara.

The committees on research of the American Philosophical Society and the University of California, Santa Barbara, and the trustees of the Huntington Library, who provided a grant-in-aid, have all assisted in helping to defray the cost of an expensive undertaking.

An editor of a work of this kind feels grateful to those whose counsel contributes to the virtues of the book. This work owes many of its virtues to such counselors but none of its defects. I am greatly indebted to my wife, whose suggestions, though not apparent to the reader, are on numerous pages. I am especially grateful to Jean Bonheim and Mary Jane Bragg for editorial assistance. Alice Kladnick, Amelia B. Bliss, and Helen L. Nordhoff have typed portions of the book.

W. R. J.

Santa Barbara, California
March 3, 1964

Contents

Introduction   1

Editorial Note   43

I FRONTIERS AND SECTIONS   45
   Introduction to a Lecture on Sectionalism   47
   Draft on Sectionalism   48
   Lecture on Sectionalism   52
   Lecture on Political Maps   70
   Democratic and Whig-Republican Areas in
     Presidential Elections   73
   Class and Sectional Struggles   77

II THE COMPLEXITY OF HISTORY   79
   On Opening a New Course   80
   Opening Remarks at the Beginning of a Course
     on the History of the United States, 1880-1920   81
   Dr. Von Holst's History of the United States   85
   What Is Colonial History?   105

III GEORGE WASHINGTON AND THE NATION   109
   Convocation Address   111

Why Did Not the United States Become
   Another Europe?   116
Washington the Nationalist   141

IV AMERICAN SOCIAL HISTORY   151
   The Hunter Type   153
   Some Sociological Aspects of American History   155
   The Development of American Society   168
   Introduction to a College History of the
      United States   191

V EDUCATION AND DEMOCRACY   193
   The State University   194
   The Idea of Service in the University   196
   The University of the Future   197
   The High School and the City   200

   Index   209

Illustrations

Frederick Jackson Turner   frontispiece

First Page of Turner's Essay "Dr. Von Holst's
    History of the United States"   87

Turner and Charles Homer Haskins   108

Turner and His Wife   108

Turner "On the Trail" in 1904   157

Turner about 1924   185

"Turner 'On the Trail' in 1904" is reproduced by courtesy of Dr. and Mrs. James G. Edinger. The other illustrations are from the Turner Collection, Huntington Library.

Frederick Jackson Turner's
Legacy

❧ Introduction

THE MATERIALS in the Frederick Jackson Turner papers at the Henry E. Huntington Library are new to most American historians, for the collection was first opened to qualified scholars on January 2, 1960. The collection is referred to in the rapidly accumulating literature on Turner, but these references have been tantalizing glimpses of a larger treasure of original documents — documents indispensable to any full appraisal of Turner's life and work.

Study of these papers, however, does not basically change our view of Turner as a historical thinker, a great teacher, and a significant figure in the academic life of two major universities. He has been portrayed as a man who inspired investigation into almost every interpretive phase of American history, far beyond the frontier theory into the complexities of sectionalism and multiple hypothesis and into the varied interrelationships between history and the whole interlocking chain of the humanities, the social sciences, and the physical and biological sciences.[1] His teachings and writings have

[1] See essays on Turner by Joseph Schafer, Avery Craven, and Merle E. Curti reprinted in *Wisconsin Witness to Frederick Jackson Turner: A Collection of Essays on the Historian and the Thesis*, comp. O. Lawrence Burnette, Jr. (Madison, 1961), pp. 25-43, 100-116, 175-204; Fulmer Mood's essays "The Development of Frederick Jackson Turner as a Historical Thinker," *Publica-*

been seen as providing a powerful impetus to the study of social and economic history and as having been partly responsible for awakening interest in the whole field of intellectual history. His frontier hypothesis in particular provoked a lively controversy which exploded in essays and pamphlets.[2]

While Turner's personal papers do not change our basic ideas about him, they do reveal the interesting story of his formative period, the influence of his teachers and associates, and the kind of books and pamphlets he read. Through examination of this collection we can see more clearly why Turner wrote no more than he did. We can form better answers to such questions as what were his research and writing techniques and what were his points of emphasis in writing and teaching as they developed throughout his long career. We also learn more about his intimate associates, his relationships with his students, his family life, and his long battle to balance a pay check against the financial obligations of rearing a family and carrying on a program of research. His papers show his awareness of criticism as well as his desire that his work be better understood. Many of the documents disclose trends in his intellectual development through the Wisconsin, Harvard, and Huntington Library years.

---

tions of the Colonial Society of Massachusetts, Vol. XXXIV: Transactions 1937-1942 (1943), 283-352, and "Turner's Formative Period," in The Early Writings of Frederick Jackson Turner, comp. Everett E. Edwards (Madison, 1938), pp. 3-39; Carl L. Becker, "Frederick Jackson Turner," in his Everyman His Own Historian: Essays on History and Politics (New York, 1935), pp. 191-232; Edward Everett Dale, "Memories of Frederick Jackson Turner," Mississippi Valley Historical Review, XXX (1943-44), 339-358; Homer Carey Hockett, The Critical Method in Historical Research and Writing (New York, 1955), pp. 234-238; Edgar Eugene Robinson, "Frederick Jackson Turner," North Dakota Historical Quarterly, VI (1931-32), 259-261; "'Turner, As I Remember Him,' by Herbert Eugene Bolton," ed. Wilbur R. Jacobs, Mid-America, XXXVI (1954), 54-61.

[2] See Gene M. Gressley, "The Turner Thesis — a Problem in Historiography," Agricultural History, XXXII (1958), 227-249; Ray A. Billington, Norman J. Simler, and Gilman M. Ostrander, "Some Aspects of Turner's Thought," ibid., pp. 250-261. Historians now accept the frontier thesis as it was intended, as a

Briefly described, the Huntington collection falls into three broad categories. Probably the most important of these is sixty-seven boxes of indexed correspondence and other documents, detailing much of the story of Turner's life and work, and some twenty manuscript volumes, comprising such items as selected letters, scrapbooks, family diaries, and student notebooks.[3] The papers include both Turner's letters and replies from his correspondents. Many are carbons, photostats, or typescript copies of manuscripts owned by other libraries or by individuals. There are noticeable gaps, too, and some of these are filled by collections preserved at Harvard University, Johns Hopkins University, the Library of Congress, and several state universities.

The second category is the huge mass of Turner's research and teaching materials. These include, for instance, a lively series of lectures on the "History of Liberty" as well as typescript copies of lecture notes taken by students in Turner's classes. Of even more interest are dozens of manuscript lectures, speeches, and essays, most of them unpublished. Many of these are fragments which begin boldly in Turner's legible handwriting but unfortunately soon degenerate into a disappointing scrawl and finally into a scribbled outline. This material is lodged in thirty-four bulging file-cabinet drawers. Of cardinal importance in the study of Turner's writings are nineteen additional file drawers filled with thousands of

---

suggested hypothesis or interpretation, and have long since abandoned needless bickering. For recent appraisals of the frontier theory, see Billington, "The American Frontier Thesis," *Huntington Library Quarterly,* XXIII (1959-60), 201-216; N. D. Harper, "Frontier and Section: A Turner 'Myth'?" *Historical Studies, Australia and New Zealand,* V (1951-53), 135-153; Robert E. Riegel, "American Frontier Theory," *Cahiers d'Histoire Mondiale. Journal of World History. Cuadernos de Historia Mundial,* III (1956), 356-380; Jacobs, "Frederick Jackson Turner," *Encyclopaedia Britannica* (Chicago, 1961), XXII, 624-625; Ellen von Nardroff, "The American Frontier as a Safety Valve — The Life, Death, Reincarnation, and Justification of a Theory," *Agricultural History,* XXXVI (1962), 123-142.

[3] Correspondence is in Huntington Library, Turner Papers (hereafter referred to as HEH, TU), Boxes A, B, 1-52, TU-H Boxes 1-8, and several uncatalogued boxes. Items labeled "Manuscripts and Documents" are in TU Boxes 53-57. The manuscript notebooks are numbered Vols. I-XXII.

3 x 5 reference cards, chronologically arranged under topics on the growth and expansion of American civilization in the eighteenth and nineteenth centuries.

The third category includes items that Turner accumulated, such as nineteen boxes of clippings and offprints, a map collection (containing many maps made by Turner himself), and nine boxes of lantern slides for illustrating lectures. In this miscellaneous assortment are other items of value: for instance, a carton of excellent photographs of Turner and his family and a large box of student theses. More significant, perhaps, is a portion of Turner's personal library, comprising some 375 books and 300 pamphlets, many of them decorated with his marginalia. These are a part of the rare book collection of the Huntington Library.[4]

    ✵   ✵   ✵   ✵   ✵

One of Turner's manuscripts, the notes he made for a talk to students of the Harvard History Club, tells much about his family background and personal life, especially his youth.[5] "My family history," he said, "runs back to the beginnings of the Puritan migration to New England." Successive generations on both sides of his family had lived in Connecticut and western New York and, he recalled, had pioneered westward to Michigan and Wisconsin. "I am inclined to think," Turner said, "that the history of these regions and of these pioneer folk became a part of the influences that shaped my thinking toward a less sectional view and a more dominant American view . . . ."

Turner was born on November 14, 1861, in Portage, Wisconsin. He told the Harvard History Club students, "My birthplace was at the portage where Father Marquette crossed from the Fox to the Wisconsin on his journey down the Mississippi, and which was the highway of many another explorer, but I am forced to admit

[4] For further description see Billington and Jacobs, "The Frederick Jackson Turner Papers in the Huntington Library," *Arizona and the West*, II (1960), 73-77.

[5] "Draft of a lecture to the Harvard History Club, 1923 or 4," HEH, TU Box 56. Turner has identified his seventeenth-, eighteenth-, and nineteenth-century

4

that this made no impression upon my mind. I do not recall that it was ever mentioned in my school days study of American history — nor did I read any Parkman until late in my college course and not much of that masterpiece until after I myself began to lecture on Western history."

"But in those early years," Turner continued, "I was made conscious of Europe, for Europe was all about me." He then described the rural town of Portage, where he saw the mixing bowl and melting pot of the frontier, Irish raftsmen of the river, German merchants, Scotch farmers — Norwegian, Swiss, Welsh, and English settlements. "Europe," he said, "seemed familiar when I went abroad."

Turner's autobiographical notes and data compiled by Merrill H. Crissey, his secretary in later years, provide further information about his personal life.[6] The youthful Fred Turner, affectionately called "Fritz" by members of his family, attended schools at Portage, but most of his real education, he said, took place in his father's small newspaper office, where he worked as a typesetter. Here he learned about Wisconsin government and politics from his father, "editor & politician of N[ew] Y[ork] stock — A Republican, who had been brought up as a Dem[ocrat] & was named Andrew Jackson because he was born [in] 1832."

Andrew Jackson Turner, the historian's father, emerges from the early letters between himself and his son as a strong, articulate figure, guiding his son firmly but judiciously, extolling the virtues of hard work, self-sufficiency, and wise utilization of one's time. The father's letters, together with Turner's explanatory notes attached to some of the manuscripts (for Turner exhibited an unexpected lack of modesty in identifying many of his papers for a biographer), reveal a figure that the son admired and respected, a self-made man, a competent journalist and political leader of a

---

New England and New York ancestors in his copy of *The Turner Family Magazine,* I, No. 1 (New York, Jan. 1916), 1, 6, 12, 13. TU uncatalogued materials.

[6] "Autobiographical data: rough notes," ca. 1929, and Crissey, "Drafts of biographical data on Frederick J. Turner," 1932-44, HEH, TU Box 57.

frontier community. In one of his letters Turner affectionately recalled his father's "strong, gentle presence" and his reputation as
"one who helped his fellows, and stood for good things." "That," he
wrote, "is the kind of legacy that is best worth having."[7] These
traits also appear to have developed in Turner's personality, characterizing his life as a father, a teacher, and a writer.

After graduating from the University of Wisconsin in 1884,
Turner was for a brief period a correspondent on Chicago and
Milwaukee newspapers. In his autobiographical notes Turner re-
calls his unhappiness with reporting and his desire to study history,
which brought him back to the university to prepare for a career
in college teaching. After completing his M.A. degree Turner went
in 1888 to the Johns Hopkins University for his doctorate, and the
following year he married Caroline Mae Sherwood of Chicago. Two
boxes of "love letters," written during the period preceding their
marriage, are filled with the sentiments we might expect from a
young man looking forward to marriage, but they also describe his
Johns Hopkins experiences of 1888-89.[8] Some of these letters, fifteen
to twenty pages in length, include accounts of the Herbert Baxter
Adams seminary and skillfully written profiles of his teachers and
fellow students. The Turners had three children. Dorothy, or
"Peggy," became the joy of her father's life, but both parents were
greatly saddened by the loss of a daughter and a son who did not
survive childhood illnesses. After the death of his seven-year-old
son, Turner wrote his close friend and former student, Carl Becker,
"I have not done anything, and have not the heart for anything."[9]

Although he had been a tutor in rhetoric and oratory at his alma
mater before attending Johns Hopkins and had produced a doctoral

[7] Turner to Max Farrand, Nov. 16, 1908, HEH, TU Box 10. The obituary on
A. J. Turner in *The Portage Democrat*, June 12, 1905, describes him as "a
force in politics," "a great lover of the game of politics," and "no amateur at
the profession." TU uncatalogued materials.

[8] HEH, TU Boxes A and B.

[9] Nov. 17, 1899, HEH, TU Box 2. Jackson Allen, Turner's son, was born in
1892 and died in 1899. Mae Sherwood was born in 1894 and also died in 1899.
Dorothy Kinsley (later Mrs. John S. Main) was born in 1890. Crissey, "Drafts
of biographical data," TU Box 57.

dissertation, *The Character and Influence of the Indian Trade in Wisconsin*[10] (showing the trading post to be a frontier institution that had evolved from ancient times), Turner's academic career really began in 1889 with his appointment as assistant professor of history at the University of Wisconsin. Blond and handsome, with a pleasing voice and a quiet sense of humor, Turner was a skilled teacher and likable colleague who moved easily up the academic ladder. He taught with distinction at Madison for twenty-one fruitful years, and it was during this period, in 1893, that he delivered before members of the American Historical Association his paper entitled "The Significance of the Frontier in American History," in which the frontier hypothesis was clearly set forth. *Rise of the New West, 1819-1829* (New York) appeared in 1906 in the American Nation series. In 1910, the same year as his election to the presidency of the American Historical Association, he moved to Harvard University. His first book of essays, *The Frontier in American History*, was published in 1920, which resulted in a wider audience for his theories and began a decade of controversy among American historians about his work. Following retirement in 1924 and temporary residence in Madison, Wisconsin, Turner became a research associate at the Huntington Library in 1927, spending his twilight years in research and writing. Twelve more essays appeared in his *The Significance of Sections in American History* (New York, 1932), which was awarded a Pulitzer prize. Turner died on March 14, 1932.[11] His last book, *The United States, 1830-1850: The Nation and Its Sections* (New York, 1935), as well as *The Significance of Sections*, appeared posthumously.

✴   ✴   ✴   ✴   ✴

The most valuable material relating to Turner's formative years

[10] Published in Baltimore in 1891 as Johns Hopkins University Studies in Historical and Political Science, Ninth Series, Nos. 11-12.

[11] From heart failure, according to Farrand in a telegram to Abbott Lawrence Lowell, March 14, 1932, HEH, TU Box 47. "Cards in Professor Turner's desk at the Huntington Library at the time of his death — with explanatory notes by Fulmer Mood," March 14, 1932, TU Box 47, mention that one of the last

is probably found in his classroom notebooks,[12] his commonplace books,[13] his syllabuses,[14] and his correspondence with William F. Allen and Herbert B. Adams, the two teachers who had much to do with shaping his intellectual development.[15] The three cardboard-covered commonplace books, largely composed of reading references, quotations, and drafts of college orations, record books he read in successive years. We know from these lists that he was an eager reader. In 1880, a youth of nineteen, he read some thirty-three volumes, concentrating on novels by Dickens, Swift, and Cooper and the works of Milton, Macaulay, and Irving. His lists for the next three years include writings of Carlyle, Horace "in original Latin," Tacitus, Emerson, Parkman, Shelley, Dante, Herbert Spencer, Darwin, and Lucretius.[16]

In these early notebooks Turner shows himself to have been interested in the literature of protest against conformity and authority. Much of the background reading for Turner's college orations focuses on man's place in the universe, his struggle for freedom in a world governed by Darwinian concepts of natural law.

As early as 1878, in his high school graduation oration on "The Power of the Press," Turner concluded that "the Press joined the Past and the Present and made them one."[17] The idea of linking the past with the present becomes a theme in many of Turner's later writings. One of his college orations for which he made notes dealt with " 'Imaginativeness of Present' or its general worth as contrasted

books he used was Walter Prescott Webb's *The Great Plains,* published in Boston in the summer of 1931.

[12] Covering undergraduate and graduate years at the University of Wisconsin, 1883-88, HEH, TU Vols. XIII-XVIII.

[13] Three manuscript notebooks covering the years 1880-87, HEH, TU Vol. III.

[14] Used for classroom teaching of English history, the colonization of North America, and the history of the West, ca. 1893-1909, HEH, TU Vol. VI.

[15] HEH, TU Boxes 1 and 2.

[16] Commonplace Book No. 1, labeled "F. J. Turner — 1881," HEH, TU Vol. III.

[17] Turner's newspaper scrapbook inscribed "F.J.T. Scrap Book F. J. Turner, 1876," HEH, TU uncatalogued materials.

with past."[18] In casting about for ideas for this oration Turner delved into Lucretius, *De rerum natura*, the fifth book of which contains a theory of incipient evolutionism, a genetic concept of sociological growth. Lucretius here develops the idea that men were naturally stimulated by environmental experiences to advance from primordial existence. Such natural environmental contacts, according to Lucretius, encouraged the first glimmerings of civilization and spurred the development of governmental forms. This theory of historical causation is not unrelated to themes of social evolution expressed in Turner's frontier theory.

Other authors, too, contributed to his growth as a historian. Turner was not as self-pollenizing as he has often been portrayed. In thumbing through Franklin's writings, Turner was struck by a quotation about the new conditions existing in America: "The boundless woods . . . are sure to afford freedom and subsistence to any man who can bait a hook or pull a trigger."[19] There is little doubt that the gentle mysticism of Emerson's essays also inspired him, for he read them all, and drafts of his orations are highlighted by phrases about human dignity, self-reliance, and "life in harmony with nature." Turner was struck with Emerson's dictum that nations evolve from "brute youth" to a stage when mankind's perceptive powers reach their ripeness, "the moment of adult health."[20]

Herbert Spencer and Charles Darwin gave him further incentive to study the changing forces of history. "New poets," he wrote in the second commonplace book, "will read a lesson from Spencer & Darwin & sing Man and Nature." "Evolution & its accompanying features," he declared, "is now in the intellect, when it reaches the hearts of men, then may we not look for a new age, a renaissance in thought."

Turner's orations consistently return to the theme that reason and imagination are needed to understand the evolution of civilization. It was time, he believed, to make a reappraisal of history in the

---

[18] Commonplace Book No. 2, HEH, TU Vol. III.

[19] Commonplace Book No. 3, HEH, TU Vol. III. The editor has not located this quotation, although the theme is present in Franklin's writings.

[20] Commonplace Book No. 2, HEH, TU Vol. III.

light of present conditions. More insight was needed to tell the story of what he called "the common people; the lowly toilers of the soil." "By far the greatest problem bequeathed to this age," he wrote, "is the social problem. In the past the lower classes have been so completely in ignorance as well as oppression that their condition did not fully make itself known to them — but now as men grow in knowledge . . . the question reaches critical importance. Even among the common people rests the arbitration of questions. They are becoming discontented."[21]

Turner discovered more coloration for his theme in reading and rereading Shelley's *Prometheus Unbound* and *Queen Mab*. Shelley's eloquent, passionate lines exposing cruelty and oppression in history moved Turner to write about the hope of "the ultimate renovation of man & of the world" and "the beginning of a modern life."[22] As Shelley's plea for freedom for the oppressed stimulated the thought of Turner, so did the evolutionism of Lucretius, Emerson, Spencer, and Darwin shape his view of historical causation and the true meaning of history.

Still another influence in his early years was the liberalism of Unitarianism. His commonplace books abound with phrases like "broader ideas of religion," "half worn religion," "the anthropomorphic God," and the "democratic, ethical, spirit of Christ."[23] Turner's emphasis on self-reliance and on individualism in his later writings may be indirectly traceable to Emersonian Unitarianism. Certainly he seems to have accepted the Unitarian tenet that one should not be subservient to the tyranny of outmoded doctrines.

Turner's debt to his teacher William F. Allen, one of the leading Unitarians of Madison, has been stressed by Fulmer Mood[24] and by Turner himself in autobiographical letters.[25] Allen appears to have

[21] Ibid.

[22] Ibid.

[23] Ibid.

[24] "Turner's Formative Period," in *The Early Writings of Frederick Jackson Turner*, pp. 9-12.

[25] The following letters, which are Turner's most important autobiographical ones, refer to his debt to Allen: Turner to Constance L. Skinner, March 15,

been one of the few men occupying chairs of history near the turn of the century who deserved the name of Renaissance scholar. His letters to Turner reveal catholic tastes in literature, for he was able to advise his protégé in almost any field of scholarship. In a letter of 1888, for example, Allen sweeps over disciplines and chronology, authoritatively suggesting books for his pupil on such varied topics as the medieval church, Asiatic studies, and primitive beliefs. It is also significant that Allen, who had studied at Berlin and Göttingen and had lectured at Johns Hopkins where Leopold von Ranke's influence was well known, emphasized what he called "scientific inquiry" in historical study. He wrote to Turner about "applying laws" and keeping research within the bounds of "scientific channels."[26]

Turner was first exposed to German "scientific" techniques of research and writing by Allen. One has the impression from reading Turner's papers that he was practically a *Herr Doktor*, saturated with *Kulturgeschichte* and German methodology, before he ever left Wisconsin for additional graduate study. Several times in his letters Turner mentions that Allen's institutional approach to medieval history encouraged him to examine the formation of American institutions. It was Allen who led him to "approach American history in the spirit of Mediaeval historians who had to deal with institutions in the formative period."[27] There is evidence

---

1922, HEH, TU Box 31; to Becker, Dec. 16, 1925, TU Box 34; to Curti, Aug. 8, 1928, TU Box 38; and "Copy" and "Rough draft" to William E. Dodd, Oct. 7, 1919, TU Box 29. Elsewhere Turner wrote: "From Allen I learned what historical scholarship meant, and I never found a master who held higher or better standards of historic truth, and devotion to the original sources, critically studied and interpreted." "Tribute to William Francis Allen, [1924]," TU Box 56.

[26] Oct. 30, 1888, HEH, TU Box 1. Allen's study of history at the universities of Berlin and Göttingen is briefly described in his *Essays and Monographs,* ed. David B. Frankenburger et al. (Boston, 1890), pp. 8-10. The fruit of this experience was made available to Turner, as his notes from Allen's classroom lectures reveal. TU Vol. XIII.

[27] Turner to Curti, Aug. 8, 1928, HEH, TU Box 38. This twenty-three-page letter provides background material for Curti's "The Section and the Frontier in American History: The Methodological Concepts of Frederick Jackson

that Turner's doctoral dissertation on the fur-trading post as an institution was virtually completed under Allen when Turner was only nineteen years of age, before he ever saw Johns Hopkins and the famed Herbert Baxter Adams seminary. His Wisconsin training appears to have given him sufficient familiarity with the history and institutions of other countries that he was able to recognize what was distinctly American. He had had scarcely one year of college work in American history but found this gap in his formal education no handicap in his own research.[28]

Allen's teachings had another effect on Turner which indirectly modified the young man's whole approach to the study of history. Allen taught by means of syllabuses with suggested study topics for pupils. Like many a junior faculty member, Turner emulated the example set by a senior professor. Even as an undergraduate Turner followed a scheme of study based on Allen's idea of picking out topics for special examination.

In a student notebook on American history he selected American colonization as one of his topics. He suggested that society should be analyzed as an organism and that the topic be studied "vertically" for its "inheritance"; "horizontally" for "interaction of conditions"; "physically" for its "environment"; and "sympathetically" for what he called its "peculiar conditions." This he labeled his "laboratory method." For each topic, the objective was to "know all about it." The "essential facts" had to be mastered.[29]

At first glance this unique method of study appears fresh and stimulating, but it resulted, for Turner, in the accumulation of

---

Turner," in Stuart A. Rice, ed. *Methods in Social Science: A Case Book* (Chicago, 1931), pp. 353-367.

[28] Turner to Becker, Dec. 16, 1925, HEH, TU Box 34. Turner wrote: "I had only on[e] term (1/3 yr), two three times a week, in American History at Wis--- and practically none at J H U." Becker used much of the material in this letter for his essay on Turner first printed in Howard W. Odum, ed. *American Masters of Social Science* (New York, 1927), pp. 273-318. "Not that there is any such thing as a Science of history, but that is no matter," Becker wrote to Turner as the book was being published. Feb. 11, 1926, TU Box 35.

[29] "American History, 1492-1763," HEH, TU Vol. XIV (1).

12

dreary compilations of chronological data. Indeed, some of his history notebooks are not unlike miniature versions of *Haydn's Dictionary of Dates,* a work frequently consulted by the youthful Turner.

This technique of amassing factual information was used by Turner as early as the 1880's, when he began his lifetime project of compiling the whole history of the United States on 3 x 5 cards, all chronologically arranged under topics. In the middle period of his life Turner decided that part of his references might be recorded on half sheets of paper, and finally during the Harvard era he turned to the use of full-size typewriter sheets. Despite the transition to different sizes of paper, Turner never abandoned his small cards, a vast storehouse of factual data which he used as a basis for all his historical writings, including his 1893 essay on the frontier (although the original copy of the famous essay is not among his papers). It is perhaps a weakness of Turner's work that, using these cards, he commented on American society as a whole, basing his arguments mainly on eighteenth- and nineteenth-century data pertaining to the territory east of the Mississippi.

The older cards, first filed in the 1880's and 1890's, are easily identified, yellow with age and dog-eared, with notations in lavender ink.[30] Turner's card files show it was no small undertaking for him to penetrate critically the historical core of an era, to weigh the issues, and to arrive at the truth by discarding the inessentials. The thousands of cards with their "subject tabs" were more than what Merrill Crissey (Turner's secretary) called a "skeleton of events." They were Turner's "raw material." Crissey wrote that Turner dictated from these cards. Chapters of the book *The United States, 1830-1850* were composed in this fashion, the early drafts typed in triple space to allow room for deletions, stylistic refinements, and interpolations.[31] The fact that critics have noticed little stylistic elegance or wit in his later works may well be traced to Turner's dependence on dictating from cards, for Turner's im-

[30] HEH, TU 3 x 5 Drawers 1 and 2.

[31] "Memorandum on Professor Turner's writing of his book *United States, 1830-1850: The Nation and Its Sections,*" July 5, 1932, HEH, TU Box 49.

promptu handwritten letters sparkle with metaphor and contain jewels of wit and humor.

Turner's chronological approach to historical study is also revealed in his lecture notes and in notes taken by students in his classes.[32] His deliberate, fact-by-fact, chronological narrative of westward expansion in his lectures was seldom relieved by interpretive judgments except at the beginning and at the end of his course. Even his most admiring students were not reluctant to comment on the dullness of his lectures. His graduate students, as Turner pointed out in his letters, were also led to approach history chronologically, examining in their papers successive periods of American history.

Turner acknowledged that papers by his advanced students exposed new problems of interpretation and were useful to him by strengthening his knowledge. Indeed, these students helped to supply Turner with the facts that he required for his interpretive essays on American social development. Turner appears to have had a gift for absorbing the best his environment offered. At the same time he was lavish with his own talents. He once complained, in mature years, that a professor is like a small mountain spring, limited in vitality. "Graduates," he said, "are expert *drinkers* and they are not satisfied with anything less than *fresh* water."[33]

Turner learned much, then, from his teachers, from his students, and from the books of great writers of the past. He also read almost every noteworthy historical book of his day and sifted the leading writers of his generation to take from them what he could. His familiarity with the works of Francis Parkman, Richard Hildreth, John A. Doyle, Alexander Johnston, George Bancroft, Justin Winsor, James Schouler, Henry Adams, Hermann von Holst, and Hubert

[32] A number of Turner's lecture notes are in HEH, TU File Drawers 1-22, especially Drawers 1, 2, 10, and 22. There are sets of student notes, by George W. Bell (1910) and by T. C. Smith (1911), for his "History of the West" course in Drawer 14. The editor has also examined sets of notes taken for the same course by Thomas P. Martin, Everett E. Edwards, and Horace J. Smith; the best single set is that of Homer C. Hockett when he was acting as an assistant to Turner in 1902. See also Jacobs, "Frederick Jackson Turner — Master Teacher," *Pacific Historical Review*, XXIII (1954), 49-58.

[33] Turner to Curti, Oct. 12, 1921, HEH, TU Box 31.

H. Bancroft indicates the thoroughness of his reading.[34] These secondary works, like the papers of his students, appear to have led Turner to new interpretations. Von Holst's *The Constitutional and Political History of the United States*, for example, occupied his attention for several years, as he plowed through volume after volume, ornamenting pages with his marginalia.[35] This experience finally provoked him in the 1890's to sit down and scrawl out a forty-six-page critique of Von Holst's volumes.[36]

Another work which influenced the young Turner and which left its mark on his frontier theory was Achille Loria's *Analisi della proprieta capitalista.*[37] The notes which Turner made on Loria refer frequently to the importance of "free land" in American history. "Too great stress has been laid on the democratic character of the immigrants to America," he wrote. "Free land is the explanation at bottom."[38]

Henry George, as well as Loria, provided basic ideas for Turner's frontier hypothesis. Upon discovering in Loria's *Analisi*[39] a quotation from *Progress and Poverty* translated into Italian, Turner jotted down the reminder: "Be sure to get this quotation from George."[40] The passage as written by George is as follows:

[34] Turner's history notebooks, HEH, TU Vols. XIII-XVIII; TU 3 x 5 Drawers 1 and 2.

[35] Turner's personal copy, tr. John J. Lalor et al. (Chicago, 1877-85), Vols. [I-V], is HEH Rare Book 212060. The full set included eight volumes, the final one published in 1892.

[36] "Essay on History of U.S. by Von Holst, 189-," HEH, TU File Drawer 15.

[37] 2 vols. (Torino, 1889). Turner's copy is HEH Rare Book 114780.

[38] "Turner: Notes on A. Loria," HEH, TU File Drawer 15. Further evidence of Loria's influence on Turner is found in Loria cards, TU 3 x 5 Drawer 1, and Lee Benson's excellent essay "Achille Loria's Influence on American Economic Thought, Including His Contributions to the Frontier Hypothesis," in his *Turner and Beard: American Historical Writing Reconsidered* (Glencoe, Ill., 1960), pp. 1-40.

[39] Vol. II, p. 45.

[40] "Turner: Notes on A. Loria," HEH, TU File Drawer 15.

This public domain has been the transmuting force which has turned the thriftless, unambitious European peasant into the self-reliant Western farmer; it has given a consciousness of freedom even to the dweller in crowded cities, and has been a well-spring of hope even to those who have never thought of taking refuge upon it. The child of the people, as he grows to manhood in Europe, finds all the best seats at the banquet of life marked "taken," and must struggle with his fellows for the crumbs that fall, without one chance in a thousand of forcing or sneaking his way to a seat. In America, whatever his condition, there has always been the consciousness that the public domain lay behind him; and the knowledge of this fact, acting and reacting, has penetrated our whole national life, giving to it generosity and independence, elasticity and ambition. All that we are proud of in the American character; all that makes our conditions and institutions better than those of older countries, we may trace to the fact that land has been cheap in the United States, because new soil has been open to the emigrant.[41]

Although Turner's indebtedness to Henry George has not previously been documented, historians have commented on the fact that both had much of the same thesis and some of the same words.[42] Turner was acquainted with Henry George's *Progress and Poverty* as early as 1887,[43] and he later owned an edition of 1883; nevertheless it was undoubtedly Loria's *Analisi* that suggested to Turner the most appropriate passages in *Progress and Poverty* for his theme of frontier expansion in American history.

One of Turner's early unpublished essays, "The Hunter Type," suggests that still another work, Theodore Roosevelt's *The Winning of the West*, may well have contributed to the frontier theory with the idea that the American character could be observed by a study of the westward movement.[44]

[41] (New York, 1880), pp. 350-351.

[42] See, for instance, Eric F. Goldman, *Rendezvous with Destiny* (New York, 1952), p. 71n; Charles Albro Barker, *Henry George* (New York, 1955), p. 300.

[43] Turner to Caroline Mae Sherwood, May 11, 1887, HEH, TU Box A.

[44] See notes in this volume accompanying Turner's essay "The Hunter Type," pp. 151-152.

Turner was a man who worked best when stimulated by contact with the ideas of others. At Johns Hopkins he absorbed Herbert Baxter Adams' theories and methods, including the "germ theory" according to which American institutions were products of European "germs"[45] — a theory that he never completely abandoned. Adams was so impressed with his pupil's essay on "Problems in American History"[46] that he took it upon himself to schedule Turner for another "such paper" at the American Historical Association's meeting in Chicago in 1893.[47]

Adams did another service for his pupil by offering him a challenge. "When Herbert Adams once told us," Turner recalled in a letter, " . . . that his seminary having dealt with American local institutions had exhausted the opportunities for new contributions in the field of U.S. history and would turn to European history for its next work, it was a challenge to me to work out my own ideas."[48] The ideas that Turner was planning to work out were not entirely his own, for at Johns Hopkins he was drawn into close and stimulating association with several other instructors. Albion W. Small, later to become one of America's leading sociologists, was a critic of American historians who narrated political events and neglected social forces. Small, Turner's teacher and a personal friend, also emphasized essential interrelationships in the whole area of the social sciences. Turner's classroom notes and correspondence indicate the extent to which Small's views affected the development of Turner's own ideas.[49]

[45] See Adams, *The Germanic Origin of New England Towns,* Johns Hopkins University Studies in Historical and Political Science, [First Series], No. 2 (Baltimore, 1882), pp. 5, 10-38; Ostrander, "Turner and the Germ Theory," in "Some Aspects of Turner's Thought," *Agricultural History,* XXXII (1958), 258-261.

[46] *Aegis* (University of Wisconsin), VII, No. 4 (Nov. 4, 1892), 48-52.

[47] Adams to Turner, Nov. 28, 1892, HEH, TU Box 1.

[48] "Rough draft" of letter, Turner to William E. Dodd, Oct. 7, 1919, HEH, TU Box 29. (A typewritten "Copy," which differs from the "Rough draft" and is probably the version sent to Dodd, is in the same folder.)

[49] "Small's method is to ask in details & then draw conclusion. He does not state a proposition & then find illustration." "Turner's Notes on A. W. Small,

Woodrow Wilson was another teacher and close friend. On the death of Turner's son Wilson wrote him, "I assure you, my dear fellow, that my feeling for you is not of the ordinary kind: separation does not seem in the least to lessen or weaken the sense of comradeship and the genuine affection you have excited in me since I first learned to know you. It is, as you know, one of the abiding disappointments of my life that we cannot be colleagues; and, now that you are in trouble, I feel more keenly than ever the pain of not being able to take you every day by the hand and help you with sympathy at least, if with nothing more."[50] Wilson had attempted in 1896 to create a chair for Turner in American history at Princeton.[51] In Turner's year at Johns Hopkins, Wilson provided keen intellectual stimulus for his friend and pupil. The two young men debated on the significance of the West and the South in American history, on politics, and on books. Turner said that out of this give-and-take he discovered "the larger meaning of sectionalism as a movement between New England, Middle, Western and Southern sections, rather than between North and South."[52]

It was Wilson who put Turner on the track of Walter Bagehot's provocative *Physics and Politics,* a well-used copy of which is still among Turner's books in the Huntington Library.[53] In this unusual

J.H.U., Lectures, 1889 – Spring," HEH, TU File Drawer 15. The Small-Turner correspondence is found in TU Boxes 1, 3, 5, 6, and 26.

[50] April 4, 1900, HEH, TU Box 3.

[51] Jacobs, "Wilson's First Battle at Princeton: The Chair for Turner," *Harvard Library Bulletin,* VIII (1954), 74-87.

[52] "Copy" of letter, Turner to Dodd, Oct. 7, 1919, HEH, TU Box 29. In the accompanying "Rough draft" of this letter, Turner mentions that Wilson suggested "the word 'hither' as descriptive of the eastern edge of the frontier!" In the "Copy" Turner wrote about Wilson's reaction to his paper on the fur trade in Wisconsin. "When I read this to the seminary at Johns Hopkins (1888-89), Mr. Wilson put new life into me by saying: 'this is the kind of atmosphere in which we can breathe.'" Wilson's participation in the Adams seminary is mentioned in "Records of the Historical Seminary 1877-92," typescript copy, Dept. of History, Johns Hopkins University.

[53] Humboldt Library of Popular Science Literature edition (New York, 1880), HEH Rare Book 124219.

book Bagehot expounds Victorian notions of natural selection and evolution and at the same time takes up questions of social psychology and history as they are shaped by innovation, rebellion, custom, and conflict. Turner recalled in a letter about Wilson, "His emphasis upon Bagehot's idea of growth by 'breaking the cake of custom' left a deep impression upon me when I came to consider what part the West had played."[54]

An inevitable consequence of Turner's sojourn at Johns Hopkins was his association with another teacher, Richard T. Ely, the economist who, according to Turner's correspondence of 1889, introduced him to the works of John Stuart Mill and Francis A. Walker. Ely's "method," Turner wrote, was "to understand Mill; then to compare him with Walker, and others."[55]

Of these economists, Walker, director of the tenth United States census, had perhaps the greatest impact on Turner's thinking. A newspaper copy of a lengthy Phi Beta Kappa address by Walker is among Turner's papers, heavily marked and annotated.[56] Here, in Walker's eloquent description of westward expansion in the nineteenth century, emerge many of the germinal ideas of the frontier theory. He talked about the "vast territory" occupied by a people who had a "genius" for adaptation and inventiveness and were lured westward by "vacant soil." He left no room for doubt about the "fire of Americanism" from the new West where men, he said, could "meet and mingle" in lands "having no history of their own." Walker also had words of praise for "the power of the statistician" in recording human history, a theme that is developed in a number of Turner's published and unpublished essays.[57]

In introducing Turner to Walker, Ely made a contribution to Turner's education in economics that is hard to overestimate. Turner was later responsible for bringing Ely to the University of Wisconsin in 1892 to establish the School of Economics, Political

[54] "Copy" of letter, Turner to Dodd, Oct. 7, 1919, HEH, TU Box 29.

[55] Turner to Allen, Oct. 31, 1888, HEH, TU Box 1.

[56] "F. A. Walker, Φ.B.K. 1889 – June 19," HEH, TU File Drawer 15.

[57] Ibid.

Science, and History.[58] With Charles Homer Haskins, another Johns Hopkins man, Ely and Turner developed at Wisconsin the Johns Hopkins technique of instruction through seminars. They were joined in 1904 by John R. Commons, who had also studied at Johns Hopkins and shared Turner's views on the significance of American social history.[59]

✿   ✿   ✿   ✿   ✿

With a Johns Hopkins doctorate, Turner soon found himself a member of a kind of exclusive academic club. Men like Wilson, Small, Ely, Haskins became friends, all of them influential in shaping his career. Other Johns Hopkins men, like J. Franklin Jameson, discreetly welcomed him into the inner circles of the American Historical Association. More than any other person, Jameson, as his long correspondence with Turner discloses, was instrumental in opening up avenues for publication in the *American Historical Review* and providing opportunities for Turner to hold offices on the association's council and editorial board.[60]

It was during his year at Johns Hopkins or shortly thereafter that Turner had the good fortune to discover a book which he said deeply affected his thinking and study, Johann Gustav Droysen's *Grundriss der Historik*.[61] In several of his letters Turner dwelled on his indebtedness to Droysen. To Merle Curti he wrote, "I early respond-

[58] Turner's correspondence relating to Ely's move to Wisconsin discloses that Ely was not backward in demanding a good salary, an expanding graduate program, and authority to put the program into operation. Turner to Ely, Dec. 1, 1891, and Feb. 19, 1892, Richard T. Ely Papers, Wisconsin State Historical Society, HEH Film No. 452.

[59] Turner to Commons, Nov. 30, 1908, HEH, TU Box 11; Jacobs, review of *The Making of an American Community*, by Merle Curti et al., *Arizona and the West*, II (1960), 294-299.

[60] Turner's correspondence with Jameson began in the 1890's and ended in 1932, the year of Turner's death. Letters relating to the American Historical Association and the *American Historical Review* are found in HEH, TU Boxes 2, 4, 5, 6, 8, 9, 10, 12, and 16.

[61] Two editions of the book from Turner's library are in the Huntington collection: *Grundriss der Historik* (Leipzig, 1882), autographed and dated by

ed to the suggestion of Droysen in his *Historik* that History was the self consciousness of humanity, — in other words the effort of the present to understand itself by understanding the past."[62] In the same vein he wrote to Carl Becker saying that after reading Droysen he "conceived of the past as the explanation of *much* of the present — not all of it however, thank God."[63] Becker had written some years earlier that Turner had in seminars used the statement "History is the self-consciousness of humanity." "The phrase," Becker recalled, "must have been working in the 'fringe' of *my* consciousness all these years."[64] Turner repeated Droysen's dictum in a letter to Arthur M. Schlesinger, along with the observation, " 'Historical mindedness' is among the most important elements needed in modern civilization."[65] Despite Turner's emphasis on "historical mindedness," he was cautious about taking lessons from the past. In a letter to an acquaintance he once remarked, "conditions in ancient history and, indeed, in much of the history of the past are so different from those in the present that lessons derived from anything but recent history are apt to be misleading."[66]

Yet Turner himself never hesitated to delve into the works of the masters of ancient history. He expected his students, as he wrote to Carl Becker, to do the same. "The idea is," he said, " . . . to read a considerable block of history by a great master — the exact period is not so important."[67] Theodor Mommsen, the great historian of Rome, was for Turner such a master, and he found time to quote

---

Turner "1890" (HEH Rare Book 124357); and *Outline of the Principles of History,* tr. E. Benjamin Andrews (Boston, 1893), autographed and dated "1893" and containing Turner's marginalia (HEH Rare Book 124480).

[62] Aug. 8, 1928, HEH, TU Box 38.

[63] Dec. 16, 1925, HEH, TU Box 34.

[64] Becker to Turner, May 16, 1910, HEH, TU Vol. I, a manuscript volume of tributes and letters presented to Turner when he left the University of Wisconsin in 1910.

[65] Oct. 22, 1922, HEH, TU Box 31.

[66] Turner to Richard Henry Dana, May 3, 1915, HEH, TU Box 24.

[67] July 3, 1896, HEH, TU Box 2.

in his commonplace books from Mommsen's philosophical observations on history.[68]

Although his correspondence shows Turner had great difficulty mastering foreign languages, he seems to have extracted what he wanted from a massive treatise written in Italian, a language unfamiliar to him. His copy of Loria's formidable two-volume *Analisi della proprieta capitalista* has marginalia limited to occasional light pencil lines in the section which he consulted.[69] Strangely enough, though Turner was probably capable of reading this work and though he was able to find and adopt a phrase like "a huge page in the history of society,"[70] still Turner was forced to ask a friend to translate a postcard he received from Loria.[71]

While his formal language training was meager, Turner was never hesitant about plunging into materials published in foreign languages. His records show reading in Latin, German, French, and Spanish as well as Italian. Over the years his linguistic abilities improved so that he was able to base a significant part of his research on conclusions reached by foreign scholars writing in their own language, and he was also able to consult material from foreign archives. Accordingly, he felt keenly the need for what he called "a basal requirement" in languages for his pupils. He wrote Carl Becker that "languages afford such essential tools for the student who means to go really into his work, and such *windows* into other literatures etc. A liberal language training is perhaps the striking difference between provincialism and real culture. The *earlier* a man gets it the better . . . ."[72]

One of his early excursions into sources in a foreign language, Turner explained in another letter to Becker, was responsible for his interest in frontier fur-trade history. Turner recalled:

[68] Commonplace Book No. 2, HEH, TU Vol. III. In a history notebook of 1882 are Turner's notes for a course in "Ancient Institutions" under Allen. Turner Papers, Wisconsin State Historical Society, HEH Film No. 452.

[69] Vol. II, pp. 42-65.

[70] Benson, *Turner and Beard*, p. 27.

[71] Ibid., p. 32.

[72] Feb. 24, 1908, HEH, TU Box 10.

Allen assigned me, in one of his classes, a thesis on the subject "Common lands in Wisconsin." ... I soon saw that it wasn't a subject which would get me far, and while I was looking over the material, Dr. Draper happened in the library ... and looking over my shoulder said that I might be interested in some old French fur traders' letters from those villages. Of course I was glad to see them, and he let me loose on a box of papers, waterstained, tied in deer skin thongs, written in execrable French which, however, did me no harm, for I was guiltless of any knowledge whatever of French. ... I found I could, with a dictionary get on .... So I learned Kanuck French, and fur trade history .... Thus while a Junior, I did the thesis, which in substance, I later turned in for my doctoral dissertation. It was my own idea — by accident.[73]

In the Draper collection at the Wisconsin State Historical Society Turner found evidence to support his portrayal of the political and social forces in American history, forces which had been at least partly suggested to him by other writers. Describing the background of his paper "Western State-Making in the Revolutionary Era,"[74] Turner wrote: "The Draper Collection has enabled me to use MS. materials to elucidate the movement. It would be my purpose to bring into a single view the various efforts at state-making in the West in that period, considering the causes, processes, theories, and economic considerations involved in the movement."[75]

[73] Dec. 16, 1925, HEH, TU Box 34. It is not clear to which piece of work Turner is referring here. His Commonplace Book of 1883 (No. 2), HEH, TU Vol. III, has a notation: "Investigate landholding peasantry about Madison ... (Census — Ag. Reports — Talks)," which may be connected with the thesis Allen assigned him. In a letter of April 16, 1883, to L. J. Porlier, Turner states that Lyman C. Draper had advised him to write for information about the Grignon claim for land at the portage of the Wisconsin and Fox rivers, the site of the city of Portage. Green Bay and Prairie du Chien Papers, Vol. 27, p. 56, Wis. MSS C, Wisconsin State Historical Society. A newspaper article by Turner, "History of the 'Grignon Tract' on the Portage of the Fox and Wisconsin Rivers," appeared in the State Register of Portage, Wis., June 23, 1883. It is possible that the "Grignon Tract" was the subject of his junior thesis.

[74] American Historical Review, I (1895-96), 70-87, 251-269.

[75] Turner to Jameson, June 9, 1895, HEH, TU Box 2.

Turner described in other letters the extent of the Draper collection, which, he proudly claimed, told a vivid story of American expansion from the Alleghenies to the Mississippi. He was not immune to the romantic, heroic saga of the Old West which had motivated Draper to gather his documents in the first place. Indeed, Turner at one time planned to follow Draper's footsteps in attempting a biography of George Rogers Clark.[76]

The Draper collection had a further influence on Turner, for its stress on certain materials led him to concentrate his own investigations. Nowhere is this more graphically illustrated than in Turner's collection of maps at the Huntington Library. Turner's maps, covered with his markings and notations, are confined to the territory east of the Mississippi River. It is also apparent from study of his research notes that he tended to place a geographic limitation on his work.

But Turner's grand area of research, as confirmed by his papers, gradually centered on America's heartland of agriculture, commerce, and industry, the Midwest. He appears to have become convinced that the Midwest of the nineteenth century was a kind of governor determining the oscillations of America's political pendulum. That this area became a producer, distributor, processor, and consumer gave impulse to his studies of the economic basis of sectionalism. Here he found the rhythmic pulse of the American spirit he liked to talk about, where the evolution of society could be studied from

---

[76] Turner to Houghton Mifflin & Co., Jan. 21, 1902(?), HEH, TU Box 3. Turner's interest in biography led him to propose the idea of the *Dictionary of American Biography*, and due credit is given him by Waldo G. Leland, secretary of the American Council of Learned Societies, in a letter to Turner, Dec. 15, 1928, pasted in the flyleaf of [John H. Finley], *Dictionary of American Biography* (New York, 1928), a booklet published in celebration of the first volume of the reference work, in the Turner book collection, HEH Rare Book 126689. In this letter Leland writes: "Amid the celebrations and rejoicings over the publication of the first volume of the American Dictionary of Biography, we have not forgotten that you were the first member of the Council of Learned Societies to suggest this undertaking. I remember the scene very vividly — we were seated in the front room on the top floor of the building occupied by the Institute of International Education, and you were

manuscripts in the Draper collection, supplemented by documents from other repositories.

A number of Turner's unpublished lectures on sectionalism testify to his interest in Midwest geography and geology. As late as 1928 he told a Pasadena, California, audience about the unusual results of his investigations. "Observe," he said, in commenting on a lantern slide, "how, in the election of 1856, the counties that voted in favor of Fremont almost exactly coincided with . . . [the] second glacial ice sheet. This was the land of the basin of the Great Lakes and the prairies rejected by the Southern settler and occupied by Greater New England."[77]

In his concentration on Midwestern history Turner almost entirely neglected the Far West, perhaps an indication that many of his generalizations, especially in the light of recent history, need re-study.

*　*　*　*　*

Turner was conscious of the fact that, in spite of his influence as a historian, his published works were few in number. Reflecting on a lifetime of research in a talk he gave at a meeting of the Pacific Coast Branch of the American Historical Association in 1928, Turner declared that he did not see himself as a "bibliophile," but as one who was "interested more in mass history than in the unique item." Turner here implies that he was concerned with the whole development of the American people. This in part explains why he never felt ready to put all his ideas in print. His task was never completed. The discovery of what he called his "treasures" or "unique material" was constantly forcing him to reappraise what he had already done,

---

on the south side of the room." Turner's work in connection with the *Dictionary of American Biography* is also recorded in a folder of correspondence on the subject, TU Vol. VIII.

[77] "American Political Sectionalism," Feb. 20, 1928, p. 20, in folder marked "Pasadena Lecture, Feb. 28, 1928, First Draft?" HEH, TU File Drawer 14. Turner's early interest in geology and its relation to American politics is revealed in "Turner's Notes on Van Hise Lecture," Nov. 1898, TU File Drawer 14.

and of course it was a joy to him to plough through source material such as letters and old newspapers.[78]

Turner was also held back in his work because of time he gave to students, advising them on their courses, reading and rereading their theses, and writing letter after letter to support their applications for fellowships or new positions, never rejecting their pleas for help. When he was attacked by a faction of the University of Wisconsin regents because of his modest publishing record, Turner defended himself in a twenty-two-page letter by pointing to the number of his students who were "saturated with 'the Wisconsin idea.'" By this he meant, as he said, "the importance of economic and social factors in American history." These students, Turner pointed out with no little pride, were teachers in major universities and colleges of the Pacific Coast as well as the Mississippi Valley. Had he shown "less interest" in his students, Turner remarked, he might have "published more books."[79]

Turner's problems as a writer are well illustrated by his project to write a college textbook, which led to plans for a high school history as well as what he called a "grammar history."[80] His penchant for detail led him to write hundreds of letters to publishers outlining his chapters, but unfortunately none of these books was ever completed.[81] His publishers at first drew back in dismay when

[78] "Talk by F. J. Turner to Pacific Coast Branch. 27 Decbr. 1928," notes following page 12 of manuscript, HEH, TU File Drawer 15. In a letter to his wife, May 13, 1907, TU Box 9, Turner described his frustration in dealing with "the treasures" of the Library of Congress.

[79] Turner to Charles Richard Van Hise, June 19, 1908, marked in Turner's handwriting "Rough Draft not sent," pp. 10, 19, 20, HEH, TU Box 10.

[80] Henry Holt & Co. (Edward N. Bristol) to Turner, May 5, and reply by Turner, Aug. 10, 1905, HEH, TU Box 5, discuss plans for publication of these textbooks. Additional correspondence with Holt and other publishers regarding these books is in TU Boxes 2 and 5, and Turner's contract with Henry Holt and Company for a "College History of the United States," dated Nov. 3, 1897, is in TU Box 2.

[81] Turner also corresponded with publishers about a projected book on "The Old West" (Macmillan & Co. to Turner, March 18 and April 4, 1896, HEH, TU Box 2) and another volume entitled "The Retreat of the Frontier" (Houghton Mifflin & Co. to Turner, June 15, 1904, TU Box 4).

they learned of Turner's demand that he "use maps pretty freely,"[82] but they overlooked this prospective expense because of what they called his "gift of generalization."[83] Turner, optimistic about completing his college and high school texts, accepted $500 as an advance royalty[84] which he later had to return.

One may ask, why did Turner consider writing textbooks? Certainly he had need of money, for his personal financial story is that of one monetary crisis after another. Yet there were other considerations. In defending himself against the criticism of the Wisconsin regents for writing textbooks, Turner hit back by replying that a textbook writer improved his teaching by giving more attention to "pedagogical questions, such as mode of presentation, selection, arrangement, and emphasis of material, perspective, etc." He pointed out that most of the "really important historical *writing* in this country has been done by men *not connected with universities*." "This ought not to be the case," he argued. "It . . . tends to limit the historians to men of private fortune."[85]

Although Turner was optimistic about financial returns he might receive from his writings, the royalties from the two books he published during his lifetime were small. There remains only a slim folder in Turner's papers to remind us of the unpublished textbooks. His correspondence about the matter, however, would fill a thick volume. The handwritten introduction to his college textbook gives us an insight into the kind of book he envisioned. "The history of the United States," he wrote, "is the history of the occupation of a vast wilderness in a brief period. . . . As American society has spread to the West, it has been obliged to adjust itself to the physical conditions and resources of diverse sections. The evolution, in-

[82] Henry Holt & Co. to Turner, Nov. 3, 1897, HEH, TU Box 2.

[83] Henry Holt & Co. (Bristol) to Turner, May 5, 1905, HEH, TU Box 5. See also Ray A. Billington's penetrating essay "Why Some Historians Rarely Write History: A Case Study of Frederick Jackson Turner," *Mississippi Valley Historical Review*, L (1963-64), 10-12.

[84] Henry Holt & Co. (Bristol) to Turner, Oct. 14, 1905, HEH, TU Box 5.

[85] Typed draft of letter, with corrections, Turner to Senator George Wylie, Feb. 22, 1906, HEH, TU Box 6.

teraction and consolidation of these sections has made an American nation, with a composite people, with institutions mainly derived from Europe . . . ."[86] His brief introduction, a summary of conclusions based on years of patient historical investigation, demonstrates how carefully Turner harmonized his frontier thesis with his studies on sectionalism and social evolution and how willingly he acknowledged the importance of a European heritage, a modification of the "germ theory."

It is a loss to American history that Turner never finished writing his college textbook. There is good reason to believe, from study of Turner's correspondence, that he simply found it difficult to sit down and write. He was not immune to the attractions of long summer vacations in the woods[87] and loved his work as a teacher. Still, Turner did on occasion become exasperated with his own lack of productivity. At one time he wrote a friend that he considered the advisability of quitting teaching and taking up writing.[88] He was so pleased with himself when he completed the draft of the last chapter of *Rise of the New West* that he exclaimed in a letter to his wife, "Whoopla! I may drink up the last bottle of . . . champagne when I revise the chapter and actually post it."[89] Yet he hinted that he might not have completed the book if it had not been for the undaunted resolution of Albert Bushnell Hart, his editor. "One thing I do owe to Hart," he wrote his friend Max Farrand, "and that is the steadfast way in which he has worked the reel and

[86] "Turner, F. J. 'College History of the United States,' " HEH, TU File Drawer 15.

[87] Turner's correspondence shows that he took vacations in the northern woods during many of the summers while he was at Wisconsin. During his Harvard years he and Mrs. Turner stayed at their seashore house at Hancock Point, Maine. Accounts of Turner's summer vacations are in Mrs. Turner's "Journal of a Camping Trip" (with Mr. and Mrs. Van Hise), Aug. 10-- Sept. 10, 1908, HEH, TU Vol. XI; her "Household account book. 1921 & 1922, Cambridge and Hancock Point," TU Vol. XII; and her "The Moorings — Hancock Point, Maine," 1919-31, TU Vol. XXI.

[88] Turner is paraphrased in a letter to him from Walter Hines Page, April 25, 1905, HEH, TU Box 5.

[89] [Dec. 7, 1905], HEH, TU Box 5.

finally landed the *MS*. It's a poor sucker instead of a trout, but it fought like the devil against coming to the landing net."[90]

Rise of the New West had been particularly difficult to write because it involved organizational problems of the first magnitude to portray the West as a "moving process" with political, economic, and social forces at work "modifying the East." In many respects, Turner's publications were held in check by those very qualities that make his work endure — his refusal to make rash or casual judgments because of his knowledge of the complexity and tremendous scope of history.[91] Turner also had a genuine feeling of responsibility to his profession which caused him to occupy himself with his students while attempting to finish his own work.

In the next few years following the completion of his book, Turner confessed to a sense of uncertainty about his future writing. "My craft," he wrote Farrand, "goes tramping about so many ports that I feel unable to chart out a sailing route."[92]

＊　　＊　　＊　　＊　　＊

Turner allowed himself to become involved in other time-consuming activities at Wisconsin, and as the years went by he began to feel fettered by various obligations that he had assumed. Whether or not Turner liked committee work or faculty intrigue, he was soon drawn into the corridors of campus politics, where he came to be quite at home. More and more he was lionized by the university, often called upon to speak for the faculty or the administration. He was, for instance, the spokesman for a committee concerned with the problem of professionalism in intercollegiate football and even attempted to get those colleges where the disease was at its worst to agree to replacing the offending football coaches.[93] But although

[90] Dec. 29, 1905, HEH, TU Box 5.

[91] Turner's views on the complexity of the historical process of westward expansion are discussed in Jacobs, "Frederick Jackson Turner, 'The Significance of the Frontier in American History,'" *The American West*, I (1964), 32-35, 78.

[92] Oct. 19, 1909, HEH, TU Box 12.

[93] Correspondence of 1905-07, HEH, TU Boxes 5-9, and Turner papers of this same period at Wisconsin State Historical Society (Wis. MSS A1, Box 2) are

Turner had some success in bringing about reforms, he himself felt that "like the poor, I expect that we shall always have the problem of athletics with us."[94]

In one of his speeches, "The University of the Future," Turner spoke of the need for "creative power" in higher education. "The State University," he declared, "is the very outcome of democracy. . . . From this fact flow its great opportunity and its gravest danger."[95] Turner hoped to protect his university from the danger of becoming a kind of popular training center for agriculture and engineering students. For this reason he helped to bring about the election of Charles Van Hise as president of the university in 1903.[96] Van Hise, an eminent geologist and a close personal friend of Turner's, proved to be a courageous executive. Through the years he often relied on Turner as one of his chief advisers.

Turner had become increasingly certain about the desirability of leaving the University of Wisconsin. A fascinating segment of his whole correspondence is the steady flow of offers that coursed into his office from leading universities of his day. Invitations from Princeton, Johns Hopkins, the University of Pennsylvania, Amherst, and the University of Chicago came first, followed by others from Stanford and the University of California. Wilson was probably responsible for Turner's declining a position at Chicago in 1900 when he cautioned his friend about that institution's "feverish progressiveness." "I should think," he wrote Turner, "Chicago a splendid place to work in a hundred years from now, when Dr. Harper was dead and the place had cooled off . . . ."[97]

---

concerned with this problem.

[94] Turner to James Alton James, Dec. 5, 1906, HEH, TU Box 6.

[95] "Turner: 'The University of the Future,' talk to alumni: 1897?" pp. 4, 5, HEH, TU File Drawer 15.

[96] James Charles Kerwin to Turner, June 10, and Turner's reply of June 11, 1902, HEH, TU Box 3; Merle Curti and Vernon Carstensen, *The University of Wisconsin: A History, 1848-1925* (Madison, 1949), II, 12-13. From Turner's correspondence of 1902 the reader has the impression that he could have promoted his own candidacy, if he had chosen to do so. TU Box 3.

[97] April 4, 1900, HEH, TU Box 3. Four letters from William Rainey Harper

Following the Chicago offer came persistent invitations from Stanford and the University of California. Turner in 1906 almost committed himself to Stanford, but the San Francisco earthquake tumbled so many university buildings that President David Starr Jordan had to suspend the offer for one year.[98] At this time Turner was seriously considering invitations which might help him improve his financial status or lighten his teaching responsibilities. He complained in his letters that he was in middle life, his house was mortgaged, and he was several thousand dollars in debt. To make ends meet he had to resort to borrowing on his life insurance.[99]

The pressure of outside offers brought the regents at Wisconsin to make a concession, not in the form of increased salary but in a reduced teaching load. A memorandum given to Turner for his approval states: "In order that Professor F. J. Turner may carry to a conclusion the very important investigations in history upon which he has been engaged for many years, and put the results of the same into form for publication, [it is resolved] that he be relieved from instructional work for such part of one semester in each year as may be necessary to that end . . . ." Turner accepted the proposal but carefully changed the language in the memorandum to read "may advantageously carry on the very important investigations," crossing out the words "to a conclusion."[100] The lack of communication between Turner and the regents is clearly illustrated by the fact that they thought he might actually bring his investigations "to a conclusion."

Why did Turner leave his alma mater in 1910 after this concession was made? He wanted more time for uninterrupted research.

to Turner, Feb. 14, 1900, to Nov. 27, 1901, TU Box 3, reveal Harper's continuing attempts to move Turner to Chicago to replace Hermann von Holst.

[98] Jordan to Turner, April 19, 1906, HEH, TU Box 6.

[99] Turner to Farrand, June 23, 1905, HEH, TU Box 5. Stanford had offered a salary of $5,000. Turner's salary at Wisconsin at this time was $4,000, which was supplemented by a "summer session provision."

[100] Resolution of a committee of the regents of the University of Wisconsin, dated by Turner Jan. 22, 1906, HEH, TU Box 7. The regents formally passed the resolution and notified Turner on April 20, 1906.

Certainly he was wearying of the constant attacks made by the regents on his light teaching assignment, which they wanted to change if his salary was raised. What was more important, however, was Turner's disgust with the political factions that insisted on favoring applied fields at the expense of the liberal arts. His departure to a chair offered him at Harvard, he concluded, would be a silent protest against such tyranny and would in years to come be a genuine benefit to his alma mater.[101] This position at Harvard had been arranged for him largely through the efforts of his former colleague Charles Homer Haskins.[102] In comparing an offer from the University of California, Turner wrote to his wife about Henry Morse Stephens of Berkeley, "I find that he really wants me for more pioneering — the joy of building up a department in a new land. I have drunk pretty deeply of this wine for twenty five or so years."[103] Turner, tired of pioneering, chose to accept the position at Harvard.

There was little enthusiasm in Madison for Turner's move to Cambridge, Massachusetts. Many of his students wrote letters of protest to him. Carl Becker expressed their sentiments about Turner leaving the Midwest for the East when he wrote about reading that "the Fellows" of Harvard, "whoever they may be," had appointed Turner. He asked if Turner had accepted. "I suppose," Becker added, "at Harvard they think that when the Fellows appoint a man the incident is closed." Turner replied that he had indeed accepted and then explained his reasons for leaving Wisconsin.[104] But one person in Madison was not entirely displeased at the course of events: President Van Hise. If Turner had to move to another university, it was better for the reputation of Wisconsin, Van Hise believed, to lose him to Harvard than to California![105]

[101] Turner to Becker, Dec. 5, 1909, HEH, TU Box 12.

[102] Haskins to Turner, Sept. 16, 1909, HEH, TU Box 12. See also Billington, "Frederick Jackson Turner Comes to Harvard," *Proceedings of the Massachusetts Historical Society*, LXXIV (1962), 51-83.

[103] Oct. 6, 1909, HEH, TU Box 12.

[104] Becker to Turner, Nov. 21, and reply, Dec. 5, 1909, HEH, TU Box 12.

[105] Turner to his wife, Oct. 7, 1909, HEH, TU Box 12.

The large correspondence of Turner's Harvard years does not tell a story of a man who was noticeably unhappy with new associations and a new environment. He knew he would meet a certain coolness because he was a Midwesterner and not, as he said, "manor born"; but he was warmly welcomed by President Abbott Lawrence Lowell, by Albert Bushnell Hart (his former editor in the American Nation series and in encyclopedia articles and the friend who had guided Turner's *Rise of the New West* into publication), and by Archibald C. Coolidge, as well as by Haskins.[106] He was sought after as a member of various clubs and literary groups and later developed friendships with members of other departments.[107] It is true that Turner's correspondence with Edward Channing, another member of the history faculty, was always reserved, even though the two collaborated, with A. B. Hart, in revising the *Guide to the Study and Reading of American History.* For Turner these seem to have been happy and fruitful years as students flocked to his seminars. He always maintained his sense of humor and did not take amiss the occasional ribbings from pupils and colleagues about his "Wild West Show," as his course on the history of the West was affectionately called.

Two segments of Turner's correspondence during his Harvard years are of special interest. One of these is a bulky group of letters of 1915-16 which Turner had sealed in separate boxes before his death. Max Farrand, director of research at the Huntington Library, who knew that the letters dealt with an unfortunate and bitter controversy in the American Historical Association, decided with some trepidation to allow these to be opened for investigators.[108] Memorandums indicate that a portion of the letters may have been destroyed, perhaps some of those written to Turner by Charles H.

---

[106] The cordial reception began before Turner actually accepted the position, as one sees from his letter to his wife, Nov. 25, 1909, HEH, TU Box 12.

[107] Recollections of Turner's Harvard friends and former students appear in a series of letters of appreciation and condolence addressed to Mrs. Turner at the time of her husband's death on March 14, 1932. HEH, TU Vol. V, a portfolio of fifty-two letters.

[108] Farrand, "Memoranda on the Turner Papers," March 4, 1933, HEH, TU Box 57.

Ambler, his former pupil, who joined a faction to "reform" the American Historical Association.[109]

Turner, completing his term as secretary of the board of editors of the *American Historical Review*, fought off the brunt of an assault led by Frederic Bancroft, member of the association's council. Bancroft, biographer of Carl Schurz, and William Seward, historian of the South and a benefactor of Columbia University, led the protests of a minority group which felt it represented the large mass of members who had little or nothing to say about the association's policies and leadership.[110] The kernel of Bancroft's charges was that the association was monopolized by a few historians from a select group of universities. Bancroft accused this elite of entrenching themselves in power by reelecting themselves to the editorial board of the *Review*. In a published pamphlet he blasted the secrecy of the board and asked to see the minutes and official contracts which enabled them to control and pilfer the association's treasury.[111] In one folder alone there are thirty-six letters and telegrams from J. Franklin Jameson, the *Review's* editor, almost all of

[109] Farrand had a rather curious attitude toward the Turner collection in spite of the fact that he had been largely responsible for collecting originals or copies of Turner's letters from those who knew him. In his memorandum of Jan. 18, 1933, HEH, TU Box 57, Farrand states that "a very large number of the purely professional letters might well be destroyed." He goes on to say, "I have that same feeling with regard to the more or less formal correspondence when he was president of the Am. Hist. Assn. There are a few series of letters from such men as Carl Fish, Paxson, Van Tyne, *et al*, that might be worth keeping for a time at least, because of the importance of the men." In his memorandum of March 4, 1933, TU Box 57, Farrand mentions the advisability of keeping the Ambler correspondence "secret." Turner, Farrand says, "felt very strongly about it." In TU Box 26 are four letters from Ambler, Jan. 16--Feb. 5, 1916, on the controversy and one reply of Feb. 9, 1916, in which Turner terminates the correspondence.

[110] Turner's voluminous correspondence on the controversy is in HEH, TU Boxes 23-26, covering the years 1915-16. A summary of the affair appears in Jacob E. Cooke, *Frederic Bancroft, Historian* (Norman, Okla., 1957), pp. 98-102.

[111] "Notes from which were prepared the Minutes of Meetings of the Board of Editors of the *American Historical Review*," 1912-15, HEH, TU Box 56; Turner to Claude H. Van Tyne, Aug. 5, 1915, TU uncatalogued photostat

them concerning Bancroft's "reform" movement.[112] Jameson, aroused to the point of white heat, indulged in a bit of healthy profanity at the gross exaggeration of Bancroft's charges. The controversy left vivid scars of enmity in the association, but it did lead to transferring the ownership of the *Review* from the board of editors to the members of the association.[113] For Turner, who had no taste for this sort of thing, the whole affair was a sad experience, much worse than the political disputes he had survived at the University of Wisconsin. Becker, in writing to Turner about the issues involved, reluctantly concluded that little could be done, for that man Bancroft was, as he said, a "subject for a psychological study!"[114]

It is refreshing to turn from the unpleasantness of this part of Turner's correspondence to the letters of Turner and Mrs. Alice Forbes Hooper, a wealthy woman who was captivated by Turner soon after his move to Harvard and who became the leading financial backer of his Harvard Commission on Western History.[115] These letters disclose a remarkable friendship which lasted until Turner's death. Perhaps nowhere else in his papers are revealed so many hitherto unknown sidelights on his personality, his reading interests, his work as a scholar and teacher, and his reaction to contemporary affairs. From these letters we know that Turner was a liberal in his politics, a Democrat who had voted for William Jennings Bryan with some misgivings.

Excerpts from some of the letters illustrate their tone. Turner usually writes to Mrs. Hooper as "Dear Lady." She responds by

---

from Claude H. Van Tyne Papers, William L. Clements Library; mimeographed copy of letter, Edgar A. Bancroft to J. Franklin Jameson, [Nov. 1915], TU Box 25; Edward Potts Cheyney to Turner, May 18, and Turner to Cheyney, May 29, 1915, TU Box 25; Frederic Bancroft to Turner, Nov. 3, 1915, TU Box 25; Charles H. Ambler to Thomas W. Page, Aug. 10, 1915, an extract in Turner's handwriting, TU Box 25.

[112] Jameson to Turner, Jan. 26--Dec. 9, 1915, HEH, TU Box 23.

[113] Report of Cheyney, chairman of the board of editors, Dec. 29, 1917, *Annual Report of the American Historical Association for the Year 1917* (Washington, D.C., 1920), pp. 68-69.

[114] Oct. 16, 1915, HEH, TU Box 25.

[115] HEH, TU-H Boxes 1-8.

addressing him as "Dear New Friend," "Dear History One," or "Dear Historicus." The frankness of these letters is apparent in a missive Turner wrote in 1912, near the beginning of his long correspondence with Mrs. Hooper. "I may not succeed in talking to you as a man to a man," he wrote, "but I shall not sacrifice any masculine candor because I am talking to a woman."[116] He had need of "candor" in those letters explaining the necessity for funds, for Turner was spending Mrs. Hooper's money purchasing books and documents for what she called "a patriotic interest in conserving & collecting."[117]

While the sheer volume of the Turner-Hooper correspondence is enough to make the investigator draw back in sudden loss of spirit, especially when he attempts to decipher Mrs. Hooper's handwriting, many other segments of Turner's letters are smaller in size and no less distinguished. One of these is a spate of manuscripts resulting from Charles A. Beard's critical review of *The Frontier in American History*. Beard wrote: "On penetrating to the heart of Mr. Turner's reflections, we find that he is in fact thinking of American history mainly in terms of economic group conflicts. . . . But strange to say he says very little indeed about the conflict between the capitalist and organized labor . . . . On this point our orthodox historians are silent. The tabu is almost perfect. The American Historical Association officially is as regular as Louis XIV's court scribes."[118] A letter to Merle Curti in the Turner papers discloses that Beard regretted the lash of his tongue in this review and that he respected Turner as a scholar who stimulated the study of economic history. "In my opinion (and you may quote this if you like)," Beard wrote, "Mr. Turner deserves everlasting credit for his services as the leader in restoring the consideration of economic facts to historical writing in America. The old Federalists and Hildreth understood and appreciated the significance of such facts, but American historians for a long time after 1865 wandered around in an arid desert of political and constitutional theorizing. It was Mr. Turner who led in putting history on a scientific plane. Besides

[116] Jan. 5, 1912, HEH, TU-H Box 1.

[117] Mrs. Hooper to Turner, June 1, 1916, HEH, TU-H Box 3.

[118] *New Republic*, XXV (1920-21), 349-350.

this, he is a scholar of fine talents and unwearying industry. His stamp is deep and indelible on historical writing in America."[119]

Turner was not unduly disturbed by the review and wrote to calm his daughter, whom he called "fighting Peggy." She had read Beard's notice and had written her father to ask if Beard was a disgruntled member of the American Historical Association. Turner replied that he was an "ex-Columbia professor, radical in tendency, but chiefly interested in urban problems and in the struggle of capital and labor." He also told his daughter, "I'm thicker skinned than you, and I enjoyed Beard's review, though I am writing him of some points of doubt about his microscope. He read the first essay at least, and that is more than can be expected of most reviewers . . . ."[120] Writing to Mrs. Hooper on the same subject, he commented: "Yesterday I replied in a purely personal letter to Professor Beard, my reviewer in the New Republic (Feb. 16) on some points of his criticisms which didn't seem to me sound. But I like real criticism better than sweetmeats, and his is one of the few reviews which have gone into the merits of my literary child of something like 30 years ago. I find myself like a great grandfather in reference to the essay on *The Frontier,* quite ready to see its imperfections myself, but disposed to pick up the cudgels when some one else finds flaws in its features."[121]

Turner did write to Beard, but all we have is the answer. Beard's reply dwelled on "the elusive character of words." After acknowledging the importance of free land in American history, he declared, "On Americanization, I surrender, for frankly I do not know what the term means or ever has meant. About the only test I can apply is that of plain loyalty in a crisis." He then turned to Turner's theory on the importance of free land. "Free land," he said, "makes free farmers; America has had more of them than any other country; hence a free farmer is more characteristically American than an industrial worker."[122]

[119] Beard to Curti, Aug. 9, [1928], HEH, TU Box 40.

[120] Turner to Dorothy Turner Main, Feb. 18, 1921, HEH, TU Box 31.

[121] Feb. [18?], 1921, HEH, TU-H Box 5.

[122] May 14, 1921, HEH, TU Box 31.

Turner was left unsatisfied by this comment and resolved to defend his views. A number of months after receiving Beard's letter he made notes for an essay, "City, Frontier, and Section, or the Significance of the City in American History." In his annotations Turner wrote: "I have written & lectured more on the subject than Beard recognizes. . . . When & how . . . did cities become densely populated and why?" Examine, Turner reminded himself, the "extent to which the cities were built up by movement from interior rural areas . . . . The city [is] dependent upon natural resources, & markets, furnished by extending frontier . . . ."[123] Had the essay been completed, it might have given us a new view of the growth of urban society.

✻   ✻   ✻   ✻   ✻

It is not easy to grasp the essence of Turner's interpretations of American history because there are modifications of his views in both his published and his unpublished writings. In contrast to his predecessors who had stressed such factors as English tyranny, slavery, religious freedom, the growth of democracy, or nationalism, Turner emphasized the significance of a transplanted civilization growing in a wilderness environment. For Turner, the individualism of the frontier stimulated democracy from the beginning of American history. The Americanism that developed was influenced by the presence of free land in the West which pulled settlers away from the East and from established patterns of thought. The frontiersman's restless energy, his self-reliance, and his love of freedom could not help but modify the American character. Great leaders like Jefferson, Jackson, and Lincoln symbolized the force of Western democracy in American life.

Turner's suggestive phrase "the significance of the frontier" has been used to describe the frontier history of other countries, including the Latin-American nations, Australia, and Russia. The idea gave new importance to the study of local history, which according to Turner was "not isolated but a fragment of the history of the

[123] HEH, TU File Drawer 14. Turner has dated the manuscript Oct. 1922. N. D. Harper, "The Rural and Urban Frontiers," *Australian Journal of Science,* XXV (Feb. 1963), 321-334, supports Turner's views.

commonwealth, the nation, the world." "Local history is therefore," Turner wrote, "the history of a locality upon which play the forces of general historic change; which is in itself a miniature of these changes, a specimen from which they can be understood by study more intimately."[124]

In his frontier hypothesis Turner stressed the importance of the modifying influences of new environments as well as free, or almost free, land. But he did not fail to recognize the persistence of habits of emigrants from older regions as pioneer settlements went through a process of social evolution. At first raw and primitive, the frontier areas witnessed generations of historic change with sectional variations partly caused by physiographic factors. After some three hundred years a new civilization emerged on American soil, a civilization which was largely molded by the passing frontier. This transformation came about through what Turner called "the frontier process," involving interrelated social, political, and economic forces over a period of years.

In commenting on Turner's frontier theory, Herbert Eugene Bolton wrote: " 'The frontier' was an intriguing phrase, and it epitomized the historical beginnings of every American area. It gave significance to the history of every township, county, territory or state. It appealed to local patriotism everywhere across the Continent, from Plymouth to San Francisco, from Florida to Los Angeles, and now, outside of our own borders, the history of the frontier illuminates the history of all the other Americas — British, Spanish, Portuguese, French and Dutch. No wonder Turner is worshipped as a prophet."[125]

Yet Turner did not claim that his frontier theory was the only key to the interpretation of American history. At Harvard, during his later years, he showed his open-mindedness by modifying some

---

[124] "Outline for address on History and the Local Historical Society — Cambridge Historical Society," April 25, 1911, HEH, TU Box 56.

[125] " 'Turner, As I Remember Him,' by Herbert Eugene Bolton," ed. Jacobs, *Mid-America*, XXXVI (1954), 59. James C. Malin has stressed the implication of the frontier hypothesis as "the doctrine of closed space," an agricultural interpretation of history in an industrial age and isolationist in an international age. "Mobility and History: Reflections on the Agricultural Policies of the

of his early generalizations, repeatedly emphasizing multiple causation in history. His stimulating essays on sectionalism, based on the idea of multiple hypothesis, showed that there were many social, economic, political, and geographical forces which divided the nation into distinct regions or sections. American history, in Turner's view, was the story of a federation of sections which gave nutriment to a complicated American spirit, "Uncle Sam's psychology."

In his essay "Sections and Nation" Turner gives us perhaps his most penetrating analysis of causal factors in American history. "No single factor," he wrote, "is determinative. Men are not absolutely dictated to by climate, geography, soils, or economic interests. The influence of the stock from which they sprang, the inherited ideals, the spiritual factors, often triumph over the material interests. There is also the influence of personality."[126] In an unpublished manuscript he again questions economic determinism or the validity of any "single formula" for writing history.[127] Elsewhere he speaks of "the mass of the evidence" or "the lack of it, the prejudices of the witnesses, the prepossessions of the society . . . , the nearness of the events."[128] All of these factors together with the complexity of what Turner called "the human spirit" repelled him from any dogmatic theory of causation. In an autobiographical letter to Merle Curti, he emphasized his idea of "multiple hypothesis," long ago borrowed from the distinguished geologist Thomas C. Chamberlin: "I, as you perhaps recall, valued Chamberlin's paper on the Multiple Hypothesis, which I have aimed to apply to history as he to Geology. . . . It is also a point to be noted that

---

United States in Relation to a Mechanized World," *Agricultural History,* XVII (1943), 177.

[126] *The Significance of Sections in American History* (New York, 1932), p. 337. Unfortunately European historians have tended to identify Turner as a proponent of the frontier theory and to neglect his wider view of historical causation and multiple hypothesis. See Roland H. Beck, *Die Frontiertheorie von Frederick Jackson Turner* (Zurich, 1955); Per Sveaas Andersen, *Westward Is the Course of Empires* (Oslo, 1956).

[127] "The Significance of the Section in the United States, May, 1922," p. 45, HEH, TU File Drawer 14.

[128] "Turner, on opening a new course, 1924," HEH, TU File Drawer 15.

I have been more interested in studying a leader's environment, the society in which he lived, the lesser men whose support he needed & whose opposition modified his policy, than in *minutiae* of his personal life."[129]

It was logical that Turner thought in terms of multiple causation, for his essays on sectionalism are predicated on this concept. As he suggested in one of them, the study of sectionalism made the investigator analyze every factor of human experience including "physical geography" and "cultural ideals and convictions of the society."[130] Turner appears more and more to have tempered the early generalizations, giving evidence of judiciousness and integrity of mind. The reader of his papers at the Huntington Library is convinced that Turner was willing and even eager to consider any interpretation of history. There were very few of these interpretations that he neglected to point out in his lectures and in his published and unpublished works.

Turner's main contribution to historical thought has been to encourage a better understanding of the American character and the varied origins of American democracy's development. He believed that historical interpretations were almost inescapable, but he never lost his zeal for complete objectivity in sifting and counterchecking the facts.

In writing to Merle Curti after retiring from teaching, Turner talked about the views he imparted to his students: "I think," he wrote, "political, economic, and social history is all tied together and the interaction of these factors must be considered in any investigation into one of them. And if I had any influence upon students it was by pounding hard on this conception, and then keeping pretty much out of their way, while they blazed out their own trails." "At any rate," Turner concluded, "they are carrying on, in many fields, widely apart, and *keeping it up* on their 'own hook' . . . ."[131]

[129] Aug. 8, 1928, HEH, TU Box 38.

[130] "The Significance of the Section in the United States, May, 1922," p. 47, HEH, TU File Drawer 14.

[131] June 11, 1927, HEH, TU Box 36.

41

His self-assumed task of examining social, economic, and political streams in American history involved him in thoughts about his country's future. One of his speeches of the 1920's gloomily forecast what portended for America: population pressures; diminishing food supply; the exhaustion of forest, oil, and coal reserves; the threat of war; the horror of a dreaded "chemist's bomb."[132] He also lamented in his addresses the increasing tendency toward conformity with an accompanying "decline in self-confidence" in America.[133] Certainly these reflections have a modern tone. Turner appears to have understood his country and her history better than any other historian of his generation.

[132] "Notes for Shop Club Lecture, 1923 — Winter," HEH, TU File Drawer 15.
[133] "Lecture: Univ. of Chicago, 1916 — June 5," HEH, TU File Drawer 15.

Editorial Note

FREDERICK JACKSON TURNER's *legacy of essays, lectures, and memorandums published in this volume are selected from the thousands of fragments of essays and unfinished manuscripts in his collected papers at the Huntington Library. One essay, "The Development of American Society," has been previously published. The version printed here incorporates Turner's last handwritten revisions and additions.*

The intent of the editor has been to make easily available these unpublished essays, lectures, and memorandums which mirror the concerns of Turner during his years as a historian and teacher. Although some of the individual pieces in this edition do not exhibit Turner at his best, the selection as a whole is representative of the most interesting unpublished material in his files. In these pieces we catch a glimpse of the historian's workshop with some of its untidiness but "where the chips were flying" and where, as Turner said, one "can see the workman cut his finger and jam his thumb."

The editor, confronted with unpublished materials amounting to tens of thousands of pages, made the decision to be selective and to avoid excerpts, to avoid publishing parts of a manuscript when the whole or almost the whole was available. Only when Turner's manuscripts degenerate into a scribbled outline or bibliographical notes, with renumbered pages, as they occasionally do, have deletions been made and indicated by a footnote.

In this edition much effort has been devoted to maintaining an accurate text, although it is impossible to reproduce interlineations and marginal notations on handwritten pages with perfect fidelity. The manuscripts in Turner's handwriting are in ink or pencil, often with numerous revisions — in red, blue, and black pencil, crayon, or ink. Revised pagination and sheets of various sizes show that Turner sometimes borrowed from earlier essays. Turner's deletions when legible are reproduced in a footnote if they show a significant trend of thought. Although Turner's orthography is not always conventional, his spelling, grammar, and punctuation are preserved as they are found in the manuscripts except for minor changes. For instance, obvious slips of the pen and typographical errors are corrected. The ampersand is changed to "and." Other abbreviations are expanded when the full word contributes to easier reading of the text. Minimum alterations in punctuation are made when necessary for intelligent reading. Titles of publications are italicized. In the few cases that Turner failed to provide a title for his unpublished writings, an individual manuscript is identified by the title appearing on the manuscript's folder.

The location of the document and available information on the probable date when it was written are given in footnotes. A number of the important quotations used by Turner have been traced to their source despite his unfortunate habit of omitting citations. The minor errors or variations in Turner's quotations have been corrected when the source has been found. Brackets indicate material supplied by the editor.

1

ᴥ Frontiers and Sections

FOR FREDERICK JACKSON TURNER, *the theory of sections was in itself a way of objecting to theories, a way of insisting on the complexity of reality and multiple causation in history as opposed to the simplicity and neatness of theory. But this particular theory made comprehensible and explorable a complicated series of historical phenomena, phenomena which without a unifying idea might seem nebulous and unimportant. It was by means of the theory of sections that Turner was able to view the whole area of the social sciences as one fertile field for research in all of American history.*

For the reader who wishes to grasp the bent of Turner's mind, who wishes to observe that most agile mind at work on the various facets of a single idea, these essays and notes, written in the 1920's and grouped together under the title "Frontiers and Sections," provide a fascinating first step.

In his "Introduction to a Lecture on Sectionalism" Turner prepares the reader for the freshness and vitality of his technique of research by insisting on the freedom of the investigator to jump boundaries. He refuses to be bound by any narrow, traditional description of the historian's domain and will if it suits his objective invade the territory of the geographer, of the sociologist, or of anyone else who might have light to shed on his subject. Sectionalism,

45

he finds, is not an American phenomenon, but one that is observable at many other times and places. Turner is appalled by the simplicity of those writers who ignore the variety of America and treat her as if she were a nation with a common landscape and common interests. This introductory lecture, as well as other pieces in the group, demonstrates how skillfully the mature Turner of the 1920's merged and even subordinated his frontier theory to his theory on sections.

In the two essays dealing primarily with political maps and presidential elections Turner again insists that we will need the help of geographers, economists, political scientists, sociologists, and historians to arrive at any valid explanation for the voting patterns which appear in clearly definable geographic areas. "One must," he says, "adopt the geologist's use of the multiple hypothesis to explain complex areas." Indeed, both of these essays deal with the immense difficulties of arriving at any valid conclusions whatsoever in this complicated field, and both pieces provide the reader with a foretaste of the problems encountered in the next group of essays and lectures on "The Complexity of History." Yet Turner does not hesitate to make tentative interpretations in these two essays to explain voting results. He suggests, for example, what now may seem self-evident but what was at the time a provocative idea, that "the geographic influence is most obvious where there is the strongest political inertia, and weakest in regions where the result is determined by reflection and conscious decision."

It is with the "Lecture on Sectionalism" that we begin to appreciate Turner's ability to explore the ramifications of his theory of sections. His broad view of the statesman as one who must adapt the interests of his section to those of the nation as a whole is further enlarged by consideration of factors that cause sectional transformations: population density, geography, the frontier advance, stages of economic development, and, as the final paper of this group indicates, factors of social class.

In this "Lecture on Sectionalism" the phenomenon as it developed in America is examined: sectional rivalry arising from the disparity between the agricultural democracy of the West and the more prosperous classes of the East, sectionalism arising from the contest for power between the colonial sections, and then sectionalism

46

*growing out of the more local rivalries of geographical regions.
Fragment though it is, the "Lecture on Sectionalism" presents
briefly most of the basic ideas Turner set forth on the subject and
illustrates with lively example the suppleness of Turner's mind, his
alertness to changing sectional forces, and his skill as a writer in
moving from events of the past to events of his own time and on
to intriguing speculations about the future.*

INTRODUCTION TO A LECTURE ON SECTIONALISM[1]

Whether to call this lecture a historical geographical, political,
economic, or sociological discussion, I do not know, and I don't
much care, for I am one of those who believes in breaking line
fences, even at the risk of arrest for trespass, or disclosure of being
an amateur, or something worse, breaking into the professional's
game.

Seriously we need correlation of our subjects in the social studies,
and until men trained in the various sciences work together, or
individually achieve competence in the respective fields, it is perhaps permissible for the explorer to report his imperfect
observations.

My title might have been "The Farmers' Bloc and its Background," or the "Geography of American Politics," or the "Geography of American Opinion," or "Uncle Sam's Complex Personality," or half a dozen other titles, but I have chosen to call it the
"Significance of the Section in American History," because it is
intended to serve as a companion piece to another paper of mine
on the "Significance of the Frontier," and because it is fundamentally a historical interpretation rather than a narrative. My
interest in the section in American history was contemporaneous
with my interest in the frontier. They are mutually interpretative,

[1] MS: HEH, TU File Drawer 14, folder marked "Talk on Sectionalism (draft),
April, 1922." A note in Turner's handwriting provides the date.

47

for up to our own day, the frontier has been passing decade after decade into new geographic Provinces or Regions, founding new regional societies, reacting with the environment to produce sectional ideals and traits differing in each region, and interplaying with each other. Now, we confront a nation with less mobility, with its unpossessed natural resources, more or less taken up; and exhibiting the larger outlines of a nation's portrait, revealing something of the America that is to be, even as a man's physiognomy takes firmer shape, as the unformed boyish face takes on the features and the lines of character of the man.

Sectionalism is no new thing in American history. That will be readily admitted. But ever since the Civil War, the word has taken on so sinister a meaning, and the phenomena have been so less obvious, that leaders in politics, and public opinion itself, have been prone to deny the existence and condemn the possibility of sectionalism in our own day. But despite the denials, I desire to show that in various forms, the thing does exist, and that it has some advantages.

ᴥ DRAFT ON SECTIONALISM[1]

About thirty years ago I ventured to set forth some ideas upon the Significance of the Frontier in American History. It had the interest to me of being a historical interpretation of forces still operative but beginning to take the form of history. At the time the essay was regarded as a curious idea in some parts of the East. But in the course of thirty years the ideas have become rather commonplace among historians. Some fifteen years ago, perhaps because the contemporary significance of the frontier was declining, I seized upon another historical topic, which indeed I had sketched in one of the later editions of the paper on the Frontier, and began to urge

[1] MS: HEH, TU File Drawer 15, folder marked "Draft, Piece on Sectionalism, 1922." Notes by Turner on the manuscript indicate that it was probably written in 1922.

the importance of the Section in American history. Not the section that is indicated simply in the struggle of North and South over slavery and the Negro question; but the more complicated and various sectionalism which has run through American development. Whether this was due to the fact that I have never been able to divorce past and present events since the days when I was newspaper reporter as well as instructor in history, and have always had a leaning to live subjects, or whether it was due to an early interest in social and institutional changes in the reactions between forming peoples and their environment derived from a training in Mediaeval history, which has much in common with American history, I cannot say. Probably it was naturally the outcome of my studies of the advancing, or retreating frontier, whichever way you look at it. For I soon found in the study of American settlement, as it pressed into new regions of the spacious wilderness domains that opened before the American people, that one must take note not only of the factor of space, the adjustment of men at the edge of free land to primitive conditions — and the changes wrought in the frontier types in successive years of the advance — factors which made the frontier line along its whole length much alike and even showed striking similarities in the character and influence of the American frontier in all eras — I soon found, I say, that the frontiers entered and crossed geographical provinces or regions which varied from the older colonizing regions; that these older regions themselves were unlike each other, and that in the extension of the older sections differing men, societies, institutions and ideals were being carried forward. In other words that the frontier advance was an advance of rival sections, Northeastern, Middle and Southern; that these sections themselves flowed into new geographic moulds. The vast space before the American advance was not a uniform area, but itself made up of different regions, which called out new activities, imposed new economic experiences, new types of society, and had new and varying effects upon the older regions and upon the nation as a whole.

So I was forced to undertake a survey of the Region in American history as well as the Frontier. I was forced to study the evolution of society and politics in the old Northwest, the Middle West, the

49

western border states like West Virginia, Kentucky, Tennessee, the Cotton Kingdom of the Southwest, in contrast to the tobacco planting states of the Old South; the opening of a New Southwest in Texas and its neighbors, the colonization of a New Northwest along the Columbia basin, the California empire along the Pacific coast; the conquest of the Great Plains and the Rocky Mountains, the dealings with Arid America; the effects of the successive additions of these regions upon the political balance of power, upon the economic life and ideals of the Union, as embodied in its cultural life and its literature.

No one could follow the advance of settlement into these numerous regions, and fail to see the evolution of new Sections, the contribution of new elements to the American nation. The more we studied the matter the more the significance of the Sections became manifest.

In recent years the significance of the advance of the frontier of older regions into new has become recognized as a world historic phenomenon. The anthropologist and archeologist traces the extensions of types of mankind, of artifacts, of lines of commerce, of adjusted institutions and cultures; the part played by such factors in Oriental and Classical history is increasingly recognized. The spread of the Slavs, the Germans, into new lands, the colonial element, in a word, in Mediaeval and modern history is seen to be at least as important and influential as the detailed evolution of institutions, and the local annals of the home lands. In our own day the struggle over frontiers in this sense, the acquisition and domination by rival nations of hinterlands and spheres of influence and mandates in Africa and Asia, the rivalry in establishing transportation routes, like the Bagdad railway, in preserving lines of communication on land and sea of the mother or master countries and these unfolding opportunities, have been forced upon our attention and the record has been written in blood, even in the greatest of all wars.

In like fashion the students of society, historians as well as geographers, demographers, and sociologists, have been paying attention to the significance of natural regions, and there is a growing literature on the subject. It is seen that there are nucleal lands, and transition zones, but that the earth's surface is divided into geographic entities, regions, where the relations of environment and peoples, resources, position, resulting economic, social, political and cultural phenomena, have affected the history of civilization and the burning questions of contemporary diplomacy and government.

The United States means much more than a single country. It is too large to treat as a unit. The libraries are full of the works of travellers who describe the United States after a visit to New York and Boston, or perhaps a hasty trip to Chicago, or even a Pullman car observation of half a week between Atlantic and Pacific. Too often they generalize for the whole continental zone from the observations at these few stations. But the American himself is prone to do quite as misleading a thing. He is prone to write of America from the prepossessions, experiences and ideals of his particular section. To conceive of America as his section writ large; even to impose his thinking and phrases upon other sections as in the national hymn of America,

> I love thy rocks and rills,
> Thy woods and templed hills,

is the New England scene. The prairie dweller near the Great Lakes, the Great Plainsman, the dweller among the valleys over topped by the snowy peaks of Rockies and Sierras, sing of templed hills, and the man of Arid America, with far horizons of level desert, chants of rills and woods, translating unconsciously perhaps into irrigation ditch and greasewood.

In fact New England finds it hard to realize that she is not America, hard to bear with sections which do not think as she thinks, whose interests are not her interests, thinks of the common well fare as demanding that the American commonwealth should be fitted with New England clothes and stand in New England shoes. But so does the planter of the South, the farmer of the Middle West, the cattle raiser of the Great Plains, and the miner of the Mountains, think of the common well fare in terms of his own section.

Nor do we fully understand each other.

51

❧ LECTURE ON SECTIONALISM[1]

From this period[2] on to the present time sectionalism in America has been due primarily to two factors: (1) the advance of these coastal sections toward the interior produced a sectionalism of East versus West, the West being at first the outer edge of the Atlantic coast colonies and changing decade by decade until the West lay along the Great Plains and the Rocky Mountains and the East shaded into the West along the Great Lakes and the upper Ohio. (2) In this movement of advance the population discovered, conquered and colonized the various geographic regions into which the United States was divided.

Until our own day the western factor has been very important. It operated both as an eastern and western sectionalism and as a treasury from which the older coastal section[s] strove to recruit their power. Now that the movement of the frontier is coming to an end the existence of varied and contrasting geographic regions in the vast spaces which the American people have colonized is becoming the important factor. As American life reaches the conditions of settled society the differences between the various societies which were formed as settlements spread into the geographic molds of the continent become more apparent. The analogies between the American section and the European nation seem likely to receive new emphasis.

Let us next examine these various factors: the sectionalism of East and West, the sectionalism arising from the struggle for power between the colonial sections, each striving to secure predominance by drawing on the growing West, and, finally, the rivalries of the

[1] MS: HEH, TU File Drawer 15, folder marked "Lecture on Sectionalism, temp. Pres. Coolidge." Internal evidence indicates that the lecture was composed in the 1920's. Page numbering of the manuscript shows it was originally part of a longer essay.

[2] An accompanying partial draft of the lecture refers to the period "that immediately followed the War of 1812."

52

natural geographic regions themselves when this western factor came to an end. The contest of coast against interior appeared almost from the beginning, but it did not become clearly evident until after the middle of the eighteenth century. By that time the back counties in all the colonies had received a sufficient population to form a western type of society, had begun to develope a self-consciousness and had created alarm in the older centers by the part which they took in legislation and by the demands which they made. Practically all of the eastern states were in control of the tidewater counties which had gerrymandered the legislature by refusing to form new counties or to award them power in proportion to their population in the legislative apportionment. This raised the question of the basis of representation and the eastern settlements laid stress upon property while the western settlements insisted that the white population ought to constitute the basis. Therefore over questions like the building of roads, creation of public schools, the levying of taxes, whether by the poll or upon real estate and personal property, violent struggles arose. In the South the existence of the Negro slaves in the tidewater counties and the absence of them in the Upland made a particularly serious problem. The man of the interior saw no reason why the planter should have representation for his slaves, and indeed, was not unwilling to tax the slave property in order to secure the funds necessary for internal improvements to give an outlet for western agricultural surplus, for education, etc. On the other hand, the planter naturally looked with concern upon the possibility of a white majority in the back country securing the control of the legislature and taxing the coastal counties in such a way that their wealth would be redistributed for the benefit of the interior. Thus the issue of the man and the dollar arose and thus the emphasis upon minority rights as a means of safeguarding property rights was early developed. When Calhoun, in the later twenties, became the political philosopher of the South, his doctrine of concurrent majority and of nullification rested upon Southern experience in the contest between the eastern seaboard counties and those of the interior. By the time of his South Carolina Exposition the problem had become a nation-wide one and the South as a whole in relation to the rest of the Union occupied a position comparable to the tidewater counties in reference to the interior counties. The right of state veto derived its significance, therefore, from the fact that it was a device to protect a section, and particularly a minority section against the rule of the majority.

The antagonism between East and West was emphasized, moreover, by the differences which existed between the rude agricultural democracy of the interior and the cultivated aristocracy of merchants and planters along the coast. The back-country was not only democratic by virtue of the fact that it was settled by the poorer classes for the most part, but it was also less English in its composition. The tide of immigration, Scotch-Irish, Irish proper, Germans, etc., had flowed to the frontier. The differences in race, in religious organizations, in industrial society, reinforced the differences which I have already mentioned. Between the coastal settlements and the back-country there lay in the South the barrier of the fall line where river communication was interrupted and the pine barrens, a strip of infertile soil which checked advance from the coast. Therefore it happened that the interior counties of the Southern states were rather the children of Pennsylvania than of the Southern colonies and that their economic relations were with Baltimore and Philadelphia rather than with the seaports of the South.

But it was not only in the South that these two sections of East and West existed. In the northern counties as well the differences between the newly settled towns of the back-country and the vested interests of tidewater were keenly felt. Gouverneur Morris of Pennsylvania said, in the Constitutional Convention of 1787, "The busy haunts of men, not the remote wilderness, was the proper school of political talents. If the western people get the power into their hands, they will ruin the Atlantic interests. The back members are always most averse to the best measures."[3] Although Morris's

[3] A favorite quotation of Turner's which is heavily marked in his copy of Jonathan Elliot, ed. *The Debates in the Several State Conventions on the Adoption of the Federal Constitution*, Vol. V: *Debates on the Adoption of the Federal Constitution* (Washington, D.C., 1845), 298, HEH Rare Book 119890 [Vol. II]. This volume, inscribed "A J Turner" (Turner's father), is filled with Turner's marginalia. Quotations from the volume repeatedly appear in Turner's published and unpublished essays because the debates clearly de-

method of safeguarding the interests of the coastal section was different from the nullification device which Calhoun later championed, it had the same object. He would so fix the ratio of representation that the number of representatives from Atlantic states should always be larger than the number from western states. This, in his opinion, would not be unjust, "as the western settlers would previously know the conditions on which they were to possess their lands."[4] On the motion that the representatives from new states should not exceed those from the old thirteen, Massachusetts, Connecticut, Delaware and Maryland, all of them later federalist strongholds, voted aye. Pennsylvania was divided; and the motion was defeated by southern states plus New Jersey. Shortly before this, in 1786, Rufus King of New York, later a senator and a minister to England, gave his opinion, "that every Citizen of the Atlantic States who emigrates to the westward of the Allegheny is a total loss to our confederacy."

"Nature," he said, "has severed the two countries by a vast and extensive chain of mountains, interest and convenience will keep them separate, and the feeble policy of our disjointed Government will not be able to unite them. For these reasons I have ever been opposed to encouragements of western emigrants. The States situated on the Atlantic are not sufficiently populous and losing our men is losing our greatest source of wealth."

In this same year John Jay attempted to negotiate in Congress a treaty with the Spanish representative by which we were to forego the navigation of the Mississippi for a period of years. This aroused the violent indignation of the West, which felt that its interests were sacrificed to those of the commercial Atlantic states. The violence of their language makes it reasonably certain that the nation might have lost the Mississippi Valley had these arrangements been made.

---

fined sectional rivalries and problems concerning the West. The quotation cited above is in *The Frontier in American History* (New York, 1920), pp. 207-208, and in *The Significance of Sections in American History* (New York, 1932), p. 26. A number of other quotations in this "Lecture on Sectionalism" also appear in these volumes.

[4] Elliot, ed. *The Debates in the Several State Conventions*, V, 279.

I have dwelt upon this aspect of the early sectionalism of the West because it is a phenomenon which meets the historian persistently in all the subsequent years down to our own time. I need only mention Jacksonian democracy, the Grangers, the Populists, the Insurgents, Progressives, the Farmers' Bloc, and the La Follette movement to remind you of this fact. But the clash of interests has been much more pervasive than these third party movements indicate. In all important legislation it has been necessary for the eastern wing of the Republican party or of the Democratic party to compromise in order to secure a united party action or it has been necessary to overbear the protests of the minority section and thus to risk the ability of the party to carry out its program. In such a case the revolting wing has formed alliances, so to speak, with other sections and parties, and these insurgents, or "blocs" have been able to shape legislation in opposition to the supposedly dominant party. To deal adequately with this aspect of our history would take many lectures so that I shall have to content myself with reminding you that there has always been a sectionalism of East against West, and that East and West have been quite different geographically as the American population spread decade after decade into the interior and thereby constituted new Easts and new Wests.

As I pointed out, however, the western factor was not only one of antagonism between the East and itself. It was also a basis for the struggle between the coast-wise sections for power. In the Virginia Ratification Convention of 1787, William Grayson, who was not a radical member said: "I look upon this as a contest for empire. . . . If the Mississippi be shut up, emigrations will be stopped entirely. There will be no new states formed on the western waters. . . . This contest of the Mississippi involves this great national contest; that is, whether one part of the continent shall govern the other. The Northern States have the majority, and will endeavor to retain it."[5]

. . . .

At first the northeastern states, particularly New England, were

[5] Elliot, ed. *The Debates in the Several State Conventions*, III (Washington, D.C., 1836), 365. Following this quotation is the sentence fragment "To

56

menaced by the way in which the South increased its power by means of new western states. The migration of the South and particularly of the southern upland had spread the population of that section north of the Ohio into the southern counties of Ohio, Indiana, and Illinois, as well as into Kentucky, Tennessee and Missouri, and into the Gulf basin, western Georgia, Alabama, Mississippi, Louisiana and Arkansas. New England had been settling the northern states of that section, Maine, New Hampshire and Vermont, had spread its population into western New York and later she had begun northern settlement in Ohio at Marietta and had occupied the western reserve. But by the time of the war of 1812 New England was still but slightly represented in the north central states and the middle region still found its own wilderness sufficient to engage its attention. It was, therefore, opposed to the rapid expansion of settlement not only because of the loss of its people and the differences that existed between westerners and itself, but even more because the West seemed to New England to be a recruiting ground for the South in the struggle for power. Among the proposals of the Hartford Convention of 1815 was that there should be a constitutional amendment providing that no new state should be admitted into the Union without the assent of two-thirds of both houses of Congress. This would have given New England, reinforced by two other states in the Senate, a power to prevent the formation of further states in the West. Professor Morison, in his *Harrison Gray Otis*, has published the schedules of Nathan Dane, the secretary of the Hartford Convention, wherein he showed that in the commercial states capital had been invested in commerce, and in the slave-holding states in western lands. When, he said, "Kentucky, Ohio & Tennessee — were raised up by this interest, & admitted into the Union — then the balance was, materially, affected . . . . Then these non commercial States pressed the admission of Louisiana" and turned the balance against the Northeast. He reasoned, therefore, that "if a bare majority in Congress can admit new States into the union, (all interior ones as they must be) at pleasure,

Monroe of Virginia, later President of the United States," and a blank numbered page.

in these immense Western regions, the balance of the union, as once fairly contemplated, must soon be destroyed."[6] There is abundant evidence that the extreme Federalists desired a new union in friendly relations with Great Britain. They dreamt of a reorganization of the Old Thirteen by which the South should lose its two-thirds representation for the slaves and the West should be allowed to fall to the victorious arms of Great Britain and thus to cease to be a menace. The victory of Jackson at New Orleans was a surprise to them. The Mississippi Valley remained within the Union, New England found in the growing West a new market for her manufactures which developed as her sea power declined, and New England people poured so rapidly into the northern half of the valley that there was established a zone of the Yankee stock, a greater New England which reached to the prairies and the shores of the Great Lakes. As a result the South began to take alarm. The formation of the Free Soil party, the Wilmot Proviso, the discontent of the northern democracy when the South failed to support their demands for Oregon up to fifty-four forty or fight, the resistance of the North to the annexation of Texas — all these things created in the South much the same sort of sectional alarm over western power that had been felt earlier by New England. "I have very great fears," wrote Justice Campbell, later of the Federal Supreme Court from Mobile in 1847, to Calhoun, "that the existing territories of the United States will prove too much for our government. The wild and turbulent conduct of the western members upon the Oregon question and their rapacity and greediness in all matters connected with the appropriation of the revenues induces great doubt of the propriety of introducing new States in the Union so fast as we do. . . . Their notions are freer their impulses stronger their wills less restrained. I do not wish to increase the number till the New States already admitted to the Union become civilized."[7]

[6] Samuel Eliot Morison, *The Life and Letters of Harrison Gray Otis, Federalist, 1765-1848* (Boston, 1913), II, 195. Turner's copy, a gift from Morison, is HEH Rare Book 138323.

[7] John A. Campbell to Calhoun, Nov. 20, 1847, in *Correspondence of John C. Calhoun,* ed. J. Franklin Jameson (Washington, D.C., 1900), p. 1141.

In commerce as well as in politics there had long been in progress a contest between the rival sections for ascendancy over the trade of the Mississippi Valley. The rival cities of the coast representing the rival sections had engaged in a contest of canal and railroad building intended to drain the rich commerce of the interior into one or another of the sections.

It must not be supposed that the West was intended to remain a tributary section either in politics or in commercial life, or even in literary lines. Senator Douglas of Illinois spoke for the West when he denied that the South had any share in the territory or the North or any other geographical division unknown to the constitution. Expecting that there would be seventeen new free states, Douglas argued that the theory of an equilibrium to be obtained by checking the growth of the West or by dividing it as the spoils of sectional warfare was a visionary one. St. Louis, Memphis and Chicago became the leaders of new western advances toward the Pacific Coast, and it was believed by a St. Louis journal that "a line of cities will arise on the banks of the Mississippi that will far eclipse those on the Atlantic coast."

This aspect of the West as a reservoir for power in the contests of rival sections is one of the most persistent features of American history. Of course it is most obvious in the slavery struggle between North and South, but it was by no means limited to that even during the period prior to the Civil War and since that war the same phenomenon is to be observed on other issues as the maps which I shall show you will reveal.

Before leaving the subject of western sectional influence I must speak of one other aspect of the frontier advance. American society passed into the interior not as a dense and highly organized population with a solid impact upon the wilderness. As is well known, it came in a series of waves corresponding to relative density of population and by consequence to different stages of economic growth. At the risk of saying to you what you already know I venture to remind you that the hunter and the fur trader who pushed into the Indian country were followed by the cattle raiser and he by the pioneer farmer whose family constituted a self-sufficing economic unit, without an interest in a market because they produced little or no surplus, raising their own food, weaving their own clothing. When this stage passed on to the remoter West, this household industry was replaced by more intensive farming and the raising of a surplus for export. The intensive farmer living in a frame house replaced the backwoodsman in his log cabin. Soon the banker came, the lawyer, the journalist, the doctor, and more complex society in general. Then followed urban life, manufactures, industrialism.

These stages were not sharply defined, they intermingled and shaded into each other and sometimes stages which I have not mentioned appeared in regions especially suited to them, for example, mining. By reason of these successive waves of economic life, what was at one time a southern pioneer society of poor whites raising wheat and corn became later a planters' society based on slavery and cotton cultivation. What was once a northern wheat zone became later a dairy or mixed farming or a manufacturing zone. The fur trading stage of the great plains was replaced by the cattle raising stage after the conquest of the Indians and the destruction of the buffalo. The great cattle ranches in turn gave way to the homesteader, and he was replaced by the bonanza farmer, or by the oil driller, etc. As these economic transformations occurred, statesmen who grew up with the changes changed their policies and voiced the demands of their changed society. Thus Calhoun, the child of pioneer parents, was a nationalist at the time of the war of 1812, anxious to reveal the full power of the central government. But in the later twenties when the region in which he lived had become a cotton planting, slave holding section, whose interests were threatened by the power of the other sections in Congress, he became the prophet of minority rights, of sectionalism, of the South against the nation.

In the years before the war of 1812, Henry Clay wore homespun clothes and supported homespun policies. No one expressed more antagonism to the Bank of the United States than did he. But when his Kentucky blue grass land passed from pioneer conditions to those of a planting gentry, interested in transportation, in manufactures, and in bank credit, Clay developed his American system in which the National Bank was one of the corner stones.

In the days when New England was dominated by commerce and by agricultural interests, Daniel Webster was a supporter of free trade. He took distinctly the Federalist position in the war of 1812, but when his constituents transferred their investments from the harbors to the waterfalls, from the ocean to the interior, when, in short, New England found that she needed a national government which should favor her manufactures by a protective system, and which should hold the nation together, and permit interstate trade, Webster became the champion of national consolidation and of the protective tariff.

On the other hand, statesmen like William Jennings Bryan, whose family had been pioneers from the colonial days, and who himself joined in the march toward the West, kept steadily in frontier society, first in the frontier state of Illinois; then when that region was passing away from frontier influences, he went to Nebraska while frontier ideals still dominated his state. He remained a frontiersman in his policies.

There has been, therefore, a sectionalism of relative density of population, of stages of economic development. In order properly to estimate the importance of the individual statesman in shaping American policies, we must give due consideration to these sectional transformations which shaped his course. His very inconsistencies were, in many cases, the real consistencies which came from representing the interest of his section. He was the outcome of deep-seated sectional changes, not the inconsistent and capricious exponent of contradictory policies.

This aspect of migratory and changing sectionalism has not yet ended. Important regions of the United States are still undergoing economic changes. There are frontiers of farming life, frontiers of urban life, frontiers of highly developed industrialism. Considering this aspect of America the question arises whether the westward march of industrialism, the increasing density of population, will wipe out the sectionalism arising from contests between East and West and will obliterate the factor of transforming sectionalism under the influence of these waves of economic change. Will the nation become all eastern in its quality? To President Coolidge, as his speech of last November shows, the United States seems likely to become an industrial nation, importing its supplies of food and resources and facing the problem of maintaining a prosperous, self reliant, confident agriculture in a country preponderantly commercial and industrial.

This brings us to a consideration of the natural physiographic regions in the United States. It brings us to a reconsideration of the fact that we are equal in area and in variety of resources not to a single nation of Europe, but to all Europe. Our agriculture, our manufacturing, our mining, our wealth are vastly greater than those of any other nation, greater, indeed, in some of these items than all of Europe. We are forced to think of ourselves continentally to compare our sections to European nations. It will be impossible for us to derive unlimited imports of food and raw material from the other parts of the earth. Europe itself is obliged to import much of its supplies. Only in this way has Europe been able to attain its present population. The American population is gaining upon that of Europe and it will not be long before we have reached the limit of population on our present standard of living, our present birth rate, and our present self-sufficing economic life. If, therefore, there are great regions in America especially suited to agricultural production, it is unlikely that industrial transformation will flow across these regions. We shall need food producing sections and certain great regions will be more suitable for agriculture than for manufactures. Whether the relationship will be that of a partnership between industrial and agricultural life or whether industrial society will give the dominant tone to America, only the future can tell.

But it seems certain that the natural differences of geographic regions in the United States will be emphasized as time goes on. There will be a decline in the movement of inter-state migration, men will be more accustomed to living provincially in their own section; the improvement of transportation will assist in breaking down the importance of the state, the radio will diminish localism, but the very fact that we are continental in our breadth will probably continue to emphasize the section as the state declines. It is at least worth consideration that in Europe the improvement of transportation facilities between nations, the increasing density of population, the multiplication of points of intercourse and by consequence points of friction have served rather to foster nationalism and subjects for controversy than the reverse.

That sectionalism is not dying away in the United States will be clear enough to anyone who examines the newspapers and reads the debates in Congress, not to speak of analysing the votes in that body. A common congressman was bold enough in 1908 to suggest that "if New England could be ceded to Canada, the legislative difficulties of the country would be cut in half." A leading Boston newspaper said, in 1912, "Let us not forget that the influence long exercised by New England in both houses of Congress to the great advantage of this section has resulted in powerful combination against us in business as well as in politics." Two or three years ago one of the leading Boston papers said, "The New England states have different governments and are separate and distinct political organizations, but they are bound together by geographic, historic, political and industrial interests. What helps one New England state in the shape of legislation originating in Washington helps all the New England states. What injures one New England state in the shape of legislation originating at Washington, will hurt all the New England states." "While certain artificial limitations exist between all the New England states," says another Boston editor, "there are no real barriers between them; essentially they are one." Western insurgency, the Progressive movement, the farmers' bloc, the movement led by La Follette, these and similar indications are all evidences that a north central group exists and especially the western half are restive under the leadership of New England in the Republican party and will hereafter demand more thoughtful consideration of their interests and their rights. In an editorial in the Chicago *Tribune*, discussing the decision of the Supreme Court against the claim of the Sanitary District of Chicago to divert water from Lake Michigan without the permission of the Secretary of War, occurs this language, "It is time for Chicago, Illinois, and the entire Mississippi Valley, to rise in revolt against a tyranny which now threatens its very existence. . . . This is neither a conquered country nor a colony, but an integral part of a nation and as such entitled to the same consideration afforded to New England and

63

to New York." The editor demanded a filibuster by his section to prevent the Houses of Congress from organizing and in another editorial in the same issue, under the title "The West is West, but the East is London," he exclaimed, "It is natural that the East should turn to London, for London policy is Atlantic policy," and he speaks of "London and its provinces in Montreal, Boston, New York and Washington."

Fortunately the north central states did not respond to this appeal to create a Congressional chaos and did not follow the editor in reading New York and New England out of the United States and into the realm of London. Indeed, some of the most violent protests against Chicago's diversion of the waters of the Great Lakes came from the north central states themselves. It is unnecessary to point out that there is a so-called solid South. If there were time to discuss southern sectionalism I should like to go over with you the evidence that the South is not and never has been so solid as has been supposed and that a great wedge of northern industrialism pushes down from the North into the heart of the South. If it were not for the problem of the Negro the solidity of the South would long ago have completely broken. But as the case stands the South still remains a section. In this connection I cannot refrain from quoting the words of Thomas Jefferson when he was informed early in the nineteenth century that the Northeast felt that the union with the South was doomed to fail. "It is true," he said, "that we are completely under the saddle of Massachusetts and Connecticut, and that they ride us very hard, cruelly insulting our feelings, as well as exhausting our strength and subsistence. Their natural friends, the three other eastern States, join them from a sort of family pride, and they have the art to divide certain other parts of the Union, so as to make use of them to govern the whole." But, "Seeing," said Jefferson, "that an association of men who will not quarrel with one another is a thing which never yet existed . . . seeing that we must have somebody to quarrel with, I had rather keep our New England associates for that purpose, than to see our bickerings transferred to others. They are circumscribed within such narrow limits, and their population so full, that their numbers will ever be the minority, and they are marked, like the Jews, with

64

such a perversity of character, as to constitute, from that circumstance, the natural division of our parties."[8]

It will be observed that although Jefferson does not extoll New England he permits her to remain within the Union.

Let us next inquire what the natural regions of the United States are. Let me recur to the fact that the spaces involved are imperial, the north central states alone could in area make room for all the powers which fought in the World War on the side of Germany; or for all the European territory of Spain, Portugal, Belgium, Roumania, the United Kingdom, Italy and France combined. Even the single state of Texas is larger than Germany before the war, and it could supply the space for seventeen of the smaller European nations. The Old Thirteen Atlantic states are greater in area than the homelands of England, France and Italy combined. The factor of space, therefore, necessarily bulks very large in American history. Basing their divisions primarily on geology, the geographers divide this vast American area into physiographic regions, such as the New England province, the Piedmont province, the Gulf plains, the lake and prairie plains, the great plains, etc.[9]

Across these geographic provinces have flowed the tides of settlement from the differing sections which I have mentioned on the Atlantic coast. The United States Census Office, influenced primarily by the statistician and the economist dealing with these facts of migration, enumerates another set of divisions or sections: the North Atlantic, made up of New England and the middle Atlantic states; the South Atlantic, the North Central and the South Central, each divided into two parts lying east and west of the Mississippi; the Mountain Division and the Pacific Division. Roughly speaking these census divisions also conform to popular usage which designates New England, the Middle States, the South, the Middle West, the Far West. In popular speech also, there are such subdivisions

[8] Jefferson to John Taylor, June 1, 1798, in *The Writings of Thomas Jefferson*, ed. Paul Leicester Ford, VII (New York, 1896), 263-265.

[9] Turner's footnote: "See *Annals of the Association of American Geographers*, VI, 1916, 19-98 and map [Nevin M. Fenneman, "Physiographic Divisions of the United States"]; also [Armin Kohl] Lobeck, *Physiographic Diagram of the United States* [(Madison?), 1922]."

as the Cotton Belt, the Border States, the Corn Belt, the Inland Empire, and Arid America. The Interstate Commerce Commission, the Federal Reserve Bank System, and various advertising agencies and regional organizations each have their own sectional mapping, all of which differ in detail but resemble each other in the large. The geographers' provinces loosely coincide with those of the Census Office. But the human factor has been at work on these geological provinces. Generally speaking they lie in zones running in a northerly and southerly direction while migration has tended from East to West athwart them. By consequence, sometimes a Census division is made up of several geographic provinces. Moreover, within the larger divisions there are such minor subdivisions as the Lexington Basin or the Kentucky Bluegrass, the Nashville Basin, the Appalachian Valley, the non-glaciated regions north of the Ohio, and the glaciated lands which constitute a kind of enlarged Great Lake Basin with lobes corresponding to the shore line of the Great Lakes themselves and bounded on the south by the terminal moraine, a kind of New England stone wall marking the outer edge of the glaciers. This terminal moraine between the older and newer ice sheets has marked and continues to mark definite social and party subdivisions, definite soil areas, and contrasting groups of counties in the matter of wealth.

Then there is the Black Belt in the Lower South, running from the Piedmont in South Carolina in a band across Georgia and Alabama, with the kindred region of rich alluvial soils along the lower Mississippi.

Most of the political and economic history of such states as Kentucky, Tennessee, Missouri, Illinois, Indiana, Alabama and Mississippi can be written in terms of geology. Indeed, it is only by full recognition of these geographic regions that we can understand the division of political parties within these states and their social structure. In the Mississippi Basin the regions of richest soils tended to be Whig or in the North in later years Republican. These regions of rich soils are also those of least white illiteracy, of relative density of population, of higher farm values, of greater wealth. On the other hand, the less fertile lands tend to the reverse of all this. But there are sufficient exceptions to prevent any interpretation of politi-

66

cal history on the basis exclusively of geography or of economic determination. The human factor has also to be reckoned with. But it is well to recall that these subdivisions within the larger sections sometimes constitute minority and dissenting regions which prevent the complete operation of the larger sections, particularly since the great sections are often very closely divided in elections.

At times, also, the attitude of the large section is shaped by the superior energy and intelligence of these nucleal lands in their midst. Such, for example, was sometimes the case in the South Central division, where Henry Clay in his Bluegrass kingdom exercised sway over unlike areas in that division. These factors will appear more clearly when I shall show you the lantern slides as I am soon to do. Before this, however, I must also note that there are degrees and kinds of sectionalism.

1. A section may act under hatred of other sections, and may forcibly demand independence. It may carry self-determination to the extreme of civil war as did the slave holding South.

2. A section may coincide with a party. This will result from resistance to the domination of another section or sections when they completely control the machinery of the victorious party. Obviously, this type of sectionalism cannot be successful short of the use of force because it is by its very nature a minority section unwilling to make sacrifices and combinations. As a rule it is a step in reorganization of parties.

3. Within the same party a section may possess the instruments of legislative power such as the speakership, the chairmanships of important committees, etc. If this ruling section has sought to use its power primarily for its own advantage, party voting will often give way to sectional voting, to the formation of alliances or working agreements between the aggrieved sectional wings, or blocs may be formed as for example by the union of insurgent Republicans in the West-North Central states with the Democratic South, or as in the case of the northern Democrats of the North Central states who voted for the Wilmot Proviso or the Randall Democrats of Pennsylvania who voted with Northeastern Republicans for a protective tariff. Though often called by names indicative of eco-

67

nomic interests, or class divisions, they are almost always sectional in composition.

4. Another type of political party sectionalism may manifest itself only in preliminary voting, as on separate schedules or a tariff bill, or on amendments to a bill, or on third readings. Having thus recorded its protest, the minority section may unite in a final vote under party pressure and loyalty. Where this occurs, there has, however, usually been a process of log-rolling, of bargaining between this and other divisions, as an agreement to vote for tariff in return for appropriations. Since it is only under great sectional stress that representatives or senators will break their party allegiance, sacrifice their right to promotion in the organization, and endanger appropriations from their districts as well as forfeit support from the campaign funds of the party, it is surprising to find as much sectional revolt as appears when the votes in Congress are analyzed geographically.

5. There is also a sectionalism in economic interests, in business, manufacture, agriculture, transportation, and even in social characteristics and ideals as expressed in popular traits, in public opinion, in literature, and even in religion. Often these are more deep seated and influential than the sectionalism which is shown in votes in Congress. For example, it is significant that the North Atlantic states have all but a small amount of the woolen manufactures of the nation, and that of these Massachusetts has a lion's share. But the great wool raising states are in the Far West, together with certain counties in Ohio and Michigan. Schedule K was the basis for a sectional tariff division between these two regions. Three fourths of the nation's boots and shoes are made in the North Atlantic states and nearly one-half were made in Massachusetts. But the supply of domestic hides came from the western states. Of the capital invested in manufactures nearly one-half is in the North Atlantic division. The east-north Central and the North Atlantic together reported three fourths of the total. In 1920 over half the income and profits tax was paid by the North Atlantic states.

Such facts as this make it certain that there will be sectional discontent over legislation; that the richer sections will feel that they are exploited for the benefit of the country as a whole in such bills

68

as those for good roads, maternity laws, etc. The demand of the states along the Great Lakes for a deep water way by way of the St. Lawrence to the ocean will be resisted by New England in behalf of the port of Boston and by the harbor of New York on the plea that the Erie Canal should be improved instead of allowing any portion of our western trade to pass through Canada and thus be subject to unfriendly legislation by that power in cases of disagreements. The final consideration to which I invite your attention arises from the fact that a section is seldom aware of the fact that it is acting sectionally. The triumphant section will conceive that its own form of society and its own interests are best for the nation as a whole, and that the opposing sections are the ones that are acting un-nationally. Similar assumptions will be made by the aggrieved sections, who will feel that their natural rights are being sacrificed not to a national end but for the benefit of an exploiting section which happens to be in control.

We are all of us disposed to think in terms of our own section, to believe that the nation and our own section are in fact the same thing. This makes of nationalism in fact a sectional mirage. In a nation made up of so many contrasting and in many ways conflicting sections it is highly important that we should not think in terms of our section alone, that we should realize that a pattern must be discovered and accepted which will provide for the various other sections of which the nation is composed. The preservation of the American peace is dependent upon an attitude of mind which accepts compromise and concession. Such an attitude is not inconsistent with sectional rights, but it is absolutely essential in a nation which is in reality a federation of sections.

❧ LECTURE ON POLITICAL MAPS[1]

The existence of persistent and non-accidental political areas seems to be demonstrated by these maps.

To give the explanation for each region and particularly for a given county at a particular election is very difficult, and usually impossible with scientific certainty. The path of interpretation in this case is beset with pitfalls. In the first place there is the fact that the issues themselves are usually somewhat too confused for a simple explanation. Politicians tend to make the planks in their platforms sufficiently numerous and varied and often sufficiently ambiguous to allow the party following to march together under various flags if not under a common banner. Leaders are often selected who do not sympathise with the platform. In the earlier period there were no formal platforms, simply general tendencies and a party record. Men often vote for a candidate regardless of the party platform, and especially for a "favorite son."

In respect to issues, however, it may be said that while in each election the issue and the candidate affects the total majority, it affects the distribution of majorities very much less, owing to the inertia of political habit in so large a part of the community where the practice prevails of taking one's politics like his religion from his father and passing it on to his son; and through a series of elections particular variations in issues tend to correct themselves, and to leave the general party attitude the significant thing.

When one takes up the local geographic conditions the difficulties are even more evident. So numerous are the factors that may have determined majority action that the interpreter may select his favorite from a crowd of candidates and, by choosing one here and another there, make a plausible case. The temptation to self

[1] MS: HEH, TU File Drawer 10, one of several items in folder marked "Notes for a Talk on Political Maps, circa 1920." Accompanying notes in the folder date the writing in the 1920's. Pagination indicates that the manuscript was taken from a lengthy essay which included the next piece on "Democratic and Whig-Republican Areas in Presidential Elections."

deception here is great, and the complexity of the problem a very real difficulty. Let us take specific illustrations.

Is the persistent Whig-Republican area on the shores of Lake Erie in New York and Ohio the geographic expression of good harbors and commercial influence? Or is it the outcome of the political inertia of the New England settlers who occupied western New York, the Connecticut Reserve and adjacent districts late in the eighteenth and early in the nineteenth century? Is it purely accidental that this earlier area of Whig interests under a primarily agricultural regime coincides with the Republican area under a dominantly manufacturing regime?

When one attempts to explain Perry County, Tennessee in 1836, as a Whig county in a region which on general considerations should be democratic by the fact that in the census of 1840 it is reported as among the few counties of Tennessee having a considerable capital invested in iron mining, he is confronted by the fact that Stewart County in which there was the heaviest investment in iron mining was democratic. If one attempts to explain the democratic vote for Van Buren in Tennessee in 1836 as the vote of the back country farmer raising corn and wheat and tobacco in a varied agriculture, and chiefly by free labor, he is met again by the fact that East Tennessee is the very home of that type of Tennessee farmer, and it voted for Van Buren's opponent, White, while at the same time the heaviest slave holding cotton raising counties, located chiefly in the extreme west of Tennessee, also voted for White, although one of the heaviest cotton counties in that district voted for Van Buren. Under these conditions it is necessary to turn to additional considerations. Hugh Lawson White was East Tennessee's favorite son; he had been a supporter of Jacksonian Democracy and in 1836 he professed to be still a democrat and a better exponent of the original democratic principles on which Jackson won his first election than Jackson himself, and he was able to appeal to State pride and prejudice against a northern candidate. But these considerations which are plausible enough and valid in some degree, no doubt, are limited by the fact that even after this particular election Eastern Tennessee continued dominantly Whig as also in later years Republican. I am inclined to explain this

71

chiefly by the superior transportation facilities of the Whig Republican area of East Tennessee as compared with the Democratic areas. West Tennessee is in a geographic sense merely the extension of the Mississippi alluvial cotton belt and black belt and it also tended to continue Whig, except for the counties within it least given to cotton cultivation and slave labor. In attempting to limit our problem by closer analysis also we are met by difficulties of lack of data. If a large producing cotton county goes democratic, one needs to enquire whether the production was in the hands of few men who controlled many slaves but not their neighbor's vote; or whether there was a potential majority of small farmers, which under normal cotton belt conditions would be swayed by the leadership of the great planters, but in the particular case was led by some effective politician in the opposition. Or was there some factor quite apart from cotton, or slavery, as for example a local economic disaster making hard times or a retrograde population in an area generally advancing in population, and thus an island of discontent; or the fact that this county was a recent settlement by democratic colonists; or was there a monopoly of political influence by some of the cotton counties neighbor to this one, and so revolt; or in spite of large cotton production was there perhaps some other and dominating interest. In a word one must first observe whether the political status is a durable one; if so he must take note of the possibility that the dominant influence at one period may not be the same as that at a later period, though the political result is the same in each case; one must adopt the geologist's use of the multiple hypothesis to explain complex areas; and must not attempt to give a decisive reason for the political complexion of a given county at a given election. Observing a series of elections, however, and noting the relation of this county to a sisterhood of counties behaving in a similar way, and where one can eliminate from the mass of them the conflicting element that made uncertainty for the particular county, one may reach certain fairly safe general considerations. These should be tested by such remains of contemporary opinion as we possess in the press, memorials to Congress, speeches, correspondence, etc. Frequently these all agree and constitute the basis for reasonable certainty as to causes. But very much remains to be done in the intensive study of the physical conditions, distribution of votes by precincts, and historical data on opinion, leadership etc., before a satisfactory scientific judgement can be pronounced.

It seems certain however that the geography of American politics demands combined research by geographers, economists, political scientists, sociologists and historians, for in matters relating to human development the field is a unit and needs cooperative study.

❧ DEMOCRATIC AND WHIG-REPUBLICAN AREAS IN PRESIDENTIAL ELECTIONS[1]

There are areas which persist for decades in which there is a normal majority or plurality for the same party or for parties having fundamentally like programmes. There is a real geography of politics. The most obvious distribution is into the North and South.

The Northern Whig-Republican area is broken chiefly by Democratic groups of counties in the back country of Pennsylvania and the Catskill area of New York, the central highlands of Ohio, an island in northwest Ohio and northeast Indiana, certain vertical columns of counties in Indiana, the wooded area of Illinois, and the German area of Wisconsin. As the silver question rises the new western mining states and the wheat area of Minnesota, Kansas, Nebraska and the Dakotas break away first into populism and then waver toward Democracy. The general tendency is for Republican strength to lie along the areas of communication and manufacturing. In the Great Lake zone and the prairie parts of the Old Northwest these are the regions settled by New England--New York stock. The Democratic areas in this Old Northwest tend to reflect the

[1] MS: HEH, TU File Drawer 10, one of several items in folder marked "Notes for a Talk on Political Maps, circa 1920." From the evidence in accompanying notes in the folder, the essay appears to have been written in the 1920's. Pagination shows that the essay was at one time part of a longer piece, which included the preceding "Lecture on Political Maps."

Southern upland migrations particularly in Missouri. But there is a strong Republican area in Missouri and Illinois about St. Louis as a center, possibly influenced by Germans.

In the South

In the Whig Democratic period from about 1836 to 1852 the Whig area is chiefly the Black Belt; and parts of the Appalachians. The Democratic counties of the lower south are the nonslaveholders counties of the northern zone of Georgia and Alabama and the eastern counties of Mississippi, while the Whigs are strongest in the black prairie belt of interior lowland north of the cuesta and in the alluvial cotton raising area along the Mississippi in Mississippi and Tennessee, together with the counties along the South of Alabama, Mississippi and Georgia where the alluvial margins of rivers allow cotton and slavery in the midst of a generally non slaveholding population of the land barrens of the coastal plain. Tennessee has three distinct areas — the Whig cotton raising west, the mixed cotton, corn and varied agriculture of middle Tennessee, where the Whigs tend to be stronger in the limestone area, and the Democrats in the enclosing region of harder rocks; and East Tennessee which tends strongly to Whig, with exceptions in the distinctly wheat raising counties.

After the war there is a period when the Negro vote carries the former cotton raising Piedmont and alluvial lands into the Republican camp; but following the reconstruction era the Southern Republican area is almost eliminated except for the Republican area of the Appalachians. Here the tendency is marked for the counties in those portions of the mountains where there are few Negroes and where there is also excellent facilities for communication,[2] particularly along the lines of the Railroads of the Tennessee Valley, Cumberland Gap and Southeast Kentucky, to go Republican and [for] this peninsula of northern types of the farmer, and of industrial development generally, to extend and take in adjoining counties. But among the mountain whites of West Virginia (except the Kanawha Valley), South West Virginia and Western North Carolina this is a tardy growth, though unmistakable. One is inclined

[2] Turner's marginal note: "The Tennessee river trying to express itself."

74

to associate it with the extension of northern capital into mining areas and to the textile mills of the mountains in the recent period. The old blue grass island in the midst of the hard rocks of Kentucky, where the slaveholders were more numerous and where the Virginia type of settler and of society was established at an early date, is resistant, remaining Democratic when the hard rocks about it become the abode of Republicans.

Perhaps the most suggestive fact is (1) the relation between the Whig-Republican party and the areas of settlers of New England ancestry, chiefly along the Great Lakes, and the Prairies of the eastern part of the North Central states. These areas are also from combined influences of geography and social origins, regions of manufacture, property, and capitalistic influences in general; and (2) the relation between Democracy and the areas of settlers of Southern upland extraction, originally coming in considerable degree by migrations from the north into the Piedmont region, and then occupying the counties adjacent to the Ohio ascending into the interior of Indiana as a hunter folk, and entering the wooded valley of the Illinois and ascending the Missouri. This is chiefly a pioneer farming stock responsive to the argument for simplicity and individualism, a conservative democracy of the common man, resistant to industrial society of the manufacturing and city type and to the tendencies of modern capitalism. The segregation of groups in the South on lines of soils, slaveholding and cotton raising into democratic poor whites and Whig planters has already been sufficiently discussed.

I have refrained from attacking the problem of the city which is too complicated a topic for discussion at this time.

We may assert therefore as proven
1. That there is a real geographical arrangement of political majorities in American elections.
2. That this is not accidental but the sections bear relations to underlying influences and that there are transition areas between the strongest opposing areas.
3. That these divisions are fairly stable, persisting in some cases for at least half a century and illustrating the fact of habit in voting.

4. Absolute geographic control cannot be asserted; certainly not in any direct and immediate form of control. The same geographic area under similar conditions in respect to issues changes its attitude, sometimes no doubt by considerations of the personality of the candidate, sometimes by the influence of new leadership, organization, or possibly corruption.[3] Areas similar geographically but differing in the stocks of the original settlers or under influence of leadership vote opposite majorities in many cases. Church affiliation sometimes shapes the action of a region. In short the geographic influence is most obvious where there is the strongest political inertia, and weakest in regions where the result is determined by reflection and conscious decision. The fact that the majority may be very great or very small and the areas remain the same makes the appearance of control in the maps somewhat deceptive and leaves play for independent voting; moreover through the series of maps the minority of white concealed by the majority of black, or the reverse, must always be borne in mind. But the striking fact is the usually small percentage of the majority. Professor Giddings has made this the theme of his valuable paper on the Conduct of Political Majorities[4] in which he points out that no national political majority is likely to be a compact and oppressive numerical majority but rather what Calhoun called a concurrent majority of more or less dissimilar local group interests loosely bound together and exhibiting such a low percentage of majority in the localities as to make the combination one of unstable equilibrium, difficult to maintain while carrying out a drastic national program.

5. But a geographic aspect there clearly is in American politics; and whether this tendency to geographic adjustment is a growing one as the nation settles down to a less migratory type of population and industry and under stable conditions allows

[3] Turner's marginal note: "Kentucky Blue Grass reverses before and after."

[4] Franklin H. Giddings, "The Nature and Conduct of Political Majorities," *Political Science Quarterly*, VII (1892), 116-132. Giddings stresses the need for sociologists to study political parties and on p. 132 maintains: "A political majority . . . has a nature that can be described in terms of the laws of social psychology."

sectional influences freer play, on the one hand; or whether the tendency will be counteracted and destroyed by the forces of national uniformity, seen in the development of means of communication, the wider national circulation of news agencies, etc., can not be asserted with confidence. Whatever is to be the future there is in our history and at present very convincing evidence that party grouping and legislation is deeply influenced by geographic factors.

CLASS AND SECTIONAL STRUGGLES[1]

Sectional contests are not inconsistent with class contests — to a considerable extent the American class struggle is itself sectional. The sections in which both capitalism and labor are most self conscious are the North Atlantic and the Mountain states, and they are frequently allied under capitalist influence. The Negro problem and cotton culture distinguish the agricultural South, especially the Lower South, from the grain raising agricultural West North Central States. But they have an economic class interest in common as the Farmers Bloc indicated. The East North Central constitute a section in which the distinguishing feature is the interpenetration of agriculture and manufacture, with a strong rural middle class as check upon the labor contest.

One can imagine such an expansive power of North Atlantic capitalism as might transform the East North Central into a section more like that of the older North Atlantic. Community of interests might be established between such trusts, or combinations as the Steel Trust, the Oil Trust, the Railroads, and perhaps the Automobiles, the Banks, the Mine operators, as would extend the capitalistic type as a great zone across North Atlantic and East North

[1] MS: HEH, TU File Drawer 14, folder marked "Sections — Kinds and Degrees — Class and Sectional Struggles." There is evidence to suggest that this essay was written as an introduction to a chapter for a book. Contents of the manuscript date it early in the 1920's.

Central states. But of course there would be a corresponding extension of labor organization. In view of the demand for food, and the suitability of large parts of this fertile North Central section for agriculture, aside from the inherited qualities and ideals of its people, it could never become quite assimilated to the North Atlantic type. But assume that it did. We should have as a result only a larger section, and sharper conflicts between the capitalist and the agricultural type of other sections. Interesting questions might then arise over redistribution of political power. The eighteen senators of the North Atlantic would combine with the ten from the East North Central, to make twenty eight of the fifty six — just half. They would control over half the nation's population as it stands today. With them would perhaps join in common capitalistic interests the wedge of districts along the Alleghanies to the South with its apex at Atlanta, and Birmingham, — the dagger of iron, coal and textile manufacture thrust into the Agricultural South. Population now increases more rapidly in highly industrialized sections than in rural lands. But this is conditioned upon the supply of food and material. Herein lies the certainty of contests between these hypothetically combined capitalistic sections and the other sections of the United States. If these other sections became an exploited minority group, they would cry out, would seek recruits among the agricultural interests within the East North Central wing. These interests might hold a balance of power. At any rate sectional contest and sectional compromise would not disappear from the picture of American society.

Let us imagine on the other hand the reverse outcome, the triumph of Bolshevistic labor ideas. New England might then divide into Northern and Southern halves according to its economic interests. Assume a combination of Southern New England, the Middle States, and West Virginia, with radical miners of the Mountain states, and of the Middle West. Add for full measure a Negro revolution in the South. What would happen? Would not race antagonism afford grounds for sectional divergence between Northeast and South? Would not the Pacific Coast and West North Central states join to resist agricultural expropriation? Russian experience would seem to say so.

2

❧ The Complexity of History

TWO OF THE FOUR PIECES *included under this heading were com-*
posed as introductions to classroom lectures at Harvard, and
two were appraisals of writings by other historians. The first two
are lecture fragments which summarize for us Turner's conscious-
ness of the difficulties in attempting to appraise historic truth: the
complexity of forces, the mass of evidence, or lack of it, bias in the
witnesses, bias of the society, the nearness of the event to the pres-
ent time, bias in one's own ideas and in the ideas of one's own
society — all of these and more interfere with the best-intentioned
searcher after historic truth. Turner knows that he cannot circum-
vent all of these problems, but he nevertheless hopes that by broad-
ening his field, by breaking down interdisciplinary barriers, and by
puncturing watertight compartments, he can include economic,
social, and geographic factors in his historical thinking. Moreover,
he strives to give his students fair and meticulous accounts of con-
troversial questions as he explores with them the interaction of his-
torical forces.

Imagine, then, the indignation of such a man who, believing it of
paramount importance to scholarship to avoid narrowness and dog-
matism, comes upon evidence of just these qualities in two highly
esteemed practitioners of his own profession. Von Holst's **The**

Constitutional and Political History of the United States, *stressing the struggle over slavery as the key interpretation of American history, offended Turner by ignoring the infinitely complex historical phenomena in the development of American democracy. Unfortunately, the reader detects in Turner's critique of Von Holst's work a minor, but clear, tone of outrage that a foreigner should have presumed to write a United States history. Even worse, Henry Adams and Henry Cabot Lodge said it was the best work of its kind that had appeared; no American could have done as well. Yet Turner's very human pique was obviously secondary to his professional assessment of what he considered to be a work distorting American history. It is in discussing these distortions that Turner provides us with an exciting description of what he believes to be the best kind of historical scholarship. Here we are given a thorough explanation of the complexity of "the frontier process" as well as other "processes" in American history.*

Turner had respect and, indeed, admiration for his old friend, Charles M. Andrews, as a historian. Nevertheless, he rejects Andrews' idea that colonial American history is best studied from the viewpoint of the mother country, believing, as one would expect, that such an approach was only one among many and, applied in isolation, might distort rather than enlighten.

These four pieces, then, provide us both with a description of Turner's views concerning the complexity of history and with illustrations of the manner in which these views influenced his attitude toward historical writing.

ON OPENING A NEW COURSE[1]

In this class I have students from South as well as North, and doubtless students from all minor sections. I have, it may be assumed, democrats, republicans, progressives, socialists, prohibitionists, etc.,

[1] MS: HEH, TU File Drawer 15, folder marked "Turner, on opening a new course, 1924." The manuscript is undated.

as well as the indifferents. Under these circumstances it is a matter of regret that such a brief course requires at times summary statement, of conclusions without the detailed examination in class of the reasons for the conclusion — the examination of the historical evidence, the analysis of the problems, often complex, the limitations of the general statement. I am aware that only by such an examination in the spirit of historical fairmindedness can a conclusion be made effective upon your minds, or produce the effects of historical study as a mental training. Two courses are open (1) to state various views on disputed points, and refrain from a conclusion. This does not appeal to me as a rule of action. The other to state my conclusions, with frank concession that they are often on controverted points, and briefly to suggest some of the points in dispute. You will take what I say therefore as an attempt to reach the truth, but subject to the difficulties, particularly as we reach our own time, which any scholar encounters by reason of conflicting evidence, at times the mass of the evidence, and at other times the lack of it, the prejudices of the witnesses, the prepossessions of the society in which the speaker has lived, the nearness of the events dealt with. Time alone can furnish a satisfactory answer to many of the questions with which we have to deal; by furnishing new material, by exhibiting the outcome of forces and policies whose full meaning can only thus be revealed.

With this premise let us consider the question of the right of secession.

OPENING REMARKS AT THE BEGINNING OF A COURSE ON THE HISTORY OF THE UNITED STATES, 1880-1920[1]

Introduction

My desire to close my teaching experience with the recent history.

[1] MS: HEH, TU Box 56, folder marked "1924, Feb., Notes for opening remarks at beginning of his course on the History of the U.S., 1880-1920, in his

Definitions of History: more than past politics; see my "Social Forces" (1910); self-consciousness — understanding present by past.

Difficulties of the period. *Recent* and so exposed to prejudice: class, region and section, party (habit), nationalism. Lack manuscript — inside view. But these manuscripts are rather questions of detail — not of large tendencies. Such detail always uncertain.

Complexity of the recent forces. But opportunity for breaking line-fences, destroying water tight compartments. Try to get general view.

I give the course because I know too little of the period. Want to know more. No period of like years more important. And I am offering you a chance to go along on the excursion, an opportunity to read: 1. Text book; 2. Biographies, Writings, Congressional Documents (a mine), Newspapers and magazines; 3. Study a topic more intensively.

Result at least a general survey and a deepening at one or more points, and a realization of interaction of forces of all kinds to make our age — and its periods.

We must take account of economics; but this is not a course on that subject, or an economic history — per se. Same of government and politics and other fields.

The point of view is the contribution in each of the fields to the common historical tendency and the respective influence of each in the various periods.

Assume that you are interested because you take the work. Midterm, final examinations — others if I wish. Read in advance — about 1 [presidential] administration per week besides text 120 pp. Thesis (3000 to 6000 words) due May 10. At least two biographies or autobiographies of importance.

Outcome of Western movement. When I began its study and why. My *Frontier*. Stages — sketch *1880-1900*. Outcome . . . .[2]

---

final year of teaching at Harvard." Turner's reference to his last year of teaching dates this manuscript 1923-24.

[2] Turner at this point outlines in headings the "outcome" of the westward movement, with mention of topics such as "land," "population," "cost of living," "labor and immigration" ("volume and change in origin and destination and quality"), and "strikes."

Resume — United States has such and such fractions of total world resources, wealth, etc., minerals, crops, etc., world gold — United States ½? *But* it is reaching the saturation point — quote alarms.

Blackwoods, 1821 — A century ago an English critic remarked: "Others appeal to history: an American appeals to prophesy; and with Malthus in one hand and a map of the back country in the other, he boldly defies us to a comparison with America as she is to be."[3]

This a text. Show census map of 1820.

Looking back over my work as a University teacher, which ends this year, I find that the central interest of my study has been that of these maps of population advance. Not as a student of a region, but of a process. From cave-man to the occupation of the planet. Study of American advance required examination of the geographic, economic, social, diplomatic advances of the frontier, leading to a paper on *Significance of the Frontier in American History*, published 1893, to studies of the diplomatic contest for the Mississippi Valley, to examination of the Sectional aspects of the advance into new geographic areas, which compelled me to study conditions in the various Atlantic Coast regions leading to migration, and into the effects of the newer regions upon these older ones, and to study the special geographic problems into which the various zones of advance brought new societies — the interaction of the various migrating stocks each in its particular geographic province, adjusting to new social types, and the resulting play of sectional forces in American politics as the old and the new sections found in Congress and in party the need of adjustment or the impulse to conflict.

As a result I have been led to a study of the various sections of the United States, both internally and in their mutual relations with each other and the federal government.

Thus by proceeding from the study of the frontier and of the section I have approached the history of the United States from

[3] The editor has not been able to find this quotation in *Blackwoods Edinburgh Magazine* for 1821.

somewhat different angles than my predecessors, but I have found it necessary to consider the history as a whole, not as the history of the West by itself.

Nevertheless I have always been interested deeply in the relation between geography and population historically considered. I began my professorship about the same year that the Superintendent of the Census announced, in 1890, that the frontier line could no longer be traced on the map[4] — and I close it with a remarkable flood of studies (most of them the aftermath of the studies in production and the food supply and the natural resources of the United States in particular and the earth in general) concerned with the relation of population to the resources for maintaining it.

Interestingly, this output of books and articles comes at a time when the census reports of the United States show that urban population (2,500+) exceeds the rural population for the first time, and that great cities, of over 250,000 population, contain over one-fifth the people of the Union, while one-third of the counties of the Union have declined in population since 1910. Large areas of wheat farmers are in such distress, owing to the fall in the price of wheat due to the decline in the effective European demand for export, that they are calling on the federal government for aid.

And yet the group of scientists, including many of the most competent in their particular fields, are warning the United States of a coming catastrophy due to the approaching insufficiency of food and natural resources to sustain the increasing population.[5]

---

[4] Turner's interlinear note: "[Show 1870, '80, '90], ca. 100 years after Massachusetts, Connecticut and Virginia designated frontier towns or forts by law."

[5] Turner's notes follow in outline form with this comment on population growth: "Beginning to grow *vertically;* show Sky Scrapers." His outline deals with the changes experienced in the United States, first by topical "stages" and then by chronological periods, and it ends with the world view and a prediction of possible "limitations" on population.

❧ DR. VON HOLST'S HISTORY OF THE UNITED STATES[1]

On the occasion of the appearance of Professor von Holst's *Constitutional History of the United States,* Henry Adams, and Henry Cabot Lodge, in *North American Review* of October 1876, declared:

"Such a work was greatly needed, and it is mortifying to be obliged to confess that we know of no American who could have done it equally well. After the flood of trash which England and France have poured out with little variety for a century past on America and her institutions, it is beyond measure refreshing to find at last a man who knows what he is talking about and who attacks his subject in a way that commands respect. . . . This book deserves to be and will doubtless become the recognized handbook for all serious students of American history."[2]

Since then the American writers Schouler and MacMaster have entered the field to cover the same epoch as Dr. von Holst, and the nine volume work of Henry Adams himself on the administrations of Jefferson and Madison has appeared, not to mention handbooks like the works of Hart and Wilson in the Epochs of Ameri-

---

[1] MS: HEH, TU File Drawer 15, folder marked "Essay on History of U.S. by Von Holst, 189-." Note in Turner's handwriting on first page: "About 1889-90?" Parts of the essay may have been written before 1890; but internal evidence indicates a portion of it was written after 1893, perhaps even as late as 1896. On April 8, 1896, William Peterfield Trent, editor of the *Sewanee Review,* wrote Turner: "By the way don't forget your promise to fix up part of your Von Holst paper into an article for me. I still remember it as admirable & I should very much like to have it." TU Box 2.

[2] CXXIII (1876), 328, 329. Notes accompanying the manuscript show that Turner had also been reading John W. Burgess, "Von Holst's Public Law of the United States," *Political Science Quarterly,* I (1886), 612-635; Albert Bushnell Hart, "Hermann von Holst," ibid., V (1890), 677-687; Albion W. Small's review of Vols. IV and V of Von Holst's *The Constitutional and Political History* in *Baptist Quarterly Review,* VIII (1886), 423-429; and a number of reviews of Von Holst's writings by William F. Allen in the *Nation.*

can History Series. The work of Dr. von Holst has now been completed to 1861, translated, and published in seven volumes aggregating over three thousand large pages, and equipped with an additional volume giving the index. The 7th volume was issued 1892. Since Dr. von Holst's first volume appeared in Germany over 20 years have passed — years that have steadily carried us away from the epoch of the civil war, and disclosed more and more the real tendencies of American history.

Perhaps it is not unfitting that the question should be raised, has the great reputation which the work made for its author been sustained, and is it likely to remain "the recognized hand book for all serious students of American history"? Particularly is the question germane in view of the fact that Professor von Holst has himself transferred his home to the American democracy of which he has been so keen a critic. After having given repeated refusals to the Johns Hopkins University he has at last yielded to the persuasions of President Harper, and taken up his abode at Chicago.

His career is a remarkable one. He was at least American in the sense of having risen by his efforts from obscurity. He was born in 1841 the son of a poor German parson in Livonia. Having taken his degree of Ph.D. at Heidelberg, he went in 1866 to a tutorship in St. Petersburg. But for his liberal speeches he was excluded from Russia and in 1867 came in the steerage as an emigrant to America. Here he engaged in multifarious occupations, from manual labor to editorial work on the *Deutsch Amerikanisches Conversations-Lexicon*.[3] He soon became a student of American politics.

At first he had come with idealistic views of the nation. Laboulaye, so he says, was the butler who had filled his knapsack of expectation.[4] The reader of his books finds it hard to believe him when he says that at first America was enveloped for him in the misty vagueness of a grand and wonderful fairy tale. But before long he got acquainted with Tammany Hall. He found that America was but one scene in the drama of western civilization. He felt him-

[3] Ed. Alexander J. Schem (New York, 1869-74).

[4] Edouard René Lefebvre Laboulaye (1811-83), French jurist and author of *Histoire politique des Etats-Unis . . . 1620-1789*, 3 vols. (Paris, 1855-66).

Dr. Von Holst's History of the United States.

About 1889-90? Never publ.

On the occasion of the appearance of Professor von. Holst's Constitutional History of the United States, (North American Review of October 1896, through Henry Adams, and Henry Cabot Lodge) declared:

"Such a work was greatly needed, and it is mortifying to be obliged to confess that we know of no American who could have done it equally well. After the flood of trash which England and France have poured out for a century past on America and her institutions, it is beyond measure refreshing to find at last a man who knows what he is talking about and who attacks his subject in a way that commands respect.... This book deserves to be and will doubtless become the recognized hand book for all serious students of American history—"

Since then the American writers Schouler and MacMaster have entered the field to cover the same epoch as Von Holst, and the nine volume work of Henry Adams on the administrations of Jefferson and Madison has appeared, not to mention handbooks like the works of Hart and Wilson in the Epoch of Am. History

The First Page of Turner's Essay "Dr. Von Holst's History of the United States" self standing in the fresh and clear air of stern historical truth. At this time he was recommended by von Sybel the German historian to a number of Bremen men who desired to have an account of the workings of popular government, designed to aid in reorganizing Germany under the North German Confederation. He began by proposing to present a picture of the American society of the type of Bryce's *American Commonwealth*. But he found that his studies must first produce a different work. He must trace the origins of the America he found before him. Therefore he proposed for his life work a magnum opus: "The Constitution and Democracy of the United States of America." Three distinct parts were to be embraced in this work. To the first part as projected by him I call your particular attention, for in his statement he lays down the purpose of the work we are now reviewing. He says that the first part had for its aim to deal with the inner history of the United States, so far as it has to do with the development and the comprehension of the Constitutional law and democracy. The second part would expound the Constitutional Law. The third, the existing political and social-political conditions. The first part of his work is completed to 1861, the second in an abridged form appears in his contribution to Marquardsen's *Handbuch des Offentlichen Rechts*.[5] It is doubtful if the third part will ever be written. Since the days when Dr. von Holst began his work Bryce has covered the second and third parts of the scheme in his *American Commonwealth* and thereby corrected in Europe many of the erroneous notions which De Tocqueville's *Democracy in America* gave rise to, and which appears to have been one of the reasons for the work which von Holst proposed. It is not likely that the learned author will attempt a rivalry in Dr. Bryce's field.

I desire now to call attention to several facts.

1. The period in which Dr. von Holst formed his impressions of America was that exceptional period of demoralization immediately following the war — the era of the carpet bagger, the whiskey ring, the era of Fiske and Tweed, Credit Mobilier, Star route frauds, and all that corruption in high places at which the nation was aghast. To

[5] Heinrich von Marquardsen, *Handbuch* . . . (Freiburg, 1887 ff.).

a writer who gained his impressions from this period American democracy would certainly prove depressing.

2. The environment under which Dr. von Holst studied America in person was New York City; and Tammany hall loomed in the foreground with portentous outlines. With the healthy democracy of the country and the west he was not familiar.

3. The historical friend who gave the impetus to his work was von Sybel, the great Prussian archivist and historian, who belonged to what Lord Acton calls "that central band of writers and states-men and soldiers, who turned the tide that had run for six hundred years and conquered the centrifugal forces that had reigned in Germany longer than the Commons have sat at Westminster." Von Holst was called to be a member of the faculty of the University of Strassburg — that child of the victory of Prussia and German centralization in the Franco-Prussian War — travelled on a stipend furnished by [the] Royal Prussian Academy of Science. He left America at a time when here also the forces of nationalism were celebrating the victories of the Civil War. Thus his mind was dom-inated by nationalism rather than by federalism, not to mention particularism. To the man of this age the nation was conceived as unitary in fact, whatever it might be in theory.

4. He had lived in Europe which was a plenum — where oppos-ing forces contended, without room for expansion and growth. In America he lived on the Atlantic coast and so did not realize in actual life the great fact of American Expansion. It was not until 1878-9 after he had completed the first two volumes of his work bringing our history to 1846, he visited as he tells us "the parts of the union not yet known to him — the southern states and the terri-tory west of the Mississippi," spending a year in the travels.

I have thus outlined the background of his experiences because it seems to me that they are important to one who would under-stand the tone of his history. In addition to the points already mentioned it may be said that Dr. von Holst is by nature analytical and critical in his treatment.[6] He is of the oratorical and dogmatic

[6] Deletion by Turner: "The natural critical bent of his mind has perhaps been emphasized by the fact that he has long been a sufferer from chronic indi-gestion."

temperament also and once convinced of the truth of his views is full of vigor and determination in his presentation of them. He has had practical legislative experience in Baden having been for many years a member of the upper legislative chamber, and at one time a candidate for parliament on the national liberal ticket. This practical experience has doubtless been of very great value to him in his work as a historian of politics — and an expounder of public law.

From some points of view Dr. von Holst's qualifications for writing a history of the U.S. are extraordinarily good. He was trained in the critical German method of research and the use of authorities; he may be said to have been the first to apply this method to the period of U.S. history which he treats; he has combined experience in public life with his labors as a historian; he is not entirely unfamiliar with American life: besides his five years residence and subsequent travels, he married an American wife — a Vassar girl. As a foreigner he should perhaps be free from bias an observer who could look at his subject objectively.

On the other hand there are dangers in each one of these qualifications. The power of critical use of original source has led him to too great dependence on printed texts, and particularly on government documents like the *Congressional Globe* — as a final source. An active part in politics leads to the argumentative rather than the judicial and purely scientific frame of mind; a few years of American residence in a restricted region might give a confidence in one's knowledge of American conditions that would be narrow and misleading. New York and New England people often speak of a thing as un-American when they mean that it differs from the practice of those limited areas. The European inheritances and environment leave their own prejudices — the unitary state, the stationary populations, the rule of classes, bureaucracy, lack of popular activity except in a revolutionary way — these are some of the difficulties. Certainly a German is no more likely to judge impartially as to the merits of Negro slavery in the 19th century than most Americans. His judgement is apt to be the harsher, he never having experienced the practical difficulties in the way of removing this deep seated economic organization.

The author himself appears to recognize this difficulty. In the preface to the first volume he declares that he has one great advantage over all his American predecessors in being a foreigner. He realizes that he may some times miss the exact mark because his flesh and blood are not filled with that indefinable something called national sentiment, but the foreigner on the other hand has only to ward off his prejudices, not the difficulties arising from national sentiment. But in the preface to his concluding volume he admits that "an essential precondition of a satisfactory solution of the problem was a constant and intimate association with the intellectual life of the American nation in its living, progressive development in all its phases and in its every direction; and," he adds, "this precondition could not, in the nature of things, be fulfilled to the extent required and in the right way, in a university of southern Germany and in a city of medium size."[7]

The task which Professor von Holst proposed to himself it will be remembered was the explanation of American Constitutional characteristics, and the American democracy. He began his task as a historical introduction to a proposed survey of the social and political conditions of the United States of 1783, having reached the conclusion that such a historical background was essential to a right understanding of existing conditions. He proposed to consider those parts of our history which explained American democracy and its political organization.

The question which I now propose is — What topics were fundamental to such an explanation. Making a survey of the existing U.S., and selecting its main features, we find that to an adequate explanation of the nation an historical account of at least the following processes is essential.

1. The evolution of a composite nationality — the race question. It is plain that if the English constitution were put into French hands it would operate differently. Race affects politics.
2. The existence of an independent American continent, free from the European state system of which it was a part in colonial days.[8]

[7] "An Open Letter to Dr. Heinrich von Sybel. (In lieu of the Preface)," *The Constitutional and Political History*, Vol. [VII]: 1859-61 (Chicago, 1892), iv-v.

[8] Turner's interlinear note "cf Sumner's Hamilton" refers to William G. Sum-

3. The spread of settlement steadily westward, and all the economic, social and political changes involved in the existence of a belt of free land at the edge of settlement; the continual settling of successive belts of land; the evolution of these successive areas of settlement through the various stages of backwoods life, ranching, pioneer farming, scientific farming, and manufacturing life. I have written of the importance of this view of our [history].[9]

. . . .

5. The evolution of a complex industrial organization in place of the simple agricultural life of the colonies.
6. The slavery struggle and the Negro suffrage problem.
7. The evolution of sectionalism, and state particularism, and the final triumph of nationalism. Nevertheless sectionalism was simply subordinated, not exterminated. Sectionalism means, moreover, not simply North and South, but New England, the Middle Region, the South and the West up to the time of the war.
8. The evolution of political institutions to meet these changes and contentions, the development of the constitution by construction, and by usage — such as the growth of committee government, the power of the speaker, the machinery of nomination, the extension of the power of interstate commerce to the new conditions involved in railroad transportation, etc. All that series of unobserved amendments of the constitution due to changes in the character of the objects entrusted to Congress. It was one thing to grant power over the interstate commerce carried by sloop, packhorse, and Conestoga wagon. It is another to grant power over interstate commerce carried on by railroad, steam boat, and, perhaps, the flying machine. In this connection also the student of the Constitutional history of U.S. who would compare our political development with

---

ner, *Alexander Hamilton* (New York, [1890]). Sumner in the second chapter of his biography touches on the thesis Turner mentions.

[9] Turner has removed a page in the manuscript, which undoubtedly dealt with point "4."

development of European nations must take account of the political history and constitutional changes of the various states, for it has been shown that out of 12 greatest subjects of legislation which have engaged England during this century only *one* would have come before Congress under the constitution as it was before the war. The rest would have fallen to state legislatures.

Summing up, an American history that should correctly interpret American political life — to say nothing of economic and social life — should deal with at least these great historical processes:

1. The evolution of a composite non-English nationality.
2. The movement away from the European state system; the rise of an American system.
3. The movement westward, including the management of the public domain, and the question of free lands.
4. The democratic movement.
5. The industrial transformations.
6. The slavery struggle.
7. The struggle of particularism, and sectionalism with nationalism.
8. The growth of the constitution by evolution of political institutions unprovided, by constitution and by the transformation of institutions provided for, by construction of the various departments of government, and by the modifications of the State Constitutions.

Each of these 8 processes is related to the others, and the list might properly be extended. I lay down the proposition that a history which aims to explain American democracy in the broad sense given to the word by De Tocqueville and von Holst, and which aims to explain and criticise the workings of the American Constitution must take account of at least these categories.

I fear that I may have wearied you in this enumeration. But the enumeration was essential to my purpose, for the main criticism which I am compelled to offer on the *Constitutional History* of Dr. von Holst is that it is not a constitutional history of the U.S. at all, but rather a history of the slavery struggle. Later I shall have something to say upon the merits of the work as a history of that struggle,

93

but first it is necessary to show how far the work is from being a constitutional history of this country.

In my opinion more harm may be done by an improper perspective or by omissions, than by defects in regard to accuracy of statement. If I aim to describe an elephant, and give only an account of his feet, alleging at the same time that this constitutes the elephant, the microscopic accuracy and keenness of criticism of these organs will not atone for the failure to speak of the rest of the animal.[10]

Professor von Holst has written the Constitutional history of the U.S. in seven volumes. The first volume, under the title *Constitution and Democracy of the U.S.A.*, extended [from] 1750 to 1832 (82 years).

The second extended from 1828 to 1846 — 18 years, the third 1846-50, the fourth 1850 to 1854, the fifth 1854-1856 (2 years), the sixth 1856 to 1859, and the 7th 1859 to 1861. The first two volumes covered the period from 1750 to 1846 — about a century; the remaining five volumes cover the period 1846 to 1861, about 15 years, or an average of about 3 years to a volume. Obviously there is a decided lack of proportion here — and there is a reason for the lack of proportion. Doubtless it is due in part to the growth of the author's own material, and to his increased grasp of detail. But there is a deeper reason. To Professor von Holst, American history is primarily the struggle of the slavery interest allied with State Sovereignty against the Nation; and secondarily it is the rise of party government and the politicians by the great mistake of 1829 whereby Jackson defeated John Quincy Adams. He is the prophet who stands in the market place and denounces the Planter, the particularist, and the politician, demands their destruction, and berates the public for not seeing the iniquity of all three. He leaves almost entirely out of consideration the other categories.

To Dr. von Holst, the question of State Sovereignty was settled by the Constitution in 1787. Evidences of particularism are therefore to be chastised as indications of the perversity and lack of logic

[10] Deletion by Turner: "Nor will it do to speak even of the feet or the trunk as seen simply in a state of rest. Unless I describe them in *action* and in *growth*, I have failed to describe the organ."

of American statesmen who were absurdly inconsistent in not accepting their own work. Particularism, to him, is an adjunct to slavery, and the warfare of the north and the south over this question constitutes our history. Acting on these assumptions he is able to compress our first century into two volumes, while he devotes the other five to the fifteen years of the slavery struggle.

But the period of 1750 to 1846 was the formative period of American history. After the interlude of the slavery struggle, American history returned to the lines laid down in this first period. Again the legislation turned on the development of the interior, and on questions arising from this movement west. In the period skimmed over in Dr. von Holst's first volume, the South did its great work for the nation. In a speech delivered in the senate of the U.S. in 1858, Hammond of S.C. was able to make this proud boast: "You complain of the rule of the South: that has been another cause that has preserved you. We have kept the Government conservative to the great purposes of the Government. We have placed her, and kept her, upon the Constitution; and that has been the cause of your peace and prosperity. The Senator from New York says that that is about to be at an end; that you intend to take the Government from us; that it will pass from our hands. Perhaps what he says is true; it may be; but do not forget — it can never be forgotten; it is written on the brightest page of human history — that we, the slaveholders of the South, took our country in her infancy; and, after ruling her for sixty out of the seventy years of her existence, we shall surrender her to you without a stain upon her honor, boundless in prosperity, incalculable in her strength the wonder and the admiration of the world. Time will show what you will make of her; but no time can ever diminish our glory or your responsibility."[11]

It is a pertinent question whether Dr. von Holst does justice to the southern Slavocrats by compressing into two volumes the half century which gave the evidences for this assertion of Senator Hammond. If he was to attack the South, he should at least have written the record of her earlier statesmanship in an appreciative way. Not

[11] James H. Hammond, remarks on bill for admission of Kansas, *Congressional Globe*, 35th Congress, 1st Session, March 4, 1858, p. 962.

only was the century 1750-1846 the era when the South showed its best statesmanship: it was the period which saw the colonies pass from isolated settlements, to settlements tied together by industrial intercourse through turnpike, steamboat and railway; from maritime colonies hugging the Atlantic coast to an inland power that found its center of gravity along the Mississippi Valley; from a people who could say "a state is my country" to a people who felt the throbs of national patriotism, and who were ready to lay down their lives for this ideal. "Physics prevailed over metaphysics" in this period. If this period be slighted the whole strength and historical validity of particularism is neglected. And it is just this error that Dr. von Holst makes. He starts with an assumption instead of an investigation.

The political effects of the immigrant, with some condemnations of the Irish and some kind words for the Germans, are considered in connection with the know-nothing agitation; but the effects of the influx of untrained immigrants upon the delicate balance of American political organization and theory he does not adequately treat. He treats our diplomatic history inadequately. It is true that whenever it becomes involved in party contentions he gives a sufficient account of it to explain the party action, but as a rule his diplomatic history is a pendant to his slavery discussion. It comes in as a part of the "unseen workings of slavery." Doubtless slavery was a factor, too, in a large part of our diplomacy, but this should not conceal from our eyes the fact that every nation, whether slave holding or not, aims to extend its territory, and has diplomatic contentions with foreign states. It is legitimate for the author of the history of the Slave Power to write his history of diplomatic action from the point of view of slavery. But even if this were the dominant influence in the diplomacy the historian of American democracy should endeavor to construct his account so as to show the action of a Democracy in Diplomacy. It cannot be said that Dr. von Holst does this. He treats the subject from the point of view of slavery — even to the extent of making our acquisitions of territory depend largely on the interests of slavery. But history will not agree that Oregon was demanded simply as an offset to Texas — a white pawn for a black one. The acquisition of Western territory was something besides the game of chess between Southern and Northern politicians. It was possible for these politicians to play their game exactly because of the expansiveness of the American people. Movement west was their very life. The slavery struggle was incidental to this expansion. This is the first thing to deal with. I cannot but lament the utter failure of the author to see the importance of this great fact of westward migration. Here was a nation which for four centuries from the time of Columbus was engaged in winning a wilderness. As I have said in another paper: "Up to our own day American history has been in a large degree the history of the colonization of the Great West. The existence of an area of free land its continuous recession, and the advance of American settlement westward, explain American development.

"Behind institutions, behind constitutional forms and modifications, lie the vital forces that call these organs into life and shape them to meet changing conditions. The peculiarity of American institutions is, the fact that they have been compelled to adapt themselves to the changes of an expanding people — to the changes involved in crossing a continent, in winning a wilderness, and in developing at each area of this progress out of the primitive economic and political conditions of the frontier into the complexity of city life. . . . Even the slavery struggle, which is made so exclusive an object of attention by writers like Professor von Holst, occupies its important place in American history because of its relation to westward expansion."[12]

As Woodrow Wilson has said: It was not "an issue of morals simply, made up between the New England conscience and the South. It was a question made up, in fact, between the South and the West. It was the men whom Lincoln represented, and not the anti-slavery societies, that pushed the question to a settlement. The New England conscience would have worked *in vacuo* if there had been no territories and no intense and expanding western life."[13]

A writer whose aim was primarily the explanation of American

[12] Quoted from "The Significance of the Frontier in American History," in *The Frontier in American History*, pp. 1-2, 3.

[13] Woodrow Wilson, "Mr. Goldwin Smith's 'Views' on Our Political History," *Forum*, XVI (1893-94), 497.

democracy might certainly have been expected to give some adequate account of the steps and causes which placed this democracy in power, and of the methods by which its will was formulated. This is perhaps the crucial test of the permanent value of his work. No amount of homily against the radical democracy, and the rule of politicians, no amount of laments that at this time the people took a "downhill road on which turning is ever hard, & in the best of cases can be only very gradual," will help us here. If this rise of popular power was a disease, which now "broke out" as the tory historian wrote of the first Legislative Assembly of Virginia, — the wise historian must correctly diagnose the disease before he applies the remedy. But what if the disease prove rather the birth pangs of a man child!

Here is Dr. von Holst's explanation of the origin of the disease of democracy in this country:

"Jackson was the man of the masses, because by his origin and his whole course of development both inner and outer, he belonged to them.

"From the mass of the population in the southern states there arose an aristocracy of large landed proprietors and slave holders, and in the northeastern states a bourgeoisie composed of merchants, those engaged in industrial pursuits and the followers of the learned professions. The struggle for political supremacy had thus far been carried on by these two strata of the population; and the plebs, with political rights, as a rule did no more than furnish the common soldiery with which the leaders fought their battles. But the heat of party struggles and their vicissitudes had already taught this same plebs, and well enough, that the power was in their hands, and that it only depended on their will, whether they would actually exercise it themselves or not. The construction of the state was based on the assumption that they were equal to the task, and the talk of their leaders had gradually clothed the theory of popular sovereignty in such a garb, that its literal execution and the idea of the republic and of freedom seemed to be coincident. All that was wanting to change the desire of making the actual condition of things harmonize better with theory, into a resolve, was an exciting cause in the shape of an opportunity. This opportunity was afforded by

Jackson's candidacy, for his name was already a very noticeable one in the history of his country. It was not the victorious general, but the man of the people . . . . "[14]

. . . .

How much more complicated a process is this than that assumed by von Holst! It shows these faults in his method:

1. A failure to take note of the expansion of settlement, the changes of population and the readjustment of political power and the extension of the franchise to correspond with this.

2. A failure to note the effect of free land in promoting democracy.

3. A failure to note the political effects of changed industrial conditions.

4. A failure to note the rise to power of the middle region. This region not being devoted to slavery, and not being filled with New England anti slavery agitation, drops from his scheme of American history though it is in fact the typical American region which most demands study.

5. A failure to give an account of the rise and influence of that most important portion of our unwritten constitution — the nominating convention. There is a beautiful example of the evolution of an institution here but it cannot be studied from the *Congressional Record*. It is possible instead to berate the trading politician on general principles, however.

6. Failure to study changes in State Constitutions.

7. These misapprehensions and omissions vitiated his whole conception of American democracy, for they show that it was the product of the existence of free land, and that it grew as the country marched toward the west. The rise of this democracy was no lapse

[14] Quoted from *The Constitutional and Political History*, Vol. [III]: 1828-46 (Chicago, 1881), 3-4. In Turner's copy of this volume, HEH Rare Book 212060, are his marginalia protesting Von Holst's interpretations (pp. 4, 19): "Inattention to *West*"; "Total misapprehension. The people were rising to self conscious activity. It is true that they did not rise *full cultured;* the phenomenon was not of a decline in political activity and interest but a rise of the common people with all their deficiencies to self conscious power."

Turner removed several pages from the manuscript at this point. After a sentence fragment ("machinery of the movement"), the essay resumes.

of the people from aristocratic virtue to be scolded at. It was the rise of the people to economic and consequently to political power and self-consciousness.[15] It had its difficulties and its dangers. It meant individualism, with the fear of overgovernment and the danger of losing adequate administration thereby. It meant a lowering for the time of the tone of state craft — the dominance of the politician — the contempt for European experience. But it meant life and growth in self-government, and at bottom this western democracy was as healthy as it was rude and energetic. It offers few warnings and few examples to European democracy for it was born from conditions that can never be possible to Europe. It was a democracy that came not from the political theorists' dreams of the primitive German forest. It came stark and strong and full of life from the American forest.

A single example must suffice to illustrate this historian's defects in failing to take account of varied and changing industrial conditions in relation to politics.

He always treats the South as a whole in discussions of slavery and southern political views. What are the facts. In the middle of the 18th century the entire region of the south beyond tidewater was occupied by small farmers, predominantly of Scotch-Irish and German stock, thrifty pioneers of the Pennsylvania type. The tobacco and indigo planting aristocracy constituted the slave holding tidewater region. Thus there were two distinct belts, the tidewater ruling the interior. But tobacco planting began to decline at the period of the Revolution and corn culture began to take its place. Abolitionist sentiment in Virginia and Maryland became prevalent, and it looked for a time as though these regions would be assimilated to the middle region. This was the period of the Old Dominion statesmen who ruled the early nation. It accounts for a large share of American politics of the period. But there came the invention of cotton textile machinery in England, the industrial

[15] Deletion by Turner: "Thank God for it." Marginal note: "It was not a 'shallowing, demoralizing, materializing transformation of the American democracy'" (a reference to Von Holst's concluding sentence in his chapter "The Reign of Andrew Jackson," *The Constitutional and Political History*, [III], 79).

revolution followed, and a demand for cotton arose. The cotton gin enabled slave labor to supply this. Slave farming began to move into the cotton areas of the midland region of the South; the states of the Gulf and lower Mississippi were settled by this economic force. This called out the demand for Texas, a demand which would have come whether cotton was cultivated by slaves or by free labor. The previous antagonism between the tidewater slaveholders and the interior farmer broke down. The south became united on an industrial issue. It was all slaveholding now. Before this the slaveholding region of the coast in Virginia and South Carolina had gerrymandered the state to protect slave property against legislative attack by taxation on the part of the more numerous West. As they became a continually diminished fraction of the population the tidewater planters had demanded more and more the control of the legislature to protect their rights. But under the influence of the spread of cotton culture by slave labor the south became solidified, and needed as a *section* the same minority protection that the tidewater portion had previously insisted on.

Thus Calhoun following these changed conditions ceased to attend to internal improvements, and other national legislation, and began to fashion with exquisite skill the chain of logic with which he proposed to bind the giant of nationalism. In this economic and social transformation lies the explanation and the defense of the systematic particularism which the South formulated. To expel slavery by the sword seemed to mean the disruption of the nation — a dreadful calamity. Such a tragedy as this needs a more sympathetic historian than von Holst.

I have taken this one illustration as a type to show von Holst misrepresents and treats superficially our political history by failing to get beyond the printed texts of public documents to the life of the people. The method is applicable in countless directions with the same result.

I come next to Dr. von Holst's failure to unite the history of development of American political institutions. The student who goes to him for a history of the evolution of party machinery, the nominating convention, the power of the speaker, committee government, the modification of the electoral system, the extension of the franchise, legislative apportionments, the spoils system, the management of the public domain, and so on will come back disappointed. Perhaps this is to be expected. But what shall be said of his total neglect of changes in State constitutions, as if these were no part of our political organism. More than this, what shall be said of his failure to realize the fundamental importance of the federal judiciary in the construction and development of the constitution. John Marshall was one of the most effective makers of the nation. In the work of nationalizing the constitution he was unexcelled. Dr. von Holst makes 12 references to him scattered through his seven volumes. Most of these references are mere footnotes. No one is a paragraph in length. One would hardly realize that there was a supreme court from the perusal of Dr. von Holst's history. It is not until he reaches the Dred Scott case that it rises to the dignity of extended criticism at his acrid pen.

It will doubtless be a relief to you to find that in my opinion Dr. von Holst does have much to say upon two of my categories of American history. Slavery and state sovereignty he treats *in extenso*.

I shall be obliged to content myself at the present time with brief reference to his treatment of the state sovereignty question, leaving for a future paper[16] the criticism of his characterization of public men, and his treatment of the history of the slavery struggle. I do this with less reluctance believing that discussion will bring out criticisms from those more competent than I to pass upon these points.

State sovereignty is but a part of a larger problem: sectionalism. To rightly interpret it, the author must trace the evolution of the various sections. Dr. von Holst does not do this; and he practically leaves two sections entirely out of his scheme of American history — the Middle States and the West.

The historian of state sovereignty must start with a firm grasp of the fact that the whole history of this country up to the beginning of the nation shows the dominance of particularism. Not even England was to be allowed to step within the charmed circle that enclosed the internal polity of the colony. With the declaration of

[16] Apparently never written; not found in HEH Turner papers.

independence the colonies destroyed the only organization that served as an effective central authority. In the revolution and the confederation state sovereignty was triumphant and was guarded as the very palladium of individual liberty. The constitution was framed by men in advance of the nation and consent to it was wrung from the grinding necessities of a reluctant people. To use the coarser expression of Callendar, "it was crammed down the gullet of America."[17] But it was only accepted on the statement that it was a government of restricted powers. The states were conceived as sovereign in respect to all powers not delegated, the nation sovereign in respect to limited powers assigned to it. There was believed to be two sovereignties with distinct spheres. As Elsworth[18] of Connecticut put it, "Each legislature has its province, their limits may be distinguished. If they will run foul of each other, if they will be trying who has the hardest head, it cannot be helped. The road is broad enough but if two men will jostle each other the fault is not in the road." At the period of the making of the constitution, the function of a supreme court as the committee of experts to interpret the constitution and set the meets and bounds of sovereignty had not been long in existence. Outside of the states it was unparalleled among all the nations of the earth. That interpretations affecting sovereignty should be decided in ordinary cases between man and man could certainly not be realized by the public. The constitution was deemed so much an experiment that the dangers to state sovereignty were not serious. The real danger was that each state would be a law to itself. The people of that age made no sharp limitations between the right of revolution and the purely legal and formal right of changing their institutions as provided by the constitution. As a question of purely legal construction of the constitu-

[17] Turner probably quotes James Thomson Callender (1758-1803), political writer.

[18] Oliver Ellsworth (1745-1807), statesman, chief justice, and delegate to the Constitutional Convention. This appears to be a quotation from Jonathan Elliot, ed. *The Debates in the Several State Conventions*, Vol. V: *Debates on the Adoption of the Federal Constitution* (Washington, D.C., 1845). Turner's copy of the book, HEH Rare Book 119890 [Vol. II], has marginalia opposite a number of statements by Ellsworth, but the editor has not found this passage.

tion I am inclined to agree with von Holst that the supreme court was made by it the final arbiter. But this would have been a worthless advantage if the states had remained in the position of power and in the frame of mind that they held when the constitution was accepted. Dr. von Holst assumes national sovereignty from the beginning.[19]

This is strong language but there is much truth in it. It was only after the transforming forces of economic nationalism and western growth had played upon the American people that the present doctrine with regard to the relation of states and nation became any thing more than a magnificent perspective. Doubtless sooner than allow the general government to coerce a group of states the men of 1789 would have shivered the union into fragments. National sentiment and power was a plant of slow growth.

Von Holst has missed this point of view, and his work therefore loses the opportunity of picturing the splendid spectacle of the real growth of national sentiment. Instead he is forced to contemptuous criticism of the American people for having framed a nation, and being unaware of what they had done.

---

[19] Turner's note at the end of this sentence: "Quote Small page 425 *Baptist Q[uarterly] Review*, [Vol.] 8." Here, in his lengthy review of Von Holst's Vols. IV and V, Small comments on the origins of "state-sovereignty and nationality" in the United States: "When the issue between state-sovereignty and nationality shall have been investigated by the generation to which the controversy is not politics, but history, the view to which von Holst is a pervert will be repudiated as emptying our national experience of its profoundest meaning. If according to this myth, American nationality sprung full-grown into life, the century whose politics von Holst professes to interpret was a period of disgraceful retrogression. If our unity was a kind of political immaculate conception, then indeed we plunged from purity into a national debauch that lasted nine decades."

WHAT IS COLONIAL HISTORY?[1]

Recently one of our distinguished colleagues has urged upon the attention of this Society a greater attention to the distinctly colonial aspects of the history of Massachusetts viewed as a part of the English empire.[2] He lays the stress upon the mother country and the relations between the colonies and that country. In other words, Professor Andrews would "study the colonies from some point outside of themselves," and he believes that "to the scholar there is only one point of observation, that of the mother country from which they came and to whom they were legally subject."[3]

If the contention is simply that in a study of colonies as colonies, in an enquiry into the colony of Massachusetts as a dependency of the British Empire, there is need of more thorough research both upon English conditions and the relations of the colonies thereto, few students would deny the importance of this view point. Nor is it to be doubted that there is in the British archives which this able scholar has listed for us under the auspices of the Carnegie Institution a mass of material as yet insufficiently explored for both administrative and economic history.

One may go farther and gladly assent to a proposition that there is need of some outside position from which to study the history of each of the colonies, in order that local history and antiquarian research may be made to contribute effectively to an understanding of historical development broadly viewed.

[1] MS: HEH, TU File Drawer 14, folder marked "Turner: What is Colonial History? 1918 — April 26." A notation in Turner's handwriting on the first page dates the manuscript.

[2] See Charles M. Andrews' remarks on the study of American colonial history, *Publications of the Colonial Society of Massachusetts*, Vol. XX: *Transactions 1917-1919* (1920), 159-163.

[3] *The Colonial Period* (New York, 1912), pp. vi-vii. Andrews' viewpoint is stated in less dogmatic terms in his *The Colonial Period of American History* (New Haven, 1934), I, xi-xiv.

I assume also that Professor Andrews with his own breadth of interest and his sound scholarship would assent to the proposition that American history as such finds fountain heads in the old thirteen colonies. That, in some measure at least, their institutional beginnings, their society and their activities are a part of American history. But should these aspects be subordinated to the technically colonial side? Should the contributions of the colonies to the main stream of American history be excluded from the province of the colonial historian?

Is it the province of students of later periods, (by way of retrospection), to gather up these origins, viewing them only as buried seeds which were to germinate in later times.

It is my purpose in this five minute note merely to raise the question whether there is not need to consider *two* vantage grounds for observation during the whole colonial era: both the English home which the colonists left and the American wilderness to which they came.

Without special qualifications in colonial history I must speak with great deference to the judgement and knowledge of our colleague whose views I have tried to state. But after all, the question is one of general perspective as well as of command of the materials. And because I have some apprehension that American scholarship may be turned so strongly in the direction of the mother country and the relations of the colonies thereto as to obscure and unnecessarily subordinate attention to the peculiarly American aspect of the subject, I venture to suggest that the experience of those Englishmen engaged in adjusting their institutions, their personal relations, even their ideas to the conditions involved in entering this wilderness are more than material for the student of later times. They seem to me to be vital factors in understanding the colonists themselves and their attitude to the British empire. Shall we not miss essential facts in explaining the attitude, the motives, the point of view of the colonists of Massachusetts if [we] look at them primarily from the English post of observation. Should we not also observe them from the Alleghanies, let us say; knowing that the significance of their actions lies in part in what they were doing as a part of that movement of expansion which spread the European men, ideas, and institutions across a continent, and modified them at each stage of their advance? Would it not be unwise to study the Massachusetts man in western New York, or Wisconsin, in the days when those regions were undergoing a process of colonization, as though he were only secondarily affected by his new environment? Would it be correct policy to study them primarily from the point of vantage of the Massachusetts which they left? Was not the more important thing the play of the new influences, the grappling with unaccustomed conditions in surroundings, economic life, the breaking of old customs, the creation of new institutions, the modification of the type?

In a word I apprehend that whether we view Massachusetts as an English colony, or an American commonwealth in the colonial era, we must have two points of observation, for the same period, the English *and* the American. They are mutually interpretative; both are essential, for the Massachusetts colonist was from the moment of his landing subject to new stimuli, forced to new ways. Whatever old names attached to his institutions they became essentially different things in their operation, their adjustments, their modification to suit the American conditions. These processes of change challenge the attention of the student of the colony. I find it difficult to believe that it is wise to separate or postpone the peculiarly American aspects in a treatment of the colonial epoch, for I am strongly inclined to believe that such separation, such subordination, would deprive the historian of some of the most essential material for enabling his readers to understand the motives and methods and machinery of colonial relations with Great Britain, even if it were conceded that the best observation tower for the survey of the colony is on the other side of the Atlantic. Massachusetts was an American commonwealth at the same time that she was an English colony. She had the American forest at her back door as well as the Atlantic ocean in front of her. She worked under both influences. Why not consider them together: the variations of type as well as the transmitted traits? Which is the more important to the American, as contrasted with the English, historian?

Turner and His Wife about 1890

Turner and His Lifelong Friend and Colleague Charles Homer Haskins about 1890

3

George Washington and the Nation

TURNER'S IMPORTANCE *as a historian does not lie in his ability to evoke the past or to create a dramatic image of America's great men. He is no Francis Parkman, no scholar-poet who is able to make of history a multicolored romantic tale, sweeping us along by the sheer fascination of seeing our national heroes as actors in the drama of history. This is not Turner's way. His talents are analytical rather than dramatic. He was attracted to the problem of untangling and tracing the complicated roots of our national history. Turner's bent toward speculative historical writing was reinforced by the foundation of theory upon which most of his writings were based, for he was convinced that underlying trends and patterns in large part shaped our past. Beside these the story of the individual man — even the great man — or the single event lapsed into relative insignificance. Turner went so far as to suggest that American great men were less interesting than those of Europe, that in the United States men should be studied for the manner in which they reflect their societies because, more clearly than European leaders, they were the products of their societies. Thus, temperament and theory combined to make of Turner an analyst of the American past rather than a master of the art of dramatic historical writing.*

The first piece in this group exemplifies Turner's problems in dealing with human character and action. In "Convocation Address" we might expect an intricate, lifelike portrait of one of our greatest presidents, full of subtle shadings. But instead Turner appears to have departed from his established principles: he has analyzed his subject almost entirely in terms of Washington's role in the westward movement, allowing an application of the frontier theory to dominate complex reality. Indeed, in this interpretation of Washington (as well as in his famous essay "The Significance of the Frontier in American History"), Turner could be accused of committing the fault which he criticized in the work of Von Holst — that of treating history from the standpoint of a fixed idea, with a resulting tendency to distort. Thus Turner writes, "If we desire to understand the true greatness of George Washington, we must know what was his attitude to the West." This seems to overstate the case.

Yet the "Convocation Address" on Washington is significant for other reasons. It illustrates Turner's view of a great man who is a product of his environment, a leader who represents the "expansive forces in American life." In the other two essays Turner enlarges on this portrayal of Washington as a national figure who rose above the politics of sectional rivalry.

But these two essays deal only indirectly with America's first president and are concerned primarily with the relationship between America and Europe. "Why Did Not the United States Become Another Europe," the major portion of which was written in 1916, suggests that we heed Washington's warning about getting involved in European alliances, rivalries, and quarrels. Moving beyond this topic, the essay expands into a lucid discussion of the probable divisions which America might have suffered (into separate colonies of European nations, into independent nations) as contrasted with those divisions which actually took place (division into sections in which political party loyalties were strong enough to overcome sectional rivalries and preserve national unity). As a result of this last kind of unity, the unity of a federation of sections held together by political party ties, Turner concluded America had had comparative freedom from the devastating wars which had been Europe's unhappy fate.

In "Washington the Nationalist" Turner reversed his tentative judgment about heeding our first president's advice. After discussing Washington's reasons for desiring to maintain American neutrality in the 1790's, Turner describes changed conditions of the new world of the 1920's, in which one could no longer claim to know what Washington would have advised. Along with Turner's convincing description of changed conditions we are left with the impression that he, at any rate, believed that Washington might have chosen to exert American moral leadership in the twentieth century to avoid the almost certain catastrophe of a modern global war.

CONVOCATION ADDRESS[1]

At the last Convocation, the students of the University had the pleasure of hearing a notable address from a great preacher on the anniversary of the birth of Abraham Lincoln. We who live in the Middle West may well be proud to reckon Lincoln as a product of this region. He was the very fruitage of the pioneer life that entered the forests of the Northwest rifle and axe in hand, and began the conquest of the wilderness.[2]

It is undoubtedly true that Lincoln represented more fully than any other American the ideals and achievements of the pioneer stock of the Mississippi Valley. In his Calendar of Great Americans, Woodrow Wilson has laid down the doctrine that the test of greatness for American heroes is their ability to understand and sympathize with the national ideals of the American people, and their services in advancing these ideals. When we inquire what have been the most abiding interests in American life, the ideals which our heroes must represent, we cannot fail to see how profound an in-

[1] MS: HEH, TU File Drawer 15, folder marked "Convocation Address, Turner, Feby 22, 19--." The manuscript is undated.

[2] Turner at this point intended to add a quotation on Lincoln from James Russell Lowell. After a sentence fragment ("No one can think of Lincoln without assenting to the noble words of Lowell, where he says:"), the manuscript continues.

fluence upon our life has been the steady march of American civilization into the West. Here was a wilderness to be won from stubborn nature, from the Indians, from the Frenchmen who seized and held it while the English colonists still clung to the Atlantic coast, and after the Revolution, from the rival nations on our flanks, England and Spain. The conquest of the continent has furnished the training to the American people, shaped their institutions, given them their most fundamental traits, developed in them that capacity for vast design, that power to deal with great spaces of the world's surface, that optimism and that will-power which are such distinctive features of this nation. It is the tremendous importance of this western movement that gives significance to the topic which I have chosen for this celebration of Washington's Birthday. If we desire to understand the true greatness of George Washington, we must know what was his attitude to the West. We desire to know something of this attitude not only because we wish to find some bond of connection between this great man and the region where he lived, but also because the inquiry raises the question of Washington's real greatness. Did he in any way represent these expansive forces in American life? Did he share in this great movement which has dominated American characteristics, or was he, as some have said, merely the last and greatest of the English colonists?

In the period of Washington's birth another Western influence was in progress — a movement that culminated and expressed itself in Andrew Jackson, and because his career typifies one of the most important phases in American expansion to the West, because it explains Western individualism and democracy, I wish next to speak of this man and of this movement.

It was in this period that the Nation turned its eyes with passionate determination toward the Mississippi valley, and the struggle between France and England gave the West to Saxon freedom. It was not only one of the decisive events in American history; it was one of those turning points in the history of the world.

In 1753 the French prepared to occupy the Ohio Valley. They called to this task the traders who had been operating in the woods of Wisconsin and Minnesota. At Ft. Le Boeuf on a portage between the sources of the Ohio and Lake Erie was stationed St. Pierre. To this representative of new France there came through the forest and the December snows a tall youth of 21, the herald of the Governor of Virginia, to bid the French withdraw, and yield possession to the English. You know this messenger of war; it was George Washington, already as a surveyor skilled in woodcraft, and well fitted by his discretion for the task confided to him. The French refused to yield possession. Washington was sent with a Virginian force to seize the forks of the Ohio, but the French had anticipated the movement, the rivals met, and the shot was fired that began the war that gave the West to the Americans. Overcome by superior force, the young soldier surrendered, and returned to Virginia. Again he appears on the scene of conflict for the Ohio Valley, at Braddock's defeat, where his frontiersmen showed what Westerners could do when rightly led, even in the face of disaster. Braddock was defeated but "Braddock of Fontenoy, stubborn and grim, carved a cross on the wilderness rim" — the clearings that his axeman made never were obliterated.[3]

It is not too much to say, then, that Washington opened that world historic war that gave to Prussia the headship among German peoples, to England India, and to Americans the Mississippi Valley. In the three years that followed Braddock's defeat, Washington and his backwoodsmen protected Virginia's frontiers against the French and Indians. He was a leader that the stalwart sons of the West might be proud to follow. One of his lieutenants describes him at the close of these campaigns, as a youth of commanding presence, straight as an Indian, six feet, two in his stockings, heavy, muscular, large boned, long armed, and broad shouldered, his head gracefully poised on a superb neck, eyes bluish-gray, penetrating and overhung by a heavy brow, with firm chin, and tightly set lips, a countenance under control, but capable of expressing the deepest feeling when moved by emotion. Such was the man that passed from the struggle for the West to his Virginia plantation, and from there to the battles of the Revolution. The duties that then fell to him took him away from Western scenes. But if tradition can be trusted

[3] The quotation, slightly modified by Turner, is from John Williamson Palmer's "Ned Braddock." See Burton E. Stevenson, ed. *Poems of American History* (Boston, 1922), p. 114.

he always kept before him the possibility of a final stand in the land beyond the Alleghanies, and among the frontiersmen with whom his military career had opened. — "What will you do if you are defeated by the British?" he was asked. "We will retire beyond the mountains and there be free," was the answer.

In the dark days of the Revolution, in the camp at Newburg, Washington turned the attention of his discontented officers to the Ohio region, as a land in which they might retrieve their fallen fortunes. He presented their petitions for a western state to Congress, and he was among the very first to urge upon that body the importance of a systematic organization of the Northwest territory. He foresaw the tide of migration that was to sweep into these fertile lands and he desired to organize it for the best results. It is one of the chief glories of Washington that the founders of Ohio and the Northwest territory declared that their attention was turned to the region by the Commander in Chief, who years before had threaded his way through those Western wilds to give his portentous message to the French.

At the close of the Revolution the West was discontented. Shut off from the Atlantic coast by the Alleghanies, deprived of their natural outlet, the Mississippi, by the Spaniards, they were contemplating withdrawal from the weak confederation. Washington's clear eye saw the danger and proposed the remedy. "The West hangs as it were upon a pivot; the touch of a feather would turn it any way," said he. And he proposed to bind it to the east by ties of interest by giving its products an outlet on the Atlantic. His first business after leaving the army at its disbandment was to visit the portages between the Mohawk and the Great Lakes in Western New York with a view to seeing how internal improvements might be made to connect East and West. In 1784 he visited his old haunts between the Potomac and Ohio, for the same purpose, and he urged the opening of a road between these rivers "as a means of becoming the channel of conveyance of the extensive and valuable trade of a rising empire." In these tours lay the germs that ripened into the Erie Canal, and the New York Central Railroad, the Old National Turnpike and the B. & O. Railway — the lines of western settlement. Washington foresaw the future — he would break down the mountains by roads and canals, and weld east and west into a nation. If living in our age he would have been [a] great railroad captain of industry. The outcome of these arguments was the well known meeting between representatives of Maryland and Virginia at Mt. Vernon which led to the Annapolis convention to promote regulations for interstate commerce. This convention revealed the need of wider powers and more radical action and the Constitutional Convention followed. Along the line of interstate commerce lay the easiest road to national political development, and in this movement Washington led the way.

Neutrality and Inclusion of West in Nation

In his presidency England was induced to relinquish her hold on the Northwest which she had held despite the treaty of peace. And his firm stand for American neutrality prevented the French republic from dragging us into war on her side, a war which had for one of its objects the capture of New Orleans and the control of the Mississippi by France. Thus the wisdom and prudence of Washington saved for us the upper and the lower courses of the Father of Waters, the noble river that now with its far stretching affluents binds the nation together.

He understood the West. He foresaw its mission and believed in it. Knowing its inevitable expansion over the Mississippi Valley, he neither feared nor sneered at this vast prospect which seemed to others fraught with danger to the Republic. He trusted in the larger lines of American growth.

He was not a colonial planter; he was no narrow provincial; he was an American, perhaps the first of our public men, who by his freedom from sectionalism, by his independence of European influence and by the continental sweep of his vision is entitled to bear that name.

❧ WHY DID NOT THE UNITED STATES BECOME ANOTHER EUROPE?[1]

Perhaps no national hero who has left a testament to his people stands the test of the years so well as does George Washington. His wide and varied experience, his disinterestedness, his lofty and well balanced character, and his far-sighted and sound judgment make the advice which he gave over a hundred years ago, vital and useful for his countrymen today.

It is not well that the words of any great man shall become a fixed and permanent standard of conduct, a fetish for his people. The great man himself usually achieves his distinction, as Washington did, by breaking with an older order, by constructing something new and more suitable for his time. In the same way, later generations should be free to adjust to new conditions, to follow new and constructive leaders. But Washington's wisdom has an enduring quality.

I have chosen for the text of my remarks the portions of Washington's Farewell Address in which he urges close union upon his countrymen. This he advised, both as a means of avoiding external attack and of securing exemption from those broils and wars between themselves which so frequently afflict neighboring countries

[1] MS: HEH, TU File Drawer 15, folder marked "Lecture, Trinity College, Durham, N.C., 1916." The first page of the manuscript has two notations in Turner's handwriting: "Trinity College 1916," and "1916 — before the American entry into World War," an indication that Turner probably revised some of his views. Further evidence is found in the addition on his carbon copy of this lecture (same folder) of a final sentence in 1921. The editor of the *South Atlantic Quarterly,* William Henry Glasson, asked to publish the lecture, but Turner, apparently planning to revise the manuscript, refused with "regrets." Glasson to Turner, March 1, 1916, TU Box 26. In a note on the last page of the carbon copy of the manuscript, Turner makes reference to his article "Sections and Nation" (printed in *Yale Review,* XII (1922-23), 1-21; reprinted in *The Significance of Sections in American History,* pp. 315-339), which enlarges on some of the themes of this lecture.

not tied together by the same governments, — wars "which their own rivalships alone would be sufficient to produce, but which opposite foreign alliances, attachments and intrigues would stimulate and imbitter." "Is there a doubt," he asks, "whether a common government can embrace so large a sphere? Let experience solve it."

"In contemplating the causes wch. may disturb our Union, it occurs as matter of serious concern, that any ground should have been furnished for characterizing parties by *Geographical* discriminations: *Northern* and *Southern; Atlantic* and *Western;* whence designing men may endeavour to excite a belief that there is a real difference of local interests and views."

"To the efficacy and permanency of Your Union, a Government for the whole is indispensable. No Alliances however strict between the parts can be an adequate substitute. They must inevitably experience the infractions and interruptions which all Alliances in all times have experienced."

"Europe has a set of primary interests, which to us have none, or a very remote relation. Hence she must be engaged in frequent controversies, the causes of which are essentially foreign to our concerns. Hence therefore it must be unwise in us to implicate ourselves, by artificial ties, in the ordinary vicissitudes of her politics, or the ordinary combinations and collisions of her friendships, or enmities:

"Our detached and distant situation invites and enables us to pursue a different course. . . . Why forego the advantages of so peculiar a situation? Why quit our own to stand upon foreign ground? Why, by interweaving our destiny with that of any part of Europe, entangle our peace and prosperity in the toils of European Ambition, Rivalship, Interest, Humour or Caprice?"[2]

In proposing the question, *Why did not the United States become another Europe?* I am not suggesting a fantastic or impossible thing. To no one did such an outcome seem more clearly possible than to

[2] Although Turner sometimes quoted Jared Sparks's edition of Washington's writings, the Fitzpatrick edition, because of its reliability, has been used for correcting errors. "Farewell Address," Sept. 19, 1796, in *The Writings of George Washington*, ed. John C. Fitzpatrick (Washington, D.C., 1931-44), XXXV, 221, 222, 223, 224, 234.

George Washington, the Father of his Country. To no generation of Americans before ourselves has the dreadful significance of such an outcome been so evident.

Washington spoke out of the fulness of his own trying experiences. It is not too much to say that during the greater part of his life the United States seemed more than likely to remain a part of the European state system. Historically, of course, it was just that. When Washington was born, England's claims still ran from sea to sea; France held the Great Lake basin and the Mississippi Valley; Spain's dominion included Florida, the Pacific coast, and the Southwest; and all these powers had conflicting boundaries and irreconcilable ambitions. Men still living at that time could remember also when Sweden's flag floated over the Delaware, and the Dutch held New York.

In his young manhood, Washington himself had followed the trails through the western wilderness as the messenger of the English of Virginia demanding that France should withdraw from the Ohio. It was his guns which opened the conflict which ended in the expulsion of France from the American mainland. He had led his countrymen in the war for independence — a war which Frederick the Great significantly called a crisis in the affairs of *Europe*, — and he had seen with grave anxiety the possibility that France might acquire a permanent hold upon the young republic at whose birth she assisted.

In the negotiations for peace at the close of that contest, France was willing to shut the United States up in the narrow space between the Alleghanies and the Atlantic, leaving to England the territory northwest of the Ohio, to Spain the control over the Mississippi as well as the vast territory beyond it and the supremacy in the lands about the Gulf of Mexico. Of the rest of the country, between the Alleghanies and the Mississippi, France would make an Indian country, divided into rival spheres of influence, or protectorates, over one of which Spain, and over the other the United States, should preside. Obviously such an outcome would have made of the United States a mere dependency of France. This was exactly what was intended. Our ally did not propose to assist us to become a great power indifferent to her protection. Breaking their instructions to be guided by France, the American commissioners made a separate and conditional treaty with England by which we gained her assent to our boundary on the Mississippi and the Great Lakes. France could not well compel us to continue to fight an enemy in order to exact from him worse terms than he was willing to grant us, and so she gracefully yielded.

Conditions at the close of the Confederation were even more menacing. The different sections of the union were bound together by merely nominal bonds. England remained on the Great Lakes in territory she had given us by treaty, and Spain continued to hold her posts east of the Mississippi and to shut the river to the commerce of the great valley. In this period some of the most prominent and trusted men in Kentucky and Tennessee corresponded with the representatives of Spain over the matter of withdrawing from the Union and accepting the sovereignty of Spain in return for freedom to navigate the Mississippi. English leaders similarly intrigued with men of prominence in Kentucky, on the Ohio, and in Vermont, hoping to secure at least the separation of these regions and to promote friendly relations on their part with England.

From this anarchy, which could only have resulted in a return to the European system, our new Constitution saved us. But the danger rather changed its face than disappeared. So long as rival European nations held our flanks, our interests as a youthful power were certain to be subordinated to European aims.

A few illustrations out of many will make this clear. In the year in which Washington became president, the Spaniards seized a fur-trading establishment of the English at Nootka Sound on what is now Vancouver Island. This remote incident was fraught with weighty consequences. It raised the whole question of the respective rights of Spain and England in the New World, and by 1790 it bade fair to result in war — a war in which France was expected to assist her Spanish ally and which was certain to involve this hemisphere. England prepared to conduct an expedition across American territory to descend the Mississippi against New Orleans, while the Venezuelan revolutionist, Miranda, then in England, raised the vision of the freedom of Latin America won by the aid of England and the United States.

But it seemed to Jefferson, then Secretary of State, that this violation of our neutrality was not only obnoxious in itself, but would result in surrounding us by the power of England, because, if victorious she would hold the Northwest beyond the Ohio and the Gulf region, besides dominating the Atlantic coast by her fleet. Such a situation would compel, he thought, either "bloody and eternal war, or an indissoluble confederacy" between us and England. It turned out that France, then on the verge of the revolution, did not give effective support to Spain and the latter was forced to agree to a peaceful recognition of England's rights. But in a short time France and Spain were at war as the French Revolution overturned old European alliances and policies, and France invited England and the United States to join her in dividing up Spanish America. Soon afterward, however, she declared war against Great Britain.

In the conflagration which followed this crusading young republic of France used every effort to draw us into her train. She proposed to use our ports as a refuge and a base of operations. She set in motion revolutionary movements on our frontier by the action [of] her minister, Genet, who found a western tool in George Rogers Clark, the hero of the Illinois campaign in the Revolution. It was the aim of these movements to free Louisiana, Florida and Canada with the design of making them substantial dependencies of France.

Toward the close of his second administration, just before he wrote his Farewell Address, Washington had seen his country torn between the partisans of France and the partisans of England. In his own cabinet Hamilton, Secretary of the Treasury, leaned to English policy and Jefferson, Secretary of State, to French. He himself had become the target of the most violent abuse for his policy of neutrality. Waves of passion sweeping over the friends of the two nations furnished the main sources of party feeling. In the year of the address, Collot, a prominent French military engineer, made a tour to the West under orders of the French minister and proposed a plan for fortifying the passes of the Alleghanies and the strategic positions on the Mississippi against the United States. Alarmed by the prospect that the Mississippi Valley might fall under the power of Napoleon, a Federalist senator Blount, of Tennessee, was found to be plotting a combined attack upon the Spaniards in New Orleans by the English and the American frontiersmen. The project involved an expedition to be made up of a contingent from Canada, including Indians under Brant, and a western army together with a British fleet to blockade the mouth of the Mississippi. In the face of this danger to her ambitions, France renewed her commission as general to George Rogers Clark and sent agents to stir up her friends in Kentucky, Tennessee, and the back country of the Carolinas and Georgia. England meanwhile endeavored to protect the Indians north of the Ohio by arranging for a neutral zone. For some time Spain had been looking toward England for help. The two powers recognized that they had a common interest in the West. When General Wayne was advancing toward Lake Erie in 1794 on his expedition against the Northwestern Indians, the Lieutenant Governor of Canada took possession of an advanced post on the Maumee to protect Detroit, and here he corresponded with the Governor of Louisiana regarding joint action of England and Spain and their Indian allies against the United States. After he defeated the Indians in the battle of Fallen Timbers, General Wayne marched his little army under the guns of the British fort, daring its commander to fire. It needed only a match to have precipitated a war of Spain, France, England and the United States on American soil.

But Washington carried out his policy of avoiding entangling alliances and pushed Europe away from our immediate flanks east of the Mississippi. By the treaty of Jay he excluded England from the Northwest and by that of Pinckney he excluded Spain from the Southwest.

Having seen the conditions somewhat as they seemed to Washington when he delivered his address, let us see how far the peril of European possession of all or part of our territory exhibited itself in the years that followed.

The significance of the Louisiana Purchase, as a part of the history of our foreign relations, lies in the fact that Napoleon gained it from Spain on the plea that France would be a "wall of brass" against the expansion of the American nation, and would shut it up within "the limits which nature seemed to have intended" for it. France meant by this that the Alleghanies furnished our natural bounds.

When he acquired Louisiana in 1800, Napoleon intended to add Florida, and thus to make a French lake of the Gulf of Mexico, for he claimed Texas in his Louisiana. He proposed to win, or force, the western settlers to accept the French flag by the control which he could exert upon them at the mouth of the Mississippi. Thus he would make a middle kingdom, such as Aaron Burr and Wilkinson are charged with planning soon after, — a realm which would extend from the Alleghanies, fortified against the Americans by his engineers, across the Mississippi to the utmost bounds of Louisiana along the crest of the Rockies, and north as far as he could push his power. Probably the failure of this undertaking was due both to the seapower of England and to the discovery that the West would fight sooner than yield the control of its river to a strong and aggressive nation. As the attempts of France to secure Louisiana from Spain had become known, leading Federalists like Rufus King and Alexander Hamilton, gave friendly attention to a plan for a combined attack by England and the United States upon all the Spanish possessions in the New World. Even so good a friend of France as was Thomas Jefferson saw that Napoleon must become our dearest enemy if he held New Orleans and that unless he gave up the river, "we must marry ourselves to the British fleet and nation, holding the two continents of America in sequestration for the common purposes of the united British and American nations." "Jefferson," confidentially wrote the French ambassador to his government, after he had bitterly reproached Washington for the terms of his Farewell Address, — "Jefferson is an American, and as such, it is impossible for him to be sincerely our friend. An American is the born enemy of European peoples."

It is certain that by the acquisition of Louisiana we took a long step in the direction of excluding Europe from America, and that the acquisition had a momentous train of consequences; for the annexations of Florida, Texas, Oregon, California and the Southwest were in a real sense echoes of the Louisiana purchase, without which they could hardly have been secured. Each annexation meant not only more American territory, but the exclusion of dangerous parts of the European state system, fragments which aroused the cupidity and intrigues of rival European states, germs of the European malady. Each of the vast additions was made possible by the advance of the American pioneer into the unoccupied or sparsely populated portions of the West. In the negotiations over a treaty of peace at the close of the War of 1812, the British representatives desired to organize the larger portion of the territory north of the Ohio into a buffer state, to be held by the Indians. They failed to enforce this because they could not meet the argument based on the solid fact of existing American settlements. This it was also which ended the joint occupation of Oregon. Before the will of the American frontiersmen who continued the advance of the American people into Texas, the plans of France and Spain to make of Texas an independent buffer state also fell. No European nation has been able to solve this problem of checking the Western advance by dense colonization across its path. The intervening ocean has so far prevented the lodgement in force by Europe in the interior.

Nevertheless European sea-power was influential. There is a series of evidences that time and time again portions of the United States turned to Europe for protection when it thought its rights invaded or its interests gravely neglected. The close of the confederation abounded in illustration of this — "Great Britain" wrote an indignant western man in 1786 in a widely distributed circular, "stands ready with open arms to receive and support us. They have already offered to open their resources for our supplies. When once reunited to them, farewell, a long farewell to all your boasted greatness." "The large states dare not dissolve the confederation," said a Delaware delegate to the Constitutional Convention the next year. "If they do the small ones will find some foreign ally of more honor and good faith, who will take them by the hand and do them justice."[3]

Calhoun told John Quincy Adams in the heat of the Missouri Controversy that if the union was dissolved the South would be compelled to form an alliance, offensive and defensive, with Great Britain, which he admitted would be substantially a return to the

[3] Turner has inserted an almost illegible interlinear notation which seems to read: "Hartford Convention — and New England relations to England."

colonial state. When Calhoun formulated the doctrine of nullification for South Carolina, President Jackson wrote (1831) to the Union committee of that state, "Every enlightened citizen must know that a separation, could it be effected, would begin with civil discord and end in colonial dependence on a foreign power, an obliteration from the list of nations." While Texas was an independent republic, its destiny still undecided, there was a very grave possibility, (as recently examined archives in that state, Mexico and Europe show), that Texas might maintain itself only as a dependent republic under England or France; and that it might on such terms extend its borders across the continent. California at the same time was about to fall from the feeble hand of Mexico, and English and French agents reported to their governments upon its suitability for a European possession. Contemporaneously the destiny of Oregon and the Northwest was at stake.

The Civil War raised a similiar situation, fraught with the danger that the South might win independence at the price of European ascendency over herself and Mexico.

Nor can we, even at the present day, be sure that European intrigue, and war for empire may not be extended into this New World and draw the United States, in effect, into the European system. This may result from the unsettled conditions in the Caribbean Sea and Central America in the vicinity of the Panama Canal, or by reason of defiance of the Monroe Doctrine in some portion of South America, or by involving ourselves in Old World wars, wantonly, or from sad necessity.

The world is shrinking in these days of electric communication, the aeroplane, and the swift ocean steamers. Adam Smith at the period of our Revolution assured the English farmer that he need fear no competition from the Irish cattle because of the protection afforded by the cost of transportation across the channel. Today Argentine and Montana cattle help to feed England. In other words, Argentina is effectively as near England as was Ireland in 1776. England is about as close to New York as is San Francisco; in effect Japan is no more remote from Seattle than was Kentucky from Philadelphia a hundred years ago.

But in spite of tendencies to break down American isolation and to sweep the United States into the world conflict, it does not follow that we should be carried into that maelstrom, and particularly not on European terms. Washington's warnings against entangling alliances still have validity and they gain new force from the awful tragedy which meets our gaze whenever we look across the Atlantic.

Looking back over the events we have traced, we reach certain conclusions — that the United States was not occupied by European nations, and that we did not become a mere part of this European territory, dependent and feeble, was due partly to the fact that European nations were, (under the conditions of the earlier years), too remote to make populous and strong colonies here, and that different areas of the United States were not persuaded by domestic ills to accept the flag of one or another of the rival nations.

The reason for this reluctance to yield to the intrigues of European governments was partly in the fact that the abundant resources of the unoccupied West furnished a safety valve and a remedy for discontent; partly that a flexible and gentle control was exercised in the United States itself under a system of free government; and also to the fact that in general the European nations were, in language, institutions, and general characteristics, too unlike Americans to win their allegiance.

This was not the case in respect to England but with England after the declaration of independence we had two wars, and thus a historic antagonism. Where the frontiers of the two people touched there were at first uncongenial conditions. English fur traders and the American pioneer farmer did not find much in common. The century of peace between England and the United States, which should have been celebrated last year, was due to some extent, no doubt, to the agreements of mutual naval disarmament on the Great Lakes, to agreements of joint occupation until the facts of actual settlement determined the issues, and to an accommodating spirit between the two English speaking people in boundary contentions, and a realization, from experience, of the unprofitableness of wars between them; that Canada became largely at the mercy of the United States by reason of its smaller population; and that the mother country was too remote for satisfactory transfer of great armies needed.

But the peace with England was even more due to the fact that there were such vast spheres of influence within which Canada and the United States could each peacefully develop without serious collisions with each other, and that there were such friendly commercial connections, ties of blood, and community of political ideas, that, in spite of misunderstandings, the English and the Americans preserved good will, and a compromising temper.[4] At each critical episode, the result was determined either by the actual advance of the American pioneer into the disputed region in such numbers as to decide the diplomatic action, or by the fact that the huge economic growth of the United States, its effective resources, made clear the advantage of retaining the United States as a peaceful friend rather than as a warlike foe. At last the tradition of peace became almost irresistible. It had a hundred years of habit behind it.

So far we have been considering the possibility that the United States might have been mere European territory, divided between one or more European nations. But the United States might have become another Europe, — that is, might have run the same general kind of course that European nations have run, — even though it remained apart from Europe itself.

Nature in fact seemed to have decreed this outcome. The United States is, in area, equal to entire Europe. Each of the various geographic provinces into which it is divided is more than sufficient in size and natural resources for one of the greater nations of Europe, indeed for some of the Empires which have arisen in Europe. Lay the map of Europe upon a map of the United States drawn to the same scale, and Constantinople will fall not far from Nashville, Tennessee; Paris will lie in Yellowstone Park; Berlin will change places with Bismarck, North Dakota; London will be not very far from Helena, Montana; and New Orleans will float in the Mediterranean near the shores of Crete, south of Greece. Either Germany or France could be accommodated in the state of Texas, with room to spare. Great Britain and Ireland could rest comfortably in New Mexico, or rattle around in California.

In such vast spaces, with such variety of sections, with such

[4] Turner's marginal note: "and need of American cotton and grain. Oregon era — corn laws. Civil War era."

natural facilities for antagonistic interests, there was abundant opportunity for European conditions to repeat themselves. Let us next briefly retrace our steps and enquire how far such a possibility was realized, how far did American sections tend to act like European nations? We shall find that disunion was not a phenomenon limited to the struggle between North and South, although that is the most obvious instance of acute sectionalism. Sectionalism is one of the oldest and most deep-seated of American phenomena. The New England Confederation and its dealings with rival nations like the Dutch and the French through their American representative, as two separate countries might deal with each other, is a seventeenth century example. In the eighteenth century from its beginnings there had been frequent proposals by responsible officers for dividing the colonies into sectional unions. Livingston of New York, in 1701, proposed to make three distinct governments by "annexing" Virginia and Maryland to North and South Carolina as one government; combining New York, the Jersies, Pennsylvania, and Delaware with part of Connecticut, as another; and making of the rest of New England a third. Franklin's Plan of Union in 1754 was, in part, due to a desire to block the plans of other commissioners to bring about sectional unions.

The most striking illustration which I have found of this early recognition of the sectional basis of American life is in a discussion by Mitchell a well-known authority on the colonies. In his *Contest in America*, which appeared in 1757, he set forth his belief that a general union was impracticable. He would, therefore, divide the colonies into separate parts, "whose situation is much the same, and whose interest, that rules everything, is more easily connected . . . ." "What mutual interest, connection, or dependance," he asked, "have *New England* and *Carolina, Virginia* and *Nova Scotia* . . . ." He then pointed out that the colonies were usually divided into northern and southern, which only regards their trade but not their security and protection. He would divide the "many colonies on the continent of North America into three, the *Northern, Middle,* and *Southern.*" "Under the first," he continues, "I include *Nova Scotia, New England, New York,* and *New Jersey.* In the middle division are *Pennsylvania, Maryland,* and *Virginia.* And in the southern division we include North and South *Carolina* and *Georgia.*

"These three divisions make three different and distinct countries; separated from one another by natural boundaries; different in situation, climate, soil, products, etc. while the several colonies included in these divisions, which we look upon as different countries, are all one and the same country in these respects . . . ."[5]

Besides such conscious recognition of groups of colonies there were very real colonial sections which were not recognized at the time because they were composed of fragments of colonies which taken together were in real unity, though apportioned among several colonies. An example of this sort is the upcountry people as compared with the seaboard. In such a colony as North Carolina or Virginia this was clearly recognized, and the grievances of the back country against the seaboard part of the colony are clearly set forth in Jefferson's Notes on Virginia, while in North Carolina the settlers wrote them themselves in the Regulation War which resulted in the battle of the Alamance. What is not so generally known is that, from Pennsylvania south, there was a kindred series of back country sections constituting as a whole a single type of society, the early West beyond the tidewater, which in many ways was in antagonism with the corresponding older parts. A similar condition existed in New England.

If the west of the early colonial period was not so much observed, the remoter West beyond the Alleghanies soon made itself strikingly manifest. Of this we have already furnished evidence, in considering the intrigues of Europe. But the Mississippi Valley was also a bone of contention between the older sections of the coast and a desirable ally of one or the other section as the political power of the West grew with its increasing population.

From the era of the Revolution the different sections began to shape their action with reference to the West as a means of acquiring political dominance. Its future as holder of the balance of power was fully perceived. In the discussions in the Continental Congress over the problem of how far to go in the matter of insisting

[5] [John Mitchell], *The Contest in America between Great Britain and France* (London, 1757), pp. 39-40.

upon our right to the great river as a boundary, and whether we should make an ultimatum of the right to navigate its course to the sea, the different sections broke apart and bitter rivalries existed, which the French minister used to his advantage. The land question gave occasion for similar sectional divisions, and threatened to wreck the possibility of union under the confederation. When Maryland was convinced by Virginia's cession of her backcountry north of the Ohio that the Old Dominion was not to become an overwhelming power in the Confederacy, she signed the Articles. But these claims of various states might have resulted in civil war, as indeed they did in the controversy between Pennsylvania and Connecticut.

When Jay, secretary of state in the Confederation, proposed to forego the navigation of the Mississippi for a period of years as a means of securing friendly commercial connections with Spain, (which would chiefly have benefitted the New England states), both South and West flamed up in opposition. Rufus King, of the Federalist Northeast, thought that every citizen of the United States who emigrated to the westward of the Alleghany was a total loss to the confederacy. "Nature," he said, "has severed the two countries by a vast and extensive chain of mountains, interest and convenience will keep them separate and the feeble policy of our disjointed government will not be able to unite them." The words are almost identical with the words of the French diplomats when they considered the severance of the Mississippi Valley from the United States as they planned to include it in Louisiana.

Monroe, on the other hand, representing the views of the planting South which found an ally in the West, charged the Northeast with a desire to break up the settlements on the Western Waters, or to promote the separation of the Westerners from the confederation, so that no future states would be formed there, — "to throw the weight of population eastward and keep it there," so as to raise the value of the unsold land of New York and Massachusetts and keep the weight of government in the Northeast. Contemporaneously Otto, the French chargé, reported that the south desired to attract population to the West as a means of controlling American politics. These examples have been taken from that troubled year 1786.

The next year the constitutional convention met and again the West played a prominent part in sectional debates. Washington believed that there was a party favorable to three distinct confederacies, at least his words after the convention seem to indicate so. In the discussions, such leaders as Charles Pinckney of South Carolina, Williamson of North Carolina, Randolph, Mason, and Madison, of Virginia, and Franklin of Pennsylvania spoke at times in favor of recognizing the three great sections, northern, middle, and southern, in the organization of the different departments of government. Finally, however, the Constitution even forbade the agreements between the states, with the idea perhaps of avoiding sectional developments. Efforts by Northeastern extremists to place the West at a permanent disadvantage in the government by means similar to those by which the coast controlled the interior counties of the South met with failure.

Perhaps the South was less inclined to draw out because it perceived that the growth of the West was making for Southern power in the Union. Jefferson has some interesting observations on sectionalism in his letter to John Taylor of Caroline, in 1798. Taylor had reported a strong feeling on the part of the Northeast to the effect that union between that section and the south was doomed to fail and he had evidently written to Jefferson his own apprehension that the time was at hand for disunion. At any rate, Jefferson answered in these words abounding in sound good sense.

"It is true that we are completely under the saddle of Massachusetts and Connecticut, and that they ride us very hard, cruelly insulting our feelings, as well as exhausting our strength and subsistence. Their natural friends, the three other eastern States, join them from a sort of family pride, and they have the art to divide certain other parts of the Union, so as to make use of them to govern the whole." He adds, if disunion once starts, it will be progressive, and says, "seeing that we must have somebody to quarrel with, I had rather keep our New England associates for that purpose, than to see our bickerings transferred to others."

"Better keep together as we are, haul off from Europe as soon as we can, and from all attachments to any portions of it; and if they show their power just sufficiently to hoop us together, it will be the happiest situation in which we can exist."[6]

The New England Federalists preserved a steady antagonism to both the South and its western allies. If Jefferson saw in them a convenient target for the surplus sectional enthusiasm of the South, they justified the confidence. Jefferson's election, the embargo, the Louisiana Purchase, the War of 1812, the Missouri Compromise, and the Hayne-Webster debates were successive chapters in the same story. The extremists of the Essex Junto in Massachusetts hoped to utilize the intense feeling in New England to bring about what Monroe had foreseen with concern in 1786, a break up of the Union, and a separate combination of New England, New York and perhaps Pennsylvania. But some of the leading federalists went for a new Union which should leave out the West, as the raw material from which the South recruited its strength, and which should include only the "good old thirteen." Thus the south would be left at the mercy of the North East and her English ally. A writer in the Boston *Advertizer* in 1814 declared that the West never could belong to the Union: "Their outlet," he said, "is through the Mississippi. They have no natural connection with the Atlantic States. . . . If the Union of the States is preserved, the Western region will drain off the Atlantic population, consume the resources of the Union, — and reward us by removing the seat of empire beyond the mountains. What, then, seems most obviously to the interest of all concerned? *Let the Western states go off*, and take care of themselves." Timothy Pickering, the former Secretary of State, and Gouverneur Morris were the leading expositors of this idea. Whether they could have carried the people of New England with them in this program is doubtful, but the latest and most thorough student of the episode declares that the leaders were more conservative than the people. The significance of their attitude toward the West becomes more startling when we recall that at this time Pakenham's British army was on its way to capture New Orleans and hardly a prominent New England man doubted that he would succeed. Then it was thought, the West would accept England's

[6] Jefferson to John Taylor, June 1, 1798, in *The Writings of Thomas Jefferson,* ed. Paul Leicester Ford, VII (New York, 1896), 263-265.

sway, and New England would institute a new Union on her own terms, and in close friendship with the mother country.

Under such conditions, our capital already captured and burned, the British in possession of part of Maine, our sea power lost, and Napoleon's empire coming to its end, while the American government had hardly a treasury or any credit, a proposition such as was made in the Hartford Convention by the New England section to refuse to pay taxes coupled with a demand that it should be allowed to defend itself and dictate a new constitution constituted a portentous illustration of what sectionalism might mean to the American people.

State sovereignty, except as a juristic question, has always been a mere sword in the hands of sectionalism. This it was which gave the doctrine significance and strength. When South Carolina failed to get sectional acceptance for her nullification program in 1833 she made terms and waited until the sectional self-consciousness and sectional feeling of the south expressed itself. We need not recount the successive stages of this development. One thing is clear the more it is studied: the story is not adequately told in terms of North against South. These sections were composed of other sections, each influential upon the course of the contest and upon its outcome. There is no certainty that the division into north and south would not have been followed by other divisions, other armed frontiers, diplomatic negotiations, alliances, wars, and international congresses.

Let us thank God that that is all a part of the history and the unfulfilled fears of a half century ago, as the Hartford convention was of a hundred years ago. And let us see to it that Washington's wisdom shall be our guide in the future occasions for counting the value of the Union.

So far we have considered together two ways in which the United States might have become another Europe. First, the possibility of European nations themselves dividing up the United States; and second, the possibility of American sections becoming independent nations, and thus reproducing European conditions.

Next, let us take brief notice of a different kind of sectionalism in the United States, less acute than those which we have just been considering, more normal and by consequence more characteristic of sectionalism as a peculiar American phenomenon.[7]

Have we, indeed, run an altogether different course from Europe? Is there in our history no counterpart of international relations? It seems to me that we have such counterparts, that we found a substitute for European nationalism. If we did not develop separate nations within the area of the United States, if the various and critical eruptions of sectional disunion which I have noted were transient and unsuccessful, we nevertheless have persistent milder sectional phenomena which may be called the wraiths or images of separate nations and their international relations within the United States. These images, these rudimentary organs, if you will, represent outgrown European types, are the evolutionary echoes of the European state system. They hold for us also an important contribution to the answer to our question why did not the United States become another Europe.

Not to be mysterious about it, I must say at once that what I have called the images of European nations are formed by sectional groupings in our party politics, our elections, our votes in Congress, and in our nominating conventions. They are revealed in our popular nomenclature, as, for example, the Lower South, the Inland Empire, the Midland Empire, the Middle States, New England, the New Northwest, the Mountain States. Our literature is federal, not national. Of course one can trace through it the especial American spirit, when compared with European literatures. I do not mean, for a moment, to deny the existence of that. But after all, our literature is a literature of great sections with a common central bond, rather than a homogeneous national literature. It is a literature which reflects the existence of New England, the South, the Prairie West, the Pacific Coast, and the other vast sections in which have long existed or are now forming special American types, each with its own material background, its home scenery, its own manners and customs, prejudices and ideals, its own psychology.

The political aspects are the easiest to depict. When party groupings are mapped either by national elections or by congressional

[7] Turner's marginal note: "Insert Immigrat[ion?]."

votes, certain persistent sections are disclosed: the Northeast stands as one; the South since the war is another; sometimes a group of states in the Middle West is a third. The Federalist States, the states which followed John Quincy Adams, the states which in the closing quarter of the nineteenth century consistently opposed any compromise with silver, and in general, those which were most respectful of vested interests have been found in the North Atlantic division, most consistently in New England. The region most concerned in preventing Negro suffrage, the South, has been proverbially "solid" since reconstruction. The same Middle Western states which produced the granger movement were also the storm center of the greenback movement, and the populistic and the progressive party development. Often a map of a presidential election when the state is taken as a unit seems to reveal a northern zone against a southern zone. But analysis always shows that these apparently unified zones are in reality divided into separate wings, held together by some agreements on essentials while tending to break apart when the compromises prove irksome.

Roosevelt, for example, held the Northeast and the Northwest together under the battle cry of "the square deal" in his election of 1904. But in 1912 when the two divisions broke apart his strength lay in the Western wing, while his Republican rival was ascendant in the east.

We may carry this analysis farther by mapping votes by counties, and this test reveals interstate areas concealed when the state alone is the unit. We find that what looked like a solid group of states north of the Ohio, for example, is really made up of subdivisions; the democratic counties extend into Indiana, Illinois and parts of Ohio like fringes from the South, while the prairie regions, later colonized and by the Yankee stock, are normally Republican. In an earlier period regions along rivers or Great Lakes, where federal internal improvements were desired, and regions where the influence of capital and credit was strong, like the blue grass country of Kentucky and Tennessee and the black belt of the Lower South, tended to be Whig, while the interior agricultural countries were more likely to be Democratic.

This means, that instead of forming separate governmental organizations and settling disputes in European fashion, American divisions have to be sought for by political analysis and mapping by votes. As soon as the test is applied the existence of long enduring and clearly defined political sections is made manifest.

We may speak of them in terms of larger sections, like the South, or the Northeast, or the Middle West, and we may also perceive that there are sections within these larger sections, running across them some times, and into other sections, when we refine the analysis.

To make this clearer and concrete let us recall that there normally runs down along the Alleghanies from Pennsylvania to Georgia a huge peninsula of republicanism denting the solid south, as a military wedge might bulge in a frontier. Year after year this thrust pushes toward the Gulf threatening the unity of the South as a political section as the Alleghanies threatened the unity of the Confederacy.

Statesmen and politicians have long recognized these sectional divisions and have accommodated their policy first to the winning of their section and next to combining their section with others to attain a national position with a platform on which the allied sections could agree.

John Quincy Adams early recognized the danger to New England arising from her political isolation, and when the opportunity presented he combined his section with Clay's political dominion in the Ohio Valley and became President. This "bargain" was not the sordid bartering for the spoils of office which it looked to the indignant eyes of Andrew Jackson. It was in fact a readjustment of sectional alliances, an attempt of New England and parts of the Middle States to dispossess the South in the sphere of influence, the hinterland, in the Ohio Valley. Under this alliance the two northern sections controlled legislation upon tariff, land, and internal improvements, until Jackson's ascendancy broke the combination.

The Hayne and Webster debate in 1830 in which the state sovereignty and nullification discussion bulk so large, in the pages of the historians, was when studied in the actual report, quite as much a conflict of sections, in which the West through Benton charged New England with antagonism to the real interests of the West; and the South through Hayne supported the contention and offered an alliance based upon federal relinquishment of the lands beyond the Alleghanies to the states in which they lay. Webster defended New England as well as Nationalism. The whole period from the close of the war of 1812 to the slavery struggle is in fact characterized by sectional contests, alignments and re-alignments over the principal topics of congressional legislation.

Clay tried to form an entente between conflicting sectional interests, and his main strength rested in the Northeast and on the Ohio. Jackson, Benton, Grundy, and their friends championed the Mississippi Valley south of Kentucky and welcomed southern aid. Calhoun, seeking the presidency, tried to find some system of sectional adjustment. He was firmly entrenched in the slave-holding region especially in the Southeast, and was ready to suggest the advantage of a separate custom house for the cotton-raising and exporting states. He would make South Carolina the outlet for the Ohio Valley by fostering railroads to Charleston; and was ready to conciliate the West by offering her what his eastern enemies called the "splendid bribe" of the public lands.

Similar sectional alliances marked the compromise platform of the Democrats in 1844, when Oregon up to fifty four forty was offered to the Northwestern Democrats, and Texas to the southern Democrats. The difficulty in carrying out the bargain fostered the split in the Democracy characterized by the Wilmot Proviso controversy. The recent history of the silver struggle, and the progressive movement, is full of illustrations of the underlying sectionalism of our parties.

Thus we may apply to our intersectional political history terms familiar in the international history of Europe. The areas devoted respectively to freedom and slavery under the Ordinance of 1787 and the Missouri Compromise were rival spheres of influence of the Atlantic sections. The struggle over Louisiana, Missouri, Texas, and Kansas, Nebraska, was a struggle for balance of power. So also was the contest over the admission of the territories of the New Northwest about 1889 and 1890. Negotiations, alliances, treaties have been concealed under sectional divisions in votes in Congress, and in the factions and the platforms of national nominating conventions. Party platforms embody the terms of agreement of inharmonious sectional wings of the same party, and sometimes cover up these differences by ambiguous, or straddling planks. Sometimes the sectional compromise takes the form of inconsistent nominations for the various offices. Often these alliances fail to stand the test in time of strain, as when the triple alliance of 1840 embracing Harrison Whigs, Clay Whigs, and Tyler Whigs broke down when Clay tried to reap the fruits of victory. A similar break-down marks the alliance of Eastern and Western Republicans under Roosevelt's gospel of the square deal, when Taft gave an eastern interpretation to its terms, and Roosevelt a western.

Nevertheless it is important to keep in mind that parties continued to be nominally national through the whole of our history, except for a brief period on either side of the civil war. Lines of counties having the same political complexion ran across the major sections. Islands of democracy existed in republican seas, and the reverse. But quite as important also is the fact that distinctly republican or democratic regions contain minorities of the opposite party, varying from close divisions to a mere party flavor. As Professor Giddings[8] has pointed out, majorities are generally so small and the separate groups that make up a section or a dominant party are in such a state of unstable equilibrium, are bound by such weak ties to the section or party as a whole, that any program of drastic oppression of one section or interest by another would quickly reveal that the differences between the allied interests were important as well as the points of agreement; and so the positive sectional or party program of exploitation would meet shipwreck, would find its own forces disintegrating and re-forming in new combinations.

With his imperfect experience with parties, Washington warned his countrymen against them; he feared parties and party spirit, because he had found them closely related to sections in his day, and because they were so violent, so saturated with the passions of rival supporters of England or of France. But in truth party ties have been profoundly influential in holding the nation together. There was an inter-sectional party patriotism, a national feeling between the differ-

[8] A reference to the Columbia University sociologist Franklin H. Giddings, whose essay "The Nature and Conduct of Political Majorities" appeared in *Political Science Quarterly*, VII (1892), 116-132 .

ent portions of the same party which, except in one tragic period, served as ligaments to hold the parts together.[9]

When North and South reproduced the conditions of Europe by engaging in Civil War, they fought because the conditions which had substituted peaceful sectional interaction for international conflicts had temporarily broken down. There was no longer room for expansion of slavery and freedom side by side. The West, that reservoir of compromise and amelioration, was being shut off to Southern advance. Parties had gradually become sectional. Sectional self-consciousness and sectional differences over the standards of ethics as well as politics had in reality brought about the existence of separate countries for the time. The constitution was re-construed (contrary to the interpretation of men like Washington) as a mere alliance of sovereign states, and behind the state stood the section giving force to its complaint. In effect the South had ceased to feel that its relations with the North were closer than with England. It had come to believe that Cotton was king and that it would better seek entangling alliances with England and France than to fall under the sway of the anti-slavery north. And all this proceeded from the fact that Negro slavery differentiated the South as a separate section, — that for the time party and section coincided, that parties as a nationalizing force had broken down.

We are now in a position briefly to reach conclusions why the United States did not become, as it might well have become, another Europe.

Separated by the ocean, when transportation was so defective that the ocean really divided us, from the Old World, we were able to exclude Europe from our own midst, and by following the ad-

[9] Turner's interlinear notation after this sentence reads: "[Insert A] [Calhoun Corr. 452]." Although no "insert" accompanies the manuscript, Turner's copy of J. Franklin Jameson's edition of *Correspondence of John C. Calhoun* (Washington, D.C., 1900), p. 452, HEH Rare Book 204788, contains his marginalia. Turner has marked a passage in a letter of April 2, 1840, from Calhoun to James H. Hammond, which gives Calhoun's view of our national political parties: "I think our natural political condition is the absence of local parties, and that past experience for the last thirty years shows it. It results from a fortunate political organization of the State Government, and is the real cause of our great relative ascendancy and influence in the Union."

vice of Washington, we were able to develop our own primary interests regardless of her quarrels. No sharp distinctions of language, race, ideals or religion characterized our separate sections, except for slavery. Where faint suggestions of such distinctions exist today their potential menace is clearly in evidence. Our governmental organs developed federally while both state and nation were in the gristle, plastic, incomplete. From the colonial beginning there had been a general government, assigned varying functions but always checking the sense of state or sectional separateness. As we grew, we found our economic interests conserved by assigning to the central government control over such important matters as the tariff and interstate commerce. In effect we created a continental *Zollverein,* a free trade customs union within the limits of the United States, and so avoided some powerful temptations to take arms.

Before the expanding nation was the great West, offering, it is true, opportunities for rivalries, but offering also, because so vast, the means of compromising the differences, and affording the opportunity to turn our energies and ambitions to peaceful construction. This vast unorganized empire was incorporated into the union under our unique federal colonial system. The American people did not extend by conquests of colonies by powerful separate states, but by the organization of territories under the system framed in the Ordinance of 1787, and by the admission of these territories as states, equal in a sisterhood of states, as they came to maturity. The public domain constitutes also a great national treasury, a common fund to be administered by the whole Union, thus forming a tie of interest. Democracy and equality of opportunity became almost the American religion and these were associated with the idea of a united nation. Finally, and perhaps quite as important as any other one factor, national parties constituted a means of common action on an interstate and intersectional scale. They divided the sections themselves at the same time that they furnished a bond between the sections. They furnished a party feeling, a party allegiance on an intersectional scale.

No mere alliance of sections would have held the Union together; no mere tribunal acting upon Confederated states, no league for the preservation of peace, could have exacted obedience to its decrees; no intersectional or international military or naval force would have sufficed to prevent wars. Rather they would have precipitated wars. But space, and time, and the freshness of youth permitted this nation to grow up remote from the tyranny of Old World customs and traditions; permitted us to bind our sections together with gentle ties of party organization, with outlets for sectional ideals and interests, sectional feeling and sectional energy under the forms of party agreements between sections, party rivalries, and peaceful voting.

Are we not fortunate in this outcome? Does it not offer opportunities for high ideals, for self sacrifice, for competition in service to humanity, as effective as the opportunity afforded by the rivalry of force, the bloody competition of warring nations? Is not the rich variety of American life, as it expresses itself in its varied sectional ideals; in its varied and yet united sectional literature; in its Southern home feeling; its New England home feeling; its Western home feeling, a providential substitute for the patriotism of separate European nations? Is not our national patriotism the better because it is made up of many sectional patriotisms all bound into one by the "mystic chords of memory," by the name, American; by love for the flag of many stars?

"Oh, how sweet is the quiet of these parts," wrote William Penn from the American woods, in the days when the armies of Louis the Fourteenth were devastating Europe, — "Oh, how sweet is the quiet of these parts, freed from the anxious and troublesome solicitations, hurries and perplexities of woeful Europe!" Have we not, indeed, solved the problem of a variety of cultures without the need of destroying civilization to maintain one variety or to provide for its unchecked development? Shall we not hold fast to that which is good, even though to maintain this American system we must build still stronger walls against the use of force by approaching Europe in this New World, and arm still more strongly the defenders of those walls?

Washington made peace possible in America by taking the sword. He cut the bonds that bound us to the Old World. We Americans will be found strong enough to forge and use a sword that shall preserve his work and his ideals[10] against European efforts to control or to divide us into social groups. Out of our own experience in a federation of sections, held together in matters of political activity by party ties which run across sectional self-consciousness, we can furnish a remedy to Europe for its national particularism and for the imperialism of immoderate nationalism.

WASHINGTON THE NATIONALIST[1]

A nation is known by the heroes which it keeps. It is well that Americans meet to celebrate their great men, and none was worthier of veneration than the man to whom the Sons of the Revolution pay tribute today. No nation has a nobler galaxy of statesmen in its history than has the United States. That we preserve their memory and seek to profit by their example is an evidence of the soundness of the American spirit and a ground for confidence in the future of this people.

What, we may ask, entitles a man to the name of great American?

First, I should say, the man must have those elemental qualities and achievements which have won the assent of the World to his right among the great ones of the earth. His greatness must be recognized by the other nations as well as by his own.

This recognition Washington has won in both hemispheres.

He must be great also in the traits which most distinguish the nation itself. He must be a great American — one who has had

[10] The original copy of the manuscript ends here. The final sentence and a half appear on the last sheet of an accompanying carbon of the manuscript and are marked "added 1921."

[1] MS: HEH, TU File Drawer 15, pages entitled "Washington the Nationalist" in an envelope laid in folder marked "Notes for an address on Washington's Birthday. Boston, Feb. 22, 1923." In this folder Turner has a notation referring the reader to the quotation of his comments in Arthur H. Vandenberg's *The Greatest American, Alexander Hamilton* (New York, 1921), pp. 19-21. Turner there concludes that Abraham Lincoln was "the greatest American."

close contact with the main currents of the life of the United States, who has reflected its aspirations and ideals in his own time, and has in addition been a leader in the movements which have continued to mould his country. He must embody in a supreme way the deeper and enduring qualities of his people. He must be a nationalist rather than a sectionalist, for while the man of a section may be a great man, he is not a great American. In the award of that distinction, the people of all the sections must unite. He must transcend the bounds of party leadership, as well, and be able to win the confidence and the respect of rival political camps.

On all these counts Washington clearly ranks as a great American, perhaps the first of those who in point of time are entitled to that name, unless we except Benjamin Franklin. In the mastery of men he was supreme. To have handled such opposing statesmen as Hamilton and Jefferson and have used them for the common service of the nation is in itself to have proved his greatness.

I suppose that among the tests of a great American are his attitude toward democracy, his confidence in the people's capacity to rule themselves under leadership. Here Washington clearly surpassed Hamilton. When some of his officers in the dark days before the Constitution proposed a dictatorship to him his indignant rejection of the suggestion placed him forever above the group of military heroes who in other lands and times have yielded to that temptation. Writing to John Jay of the fact that "even respectable characters speak of a monarchical form of Government without horror," he exclaimed: "what a triumph for our enemies to verify their predictions! what a triumph for the advocates of despotism to find that we are incapable of governing ourselves, and that systems founded on the basis of equal liberty are merely ideal and fallacious!"[2] If we contrast this with Hamilton's profound distrust of the people, his desire for an executive during good behavior, his characterization of the constitution as a frail and worthless fabric. "Our real disease is democracy" said Hamilton and he feared the "poison" of it.

On the other hand, contrast Washington with Jefferson, whose love of liberty so far transcended his love of order that he thought a

[2] Washington to John Jay, Aug. 1, 1786, in *The Writings of George Washington*, ed. Fitzpatrick, XXVIII, 503.

revolution every twenty years might be a good thing. Washington's democracy was not a revolutionary democracy; he put down the Whiskey Insurrection by force.

Not only was Washington representative of America's trust in the people, he was American and a nationalist, by his experience and sympathies. Let us recall some of the ways in which he had shared and led in the fundamental movements of American life in his time.

Born in 1732 to the life of a Virginia country gentleman, before he was seventeen he was out on the frontier of his day, as a surveyor in the wilderness, sleeping on the ground before a campfire, responding to the fascination and the inspiration to new things which the American forest exercised upon the imagination of those who penetrated within that vast empire which swept from coast to prairie. He became Western frontiersman as well as colonial gentleman. He became the herald of American advance, when as the agent of the governor of Virginia, with a frontier guide and Indian packmen, he followed Nemacolin's path to the upper waters of the Ohio and emerged from the wintry wilderness upon the French fort near Lake Erie, to warn the French that they were encroaching upon English soil. The frontier of New France in the person of Legardeur de Sainte Pierre met the frontier of Virginia in the person of George Washington, the youth of twenty one. Soon after at the forks of the Ohio Washington's guns sounded the beginnings of the fateful contest for the future of North America between the English and the French. His provincials rallied the English regulars after Braddock's defeat, along the road that was to grow into the Old National Turnpike and then the Baltimore and Ohio railroad. In fighting for the forks of the Ohio, Washington was laying the foundation for that industrial power which centers at Pittsburgh today.

In the Revolution men turned instinctively to him as the General of the American armies.

Professor Sloane,[3] once George Bancroft's secretary, tells of a conversation with the Prussian officer who spoke slightingly of the

[3] William Milligan Sloane, 1850-1928, educator and historian, and George Bancroft's secretary and research assistant in the 1870's.

northern generals in our Civil War but who affirmed that we had one military genius — saying that Washington's New Jersey campaign was a model for study. And when Mr. Sloane asked the officer's name he clicked his heels in Prussian salute and answered, "Von Moltke."

We may be confident that this is good authority on Washington's reputation as a general. But it was not only his skillful Fabian tactics and his courage and skill in seizing the moment for attack. Washington's character and wisdom constituted [the] pivot of the American cause during the revolution. Whether it was in pressing upon a divided and ineffective Congress the need of men, supplies, and plans, or in heartening the suffering soldiers during the hardships of Valley Forge, when their country seemed to have forgotten their services and their needs, it was upon Washington that the Union hinged.

We who live in the shadow of the Elm under which tradition says he took command of the American army, and who pass his residence at Craigie house in Cambridge, know of his services to Boston and to New England. When Bernard the Englishman remarked to him in his retirement at Mount Vernon upon the differences between the inhabitants of New England and the Southern states Washington replied: "I esteem those people greatly, they are the stamina of the Union and its greatest benefactors." The South, the North and the West were all embraced in Washington's experience and sympathy. He was no sectionalist who thought of the Union in terms of his own province, but a Nationalist. While at Cambridge he recommended to the President of Congress as the army uniform the hunting shirt of the frontier, saying, July 10, 1775, "I know nothing so trivial in a speculative View, that in Practice would have a happy Tendency to unite the men and abolish those Provincial distinctions which lead to Jealousy and Dissatisfaction."[4] When Morgan's men from the Virginia Valley and Cresap's rangers from Maryland, and riflemen from Pennsylvania rushed to the support of the Yankees around Boston garbed in hunting shirts and moccasins, and armed with rifles, tomahawks and hunting knives, Washington's belief

[4] *The Writings of George Washington*, ed. Fitzpatrick, III, 325.

that the frontier [and] nationalism went together was strikingly illustrated.

Washington was a nationalist, an all-American. He knew by personal experience all sections. A native of Virginia, he had spent much of his youth in West Virginia, Maryland and Pennsylvania. He travelled through the South; and lived in Cambridge, New York, Philadelphia, Mt. Vernon, and in New Jersey camps. He traversed and studied the routes between the East and the West — that rising empire as he called it. He explored the Mohawk route to the Great Lakes, which became the Erie Canal; and the line of Braddock's march which became the Old National Road, and the Potomac and Ohio canal route. From the conferences over interstate commerce and internal improvements held at Mt. Vernon came the Annapolis convention, and finally the Constitutional Convention over which he presided. We may well believe that from his chair, his approving smile encouraged all the friends of a national government and his grave seriousness checked the advocates of State selfishness. Called to the Presidency of the country he had saved he exhibited the same breadth of view, the same confident courage in his country's destiny, the same reprobation of local and sectional jealousies. The words of his farewell address still live warning us against characterizing parties by geographical discriminations and against the "misrepresentation of the opinions and aims" of different sections.

Washington was great and national too in his determination that the United States should be no mere appendage of the Old World, but should stand firmly on its own American feet.

Would Washington have favored our entering the League of Nations today? It is not the historian's business to prophesy — much less to chart the course of our great men of the past under the changed and complex conditions of the day.

When Frederick the Great learned of the Declaration of Independence he called it a crisis in the affairs of *Europe*. But Washington saw another destiny for us and would not "entangle our peace and prosperity in the toils of European ambition, rivalship, interest, humor or caprice"; and he reprobated a passionate attachment for any one European nation declaring that the nation which indulges toward another an habitual hatred or an habitual fondness is in some degree a slave.

But this the historian may do. He may depict the specific conditions of the time which called out the words of the Farewell Address and he may discuss the mental and moral qualities of the statesman himself as a basis for an opinion.

Washington was the last man to attempt to freeze American policy into a formula regardless of time and conditions. We must not let the heroes of our past destroy our own initiative and independent thought. Had Washington followed such a course he would have remained a stationary tidewater slave holding planter, a tory in the Revolution, an advocate of monarchy, a provincial Virginian indifferent to the sister colonies, indifferent to the new and finer society which together they were destined to build for a continental nation, a nation which now covers an area as large as all Europe and holds within its territory diverse sections as large as European nations.

All his life Washington had been an innovator. He had rejected old formulae and had shaped his action and his foresight to new conditions. Explorer and pioneer he had refused to remain a country gentleman and a colonial Englishman. He was the herald of English advance into the West. He was a land speculator on the largest scale in the regions into which he saw the tide of civilization would flow. He had the courage, the insight, the creative vision to see a new order of things as the inevitable sequence to this growth, and he marked out the routes of trade, the avenues of communication with a land as yet in wilderness — its infancy — and called it a "rising Empire." A rebel against the formal legalism of the mother country, he led the American army to independence; he helped to overturn that weak constitution called the Articles of Confederation, and the weight of his name aided powerfully to bring in our new republican system. He was an originator in military strategy and tactics. He evolved a new doctrine of neutrality and set the example by his strict administrative act. He was as open minded as he was sound of judgement in determining the course suited to the particular conditions.

What were the conditions fresh in Washington's mind when he

warned against involvement in the ordinary course of European politics, and against interweaving our destiny with any part of Europe?

We were then a nation almost limited to the states of the Atlantic coast, with a population of about five million. Today we span the continent, have over 100 million people, hold wealth equal to that of all Western Europe, and hold as much of the gold of the world as does Europe. In the days of the American Revolution, Adam Smith assured the English farmer that he need not fear the competition of Irish cattle because the ocean barrier afforded sufficient protection in the costs of transportation. Today cattle from our Great Plains and from Argentina furnish much of the roast beef of England. The world has shrunk. Where then it took the sailing vessel six weeks to cross the Atlantic, it now takes the steamer four or five days. By radio we hold practically instantaneous conversation with Europe. What happens in Russia, in Mesopotamia, in Japan, and China, on the Ruhr, is reflected in the markets of New York and Boston and Chicago. Even the Dakotan farmer's prosperity rises and falls with that of Europe.

We who sought neutrality found ourselves by the very force of circumstances involved in the World War. The American flag has just descended from Ehrenbreitstein on the Rhine and our dead lie buried in the fields of Flanders and of France. We have found that the embers of the European conflagration fall on our own house. Even the administration which refused the League of Nations has had its observers in European councils and their voices have been heard on the question of the merits of Reparations and on the Turkish problem. We called a conference of nations at Washington and signed agreements covering the Pacific Ocean and scrapping the Dreadnaughts of the Atlantic. We are no longer feeble, we are no longer isolated, the world is not Washington's world.

When Washington spoke his farewell words England on our northwestern border had just been aiding the Indians to hold to the Ohio river and had been tampering with the loyalty of men in Vermont, Kentucky and Ohio. Spain held the eastern banks of the lower Mississippi and its mouth and strove to disrupt the Mississippi Valley by pressure of the Indians and by seducing our leading

Westerners to her allegiance. France had sent her commissions and had raised forces in Kentucky, Tennessee and the back country of the Carolinas and Georgia to wrest Louisiana from Spain and to compel the Union to follow her policy or lose the whole Mississippi Valley eastward to the Alleghanies. In a word the powerful rival nations of Europe were lodged in our very midst; they blocked our road to the West; they used our ports for prizes and blockaded our shipping at our very doors. Americans were divided into partisans of France or partisans of England, forgetful of their own country, and with a bitterness of feeling that made mobs, and turned our domestic issues into party contests of friendship for this or that European power.

Removed from the European state system we have built up the American peace for a whole continent where sections take the place of nations, where legislation replaces war, where adjustments of differences are made in the spirit of reasonableness and compromise.

Unless Europe learns of some such way, her civilization is doomed to fall in a great catastrophy. Nor can any man say that Latin America will not become involved, nor Asia, nor Africa — for the spirit of militarism re-aroused and equipped by the efficiency of modern science applied to war will not set barriers to its march. Will the United States escape?

What Washington would do with all this power and wealth and moral force in the face of these conditions no man can say with assurance. His mantle has not descended to the most confident of the editors or the senators who would speak for him and in his name.

It is a great name! The nation which he founded has become a great nation — so great that the question turns upon whether its economic and moral force is not strong enough to impress an American system and American ways upon Europe rather than to submit to fear from the influence of Europe upon itself. Would Washington lead the way to an American solution?

This at least we may say. If Washington were living at this hour we should have a statesman who would apply to the problem a grave serenity, devoid of partizanship, a breadth of vision, a calm confidence in his country's duty and destiny, a courageous trust in her fundamental ideals as a medicine for a sick world. We should

148

have a national statesman, not the spokesman for a section, or a single party. We should have an American sound in character, sane, just, well balanced in his judgement, a man of vision but no visionary, strong in mind, in definiteness of purpose and in will; rich in soul — a man whose natal day we may celebrate with thanks to God that he gave us and the world his example and his inspiration.

4

❧ American Social History

THE FOLLOWING FOUR PAPERS *lie at the very heart of Turner's work. In them he devotes himself to exploring the broad developments of American history and in particular the way in which the constantly advancing frontier helped to form regions of varying stages of evolutionary development, all in a state of flux.*

In the first of these selections Turner describes in some detail a pioneer of the backwoods. "The Hunter Type," an early draft of an essay, is by no means typical of Turner, tending as it does to romanticize the subject in the mode of Theodore Roosevelt's The Winning of the West. *Turner seems to have been aware of this, for sentences he tentatively deleted as he reread and marked the manuscript were those glorifying the backwoodsmen or attributing to them sentiments they might not have had: "They loved to hear the crack of their long rifles, and the blows of the ax in the forest." Turner's idea that the* type *more than the* individual *should concern the investigator of American history is clearly evidenced here. Although the theory is advanced with assurance in other Turner essays, it seems to falter in its argument to convince in this early piece, written about 1890.*

But "The Hunter Type" has other interesting features. If we examine Turner's description of the backwoodsman and then read

151

his essay "The Development of American Society," which raises the modern problem of American individualism faced with state intervention, we cannot avoid observing that his knowledge and admiration of the "hunter type" coexists with his knowledge that modern America requires the individual to accept the intervention of the state in certain areas in the interests of good government. Turner's sympathies — and his understanding — are wide.

All the essays reveal the extent to which Turner ignored the established boundaries separating the academic disciplines, the extent to which he thought of himself as sociologist as well as historian, therefore concerned with the present as well as the past. These pieces also illustrate Turner's refusal to identify himself with any one school of historical thought. Scholars have increasingly made themselves specialists in limited fields of knowledge, but Turner was moving in the other direction. He was one of the very few modern scholars who have attempted to bring together the disciplines. Gifted with an extraordinarily broad range of interests, he refused to accept arbitrary rules limiting the scope of his investigations.

Turner was fascinated by the way in which the past clarifies the present. The study of the American past he found particularly valuable, for through it certain universal patterns of evolution could be traced and identified. America was a microcosm in which the development of a society from primitive beginnings to its complex industrial state could be studied in detail. Under his microscope Turner could examine the European immigrant and his reaction to the wild American environment; moreover, the changes which the environment wrought on the immigrant as well as those which he wrought on the environment might be charted. His traits of character, those that are representatively American, could be identified and traced back to their origins in the more primitive life lived by early Americans. Such an approach, emphasizing as it does the sociological factors that formed our society, is one which readers familiar with Turner's published work will associate particularly with his important presidential address before the American Historical Association in 1910 on "Social Forces in American History."

❧ THE HUNTER TYPE[1]

On the western outskirts of the Atlantic colonies, pressing continually toward the West, dwelt the American backwoodsmen.[2] (They found too little elbow-room in town-life. They loved to hear the crack of their long rifles, and the blows of the ax in the forest. A little clearing, edged by the woods, and a log house, — this was the type of home they loved.)[3] All along the uplands from Pennsylvania to Georgia, forming a cordon of defence to the colonists of the lower lands toward the east, lived these pioneers. They had come from various nations. Louis the XIV, the Grand Monarch of France, had revoked the Edict of Nantes, and thereby forced thousands of his Huguenot subjects into exile. Some of them found their way to the American backwoods, among them the ancestors of John Sevier . . . .[4]

What was the life of the backwoodsman?

The backwoodsman arrayed himself in fur cap, moccasins, or leggins, as did the Indian he met. The most distinctive part of his

[1] MS: HEH, TU File Drawer 15, folder marked " 'The Hunter Type,' 1890." Turner's accompanying notations indicate that the essay was written about 1890 and that it was largely based on the first volume of Theodore Roosevelt's *The Winning of the West*. Turner's annotated copy of this work, 4 vols. (New York, 1889-96), HEH Rare Book 139455, has a number of marked passages which suggest that Roosevelt's first two volumes provided a romantic inspiration for the frontier hypothesis. Roosevelt, for instance, in a passage marked by Turner (Vol. I, p. 7), writes eloquently about the "true significance" of "the vast movement by which this continent was conquered and peopled." See also Turner's review of Vols. I and II of this work in *Dial*, X (1889-90), 71-73.

[2] This sentence was deleted by Turner but has been restored to introduce the essay.

[3] Diagonal pencil lines across the first page indicate that Turner probably deleted the next four sentences.

[4] Turner has renumbered the pages in the manuscript, and part of the essay at this point may be missing.

garment was the hunting shirt. This was a "kind of loose frock of cloth or deerskin," reaching "nearly to the knees," "open before, and so wide as to lap over a foot or two when belted." The cape was large and sometimes handsomely fringed. The bosom served as a wallet to hold a chunk of bread, and the tow for wiping out the rifle. On the belt were hung the bullet bag, the tomahawk and the scalping knife. A long rifle and an ax completed his equipment.[5]

The woodsmen lived remote from city life. Continually they kept pushing by families or small groups of families, toward the west. They moved by the aid of packhorses carrying their household goods which included the few kitchen utensils and flour and bacon, salt and seed corn, and some changes of clothes. As they journeyed the daughters walked beside the mother, who rode on the horse. In front came the father and the stalwart sons. Generally they settled in small groups of families and built a palisaded log fort. A range of cabins made one side of the fort, and stockades the rest. At the angles of the fort were blockhouses of logs. Such defenses were common in New England and among the French traders as well. As a rule the settlers lived outside and only collected in the stockade when the Indian was on the war path. The cabin was of rough logs and had a solid plank door and two or three little windows, in which *oiled paper* took the place of *glass*. The roof was covered with cut saplings; and the so called "puncheon floor" was made of split logs, with the flat side up. A chimney of sticks and stones laid in clay was built up against the side. The deep open fireplace was the center of the home-life. About it on wooden pegs hung the weapons, the utensils, and the family wardrobe. Display of clothes indicated wealth. The bed was covered with furs. Three legged stools furnished seats, and in the corner was the water bucket with a gourd for drinking cup. Hog and hominy and corn pone made a substantial if not delicate diet. Such houses are not unknown in the woods of northern Wisconsin today.

And though their life was rugged and the men were like their surroundings, yet the element of fun was not lacking. The boys loved to contend in wrestling, running and jumping. They learned

[5] Turner's marginal note: "Hatred of Indian."

to throw the tomahawk, and to hunt. They learned to mimic the noise of bird and beast and by imitating the gobble of the turkeys, or the bleat of the fawn, they often brought them in range of their rifles. For the older ones there was the log-rolling, the corn-shucking, the house-raising, and the quilting bee. They loved to dance, especially the rollicking Irish trot, and not seldom they loved to fight.[6]

They spun their own wool and flax and tanned the leather for their clothing. Ground their corn in hand mill. General home industries. Need of salt, and iron. The pack train — after fall seeding.[7]

SOME SOCIOLOGICAL ASPECTS OF AMERICAN HISTORY[1]

In a recent paper on the requirements for the historical doctorate, Professor Emerton, of Harvard, dismisses American history as a subject for historical investigation, with the remark that the narrowest of all fields is the history of our own country.[2]

The observation will commend itself to many. It is easy to see the reasons for such a view. America's chronology is brief; her story at first sight seems to lack in color, in richness and complexity. She can show no such many-sided wealth of institutional life, of human thought and endeavor in many of its relations, as appear in the history of Old World nations. It is not surprising that the historian

[6] Turner has decorated the above paragraph with a series of diagonal and circular lines without clearly deleting it.

[7] Turner cites Roosevelt, *The Winning of the West*, I, 121.

[1] MS: HEH, TU File Drawer 15, folder marked "Some Sociological Aspects of Am. History. Lake Forest Col., Lecture. 1895 — April 13." A notation in Turner's handwriting provides the date.

[2] Ephraim Emerton, "The Requirements for the Historical Doctorate in America," *Annual Report of the American Historical Association for the Year 1893* (Washington, D.C., 1894), pp. 79-90.

who unrolls the gorgeous vellum of mediaeval history fails to appreciate the importance of American history.

Nevertheless, I do not think it can be justly said that our history is narrow. It has been made to appear narrow, with its emphasis upon Pocahontas, and the town-pump. But these things are the faults of the historians, not of the history. From the University at Padua come these words of Achille Loria: "America has the key to the historical enigma which Europe has sought for centuries in vain; and the land which has no history, reveals luminously the course of Universal history."[3] These are the convictions of a sociologist, and it is from the sociological point of view that American history becomes of profound significance. Missing this point of view our historians have failed to present their subject in its real dignity. Henry Adams has well said: "The scientific interest of American history centred in national character, and in the workings of a society destined to become vast, in which individuals were important chiefly as types. Although this kind of interest was different from that of European history, it was at least as important to the world. Should history ever become a true science, it must expect to establish its laws, not from the complicated story of rival European nationalities, but from the methodical evolution of a great democracy. North America was the most favorable field on the globe for the spread of a society so large, uniform, and isolated as to answer the purposes of science."[4]

This, then, is the justification for the study of American history, and this, it seems to me, gives the point of view from which this history may be most profitably approached. If in other countries men may be studied for themselves, and for their influence on their time, in America men are to be studied primarily as expressions of the development of a great democracy in a given age and environ-

[3] This passage is marked in Turner's copy of *Analisi della proprieta capitalista* (Torino, 1889), II, 15, HEH Rare Book 114780. The translated quotation appears also in *The Frontier in American History*, p. 11.

[4] Adams, "American Character," in his *History of the United States of America* (New York, 1891), IX, 222. The quotation, without citation, appears in the chapter "Problems in American History," in Turner's *The Significance of Sections in American History*, p. 7.

Turner "On the Trail" in 1904 with His Daughter, Dorothy

ment. I would not seek to diminish the study of our history as a fountain of patriotism. The story of its statesmen and heroes is well worth the reading and the teaching. It is important, also, to know the history of its governments, local, state and national. These things are essential to the exercise of intelligent citizenship. But deeper than the facts of individual life and political institutions are the great undercurrents of society, that ocean that moves, and changes, and surges evermore beneath the ships of state that float on its bosom. It is only by understanding the reactions between American society and the American environment that we shall be able rightly to estimate the significance of American political history. The subject has been pigeon holed into divisions based on state geography, or the four-year periods of presidential administrations. Of America as a social organism growing and changing in reaction with its environment, we hear very little.[5]

If we turn to consider what have been the most essential features in American development we are met at the outset with the fact that here was a continent sparsely inhabited by a primitive people. To this continent came Europeans bringing with them ideas, institutions and social traits from the Old World. At once a most interesting interaction occurred. A highly developed civilization was sharply precipitated into a Wilderness environment. Obviously the outcome of this phenomenon will be a resultant of three forces: the European germs; the native races; and the physiography of the new continent. To neglect any one of these factors is to miss the truth. Our history is one of social and institutional modification. First of the modification of European material under the new American conditions. Second of the modification of Eastern material by the West. America has been a transforming agent bringing forth continually new products from the elements she has received.

The early history of our country — the colonial period proper — is a history of European germs developing in an American environ-

[5] Deletion by Turner: "The work of the historian of the United States should account for and explain the characteristics of the United States of today; it should enable the present age to understand itself by understanding its development from the past. To state this fact is to show the inadequacy of our histories."

ment. The usually dull pages of Colonial history become full of interest and instruction when studied from this point of view. We see in the Seventeenth century the planting of these germs, the struggle of them for existence in a new environment. From the earliest days a process of transformation, a process of Americanization begins. In the course of the first half of the Eighteenth century these modified forms of English institutions have become clearly developed.[6] We have ideas and institutions that are to some extent American. This colonial process occurred on the coast area, between the Atlantic and the "fall line"; the tidewater region. In this period England had extended her borders to include the better part of our Atlantic coast; she absorbed it into her state system, and worked it like a farm for the benefit of the mother country. The ships that sailed between the ports of England and those of her colonies were like shuttles, weaving close the warp of a common life. The colonist read the English news, and the English books. The merchants were the agents of English firms. The connection between the Old World and the tidewater area of the New World was close and constant; and so in spite of all the modifying forces of the new land, the coast area was profoundly influenced by England, and reflected English characteristics. Even the wilderness environment and the dividing ocean could not transform a section continually in touch with the Old World. Before the wilderness could remodel these earliest colonists, the wilderness itself had fallen before the assaults of the continually recruited European civilization. Thus the coast area seemed likely to produce institutions and men who were but partly modified shoots from the parent tree. Even the physical features of the colonial Americans of the coast are described as English by travellers of the Eighteenth century. The ruddy complections, without delicacy of feature or play of expression are noted, and the phlegmatism of the colonists is frequently commented upon.

Thus in the early phases of the evolution of American society we

[6] Deletion by Turner: "and to English ideas, and men, have been added Scotch-Irish, German, and French ideas and men. Blending, these elements wrought a further modification of the English type, and gave new characteristics to the American society that was developing."

see formed along the Atlantic coast an aggregate of European populations with institutions representing modifications of those of the Old World. We can hardly call this social aggregate a unit, for the circumstances of colonization as well as the physiography had caused the recognition, even in colonial days that there were three fairly well defined sections in the coast region. The *Southern* section of the tidewater area was occupied chiefly by Englishmen modified by a warm climate, and the utilization of slave labor. The planter and his household living on a large estate, in a life comparable to that of the English country gentleman, made the social unit. The raising of staples like tobacco and rice for exportation was the typically colonial industrial interest. Settlement was rural rather than urban.

In *New England* we have radically a different environment, — a broken coast line full of little harbors, the hills near the sea, the rivers short and tumbling, a land suited to the raising of a race of fishers and sailors, merchants, and hardy farmers. Here we have the Englishman with an ideal, — Puritanism. This religious and social ideal dominated and distinguished the section. The town, a compact settlement, with congregation and town meeting took the place of the plantation as the social unit.

Between these two sections lay still a third section, the middle region. New York harbor was an open door to all Europe; the middle region was less English than the other sections. "It had a wide mixture of nationalities, a varied society, the mixed town and county system of local government, a varied economic life, many religious sects. In short, it was a region mediating between New England and the South . . . . It represented that composite nationality which the contemporary United States exhibits, that juxtaposition of non-English groups, occupying a valley or a little settlement, and presenting reflections of the map of Europe in their variety. It was democratic and nonsectional, if not national; 'easy, tolerant, and contented'; rooted strongly in material prosperity. It was typical of the modern United States."[7]

[7] This quotation is the first of a number of clippings which Turner inserted in the manuscript from a printed copy of "The Significance of the Frontier in American History," *Annual Report of the Amer. Hist. Assoc. . . . 1893,*

These sections are therefore real social factors in American history. The history of such groups as these is necessarily a more fundamental fact than the facts of separate colonies or states. If these sections had been unable to expand, we should have had to study the interactions of the three sections with each other and with Europe. This, indeed, is the work to which most of our historians have devoted themselves. But in fact these three sections were expanding and this fact our historians have neglected. The tidewater settlements had in the rear a vast unoccupied continent, a treasure house of opportunities. Here were lands, and mines, and forests, and material resources innumerable, enticing men continually to the wilderness. The tidewater society with its modified Old World traits was on the march toward the West. Each of these tidewater sections was spreading to the interior; there to undergo transformations, to meet and interact with the other sections.

This, then, is the second phase of American social growth, the occupation of the West.

"Behind institutions, behind constitutional forms and modifications, lie the vital forces that call these organs into life and shape them to meet changing conditions. The peculiarity of American institutions is, the fact that they have been compelled to adapt themselves to the changes of an expanding people — to the changes involved in crossing a continent, in winning a wilderness, and in developing at each area of this progress out of the primitive economic and political conditions of the frontier into the complexity of city life. Said Calhoun in 1817, 'We are great, and rapidly — I was about to say fearfully — growing!' So saying, he touched the distinguishing feature of American life. All peoples show development; the germ theory of politics has been sufficiently emphasized. In the case of most nations, however, the development has occurred in a limited area; and if the nation has expanded, it has met other growing peoples whom it has conquered. But in the case of the United States we have a different phenomenon. Limiting our attention to the Atlantic coast, we have the familiar phenomenon of the evolution

pp. 199-227. The first clipping is from p. 220. Quotation marks are supplied by the editor. "The Significance of the Frontier in American History" is reprinted in *The Frontier in American History*, pp. 1-38.

of institutions in a limited area, such as the rise of representative government; the differentiation of simple colonial governments into complex organs; the progress from primitive industrial society, without division of labor, up to manufacturing civilization."[8]

But in addition to this in this *second* phase of our social development we have the striking and peculiar fact that there has been a recurrence of the process of evolution in each area of the West reached in the course of expansion. "Thus American development has exhibited not merely advance along a single line, but a return to primitive conditions on a continually advancing frontier line, and a new development for that area. American social development has been continually beginning over again on the frontier. This perennial rebirth, this fluidity of American life, this expansion westward with its new opportunities, its continuous touch with the simplicity of primitive society, furnish the forces dominating American character. The true point of view in the history of this nation is not the Atlantic coast, it is the great West."[9] This flow of population along the river valleys and through the mountain passes ever to the West has gone on up to our own day. The colonization of America did not end with the planting of Georgia. To trace the successive stages of this occupation of the continent, and the consequent transformations of American society, is the task of the future historians who shall give an adequate explanation of the America of today, its men, its institutions, and its ideas.

There are successive stages of this advance, each stage related to a natural territorial area. The first stage was the occupation of the oldest "West," the land between the Blue Ridge and the "fall line," in other words the land between the mountains and the settled area of the coast. When this was partly occupied, settlement flowed across the mountains and possessed the region between the Mississippi and the Alleghanies. These successive movements are closely related, and they are so important that I shall ask your attention to

[8] Clipping from *Annual Report of the Amer. Hist. Assoc. . . . 1893*, pp. 199-200.

[9] Ibid., p. 200.

some of the social characteristics resulting from this spread of settlement from the coast to the Mississippi.[10]

.   .   .   .

Obviously we have here a region decidedly different from the sections of the Atlantic coast. But a most obvious and important fact in this connection is the fact that this region is one that is steadily growing. "The *West*" which began with the fall line near the Atlantic has finally so expanded that it is becoming the Nation. The old East has become a fringe on the edge of the map.

Not only has this spread of population made the West almost synonymous with the nation, the West has acted as the great *de-sectionalizing* force. As New England and the South marched westward they lost the acuteness of their sectionalism, they became more and more Western. On the tide of the father of waters, North and South met and mingled into a nation. Interstate migration went steadily on, a process of cross fertilization of ideas and institutions. The struggle of the sections over slavery on the Western frontier does not diminish the truth of this statement, it proves the truth of it. Slavery was a sectional trait that would not down. But in the West slavery could not remain sectional. It was the greatest of frontiersmen, Abraham Lincoln, who declared " 'I believe this Government can not endure permanently half slave and half free. It will become all of one thing or all of the other.' Nothing works for nationalism like intercourse within the nation. Mobility of population is death to localism, and the western frontier worked irresistibly in unsettling population."[11] Thus the expansion of New England, the Middle Region and the South into the Mississippi valley led to a blending of these sections. The different sectional colorings were mixed in this palette of the West into a common national hue, but one section gave the tint to the new color. This section was the Middle Region.

The Middle Region was not cut off from the West by the moun-

[10] Turner has removed several pages from the manuscript and substituted a sheet marked "Insert Jackson," possibly a reference to inserting a quotation from "The Significance of the Frontier in American History" concerning Jacksonian democracy and the West.

[11] Clipping from *Annual Report of the Amer. Hist. Assoc.* . . . *1893*, p. 221.

tains, as was New England and the South. It was pre eminently the expanding section, mediating between East and West as well as between North and South. Its composite nationality, its democratic social structure, and its natural tendencies were all reflected in the Great West, and thus the Middle Region merged with the West and became the type of American society. It was from this stage of our social development that some of our greatest Americans came. Andrew Jackson had lived his life in this backwoods society. He represented it. All of its rudeness, and rashness, its vehemence and its daring, its democracy and its nationalism, were personified in this backwoods leader of men. From this same frontier society in a later stage of its advancement came Abraham Lincoln. And these two men are perhaps the most distinctively American of our national heroes.

I shall not attempt to estimate the characteristics and the results of the later stages of this westward march of the American people. Each stage made a contribution to the character of American society, and each stage has its own lessons for the student of sociology. What problems in social aggregation, in city evolution, in transportation, in all the phases of descriptive sociology do the young communities which have sprung up from the prairies and the mountains west of the Mississippi offer to the student of social evolution, and how unworked is all this material for the historian, the economist, the political scientist! We have lessons here that may serve to interpret the evolution of the Old World as well as that of the New.

I turn next to call your attention to some other aspects of this flow of population.

Not only were various sections expanding to the west and merging into each other; there were various waves of social development crossing the continent. The Atlantic coast was first occupied by fishermen, fur traders, miners, cattle raisers and farmers. Excepting the fisherman, each type of industry was moving toward the West, drawn by an irresistible attraction. If at any date in our national history we were to travel from the West to the Atlantic coast we should have met these successive waves of social development, first the Indian, then the furtrader and hunter, then the cattle raiser, then the farmer, and finally the manufacturer. In other words we have the stages of the industrial evolution of society, here arranged horizontally instead of vertically, spread out across the country. The hunting stage, the pastoral, the agricultural, and the manufacturing stage. Not every area has passed through each of these stages, though many of them have. But all have evolved through some of these separate social developments. What is now the manufacturing state of Ohio was earlier almost entirely given over to farming, with diversified crops, still earlier it had been an area of almost exclusive wheat cropping, earlier yet the range with cattle herder was its industrial type, and still earlier Ohio was a furtrading and hunting region. The same is true for parts of Illinois, of Wisconsin, of many of the states of the middle West. Indeed within various states we can still trace these advancing waves of successive industrial phases. Each of these social areas has had an influence in our economic and political history.

To take an example: "The colonial and revolutionary frontier was the region whence emanated many of the worst forms of an evil currency. The West in the war of 1812 repeated the phenomenon on the frontier of that day, while the speculation and wild-cat banking of the period of the crisis of 1837 occurred on the new frontier belt of the next tier of States. Thus each one of the periods of lax financial integrity coincides with periods when a new set of frontier communities had arisen, and coincides in area with these successive frontiers, for the most part. The recent Populist agitation is a case in point. Many a State that now declines any connection with the tenets of the Populists, itself adhered to such ideas in an earlier stage of the development of the State. A primitive society can hardly be expected to show the intelligent appreciation of the complexity of business interests in a developed society."[12]

The United States is at once a developed country and a primitive one. The same political questions have been put to a society advanced in some regions, and undeveloped in others — to the manufacturing areas, to the farming areas, to the grazing and the mining areas. This fact in our social structure is of profound political importance. On specific political questions each area has reflected the

[12] Clipping from *Annual Report of the Amer. Hist. Assoc.* . . . *1893*, p. 223.

ideas natural to its social structure. Moreover as we have seen, in a given area there have been successive stages of social evolution. With each change in social development the region has shown changed political views: thus Wisconsin, once a "Granger" state, has now little sympathy with the Western populists. We shall never understand our political history until we give due study and weight to these different economic areas and economic changes.

American historians ought to make an attempt to map the natural social and industrial areas of the country. Deeper than the facts of state lines lie the facts that there are in America social and economic units which pay little or no attention to boundary lines. For each stage in our history these areas should be mapped and studied. I have placed before you one such map — a map to show the social and economic groupings at the time of the ratification of the federal constitution in 1787-8.

In conclusion let me sum up some of the aspects of American history which are of interest to the sociologist:

First we have the evolution of the society of the Atlantic coast, with its modified European ideas and institutions, and with three well marked sections.

Second we have the expansion of these sections to the West, — the blending of the sections, the transformation of the institutions and ideas of the coast by the backwoods. American society became formed, as settlement flowed west.

Third this movement westward occurred with successive waves of social development: the hunter was followed by the rancher, the rancher by the farmer, the farmer by the manufacturer. Each new area received contributions from the areas to the east; the rancher of the great plains learned his lessons from the rancher of the Cow-pens of the Carolinas; the constitutions of the Dakotas bear the marks [of] the constitutions of the Eastern states. There was social continuity in this advance, but each new area gave opportunity for experimentation as well, and so American society was in continual change.

Fourth each area reached by these successive waves changed its social and political ideals as it underwent these economic changes.

And finally the Continent was crossed by settlement. American character has been formed by this expansion of the American social organism. Moving westward the European became more and more Americanized. As successive terminal moraines result from successive glaciations, or as successive shore lines mark a receding lake, so each frontier of American expansion left behind it traces which persisted in the character of the people. That coarseness and strength combined with acuteness and "inquisitiveness; that practical, inventive turn of mind, quick to find expedients; that masterful grasp of material things, lacking in the artistic but powerful to effect great ends; that restless, nervous energy; that dominant individualism, working for good and for evil, and withal that buoyancy and exuberance which comes with freedom — these are traits of the West, or traits called out elsewhere because of the existence of the West. Since the days when the fleet of Columbus sailed into the waters of the New World, America has been another name for opportunity, and the people of the United States have taken their tone from the incessant expansion which has not only been open but has even been forced upon them. He would be a rash prophet who should assert that the expansive character of American life has now entirely ceased. Movement has been its dominant fact, and, unless this training has no effect upon a people, the American energy will continually demand a wider field for its exercise. But never again will such gifts of free land offer themselves. For a moment, at the frontier, the bonds of custom are broken and unrestraint is triumphant. There is not *tabula rasa*. The stubborn American environment is there with its imperious summons to accept its conditions; the inherited ways of doing things are also there; and yet, in spite of environment, and in spite of custom, each Western advance did indeed furnish a new field of opportunity, a gate of escape from the bondage of the past; and freshness, and confidence, and scorn of older society, impatience of its restraints and its ideas, and indifference to its lessons, have accompanied the Western march."[13]

And now four centuries from the discovery of America, at the end of one hundred years of life under the Constitution, the line

[13] In this clipping, *Annual Report of the Amer. Hist. Assoc. . . . 1893*, p. 227, Turner has deleted the word "frontier" to substitute "West," "Western advance," and "Western march."

of settlement has crossed the continent. We have reached another stage of American social development. The free lands are gone; the labor problem is upon us. We cease to be an isolated state and are beginning to meet questions of foreign relations. For a century the United States has been what John Randolph called it: "The mammoth of the American forest."[14]

. . . .

One of the first steps to be taken is to understand this present day America by seeing how it has come to be what it is, by taking account of the complex and changing social life of America. And after all this is done, capitalist and laboring man, reformer and conservative, will find that Time *alone* is the great transformer; that many of the problems that meet us are only to be settled by these unresting, these unhastening processes of social change.

❧ THE DEVELOPMENT OF AMERICAN SOCIETY[1]

Introduction

It is not without significance that when nations have reached a high level of achievement, when the energy of national life is at full tide, they turn with an irresistible longing to learn more of their history.

It is a profound saying of a German historian that "history is the self-consciousness of humanity."[2] It is humanity's effort to under-

[14] A portion of the manuscript was removed by Turner at this point. The paragraph below follows a sentence fragment ("be a task worthy of the highest endeavor to effect this reconciliation") on a renumbered page.

[1] Source: A copy of the printed article "The Development of American Society," *Alumni Quarterly of the University of Illinois*, II, No. 3 (July 1908), 120-136, with revisions and additions by Turner, HEH Rare Book 126668. Turner's notes on the cover of the article suggest that further revisions might include economic factors stressed by John B. Clark in his introduction to *A Documentary History of American Industrial Society*, ed. John R. Commons et al., I (Cleveland, 1910), 33-53.

[2] A dictum by Johann Gustav Droysen. See pp. 20-21.

stand itself by understanding its origins, by taking stock of the forces that have made a nation what it is, by considering the elements in its development that have been outgrown and laid aside, as well as the institutions, forces and ideas that persist as controlling influences in the life of today.

The things that have been outgrown still serve to interpret us to ourselves, by the contrast which they afford, and by bases which they supply for measuring historical change. The things that persist enable us to see that the present does not shape its own course, but is weighed upon by customs, prepossessions, and tendencies as well as steadied by institutions and inspired and guided by historic leaders and ideas. The nation is builded by successive generations, like the cathedrals of Europe still in process of completion and reflecting the varying tastes of the revolving years.

There is a charm in restoring the past, in compelling the procession of leaders of human thought and action again to traverse the stage of human consciousness, in rescuing from oblivion what is worth the memory of the present day. The events of past years, the institutions that have passed away, the life and manners of societies that have gone are a precious heritage, not to be wantonly ignored in the heat and bustle of the day. Life becomes a richer thing when it is viewed largely, when it is seen as a continuous movement, reaching back to generations that are gone.

When the historian enters upon the task of examining the record of other times, when he confronts the vast accumulation of material for history, he may well be appalled at the magnitude and the difficulty of his task. The materials of history are a great heap of fragments which must be made into a mosaic. Perhaps the supreme task of the historian is that of finding the essential, the really typical and vital in the mass that lies before him. The history of the United States is so brief that this problem of synthesis, this determination of what is worth while to relate, this effort to find the larger lines of development whose origins must be traced back, might seem to be a simple one; but it is not so.

It is said of one of the best of American historians that he ceased writing because he was unable to fashion for himself a criterion of what was relatively important in historical composition. Why should certain things be told and certain other things be left untold? What were the really significant lines of American growth? What, after all, was really worth the telling?

Keys

There have been many *keys to American history;* some writers have found the dominant element in the contest between Puritan and Cavalier; others in the slavery struggle; others in the contests between state and nation; others in the rise of democracy. These are but a few of the solutions. In truth there is no single key to American history. In history, as in science, we are learning that a complex result is the outcome of the interplay of many forces. Simple explanations fail to meet the case. But with all due recognition of the complexity of the historical processes in the United States, it is clear that unless more attention is paid to the essentials, unless more effort is made to discern the really influential forces at work, we shall weave but a tangled web, interesting may be, but without significance.

Society

To him who looks below the surface of things, *the history of the United States derives its interest from the development of its society.* This society is a human sea, — mobile, ever-changing, restless; a sea in which deep currents run, and over the surface of which sweep winds of popular emotion, a sea that has been ever adjusting itself to new shore lines, and new beds. By the side of this mighty movement the story of *individual leaders,* and the narrative of *events* sink into insignificance. For, in America, whatever be the case elsewhere in history, society has shaped its men.

In America, as perhaps nowhere else in the world, we may trace the evolution of a vast population, almost under our gaze, from a handful of colonists lodged in the wilderness, in the presence of untold natural resources, up through a swift succession of changes social and industrial, to a democracy of nearly ninety million souls; from a thin line of European settlement fighting for existence on the edge of the Atlantic to a broad zone of civilization stretching across a continent and finding new problems beyond the rim of the Pacific. Three hundred years ago the successors of the Elizabethans followed Captain John Smith as he struck those first daring blows at

170

the American forest which stretched almost impenetrable across the continent. Yesterday the President of the United States summoned the governors of forty-six states to deliberate upon the danger of the monopoly and exhaustion of the natural resources of the nation. The timber supply was declared to be endangered unless measures were taken for its conservation, and it was said that the depletion of the anthracite coal fields would be effected well within the century, even at its present rate. The duration of the supply of high grade iron ores that had been the basis for so much of the industrial civilization of the United States, and for its economic power in our own day, was shown to be measurable in years instead of the ages which it had taken to create them. The arable public domain that seemed to statesmen like Henry Clay certain to last for ages has now almost passed into private possession, and the nation turns to reclaim the deserts by costly projects of irrigation wherewith to provide 20 acre farms for a people who once thought little of a thousand acres. Truly these three centuries of the unresting toil of the American democracy to master the wilderness have brought an outcome which would have been incredible to John Smith and Governor Bradford.

The time is fitting, therefore, to turn to consider some of the phases of the development of American society in the course of the industrial conquest of the continent. And first I would direct your attention to the fact, so familiar that we may lose its significance in the shaping of this society; that it is indeed a continental phenomenon which we have to observe. As Vidal de la Blache, the geographer, has well said, "The history of a people is inseparable from the country which it inhabits. The Greek people can be represented only in the midst of their seas, the English people only on their island, and the American only in the vast spaces of the United States."

The American had continually before him the vision of a continent to be subdued, challenging his courage and ambition, calling out his endeavor in the presence of unparalleled opportunities, raising the competitive spirit to its highest point, stimulating nervous energy, inventiveness, optimism, practical capacity and largeness of design. This society was compelled from its early days, to grapple with the problem of magnitude. The influence of these far horizons, this amplitude of space upon the American mind, and upon our social development can best be understood by imagining the United States laid down upon Europe. The coasts of Spain and Southern California would then coincide while Constantinople and Charleston, South Carolina, lay near together; Southern Italy and New Orleans would be side by side, and the southern coast of the Baltic and the southern shore of Lake Superior would fall in line. In other words, American society has shaped itself in an area comparable not with a single European nation, but with Europe itself.

The task which confronted American society differed, therefore, from that which has confronted all other democracies, first in the element of spaciousness. The Mississippi Valley alone could engulf the combined nations of France, Germany, Italy and Austria-Hungary, and it is estimated that this valley can sustain a population of three hundred millions. And yet, through all those ages while the Old World was making its history and evolving its society, this huge, shaggy continent, a world of gloomy forests, vast, empty, wind-swept plains, and forbidding mountain masses, lay shrouded in mystery, showing daily to the sun only a few scattered folk of the stone age, struggling from the degradation of brutal savagery.

Space Expansion

The first and fundamental fact in the development of American society is, therefore, the *imperial area* with which this society has had to deal. The second fact is that this society did steadily *expand* for three centuries into the western wilderness. The most impressive series of maps with which I am familiar is that published by the United States census office, exhibiting decade by decade the spread of our population. The frontier now pushed forward a projection of settlement as superior energy of the people determined, or as the attractiveness of soils or mines invited; now showed indentations where physical obstacles, or Indian barriers, retarded the advance. "This gradual and continuous progress of the European race toward the Rocky Mountains," wrote De Tocqueville, 1833, "has the solemnity of a providential event. It is like a deluge of men, rising unabatedly and driven daily onward by the hand of God."

Talleyrand, who shaped the foreign relations of France during so much of the Napoleonic era, was impressed by the same phenomenon, though in a different way, according to the difference of his temperament. Traveling over central Pennsylvania in the period of his exile in 1796, he writes: "I was struck with astonishment; at less than a hundred and fifty miles distance from the capital; all traces of men's presence disappeared; nature in all her primeval vigor confronted us, forests as old as the world itself. . . . On reaching higher ground, our eyes wandered, as far as the sight could range, over a most varied and pleasant picture. . . . In the face of these immense solitudes we gave free vent to our imagination; our mind built cities, villages and hamlets; the mountain forests were to remain untouched, the slopes of the hills to be covered with luxuriant crops, and we could almost fancy we saw immense herds of cattle grazing in the valley under our eyes. There is an inexpressible charm in thinking of the future when traveling in such countries. Such, said I to myself, was the place where not very many years ago, Penn and two thousand emigrants laid the foundations of Philadelphia where a population of eighty thousand people is now enjoying all the luxuries of Europe. . . . It is impossible to walk a few miles away from seaside towns without learning that the lively and fertile fields we now admire were, but then, but five, but a couple of years ago, mere wildernesses of forest. Similar causes produce similar effects, especially when acting with ever increasing power."[3]

What did they represent, these spreading zones of population? First of all they represent war, war against nature, and against the nature-people whom civilization pressed before them. This far-flung line of the frontier was a line of fire, its advance-guard attacked the forests from the days of the palisaded forts at Jamestown and Plymouth onward. Before the ax and the torch of the settler the noble forests gave way, but even in their surrender they shaped a social type, they transformed the European into the backwoodsman, trained generation after generation, from John Smith to Abraham Lincoln to let in the sunlight on a clearing, to build a log cabin, to

[3] This passage in the original French is in *Mémoires du Prince de Talleyrand*, [ed. Paul Léon], [I] (Paris: H. Javal, 1953), 134-135.

make a seed plot for civilization. Trained also in a sterner warfare against the Indian, hand to hand, frontier after frontier, the backwoodsmen fought Powhatan, King Philip, Pontiac, Brant, Little Turtle, Tecumtha, Red Cloud, and Sitting Bull. Each chief in turn rallied his tribesmen and strove to make alliances to stem the tide, but only succeeded in making life in the west a peril, a discipline in courage, a training school for a hardy and conquering stock.

Hard on the heels of the retreating Indian followed the cattleman. Now he planted his cowpens just beyond the tidewater, and great droves of wild horses and herds of branded cattle roamed just beyond the settlements of the coast. Now he pushed forward to the foothills of the eastern Alleghanies, and the cattle trail ran from the Carolinas north to Baltimore and Philadelphia. In the early years of the nineteenth century the cattle area passed on to the Ohio Valley, and the drovers took their way along the roads that led to the feeding ground of the Potomac River, where they fattened their herds for the markets of the seaboard; and in the middle of the nineteenth century, as the buffaloes yielded up their grazing grounds, the ranches occupied the Great Plains, the cattle trail ran from Texas to Wyoming.

As the means of transportation by steamboat, canal and railway penetrated to the west, the farmer could raise a surplus for the market, and was no longer obliged to depend upon a product which could walk to a market. The corn belt, the wheat belt and the cotton belt followed in their respective zones, the same law of western advance. As these centers of agricultural production passed to the west, social and political as well as industrial transformations followed.

The northeast feeling the competition of the western lands, and perceiving the rich field opened by the growing west, developed a manufacturing life, which in turn spread to states like Ohio, Indiana and Illinois, once so characteristically western, and the competition for the markets of the interior took the place in the activities of cities like New York, Philadelphia, and Baltimore, which once had been filled by the interest in foreign trade.

American society was developing in a series of industrial waves rolling successively toward the west. Each older area was changing

in turn from primitive industrial conditions by gradual processes
to a complex and advanced economic civilization. As Kipling wrote
of the pioneer:

> He shall desire loneliness
> And his desire shall bring
> Hard on his heels a thousand wheels
> A people and a king.

But always there remained an unconquered west at the border,
a treasure house of new resources, a reservoir of opportunity. This
characteristic of American social development, this continual process of beginning under primitive conditions in one area while society advanced in another has given tone to our whole history and has
postponed to our own time those social problems which now give
us so much concern.

Colonization of Sections

Moreover it was not possible that American society should reach
settled conditions, and homogeneity while these processes of expansion were at work. The first clearly marked social integration
took place in *sections* rather than in the nation as a whole. Any
survey of the development of the United States which did not emphasize this fact would be fatally defective; for in truth, up to the
present time at least, the United States has been a combination of
sections rather than a single society. That this must have been the
case is clear when we reflect upon the facts which we have been
considering.

The mere existence of areas of primitive social conditions, in contrast with older and more highly developed areas, made a sectional
grouping in American society — a division between east and west.
But there was also a geographical fact of a different nature which
tended in the same direction, and was likely to be more enduring
than the divisions due to the incomplete processes of social evolution.

The area into which American society was expanding and to
which it was adjusting itself was, as I have said, comparable not to
a European nation, but to all Europe. In resources and varieties of
physical geography, the continent was potentially the basis for many
nations; it presented a complex of physiographic provinces, each

175

sufficiently ample in area and different in physical conditions to have been the home of an independent nation. These facts of climate, topography, and geology alone would constitute the basis for the development of contrasted sections; and they were re-inforced by the settlement of people of different origins and under different social and economic ideals in the different areas. It is to this aspect of my subject that I next invite your attention.

Along the Atlantic coast three sections developed each with its own social organization and ideals; and these sections, expanding into the interior, colonized successively geographic provinces unlike those from which they came and developed sectional social conditions of their own. The United States is today a combination of these social sections, imperfectly assimilated into a single people.

New England

It would be an unnecessary task to dwell upon the natural conditions, the composition and traits of the people which made New England, the south and the middle region so unlike. The first was almost exclusively of English stock in origin and was dominated by Puritan ideals of politics and religion. It was shaped by Calvinistic theology which involved the self-scrutiny of the individual to determine his relations to his Creator, and at the same time the pervading community interest in its members, and the community sense of responsibility for their conduct. It was developed in a geographic province which is known as the New England plateaus, and which gave form to the economic life of the section as an isolated area, engaged in fishing, shipping and commerce in its coastal portions, and (as waterfalls were utilized), in manufacture in little cities; while the agricultural communities wrung a hard living from its stubborn soil; out of these conditions developed a society, by no means entirely homogeneous, but one readily recognized as distinct in American life, and which the term "Yankee" designates. It was the strong hold of federalism in politics, and it became by preeminence the center of literary and educational influence.

South

The south, originally limited to the seaboard, was shaped under its peculiar conditions of climate and products, and above all by the

176

acceptance of the Negro as the labor element under the system of slavery. Here the plantation took the place of the town, life was rural rather than urban, and a caste system, as it may not unfairly be called, developed, owing to the status of the Negro slave. This set apart the south as a region of a separate social type. Its economic interests as a section engaged in producing staples for foreign export increased its individuality.

Middle

The middle region was so complex in its composition that it had little social self-consciousness as a section. Nevertheless this region of many nationalities, creeds, and industries became, during a considerable part of its history, a more characteristically democratic region than either of the others. Tolerance of difference of opinion was pronounced, and, in the course of time, individualism and lack of social control became marked features of the section. Freedom of competition in the midst of exceptional industrial opportunities brought material prosperity to the section as a whole; but it also brought in the end the great inequalities in wealth which characterize the section in which such industrial cities as New York, Philadelphia and Pittsburgh hold sway.

Piedmont and Alleghany

Behind the seaboard south there grew up another section, which came to embrace the Alleghanies and their foothills on either side, with colonies pushed out into the hill and pine belt regions of the Gulf Plains, into the regions of Missouri and Arkansas adjacent to the Ozark Mountains, and into the hardwood forest of Ohio, Indiana, and Illinois. This was the section originally occupied by the upland south and its colonies. Through most of our history it has been a region of pioneer farmers, "poor whites" as the southern planters called them. It was distinctively the backwoodsman's section, militant, rude, and individualistic, as Roosevelt has described it in his *Winning of the West.*

In 1700 when the seaboard south first seriously considered ways and means for colonizing the land beyond the tidewater, the gentry of the Virginia assembly had enacted a quaint statute for the purpose of attracting military colonists to settle at the head of the tide water to serve as a protection against the Indians. It was provided that for every five hundred acres granted for such settlements there must reside in the town:

"One christian man between sixteen and sixty years of age, perfect of limb, able and fit for service who shall also be continually provided with a well fixt musquett or fuzee, a good pistoll, short simiter tomahawk and five pounds of good clean pistoll powder and twenty pounds of sizable leaden bullets, or swan or goose shot to be kept within the fort directed by this act besides the powder and shot for his necessary or useful shooting at game. Provided also that the said warlike christian man shall have his dwelling and continual abode within the town itself and near the palisaded fort."

But the warlike christian men who in reality became the defense of the back country and the strength of the firing line in America's advance to Kentucky, Tennessee, Missouri, Texas and on to the Pacific were the Scotch-Irish frontiersman and the solid German farmers who came into the back country principally by emigration from Pennsylvania.

If the men of this section were ready with the rifle and partial to whisky, in those days, they were equally given to turbulence of religious fervor in the campmeeting. Democratic sects like the Presbyterians, Baptists and Methodists planted deep in the hearts of this people an emotional attitude that affected its whole social trend. Their movements whether political or military had a flavor of religious zeal. This society gave birth to Andrew Jackson, Calhoun, Benton, Polk, Zachary Taylor, Jefferson Davis and Abraham Lincoln. In the stern determination, the fiery conscientiousness of these men, — in their individualism, their fighting power, their devotion to expansion, may be read, some of the characteristics of the society that produced them. "Warlike christian men" were they, indeed. For a generation this section furnished the political energy and the effective rule of the nation.

This section may still be traced by its intellectual and emotional attitude. In the recent wave of anti-saloon agitation the maps of dry districts showed that the strength of the movement lay in the regions where these people went. They have thrust out colonies into the non-prairie lands of Illinois, and these were the counties that went dry in this state. They can be traced in the highlands of Kentucky, Tennessee, Arkansas and Missouri, as well as in the hill regions and less fertile districts of Mississippi, Alabama, and Georgia, where the Negroes were inferior in numbers, and here too they showed the same tendency in spite of the traditional attitude of the people toward drinking.

I have dwelt somewhat upon this section in the composition of American society, because it has been too little appreciated as a factor of our life. In the course of the reconstruction era this democracy of poor whites achieved the control of the old south, except where the northern type of industrial organization planted cities in the mineral lands of the Southern Appalachians. The ideals of its children in the west are to be read in the laws of Texas and Oklahoma.

Northwest and North Central

The other sections I must content myself with hardly more than mentioning. Greater New England was formed along the basin of the Great Lakes and on the prairies of the middle west, by the migration of Yankees to western New York and into the old northwest searching for better wheat lands. This society was formed early in the nineteenth century, and gained headway when the Erie Canal and lake navigation by steamer opened the prairies to the settlers. With the completion of railroad connection between the Mississippi Valley, New York and New England the stream became a flood. The prairies offered rich soils in regions which dwarfed the parent section. Soon New England and New York communities were established through the whole northwest. The southern current which had flowed along the hardwood forest areas was checked at the prairies, and rival social types met each other. Meantime the immigration of Germans and Scandinavians to the northwest went on apace in the regions into which the Yankees of New York and New England were settling. These various types each contributed something to the industrial democracy that was growing up in this section, and the outcome was a compromise of ideals and an assimilation of stocks. The New England Puritan learned much from the German.

Gulf Plains

The lines of economic life gradually bound the northwest to the northeast, and a northern section was established contemporaneously with the increasing unity of the south, where slavery spread across the Gulf Plains.

The northern section shaded off from the stage of the prairie pioneer farmer, through various economic gradations until the highly developed capitalistic industrial society of the eastern seaboard was reached. The transition extended from Kansas populism to the capitalism of Wall street. The section was engaged in an internal contest over social and industrial ideals in which the newer regions represented conditions and convictions that had gone down before the growth of industrial society in the older areas. In addition, the labor class of the older areas of the north was now composed of the multitude of alien immigrants who rushed to the New World, and whose lower standards of comfort, lack of homogeneity made easier the triumph of capital. In a word, the western part of this northern section began to strive to erect barriers against the flood of industrial organization that threatened as it flowed toward the interior, to submerge the old social institutions and ideals of the people.

Pacific Coast

On the Pacific coast a still different society was in process of formation, a society that in many ways contrasted with the vast industrial democracy of the northern zone of the Mississippi Valley. The northern industrial society resembled the prairies in its tendency to uniformity — in the spacious levels of its life. In the long run it bid fair to reach homogeneity and to act as a vast mass where the individual counted less than society. It acted with effectiveness, but it acted with the momentum of a mass. It acted with an earnestness, but aside from its interest in shaping its economic life, and its democratic political structure, it had but few ideals. It somewhat lacked in richness of human interests.

The Pacific coast was different. Nature itself seemed to foretell the development of a society there which should be unlike the rest of America. The man who having lived all his life on the prairies travels from the broad, level, wheat and corn fields of the northwest, across the solemn monotony of the Great Plains, and sees far on the horizon the silver shimmer of white clouds that gradually take form as glistening mountain peaks, feels an unaccustomed thrill. He is aware of unknown stimuli, — of chords in his nature not hitherto struck, and as he passes beyond the mountain ranges, and puts the sunswept and mysterious desert behind him, the impression of newness, the call to the unfolding of his individual nature becomes imperious. As he sees the separate volcanic peaks, Rainier, Hood, Adams and Shasta rise one after the other, "clothed in white samite, mystic, wonderful," they seem to beckon to a new life on the coast of that ocean whose farther waves break on the shores of Asia.

Individualism, lack of social unity and control, impatience of old standards, are preeminently characteristic of the Pacific coast as a whole, and in California where nature has combined Italy and Greece, the spirit of man responds to the invitation of nature and a more sensuous pleasure-loving life characterizes the society — in spite of its practical materialism. Here, one perceives, must be the home of new movements in literature and in art. Here, as no otherwhere in American society, is a section of complex, individual ideals, without unity of action. Here American society may dream as well as work.

Arid Region

Between the Pacific coast and the Mississippi Valley, lies the newest section of the country, the arid region and the Rocky Mountains — the section which the America of today is colonizing and exploiting.

In the development of American society, the problem of magnitude has been increasingly important. The social organization of a petty locality, however densely populated, is one thing; the operation of a democratic society on a vast scale is a different thing. When the phenomena of social evolution are magnified, certain aspects are brought more clearly into view. This is one of the most significant aspects of the social conditions that are forming in this newest American section. As in the Grand Canon of the Colorado, under the crystal sky of the Great American Desert, the laws of erosion were written so plainly that American geologists were able

181

to give new interpretations to that science, so in the arid west, contemporaneous social forces stand out in clear relief. Here nature was too vast, the problem of occupation too difficult, to be dealt with by the individual. The modern mining and smelting methods, and above all the irrigation works demanded co-operation. The railroads which push their way across these vast wastes must be heavily financed. The conditions all compelled consolidation.

As a result we can see two antagonistic purposes at work. On the one side is the old American tendency of individualism reshaped into competing and finally into combining corporations formed to acquire and operate mines and transportation systems, forests and the water rights which control the dependent arid lands. Here American capital has achieved its most daring conquests, and its promoters have shown a vision and initiative unsurpassed in the history of the world.

Here also labor has organized in extreme socialistic forms, and actual warfare has been waged between capital and labor thus organized. The "bull pens" of Colorado, and the contests in Nevada, where political institutions broke down before the naked force of opposing social conditions amply illustrate the process. There are in Arizona whole cities owned by corporations into which organized labor is not admitted, and where government is a mere by-product of the industrial institutions.

Side by side with these logical tendencies of unrestrained American competition we may also see another social process. In the arid west, as in no other section, the government has taken on industrial functions. The Reclamation Act of 1903, combined with the earlier policy of forestry reserves, has placed in the hands of the federal government a vast domain which it no longer offers as a gift to whomsoever would possess it. The government now builds mammoth irrigation reservoirs for the reclamation of the arid lands. It disposes of the land and water privileges in such a way as to foster the small land holder and to preserve to the community itself the advantages of the natural resources. It owns and operates quarries, coal mines and forests with the same end in view. It experiments with new crops and advises the farmer what and when and how to plant. It contemplates the rental to manufacturers of the surplus water and steam power, which it generates for irrigation uses, and it is even considering the utilization of this power to extract nitrates from the air to replenish the wornout soils of other areas.

Socialism versus Individualism

In a word this newer west exhibits democracy in conflict with competition — two traditional American tendencies developed to a logical extreme and shown to be antagonistic. In the arid west we are fighting out the issue of social regulation against individualism. The results will be important in the history of the evolution of American society.

Up to the present time the sections of which I have been speaking, each with its own physical conditions and nativities, its own fundamental assumptions, its own social forms and ideals, have prevented the United States from being a homogeneous society. Our laws, our industrial life, our intellectual traits have been the outcome of these dissimilar sectional conditions. Political leaders have arisen in the various sections, because they represented the fundamental ideas and interests of these sections. They have achieved their national status by combinations and by compromises with the leaders of other sections. Votes in Congress and in elections all show the profound importance of the forces that have made and preserved these sectional groupings in American society.

Nationalism

But the development of *national self-consciousness* and national unity went on with the development of sectionalism. Indeed in one respect sectionalism may be regarded as a stage in the process of the increasing consolidation of American society. Beginning with the integration of the little communities of a colony or state, gradually Americans came to have sectional unity and self-consciousness which finally dominated even the state feeling, and at last, partly as the result of sectional conflict itself, national self-consciousness became ascendant. Just as the breaking down of social isolation by the spread of population and the increase of lines of communication gave real unity to state life, so the sections, as population grew, as the intervening spaces were occupied and transportation systems multiplied and improved, tended to coalesce and to break down

183

before a common national feeling and organization. Deepest of all influences in this direction were internal improvements opening the way for commerce and intercourse. This was the line of least resistance in the days when the constitutional convention came about by consultations over interstate commerce, as it is in our own time. "Let us bind the Republic together by roads and canals," exclaimed Calhoun in the days of his national feeling; and roads and canals, the nerves and arteries of the body politic, proved to be too vital connection between the Mississippi Valley and the east to permit the south to draw away the west when the supreme test of sectionalism came.

Today the transportation systems have so multiplied that they form a net work, affording avenues of intercourse throughout the whole nation, and one of the most significant features of our time is the steady consolidation of the railroad systems. Fundamental industries like iron and steel are absorbed into great trusts organized on a national basis. Banking shows a similar tendency. Labor organizations are national in their scope. The telegraph, post office, all the agencies of communication are national in organization. News agencies collect and transmit the report of the daily life of the whole people, and national chains of newspapers give simultaneous expression to editorial opinion from Atlantic to Pacific. Public opinion thus is impelled to assume national dimensions. Cities are growing at a rate disproportionate to the general increase in population, and their numerical growth is only a partial index of their influence upon the society about them. In spite of commercial rivalry between the sections which find in these cities their business capitals, the cities themselves tend to act nationally and to promote homogeneity. The increase in all directions of national conventions shows the same tendency. The larger universities form centers of national influence by bringing together students from all parts of the country. Even the churches are nationally organized. In general, it may be said that the forces of civilization are working toward uniformity, and that these forces tend strongly to counteract sectionalism in the United States and to promote social unity. But as yet these forces of sectionalism and nationalism are both clearly in evidence,

Turner about the Time of His Retirement from Harvard in 1924

and it is too early to predict an American society in which the vast spaces of the United States will be occupied by a uniform type.

I have now rapidly traced what seems to me to have been some of the fundamental forces in the development of American society — the *vastness of the area,* the *expansion of settlement,* the colonization of successive *geographic provinces,* the development of special social conditions in each, and the growing, but far from complete, movement to shape this society to a single *national life.*

Stratification

It remains to point out a final and very important phase of our development, namely, the steady *stratification of our society* by the development of contesting social classes. It is hard to realize how recently it has become possible to use the words proletariat and capitalistic classes in reference to American conditions. They still have an alien sound and grate upon our ears. But no one doubts that American social development has brought with it a profound invasion of equality.

Ranks and classes were familiar to the English colonists who occupied the Atlantic coast; but the economic development tended to break down the traditional divisions. The free lands were too close at hand, the opportunities for advancement too numerous for social stability. The indented servant of Virginia passed to the frontier at the end of his term of service, and colonial governors like Spotswood made bitter complaint of the democracy that was growing into power.

But it was the American Revolution that brought these tendencies to a focus, and formulated the theory that all men were created equal. The doctrine of the rights of man acquired a rapid ascendancy in this land which has displayed ever since colonial times a readier response to general ideas than the mother country. The Revolution was not simply a war for independence; it was a social revolution as well. The upper classes and the wealthy found the support of their special interest in English control and, as a rule, became Tories. In the destruction of the aristocratic land tenure, in the breaking down of the ascendancy of the well born and the wealthy, in the mob violence that brought ruin to the Tory squires and merchants, one must perceive a reorganization of society in the interests of the democracy.

But the enduring influence promotive of democracy was the great area of free land, the wilderness that bordered all the settlements. When in the years of the revolutionary movement the Alleghanies were crossed these forces became fully operative and shaped American ideals. In the freedom of the west, with its primitive society, absence of restraint, and a wealth of opportunities, the fundamental social ideals of America were established; individualism, equality and democracy.

It seemed to the American that these things were due to the doctrines of the Revolution and to the Constitution made by the fathers. But in fact they were born of the wilderness environment, where every man was free to hew out his own destiny, and where under this competitive society of a primitive economic type, equality of opportunity meant equality of condition. So the American became a democrat, convinced of the dignity and worth of the man, believing in the plain people, glorying too, in the triumphs of the self made man, whose achievement of preeminence under these free competitive conditions seemed to prove the truth of the gospel of democracy, and to typify the success that was the birthright of the American.

And yet, even in these days of optimism, the American evinced an unformulated apprehension lest he should fall behind in the ascending movement of society. He believed in equality; but it must be equality with the highest. This led him on in feverish haste as though he only half believed his dream of equality. "Before him lies a boundless continent," wrote De Tocqueville in the Jacksonian era, "and he urges forward as if time pressed, and he was afraid of finding no room for his exertions."

From the beginning, the competitive conditions resulted in inequalities; even in the days of Washington, corporations began to form; speculation in public lands, and bank stock, internal improvement enterprises brought together increasing masses of capital. The profits of the merchant, whose ships gathered the fruits of American trade in the days of the Napoleonic wars, became a fund for financing railroads, and so capital has steadily grown. In the era following the Civil War, as the nation turned passionately to the development of the resources of the west, society showed a clearly marked class of capitalists. The "newly rich" man became a type. The panic of 1873 saw the development of the corporations to a degree before unknown. The panic of 1893 was followed by an extraordinary development of corporate combinations in pools, and trusts, agreements and combined ownership, until it seemed as if the end of free competition under individualism was to be monopoly of all the great industrial resources and processes by a little group of men, whose vast fortunes were so invested in allied industries that they controlled the industrial life of the nation. The development of large scale machine production, the advantage of combination in the competitive struggle, were so great that vast accumulations of capital became a necessity. Alliances of railway leaders, banks, insurance companies and industrial trusts and public utility corporations in general secured this concentration. The world has never seen such huge fortunes exercising combined control of the economic life as the individualistic American democracy has produced under its competitive system.

Labor also has shown an increasing class consciousness. There were labor classes in the colonial times. The indented servants and the slaves were the most marked illustration of these conditions. In the few large cities from the early days of our national existence, labor unions existed and a democracy of laboring men demanded the ballot and proclaimed their grievances and rights. By the thirties a well established labor movement existed, with political parties, and a press, with strikes and bread mobs, with denunciation of credit currency, demands for homesteads on the public lands, a freer public school system and in general a fuller share in American prosperity. But this was only a temporary upheaval.

The European labor movements were in sharp contrast. As a French traveler in the thirties declared: The Old World workman said to his employer, "Give me bread, or I must starve or fight." The American workman said, "Give me bread, or I shall go west." The manufacturing interests were unfriendly to the opening of the public land by gift to the people, for it would increase the cost of labor. But just when the railroads fully opened the communication between the old industrial centers and the Mississippi Valley, the flood of European immigration set in and has ever since furnished a labor supply; a supply, however, which still further broke down the old American equality by its lower standard of comfort, and by its adaptation to mobilization and transfer from center to center. As the laboring class tended to belong to the foreigners, class distinctions were accentuated by race and nationalistic antipathies, and by indifference to the hardships of aliens.

The labor movement reached its height contemporaneously with capitalistic concentration, and that concentration was contemporaneous with the exhaustion of the free lands. Already the labor movement shows signs of passing over into a socialistic movement, and "the plain people," of Lincoln's phrase, are confronted with the question of whether individualistic society under free competition and democratic ideals means in its outcome the subjugation of the individual by society itself.

Thus the American of today, at the end of the era of free land, at the end of the old economic life of the American people, sees the formation of social conditions which resemble those of Europe, and he is turning to legislation to preserve the ideals formed under pioneer conditions in a continental wilderness.

The Greenback movement of the days of reconstruction became the Granger movement of the seventies. The Granger movement ran into the Populist movement. The Populist movement under Mr. Bryan captured the democratic party. The program of social regulation professed by these parties was taken up and reshaped to meet new exigencies by President Roosevelt, and today, all parties profess allegiance to the ideals of social control of industrial life to the end that the American type of civilization may be preserved.

To captains of industry who engage in the old time rivalry for the natural resources under the lax social ideals of the time, and who played the game in winning the oil fields, the ore beds, the forests and the routes of transportation, this seems a reversal of American ideals. These men of constructive imagination and will power, of audacity and energy, are a natural outcome of the conditions of society that was born on the frontier.

"This country," said Mr. Harriman to an interviewer last year, "has been developed by a wonderful people, flush with enthusiasm, imagination and speculative bent." "They have been magnificent pioneers. They saw into the future and adapted their works to the possibilities." "Stifle that enthusiasm, deaden that imagination and prohibit that speculation by restrictive and cramping conservative law, and you tend to produce a moribund and conservative people and country." "There is much left to be developed in this country. Towns are growing like magic and its people are toiling like the Aladdin lamp genii."

But Mr. Harriman does not tell us who rubs the lamp and who will possess the palace, and it is this, in truth, which disturbs American society. This "superbly capable people" have been learning the lesson of collective social control as well as the lesson of individualism. The very magnitude of the opposing interests has made legible the issues, and it is this that has brought such unanimity of opinion to the support of the dominant political leaders of the two great parties in their challenge to the economic processes.

This progress of society from pioneer life on a seashore, to the colonization of successive sections, and to the final occupation of a continental empire, capable of furnishing the basis for many European nations, is one of the most wonderful chapters in human history. If, at last, our democracy is confronted with a task incomparably larger than any democracy ever dealt with before, we may take heart from the past. Deeper even than the love of "the square deal" is the passion of this people for preserving a society in which there shall still be freedom for the individual to work out the best there is in him, so long as he shall labor under supreme allegiance to the ideal of democracy, the good of the whole.

American society is called to solve the problem of social justice in the spacious domain which has been given us. To no other institution does the call come with greater force than to the State Universities, for they open to every class the opportunity for education. They are the prospectors who drill deep through the strata of society to find the undeveloped genius among the masses. They are the manufacturers of trained citizens, who shall lead their fellows with intelligence and with the ideal of service to the state; they are the producers of disinterested and impartial experts who shall intervene between contending interests to give just judgment and enforce the law in the interests of that social development which the fathers saw as in a vision and which the sons must bring to pass in the new America that is replacing the old.

ᴥ INTRODUCTION TO A COLLEGE HISTORY OF THE UNITED STATES[1]

The history of the United States is the history of the occupation of a vast wilderness in a brief period. Nearly one hundred centuries[2] of recorded history passed while America lay unknown to the Old World, concealed in the wastes of the Ocean. It is only four centuries since Columbus planted the standards of Spain in the New World, and but three since England laid the foundations of the present United States by the settlement at Jamestown, Virginia.

But, though the time is brief, the nation which has evolved is as remarkable in its power and in its contributions to civilization, as it is in its youth. The area which it has occupied is vast. If Europe were placed upon the United States, the western coast of Spain would coincide with the coast of Southern California; Constantinople[3] would lie near Charleston, South Carolina; the southern extreme of the Italian peninsula would touch New Orleans; and the Baltic coast would be in the latitude of the southern shore of Lake Superior. In other words, the United States is, in its area, its resources, and its geographical divisions, not like a European nation, but like all Europe. It is potentially an empire, wherein vast geo-

[1] MS: HEH, TU File Drawer 15, one of several items in a manila envelope marked "Turner, F. J. 'College History of the United States.'" The manuscript is undated, but a note in Turner's handwriting elsewhere in the folder identifies it as his "College History." Turner's contract for the text with Henry Holt and Company was dated Nov. 3, 1897. TU Box 2.

[2] Turner has questioned this figure in the margin of the manuscript.

[3] Turner's notes on the manuscript: "farther" and "Revise. It takes in more."

graphic sections, each capable of furnishing the territory for several European states, take the place of Kingdoms.

The history of the United States involves an area equal to the area involved in [the] history of Europe proper. In the occupation of the successive geographic provinces we have a process of colonization which, except for the fortunate course of American development, might have produced independent nations; for the various provinces have all the physical qualifications for separate nations. As American society has spread to the West, it has been obliged to adjust itself to the physical conditions and resources of diverse sections. The evolution, interaction and consolidation of these sections has made an American nation, with a composite people; with institutions mainly derived from Europe and deeply modified to meet American conditions; and with an American spirit and democratic ideals differing from Europe, and fundamentally due to the experience of the people in occupying a new continent.

Important as are the beginnings of our history in laying the foundations of national life, we must bear in mind that there have been successive colonizations of the interior, which must also be dealt with, and that the course of settlement has called upon the American people "to occupy territory as extensive as Switzerland, as England, as Italy, and latterly as France or Germany every ten years." The result is the production of a democratic nation of over seventy million peoples, holding one of the most extensive and richest regions of the world. The future will reveal how well they will use their power. It is the purpose of this book to show how this nation came to be what it is.

5

❧ Education and Democracy

THE FOUR BRIEF PIECES *which follow demonstrate Turner's lively concern with education and the dangers which face it in a democracy with egalitarian ideals and tendencies toward conformity. All four essays make it clear that Turner's loyalty to his country did not blind him to its shortcomings — the malignant materialism of its people and an indifference to beauty and to intellectual and spiritual excellence.*

The first three pieces are all pleas that the university devote itself to educating the spirit. Turner was only too well aware of the demands that a state university offer a utilitarian curriculum, fostering a materialistic outlook among the students, even an attitude of anti-intellectualism. Indeed, Turner's correspondence shows that his eventual move to Harvard was in large part a protest against this tendency at Wisconsin.

The fourth piece, an address to a graduating high school class in Madison, Wisconsin, in 1895, gives some indication of Turner's personal efforts to improve the tone of the society in which he lived. It is a direct attempt to pierce and scatter the clouds of indifference, a plea to the young people themselves to rise above the tendencies of their environment. Turner asks the students to include, in their very American desire to better themselves, a resolution to work for

193

the improvement of their city, which had provided them with the education whose completion they were that day celebrating.

In his statements about cities of antiquity and the Middle Ages, Turner makes generalizations that might be questioned because of recent scholarship. But Turner rightfully stressed the immense civic pride felt by peoples of the past.

All the essays show that Turner believed in the effectiveness of ideas in transforming society and conserving its gains. Although Turner was critical of his society, he found comfort in tendencies which he thought would lead in a healthier direction, for he was a firm believer in the ultimate ability of American democracy to change and improve itself. Turner saw that the schools and universities of America, growing out of the societies that supported them, exhibited the faults and virtues of those societies, and that to better these schools and universities it was necessary to better American society itself.

🌿 THE STATE UNIVERSITY[1]

A recent writer says that the charge that for things of the spirit, "for the cultivation of intellectual independence, for the pursuit of knowledge which seems to have no direct utilitarian application, we must look to those institutions which depend for their existence on private beneficence" is ridiculous because it involves the two assumptions (1) that in private foundations are to be found more of these choice spirits; (2) that the democratic majority refuses to have culture in its state universities.[2]

Now I fear that it is not so clear that these assumptions are ridiculous. If we enquire where the best criticism of life, and literature, where the most fertilizing influences in philosophy, and art, are

[1] MS: HEH, TU File Drawer 15, folder marked "The State University." A quotation dates the essay about 1908.

[2] See David Kinley, "Democracy and Scholarship," *Science*, New Series XXVIII (1908), 500.

to be found, it is doubtful to say the least if the State Universities could show their due share. Moreover the argumentation before the legislatures, the budgetary proposals and sometimes the budgetary erasure as well as emphasis, shows clearly the difficulties of persuading democracy to deal liberally with the less obviously utilitarian interests in a University. The most effective argument here is that in the utilitarian development democracy is laying a broad foundation on which to build higher, that it must first have its intellectual interests quickened and its appetite developed by the influences and food which it can receive and assimilate. That the immediate task is to ennoble and moralize professional, technical and industrial education (including the drain man) so that it will see its task largely, as social service, and as related to the beautiful as well as to the useful.

Let us grant then that democracy does not yet spontaneously rise to appreciation of the higher functions of education, that it is more concerned with livelihood than with life, and that the line of least resistance is innoculating its utilitarian interests with the ichor of the things that make for higher living. Shall it follow that the Universities must surrender to these conditions entirely. Must libraries be locked up that the drain men may be active; shall music be silent that the hammer and the reaper may sound more cheerily and more effectively.[3]

Obviously it is not necessary to decry the excellence of the hog, the importance of comfort and prosperity, the legitimacy of the interest of the State University in the material uplift of its people in order to insist upon the fact that the University is also bound to try to lead the people also to the higher levels of all the interests of society; to urge that the torch of the Promethean fire shall be fed so that its flames burn brightly, with that cheering, ennobling light that lends dignity and worth to life, at the same time that the search light is turned upon the dark corners of nature's productivity in order that fuller resources of comfort and health may be opened

[3] Sentence fragment follows: "Shall look for Kansas on the rind' replace the motto: ———."

195

to the mass of men.[4] Even on the assumption of the persistence of pioneer ideals, the University is essential. For more and more society depends upon the trained man to conquer nature, to reveal new opportunities, and the work of the pioneer in finding the best lands, opening to settlement the most eligible sites, finding and exploiting the best timber forties, the best coal, iron, gold, silver mines, — has its companion piece in the work of the curious, questful, adventurous scholar, the pioneer in the field of knowledge, seeking new horizons, discovering new lands of the spirit, new avenues of the intellect, new opportunities for the unfolding of the human spirit. The scholars are the Columbuses, the Magellans, of social, intellectual, artistic advance.

In a complex, highly developed civilization, more and more dependent upon training in the processes of nature, the conditions of social development, a training in technique is essential. The simplicity of early squatter exploration is replaced by the complexity of knowledge of scientific processes.

❧ THE IDEA OF SERVICE IN THE UNIVERSITY[1]

The idea of service in the University should include not only the training for social efficiency in relation to the comforts and good government of society; but also individual character, richness, ideals, the higher things.

The University should make an atmosphere friendly to the unfolding of the individual under conditions of freedom, in all of his powers, with nourishment for each line of growth.

Social service is not to be considered narrowly, under conceptions of a disciplined army; a standardized mass; but with full realization

[4] Sentence fragment follows: "At worst we may recall the story told by a friend of mine (poorhouse)."

[1] MS: HEH, TU File Drawer 15, folder marked "Turner, 'The Idea of Service in the University.' Period 1901-1908." The manuscript is undated.

that social efficiency includes the free individual, undominated by the mass, as well. It looks to the production not of a deadening uniformity but of a congeries of individuals each instinct with life, eager to grow in spiritual life and by growing to enrich and vivify all society: to make society itself worthy and progressive and complex in its intellectual and moral richness.

THE UNIVERSITY OF THE FUTURE[1]

Fellow graduates:

A noble past is an inspiration to a university; but even such venerable institutions as Columbia, Yale and Harvard, Princeton and Pennsylvania are learning that they cannot live by traditions alone. They see that they must adjust themselves to changed conditions of today. Pennsylvania and Columbia are in important respects almost as modern as Chicago and Leland Stanford. Princeton's sesquicentennial was the occasion of her proclaiming a new policy with her new name; Harvard's stately educational structure has been hausmannized by the genius of President Eliot, and Yale, — if Yale rests content with muscular glory and the most splendid trophy room in America, she will never rank among the universities of tomorrow.

The question is less of the University of yesterday than of the University of tomorrow.

Wisconsin has her own brief past — brief in years, long in stages of development. A past, that, as we have heard, from the venerable Nestors of our alumni had its own charms, its own inspirations, its noble men. But our catalogue of 1870 is twin sister to the catalogue of a Dakota or Wyoming college of 1897. Hardly more than a quarter of a century marks the educational transition from the frontier college to the University of to-day; and the question is imperative:

[1] MS: HEH, TU File Drawer 15, folder marked "Turner: 'The University of the Future,' talk to alumni: 1897?" Turner has dated the manuscript "1897?" and identified it "University of Wisconsin, Alumni dinner speech."

197

what of the University of tomorrow? I believe that the universities of the middle west have a splendid opportunity. Into this region while it was still prairie and forest poured the children of the Atlantic states, carrying with them ideals of democracy, equality, freedom of opportunity for all men. The wilderness taught them audacity in social development. In the old centers of settlement society is becoming less plastic, the tendencies toward social stratification are accentuated and the problem for the Middle West is Can these early American ideals be conserved and adapted to the changed conditions of contemporary society. It is the mission of the State University of tomorrow to grapple with this problem. It must not servilely aim to imitate the universities of the East. It must proudly conserve what is best and original in its own experience, it must seek with independence for the best in the older institutions, and it must build freely and fearlessly. It must express the highest creative power of the center of the republic.

The State University is the very outcome of democracy. Institutions on private foundations may influence democracy from the outside; but the State University *is* democracy in its higher educational aspect. From this fact flow its great opportunity and its gravest danger. As the plain people come more and more into self consciousness and into determination to exert their power, they expose the university to two dangers. On the one hand there is the danger that democracy may not realize that education — the highest education — is essential to its own safety. The man who would turn the University over to the leisure classes and to the generosity of wealthy men alone should ponder Bacon's golden words:

"The learning of the few is despotism, the learning of the many is liberty, and intelligent and principled liberty is fame & wisdom & power."

But whatever be the *immediate* future it is safe to say that democracy will come to recognize the need of the University as essential to its own security. The greater danger is that democracy will wish to level the University down to its own ideals. If the State University of tomorrow is to be representative of the ideals of the masses, its day is done. A sapping process will have been at work upon the University ideals. Palpable and showy results will be called for in place of the subtler contributions of culture. Buildings, numbers, victories will take the place of educational power. The worth of the professor will be reckoned by the length of his office hours and by the size of his classes rather than by his contributions to knowledge.

In the face of this danger the duty of the University is clear. It was recently set forth with dignity and power by President Adams in his baccalaureate. Its duty is to find and to hold high and helpful ideals, to stand for them so persuasively, so imperatively that its sons and daughters will be the leaders of thought in this democracy. Ideals and leadership! These are the watch words of the hour. With them the future is secure. Without them, all victories on the athletic field, all budgetary glories, all lofty buildings and all crowds of students are but food for powder.

I have faith in the University of tomorrow. I believe that it will remain the unprejudiced sanctuary for the finding of truth in the midst of contending parties; that it will broaden and deepen its investigations into the fields of nature and of society; and that it will render its discoveries indispensable to democracy.

I know of no more encouraging indication in this direction than the recent growth of graduate studies. Ten years ago we had but four graduate students; in six years they had grown to more than forty and today there are 70. But the growth in numbers is not so significant as the growth in the spirit of investigation — that search for new truth by professor and student, that creative work which is the truest function and most useful service of the University.

By developing our forces of devoted graduate students we shall raise the scholarly ideals of the undergraduates with whom they mix; we shall send out a band of missionaries to the schools, the pulpit, the press, and the forum of the state, men who shall stand for the most careful research, the highest ideals, the noblest achievement of the University of tomorrow. It is for the alumni to foster and support this great work. Other institutions have recognized the power of graduate work more fully than have we. Cornell and Pennsylvania each have about forty fellowships and scholarships; Harvard has a hundred. We have ten.

Let us build the University of tomorrow. Founded on the high school and the Normal school, working gladly together, — expressing and directing the great democracy of the Middle West, — seeking the goal of spiritual power rather than that of material success, the University of tomorrow will be worthy of this place in which its lot is cast.

🐌 THE HIGH SCHOOL AND THE CITY[1]

"If a nation expects to be ignorant and free in a state of civilization, it expects what never was and never will be."

These are the words of Thomas Jefferson, the American exponent of the rule of the people. It would be *superfluous* to dwell on the obligation of the state to educate. Perhaps it is not superfluous to point out the obligation of the student toward the power that educates him. That it is the duty of the state to support education in no way diminishes the debt due to the state from those who are the especial recipients of her bounty. Next week the graduates of the University of Wisconsin will assemble on the University hill, and look across the city to the white dome of the state house. *There* is the symbol of their real alma mater — the mother whose generous hand opens the gates to the treasure house of learning. To her they owe the service of good citizenship. Patriotic, intelligent devotion to the state of Wisconsin is the right return for the bounty of the state.

To-day the city of Madison graduates from her high school this class of young men and young women. It may be taken for granted that they realize that they owe to the nation and the state a patriotic return for the benefits conferred upon them; but do they realize that they owe a particular return to the city of Madison?

The patriotism which this occasion calls for is preeminently civic patriotism, loyalty and gratitude to the city which has educated them. This type of patriotism is too little felt in America. There are germinal indications of the feeling. Americans point with pride to

[1] MS: HEH, TU Box 54, folder marked "The High School and the City: Commencement address, Madison High School, 1895, June 14. Madison, Wis." A note in Turner's handwriting dates the manuscript.

the price of local real estate; they rejoice in belonging to a boom town, they glory in platting suburb after suburb, they vie with their rivals on the census list, they struggle with each other for the possession of the normal school or the home for the feeble minded. But of deep seated devotion to the city as an institution there is but little.

To the man of the ancient world, civic emotion rose spontaneously, with overmastering power. Think for a moment what the city meant to the Greek. To him the city was founded by a god or a divine hero. Within its walls the gods made their abode. As generations went and came the city was peopled by ancestral deities as well. The city of the present was but a phase of the immemorial city, running back through ancestral deities to the god who founded it, running on through the generations to come.

Into this divine companionship the man was born. And here he lived. To lose his citizenship was to become a homeless wanderer, a man without a nation. The spell of religion was cast about the city. To pollute the waters was to offend the gods who there had their abode. To defile the city in any way was to call down the vengeance of an offended deity. On the city height, the acropolis, rose noble buildings, simple and stately, devoted to the gods. Up the rocky summit wound the solemn procession. In the open theater were performed supreme efforts of dramatic genius. On the rocky height orators addressed the whole body of citizens. Under the open sky philosophers walked and talked. As one looks back in imagination to a city like Athens, bathed in translucent atmosphere, abode of men like Phidias, Demosthenes, Socrates, Pericles, Aeschylus, standing for a great ideal of freedom, fronting the hosts of oriental power, lighting the torch of liberty, intellectual and political — that unquenchable flame that still burns and beams wherever civilization is — one is tempted to wish that he too were an Athenian, living in the city of the Violet crown, sharer in a common life, artistic, religious, political. The man of Athens knew what civic pride meant. His country was bounded by the city wall. Even in the days of her imperial glory, Athens was a city bearing rule over other cities, not the capital of a wide domain. This gave intensity to politics, and patriotism, concentrated on this one glorious city, burned with a fierce intensity. And Athens, the eye of Greece, the supreme type of the Hellenic city, was one of a noble sisterhood in the ancient world, where city and nation were one. Even Rome, the eternal city which spread its ring wall until the civilized world lived within its limits, still illustrates the devotion to the city. As the Roman household had its altars and its household gods, so the city of Rome had its temple of Vesta and its vestal virgins guarding the sacred city fire that was to Rome what the household altar was to the family. Her citizens worshipped at a civic shrine and gloried in the Roman name. Rome had no Phidias to raise a Parthenon, nor chisel perfect forms from marble, but she became the mistress of the world. Hear the words in which her poet Virgil celebrates her glories:

"Others I grant shall with more delicacy mould the breathing brass; from the marble draw the features to the life; plead causes better; describe with the rod the courses of the heavens, and explain the rising stars: to rule the nations with imperial sway be thy care. O Romans, these shall be thy arts: to impose terms of peace, to spare the humbled, and to crush the proud."

In the middle ages we have again the splendid spectacle of the city-state. You recall at once the imperishable glories of Venice, the bride of the Adriatic, Florence the home of art and letters, where the mighty Petrarch whispered the magic word beauty in the ear of sleeping Europe, where the divine Dante, sable-stoled and stern, walked the streets with his deep unfathomable song in his heart, and on his brow the bitter scorn of fate, where Savonarola raised his prophetic voice. The man of Florence knew what civic pride meant. And so, too, civic spirit can be seen in the cities of mediaeval Germany, surrounded with huge walls and moats, and battlements. Within these grim defenses, the citizens built those miracles of architecture, the cathedrals, whose lofty spires rose over the landscape, a perpetual memorial of the devotion of a whole city. And as the chimes of bells rang from the city's towers, they made sweet music in the ears of the burghers who called that city home, and aroused emotions of civic pride that the modern man can hardly understand.

It is not difficult to explain the lack of civic patriotism in America. In part it is due to the general spirit of individualism. The ancient and the mediaeval city were the outcome of social effort, of combined sacrifice and of pleasures found in exalting the glory of the city, rather than the individual glory of the citizens. And this social effort is not the characteristic of American life. Here the aim has been to build up the individual citizen. Government has been pictured as a necessary evil and taxation a thing to be endured. It is not easy to bring Americans to make liberal expenditures for the promotion of the interests of the whole. Again patriotism in America has been a divided thing. In colonial days it was England the mother country that aroused the patriotism of the people. Then men gave to their new states the devotion formerly given to England. As the national feeling grew it came to struggle with the patriotism toward the state, and the affections of the citizens "perceived a divided duty." And at best devotion to the nation has overmastered devotion to the states. In all this shifting of the object of patriotic sentiment, the city has steadily lost ground, and the sentiment of patriotism itself has suffered. Again the city is a mere *local government*. It is an administrative division in sharp contrast with the old city-state which sent its ambassadors, marshalled its army, fought with rival cities, made laws, and developed *intensity* of political activity because of the very *concentration* of this activity. Think, too, of the way population shifts in America. The citizen of Boston today may be a dweller in Tacoma in a fortnight. Cities themselves spring from the ground in a generation, — busy, populous, made up of men who come and go. Contrast this with the Greek city where families had dwelt for twenty generations.

It is not easy to arouse enthusiasm for mushroom cities, nor for a city in continual change.

Add to these explanations the fact that American cities lack individuality — and picturesqueness. The idea of *defense* was prominent in the ancient city. On the hill tops were the ring walls to which the shepards and tillers of the soil fled for refuge. Little by little the city grew about these citadels, and was picturesquely crowned with temples, or fortresses. In the modern America the conditions of *trade* have preponderated in forming the cities. At the junction of railroad systems on the plains, at the confluence of rivers, at a harbor on lake or ocean, have been built the cities of America, and the result is as monotonous and uninteresting as could have been expected. The *business* basis of the city explains not only its unpicturesqueness but the neglect of its government as well. In American cities the energetic and intelligent citizens have been so devoted to amassing wealth that they have attended to their own business blocks, and their own residences, and let the general management of the city fall into the hands of the less worthy.

But there is I think ground for hope of better things in the American city.

With the passing away of the days when there were unlimited opportunities for individual activity there is coming to America an increase of the social sense, an increased feeling of social responsibility. No longer are there millions of acres of free lands, mines to be pre-empted, great railroads to be built. Population becomes denser. There are signs that co-operation is beginning to supersede individuality.

Movement of population too is likely to *de*crease in this country. As the conditions of life become more stable men will live their lives in one city, and their children will follow them. Thus city life will gain continuity; and one generation will be the more ready to build for its successors, when its successors are likely to be its own children. As wealth accumulates, as Americans cease their feverish rush for exploiting the country, and begin [to] look for means of life as well as means of livelihood, they will more and more combine their activities to make the city a worthier place. We may expect more and more the development of public libraries, museums, art galleries; public control of transportation, lighting, water, and so on.

In the direction of better *city government* there is already to be traced a healthy spirit of reform. Civic federations are forming, men are giving scientific study to European systems of municipal government, and municipal activity. College settlements are working in the city slums. Men of wealth are endowing institutes of learning, and of practical arts for the development of a richer life among the common people. In a hundred ways the last few years have shown most encouraging signs that men are coming to realize their civic responsibility and the need of applying community of effort to the development of the city.

The old city-state is gone forever. City and nation can never again be one. The glories of Athens, of Rome, of Florence, as municipal republics, are the precious possessions of history. But they can never be repeated. Nor is it altogether a matter for regret. The very intensity of rivalry within such little states which made such a brilliant life possible brought with it equally intense antagonisms, and bitterness of faction. What was gained in variety and individuality of life was partly lost by an unworthy narrowness and provincialism.

We should strive to retain what was best in that old city life. The patriotism that belongs to one's *country* is not the feeling that we have or should have for the city; but the patriotism that consists in pride in the peculiar excellencies of the city, the patriotism that demands a pure and intelligent administration of city government, the patriotism that resents any violation of the municipal rights of the citizen, the patriotism that makes a man give freely to the support of improvements in his city, this we may well possess.

Let us congratulate ourselves upon living in a city which is so well designed to call out these worthy sentiments. If many American cities are lacking in individuality, in attractiveness, it is not so with ours. Stand on one of the hills that surround her, and count the glories of Madison. On either hand lie her matchless lakes, silver in the sunshine, golden in the moon light, opalescent, rainbow like at sunset hour. If a man is stirred by beauty he will be stirred by these lakes of ours. And there between them stands the capitol, emblem of her queenly position in Wisconsin, with its stately dome of white visible from afar. On another height rises the University. Within a decade this has grown from a little college into rivalry with the greatest Universities of the country. We shall soon count her students by the thousands. Other cities give bonuses for little schools. Madison has but to open her doors to this stream of students from all parts of the state, — from *many* states. Hospitality, mere self interest, indeed, demands that we give these guests of the city the best of sanitary conditions the best conditions of urban life in all ways.

Here too is our Historical Library, soon to be housed in fitting form near to the buildings of the University. From the Alleghanies to the Pacific there is no such library in American history as this.

It has but three or four rivals in the country. As years go on, and as the nation becomes interested in her past as well as in her present and her future, Madison will be sought by increasing numbers of scholars for this priceless possession.

But it is needless for me [to] continue this enumeration. We are indeed happy in such a city. Beauty, political life, learning have here taken their abode. Let us see to it that we do our work as citizens.

These lakes of ours like crystal beakers brimming full should sparkle unpolluted. When Longfellow wrote of our limpid lakes with sylvan deities, he could hardly have expected us to empty into these lakes the city sewage. Here at least we might borrow from the city religion of the Greek, and shrink from the anger of the offended deities of the waters. We ought to drive away the spectres from our marshes. Intelligent and patriotic action would drain them and remove the menace to the city health. We ought never to allow the central part of our city to be overhung with smoke, and the air choked with its odors. Here in our country town we have a right to pure air as well as pure water. We ought to have here the cleanest city in Wisconsin, the best roads, the best schools, the best government, and we might have all of these if we had but a little of the spirit of civic patriotism. Here is our home; let us make it worthy of the beauties with which nature dowered it.

Members of the graduating class, you have received the bounty of this beautiful city. Repay these gifts by patriotic, disinterested, vigorous citizenship. You owe to Madison a filial devotion. In a large degree the city will reflect the ideals of those who year by year pass from the high school to active citizenship. Let those ideals be high ideals. And remember that it is the wise choice of the highest things day by day that elevates the civic character.

> Daughters of Time, the hypocritic Days,
> Muffled and dumb like barefoot dervishes,
> And marching single in an endless file,
> Bring diadems and fagots in their hands.
> To each they offer gifts after his will,
> Bread, kingdoms, stars, and sky that holds them all.

I, in my pleached garden, watched the pomp,
Forgot my morning wishes, hastily
Took a few herbs and apples, and the Day
Turned and departed silent. I, too late,
Under her solemn fillet saw the scorn.[2]

---

[2] See Emerson's "Days," in *The Complete Works of Ralph Waldo Emerson,* ed. Edward W. Emerson, IX (Cambridge, Mass., 1904), 228.

Index

Acton, John Emerich Edward Dalberg (Lord Acton), 89
Adams, Henry, 14, 80, 85, 156
Adams, Herbert Baxter, 6, 8, 12, 17
Adams, John Quincy, 94, 123, 134, 135
Alabama, 179
Alamance, battle of, 128
Albany Plan (Franklin's Plan of Union), 127
Allen, William F., 8, 10-12, 22n, 23
Ambler, Charles H., 33-34
American Commonwealth (Bryce), 88
American Historical Association, 7, 17, 20, 25, 33-35, 36
American Historical Review, 20, 34-35
American nationality, origins of, 104
American Nation Series, 7, 33
American Revolution, 186-187
American system (Clay's), 60
Americanization, meaning of, 37
Amherst College, 30
Analisi della proprietà capitalista (Loria), 15, 16, 22, 156
Andrews, Charles M., 80, 105, 106
Annapolis convention, 155
Apportionment, legislative, 102
Argentina, 124
Arid region, 181-183
Arkansas, 179
Articles of Confederation, 146
Athens, Greece, 201, 202, 205
Australia, frontier history of, 38

Backwoodsmen, 151-152, 153-155, 177-178. *See also* Pioneers
Bacon, Francis, 198

Brant, Joseph, 121
British empire, 105
Bryan, William Jennings, 35, 61, 189
Bryce, James, 88
Burr, Aaron, 122

Calhoun, John C., 53, 55, 58, 60, 76, 101, 123-124, 136, 138n, 161, 178
California, 122, 124, 181
Callender, James Thomson, 103
Calvinism, 176
Campbell, John A., 58
Canada, 125, 126
Canal building, 59
Capitalism, American, 75, 77-78, 182, 187-188
Carnegie Institution, 105
Carolinas, 148
Cattlemen, 174
Causation, historical, 9, 10, 40. *See also* Multiple hypothesis
Bagehot, Walter, 18-19
Bancroft, Frederic, 34-35
Bancroft, George, 14
Bancroft, Hubert H., 14-15
Bank of the United States, 60
Baptists, 178
Beard, Charles A., 36-38
Becker, Carl, 6, 21, 22, 32, 35
Benton, Thomas Hart, 135-136, 178
Blache, Vidal de la, 171
Blocs, 56, 67
Blount, William, 120
Bolshevistic labor ideas, 78
Bolton, Herbert Eugene, 39
Boston *Advertiser*, 131
Braddock, Edward, 113
Bradford, William, 171

Census Office, U.S., 65-66, 84, 172

Chamberlin, Thomas C., 40

Channing, Edward, 33

Chicago, Illinois, 59, 63

Chicago *Tribune,* 63-64

Church affiliation and politics, 76

Cities, 38, 184, 201-204

Civic patriotism, 200-203, 205, 206

Civil War, 48, 89, 124, 138

Clark, George Rogers, 24, 120, 121

Class consciousness, 188

Clay, Henry, 60, 67, 136, 137, 171

Collective social control, 189, 190

Colonial history. *See* History, colonial

Columbia University, 197

Committee government, growth of, 92

Commons, John R., 20

Communications, 62, 124, 184, 186

Concurrent majority, doctrine of, 53, 76

Conformity, 8, 193, 195, 196-197, 198

Congressional Globe, 90

Constitution (United States), 119, 130, 138, 187

Constitutional Convention of 1787, 54-55, 115, 130, 145

Constitutional History of the United States (von Holst), 85-104

Constitutions, state, 99, 102, 166

Contest in America between Great Britain and France (Mitchell), 127-128

Coolidge, Archibald C., 33

Coolidge, Calvin, 61

Cornell University, 199

Corporations, 188

Crissey, Merrill H., 5, 13

Curti, Merle, 20, 36, 40, 41

Custom, 19; broken on frontier, 167

Dane, Nathan, 57

Darwin, Charles, 9, 10

Davis, Jefferson, 178

Declaration of Independence, 145

Democracy: origins of, 41; Jacksonian, 71; elements of in America, 91, 92, 93; expansion of in America, 98, 99, 100; associated with national unity, 139; Washington on, 142; Hamilton on, 142; in relation to historical studies, 156; in conflict with competition, 183; influence of free land on, 187; and education, 193-207

Democracy in America (De Tocqueville), 88

Democratic party, 56, 67, 73-75, 134, 136

De rerum natura (Lucretius), 9

De Tocqueville, Alexis, 88, 93, 172, 187

Deutsch Amerikanisches Conversations-Lexicon, 86

Douglas, Stephen A., 59

Doyle, John A., 14

Draper collection (Wisconsin State Historical Society), 23, 24, 25

Draper, Lyman C., 23 and n

Dred Scott case, 102

Droysen, Johann Gustav, 20, 21, 168 and n

East, conflict with West, 54

Economic determinism, 40, 67

Economics, role of, 82

Edict of Nantes, revocation of, 153

Electoral system, modification of, 101

Eliot, Charles W., 197

Ellsworth, Oliver, 103

Ely, Richard T., 19, 20

Emerson, Ralph Waldo, 9, 10, 206-207

Emerton, Ephraim, 155

Environmental theory of history, 9

Epochs of American History Series, 85-86

Equality of opportunity, 139, 186-187, 190, 198

Erie Canal, 179

Essex Junto, 131

Europe, compared with U.S., 62, 126, 132-133

Evolution, 152, 163, 164, 165, 166, 167; social, 9, 10, 28, 49, 92, 99, 158, 159, 162, 163, 164, 165, 166, 167, 168, 170; patterns of, 151-162; in urban areas, 164; stages of, 165, 166; industrial waves in, 174-175

Fallen Timbers, battle of, 121

Farmers' bloc, 56, 63, 67

Farrand, Max, 28, 29, 33, 34n

Far West, 25

Federalists, 58, 131

Florence, Italy, 202, 205

Florida, 122

Ft. Le Boeuf, 112

France, 120

Franchise, extension of, 101-102

Franklin, Benjamin, 9, 127, 130, 142

Frederick the Great, 118, 145

Freedom, 10, 38

Free land, 15, 38, 49, 92, 97, 99, 167, 168, 186, 187, 189

Free Soil party, 58

French and Indian War, 113, 118

French in Ohio Valley, 112

French Revolution, 120

Frontiers: expansion of, 59-60, 61; types of, 61; life on, 153-155

Frontiersmen. See Pioneers, Backwoodsmen

Frontier theory, 1, 2, 16, 19, 28, 38-39, 45-61 passim, 83, 92, 97, 106-107, 110, 112, 153n, 161-167, 173-175, 187, 192. See also West

Geology, 181-182

George, Henry, 15-16

Georgia, 148, 179

Genet, Edmond Charles, 120

Geography: influence on politics, 46, 70-73, 75, 76, 77; relation to sectionalism, 62, 175-183; influence on history, 65-66, 67, 83; and population, 84; role in social evolution, 158, 160. See also United States

Germ theory of history, 17, 28, 158-159, 161

German method of research, 90

Germans, 54, 100, 178, 179

Giddings, Franklin H., 76, 137

Graduate studies, 199

Granger movement, 56, 134, 166, 189

Grayson, William, 56

Great Britain, 58, 105, 107, 119, 125, 126, 159

Great Lakes, 179

Great Plains, 147

Greenback movement, 134, 189

Grundriss der Historik (Droysen), 20

Grundy, Felix, 136

Guide to the Study and Reading of American History, 33

Gulf basin, 57

Gulf Plains, 180

Hamilton, Alexander, 120, 122, 142

Hammond, James H., 95, 138n

Handbuch des Offentlichen Rechts (Marquardsen), 88

Harper, William Rainey, 30, 57, 86

Harriman, Edward Henry, 189-190

Harrison, William Henry, 137

Hart, Albert Bushnell, 28, 33, 85

Hartford Convention, 57, 132

Harvard Commission on Western History, 35

Harvard University, 3, 7, 13, 32-33, 35, 38-39, 79, 193, 197, 199

Haskins, Charles Homer, 20, 32, 33

Haydn's Dictionary of Dates, 13

Hayne, Robert Young, 135

Hayne-Webster debates, 131, 135

Heidelberg University, 86

High schools, 200-207

Hildreth, Richard, 14

History: environmental theory of, 9; evolution and, 9, 10; historical causation, 9, 10, 40; human factor in, 10, 67; as science, 11; ancient, 21; writing of, 27, 91, 94; local, 38-39; medieval, 49; American, 80, 169, 170; imperial interpretation of, 80, 105, 106, 107; definitions of, 82; economics in, 82; race and, 91; historical processes, 91, 93; American diplomatic, 96; colonial, 105-107, 158-159; study of, 152, 155-156, 158; and patriotism, 158; and the sociologist, 166; significance of, 168-169

Holst, Hermann von, 14, 15, 79-80, 85-104

Hooper, Mrs. Alice Forbes, 35-36, 37

Huguenots, 153

Huntington Library, 1, 3, 4, 7, 18, 24, 33, 41, 43

Illinois, 178

Immigration, 54, 96, 189

Indians, 174

Individualism, 10, 75, 100, 152, 177, 178, 181, 182, 183, 187, 189, 202-203, 204

Industrialism, 61-62

Insurgents, 56, 63

Interdisciplinary research, 17, 41, 42, 45, 46, 47, 50, 73, 79, 152. 156

Interpretations of history, 41. *See also* History

Interstate commerce, 92, 115

Irish, immigration of, 54

Jackson, Andrew, 38, 56, 58, 71, 94, 98, 99, 112, 124, 135, 136, 164, 178

Jameson, J. Franklin, 20, 34-35

Jay, John, 55, 129

Jay's treaty, 121

Jefferson, Thomas, 38, 64, 120, 122, 128, 130-131, 142-143, 200

Johns Hopkins University, 3, 6, 11, 12, 17, 18, 20, 30, 86

Johnston, Alexander, 14

Jordan, David Starr, 31

Kentucky, 60, 147, 148, 179

King, Rufus, 55, 122, 129

Know-nothing movement, 96

Labor, 77, 78, 182, 188-189

Laboulaye, Edouard René Lefebvre, 86

La Follette movement, 56

La Follette, Robert, 63

Latin America, frontier history of, 38

League of Nations, 145, 147

Liberalism, 10

Library of Congress, 3
Lincoln, Abraham, 38, 97, 111, 141n, 163, 164, 173, 178
Literature, American, 133, 140
Livingston, Robert, 127
Local history, 38-39
Localism and the radio, 62
Lodge, Henry Cabot (1850-1924), 80, 85
London, England, 64
Longfellow, Henry Wadsworth, 206
Loria, Achille, 15, 16, 22, 156
Louisiana, 148
Louisiana Purchase, 121, 122, 131
Lowell, Abbott Lawrence, 33
Lucretius, 8, 9, 10

McMaster, John Bach, 85
Madison, James, 130
Madison, Wisconsin, 205, 206
Mandates, 50
Maps, political, 70-73
Marquardsen, Heinrich von, 88
Marshall, John, 102
Mason, George, 130
Massachusetts, colonial history of, 105, 106, 107
Memphis, Tennessee, 59
Methodists, 178
Mexico, 124
Middle region, 99, 160, 163-164, 177
Middle West, 24, 111, 165. See also Middle region
Militarism, 148
Mill, John Stuart, 19
Miranda, Francisco, 119
Mississippi, 179
Mississippi River, 55, 56
Mississippi Valley, 55, 58, 59, 63, 111, 112, 128, 147, 148, 163, 172, 179, 180, 189

Missouri, 179
Missouri Compromise, 131, 136
Missouri controversy, 123
Mitchell, John, 127-128
Mommsen, Theodor, 21-22
Monroe, James, 129
Monroe Doctrine, 124
Montreal, Canada, 64
Mood, Fulmer, 10
Morison, Samuel Eliot, 57
Morris, Gouverneur, 54-55, 131
Multiple hypothesis in historical causation, 1, 40, 41, 46, 72

Napoleon, 121-122
Nationalism, 63, 69, 89, 92, 96, 101, 104, 133, 163, 183-186
Nations: evolution of, 9; compared to sections, 133
Negroes, 179. See also Slavery
Negro suffrage, 134
Neutrality, 111, 117-118, 120, 121, 124-125, 139, 145-147
New England, 51, 57-58, 63, 64-65, 73, 131, 132, 160, 176
New England Confederation, 127
New England conscience, 97
Nominating conventions, 99, 101
Nootka Sound, 119
North, 54. See also New England
North American Review, 85
North Carolina, 128
North Central section, 179
Northwest, 124, 179
Notes on Virginia (Jefferson), 128
Nucleal lands, 50, 67
Nullification, doctrine of, 53, 54, 55, 124, 132, 135

Ohio, 147, 165
Ohio Valley, 112

Oklahoma, 179
Opportunity in America, 167, 175
Ordinance of 1787, 136, 139
Oregon, 58, 122, 124, 136
Otis, Harrison Gray, 57

Pacific Coast, 180-181
Panama Canal, 124
Parkman, Francis, 5, 14, 109
Particularism, 89, 92, 94-95, 96, 102. See also State sovereignty
Patriotism, 96, 140, 158, 200-203, 205, 206
Penn, William, 140
Physics and Politics (Bagehot), 18-19
Physiographic regions, 62. See also Geography
Pickering, Timothy, 131
Piedmont and Alleghany, 177
Pinckney, Charles, 130
Pinckney treaty, 121
Pioneers, 123, 126. See also Backwoodsmen
Political institutions, 92, 101
Political parties, 56, 66-68; 70-77, 110, 133-134, 135, 136-137, 137-138, 139, 140, 189; Washington's view of, 137; Calhoun's view of, 138n. See also Geography
Polk, James N., 178
"Poor whites," 177, 179
Population: density, 59, 61, 62, 66; increase, 62, 83, 84; changes, 62, 99, 163; relation to sectionalism, 183-184, 186
Populist movement, 56, 73, 134, 165, 166, 189
Portage, Wisconsin, 4, 5
Presbyterians, 178
Princeton University, 18, 30, 197
Progress and Poverty (George), 15

Progressive movement, 56, 63, 136
Progressive Party, 134
Public domain, 102, 139
Pulitzer prize, 7
Puritanism, 160, 176

Railroads, 69, 179, 182. See also Transportation
Randall Democrats, 67
Randolph, Edmund, 130
Randolph, John, 168
Ranke, Leopold von, 11
Reclamation Act of 1903, 182
Regulator movement, 128
Republican party, 56, 63, 66, 67, 71, 72, 73-75, 134, 137
Rome, Italy, 202, 205
Roosevelt, Theodore, 16, 134, 137, 151, 153n, 177, 189, 190
Royal Prussian Academy of Science, 89
Russia, frontier history of, 38

Safety-valve theory (frontier as a reservoir of opportunity), 59, 125, 138, 139, 167, 175, 186, 188
Sainte Pierre, Legardeur de, 112, 143
St. Louis, Missouri, 59
Scandinavians, 179
Schlesinger, Arthur M., 21
Schouler, James, 14, 85
Scotch-Irish, immigration of, 54, 100, 178
Sectionalism, 1, 18, 24, 27-28, 40, 41, 45-78, 83, 92, 97, 101, 102, 110, 115, 126-142 passim, 160-161, 163, 164, 175-183, 184, 186, 192
Self-reliance, 10
Sevier, John, 153
Shelley, Percy Bysshe, 10

Silver struggle, 136

Slavery, 49, 53, 64, 71, 72, 74, 78, 80, 90, 92, 93, 94, 95, 96-97, 99, 100, 101, 102, 138, 163, 177, 180

Slavocrats, 95

Sloane, William Milligan, 143-144

Small, Albion W., 17, 20

Smith, Adam, 124, 147

Smith, John, 170, 171, 173

Social change in history, 168

Socialism, 182-183

Social justice, 190

Social sciences. See Interdisciplinary research

Social service, 196-197

Sociologist as historian, 166

Sons of the American Revolution, 141

South: tidewater counties of, 53, 54, 160; migration from, 57; power of, 57; fails to support demands for Oregon, 58; alarm over West, 58; northern industrialism in, 64; political parties in, 71, 72, 74, 75; statesmanship of, 95-96, 100; Von Holst on, 100, 101; industrial revolution in, 100-101; political developments in, 100-101; threatens alliance with Great Britain, 123; as political ally of West, 130, 131; political unity of, 135; in Civil War, 138; characteristics of, 176-177; reconstruction in, 179

South Carolina, nullification program of, 132

South Carolina Exposition, 53

Southern Appalachians, 179

Southwest, annexation of, 122

Space expansion in U.S. history, 172

Spain, 112, 119, 120

Spencer, Herbert, 9, 10

Spheres of influence, 50

Spoils system, 102

Spotswood, Alexander, 186

"Square deal," 190

Stanford University, 30, 31, 197

State constitutions, 99, 102, 166

State sovereignty, 94-95, 98, 102-104, 132, 135

State universities, 30, 190-191, 193, 194-196, 198. See also Universities

States, decline of, 62

States and territories, organization and admission of, 139

Stephens, Henry Morse, 32

Stratification. See Equality of opportunity

Supreme Court, 102, 103, 104

Sybel, Heinrich von, 88, 89

Taft, William Howard, 137

Talleyrand-Périgord, Charles Maurice de, 173

Tammany Hall, 86, 89

Taylor, John, 130

Taylor, Zachary, 178

Tennessee, politics in, 71-72, 148, 179

Texas, 58, 122, 124, 136, 179

Tidewater area, 159-160, 161

Time and social change, 168

Trading post, evolution of, 7

Transition zones, 50

Transportation, 62, 174, 183-184

Trusts. See Capitalism, American

Turner, Andrew Jackson, 5-6

Turner, Caroline Mae Sherwood, 6

Turner, Dorothy ("Peggy"), 6, 37

Turner, Frederick Jackson: papers of, 1-4, 43-44; correspondence of, 3-41 passim; background and early life, 4, 5; education of, 5, 6, 8, 12, 17, 18, 19, 23; marriage and children of, 6; as newspaper correspondent, 6, 49; at University of Wisconsin, 6, 7, 19, 26, 29, 30, 31, 32, 35; students of, 6, 14, 21, 26, 32, 33, 34, 41; awarded Pulitzer prize, 7; at Huntington Library, 7; death of, 7; commonplace books of, 7, 8, 9, 10, 22; doctoral dissertation of, 7, 12, 20, 23; and American Historical Association, 7, 20, 34; at Harvard, 7, 32-33, 35, 38-39, 79, 193; classroom notebooks and syllabuses of, 8, 12; personal reading of, 8, 9, 10, 14, 19, 21; teachers of, 8, 10, 11, 17, 18, 19, 23; "laboratory method" of, 12; writing techniques of, 13; at Johns Hopkins University, 17, 18, 20; economics and, 19; assists in developing seminar instruction, 20; his "historical mindedness," 21; and study of foreign languages, 22; research of, 22-23, 24, 25-26, 31; map collection of, 4, 24; interest in Midwest, 24; geographic limitations on work of, 24; interest in Far West, 25; interest in "mass history," 25; geographical and geological interests of, 25; and publication, 25-29; on university historians, 27; financial problems of, 27, 31; devotion to teaching, 28; on intercollegiate athletics, 29; on higher education, 30; employment offers to, 30, 31; liberal arts and, 32; political views of, 35; as a historian, 41, 109, 152; predicts future national problems, 42; on medieval history, 49; style of writing, 109; on American neutrality, 111, 125; on role of

historian, 145, 146, 158, 162, 169; urges societal transformations, 193-194
——The Character and Influence of the Indian Trade in Wisconsin, 7; "City, Frontier, and Section, or the Significance of the City in American History," 38; "Development of American Society," 43, 152; The Frontier in American History, 7, 36; "History of Liberty," 3; "The Hunter Type," 16, 151-152, 153-155; "Introduction to a Lecture on Sectionalism," 45-46, 47-48; "Power of the Press," 8; "Problems in American History," 17; Rise of the New West, 1819-1929, 7, 28-29, 33; "Sections and Nation," 40; "Significance of the Frontier in American History," 7, 37, 47, 48, 82, 83, 110; The Significance of Sections in American History, 7, 47; "Social Forces in American History," 152; The United States, 1830-1850: The Nation and Its Sections, 7, 13; "Washington the Nationalist," 110-111; "Western State-Making in the Revolutionary Era," 23; "Why Did Not the United States Become Another Europe," 110

Tyler, John, 137

Unitarianism, 10
United States: geographic comparison with Europe, 65, 126, 172, 191; geographic divisions of, 65-66, 67; constitution of, 93, 94, 95, 103; natural resources of, 171, 189. See also Public domain
United States Census Office, 65-66, 84, 172
Universities, 30, 184, 193-200. See also State universities

University of California, 30, 31, 32

University of Chicago, 30, 31, 86, 197

University of Pennsylvania, 30, 197, 199

University of Strassburg, 89

University of Wisconsin, 6, 7, 11, 12, 19, 26, 29, 30, 31, 193, 197, 199, 200, 205

Van Buren, Martin, 71

Vancouver Island, 119

Van Hise, Charles, 30, 32

Venice, Italy, 202

Vermont, 147

Virgil, 202

Virginia, 128, 177, 186

Virginia Ratification Convention of 1787, 56

Voting patterns, 46

Walker, Francis A., 19

War of 1812, 123, 131

Washington Conference, 147

Washington, George: neutralism of, 111, 115, 117-118, 120, 121, 139, 145-146, 146-147; view of the West, 110, 112, 114-115, 146; at Ft. Le Boeuf, 112-113, 118; at Braddock's defeat, 113; in French and Indian War, 113; appearance of, 113; in American Revolution, 114-115, 140, 144; urges organization of Northwest territory, 114; greatness of, 116, 132, 141, 142, 144; Farewell Address of, 116-117; on political parties, 137, 145; interpretation of Constitution, 138; ideals of, 141-149; nationalism of, 142, 143, 144-145, 148-149; view of democracy, 142, 143; influence of frontier on, 143; lays historical foundation for Pittsburgh, 143; youth of, 145; as an innovator, 146

Wayne, Anthony, 121

Webster, Daniel, 61, 135, 136

West, 54, 153-155; and the Mississippi River, 55; growth of, 59; as a reservoir for political power, 59; acquisition of, 96-97; resources of, 125; as balance of political power, 128-130; as political ally of South, 130-131; as focal point of American history, 162; as almost synonymous with the nation, 163; slavery in, 163; industry moves toward, 164; traits of, 167. *See also* Frontier theory

Western reserve, 57

Westward movement, 166

Whig party, 66, 71, 72, 73-77, 137

White, Hugh Lawson, 71

Wilkinson, James, 122

Williamson, Hugh, 130

Wilmot Proviso, 58, 67, 136

Wilson, Woodrow, 18, 20, 30, 85, 97; *Calendar of Great Americans,* 111

Winning of the West (Roosevelt), 16, 151, 153n, 177

Winsor, Justin, 14

Wisconsin, 154, 166

Wisconsin State Historical Library, 205-206

Wisconsin State Historical Society, 23

World War I, 147

Yale University, 197

Zollverein, 139

Frederick Jackson Turner's Legacy
was designed by Paul Weaver,
set in Caledonia type, and printed on
Warren's Olde Style paper at Northland Press
Flagstaff, Arizona
1965

Walker Lewis has had a long legal career in Baltimore, Maryland, and Washington, D.C. Writing is his chief extra-curricular activity, and he is Recording Secretary of the Maryland Historical Society. His life of Chief Justice Roger Brooke Taney, *Without Fear or Favor*, was published by Houghton Mifflin Company in 1965.

SPEAK
for YOURSELF,
DANIEL

A Life of Webster
in His Own Words

ALSO BY WALKER LEWIS

*Without Fear or Favor: A Biography of
Chief Justice Roger Brooke Taney*

SPEAK
for YOURSELF,
DANIEL

A Life of Webster
in His Own Words

Edited and Arranged by

WALKER LEWIS

Illustrated with Photographs

19 69

NOTE AS TO FORMAT AND SOURCES

Quotations from Webster are in Roman type, other material in italics, with obvious exceptions to take care of emphasis, certain sub-quotations, etc.

In the interest of readability, deletions from the quoted text have not been indicated except where necessary for clarity.

Source and explanatory references are given in notes at the back of the book, keyed to the text by page number.

CONTENTS

Introduction

I

1782–1801   Family — Childhood — Dartmouth   1

II

1801–1805   Preparation for the Law   14

III

1805–1817   Early Practice   38

IV

1817–1819   The Dartmouth College Case   58

V

1819–1820   Supreme Court Practice — Plymouth Oration   73

VI

1821–1824   Congressman from Massachusetts — Speech on the Greek Revolution   87

VII

1824–1825   Marshfield — Visit to Madison and Jefferson — Bunker Hill Oration   104

VIII

1825–1827   Niagara Falls — Adams–Jefferson Oration — Election to Senate   126

IX

1827–1829   Death of Wife and Ezekiel — Remarriage   150

CONTENTS

X

1830   The Debate with Hayne: First Speech
on Foote's Resolution   176

XI

1830   The Debate with Hayne: Second Speech
on Foote's Resolution   190

XII

1830–1834   Reply to Calhoun — The Bank War   208

XIII

1830   The Murder of Captain Joseph White   223

XIV

Frustrations and Frailties   243

XV

1833–1839   Travels and Political Aspirations   259

XVI

1839   Visit to England   276

XVII

1840–1842   Secretary of State under Harrison and Tyler —
The Webster–Ashburton Treaty   292

XVIII

1842–1845   Return to Private Life   322

XIX

1845–1848   War with Mexico — Trip to the South   341

XX

1848–1849   Death of Edward and Julia — Trip
to Martha's Vineyard   366

XXI

1850   The Seventh of March Speech   393

XXII

1850   Seventh of March Speech — The Aftermath   410

CONTENTS

XXIII
1850–1852 The Hülsemann Letter — Bid for the Presidency 423

XXIV
1852 The End 443

Biographical Notes on Principal Correspondents 455

Notes and Sources 468

Index 495

ILLUSTRATIONS

DANIEL WEBSTER AT TWENTY-TWO: Engraving by J. A. J. Wilcox from a miniature by an unknown artist. Webster had it painted while a law student at Salisbury, New Hampshire, as an engagement gift to Grace Fletcher. After her death he gave it to her sister, Rebecca, wife of Israel Webster Kelley of Salisbury, with whom Grace had been living at the time of their courtship. (*Courtesy of the Trustees of Dartmouth College*)

WEBSTER AT FORTY-TWO: Portrait by Joseph Wood, painted in 1824. (*Courtesy of the Trustees of Dartmouth College*)

WEBSTER AT FORTY-NINE: Drawing by David Claypoole Johnston. (*Courtesy of the Trustees of Dartmouth College*)

WEBSTER AT FIFTY-THREE: Portrait by Francis Alexander, painted at Boston, December 1835 for Dartmouth College, entitled "Black Dan." (*Courtesy of the Trustees of Dartmouth College*)

WEBSTER AT SIXTY-TWO: Portrait by Thomas Bayley Lawson, painted at Washington, 1844. Webster is reported to have said that this portrait may have saved his life, as he remained at home on February 28, 1844, to give Mr. Lawson a sitting instead of accepting an invitation to join a Presidential party aboard the warship *Princeton* on the day that the explosion of its big gun killed several persons, including Secretary of State Abel P. Upshur (Webster's successor) and Secretary of the Navy Thomas W. Gilmer. The portrait was exhibited in the rotunda of the Capitol; Webster's comment was, "That is the face I shave." (*Courtesy of the Trustees of Dartmouth College*)

WEBSTER AT SIXTY-THREE: Portrait by Chester Harding, believed to have been painted at New Bedford, Massachusetts, in 1845. Harding painted other copies and Webster's widow kept one in the hotel room in which she lived in New York, saying that she regarded it as the most satisfactory of the portraits of her husband. (*Courtesy of the Trustees of Dartmouth College*)

WEBSTER IN HIS SIXTIES: Engraving by John Chester Buttre. (*Courtesy of the Trustees of Dartmouth College*)

WEBSTER AT SEVENTY: Head by Joseph Alexander Ames, forming part of a portrait painted in 1852. (*Courtesy of the Trustees of Dartmouth College*)

WEBSTER'S BIRTHPLACE AT SALISBURY (NOW FRANKLIN), NEW HAMP-SHIRE: Engraving by E. A. Fowle after drawing by H. Billings. This engraving was used as a frontispiece in the earliest edition of Webster's *Works*, published under his overall supervision. It differs in details from a drawing which Charles Lanman prepared pursuant to Webster's directions, and also from the later reconstruction of the house. (*Courtesy of the Library of Congress*)

SKETCH OF WEBSTER ESTATE AT MARSHFIELD, MASSACHUSETTS: This sketch was published shortly after Webster's death, in the December 1852 issue of *Harper's Monthly Magazine*. (*Courtesy of the Library of Congress*)

PHOTOGRAPH OF WEBSTER'S HOUSE AT MARSHFIELD: Two of the croquet players are said to have been grandchildren of Daniel Webster: Caroline, on the left, and Ashburton, on the right, children of Fletcher Webster. The house burned in February 1878 and was rebuilt in a different style. (*Courtesy of the Library of Congress*)

MRS. GRACE FLETCHER WEBSTER: Portrait by Chester Harding, painted at Boston in 1827. Mrs. Webster, then forty-six, is portrayed in the costume which she had worn two years earlier at the Bunker Hill celebration. (*Courtesy of the Trustees of Dartmouth College*)

MRS. CAROLINE LE ROY WEBSTER: Portrait painted by George Peter Alexander Healy when Mrs. Webster was in her mid-forties. (*Courtesy of the Trustees of Dartmouth College*)

DANIEL FLETCHER WEBSTER: Drawing of Daniel Webster's eldest son in his Civil War military cap. (*Courtesy of the Trustees of Dartmouth College*)

EDWARD WEBSTER: Portrait by Healy of Daniel Webster's second son in his Mexican War uniform. (*Courtesy of the Trustees of Dartmouth College*)

FACSIMILE OF LETTER OF FEBRUARY 2, 1819, TO DANIEL'S BROTHER EZEKIEL: This letter tells of the favorable decision of the U.S. Supreme Court in the Dartmouth College case. The letter is printed in the text, at page 70. (*Courtesy of the Trustees of Dartmouth College*)

WEBSTER REPLYING TO HAYNE: Section of Healy painting in Faneuil Hall, Boston, portraying Webster delivering his reply to Hayne in the U.S. Senate on January 26, 1830. (*Courtesy of the Trustees of Dartmouth College*)

CAMPAIGN PICTURE: This portrays Webster as New England's favorite son for the Whig nomination for the Presidency in 1848. He was defeated for the nomination by General Zachary Taylor, who became twelfth President of the United States. (*Courtesy of the Trustees of Dartmouth College*)

GIFT COACH: Presented to Webster by admirers in New York City. (*Courtesy of the Trustees of Dartmouth College*)

DE SOTO, NEBRASKA, BANK NOTE: Someone, at least, must have thought that Webster's credit was good. (*Courtesy of the Trustees of Dartmouth College*)

ILLUSTRATIONS

CHRISTOPHER GORE: Portrait by John Trumbull. (*Courtesy of Harvard University*)

JEREMIAH MASON: Portrait by Gilbert Stuart. (*Courtesy of Harvard Law School*)

JOSEPH STORY: Engraving by A. B. Waller of drawing by J. E. Johnson. (*Courtesy of Harvard Law School*)

GEORGE TICKNOR: Portrait by Thomas Sully in 1828. (*Courtesy of the Trustees of Dartmouth College*)

ROBERT Y. HAYNE: Engraving by J. B. Longacre from drawing by H. B. Hall. (*Courtesy of the Library of Congress*)

JOHN C. CALHOUN: Portrait by Healy painted after Calhoun's death from a sketch made by the artist from life in the course of painting "Webster Relying to Hayne." Calhoun, as Vice President, presided over the Senate on that occasion. (*Courtesy of the Virginia Museum*)

WILLIAM HENRY HARRISON: Engraving by R. W. Dodson from painting by J. R. Lambdin. (*Courtesy of the Library of Congress*)

JOHN TYLER: Engraving by H. W. Smith from painting by Healy. (*Courtesy of the Library of Congress*)

LORD ASHBURTON (ALEXANDER BARING): Portrait by Healy. (*Courtesy of the Trustees of Dartmouth College*)

HENRY CLAY: Engraving by Martin and Johnson. (*Courtesy of the Library of Congress*)

EDWARD EVERETT: Engraving by J. C. Buttre from photograph by Brady. (*Courtesy of the Library of Congress*)

MILLARD FILLMORE: Lithograph by F. D'Avignon from daguerreotype by Brady. (*Courtesy of the Library of Congress*)

INTRODUCTION

FEW AMERICANS have had greater impact on their contemporaries than Daniel Webster. "A natural Emperor of men," said Ralph Waldo Emerson. "The Godlike One," chorused the press. "A steam engine in trousers," commented the Very Reverend Sydney Smith, Canon of St. Paul's Cathedral, in London. Yet of all that has been written about him, only Stephen Vincent Benét's *The Devil and Daniel Webster,* a work of fiction, seems truly to have caught his spirit. Why?

When a great man dies, he is first eulogized, then dissected. His admirers consign him to sainthood, and later commentators rip away the halo. After a few critical biographies, he is lucky if he does not resemble a corpse with the spleen and liver showing.

Like all men, Webster had his frailties. Some of his biographers have dwelt on these unduly, leading us to question how such a man could have been deemed so great. For in focusing on the flaws, we lose sight of the zest, the humor, and the earthiness that cast such a magic spell.

We can no longer recapture Webster's voice, or the excitement of his presence. But we can at least catch the words by which contemporaries knew him, and in doing so come closer to a realization of his charm.

At any rate, this is the object of the present work. It is not critical, or even impartial. In essence it is an autobiography. Webster himself does most of the talking, with only such additions as seem desirable to splice the pieces together.

As published in 1903, in what was called the National Editon, the Writings and Speeches of Daniel Webster fill eighteen large volumes. Even these are not complete. The thirty some books that have been written about him include other Webster items, and manuscript collections hold more. As I have chosen only the bits I liked most, the result is highly personal. It is like sampling a box of assorted chocolates. I go for the chewy kind myself, but I realize there may be other individuals with less exalted tastes; some, even, who like pistache.

From all of Webster, no two admirers would select exactly the same. The best cure for dissatisfaction is to pick for yourself. I recommend this. It takes time, but I can guarantee it to be fun.

Although Webster had words for most things that came within his view, he did not describe himself. As a preliminary, therefore, let us consider how he looked to those who knew him at different periods of his life.

1796–1801 — *James Hervey Bingham*

"Our first acquaintance was at the academy, at Exeter, in 1796. I went there, in July of that year, and found him there. He was then a lad of about fourteen years. He had an independent air and was rather careless in his dress and appearance, but showed an intelligent look. He left in the fall of that year. I remained at Exeter till July, 1798, then entered the Freshman Class in Dartmouth College, where I found Daniel Webster. An intimacy increased between us from that time till we left college. . . . He was a favorite with the class generally; interesting and instructive in conversation; social and very kind in his feelings; not intimate with many."

1802 — *Jacob McGaw*, at Fryeburg

"His cheeks were thin and his cheek bones prominent. There was nothing especially noticeable about him except his full, steady, large, and searching eyes. Nobody could see those eyes and ever forget their appearance or him who possessed them."

1808 — Mrs. E. Buckminster Lee

"My earliest recollection of Mr. Webster is when he came to Portsmouth in 1808 to open his law office. His appearance was very striking. Slender and apparently of delicate organization, his large eyes and massive brow seemed very predominant above other features, which were sharply cut, refined and delicate. . . . He had arrived in Portsmouth at the close of the week, and the next day being Sunday, the sexton, as was the custom in those days, introduced the stranger to the minister's pew. My eldest sister was at church, and when she came home she said there had been a remarkable person in the pew with her, that he riveted her attention, and that she was sure he had a most marked character for good or for evil.

"My father, Dr. Buckminster, took the liveliest interest in Mr. Webster, and as he remarked at this time the apparent frailty of his constitution, he urged upon his young friend his sure remedy for slight indisposition. This was half an hour of wood-sawing before breakfast, with a long two-handed saw, himself holding the end opposite to that of his young friend. We young people were always delighted when this strong medicine was taken before breakfast, for however disagreeable in itself, Mr. Webster appeared at our breakfast afterwards with his genial humor unimpaired."

1834 — Thomas Hamilton, a visiting Englishman

"I had never seen any countenance more expressive of intellectual power. The forehead of Mr. Webster is high, broad, and advancing. The cavity beneath the eyebrow is remarkably large. The eye is deeply set but full, dark, and penetrating; the nose prominent, and well defined; the mouth marked by that rigid compression of the lips by which the New Englanders are distinguished. When Mr. Webster's countenance is in repose, its expression struck me as cold and forbidding, but in conversation it lightens up; and when he smiles, the whole impression it communicates is at once changed. His voice is clear, sharp, and firm, without much variety of modulation; but when animated, it rings on the ear like a clarion. . . .

"His speeches have nothing of gaudiness and glitter. Words with him are instruments, not ends; the vehicles, not of sound merely, but of sense and reason. . . .

"In conversation Mr. Webster is particularly agreeable. It seems to delight him, when he mingles with his friends, to cast off the trammels of weighty cogitation, and merge the lawyer and the statesman in the companion; a more pleasant and instructive one I have rarely known in any country. . . ."

1834 — *Harriet Martineau*

"We saw Webster standing firm as a rock, his large, deep-set eyes wide awake, his lips compressed, and his whole countenance in that intent stillness which easily fixes the eye of the stranger. . . . Our pleasantest evenings were spent at home in a society of the highest order. . . . Members of Congress would repose themselves by our fireside. . . . Mr. Webster, leaning back at his ease, telling stories, cracking jokes, shaking the sofa with burst after burst of laughter, or smoothly discoursing to the perfect felicity of the logical part of one's constitution. . . ."

1839 — *Henry W. Hilliard*

"He recalled to me the idea of classic grandeur; there was in him a blended dignity and power . . . it seemed as if the whole weight of the government might rest securely on his broad shoulders. His large, dark eyes were full of expression, even in repose; the cheeks were square and strong; his dark hair and swarthy complexion heightened the impression of strength. . . . There was in his appearance something leonine."

1839 — *Thomas Carlyle,* writing to Emerson from England

"Not many days ago I saw at breakfast the notablest of all your notabilities, Daniel Webster. He is a magnificent specimen. . . . The tanned complexion; that amorphous craglike face; the dull black eyes under the precipice of brows, like dull anthracite furnaces needing only to be blown; the mastiff mouth, accurately closed; I have not traced so much of silent Berserkir rage that I remember of, in any other man."

SPEAK
for YOURSELF,
DANIEL

A Life of Webster
in His Own Words

THE IMMEDIATE FAMILY OF DANIEL WEBSTER

FATHER *Ebenezer Webster* (1739–1806), of New Hampshire; served in
Rogers' Rangers during French wars and mustered out as a captain, in which rank he served in the American Revolution; magistrate, member of both houses of N.H. Legislature, and a judge.
Married twice:

(1) *Mehitable Smith*, who died in 1774; five children:
Olle, or Olivia, b. Jan. 28, 1762, died in infancy
Ebenezer, b. July 16, 1764, died in infancy
Susanna, b. Oct. 25, 1766; married John Colby; died 1804
David, b. May 1, 1769; moved to Canada
Joseph, b. Mar. 25, 1772, d. 1810, unmarried

MOTHER (2) *Abigail Eastman*, who died in 1816; five children:
Mehitable, b. 1775, died unmarried at 39
Abigail, b. 1778; married William Haddock; died at 27
Ezekiel, b. Mar. 11, 1780, d. Apr. 10, 1829
Daniel, b. Jan. 18, 1782, d. Oct. 24, 1852
Sarah, b. 1784; married cousin, Ebenezer Webster; died 1811

WIVES (1) *Grace Fletcher* (1781–1828) of Hopkinton, N.H.; five children:
Grace Fletcher Webster (Apr. 29, 1810 — Jan. 23, 1817)
Daniel Fletcher Webster (July 23, 1813 — Aug. 30, 1862); killed
in second Battle of Bull Run; married Caroline Story White
— six children, all of whom died without issue
Julia Webster (Jan. 16, 1818 — Apr. 28, 1848); married Samuel
Appleton Appleton; five children, three of whom left issue
Edward Webster (July 20, 1820 — Jan. 23, 1848); unmarried
Charles Webster (Dec. 31, 1822 — Dec. 18, 1824)
(2) *Caroline Le Roy* (1797–1882) of New York City — no children

I

1782–1801

FAMILY — CHILDHOOD — DARTMOUTH

MY EARLIEST ANCESTOR of whom I possess at present any knowledge, was Thomas Webster. He was settled in Hampton, New Hampshire, as early as 1636, probably having come thither from or through Massachusetts, though he may have come by way of Piscataqua. From him to myself the descent may be found regularly recorded in the church records and town records of Hampton, Kingston, now East Kingston, and Salisbury.

The family is, no doubt, originally from Scotland, although I have not been able to learn how far back any Scotch accent was found lingering on our tongue. Probably enough, the emigrants may have come last from England. The characteristics of the personal appearance of the Websters are pretty strongly marked, and very generally found with all who bear the name in New England. They have light complexions, sandy hair, a good deal of it, and bushy eyebrows; and are rather slender than broad or corpulent.

My uncles were formed and marked in the same manner. No two persons looked more unlike than my father and either of his brothers. His mother was a Bachelder, a descendant of the Rev. Stephen Bachelder, a man of some notoriety, in his time, in the county of Rockingham. This woman had black hair, and black eyes, and was, besides, as my father, who was her eldest son, has told me, a person of uncommon strength of character. I learn the same thing from the elderly inhabitants of Kingston. My father resembled, in complexion and appearance, his mother; his brothers

1

resembled their father. Of my own brothers, only one had the Bachelder complexion; the others, three, ran off into the general characteristics belonging to the name.

My first clear and distinct recollection of my father's appearance was when he was at the age of fifty; tall, six feet, erect, with a broad and full chest, hair still of an unchanged black, features rather ⸴ large and prominent, a Roman nose, and eyes of brilliant black. He had a decisive air and bearing, partly the effect, I suppose, of early soldiership. He was the handsomest man I ever saw, except my brother Ezekiel, who appeared to me the very finest human form that ever I set eyes on.

He was born at Kingston, now East Kingston, in 1739; the eldest son of Ebenezer Webster and Susannah Bachelder. His father was a farmer, as we somewhat improperly call persons of his condition; that is to say, he was a small freeholder, tilling his own acres with his own hands, and those of his boys, till they grew up to manhood, when they were to look out, in the country round them, for acres of their own to till.

After the age of twelve or fifteen, he lived several years in the family of Colonel Stevens, the most considerable person in the vicinity; and then, as Major Dalgetty would say, he took service in the troops raised in the Provinces to carry on the French war. His first engagement, I believe, was in Robert Rogers's company of Rangers. He was with the army of Gen. Amherst, when that commander made his way by Albany, Oswego, Ticonderoga, &c., into Canada. When Canada was conquered, his occupation was gone; but that event opened new scenes of enterprise, more pacific, but promising more permanent good, to those who had strong hands and determined purpose.

Previous to the year 1763, the settlements in New Hampshire had made little or no progress inward into the country, for sixty or seventy years, owing to the hostility of the French, in Canada, and of the neighboring Indians, who were under French influences. This powerful cause of repression being effectually removed by the cession of Canada to England, by the Peace of Paris in 1763, companies were formed, in various parts of New England, to settle the wilderness, between the already settled parts of New England and New York and Canada. Colonel Stevens, already mentioned, and other persons about Kingston, formed one of these companies, and obtained from Benning Wentworth, Governor of the Province of New Hampshire, a grant of the township of Salisbury, at first called Stevenstown. It is situated exactly at the head of the Merrimac River, and very near the centre of the State. My father joined this enterprise, and about 1764, the exact date is not before me, pushed into the wilderness. He had the discretion to take a wife along with him, intending whatever else he might want, at least, not to lack good company. The party *travelled out the road,* or path, for it was no better, somewhere about Concord or Boscawen; and they were obliged to make their way, not finding one, to their destined places of habitation. My father *lapped on,* a little beyond any other comer, and when he had built his log cabin, and lighted his fire, his smoke ascended nearer to the North Star than that of any other of his Majesty's New England subjects. His nearest civilized neighbor on the north was at Montreal.

His story of this early settlement was interesting, at least, to me. The settlers, doubtless, suffered much. The mountainous nature of the country, the very long winters, with prodigious depth of snow, and the want of all roads to communicate with the country below, often induced great hardships. The settlement increased, and when the revolutionary war broke out, ten or eleven years after, the town contained nearly two hundred men capable of bearing arms. My father was their Captain, and he led them forth, with the other New Hampshire troops, almost every campaign. He commanded a company at Bennington, at White Plains, at West Point, at the time of Arnold's defection, &c. I have some little articles, the *spolia prœlii* of Bennington, which I keep, *honore parentis.*

The last time I ever saw Gen. Stark, he paid me the compliment of saying, that my complexion was like that of my father, and that his was of that cast, so convenient for a soldier, that burnt gun-powder did not change it.

My father used to tell a story on himself, about his reputation as a marksman. A few rods from the bank of the Merrimac River was a small tuft of an island, upon which stood a solitary tree. This tree used to be a favorite mark in the target-practice of the band of minute men who chose my father as their captain. These men, trained in the hard experiences of frontier life, took no little pride in their guns and in their skill in handling them. This tree was a target for them; and here they would come and exercise their skill. Being at a long distance, the thing to be done was to hit the body of the tree itself; and the way in which they determined whether the tree was hit was rather a novel one. If the bullet did not strike the tree it would fall into the water, and the splash would readily be noticed; but, if there was no splash, it was taken for granted that the ball had struck the tree itself. My father used to describe these matches among the frontier marksmen, and would say that when his turn came, he never failed of being set down as having hit the tree — as there never was any splash in the water after his shot, he got the credit of being the best marksman among them all.

"How did you manage to do it?" I once asked him.

"Oh, simply enough," he replied with a laugh. "The fact is, I never used to put any bullet into my gun."

I was born January 18, 1782. My father, by two marriages, had five sons and five daughters. I am the youngest son. I have nephews and nieces, both of the whole and half blood; that is to say, sons and daughters of my brothers and sisters, of both my father's wives.

The year following my birth, my father removed from his first residence, which was a log house on the hill, to the river side, in the same town; a distance of three miles. Here, in the meadow land, by the river, with rough high hills hanging over, was the scene of my earliest recollections; or, as was said in another case, "Here I found myself." I can recollect when it was 1790; but cannot say that I can remember further back. I have a very vivid impression, indeed, of

4

something which took place some years earlier, especially, of an extraordinary rise in the river. I remember how the deluge of rain beat, for two days, on the house; how all looked anxiously to see the river overflow its banks, how the waters spread over the meadows, how the boat coming from afar, on the other side of the river, was rowed up till it almost touched the door-stone. How Mr. G.'s great barn, fifty feet by twenty, full of hay and grain, sheep, turkeys, and chickens, sailed down the current majestically before our eyes, and how we were all busy preparing to fly to the mountains, as soon as our house should manifest a disposition to follow Mr. G.'s barn. I remember, or seem to remember all these things; I did indeed see as much of them as a child of five years could see, for I think it was in 1787, but still I am of opinion that my impression is from narrative, and not from remembrance of the vision. Plain, intelligible, and striking things of this kind, I have learned, make an impression on young minds in recital, which it is difficult afterwards to distinguish from actual personal recollection.

I do not remember when or by whom I was taught to read; because I cannot and never could recollect a time when I could not read the Bible. I suppose I was taught by my mother, or by my elder sisters. My father seemed to have no higher object in the world, than to educate his children, to the full extent of his very limited ability. No means were within his reach, generally speaking, but the small town schools. These were kept by teachers, sufficiently indifferent, in the several neighborhoods of the township, each a small part of the year. To these I was sent, with the other children.

William Hoyt was for many years teacher of our country school in Salisbury. I do not call it village school, because there was at that time no village; and boys came to school in the winter, the only season in which schools were usually open, from distances of several miles, wading through the snow, or running upon its crust, with their curly heads of hair often whitened with frost from their own breath. I knew William Hoyt well, and every truant knew him. He was an austere man, but a good teacher of children. He had been a printer in Newburyport, wrote a very fair and excellent hand, was a good reader, and could teach boys, and did teach boys that which so few masters can, or will do, to read well themselves. Beyond this, and, perhaps, a very slight knowledge of grammar, his attainments did not extend. He had brought with him into the town a little property which he took very good care of. He rather loved money; of all the cases of nouns preferring the possessive. He also kept a little shop for the sale of various commodities, in the house exactly over the way from this. I do not know how old I was, but I remember having gone into his shop one day, and bought a small cotton pocket handkerchief with the constitution of the United States printed on its two sides. From this I first learned either that there was a constitution, or that there were thirteen States. I remember to have read it, and have known more or less of it ever since. William Hoyt and his wife lie buried in the grave-yard under our eye, on my farm, near the graves of my own family. He left no children. I suppose that this little handkerchief was purchased about the time that I was eight years old.

At a very early day, owing I believe mainly to the exertions of Mr. Thompson, the lawyer, the clergyman, and my father, a very small circulating library had been bought. These institutions about that time received an impulse from the efforts of Dr. Belknap, our New Hampshire historian. I obtained some of these books, and read them. I remember the Spectator among them; and I remember, too, that I turned over the leaves of Addison's criticism on Chevy Chase, for the sake of reading connectedly the song, the verses of which he quotes from time to time as subjects of remark. It was, as Doctor Johnson said in another case, that the poet was read and the critic was neglected. I could not understand why it was necessary that the author of the Spectator should take such great pains to prove that Chevy Chase was a good story; that was the last thing I doubted.

I was fond of poetry. By far the greater part of Dr. Watts's

Psalms and Hymns I could repeat *memoriter,* at ten or twelve years of age. I am sure that no other sacred poetry will ever appear to me so affecting and devout.

I remember that my father brought home from some of the lower towns Pope's Essay on Man, published in a sort of pamphlet. I took it, and very soon could repeat it, from beginning to end. We had so few books that to read them once or twice was nothing. We thought they were all to be got by heart. I have thought of this frequently since, when that sagacious admonition of one of the ancients (was it Pliny?) has been quoted, *legere multum non multa.*

I remember one occurrence, that shows the value then attached to books. The close of the year had brought along the next year's almanac. This was an acquisition. A page was devoted to each month, and on the top of each page were four lines of poetry; some moral, some sentimental, some ludicrous. The almanac came in the morning, and before night my brother and myself were masters of its contents, at least of its poetry and its anecdotes. We went to bed upon it; but awaking long before the morning light, we had a difference of recollection about one word, in the third line of *April's* poetry. We could not settle it by argument and there was no umpire. But the *fact* could be ascertained by inspection of the book. I arose, groped my way to the kitchen, lighted a candle, proceeded to a distant room, in search of the almanac, found it, and brought it away. The disputed passage was examined, I believe I was found to be in the wrong, and blew out my candle and went to bed. But the consequence of my error had wellnigh been serious. It was about two o'clock in the morning, and just as I was again going to sleep, I thought I saw signs of light in the room I had visited. I sprang out of bed, ran to the door, opened the room, and it was all on fire. I had let fall a spark, or touched the light to something which had communicated fire to a parcel of cotton clothes, they had communicated it to the furniture, and to the sides of the room, and the flames had already begun to show themselves through the ceiling, in the chamber above. A pretty earnest cry soon brought the household together. By great good luck we escaped. Two or three minutes more and we should all have been in danger of burning together. As it was, I think the house was saved by my father's presence of mind. While others went for water, he seized every thing movable which was on fire, and wrapped it up in woollen blankets. My maternal grandmother, then of the age of eighty, was sleeping in the room.

I recollect no great changes happening to me till I was fourteen years old. A great deal of the time I was sick, and when well was exceedingly slender, and apparently of feeble system. I read what I could get to read, went to school when I could; and when not at school, was a farmer's youngest boy, not good for much, for want of health and strength, but was expected to do something.

At one time I was put to mowing and made bad work of it. My scythe was sometimes in the ground, and sometimes over the top of all the grass. I complained to my father that my scythe was not hung right. Various attempts were made to hang it better, but with no success. My father told me, at length, that I might hang it to suit myself, whereupon I hung it upon a tree and said, "There, that's just right." Father laughed, and told me to let it hang there. My brother Joe used to say, that my father sent me to college in order to make me equal to the rest of the children!

Of a hot day in July, it must have been in one of the last years of Washington's administration, I was making hay with my father, just where I now see a remaining elm tree. About the middle of the afternoon, the Honorable Abiel Foster, M. C., who lived in Canterbury, six miles off, called at the house, and came into the field to see my father. He was a worthy man, college learned, and had been a minister, but was not a person of any considerable natural power. My father was his friend and supporter. He talked awhile in the field, and went on his way. When he was gone, my father called me to him, and we sat down beneath the elm, on a haycock. He said, "My son, that is a worthy man, he is a member of Congress, he goes to Philadelphia, and gets six dollars a day, while I toil here. It is because he had an education, which I never had. If I had had his early education, I should have been in Philadelphia in his place. I came near it as it was. I could not give your elder brothers the advantages of knowledge, but I can do something for you. Exert yourself, improve your opportunities, learn, learn, and when I am gone, you will not need to go through the hardships which I have undergone, and which have made me an old man before my time."

The next May he took me to Exeter, to the Phillips Exeter Academy, placed me under the tuition of its excellent preceptor, Dr. Benjamin Abbott. I had never been from home before, and the change overpowered me. I hardly remained master of my own senses, among ninety boys, who had seen so much more, and appeared to know so much more than I did. I was put to English grammar, and writing, and arithmetic. The first, I think I may say, I fairly mastered between May and October; in the others I made some progress. In the autumn, there was a short vacation. I went home, stayed a few days, and returned at the commencement of the quarter, and then began the Latin grammar. My first exercises in Latin were recited to Joseph Stevens Buckminster. He had, I think, already joined college, but had returned to Exeter, perhaps in the college vacation, and was acting as usher, in the place of Dr. Abbott, then absent through indisposition.

I believe I made tolerable progress in most branches which I attended to, while in this school; but there was one thing I could not do. I could not make a declamation. I could not speak before the school. The kind and excellent Buckminster sought, especially, to persuade me to perform the exercise of declamation, like other boys; but I could not do it. Many a piece did I commit to memory, and recite and rehearse, in my own room, over and over again; yet when the day came, when the school collected to hear declamations, when my name was called, and I saw all eyes turned to my seat, I could not raise myself from it. Sometimes the instructors frowned, sometimes they smiled. Mr. Buckminster always pressed, and entreated, most winningly, that I would venture; but I could never command sufficient resolution. When the occasion was over, I went home and wept bitter tears of mortification.

At the winter vacation, December, 1796, or January, 1797, my father came for me, and took me home. Some long-enduring friendships I formed in the few months I was at Exeter. J. W. Bracket, of New York, William Garland, of Portsmouth, Gov. Cass, of Michigan, Mr. Saltonstall, and James H. Bingham, of Claremont, New Hampshire, are of the number. In February, 1797, my father carried me to the Rev. Samuel Wood's, in Boscawen, and placed me under the tuition of that most benevolent and excellent man. It was but half a dozen miles from our own house. On the way to Mr. Wood's, my father first intimated to me his intention of sending me to college. The very idea thrilled my whole frame. He said he then lived but for his children, and if I would do all I could for myself, he would do what he could for me. I remember that I was quite overcome, and my head grew dizzy. The thing appeared to me so high, and the expense and sacrifice it was to cost my father, so great, I could only press his hands and shed tears. Excellent, excellent parent! I cannot think of him, even now, without turning child again.

Mr. Wood put me upon Virgil and Tully; and I conceived a pleasure in the study of them, especially the latter, which rendered application no longer a task. With what vehemence did I denounce Catiline! With what earnestness struggle for Milo! In the spring I began the Greek grammar, and at midsummer Mr. Wood said to me: "I expected to keep you till next year, but I am tired of you, and I shall put you into college next month." And so he did, but it was a mere breaking in; I was, indeed, miserably prepared, both in Latin and Greek; but Mr. Wood accomplished his promise, and I entered Dartmouth College, as a Freshman, August, 1797. At Boscawen, I had found another circulating library, and had read many of its volumes. I remember especially that I found Don Quixote, in the common translation, and in an edition, as I think, of three or four duodecimo volumes. I began to read it, and it is literally true that I never closed my eyes till I had finished it; nor did I lay it down for five minutes; so great was the power of that extraordinary book on my imagination.

I was graduated, in course, August, 1801. Owing to some difficulties, *hæc non meminisse juvat,* I took no part in the commencement exercises. I spoke an oration to the Society of the United Fraternity, which I suspect was a sufficiently boyish performance.

My college life was not an idle one. Beside the regular attendance on prescribed duties and studies, I read something of English history and English literature. Perhaps my reading was too miscellaneous. I even paid my board, for a year, by superintending a little weekly newspaper, and making selections for it, from books of literature, and from the contemporary publications. I suppose I sometimes wrote a foolish paragraph myself. While in college, I delivered two or three occasional addresses, which were published. I trust they are forgotten; they were in very bad taste. I had not then learned that all true power in writing is in the idea, not in the style, an error into which the *Ars rhetorica,* as it is usually taught, may easily lead stronger heads than mine.

The opinion of my scholarship was a mistaken one. It was overestimated. I will explain what I mean. Many other students read more than I did and knew more than I did. But so much as I read, I made my own. When a half hour or an hour, at most, had elapsed, I closed my book and thought over what I had read. If there was anything peculiarly interesting or striking in the passage, I endeavored to recall it and lay it up in my memory, and commonly could effect my object. Then, if in debate or conversation afterwards, any subject came up on which I had read something, I could talk very easily so far as I had read, and then I was very careful to stop. Thus, greater credit was given me for extensive and accurate knowledge than I really possessed.

I must now go back, a little, to make mention of some incidents connected with my brother, Ezekiel Webster. He was almost two years older than myself, having been born March 11, 1780. He was a healthy, strong-built, robust boy. His intellectual character, as it afterwards developed itself, was not early understood, at least in its full extent. He was thought to have good sense, but not to have, and perhaps had not, great quickness of apprehension. The older brothers were married and settled. My father's plan was that this brother should remain with him.

This was the domestic state of things, when I went to college in August, 1797. But I soon began to grow uneasy about my brother's situation. His prospects were not promising, and he himself saw and felt this, and had aspirations beyond his condition. Nothing was proposed, however, by way of change of plan, till two years after. In the spring of 1799, at the May vacation, being then Sophomore, I visited my family, and then held serious consultation with my brother. I remember well when we went to bed, we began to talk matters over, and that we rose, after sunrise, without having shut our eyes. But we had settled our plan.

He had thought of going into some new part of the country. That was discussed and disagreed to. All the *pros* and *cons* of the question of remaining at home were weighed and considered, and when our council broke up, or rather got up, its result was that I should propose to my father, that he, late as it was, should be sent to school, also, and to college. This, we knew, would be a trying thing to my father and mother, and two unmarried sisters. My father was growing old, his health not good, and his circumstances far from easy. The farm was to be carried on, and the family taken care of; and there was nobody to do all this, but him, who was regarded as the main stay, that is to say, Ezekiel. However, I ventured on the negotiation, and it was carried, as other things are often, by the earnest and sanguine manner of youth. I told him that I was unhappy at my brother's prospects. For myself, I saw my way to knowledge, respectability, and self-protection; but as to him, all looked the other way; that I would keep school, and get along as well as I could — be more than four years in getting through college, if necessary, provided he also could be sent to study.

12

He said at once he lived but for his children; that he had but little, and on that little he put no value, except so far as it might be useful to them. That to carry us both through college would take all he was worth; that for himself he was willing to run the risk, but that this was a serious matter to our mother and two unmarried sisters; that we must settle the matter with them, and if their consent was obtained, he would trust to Providence, and get along as well as he could. The result was, that, in about ten days, I had gone back to college, having first seen my brother take leave of the meadows, and place himself in school, under a teacher in Latin. Soon afterwards he went to Mr. Wood's, and there pursued the requisite studies, and my father carried him, with me, to college in March, 1801, when he joined the then Freshman class.

II

1801–1805

PREPARATION FOR THE LAW

BEING GRADUATED IN AUGUST, 1801, I immediately entered the office of Thomas W. Thompson, in Salisbury, next door to my father's house, to study law.

The following letters to James Hervey Bingham give further details.

[Sept. 22, 1801]

I have precipitated myself into an office, with how much prudence I do not now allow myself to reflect. I am not like you, harassed with dreams, nor troubled with any waverings of inclination; but am rather sunken in indifference and apathy. I have read some since Commencement, learned a little, forgotten a good deal, and should be glad to forget much more. As to Coke and Blackstone, whom you mention as my probable intimates, "I tender them the homage of my high respects," and leave the "tenure of their position undisturbed."

I expect to meet many disappointments in the prosecution of the law. I find I have calculated too largely on the profession.

For this reason I have engaged a new auxiliary to support me under mortification; it is tobacco. I have heard much of philosophical fortitude, but never knew what it was, unless it be a sullen unfeelingness, a cold temper, or inhuman heart. But tobacco inspires courage of another kind, deliberate, yet immovable; affectionate and feeling, yet despising danger. Since I have used this great catholicon, I suspect that Cato and John Rogers were not unacquainted

14

with the virtues of the goodly leaf; else whence derived they their firmness? Oh! tobacco, how many hearts hast thou saved from the destructions of coquetry! How many throats of bankrupts hast thou preserved from their own penknives!

> Come, then, tobacco, new-found friend,
> Come, and thy suppliant attend
>   In each dull, lonely hour;
> And though misfortunes lie around,
> Thicker than hailstones on the ground,
>   I'll rest upon thy power.
> Then, while the coxcomb pert and proud,
> The politician learned and loud,
>   Keep one eternal clack,
> I'll tread where silent nature smiles,
> Where solitude our woes beguiles,
>   And chew thee, dear tobac.

If you will write me immediately, dear Hervey, and inform me where I shall find you, I will set out in the course of a few weeks. I would not ride forty miles to see anybody living but yourself; but since 'tis you, I will do it gladly. I have a thousand things to talk about beside my tobacco.

I hope to squeeze your hand soon; till when I have no other enjoyment than books afford, together with the society of Mr. Abbott and Mr. Thompson, who, when he relaxes from business, which he prosecutes with unwearied attention, is entertaining and instructive.

[Oct. 26, 1801]

Mr. Thompson has gone to Boston, Mr. Abbott to Salem, and I am in consequence alone, and shall be probably for some weeks. I have made some few writs, and am now about to bring an action of trespass for breaking a violin. The owner of the violin was at a husking, where "His jarring concord, and his discord dulcet" were making the girls skip over the husks as nimbly as Virgil's Camilla over the tops of the corn, till an old surly creature caught his fiddle and broke it against the wall. For the sake of having plump witnesses, the plaintiff will summon all the girls to attend the trial at Concord.

Mr. Thompson is made trustee of Dartmouth College.

I thank you for your receipt for greasing boots. Have this afternoon to ride to the South road, and in truth my boots admit not only water, but peas and gravel-stones. I wish I had better ones. As for my new "friend tobacco," he is like most of that name; has made me twice sick and is now dismissed.

Heigho! A man wants a remedy against his neighbor, whose lips were found damage feasant on his, the plaintiff's, wife's cheek! What is to be done? But you have not read the law about kissing. I will write for advice and direction to Barrister Fuller.

[Autobiography]

In January, 1802, the necessity of the case required that I should go somewhere and gain a little money. I was written to, luckily, to go to Fryeburg, Maine, to keep school. I accepted the offer, traversed the country on horseback, and commenced my labors. I was to be paid at the rate of three hundred and fifty dollars per annum. This was no small thing, for I compared it not with what might be before me, but what was actually behind me. It was better, certainly, than following the plough. But let me say something in favor of my own industry, not to make a merit of it, for necessity sometimes makes the most idle industrious.

It so happened that I boarded, at Fryeburg, with the gentleman, James Osgood, Esq., who was Register of Deeds of the then newly created County of Oxford. He was not clerical, in and of himself; and his registration was to be done by deputy. The fee for recording at full length a common deed, in a large fair hand, and with the care requisite to avoid errors, was two shillings and three pence.

PREPARATION FOR THE LAW

Mr. Osgood proposed to me that I should do this writing, and that of the two shillings and three pence for each deed, I should have one shilling and sixpence, and he should have the remaining nine-pence. I greedily seized on so tempting an offer, and set to work. Of a long winter's evening I could copy two deeds, and that was half a dollar. Four evenings in a week earned two dollars; and two dollars a week paid my board. This appeared to me to be a very thriving condition; for my three hundred and fifty dollars salary as a school-master was thus going on, without abatement or deduction for *vivres*. I hope yet to have an opportunity to see, once more, the first volume of the Record of Deeds, for the County of Oxford. It is now near thirty years since I copied into it the last "witness my hand and seal"; and I have not seen even its outside since. But the ache is not yet out of my fingers; for nothing has ever been so laborious to me as writing, when under the necessity of writing a good hand.

In May, 1802, having a week's vacation, I took my quarter's salary, mounted a horse, went straight over all the hills to Hanover, and had the pleasure of putting these, the first earnings of my life, into my brother's hands, for his college expenses. Having enjoyed this sincere and high pleasure, I hied me back again to my school and my copying of deeds.

[*Letter to Bingham, May 18, 1802*]

About three weeks ago we had our semi-annual exhibition. The performances of the school were such, I believe, as gave satisfaction to the Trustees. In truth, I was not much ashamed of their appearance. The Trustees were pleased to pass a vote of thanks, as also to present their preceptor a small extraordinary gratuity. Following exhibition was a vacation of 2½ weeks. Forgive me for writing in figures. I shall be glad if I can find paper for all I have to say to you, without stating my ideas by Algebra. This vacation I had devoted to the reading of Sallust, but on the day of Exhibition I had a letter informing me that "Zeke" was very sick at college. I had heard also that a young man at Salisbury, who was just about marrying my oldest sister, was on the verge of death, and had expressed very particular and urgent reasons for seeing me once more. Under these circumstances I immediately set out for New Hampshire. I went directly to Hanover, where I found my brother on the recovery, though much out of sorts. There also I saw Fanny and kissed her, nobody else. She was in decent health when I first saw her, but was taken with the cramp the night I arrived. I said but little to her. I also saw Sophia; the palpitation at her heart will not, I fear, suffer her to be a great while company for us mortals. She has frequently, you know, been charged with having palpitations of that organ, but I think she has one attached to her now that may produce greater evils than any preceding one. I had not opportunity to chat with her save in company. Mary Woodward I shook by the hand, and was treated by her with more respect than that family have ever before shown me. Nabby was at Woodstock.

When I reached Salisbury, I found that the young man whom I mentioned in the first page of this document had been dead several days. To the last he appeared oppressed with something he would reveal to no one living but myself, and that opportunity never occurred. What this was, I cannot conjecture; it might be something important, and it might be a whim of a sick man's fancy. If he had done me any injury for which he wished forgiveness, God knows I heartily forgive him. Peace to him!

I spent a few days at Salisbury, and thence took my departure again for this place. Had a pleasant journey, save the inconvenience which arose from bad roads and bad taverns. I came to one innkeeper's by name Knight. From his appearance I thought he could be no Knight of the Bath.

I arrived here last night; but must fill this page by relating a little anecdote that happened yesterday. I accidentally fell in with one of my scholars, on his return to the academy. He was mounted on the ugliest horse I ever saw or heard of, except "Sancho Panza's" pacer.

As I had two horses with me, I proposed to him to ride one of them, and tie his bag fast to his Bucephalus; he did accordingly, and turned her forward, where her odd appearance, indescribable gait, and frequent stumblings afforded us constant amusement. At length we approached Saco River, a very wide, deep, and rapid stream, when this satire on the animal creation, as if to revenge herself on us for our sarcasms, plunged into the river, then very high by the freshet, and was wafted down the current like a bag of oats! I could scarcely sit on my horse for laughter. I am apt to laugh at the vexations of my friends. The fellow, who was of my own age, and my room-mate, half checked the current, by oaths as big as lobsters, and the old Rosinante, who was all the while much at her ease, floated up among the willows far below on the opposite shore.

I will in this volume, my dear Hervey, give you some account of my circumstances, feelings, and prospects. The salary afforded me is three hundred and fifty dollars exclusive; board is one dollar and seventy-five cents; this is my academic engagement. Fortune, like other females, does not always frown. My landlord is Register; and as he is extensively in business I do the writing of his office; this is a little decent perquisite. If I will tarry, the Board will increase my salary, and do every thing for me in their power. A compensation annually of five or six hundred dollars, a house to live in, a piece of land to cultivate, and, *inter nos solos,* a clerkship of the Common Pleas, are now probably within the reach and possession of your friend, D. W.

What shall I do? Shall I say "Yes, Gentlemen," and sit down here to spend my days in a kind of comfortable privacy, or shall I relinquish these prospects, and enter into a profession where my feelings will be constantly harrowed by objects either of dishonesty or misfortune; where my living must be squeezed from penury (for rich folks seldom go to law) and my moral principle continually be at hazard? I agree with you that the law is well calculated to draw forth the powers of the mind, but what are its effects on the heart; are they equally propitious? Does it inspire benevolence and awake tenderness; or does it, by a frequent repetition of wretched objects, blunt sensibility and stifle the still, small voice of mercy?

The talent with which Heaven has intrusted me is small, very small, yet I feel responsible for the use of it, and am not willing to pervert it to purposes reproachful or unjust, nor to hide it, like the slothful servant, in a napkin.

Now, I will enumerate the inducements that draw me towards the law. First and principally, it is my father's wish. He does not dictate, it is true, but how much short of dictation is the mere wish of a parent, whose labors of life are wasted on favors to his children? Even the delicacy with which this wish is expressed gives it more effect than it would have in the form of a command. Secondly, my friends generally wish it. They are urgent and pressing. My father even offers me — I will some time tell you what — and Mr. Thompson offers my tuition gratis, and to relinquish his stand to me.

On the whole, I imagine I shall make one more trial in the ensuing autumn. If I prosecute the profession, I pray God to fortify me against its temptations. To the winds I dismiss those light hopes of eminence which ambition inspired and vanity fostered. To be "honest, to be capable, to be faithful" to my client and my conscience, I earnestly hope will be my first endeavor. I believe you, my worthy boy, when you tell me what are your intentions. I have long known and long loved the honesty of your heart. But let us not rely too much on ourselves; let us look to some less fallible guide, to direct us among the temptations that surround us.

[Letter to Thomas A. Merrill, June 7, 1802]

Fame has told me, though she is said to be a notorious liar, that you are a finished gallant; it will be natural therefore for you to inquire about the number and beauty of our Misses. You know that new towns have usually more males than females, and old commercial towns the reverse. In Salem and Newburyport, I am told, the majority of females is immense. When I resided at Exeter I thought petticoats would overrun the nation. In Fryeburg I hope our sex will continue the mastery, though the female squadron is by no means contemptible. I have seen nearly thirty white muslins trail across a ball room on an evening. In point of beauty, I do not feel competent to decide. I cannot calculate the precise value of a dimple, nor estimate the charms of an eyebrow, yet I see nothing repulsive in the appearance of Maine Misses.

[*Autobiography*]

I stayed in Fryeburg only till September. My brother then came to see me, we made a journey together to the lower part of Maine, and returned to Salisbury. I resumed my place in Mr. Thompson's office, and he went back to college.

From September, 1802, to February or March, 1804, I remained in Mr. Thompson's office, and studied the law. He was an admirable man, and a good lawyer himself; but I was put to study in the old way, that is, the hardest books first, and lost much time. I read Coke Littleton through, without understanding a quarter part of it. There are propositions in Coke so abstract, and distinctions so nice, and doctrines embracing so many conditions and qualifications, that it requires an effort, not only of a mature mind, but of a mind both strong and mature to understand him. Why disgust and discourage a boy, by telling him that he must break into his profession, through such a wall as this? I really often despaired. I thought I never could make myself a lawyer, and was almost going back to the business of school-keeping.

[*Letter to Bingham, Dec. 21, 1802*]

The best way to study law is in relation to particular points. I had read the statute of limitations, I do not know how many times, nor how many times more I might have read it among others, without discovering that it did not affect a sealed instrument, unless I had looked in reference to that particular inquiry. It is very much so, I believe, with history. We read page after page, and retaining a slender thread of events, everything else glides from the mind about as fast as the eye traces the lines of the book. Yet, when we examine a particular occurrence, or search after a single date, the impression is permanent, and we have added one idea to the stock of real knowledge.

Lovers, I have heard it said, are apt to write with trembling hand. If that circumstance alone be sufficient to constitute one, I am as valiant a lover as ever made a vow. My hand does indeed tremble, and my brain dances with twice as much giddiness as ever. But what would be imputed to love, if you were a lady, may now very fairly be ascribed to the measles. This ugly disorder attacked me about a fortnight since, and has formed a great syncope in my health and happiness. I am now convalescent, as the faculty say, and am today just able to scrawl you this; if it be very dull, pray do not blame me, but the measles; if you will agree to this, I shall shift much responsibility from my own shoulders.

[*Letters to Merrill, 1803*]

This law-reading, Thomas, has no tendency to add the embellishments of literature to a student's acquisitions. Our books are written in a hard, didactic style, interspersed on every page with the mangled pieces of murdered Latin, and as perfectly barren of all elegance as a girl's cheek is of beard; you see I can't keep entirely off the girl's cheeks. The morality of the profession is, too, a matter of doubt, or rather it is a matter of no doubt at all. Mr. Bennett says that a lawyer, who preserves his integrity unspotted, deserves a place in the calendar of saints. If this calendar were entirely made up of lawyers, I fancy it would be a short, a very short list.

Accuracy and diligence are much more necessary to a lawyer, than great comprehension of mind, or brilliancy of talent. His business is to refine, define, and split hairs, to look into authorities, and compare cases. A man can never gallop over the fields of law on Pegasus, nor fly across them on the wing of oratory. If he would stand on *terra firma* he must descend; if he would be a great lawyer, he must first consent to be only a great drudge.

John Porter, in his official capacity, has notified me of the wishes of the P. B.* to write them a poem. If six of the nine Muses were to stand at my elbow and promise that, according to their best skill and discretion, they would inspire every line, word, and syllable, semi-colon, and comma, I should not choose to undertake to write a poem. I left making rhymes when I left college; and as to poetry, I do not know that I ever made any.

I do wrong to tell you that I have made no rhymes since I was graduated. Two great occasions have called forth each a wondrous piece of verse; one, I shall some time show you, to make you laugh; the other, I have put down to make you cry; for, if an author may judge his own works, it is by far the most sublime and pathetic I ever wrote. But I must disclose the occasion of such a daring effort. On the afternoon preceding the evening of a ball, a lady of my acquaintance trod upon some sharp tool and cut her foot. On this, my Muse, who had slept some years, broke out, "like an Irish rebellion," when nobody expected it, and produced the following, which in point of sentiment and language, I know you will think equal to any thing in Homer!! Here it is, read it.

> Rust seize the axe, the hoe, or spade,
> Which in your foot this gash has made!
> Which cut thro' kid and silk and skin,
> To spill the blood that was within;
> By which you're forced to creep and crawl,
> Nor frisk and frolic at the ball!
>
> But Clara, Clara! were thy heart
> As tender as thy pedal part;

* The Phi Beta Kappa Society.

SPEAK FOR YOURSELF, DANIEL

From thy sweet lips did love but flow,
Swift as blood gushes from thy toe,
So many beaus would not complain
That all their bows and vows are vain!

There, Merrill, is not this Homerican? Adieu!

[*Letters to Bingham, Dec. 23, 1803 and April 3, 1804*]

Frequent letters are not, perhaps, absolutely essential to friendship; but they are the best and most natural consequence of it. You and I should certainly be always friends, if we never wrote another syllable to each other; but we should be friends to little purpose, if we never mutually contributed any thing to soften care and cheer the heart. Your letters have become a settled portion of my happiness; the force of habit is added to the force of esteem, and if you should intermit writing for a long time, there would be a kind of vacuum in my pleasures that I could not handily fill with any thing else.

I have had a letter from Fuller, and one from Freeborn. The former can't help saying a little about the girls, and after praising them very judiciously, concludes by saying he sees them very seldom. You and I make no such pretensions to philosophy. If I could be more among good girls than I can, I should certainly avail myself of the opportunity. I consider such company the school of refinement, and quite necessary to prevent those roughnesses of temper and manners that a clouted student and a man absorbed in business are certain to contract. It is not he who spends most hours over his books that is the most successful student. It is impossible to keep the mind on the stretch forever; it will sometimes relax; and though we may keep our eyes on our books, it will steal away to easier contemplations, and we may run over pages without receiving an idea. I know this is the case with myself, and believe it is with others. The true science of life is to mingle amusement and business, so as to make the most of time. "Every man," says Johnson, "must some-times trifle; and the only question is, whether he shall do it alone or in company."

I am now going, James, to give you a full survey of the "whole ground," as it respects my prospects, hopes, and wishes. The great object of a lawyer is business; but this is not, or ought not to be, his sole object. Pleasant society, an agreeable acquaintance, and a de-gree of respectability, not merely as a lawyer, but as a man, are other objects of importance. You and I commenced the study, you know, with a resolution which we did not say much about, of being honest and conscientious practitioners. Some part of this resolution is, I hope, still hanging about me, and for this reason I choose to settle in a place where the practice of the bar is fair and honorable. The Cheshire bar, as far as I have learned, is entitled to a preference in these respects over that of any county in the State. You know my partiality for Connecticut River folks generally. Their information and habits are far better, in my opinion, than those of the people in the eastern part of the State. These reasons compel me to say with you, "it is a goodly land," and to make it my wish to settle therein.

E contrà. Many of my friends are desirous that I should make an attempt to live in Portsmouth. Mr. Thompson, my good master, knows every thing about the comparative advantages of different places, everywhere in New Hampshire, except Cheshire county. He has frequently suggested to me that Portsmouth would be a good place for a young man, and the other evening when I hinted my inclination for Cheshire, he said he had a high esteem for the people that way, but added that he still wished me to consider Portsmouth. He says there are many gentlemen of character there, who would patronize a young lawyer, and thinks that even Mr. Attorney-Gen-eral would be fond of the thing.

Mr. T. will have business, on which I shall be at Portsmouth as soon as the roads are passable, and out of respect to his opinion, I shall make no certain arrangements for my future reading till that time. At present, I do not feel that Portsmouth is the place for me.

SPEAK FOR YOURSELF, DANIEL

[Autobiography]

I do not know whether I read much, during this year and a half, beside law books, with two exceptions. I read Hume, though not for the first time; but my principal occupation with books, when not law books, was with the Latin Classics. I brought from college a very scanty inheritance of Latin. I now tried to add to it. I made myself familiar with most of Tully's orations, committed to memory large passages of some of them, read Sallust, and Cæsar and Horace. Some of Horace's odes I translated into poor English rhymes; they were printed; I have never seen them since. My brother was a far better Latin scholar than myself, and in one of his vacations we read Juvenal together. But I never mastered his style so as to read him with ease and pleasure.

At this period of my life I passed a great deal of time alone. My amusements were fishing, and shooting, and riding; and all these were without a companion. I loved this occasional solitude then, and have loved it ever since, and love it still. I like to comtemplate nature, and to hold communion, unbroken by the presence of human beings, with "this universal frame, thus wondrous fair"; I like solitude also as favorable to thoughts less lofty. I like to let the thoughts go free, and indulge in their excursions. And when *thinking* is to be done, one must of course be alone. No man knows *himself* who does not thus, sometimes, keep his own company. At a subsequent period of life, I have found that my lonely journeys, when following the court on its circuits, have afforded many an edifying day.

It would not have been possible for us to have got along, had it not been for the small income derived from my father's official situation. As soon as the war of the Revolution was over, and the pursuits of peace returned, he was elected into such public offices as it might be supposed he was qualified to fill. His qualities were integrity, firmness, decision, and extraordinary good sense. His defect, the want of early education. He never saw the inside of a schoolhouse, in the character of a learner; and yet the first records, or some among the first, of the town of Salisbury, are in his handwriting. What he knew, he had taught himself. His character was generous and manly, and his manner such as gave him influence with those around him. Early and deeply religious, he had still a good deal of natural gayety; he delighted to have some one about him that possessed a humorous vein.

A character of this sort, one Robert Wise, with whose adventures, as I learned them from himself, I could fill a small book, was a near neighbor, and a sort of humble companion for a great many years. He was a Yorkshire man; had been a sailor; was with Byng in the Mediterranean; had been a soldier; deserted from the garrison of Gibraltar; travelled through Spain, and France, and Holland; was taken up afterwards, severely punished, and sent back to the army; was in the battle of Minden; had a thousand stories of the yellow-haired Prince Ferdinand; was sent to Ireland, and thence to Boston, with the troops brought out by Gen. Gage; fought at Bunker Hill, deserted to our ranks, served with the New Hampshire troops in all the succeeding campaigns, and at the peace, built a little cottage in the corner of our field, on the river's bank, and there lived to an advanced old age.

He was my *Izaak Walton*. He had a wife, but no child. He loved me, because I would read the newspapers to him, containing the accounts of battles in the European wars. He had twice deserted from the English king, and once, at least, committed treason, as well as desertion, but he had still a British heart. When I have read to him the details of the victories of Howe, and Jervis, &c., I remember he was excited almost to convulsions, and would relieve his excitement by a gush of exulting tears. He finally picked up a fatherless child, took him home, sent him to school, and took care of him, only, as he said, that he might have some one to read the newspaper to him. He could never read himself. Alas, poor Robert! I have never so attained the narrative art as to hold the attention of others, as thou, with thy Yorkshire tongue, hast held mine. Thou hast carried me many a mile on thy back, paddled me over, and over, and up and down the stream, and given whole days, in aid of my boyish sports, and asked no meed, but that, at night, I would sit down at thy cottage door, and read to thee some passage of thy country's glory! Thou wast, indeed, a true Briton.

My father was of such consideration among his neighbors, that he was usually in such public employment as they had to bestow. He was a member of the Legislature, and a Senator; and about the year 1791, I think, appointed a judge of the Court of Common Pleas for the county. This place afforded three or four hundred dollars a year, a sum of the greatest importance to the family. He lived just long enough to witness my first appearance, and hear my first speech in court.

In the winter of 1804, it had become necessary for either my brother or myself to undertake something that should bring us a little money, for we were getting to be "heinously unprovided." [*This was not exactly novel. For example:*]

[*Letter to Ezekiel, Nov. 4, 1802*]

Now, Zeke, you will not read half a sentence, no, not one syllable, before you have thoroughly searched this sheet for scrip; but, my word for it, you will find no scrip here. We held a sanhedrin this morning on the subject of cash, could not hit upon any way to get you any; just before we went away to hang ourselves through disappointment, it came into our heads that next week might do. The truth is, father had an execution against Hubbard, of N. Chester, for about one hundred dollars; the money was collecting and just ready to drop into the hands of the creditors, when Hubbard suddenly died. This, you see, stays the execution till the long process of administering is completed.

I have now by me two cents in lawful federal currency; next week I will send them, if they be all; they will buy a pipe; with a pipe you can smoke; smoking inspires wisdom; wisdom is allied to fortitude; from fortitude it is but one step to stoicism; and stoicism never pants for this world's goods; so perhaps my two cents, by this process, may put you quite at ease about cash. Write me this minute, if you can; tell me all your necessities; no, not all, a part only, and any thing else you can think of to amuse me.

[*Letter from Ezekiel, Nov. 6, 1802*]

Money, Daniel, money. As I was walking down to the office after a letter, I happened to find one cent, which is the only money I have had since the second day after I came on. It is a fact, Dan, that I was called on for a dollar, where I owed it, and borrowed it, and have borrowed it four times since, to pay those I borrowed of.

[*Autobiography*]

To find some situation for one or the other of us, I set off in February, and found my way to Boston. My journey was fortunate. Dr. Perkins had been in the instruction of a school, in Short* street: he was about leaving it, and proposed that my brother should take it. I hastened home, and he had just then finished a short engagement in school-keeping, at Sanbornton, or was about finishing it, it being near the end of the winter vacation; and he readily seized the opportunity of employment in Boston. This broke in upon his college life, but he thought he could keep up with his class. A letter, stating the necessity of the case, was sent to the authorities of the college, and he went immediately to Boston. His success was good, nay great; so great, that he thought he could earn enough to defray, in addition to debts and other charges, the expense of my living in Boston, for what remained of my term of study.

Accordingly, I went to Boston, in July, 1804, to pass a few months in some office. I had not a single letter, and knew nobody, in the

* Now Kingston Street.

place to which I was going, except Dr. Perkins, then a very young man, and like myself struggling to get on. But I was sanguine, and light-hearted. He easily persuades himself that he shall gain, who has nothing to lose, and is not afraid of attempting to climb, when, if he fail in his first step, he is in no danger of a fall. Arrived in Boston, I looked out for an office, wherein to study. But then, as I knew none of the legal gentlemen, and had no letter, this was an affair of some difficulty. Some attempts to be received into a lawyer's office failed, properly enough, for these reasons; although the reminiscence has since sometimes caused me to smile.

Mr. Gore had just then returned from England, and renewed the practice of the law. He had rooms in Scollay's building, and as yet had no clerk. A young man, as little known to Mr. Gore as myself, undertook to introduce me to him! In logic, this would have been bad. *Ignotum per ignotum.* Nevertheless it succeeded here. We ventured into Mr. Gore's rooms, and my name was pronounced. I was shockingly embarrassed, but Mr. Gore's habitual courtesy of manner gave me courage to speak. I had the grace to begin with an unaffected apology; told him my position was very awkward, my appearance there very like an intrusion, and that, if I expected any thing but a civil dismission, it was only founded in his known kindness and generosity of character. I was from the country, I said; had studied law for two years, had come to Boston to study a year more; had some respectable acquaintances in New Hampshire, not unknown to him, but had no introduction; that I had heard he had no clerk, thought it possible he would receive one; that I came to Boston to work and not to play; was most desirous, on all accounts, to be his pupil; and all I ventured to ask, at present, was, that he would keep a place for me in his office, till I could write to New Hampshire for proper letters, showing me worthy of it. I delivered this speech *trippingly* on the tongue, though I suspect it was better composed, than spoken.

Mr. Gore heard me with much encouraging good-nature. He evidently saw my embarrassment, spoke kind words, and asked me to sit down. My friend had already disappeared! Mr. Gore said, what I had suggested was very reasonable, and required little apology; he did not mean to fill his office with clerks, but was willing to receive one or two, and would consider what I had said. He inquired, and I told him, what gentlemen of his acquaintance knew me and my father, in New Hampshire. Among others, I remember, I mentioned Mr. Peabody, who was Mr. Gore's classmate. He talked to me pleasantly, for a quarter of an hour; and when I rose to depart, he said: "My young friend, you look as though you might be trusted. You say you came to study, and not to waste time. I will take you at your word. You may as well hang up your hat, at once; go into the other room; take your book and sit down to reading it, and write at your convenience to New Hampshire for your letters."

[*Letter to Merrill, Nov. 30, 1804*]

Now hear me talk a little about myself. I am in the office of Christopher Gore, Esq., who has lately returned from London, where he has resided for eight years, as an American commissioner, to settle commercial claims between the two nations. He is a lawyer of eminence, and a deep and various scholar. Since I left John Wheelock, I have found no man so indefatigable in research. He has great amenity of manners, is easy, accessible, and communicative, and, take him all in all, I could not wish a better preceptor. My acquaintance here does not extend very far. It were much easier for me to form connections than to support them. There are many young men of my own age with whom it would be easy to associate; but a young man who has a fortune to spend, is not a proper companion for another who has a fortune to make. There are, however, some families into which I have free ingress here. I resort sometimes to play backgammon with the girls, in order to keep off the glooms.

As far as my circumstances will admit, 'tis my endeavor to become acquainted with the aboriginal Bostonians. It is not the locality of the town, it is not a sight of Beacon Hill, or the Long Wharf, that renders Boston useful as a place of residence for a stranger; but the conversation, the acquaintance, the connection, the intimacy which one has with the Boston folks. An English lord, when he travels to view the continent, carries with him English companions, English servants, and English books. He will stop nowhere but at an English inn, and converse with nobody but his countrymen. How superlatively ridiculous this is! What use is there in going to France, if he must carry England with him? Now this is quite too much the case with young gentlemen who come here from the country to read professions. They associate together; they almost invariably fall into the same boarding-houses; and of the manners of Boston folks they catch none hardly of the spirit; of their habits they learn few beside the bad ones.

[Letter to Bingham, Jan. 2, 1805]

A letter from you always gives me two happy half hours, one when it is received, and another when it is answered. Figure to yourself, then, a large room in the third story of a brick building, in the centre of Boston, a sea-coal fire, and a most enormous writing-table with half a cord of books on it. Then figure further to yourself your most obedient, with his back to the fire, and his face to the table, writing by candlelight, and you will precisely see a "happy fellow." There, now, is a famous dash at description! Now let me try my talents at narration. Well, then, on the fifth day of November, being election day, at just twenty-seven minutes and a half past twelve, I left Mrs. Whitwell's, Court street, Boston, and on the twenty-eighth day of the same month, at one o'clock, P. M., arrived at the same Mrs. Whitwell's, in the same Court street. You can easily determine, from the above account, where I went!! If, however, you should be puzzled, I will tell you; to Albany. Yes, James, I have even been to Albany. I cannot now tell you why, nor for what, but it was in a hackney coach, with a pair of nimble trotters, a smart coachman before, and a footman on horseback behind. There's style for you! More than all this, I had my friend at my elbow. Now why the deuce must I ruin this account by informing you that it was a male friend? Yet this regard to truth must be kept up, though it is a shackling thing. Well, to proceed: my expenses were all amply paid, and on my return, I put my hand in my pocket, and found one hundred and twenty dear delightfuls! Is not that good luck? And these delightfuls were, 'pon honor, all my own; yes, every dog of 'em. Now don't you think I would jump to go to Albany again? But to be serious. I really went to Albany, in November, with a gentleman of this town, for which I received the above reward; and I'm so proud to have a dollar of my own, I was determined to tell you of it. Of my journey and all that I saw and heard, I cannot give you a particular account now.

[*Letters to Habijah Weld Fuller, Mar. 10, 1805 and Oct. 17, 1804*]

The discussion you had with the "five ladies in Boston," on the question whether Mr. W. was a "plain man," must have been, I think, very edifying. If, however, you will admit the reasoning of Granger, the Parisian, I can easily prove that I am the handsomest man in New England. This is the process: Boston is the handsomest town in New England; Tremont is the handsomest street in Boston; Scollay's are the handsomest buildings in Tremont street; Christopher Gore's office is the handsomest room in Scollay's buildings; and I am (now) the handsomest man in Christopher Gore's office, *ergo*, I am the handsomest man in New England; Q. E. D.

Day before yesterday I had a letter from brother Davis; all finely at Hanover; pumpkin pie and professors plenty; wheat and poetry a good deal blasted; girls and gingerbread as sweet as ever. Last Sunday evening, to-day is Wednesday, I had the pleasure of a moment's chat with ——— ———. I was obliged to tell all I knew, how could a body help it? One cannot get rid of a lady's question by evasion; she will immediately assail in another shape; she will know the truth and the whole truth. Even if I had the honor of being interrogated by a female with respect to any affair of my own, I should recite the facts and answer her questions in as simple and plain a style as John Bunyan's; for I hold it an established point, that when a woman has a right to know a thing, you cannot content her with any thing short of the whole matter.

Once or twice I have had the honor of bowing to Miss Paine in the streets. Possibly, it may be well that I am not in a way to cultivate the acquaintance to which you introduced me. She might perhaps write her name upon my heart as fairly as I can write it upon paper. Yet that would not be a singular case, for there has been many a lover before me, who has had Pain in his heart.

[*Autobiography*]

In January preceding my admission, I was the subject of a great honor. The clerk of the Court of Common Pleas for the county of Hillsborough resigned his place. My father was one of the judges of the court, and I was appointed to the vacant clerkship. This was equal to a Presidential election. The office had an income of fifteen hundred dollars a year. It seemed to me very great, and indeed it was so, *rebus consideratis*. The obtaining of this office had been a darling object with my father. Its possession would make the family easy, and he hastened to send me tidings that the prize was won. I certainly considered it a great prize, myself, and was ready to abandon my profession for it; not that I did not love my profession; and not that I did not hate the clerkship, and all clerkships; but simply from a desire to reach that high point of terrestrial bliss, at which I might feel that there was a *competency* for our family, myself included.

I had felt the *res angusta* till my very bones ached. But Mr. Gore peremptorily shut me out from this opening paradise. When I went to him, with my letter in my hand, to communicate the good news, he said it was civil in their Honors of the Bench, and that I must write them a respectful letter; that they intended it as a mark of confidence in me, and of respect, probably, for my father, and that I was bound to make civil acknowledgments. This was a shower bath of ice water. I was thinking of nothing but of rushing to the immediate enjoyment of the proffered office; but he was talking of civil acknowledgment and decorous declension.

Finding my spirits, and face too, I suppose, falling, he found out the cause, and went on to speak, in a serious tone, against the policy and propriety of taking such an office. To be sure, his reasons were good, but I was slow to be convinced. He said, I was nearly through my professional preparation, that I should soon be at the bar, and he saw not why I might not hope to make my way as well as others; that this office was in the first place precarious, it depended on the will of others; and other times and other men might soon arise, and my office be given to somebody else. And in the second place, if permanent, it was a stationary place; that a clerk once, I was probably nothing better than a clerk, ever; and, in short, that he had taken me for one who was not to sit with his pen behind his ear. "Go on," said he, "and finish your studies; you are poor enough, but there are greater evils than poverty; live on no man's favor; what bread you do eat, let it be the bread of independence; pursue your profession, make yourself useful to your friends, and a little formidable to your enemies, and you have nothing to fear."

I need hardly say that I acquiesced in this good advice; though certainly it cost me a pang. Here was present comfort, competency, and I may even say riches, as I then viewed things, all ready to be enjoyed, and I was called upon to reject them for the uncertain and distant prospect of professional success. But I did resist the temptation; I did hold on to the hope which the law set before me.

One very difficult task remained, however, to be performed; and that was to reconcile my father to my decision. I knew it would strike him like a thunderbolt. He had long had this office in view for me; its income would make him, and make us all, easy and comfortable; his health was bad, and growing worse. His sons were all gone from him. This office would bring me home, and it would bring also comfort and competency "to all the house." It was now mid-winter; I looked round for a country sleigh (stage-coaches, then, no more ran into the centre of New Hampshire than they ran to Baffin's Bay,) and finding one that had come down to the market, I took passage therein, and in two or three days, was set down at my father's door. I was afraid my own resolution would give way, and that after all I should sit down to the clerk's table. But I fortified myself, as well as I could; I put on, I remember, an air of confidence, success, and gayety. It was evening. My father was sitting before his fire, and received me with manifest joy. He looked feebler than I had ever seen him, but his countenance lighted up on seeing his clerk stand before him, in good health, and better spirits.

He immediately proceeded to the great appointment, said how spontaneously it had been made, how kindly the Chief Justice proposed it, with what unanimity all assented, &c., &c., &c. I felt as if I could die, or fly; I could hardly breathe. Nevertheless, I carried it through, as we say, according to my plan. Spoke gayly about it; was much obliged to their Honors; meant to write them a respectful letter. If I could consent to record anybody's judgments, should be proud to record their Honors, &c., &c., &c. I proceeded in this strain, till he exhibited signs of amazement; it having occurred to him at length, that I might be serious in an intention to decline the office, a thing which had never entered into his imagination. "Do you intend to decline this office?" said he, at length. "Most certainly," said I. "I cannot think of doing otherwise; I should be very sorry, if I could not do better at present than to be clerk, for fifteen hundred dollars a year, not to speak of future prospects! I mean to use my tongue in the courts, not my pen; to be an actor, not a register of other men's actions. I hope yet, sir, to astonish your Honor, in your own court, by my professional attainments!"

PREPARATION FOR THE LAW

For a moment, I thought he was angry. He rocked his chair, slightly; a flush went over an eye, softened by age, but still as black as jet; but it was gone, and I thought I saw that parental partiality was after all a little gratified at this apparent devotion to an honorable profession, and this seeming confidence of success in it. "Well, my son, your mother has always said you would come to something or nothing, she was not sure which; I think you are now about settling that doubt for her." This he said, and never a word spoke more to me on the subject. I stayed at home a week, promised to come to him again as soon as I was admitted, and returned to Boston.

In March, 1805, I was admitted to practice in the Suffolk Court of Common Pleas. The practice then was for the patron to go into court, introduce the pupil to the judges, make a short speech, commending his diligence, &c., and move for his admission to the bar. I had the honor to be so introduced by Mr. Gore. I remember every word of his speech. It contained a prediction, which I firmly resolved, *quantum in me fuerit,* should not go entirely unfulfilled.

My design was to settle in practice at Portsmouth; but I determined not to leave my father, during his life. Accordingly, I took a room in the little village of Boscawen [adjoining Salisbury], and there commenced the practice of the law. My father lived but another year. He died in April, 1806, and lies in the burial-ground, in his own field, just at the turn of the road, beneath the shadow of a tall pine. Beside him repose my mother, my three own sisters, and Joseph, my youngest half brother.

III

1805–1817

EARLY PRACTICE

[*Letters to Bingham: May 4, 1805*]

YOU MUST KNOW that I have opened a shop in this village [Boscawen] for the manufacture of justice writs. Other mechanics do pretty well here, and I am determined to try my luck among others. March 25, I left Boston, with a good deal of regret, I assure you. I was then bound for Portsmouth, but I found my father extremely ill and little fit to be left by all his sons, and therefore partly through duty, partly through necessity, and partly through choice, I concluded to make my stand here.

[*Jan. 19, 1806*]

My business has been just about so, so; its quantity less objectionable than its quality. I shall be able at the end of the year to pay my bills, and pay perhaps sixty pounds for my books. I practise in Hillsborough, Rockingham, and Grafton. Scattering business over so much surface is like spilling water on the ground. In point of profit I should do better, much better, if it were convenient to attend the courts in one county only.

I make no poetry; five lines to D. Abbott are the Alpha and the Omega of my poetical labors for a year. In this particular, however, I mean to reform. How would it do, think ye, to write writs in verse? For instance, let one be *clausum in his verbis,* that is to say, being interpreted, wrapt up in these words: —

EARLY PRACTICE

All good sheriffs in the land,
　　We command,
That forthwith you arrest John Dyer,
　　Esquire,
If in your precinct you can find him,
And bind him, &c., &c., &c.

If the legislature will but put our writs into a poetical and musical form, it will certainly be the most harmonious thing they ever did, and you and I shall like them vastly better than we do now.

Study is truly the grand requisite for a lawyer. Men may be born poets, and leap from their cradle painters; nature may have made them musicians, and called on them only to exercise, and not to acquire, ability. But law is artificial. It is a human science to be learnt, not inspired. Let there be a genius for whom nature has done so much as apparently to have left nothing for application, yet to make a lawyer, application must do as much as if nature had done nothing. The evil is, that an accursed thirst for money violates everything. We cannot study, because we must pettifog. We learn the low recourses of attorneyism, when we should learn the conceptions, the reasonings, and the opinions of Cicero and Murray. The love of fame is extinguished; every ardent wish for knowledge repressed; conscience put in jeopardy, and the best feelings of the heart indurated, by the mean, money-catching, abominable practices, which cover with disgrace a part of the modern practitioners of the law. The love of money is the ruling passion of this country. It has taken root deeply, and I fear will never be eradicated. While this holds everything in its gripe, America will produce few great characters. We have no patronage for genius; no reward for merit. The liberal professions are resorted to, not to acquire reputation and consequence, but to get rich. Money is the chief good; every eye is on it; every heart sighs for it. When the day will come when these things shall be ordered better, you and I cannot tell, but will hope that it will come some time.

39

SPEAK FOR YOURSELF, DANIEL

[Letter to Jacob McGaw, Jan. 12, 1807]

You call yourself such hard names in your letter that I begin to think they are well applied. I was entirely unsuspicious before, but I know nothing against your credit as a witness, and if you affirm that you are a "lazy scoundrel," the point must be considered as proved. But I forgive you, fully, freely, frankly. A man that hath both a fame to regard, a purse to regard, and a wife to regard, must be excused from any particular attention to his friends. A wife, I take it, reverently be it spoken, is like a burning-glass, which concentrates every ray of affection that emanates from a husband's heart. We single dogs have attachments which are dispersed over society, our friendships are scattered all over the world, and we love at a thousand places at the same moment; but you husbands carry all your wares to the same market. You have one bank, in which you deposit all your tender sentiments, wherefore I hold you all pardonable for forgetting your friends.

Will you be pleased to ascertain how much of my love it is lawful for me to send to your wife, and when you have settled the quantity to a scruple, I pray you give it to Phebe, with the lowest bow you can make.

[Letters to Bingham, from Portsmouth, N. H.: Feb. 27, 1808]

Since I have seen you and written you, I have changed my residence from Boscawen to this place. Some brief narration of my life since June, 1806, seems necessary to bring up the view of the present, so that we may go on in the old way of correspondence; for if I ever neglect writing you so long a time again, I shall have lost my senses.

My business at Boscawen was tolerable, but not altogether to my mind. A little money might be made there, but no pleasure of a social sort enjoyed. My brother Ezekiel was admitted to the bar in September last, and to him I made an offer of my office. The truth is, our family affairs at Salisbury rendered it necessary for one of us to reside in that neighborhood, and not being very willing to take charge of the farm, I concluded to indorse over to my brother both farm and office, if he would take both together. Being thus left to seek a new place of abode, I came to this town, a measure which I had in some degree contemplated for a length of time. I found myself here the latter part of September. I knew few people here, and Mr. Adams was the only person who advised to the measure.

Hitherto, I have done as much business as I ought to expect. There are eight or nine of us who fill writs, in town. Of course my share cannot be large, even if I should take my equal dividend. On the whole, however, I am satisfied that I did right to come, and suppose I shall meet as much success as I deserve. I have a pleasant room, in a good situation; have made some additions to my library, which is, nevertheless, yet very small; have some pleasant acquaintances in town, and time rolls along pretty agreeably; *"jam satis est."* I will expatiate no further on that endearing subject, self.

[*May 5, 1808*]

N. B. I forgot to tell you, that in June next, I contemplate to set my bachelor friends a laudable example.

On May 29, 1808, Webster married Grace Fletcher, youngest daughter of the Rev. Elijah Fletcher of Hopkinton, N. H. A friend of the Websters, Mrs. E. Buckminster Lee, said of her: "Uniting with great sweetness of disposition, unaffected, frank and winning manners, no one could approach her without wishing to know her, and no one could know her well without loving her."

They had five children: Grace, born April 29, 1810; Daniel Fletcher, July 23, 1813; Julia, January 16, 1818; Edward, July 20, 1820; and Charles, December 31, 1822. Only Daniel Fletcher, whom they called "Fletcher," survived his father.

SPEAK FOR YOURSELF, DANIEL

[*Autobiography*]

I lived in Portsmouth nine years, wanting one month. They were very happy years. Circumstances favored me, at my first beginning there. Owing to several occurrences, there happened to be an unfilled place among leading counsel at that bar. I did not fill it; but I succeeded to it.

For the nine years I lived in Portsmouth, Mr. Mason and myself, in the counties where we both practised, were on opposite sides, pretty much as a matter of course. He has been of infinite advantage to me, not only by his unvarying friendship, but by the many good lessons he has taught and the example he set me in the commencement of my career. If there be in the country a stronger intellect, if there be a mind of more native resources, if there be a vision that sees quicker or sees deeper into whatever is intricate or whatsoever is profound, I must confess I have not known it.

Before I went to Portsmouth my style was florid, and I was apt to make longer sentences and to use longer words than were needful. I soon began, however, to notice that Mr. Mason was a cause-getting man. He had a habit of standing quite near to the jury, so near that he might have laid his finger on the foreman's nose, and then he talked to them in a plain conversational way, in short sentences, and using no word that was not level to the comprehension of the least educated man on the panel. This led me to examine my own style, and I set about reforming it altogether.

My professional practice, while living in Portsmouth, was very much a circuit practice. I followed the superior court, in most of the counties of the State. It was never lucrative. There was a limit, and that a narrow one, beyond which gains could not be made from it. I do not think it was ever worth fairly two thousand dollars a year.

Business, too, fell off much, by the war; and, soon after that event, I determined on a change of residence.

I have never held office, popular or other, in the government of New Hampshire. My time was always exclusively given to my profession till 1812, when the war commenced. I had occasionally taken part in political questions, always felt an interest in elections, and contributed my part, I believe, to the political ephemera of the day. Indeed, I always felt an interest in political concerns.

Like other young men, I made Fourth of July orations; at Frye-burg, 1802; at Salisbury, 1805; at Concord, 1806, which was published; and at Portsmouth, 1812, published also.

In August 1812, Webster wrote the "Rockingham Memorial," addressed to the President of the United States on behalf of the inhabitants of the County of Rockingham who met together on August 12, 1812, to voice their protest against the actions and policies of the Administration. It said in part:

We have witnessed, with sincere and deep regret, a system of policy pursued by the General Government, from the Embargo of 1807, to the present time, tending most obviously, in our view, to the destruction of the commerce of these states.

When we assented to the National Constitution, it was among other, (but none more important) reasons, to the end that our commerce might be better protected, and the farther extended. Taught to regard our right of traversing the seas, as sacred (and it is to us as important), as our right of tilling the ground, we have supposed that we should never be deprived of the former, but for reasons, so weighty and important, as would equally justify the prohibition of the latter. We originally saw nothing, and can now see nothing, either in the letter, or the spirit, of the national compact, which makes it our duty, to acquiesce in a system, tending to compel us to abandon our natural and accustomed pursuits. We regard the Constitution as "an instrument of preservation, not of change." We take its intention to have been, to protect, by the strong arm of the whole nation, the interests of each particular section. It could not therefore be without alarm and apprehension, that we perceived in the General Government a disposition to embarrass and enthrall commerce by repeated restrictions, and to make war, by shutting up our own ports.

The alarm excited in our minds by the favorite and long continued "Restrictive System," is raised still higher, by the late declaration of war against Great Britain, an event which we believe, in the present defenceless circumstances of the country, will be productive of evils of incalculable magnitude.

The impressment of our seamen, which forms the most plausible and popular of the alleged causes of war, we believe to have been the subject of great misrepresentation. The number of these cases has been extravagantly exaggerated. Every inquiry on the subject strengthens our conviction, that the reputed number bears little relation to the true number. We are among those, to whom instances of impressment, if they did actually exist to any considerable extent, must be known. Yet we cannot find them out. Some of the members of this meeting have been constantly employed in commercial pursuits, and have had ships on the ocean from the Peace of 1783, until the ocean became unnavigable, as to us, by the Embargo of 1807, and yet during all that time have never suffered the loss of one native American seaman, by impressment. Other members of this meeting have, as masters of vessels, long inhabited, as it were, on the seas, and have been visited hundreds of times by British ships of war, and never had an American seaman taken from them by impressment.

It is well known that England pretends to no right of impressing our seamen. She insists, only, that she has a right to the service of her own subjects, in time of war, even though found serving on board the merchant ships of other nations. This claim we suppose to be neither unfounded, nor novel. It is recognized by the public law of Europe, and of the civilized world. Writers of the highest authority maintain, that the right belongs to all nations. For the same reason, say they, that the father of a family may demand the aid of his children to defend himself and his house, a nation may call home her subjects to her defence and protection, in time of war.

On the subject of naval defence, we do not feel ourselves confined to the mere language of supplication. On that topic we do not address ourselves to the favor and clemency only, of any Administration. We hold it to be our right, to demand, at the hand of the General Government, adequate protection to our lawful commerce. When the Constitution empowered the Government to build and maintain a navy, it was not supposed, that that provision would remain inoperative parchment, and a dead letter. On the contrary, it was confidently expected that that power would be exercised, as cheerfully as the power to levy and collect taxes. We consider protection on the sea to be as solemnly guaranteed to us by the Constitution, as protection on the land.

We shrink from the separation of the states, as an event fraught with incalculable evils, and it is among our strongest objections to the present course of measures, that they have, in our opinion, a very dangerous and alarming bearing on such an event. If a separation of the states ever should take place, it will be, on some occasion, when one portion of the country undertakes to control, to regulate, and to sacrifice the interest of another; when a small and heated majority in the Government, taking counsel of their passions, and not of their reason, contemptuously disregarding the interests, and perhaps stopping the mouths, of a large and respectable minority, shall by hasty, rash, and ruinous measures, threaten to destroy essential rights; and lay waste the most important interests.

It only remains for us, to express our conscientious convictions, that the present course of measures will prove most prejudicial and ruinous to the country, and to supplicate the government to adopt such a system as shall restore to us the blessings of peace and of commerce.

SPEAK FOR YOURSELF, DANIEL

As a result of his Portsmouth Fourth of July speech in 1812 and his authorship of the Rockingham Memorial, Webster was elected in November as a Representative of New Hampshire in Congress, and took his seat at the Special Session in May 1813.

[Letters from Washington: To Ezekiel, May 24, 1813]

We got into this city, so called, Saturday Eve'. The House are getting together this morning. I have marked myself a seat; or rather found one marked for me, by some friend who arrived here before me. I am in good company.

[To Edward Cutts, Jr., May 26, 1813]

I went yesterday to make my bow to the President. I did not like his looks, any better than I like his Administration.

[To Charles March, May 31, 1813]

Every one is for taxing every body, except himself and his constituents.

[To Bingham, then a member of the New Hampshire Legislature, June 4, 1813]

In our political capacity, we, that is, the House of Representatives, have done little or nothing. The time for us to be put on the stage and moved by the wires, has not yet come. I suppose the "show" is now in preparation, and at the proper time the farce of legislating will be exhibited. I do not mean to say that the "projects" will not be opposed, as far as they may be, nor is it certain that all the Democrats will "hang together," on the great subject of taxes; but before any thing is attempted to be done here, it must be arranged elsewhere.

46

Thus far the weather has been comfortable, and so long as one keeps within doors, the heat is not oppressive. Much walking, however, is not practicable, especially as there are few trees in this city, to keep off the sun. We have the advantage of you, in a better room to sit in, in having less to do, and in the means of acquaintance with a greater variety of characters. You have over us the advantage of having a majority on your side, as I trust; the prospect of a short session; the hope of doing some good, and a little society, pleasantly mixed, instead of the unvarying masculinity of our circles here. A few ladies, indeed, are to be seen by going to the weekly rout at the palace; but they are there only as so many curiosities — *rare aves* — fit for all the purposes of social life, save only the unimportant particulars of speaking and being spoken to. I understand that in the winter session, when there are more ladies in the city, the aforesaid evil is in some degree mitigated.

I have been to the levee or drawing room, but once. It is a mere matter of form. You make your bow to Mrs. Madison, and to Mr. M., if he comes in your way, but he being there merely as a guest, is not officially entitled to your *congé*. Monsieur Serurier, Madame Bonaparte, the Russian Minister, heads of departments, and tails of departments, members of congress, &c., &c., here and there, interspersed with military and naval hat and coat, make up the group. You stay from five minutes to an hour, as you please; eat and drink what you can catch, without danger of surfeit, and if you can luckily find your hat and stick, then take French leave; and that's going to the "levee."

On June 10, 1813, Webster introduced resolutions calling upon President Madison for information allegedly withheld from Congress concerning decrees of the French Government affecting the War of 1812. After a short but spirited fight the resolutions passed, and he wrote about them on June 24 to his friend Charles March.

I went on Tuesday to the Palace to present the Resolutions. The Presidt was in his bed, sick of a fever. His night cap on his head —

his wife attending him, &c. &c. I think he will find no relief from my prescription.

The news is, that the British have recd a vast reinforcement in the Bay, and the lower Country is greatly alarmed. You will see there has been a battle between a frigate & some Gun Boats.

Webster spent the summer and fall of 1813 with his family, returning to Washington for the regular session of Congress in December. Shortly after he left Portsmouth a conflagration swept over part of the town, as described in his letter of December 29, 1813, to Ezekiel:

I arrived here last evening, and here learned of the Portsmouth fire and the consumption of my house. I have only time to say, that the safety of my family compensates the loss of the property. Mr. Mason urges me that Mrs. Webster may remain at his house till spring; I think this will be best, except perhaps a short visit, if the travelling should be good, into your quarter. I have not time to say more, but thought you would be glad to hear that I am in possession of myself after the knowledge of such a loss.

Years later the fire became a subject of table conversation, reported as follows in the journal of Josiah Quincy:

"On Friday, Feb. 17 (1826) I had dinner at Mr. Webster's. Webster carved the beef and was in a charming humor. He told some good lawyer's stories, and gave us a graphic account of the burning of his house in Portsmouth in the winter of 1813. 'Though I was in Washington at the time,' he said, 'I believe I know more about the fire than many who were actively at work on the spot. Besides, here is Mrs. Webster, who was burned out. She will correct me if I am wrong.' He told us that all he possessed in the world was lost, there being no insurance upon house or furniture; but as more than two hundred buildings were consumed in the fire, some of them belong-

ing to those less able to make a living than himself, he felt he had no right to murmur. He was, nevertheless, troubled about the loss of his library. His books were full of notes and associations, and could not be replaced.

" 'I think there was something in the house which Mr. Webster regretted more than his books,' said his wife, with an amused expression. 'There was a pipe of wine in the cellar, and I am sure Mr. Webster's philosophy has not yet reconciled him to its loss. You see we were young housekeepers in those days. It was the first pipe of wine we ever had, and getting it was a great event.'

" 'Let us be accurate, my dear,' said Mr. Webster, with one of those pleasant smiles of his which fairly lit up the room. 'Undoubtedly it was a pipe of wine when we bought it; but then it had been on tap for some time, and our table was not without guests. If I had you upon the witness stand, I think I should make you confess that your pipe of wine could scarcely have been more than half a pipe at the time of the fire.' "

In April 1814 Congress repealed the hated Embargo against which the Rockingham Memorial had inveighed. In rising to the occasion on April 6, 1814, Webster expressed sentiments which were to haunt him in his later support of tariff protection for Massachusetts manufacturers.

I am happy to be present at the office now to be performed, and to act a part in the funeral ceremonies of what has usually been called the restrictive system.

The occasion, I think, will justify a temperate and moderate exultation on the part of those who have constantly opposed this system of politics, and uniformly foretold its miserable end. I congratulate my friends on this triumph of their principles.

It is the true policy of government to suffer the different pursuits of society to take their own course, and not to give excessive bounties or encouragements to one over another. This, also, is the true spirit of the Constitution. It has not, in my opinion, conferred on the Government the power of changing the occupations of the people of different States and sections, and of forcing them into other employments. It cannot prohibit commerce any more than agriculture; nor manufactures any more than commerce. It owes protection to all. I rejoice that commerce is once more permitted to exist; that its remnant, as far as this unblessed war will allow, may yet again visit the seas, before it is quite forgotten that we have been a commercial people. I shall rejoice still further, when I see the Government pursue an independent, permanent, and steady system of national politics; when it shall rely for the maintenance of rights and the redress of wrongs on the strength and resources of our own country, and break off all measures which tend, in any degree, to connect us with the fortunes of a foreign Power.

On August 24–25, 1814, the British captured Washington and burned most of the public buildings. Webster was in Portsmouth at the time, and was reelected to Congress on August 29. In October he returned to Washington, from where the following letters were written.

[*To Ezekiel: Oct. 20, 1814*]

I left home on the 7th, & arrived here on the 14 — just in season to give an unavailing vote on the question of removal [of the seat of government from Washington]. It is probable we shall hear of that question again before the session closes.

We have as yet heard nothing of the British forces under Lord Hill. It is thought here that New Orleans is his object. If he should take that city, & he will if he tries, & hold it, the Western States in one year would make their peace with England. Of this I have no doubt, from what I see & hear. I rather expect myself, that Lord Hill will first come into the Chesapeake & make a new attempt on Baltimore.

[Oct. 30, 1814]

The terms offered by England, struck our folks differently at first from what they do on reflection. For my part, I expected no better; so feeble has the government shown itself, and so little able to carry on the war successfully.

[Nov. 29, 1814]

We are here on the Eve of great events — I expect a blow up soon. My opinion is, that within sixty days Govt. will cease to pay even Secretaries, Clerks & Members of Congress. This I expect & when it comes we are wound up.

Everything is in confusion here. The Bank bill finally lost — 104 to 49 — after a day of the most tumultuous proceedings I ever saw.

The conscription has not come up, if it does it will cause a storm such as was never witnessed here.

In short, if Peace does not come this winter, the Govt. will die in its own weakness.

[Dec. 22, 1814]

We are expecting every day to hear from New Orleans. It seems certain that the English have sent an expedition thither; on its result, perhaps, the question of peace may depend.

[To Moody Kent: Dec. 22, 1814]

I do not intend spending another winter in this Great Dismal.

Things look very bad here, & I confess I have no expectation of their growing better while this War lasts. The *People cannot* pay the Taxes proposed; especially in the South. The Govt. *cannot* execute a Conscription Law, if it should try. It cannot enlist soldiers. It cannot borrow money — what can it do?

The Govt. *cannot last,* under this war, & in the hands of these men another twelve month. Not that opposition will break it down, but it will break itself down. It will go out. This is my sober opinion.

[*Jan. 14, 1815*]

Nothing yet decisive of the fate of N. Orleans — considerable reinforcements were likely to arrive in season.

The decisive engagement in the Battle of New Orleans was fought on Jan. 8, 1815. Meanwhile, unknown to the participants or to the government in Washington, the war had been terminated by the Treaty of Peace signed at Ghent on Dec. 24, 1814.

It was at this time that dissident leaders of New England met in what has come to be known as the Hartford Convention, Dec. 15, 1814–Jan. 5, 1815. In response to repeated rumors and charges of his participation, Webster later wrote an undated letter as follows to his friend Hiram Ketchum:

The Hartford Convention was holden in the winter of 1814–1815. I was then a member of Congress. Congress assembled on the proclamation of Mr. Madison, in September, and I was in my seat early in the session. When I left New Hampshire, where I then lived, no proposal had been made by any State, so far as I remember, — and I believe I am quite correct, — to hold such, or any convention; nor had such a project been proposed or agitated by individuals so far as I know.

The government of the State of New Hampshire had no part in the convention. Two counties on the river sent delegates; but as a State, New Hampshire had no concern in it.

I remained here through the session, or until one of its last days, until the Hartford Convention was over, and until the news of peace arrived.

I lived at Portsmouth, a hundred miles from the counties of Cheshire and Grafton, which sent delegates.

You will see by this that I really had nothing at all to do with the convention. I had no participation in its counsels, corresponded with none of its members, but in all respects kept entirely aloof from it. Infinite pains have been taken, for the last ten years, to find something to connect me with this assemblage, but all in vain.

[*Letter to Ezekiel: Mar. 26, 1816*]

I have settled my purpose to remove from New Hampshire in the course of the summer. I have thought of Boston, New York, and Albany. On the whole I shall, probably, go to Boston; although I am not without some inducements to go into the State of New York. Our New England prosperity and importance are passing away. This is fact. The events of the times, the policy of England, the consequences of our war, and the Ghent Treaty, have bereft us of our commerce, the great source of our wealth. If any great scenes are to be acted in this country within the next twenty years, New York is the place in which those scenes are to be viewed. More of this hereafter.

During the consideration of a tariff bill in the early part of 1816 Webster refused to agree, as a matter of courtesy, to an amendment proposed by John Randolph of Roanoke to impose a tax on sugar, and that eccentric individual, as too often was his wont, challenged him to a duel. Webster's reply (undated) was as follows:

For having declined to comply with your demand yesterday in the House, for an explanation of words of a general nature, used in debate, you now "demand of me that satisfaction which your insulted feelings require," and refer me to your friend, Mr. ——, I presume, as he is the bearer of your note, for such arrangements as are usual.

This demand for explanation, you, in my judgment, as a matter of right, were not entitled to make on me; nor were the temper and style of your own reply to my objection to the sugar tax of a character to induce me to accord it as a matter of courtesy.

Neither can I, under the circumstances of the case, recognize in you a right to call me to the field to answer what you may please to consider an insult to your feelings.

It is unnecessary for me to state other and obvious considerations growing out of this case. It is enough that I do not feel myself bound at all times and under any circumstances, to accept from any man, who shall choose to risk his own life, an invitation of this sort; although I shall be always prepared to repel in a suitable manner the aggression of any man who may presume upon such a refusal.

[*Autobiography*]

I could carry my practice in New Hampshire no further; I could make no more of it, and its results were not competent to the support of my family. Having resolved on a change, I accomplished it at once. On the 16th of August, I left Portsmouth forever, and the same day arrived, with my wife and children, at Boston. My children were then Grace and Daniel Fletcher. We stayed two or three weeks at Mrs. Delano's, and then went to housekeeping, in a house of Mr. J. Mason's, on Mount Vernon street.

I think I never went into court in New Hampshire again, except when I went down the following September in the Dartmouth College cause.

When I moved to Boston, I had still one session to serve in Congress. Mr. Mason was a Senator at that time. We went to Washington in November with our families, and took lodgings together.

[*Letter to Mason, Oct. 29, 1816*]

Mrs. Webster thinks she cannot be ready for her departure till Monday the 11th & I should think that would be in tolerable season, as it wd give us three full weeks. My plan is to make some bargain for myself & wife to be conveyed to Hartford, independent of your carriage. It is a long & heavy road to Hartford, & I should not think it would be well to add anything to the burden of your new horses, at their first setting out, & over so hilly a road. I can easily take either a hack, or a gig, & in the last case send our baggage by stage. It will be three days to Hartford, by way of Worcester, & Stafford, & not much less on any road. One day from Hartford to New Haven, & two thence to New York. We shall then have a week to go to & stay in Philadelphia, & another to get to Washington. If we go from here the 7th or 8th (Thursday or Friday) as you propose, we shall find ourselves in Connecticut at a time of the week, when we could not travel if we would.

Our daughter is yet not well. She has a tumor on her neck which we thought the mumps, but it has remained too long for that. It has for some days appeared to be better, & we believe it is going off. We have made an arrangement to leave our children with Mrs. Webber, at Cambridge.

[Letter to Justice Joseph Story, Dec. 9, 1816]

For my part, my dear Sir, I am very glad to find myself so near the close of the short period of my public engagements. And tho' I would willingly fill up the little remnant with some effort for the general good I shall see the sun go down on the third of March with unusual cheerfulness.

[Letter to William Sullivan, Jan. 2, 1817]

I am glad to find you so well employed as in chasing whales, though they be dead whales. Having seen you last in your own chamber, I was glad to learn that you have got into court, and are fit to engage in such arduous enterprises as whaling.

Your account reminded me of some very ingenious and laughable remarks of Lord Erskine, in a *crim. con.* case, some twenty years ago. They are in one of the volumes of the Annual Register. Mr. Erskine was for the defendant; his defence was that the plaintiff had abandoned his wife, and put her to separate maintenance, and having thus voluntarily relinquished the comfort and society of his wife, he could not pretend that the defendant, by his interposition, had deprived him of these enjoyments. He then went on to say that the law of England in respect to wives, was just like the law of the Greenland fishery in respect to whales; whoever struck the whale, had a right to him, so long as he held on by the line; but the moment he let go his line, the animal, in the eye of the law, was *feræ naturæ,* and became the rightful property of the first taker. So, in the case of wives; while the husband holds on by his matrimonial string, however far the wife strays, to whatever great distances she may run out from the path of duty, or however crooked and eccentric her course, the law still regards her in *custodia viri,* and will allow no interference of third persons; but if the husband will choose to let this little cord drop out of his hand, in an instant all is over! The wife then runs "unclaimed of any man," and like the wounded whale, becomes the property of the next striker.

We are doing nothing now but to quarrel with one of our laws of the last session, called the horse law (not because horses made it, for it was made by asses).

I must add also, which you will be sorry to hear, that the illness of our little daughter at Cambridge, has very much alarmed us, and we are in expectation that Mrs. Webster will be compelled to return. If so, she will be accompanied by her brother, to whom I have written to come here for that purpose, unless I should make such disposition of my business at the court as to permit me to return with her, which I do not expect.

[*Letters to Ezekiel: Jan. 19, 1817*]

Grace's illness has brought me home. We arrived four days ago. She has been declining almost ever since we left her, the middle of

November, and was so low on our arrival, that we entertained very faint hopes of her recovery. Her case is consumption, and seems a good deal like dear little Mary's. Since our return, her symptoms have been a little more favorable, and might almost encourage a slight hope of ultimate recovery. Dr. Warren thinks, at least, that for a week she is no worse. She seems a little less languid, and has coughed less to-day than any day for a fortnight. My engagements in the court at Washington are such that, if possible, I must return. If Grace should grow no worse, I intend going about Thursday or Friday. We found little trouble in opening our house and collecting our family. Eliza Buckminster is coming to stay with us awhile. We came home very quickly from Philadelphia, in four days. Mrs. W. stood the journey wonderfully well and took no cold. I have not been out so much as to my office.

[Jan. 26, 1817]

Our dear little daughter has followed yours. She died on Thursday evening at eleven o'clock, and was interred yesterday. Her death, though I thought it inevitable, was rather sudden when it happened. Her disease, the consumption, had not apparently attained its last stages. She had suffered very little. The day of her death, she was pretty bright in the forenoon, though weak. In the afternoon she grew languid and drowsy. She, however, desired her friends to read and talk with her until a few minutes before eleven, when her countenance suddenly altered, and in five or six minutes she expired.

Mrs. Webster, though in great affliction, is in tolerable health. Our little boy is very well. To-morrow morning I set out on my return to Washington.

IV

1817–1819

THE DARTMOUTH COLLEGE CASE

In Mid-Eighteenth Century, Eleazar Wheelock, a Presbyterian minister, established a wilderness school for Indians, and in 1765 sent one of his pupils, Samson Occum, to England to raise funds. The Earl of Dartmouth and others contributed over eleven thousand pounds, and on December 13, 1769, a royal charter was granted creating Dartmouth College and entrusting its management to a self-perpetuating board of twelve trustees. The charter named Wheelock as President and gave him the right of appointing his successor by will. When he died in 1779, at age 68, he named his son, John Wheelock, in his stead.

About the turn of the century, the Trustees developed sectarian and personal differences. By 1815 the anti-Wheelock faction, with the backing of the Federalists and of orthodox Congregationalists, gained control, and Wheelock carried his woes to the New Hampshire Legislature. Meanwhile, he had asked Webster to represent him and had paid a twenty dollar retainer, but when Webster learned the nature of the controversy and that his own personal and political friends were on the other side, including his former mentor, Thomas W. Thompson, he did not appear at the legislative committee hearing. One of Wheelock's friends, Josiah Dunham, took Webster to task for this, and on August 25, 1815, he replied:

On the subject of the dispute between the President and the Trustees, I am as little informed as any reading individual in society; and I have not the least inclination to espouse either side,

58

except in proceedings in which my services may be professional. It was intimated to me last spring, that the President might possibly institute process against the trustees for the recovery of money due him from them; and that in case these events should happen, the President would be glad to engage my assistance as counsel. At Concord, the President suggested, in general terms, that he might wish to obtain my professional assistance on some future occasion, which I readily promised him.

I received the President's letter, desiring me to be at Hanover at a time which had then already elapsed. If I had received it earlier, I could not have attended, because the court engaged me at home; and I ought to add here, that if I had had no other engagements at the time, and had also been seasonably notified, I should have exercised my own discretion about undertaking to act a part before the committee at Hanover. I regard that as no professional call, and should consider myself as in some degree taking side personally and individually for one of the parties, by appearing as an advocate on such an occasion. This I should not desire to do, until I know more of the merits of the case.

I am not quite so fully convinced as you are, that the President is altogether right and the trustees altogether wrong. When I have your fulness of conviction, perhaps I may have some portion of your zeal. Whenever I have said any thing to either side, it has been to impress the necessity of moderation and candor, as they will do me the justice, I trust, to acknowledge.

In the March 1816 elections the Jefferson Republicans swept New Hampshire, gaining a majority of the Legislature as well as the governorship. They promptly adopted statutes reorganizing the College: changing its name to Dartmouth University, increasing the number of trustees from twelve to twenty-one, creating a Board of Overseers, and empowering the Governor and Council of the State to fill all vacancies. In effect the State took control of what previously had been a private educational institution.

The old trustees refused to accept these changes and instituted suit to recover the books and seal of the College from Judge William H. Woodward, its former secretary and treasurer, who had sided with Wheelock and had accepted office in the new regime. The students remained loyal to the old.

In its initial stages the Trustees' suit was handled by Jeremiah Smith, former Chief Justice of New Hampshire, and Jeremiah Mason. Webster joined them on the second argument of the case before the New Hampshire Superior Court of Appeals, and, after the adverse decision of that court, undertook the appeal to the United States Supreme Court in Washington.

Coming, as it did, from a State court, rather than from a lower Federal court, the appeal was limited to the Constitutional issue of whether the Acts of the New Hampshire Legislature impaired the obligation of a contract.

[*Letter to Mason, Sept. 4, 1817, after the first argument and before the second*]

Judge Smith has written to me, that I must take some part in the argument of this college question. I have not thought of the subject, nor made the least preparation; I am sure I can do no good, and must, therefore, beg that you and he will follow up in your own manner the blows which have already been so well struck. I am willing to be considered as belonging to the cause and to talk about it, and consult about it, but should do no good by undertaking an argument. If it is not too troublesome, please let Mr. Fales give me a naked list of the authorities cited by you, and I will look at them before court. I do this that I may be able to understand you and Judge Smith.

[*Letter to Mason, Nov. 27, 1817*]

President Brown has written to me respecting the college cause in its further progress. I have engaged to keep hold of it if I go to Washington this winter. I must also have somebody to help me at Washington. I can think of nobody better for such a question than Hopkinson.

[Letter to Jeremiah Smith, Dec. 8, 1817]

It is our misfortune that our cause goes to Washington on a single point. I wish we had it in such shape as to raise all the other objections, as well as the repugnancy of these acts to the constitution of the United States. I have been thinking whether it would not be advisable to bring a suit, if we can get such parties as will give jurisdiction in the circuit court of New Hampshire. I have thought of this the more, from hearing of sundry sayings of a great personage. Suppose the corporation of Dartmouth College should lease to some man of Vermont (e.g. C. Marsh) one of their New Hampshire farms, and that the lessee should bring ejectment for it. Or suppose the trustees of Dartmouth College should bring ejectment in Vermont in the circuit court for some of the Wheelock lands. In either of these modes the whole question might get before the court at Washington.

If I argue this cause at Washington, every one knows I can only be the reciter of the argument made by you at Exeter. You are, therefore, principally interested, as to the matter of reputation, in the figure I make at Washington. Nothing will be expected of me but decent delivery of your matter.

[Letter to Mason, Boston, January 1818]

I must either accept your proposition to meet you at Newburyport or persuade you to come here. I hope you will find it convenient to come here. On any other occasion, or at any other time, I would go a hundred miles to see you. I profess to be a sort of attendant on your course, in your orbit. But at present, if you can vary a little to accommodate the secondary planet, it would be a great favor.

SPEAK FOR YOURSELF, DANIEL

[Letter to Mason, Feb. 22, 1818]

The college case is not yet argued; we expect it on this week. Wirt and Holmes are for defendant. Wirt is a man of a good deal of ability; he is rather more of a lawyer than I expected.

[Letter to Sullivan, Feb. 27, 1818]

Court meets at eleven, hears long speeches till four, and adjourns. I have dined abroad every day since I came but one; and the principal reason is, that the only boarding-house where I could get a seat at table, is one in which one would seldom wish to dine at home. I have a room and a bed at a friend's house, Dr. Hunter's, and get my coffee in the morning with his family. So, on the whole, I am better off than most of my neighbors.

The Dartmouth College case was argued before the Supreme Court of the United States, with Chief Justice John Marshall presiding, for three days, commencing March 10, 1818. Webster opened, his argument taking substantially the whole first day. The following are brief excerpts:

Eleemosynary corporations are for the management of private property, according to the will of the donors. They are private corporations. The case before the court is clearly that of an eleemosynary corporation. It is, in the strictest legal sense, a private charity. Dr. Wheelock is declared by the charter to be its founder. It was established by him, on funds contributed and collected by himself.

As such founder, he had a right of visitation, which he assigned to the trustees, and they received it by his consent and appointment, and held it under the charter. Little, probably, did he think at that time, that the legislature would ever take away this property and these privileges, and give them to others. Little did he suppose that this charter secured to him and his successors no legal rights. Little did the other donors think so. If they had, the college would have been, what the university is now, a thing upon paper, existing only in name.

The numerous academies in New England have been established substantially in the same manner. They hold their property by the same tenure, and no other. Nor has Harvard College any surer title than Dartmouth College. It may to-day have more friends; but to-morrow it may have more enemies. Its legal rights are the same. So also of Yale College; and, indeed, of all the others.

Individuals have a right to use their own property for purposes of benevolence, either towards the public, or towards other individuals. They have a right to exercise this benevolence in such lawful manner as they may choose; and when the government has induced and excited it, by contracting to give perpetuity to the stipulated manner of exercising it, it is not law, but violence, to rescind this contract, and seize on the property. Whether the State will grant these franchises, and under what conditions it will grant them, it decides for itself. But when once granted, the constitution holds them to be sacred, till forfeited for just cause.

Of all the attempts of James the Second to overturn the law, and the rights of his subjects, none was esteemed more arbitrary or tyrannical than his attack on Magdalen College, Oxford; and yet that attempt was nothing but to put out one president and put in another. Because the president, who was rightfully and legally elected, would not deliver the keys, the doors were broken open. "The nation as well as the university," says Bishop Burnet, "looked on all these proceedings with just indignation. It was thought an open piece of robbery and burglary when men, authorized by no legal commission, came and forcibly turned men out of their possession and freehold."

This measure King James lived to repent, after repentance was too late. When the charter of London was restored, and other measures of violence were retracted, to avert the impending revolution, the expelled president and fellows of Magdalen College were permitted to resume their rights. It is evident that this was regarded as an arbitrary interference with private property. Yet private property was no otherwise attacked than as a person was appointed to administer and enjoy the revenues of a college in a manner and by persons not authorized by the constitution of the college.

The plaintiffs contend that the acts in question are repugnant to the tenth section of the first article of the Constitution of the United States. The material words of that section are: "No State shall pass any bill of attainder, ex post facto law, or law impairing the obligation of contracts."

It has already been decided in this court, that a grant is a contract, within the meaning of this provision; and that a grant by a State is also a contract, as much as the grant of an individual. It has also been decided, that a grant by a State before the Revolution is as much to be protected as a grant since.

This court, then, does not admit the doctrine, that a legislature can repeal statutes creating private corporations. If it cannot repeal them altogether, of course it cannot repeal any part of them, or impair them, or essentially alter them, without the consent of the corporators. If, therefore, it has been shown that this college is to be regarded as a private charity, this case is embraced within the very terms of that decision. A grant of corporate powers and privileges is as much a contract as a grant of land. What proves all charters of this sort to be contracts is, that they must be accepted to give them force and effect.

The case before the court is not of ordinary importance, nor of every-day occurrence. It affects not this college only, but every college, and all the literary institutions of the country. They have flourished hitherto, and have become in a high degree respectable and useful to the community. They have all a common principle of existence, the inviolability of their charters. It will be a dangerous, a most dangerous experiment, to hold these institutions subject to the rise and fall of popular parties, and the fluctuations of political opinions. If the franchise may be at any time taken away, or impaired, the property also may be taken away, or its use perverted. Benefactors will have no certainty of effecting the object of their bounty; and learned men will be deterred from devoting themselves to the service of such institutions, from the precarious title of their offices. Colleges and halls will be deserted by all better spirits, and become a theatre for the contentions of politics. Party and faction will be cherished in the places consecrated to piety and learning. These consequences are neither remote nor possible only. They are certain and immediate.

Webster had completed his legal argument, but there was more in his heart. Rufus Choate, in his Eulogy on Webster at Dartmouth, July 27, 1853, said that he well remembered "how it was written home from Washington that 'Mr. Webster closed a legal argument of great power by a peroration which charmed and melted his audience.' I was aware," he continued, "that the report of his argument as it was published did not contain the actual peroration, and I supposed it lost forever. By the great kindness of a learned and excellent person, Dr. Chauncy A. Goodrich, a professor in Yale College, I can read to you the words whose power, when those lips spoke them, so many owned, although they could not repeat them."

Dr. Goodrich's account was as follows:

"The Supreme Court of the United States held its session that winter in a mean apartment of moderate size — the Capitol not having been built after its destruction in 1814. The audience, when the case came on, was therefore small, consisting chiefly of legal men, the élite of the profession throughout the country. Mr. Webster entered upon his argument in the calm tone of easy and dignified conversation. His matter was so completely at his command that he scarcely looked at his brief, but went on for more than four hours with a statement so luminous, and a chain of reasoning so

easy to be understood, and yet approaching so nearly to absolute demonstration, that he seemed to carry with him every man of his audience without the slightest effort or weariness on either side. It was hardly eloquence, *in the strict sense of the term; it was pure reason.*

"I observed that Judge Story, at the opening of the case, had prepared himself, pen in hand, as if to take copious minutes. Hour after hour I saw him fixed in the same attitude, but, so far as I could perceive, with not a note on his paper. The argument closed, and I could not discover that he had taken a single note. *Others around me remarked the same thing; and it was among the* on dits *of Washington, that a friend spoke to him of the fact with surprise, when the judge remarked, 'Everything was so clear, and so easy to remember, that not a note seemed necessary, and, in fact, I thought little or nothing about my notes.'*

"The argument ended. Mr. Webster stood for some moments silent before the Court, while every eye was fixed intently upon him. At length addressing Chief Justice Marshall, he proceeded thus: —

" 'This, sir, is my case! It is the case, not merely of that humble institution, it is the case of every college in our land. It is more. It is the case of every eleemosynary institution throughout our country — of all those great charities founded by the piety of our ancestors to alleviate human misery and scatter blessings along the pathway of life. It is more! It is in some sense the case of every man among us who has property of which he may be stripped; for the question is simply this: Shall our State Legislatures be allowed to take that which is not their own, to turn it from its original use, and apply it to such ends or purposes as they, in their discretion, shall see fit!

" 'Sir, you may destroy this little institution; it is weak; it is in your hands! I know it is one of the lesser lights in the literary horizon of our country. You may put it out. But if you do so, you must carry through your work! You must extinguish, one after an-

other, all those great lights of science which, for more than a century, have thrown their radiance over our land!

" '*It is, sir, as I have said, a small college. And yet there are those who love it —*'

"*Here the feelings which he had thus far succeeded in keeping down broke forth. His lips quivered; his firm cheeks trembled with emotion; his eyes were filled with tears, his voice choked, and he seemed struggling to the utmost simply to gain that mastery over himself which might save him from an unmanly burst of feeling.*

"*The court-room during these two or three minutes presented an extraordinary spectacle. Chief Justice Marshall, with his tall and gaunt figure bent over as if to catch the slightest whisper, the deep furrows of his cheek expanded with emotion, and eyes suffused with tears; Mr. Justice Washington at his side — with his small and emaciated frame, and countenance more like marble than I ever saw on any other human being, leaning forward with an eager, troubled look; and the remainder of the court, at the two extremities, pressing, as it were, toward a single point, while the audience below were wrapping themselves round in closer folds beneath the bench to catch each look, and every movement of the speaker's face.*

"*Mr. Webster had now recovered his composure, and fixing his keen eye on the Chief Justice, said, in that deep tone with which he sometimes thrilled the heart of an audience —*

" '*Sir, I know not how others may feel*' (*glancing at the opponents of the college before him*), '*but for myself, when I see my Alma Mater surrounded, like Caesar in the senate-house, by those who are reiterating stab upon stab, I would not, for this right hand, have her turn to me, and say,* Et tu quoque, mi filii! *And thou too, my son!*'

"*He sat down. There was a deathlike stillness throughout the room for some moments; every one seemed to be slowly recovering himself, and coming gradually back to his ordinary range of thought and feeling.*"

67

SPEAK FOR YOURSELF, DANIEL

[Letter to Mason, Mar. 13, 1818]

The argument in the college case terminated yesterday, having occupied nearly three days. On being inquired of by defendant's counsel whether the court would probably give a decision at this term, the chief justice answered "that the court would not treat lightly an act of the legislature of a State and the decision of a State court, and that the court would not probably render any judgment at this term." The cause was opened on our side by me. Mr. Holmes followed. Upon the whole, he gave us three hours of the merest stuff that was ever uttered in a county court.

Wirt followed. He is a good deal of a lawyer, and has very quick perceptions, and handsome power of argument; but he seemed to treat this case as if his side could furnish nothing but declamation. He undertook to make out one legal point on which he rested his argument, namely, that Dr. Wheelock was not founder. In this he was, I thought, completely unsuccessful. He abandoned his first point, recited some foolish opinions of Virginians on the third, but made his great effort to support the second, namely, that there was no contract. On this he had nothing new to say. The old story of the public nature of the use — a charter for the ultimate benefit of the people — in the nature of a public institution — like towns, &c. He made an apology for himself, that he had not had time to study the case, and hardly thought of it, till it was called on.

Upon the whole, no new matter or reasoning was brought forward; and, in my opinion, the argument upon the law of the case on our side is not answered. Mr. Hopkinson made a most satisfactory reply, keeping to the law, and not following Holmes and Wirt into the fields of declamation and fine speaking.

[Letter to Smith, Mar. 14, 1818]

I have no accurate knowledge of the manner in which the judges are divided. The chief and Washington, I have no doubt are with us. Duval and Todd perhaps against us; the other three holding up. I cannot much doubt but that Story will be with us in the end, and I think we have much more than an even chance for one of the others. I think we shall finally succeed.

We finished with the third day. The next morning, yesterday, the chief justice told us the court had conferred; that there were different opinions, and that some judges had not formed opinions; consequently, the cause must be continued.

[Letter to Mason, Apr. 23, 1818]

As to the college cause, I cannot argue it any more, I believe. I have told you very often that you and Judge Smith argued it very greatly. If it was well argued at Washington, it is a proof that I was right, because all that I said at Washington was but those two arguments, clumsily put together by me. I do not mean to hold you answerable for any deficiencies; but in truth have little right to claim the merit, if there be any, in the opening of our case.

[Letter to Story, Sept. 9, 1818]

I send you five copies of our argument. If you send one of them to each of such of the judges as you think proper, you will of course do it in the manner least likely to lead to a feeling that any indecorum has been committed by the plaintiffs. The truth is, the New Hampshire opinion is able, ingenious, and plausible. It has been widely circulated, and something was necessary to exhibit the other side of the question.

[Letter from Hopkinson to Webster, Nov. 17, 1818]

In my passage through Baltimore, I fell in with Pinkney, who told me he was engaged in the cause by the present University, and that he is desirous to argue it, if the court will let him. I suppose

*he expects to do something very extraordinary in it, as he says Mr.
Wirt "was not strong enough for it, has not back enough."*

*I think if the court consents to hear Mr. Pinkney, it will be a
great stretch of complaisance, and that we should not give our
consent to any such proceeding; but if Mr. Pinkney, on his own
application, is permitted to speak, we should claim our right of
reply. The court cannot want to have our argument repeated; and
they will hardly require us to do it for the accommodation of Mr.
Pinkney.*

[*Letter to Mason, Feb. 4, 1819*]

Most of the judges came here with opinions drawn in the College
cause. On the other side a second argument, as you know, was expected. Dr. Perkins had been a week at Baltimore, conferring with
Mr. Pinkney. Mr. Pinkney came up on Monday. On Tuesday
morning, he being in court, as soon as the judges had taken their
seats, the Chief Justice said that in vacation the judges had formed
opinions in the College cause. He then immediately began reading
his opinion, and, of course, nothing was said of a second argument.

[*Letter to Ezekiel, Feb. 2, 1819*]

All is safe. Judgment was rendered this morning, reversing the
judgment in New Hampshire. Present: Marshall, Washington,
Livingston, Johnson, Duval, and Story. All concurring but Duval;
and he giving no reason to the contrary. The opinion was delivered
by the Chief Justice. It was very able and very elaborate; it goes
the whole length, and leaves not an inch of ground for the University to stand on.

[*Letter from Hopkinson to Brown, Feb. 2, 1819*]

*I have the pleasure of enclosing you a letter informing you of
great matters. Our triumph in the college cause has been complete.*

Five judges, only six attending, concur not only in a decision in our favor, but in placing it upon principles broad and deep, and which secure corporations of this description from legislative despotism and party violence for the future. The Court goes all lengths with us, and whatever trouble these gentlemen may give us in future, in their great and pious zeal for the interests of learning, they cannot shake those principles which must and will restore Dartmouth College to its true and original owners. I would have an inscription over the door of your building, "Founded by Eleazar Wheelock, Refounded by Daniel Webster."

[Letter to Hopkinson, Mar. 22, 1819]

You must write out your argument. I will examine, compare, correct, & edit it; & take any other labor about it; *but you must write it, & give it the impress of your own style & manner.* This is a work which you must do for *reputation.* Our College cause will be known to our children's children. Let us take care that the rogues shall not be ashamed of their grandfathers. We shall want your argument for the press in about three weeks — or a month. Three mornings will give you time to complete it.

I believe we shall have little further trouble with the University, altho she does not seem to die with grace. The instruction in it is broken up, & the College scholars are in possession of the buildings. The story is, that a Gentleman, coming that way, brought off *two* of the classes of the University in his *gig.*

[Letter from Hopkinson to Webster, Apr. 19, 1819]

It is but time and labor thrown away to attempt to do that which we know to be impossible. The chain of connection, the whole course of thought, are now so entirely lost and gone with the things "beyond the flood," that they are as much out of my power as Noah's ark, or Jacob's ladder. All I can do is to give good counsel instead of a bad speech, to wit, that it be stated in its proper place in the big book, that the argument of Mr. Hopkinson at large could not be obtained, but that it consisted of a repetition of the principles opened by Mr. Webster, enforcing and illustrating them by various cases and arguments; and giving full and satisfactory answers to the arguments urged by the counsel on the other side. Something of this, spiced a little, if you please, with compliment so far as your conscience will allow, will answer all the purpose.

God bless you, — yours,

J. HOPKINSON

[*Letter to Mason, Apr. 10, 1819*]

My own interest would be promoted by *preventing* the Book. I shall strut well enough in the Washington Report, & if the "Book" should not be published, the world would not know where I borrowed my plumes. But I am still inclined to have the Book. One reason is, that you & Judge Smith may have the credit which belongs to you. Another is, I believe, Judge Story is strongly of opinion it would be a useful work.

V

1819–1820

SUPREME COURT PRACTICE —
PLYMOUTH ORATION

Webster's handling of the Dartmouth College case placed him in the front rank of the American bar. Probably no non-governmental lawyer, before or since, has argued so many cases before the United States Supreme Court, or such a high proportion freighted with constitutional significance.

Within three weeks of the Dartmouth College decision he participated in the argument of McCulloch v. Maryland, involving the constitutionality of the Second Bank of the United States and giving rise to what many have thought to be Chief Justice Marshall's greatest judicial opinion. In this case he was junior to William Pinkney. In nearly all his other cases he acted as senior counsel. Perhaps the most important was Gibbons v. Ogden (sometimes called the Steamboat Case), which became the foundation stone for the Supreme Court's later decisions on interstate commerce. Peter Harvey quotes Webster on this case as follows:

The two arguments that have given me the most satisfaction were the argument in the "steamboat case," and the Dartmouth College argument. The steamboat case, you remember, was a question of the constitutionality of the right of New York State to give a monopoly to Fulton, and his heirs for ever, of the privilege of plying the waters of the Hudson with his steamboats. The value of such a right was not then and could not have been, from the nature of the case, fully understood. But it seemed to me to be against the very essence of State rights, and a virtual dissolution of the Union in a commercial sense. If New York had a right to lay tolls upon her rivers for everybody that should pass, then all the other great international rivers and lakes would have the same right, and we could not be one as a commercial people. The people of New York felt that their rights were at stake in the contest; and their great lawyers — and they had many of them — were engaged on that side; the Livingstons and Clintons and others of like calibre. Mr. Wirt and myself were employed against the monopoly. When the case came to be argued before the supreme court at Washington, Chief Justice Marshall presiding, Mr. Wirt and myself met for consultation. Mr. Wirt asked me upon what grounds I based my case, upon what clause of the Constitution. He had a right to ask, as he was my senior in years and professional fame. My reply was, that the clause of the Constitution which ceded to the general government the right to regulate commerce was that upon which I based my defence. Mr. Wirt's reply to that was, that he did not see, in that line of argument, any ground for our case to rest upon. I said: "Very well; what is yours?" So he told me. I do not recollect what it was, but it was a totally different clause in which he found the grounds for his argument. I said to him: "Mr. Wirt, I will be as frank with you as you have been with me, and say that I do not see the slightest ground to rest our case upon in your view of it." "Very well," replied Mr. Wirt, "let us each argue it in his own way, and we will find out which, if either, is right."

The case came on for argument. Mr. Wirt made one of his brilliant arguments before the court. I followed with my view.

I can see the chief justice as he looked at that moment. Chief Justice Marshall always wrote with a quill. He never adopted the barbarous invention of steel pens. That abomination had not been introduced. And always, before counsel began to argue, the chief justice would nib his pen; and then, when every thing was ready, pulling up the sleeves of his gown, he would nod to the counsel who was to address him, as much as to say, "I am ready; now you may go on."

74

I think I never experienced more intellectual pleasure than in arguing that naval question to a great man who could appreciate it, and take it in; and he did take it in, as a baby takes in its mother's milk.

The result of the case was just this: the opinion of the court, as rendered by the chief justice, was little else than a recital of my argument. The chief justice told me that he had little to do but to repeat that argument, as that covered the whole ground. And, which was a little curious, he never referred to the fact that Mr. Wirt had made an argument. He did not speak of it once.

Then Mr. Webster added:

That was very singular. It was an accident, I think. Mr. Wirt was a great lawyer, and a great man. But sometimes a man gets a kink, and doesn't hit right.

Some indication of the broad, national thrust of Webster's argument, which proved so persuasive to Marshall, can be gained from the following brief excerpts:

Few things are better known than the immediate causes which led to the adoption of the present Constitution; and there is nothing, as I think, clearer, than that the prevailing motive was *to regulate commerce;* to rescue it from the embarrassing and destructive consequences resulting from the legislation of so many different States, and to place it under the protection of a uniform law. The great objects were commerce and revenue; and they were objects indissolubly connected. By the Confederation, divers restrictions had been imposed on the States; but these had not been found sufficient. No State, it is true, could send or receive an embassy; nor make any treaty; nor enter into any compact with another State, or with a foreign power; nor lay duties interfering with treaties which had been entered into by Congress. But all these

75

were found to be far short of what the actual condition of the country required. The States could still, each for itself, regulate commerce, and the consequence was a perpetual jarring and hostility of commercial regulation.

In the history of the times, it is accordingly found, that the great topic, urged on all occasions, as showing the necessity of a new and different government, was the state of trade and commerce. To benefit and improve these was a great object in itself; and it became greater when it was regarded as the only means of enabling the country to pay the public debt, and to do justice to those who had most effectually labored for its independence.

It should be repeated, that the words used in the Constitution, "to regulate commerce," are so very general and extensive, that they may be construed to cover a vast field of legislation, part of which has always been occupied by State laws; and therefore the words must have a reasonable construction, and the power should be considered as exclusively vested in Congress so far, and so far only, as the nature of the power requires. And I insist, that the nature of the case, and of the power, did imperiously require, that such important authority as that of granting monopolies of trade and navigation should not be considered as still retained by the States.

Webster had not yet resigned himself to Washington. On February 23, 1819, he wrote Mason:

A month is as long as Washington wears well. I hope to get away on the 5th or 6th of March.

[*Letter to Mason, Boston, Aug. 10, 1819*]

We have at length returned from an unexpectedly long journey. Our trip extended to Philadelphia, and on our return, we went up the North River as far as Albany, from which place we came home without finding it necessary on account of health to drink the Spring waters. Mrs. Webster is for the present satisfied with riding and will not think of going to Hanover; I believe I shall attempt it. As you have been somewhat stationary through the summer, I hope you will come up. I propose to go from here in such season as to be at Concord or Boscawen on Sunday evening. It is then an easy day's ride to Hanover; I shall go up in my chaise, and should be particularly glad to meet you at Concord. I do not think Judge Story will go up; he has engagements here which he cannot well leave.

By December 1819, during the controversy over the admission of Missouri to the Union as a slave State, Webster addressed a citizens' meeting at the Massachusetts State House and was made chairman of a committee of five to draft a memorial to Congress. Others participated in the preparation of this, but the following is generally attributed to Webster:

The laws of the United States have denounced heavy penalties against the traffic in slaves, because such traffic is deemed unjust and inhuman . . . We have a strong feeling of the injustice of any toleration of slavery. Circumstances have entailed it on a portion of our community which cannot be immediately relieved from it without consequences more injurious than the suffering of the evil. But to permit it in a new country, where yet no habits are formed which render it indispensable, what is it, but to encourage that rapacity, fraud, and violence against which we have so long pointed the denunciations of our penal code?

Increasingly, Webster was called upon to deliver keynote addresses on national subjects. At a meeting of merchants at Faneuil Hall, Boston, on October 2, 1820, he spoke in favor of free trade, saying in the course of a long speech:

77

A system of artificial government protection leads the people to too much reliance on government. If left to their own choice of pursuits, they depend on their own skill and their own industry. But if government essentially affects their occupations by its systems of bounties and preferences, it is natural, when in distress, that they should call on government for relief.

During the last two months of 1820 Massachusetts held a Constitutional Convention to consider problems precipitated by the formation of Maine (formerly a province of Massachusetts) as a separate state. Webster was elected a delegate from Boston, and his part in the Convention is described by Story in a letter of January 21, 1821, to Mason:

"Our Friend Webster has gained a noble reputation. He was before known as a lawyer; but he has now secured the title of an eminent and enlightened statesman. It was a glorious field for him, and he has had an ample harvest. The whole force of his great mind was brought out, and in several speeches he commanded universal admiration. He always led the van, and was most skilful and instantaneous in attack and retreat. He fought, as I have told him, in the 'imminent deadly breach'; and all I could do was to skirmish in aid of him upon some of the enemy's outposts. On the whole, I never was more proud of any display than his in my life, and I am much deceived, if the well-earned popularity so justly and so boldly acquired by him on this occasion, does not carry him, if he lives, to the Presidency."

Among other interesting and important topics, Webster spoke at the Convention in opposition to the requirement of a declaration of a belief in the Christian religion as a qualification for certain elective offices. He considered that such a requirement, though valid, was inexpedient, his argument being in part as follows:

This qualification is made applicable only to the executive and the members of the legislature. It would not be easy, perhaps, to say why it should not be extended to the judiciary, if it were thought necessary for any office. There can be no office in which the sense of religious responsibility is more necessary than in that of a judge; especially of those judges who pass, in the last resort, on the lives, liberty, and property of every man. There may be among legislators strong passions and bad passions. There may be party heats and personal bitterness. But legislation is in its nature general: laws usually affect the whole society; and if mischievous or unjust, the whole society is alarmed, and seeks their repeal. The judiciary power, on the other hand, acts directly on individuals. The injured may suffer, without sympathy or the hope of redress. The last hope of the innocent, under accusation and in distress, is in the integrity of his judges. If this fail, all fails; and there is no remedy, on this side of the bar of Heaven. Of all places, therefore, there is none which so imperatively demands that he who occupies it should be under the fear of God, and above all other fear, as the situation of a judge.

Earlier in the same year Webster had been asked by the Pilgrim Society to deliver an address at Plymouth on December 22 in commemoration of the 200th anniversary of the landing of the Pilgrims. The Constitutional Convention was still sitting, but Webster had prepared himself carefully in advance and on the date chosen delivered what many considered the finest of all his speeches. His friend George Ticknor gives a first-hand account of the setting:

"I went to Plymouth on the 21st of December, 1820, with Mr. and Mrs. Webster, Mr. and Mrs. I. P. Davis, Miss Stockton, Mr. F. C. Gray, and Miss Mary Mason. Where we stopped to dine we overtook fifty or sixty persons, among whom were Colonel Perkins, Mrs. S. G. Perkins, Mr. E. Everett, and many others of our acquaintance. Mr. Webster had been a little uninterested during the morning drive, wearied perhaps by his labors in the convention, and partly occupied with thoughts of the following day. But at the

little half-way house, where we all crowded into two or three small rooms, we had a very merry time, and Mr. Webster was as gay as any one.

"In the evening at Plymouth every thing had the air of a fete; the houses of the principal street — in one of which we lodged — were all lighted up, so that the street itself was illuminated by them, and a band of music went up and down, followed by a crowd, while it serenaded the many strangers already collected from a distance for the great centenary anniversary.

"In the morning I went with Mr. Webster to the church where he was to deliver the oration. It was the old First Church — Dr. Kendall's. He did not find the pulpit convenient for his purpose, and after making two or three experiments, determined to speak from the deacon's seat under it. An extemporaneous table, covered with green baize cloth, was arranged for the occasion, and, when the procession entered the church, every thing looked very appropriate, though, when the arrangement was first suggested, it sounded rather odd. The building was crowded: indeed the streets had seemed so all the morning, for the weather was fine, and the whole population was astir as for a holiday.

"The oration was an hour and fifty minutes long, but the whole of what was printed a year afterward (for it was a year before it made its appearance) was not delivered. His manner was very fine — quite various in the different parts. The passage about the slave-trade was delivered with a power of indignation such as I never witnessed on any other occasion. That at the end, when, spreading his arms as if to embrace them, he welcomed future generations to the great inheritance which we have enjoyed, was spoken with the most attractive sweetness, and that peculiar smile which in him was always so charming. The effect of the whole was very great. I never saw him at any time when he seemed to me to be more conscious of his own powers, or to have a more true and natural enjoyment from their possession.

"At the public dinner the same day, he was not much moved by

the great enthusiasm around him, which had chiefly been excited by himself. At the ball that followed, he was agreeable to everybody and nothing more; but when we came home he was as frolicsome as a school-boy, laughing and talking, and making merry with Mrs. Webster, Mrs. Davis, and Mrs. Rotch, the daughter of his old friend Stockton, till two o'clock in the morning. The next day we came back to Boston, but I remember nothing of the return."

The speech itself occupies forty-five pages in the National Edition of Webster's Writings and Speeches. *The following are brief excerpts:*

Let us rejoice that we behold this day. Let us be thankful that we have lived to see the bright and happy breaking of the auspicious morn, which commences the third century of the history of New England.

It is a noble faculty of our nature which enables us to connect our thoughts, our sympathies, and our happiness with what is distant in place or time; and, looking before and after, to hold communion at once with our ancestors and our posterity. Human and mortal although we are, we are nevertheless not mere insulated beings, without relation to the past or the future. Neither the point of time, nor the spot of earth, in which we physically live, bounds our rational and intellectual enjoyments. We live in the past by a knowledge of its history; and in the future by hope and anticipation.

There is a local feeling connected with this occasion, too strong to be resisted; a sort of *genius of the place,* which inspires and awes us. We feel that we are on the spot where the first scene of our history was laid; where the hearths and altars of New England were first placed; where Christianity, and civilization, and letters made their first lodgement, in a vast extent of country, covered with a wilderness, and peopled by roving barbarians. We are here, at the season of the year at which the event took place. The imagination irresistibly and rapidly draws around us the principal features and the leading characters in the original scene. We cast our eyes abroad on the ocean, and we see where the little bark, with the interesting group upon its deck, made its slow progress to the shore. We look around us, and behold the hills and promontories where the anxious eyes of our fathers first saw the places of habitation and of rest. We feel the cold which benumbed, and listen to the winds which pierced them. Beneath us is the Rock, on which New England received the feet of the Pilgrims. We seem even to behold them, as they struggle with the elements, and, with toilsome efforts, gain the shore. We listen to the chiefs in council; we see the unexampled exhibition of female fortitude and resignation; we hear the whisperings of youthful impatience, and we see, what a painter of our own has also represented by his pencil, chilled and shivering childhood, houseless, but for a mother's arms, couchless, but for a mother's breast, till our own blood almost freezes.

They came hither to a land from which they were never to return. Hither they had brought, and here they were to fix, their hopes, their attachments, and their objects in life. Whatever constitutes *country*, except the earth and the sun, all the moral causes of affection and attachment which operate upon the heart, they had brought with them to their new abode. Here were now their families and friends, their homes, and their property. Before they reached the shore, they had established the elements of a social system, and at a much earlier period had settled their forms of religious worship. At the moment of their landing, therefore, they possessed institutions of government, and institutions of religion: and friends and families, and social and religious institutions, framed by consent, founded on choice and preference, how nearly do these fill up our whole idea of country!

Under the influence of these causes, it was to be expected, that an interest and a feeling should arise here, entirely different from the interest and feeling of mere Englishmen; and all the subsequent history of the Colonies proves this to have actually and gradually taken place. With a general acknowledgment of the supremacy of the British crown, there was, from the first, a repugnance to an entire submission to the control of British legislation. The Colonies stood upon their charters, which, as they contended, exempted them from the ordinary power of the British Parliament, and authorized them to conduct their own concerns by their own counsels.

I have dwelt on this topic, because it seems to me, that the peculiar original character of the New England Colonies, and certain causes coeval with their existence, have had a strong and decided influence on all their subsequent history, and especially on the great event of the Revolution. Whoever would write our history, and would understand and explain early transactions, should comprehend the nature and force of the feeling which I have endeavored to describe. As a son, leaving the house of his father for his own, finds, by the order of nature, and the very law of his being, nearer and dearer objects around which his affections circle, while his attachment to the parental roof becomes moderated, by degrees, to a composed regard and an affectionate remembrance; so our ancestors, leaving their native land, not without some violence to the feelings of nature and affection, yet, in time, found here a new circle of engagements, interests, and affections; a feeling, which more and more encroached upon the old, till an undivided sentiment, *that this was their country,* occupied the heart; and patriotism, shutting out from its embraces the parent realm, became *local* to America.

But if our ancestors at the close of the first century could look back with joy, and even admiration, at the progress of the country, what emotions must we not feel, when, from the point on which we stand, we also look back and run along the events of the century which has now closed!

New England farms, houses, villages, and churches spread over and adorn the immense extent from the Ohio to Lake Erie, and stretch along from the Alleghany onwards, beyond the Miamis, and toward the Falls of St. Anthony. Two thousand miles westward from the rock where their fathers landed, may now be found the sons of the Pilgrims, cultivating smiling fields, rearing towns and villages, and cherishing, we trust, the patrimonial blessings of wise institutions, of liberty, and religion. The world has seen nothing like this. Regions large enough to be empires, and which half a century ago, were known only as remote and unexplored wildernesses, are now teeming with population, and prosperous in all the great concerns of life; in good governments, the means of subsistence, and social happiness. It may be safely asserted, that there are now more than a million of people, descendants of New England ancestry, living, free and happy, in regions which scarce sixty years ago were tracts of unpenetrated forest. Nor do rivers, or mountains, or seas resist the progress of industry and enterprise. Ere long, the sons of the Pilgrims will be on the shores of the Pacific. The imagination hardly keeps pace with the progress of population, improvement, and civilization.

Of our system of government the first thing to be said is, that it is really and practically a free system. It originates entirely with the people, and rests on no other foundation than their assent. To judge of its actual operation, it is not enough to look merely at the form of its construction. The practical character of government depends often on a variety of considerations, besides the abstract frame of its constitutional organization.

A republican form of government rests not more on political constitutions, than on those laws which regulate the descent and transmission of property. Governments like ours could not have been maintained, where property was holden according to the principles of the feudal system; nor, on the other hand, could the feudal constitution possibly exist with us.

The history of other nations may teach us how favorable to public liberty are the division of the soil into small freeholds, and a system of laws, of which the tendency is, without violence or injustice, to produce and to preserve a degree of equality of property. Here we have had that experience; and we know that a multitude of small proprietors, acting with intelligence, and that enthusiasm which a common cause inspires, constitute not only a formidable, but an invincible power.

The true principle of a free and popular government would seem to be, so to construct it as to give to all, or at least to a very great majority, an interest in its preservation; to found it, as other things are founded, on men's interest. The stability of government demands that those who desire its continuance should be more powerful than those who desire its dissolution.

But this state of things is not brought about solely by written political constitutions, or the mere manner of organizing the government. The freest government, if it could exist, would not be long acceptable, if the tendency of the laws were to create a rapid accumulation of property in few hands, and to render the great mass of the population dependent and penniless. In such a case, the popular power would be likely to break in upon the rights of property, or else the influence of property to limit and control the exercise of popular power. Universal suffrage, for example, could not long exist in a community where there was great inequality of property. The holders of estates would be obliged, in such case, in some way to restrain the right of suffrage, or else such right of suffrage would, before long, divide the property.

I deem it my duty on this occasion to suggest, that the land is not yet wholly free from the contamination of a traffic, at which every feeling of humanity must for ever revolt — I mean the African slave-trade. Neither public sentiment, nor the law, has hitherto been able entirely to put an end to this odious and abominable trade. At the moment when God in his mercy has blessed the Christian world with a universal peace, there is reason to fear, that, to the disgrace of the Christian name and character, new efforts are making for the extension of this trade by subjects and citizens of Christian states, in whose hearts there dwell no sentiments of humanity or of justice, and over whom neither the fear of God nor the fear of man exercises a control. In the sight of our law, the African slave-trader is a pirate and a felon; and in the sight of

Heaven, an offender far beyond the ordinary depth of human guilt.

Finally, let us not forget the religious character of our origin. Our fathers were brought hither by their high veneration for the Christian religion. They journeyed by its light, and labored in its hope. They sought to incorporate its principles with the elements of their society, and to diffuse its influence through all their institutions, civil, political, or literary. Let us cherish these sentiments, and extend this influence still more widely; in the full conviction, that that is the happiest society which partakes in the highest degree of the mild and peaceful spirit of Christianity.

Advance, then, ye future generations! We would hail you, as you rise in your long succession, to fill the places which we now fill, and to taste the blessings of existence where we are passing, and soon shall have passed, our own human duration. We bid you welcome to this pleasant land of the fathers. We bid you welcome to the healthful skies and the verdant fields of New England. We greet your accession to the great inheritance which we have enjoyed. We welcome you to the blessings of good government and religious liberty. We welcome you to the treasures of science and the delights of learning. We welcome you to the transcendent sweets of domestic life, to the happiness of kindred, and parents, and children. We welcome you to the immeasurable blessings of rational existence, the immortal hope of Christianity, and the light of everlasting truth!

VI

1821–1824

CONGRESSMAN FROM MASSACHUSETTS — SPEECH ON THE GREEK REVOLUTION

For the next two years Webster devoted himself to the practice of law, with earnings that enabled him to live well and to assume the debts of his father's estate. His practice centered in Boston, but part of each year found him in Washington, as we may see from the following letters to Justice Story:

[Philadelphia, January 3, 1821]

I am not content to wait till I get to Washington, without giving you some account of myself and my travels. I left Boston in the mail stage-coach Saturday noon the 29th, with Mr. Perkins, T. Parsons, and William Gardiner. We kept with the mail to New Haven, where we found ourselves Sunday, 3 o'clock. Here we remained through that day, and finding an accommodation stage-coach going the next day to New York, we took it to ourselves, and reached that city early the evening of the same day. From New York we came hither in a new line of stage-coaches, called the Union line, which we are bound to speak well of. It gave us a whole coach for forty dollars, and allowed us to take our own hours. We left New York at three or four o'clock Tuesday afternoon, lodged at New Brunswick, and arrived here to dine Wednesday, yesterday. Our journey was safe and expeditious. I mention these circumstances for your benefit, knowing that in three weeks you are to be on our track, although I am well aware that Mrs. Story would scold me, if she could scold, for adverting to such a disagreeable topic.

[*Dec. 18, 1822*]

The good creature, I. P. D., has put a cask of excellent wine at 4.25 per gallon into Mr. Blake's cellar for J. S., I. P. D., G. B. & D. W.* in equal quarter parts. He has also, I believe, a couple of dozen for you which is old & excellent.

In 1822 Webster served briefly in the Massachusetts House of Representatives. He later claimed that his sole accomplishment was the passage of a bill making it illegal "to take or catch any pickerel or trout in any of the rivers, streams, or ponds within this Commonwealth, by day or by night, in any other way or manner than by hooks and lines."

In the fall of that year a meeting of Federalists urged his candidacy for Congress, from Boston, and on October 18, 1822, a committee of prominent citizens waited upon him with the following notification:

DEAR SIR, — We, the undersigned, having been chosen at a meeting of delegates from all the wards, held at Concert Hall on Thursday evening last, a committee to acquaint you, that at that meeting you were unanimously selected to be recommended to the support of their fellow-citizens, to represent the District of Suffolk, in the next Congress of the United States; and having been, by your absence from town, unable to wait upon you personally, have the pleasure to address you, to communicate the above fact; and we beg you to be assured, that in the performance of this duty we experience a peculiar satisfaction, which will be greatly enhanced by the knowledge of your consent to conform, upon this occasion, to the wishes of your friends, in the number of which we hope to be considered, and are with the highest respect and esteem,

    Your obedient servants,

                T. H. PERKINS, ⎫
                WM. SULLIVAN, ⎪
                BENJ. RUSSELL, ⎬ Committee.
                WM. STURGIS, ⎪
                J. W. T. APTHORP, ⎭

* Joseph Story, Isaac P. Davis, George Blake, and Daniel Webster.

There is every reason to believe that Webster regretted this call to duty. He was forty, he was fond of expensive living, and he had a growing family to support. The Congressional salary of $1,800 a year would mean a large financial sacrifice, and he had not yet admitted that he could endure Washington. Nevertheless, he accepted the nomination and, after a spirited contest, was elected. Perhaps, as he had written Story earlier, "A man of forty is a fool to wonder at any thing."

The Eighteenth Congress, to which Webster had been elected, would not convene for over a year, in December 1823. For him the interval was a period of political despondency, as appears from his letter of May 12, 1823, to Justice Story:

I never felt more down sick on all subjects connected with the public, than at the present moment. I have heretofore cherished a faint hope that New England would some time or other get out of this miserable, dirty squabble of local politics, and assert her proper character and consequence. But I at length give up. I feel the hand of fate upon us, and to struggle is in vain. We are doomed to be hewers of wood and drawers of water. There is a Federal interest, a Democratic interest, a Bankrupt interest, an Orthodox interest, and a Middling interest, but I see no national interest, nor any national feeling in the whole matter.

I am, dear Sir, your true but despairing friend,

But there were redeeming moments. On December 31, 1822, to the great joy of the family, a third son was born, in Boston. On February 6, 1823, Webster, in Washington, wrote his wife:

P. S. Little Baby's name, I have no choice between two or three. I do dislike double names, unless given for some friend. There seems to be a show about it. If you would incline to call him simple *William,* I am perfectly content. It is a good name, & would respond to the name of my uncle, & his uncle.

Mrs. Webster named the baby Charles.

SPEAK FOR YOURSELF, DANIEL

[Letter to Mason, Washington, Nov. 30, 1823]

We arrived here on Wednesday evening safe and well, after a journey which, on the whole, was pleasant and agreeable. Our lodgings were ready and are very comfortable.

The attendance of members is uncommonly large, and we shall have a quorum, no doubt, to-morrow. Mr. Clay arrived last evening. He will doubtless be Speaker, although I understood Mr. Barbour's friends intend to run him. It will not go. Mr. Clay's popularity as Speaker is great, and he is in many respects a liberal and honorable man. His health is not good, but I fancy not so bad as to induce him to decline the chair.

[Letter to Ezekiel, Dec. 4, 1823]

It is time to put an end to caucuses. They make great men little, and little men great. The true source of power is the people. The Democrats are not democratic enough. They are real Aristocrats. Their leaders wish to govern by a combination among themselves, and they think they have a fee-simple in the people's suffrages.

Meanwhile, Webster had been searching for an appropriate subject for a speech with which to signalize his return to Congress. From New York, on his way to Washington, he wrote his friend Edward Everett who had recently returned from Greece and was an enthusiastic supporter of its revolt against Turkish dominion.

[Nov. 16, 1823]

I have found leisure here, and not until now, to read your admirable article on the Greeks. Since I left Boston, also, we have had important information from them. I feel a great inclination to say or do something in their behalf early in the session, if I know what to say or to do. If you can readily direct me to any source from which I can obtain more information than is already public respecting their affairs, I would be obliged to you so to do.

[*To Everett, Washington, Dec. 5, 1823*]

I have gone over your two manuscripts with the map before me, and think I have mastered the campaigns of 1821–1822, historically and topographically. My wonder is, where and how your most extraordinary industry has been able to find all the materials for so interesting and detailed a narrative. I hope you will send me a digested narrative of the events of this year, so far as they are to be learned from the last accounts.

I have spoken to several gentlemen on the subject of a motion respecting Greece, and all of them approve it. The object which I wish to bring about, and which I believe may be brought about, is the appointment of a commissioner to go to Greece.

On this trip to Washington, Webster had been accompanied by Mrs. Webster and two of their children (Julia and Edward), leaving the other two (Fletcher and Charles) in Massachusetts with their nurse Hannah. On December 20, 1823, Webster wrote his friends Mr. and Mrs. George Blake, separately:

[*To George Blake*]

I believe Mrs. W. is meditating a letter to Mrs. B. to-day; but as she told me this morning it was uncertain whether engagements of business would allow her time to write, she directed me to indite a line to Mrs. B. to be inclosed in this, which I told her I was about writing to you.

As to the business of the court, I have not yet paid much attention to it. My Spanish claims have called for all the time at my command. They are now pretty much finished, at least so far as not to be extremely burdensome on my time.

I write this in the House, not now in session, and your friend, Mr. Buchanan, is here, and he desires me to make his remembrances to you and Mrs. Blake. He means to write to you soon, and he just now says, "Mr. Blake is one of the most agreeable men I have ever known." What a poor judge of such matters he is! If he always judges so wrong he will not do to be followed!

[To Mrs. Blake]

I really think Mrs. Webster likes Washington tolerably well. Nevertheless, we need your and Mr. Blake's society very much. There is nobody here to come in of an evening, and pull off his overshoes, coats, and handkerchiefs, and sit down to a regular social talk, like your husband. For my part I would give something just to see that blue handkerchief. Our evenings are sometimes not a little lonesome. However, I occasionally, though seldom, take a nap; and as you speak of dreaming away the long nights, you hit me on a tender point, since I am always accused, very unjustly of course, of no little love of the good thing, sleep. However, I will not altogether deny it, and in respect to good dreams, I am, I am sure, surpassed by nobody; I believe I have a talent that way. Our evening parties are not yet numerous; we have been but to two, one at General Brown's, the night before last, and one at Mrs. Adams, ten days ago. Report runs that the drawing room at the White House will be opened on New Year's day, and afterward as usual. There are several handsome female faces here that I have not seen before; especially two or three ladies from the South. We may be in some danger, my dear lady, of losing the reputation of the North, if you do not come on to sustain us against this southern competition. You must remember that our northern forces are much weakened since your beautiful friend Miss Dickinson stays out of the combat. For this, as well as other reasons, I hope you will allow me to entreat you to accompany your husband.

SPEECH ON GREEK REVOLUTION

On December 8, 1823, Webster introduced a resolution in the House authorizing "the expense incident to the appointment of an agent or commissioner to Greece, whenever the President shall deem it expedient to make such appointment," and on December 21 he wrote to Everett:

The resolution will be taken up tomorrow fortnight. I find your communications of the utmost utility. In regard to the history of the campaigns, I could have done nothing without your aid.

My intention is to justify the resolution against two classes of objections, those that suppose it not to go far enough, and those that suppose it to go too far. Then, to give some little history of the Greek revolution, express a pretty strong conviction of its ultimate success, and persuade the House, if I can, to take the merit of being the first government, among all the civilized nations, who have publicly rejoiced in the emancipation of Greece.

P. S. I feel now as if I could make a pretty good speech for my friends the Greeks, but I shall get cool in fourteen days, unless you keep up my temperature.

Webster apparently found ways to keep up his temperature, if we may judge from this letter of January 6, 1824, from his friend Isaac P. Davis in Boston:

"I feel greatly obliged by your kind attention in sending the canvas-back ducks. They arrived in excellent order, in a very short passage from Baltimore. I made the distribution as you directed. Your club met with Mr. Dutton, and they made a very favorable report of the good quality of the birds. Gorham, who is now called an excellent judge, decides them to be the very best ever seen this side of Havre de Grace.

We drank your health and a happy New Year in a bumper of 'Black top.' I sent a very fine pair to our friend Blake. As he leaves this to-morrow for Washington, he will make his own report.

SPEAK FOR YOURSELF, DANIEL

Mr. Lowell has been writing on the subject of the Greeks; his signature is 'A Calm Man.' It appears to me he is the only one that is not perfectly so among us."

On January 19, 1824, Webster addressed the House of Representatives in support of his Greek resolution, saying, among other things:

I have not introduced this motion in the vain hope of discharging our accumulated debt of centuries to Greece. My object is nearer and more immediate. I wish to take occasion of the struggle of an interesting and gallant people, in the cause of liberty and Christianity, to draw the attention of the House to the circumstances which have accompanied that struggle, and to the principles which appear to have governed the conduct of the great states of Europe in regard to it; and to the effects and consequences of these principles upon the independence of nations, and especially upon the institutions of free governments. What I have to say of Greece, therefore, concerns the modern, not the ancient; the living, and not the dead. It regards her, not as she exists in history, triumphant over time, and tyranny, and ignorance; but as she now is, contending, against fearful odds, for being, and for the common privileges of human nature.

It cannot be denied that the great political question of this age is that between absolute and regulated governments. The substance of the controversy is whether society shall have any part in its own government. Whether the form of government shall be that of limited monarchy, with more or less mixture of hereditary power, or wholly elective or representative, may perhaps be considered as subordinate. The main controversy is between that absolute rule, which, while it promises to govern well, means, nevertheless, to govern without control, and that constitutional system which restrains sovereign discretion, and asserts that society may claim as matter of right some effective power in the establishment of the laws which are to regulate it.

What part it becomes this country to take on a question of this sort, so far as it is called upon to take any part, cannot be doubtful. Our side of this question is settled for us, even without our own volition. Our history, our situation, our character, necessarily decide our position and our course, before we have even time to ask whether we have an option. Our place is on the side of free institutions.

I will now, Mr. Chairman, advert to those pretensions put forth by the allied sovereigns of Continental Europe, which seem to me calculated, if unresisted, to bring into disrepute the principles of our government, and, indeed, to be wholly incompatible with any degree of national independence. I do not introduce these considerations for the sake of topics. I am not about to declaim against crowned heads, nor to quarrel with any country for preferring a form of government different from our own. The right of choice that we exercise for ourselves, I am quite willing to leave also to others. But it appears to me that new and dangerous combinations are taking place, promulgating doctrines and fraught with consequences wholly subversive in their tendency of the public law of nations and of the general liberties of mankind.

Every body knows that, since the final restoration of the Bourbons to the throne of France, the Continental powers have entered into sundry alliances, which have been made public, and have held several meetings or congresses, at which the principles of their political conduct have been declared.

The first of these principles is, that all popular or constitutional rights are held not otherwise than as grants from the crown. Society, upon this principle, has no rights of its own; it takes good government, when it gets it, as a boon and a concession, but can demand nothing. It is to live by that favor which emanates from royal authority, and if it have the misfortune to lose that favor, there is nothing to protect it against any degree of injustice and oppression. It can rightfully make no endeavor for a change, by itself; its whole privilege is to receive the favors that may be dispensed by the sovereign power, and all its duty is described in the single word *submission*. This is the plain result of the principal Continental state papers; indeed, it is nearly the identical text of some of them.

I need not stop to observe, Mr. Chairman, how totally hostile are these doctrines of Laybach to the fundamental principles of our government. They are in direct contradiction; the principles of good and evil are hardly more opposite. If these principles of the sovereigns be true, we are but in a state of rebellion or of anarchy, and are only tolerated among civilized states because it has not yet been convenient to reduce us to the true standard.

But the second, and, if possible, the still more objectionable principle, avowed in these papers, is the right of forcible interference in the affairs of other states. A right to control nations in their desire to change their own government, wherever it may be conjectured, or pretended, that such change might furnish an example to the subjects of other states, is plainly and distinctly asserted. The same Congress that made the declaration at Laybach had declared, before its removal from Troppau, "that the powers have an undoubted right to take a hostile attitude in regard to those states in which the overthrow of the government may operate as an example."

There cannot, as I think, be conceived a more flagrant violation of public law, or national independence, than is contained in this short declaration.

No matter what be the character of the government resisted; no matter with what weight the foot of the oppressor bears on the neck of the oppressed; if he struggle, or if he complain, he sets a dangerous example of resistance — and from that moment he becomes an object of hostility to the most powerful potentates of the earth. I want words to express my abhorrence of this abominable principle. I trust every enlightened man throughout the world will oppose it, and that, especially, those who, like ourselves, are fortunately out of the reach of the bayonets that enforce it, will proclaim their detestation of it, in a tone both loud and decisive. The avowed object of such declarations is to preserve the peace of the world. But by what means is it proposed to preserve this peace? Simply, by bringing the power of all governments to bear against all subjects. Here is to be established a sort of double, or treble, or quadruple, or, for aught I know, quintuple allegiance. An offence against one king is to be an offence against all kings, and the power of all is to be put forth for the punishment of the offender.

It may now be required of me to show what interest *we* have in resisting this new system. What is it to *us*, it may be asked, upon what principles, or what pretences, the European governments assert a right of interfering in the affairs of their neighbors? The thunder, it may be said, rolls at a distance. The wide Atlantic is between us and danger; and, however others may suffer, *we* shall remain safe.

I think it is a sufficient answer to this to say, that we are one of the nations of the earth; that we have an interest, therefore, in the preservation of that system of national law and national intercourse which has heretofore subsisted, so beneficially for all. Our system of government, it should also be remembered, is, throughout, founded on principles utterly hostile to the new code; and if we remain undisturbed by its operation, we shall owe our security either to our situation or our spirit. The enterprising character of the age, our own active, commercial spirit, the great increase which has taken place in the intercourse among civilized and commercial states, have necessarily connected us with other nations, and given us a high concern in the preservation of those salutary principles upon which that intercourse is founded. We have as clear an interest in international law, as individuals have in the laws of society.

It is neither ostentation nor boasting to say that there lies before this country, in immediate prospect, a great extent and height of power. We are borne along towards this, without effort, and not always even with a full knowledge of the rapidity of our own motion. Circumstances which never combined before have coöperated in our favor, and a mighty current is setting us forward which we could not resist even if we would, and which, while we would stop to make an observation, and take the sun, has set us, at the end of the operation, far in advance of the place where we commenced it. Does it not become us, then, is it not a duty imposed on us, to give our weight to the side of liberty and justice, to let mankind know *1* that we are not tired of our own institutions, and to protest against the asserted power of altering at pleasure the law of the civilized world?

I close, then, with repeating, that the object of this resolution is to avail ourselves of the interesting occasion of the Greek revolution to make our protest against the doctrines of the Allied Powers, both as they are laid down in principle and as they are applied in practice. I think it right, too, Sir, not to be unseasonable in the expression of our regard, and, as far as that goes, in a manifestation of our sympathy with a long oppressed and now struggling people. I am not of those who would, in the hour of utmost peril, withhold such encouragement as might be properly and lawfully given, and, when the crisis should be past, overwhelm the rescued sufferer with kindness and caresses.

The Greeks address the civilized world with a pathos not easy to be resisted. They invoke our favor by more moving considerations than can well belong to the condition of any other people. They stretch out their arms to the Christian communities of the earth, beseeching them, by a generous recollection of their ancestors, by the consideration of their desolated and ruined cities and villages, by their wives and children sold into an accursed slavery, by their blood, which they seem willing to pour out like water, by the common faith, and in the name, which unites all Christians, that they would extend to them at least some token of compassionate regard.

Webster later said of his Greek speech: "I think I am more fond of this child than of any of the family."

His friend Joseph Hopkinson wrote to congratulate him, saying:

"The report of your speech, meagre as it is, shows the foot of Hercules; but we want the whole body and soul, and trust you will give it to us. Mr. Hempbill wrote me it was the best he ever heard.

"By your letter to our friend Walsh, I find you are preparing a proper publication of your speech. I pray you to take pains with it. You are generally too careless of yourself and your reputation; and, content with doing a thing well, you have too little solicitude about the proof of it to the world. It is, in one respect, a misfortune for a man to obtain a high eminence of character; he is required always to maintain it, and this calls for a constant vigilance and effort which are not always convenient. Besides, few have judgment to know of what a subject is capable, and expect to see the same power displayed, whether an oak is to be uprooted, or a rose plucked from its bush."

Although the speech enhanced Webster's reputation, it had little effect on Congress, which was too preoccupied with other matters. The most engrossing was the battle already shaping up for the 1824 presidential election. On this Webster himself had much to say:

[*To Mason, Feb. 15, 1824*]

I fully believe that the election must come into the House of Representatives. The Pennsylvania Convention will meet the 4th of March, and I presume will nominate either Jackson or Calhoun, and probably the former. If so, Mr. Calhoun will be no longer a candidate. Then the question is, who will be the three candidates presented to the House. Mr. Adams certainly will be one. If Mr. Crawford gets New York, he will be one: but if he should not, and I doubt whether he will, he will not come in to nomination, in which case the other two will be Clay and Jackson.

[*To Ezekiel, Feb. 22, 1824*]

Mr. Adams's chance seems to increase, and he and General Jackson are likely to be the real competitors at last. General Jackson's man-

78091

ners are more presidential than those of any of the candidates. He is grave, mild, and reserved. My wife is for him decidedly.

[*To Ezekiel, Mar. 14, 1824*]

As to President, Jackson seems to be making head yet, Arbuthnot and Ambrister notwithstanding. The truth is, he is the people's candidate in a great part of the southern and western country. I hope all New England will support Mr. Calhoun for the Vice-Presidency. If so, he will probably be chosen, and that will be a great thing. He is a true man, and will do good to the country in that situation.

[*To Mason, May 9, 1824*]

The novelty of General Jackson is wearing off, and the contest seems to be coming back to the old question between Mr. Adams and Mr. Crawford. They, with Jackson, will, I think, come into the House; and my belief at present is that Mr. Adams will be chosen.

Webster's predictions proved remarkably accurate. The electoral votes for President were Jackson 99, Adams 84, Crawford 41, and Clay 37. As no candidate had a majority, the election moved into the House of Representatives, where Adams was chosen. Calhoun became Vice President.

The other great subject of current controversy was Clay's so-called "American System" embodying a protective tariff, as to which Webster wrote:

[*To Everett, Feb. 13, 1824*]

On this same tariff we are now occupied; it is a tedious, disagreeable subject. The House, or a majority of it, are apparently insane, at least I think so. Whether any thing can be done to moderate the disease, I know not. I have very little hope. I am aware that something is expected from me, much more than I shall perform. It would be easy to make a speech, but I am anxious to do something better, if I can, but I see not what I can do.

[*To Ezekiel, Mar. 14, 1824*]

The tariff is yet undecided. It will not pass, I think, in its present shape, and I doubt if it will pass at all. As yet I have not interfered much in the debate. I should prefer it should die a natural death, by postponement or other easy violence.

On April 1 and 2, 1824, Webster spoke on the tariff, in reply to Clay, and on April 19 he described his speech in a letter to Mason.

We have heard a good deal of nonsense on this subject, and some of it from high quarters. I think you will be surprized at Mr. Clay's speech. It is printed, and I shall send you a copy. My speech will be printed, and you will get it. Whatever I have done in other cases, I must say that in this I have published it against my own judgment. I was not expecting to speak at that time, nor ready to do so. And from Mr. Clay's ending, I had but one night to prepare.

The best description of Webster's efforts and their effect, however, comes from William Plumer, Jr., a Congressman from New Hampshire, who wrote:

"On the feelings of his opponents I know of no man whose arguments produce so painful an effect as those of Webster. During the greater part of his Tariff speech, the friends of the bill seemed to feel as if the whole fabric on which they had long labored was tumbling in ruins about their heads; others had spoken well and ingeniously on the subject; some with much knowledge of fact, others with a great display of philosophical principles. Still the system

seemed unimpaired, or but slightly affected; till Webster, in the pride of conscious power came into the field beating down as with a giant's club, the whole array of his opponents' force. They never fully recovered from this deadly assault.

"He told me that immediately after the bill was reported to the House, he obtained from the printers 50 copies of it. These he sent to the best informed merchants, manufacturers, agriculturalists, and speculative men, requesting their opinions and remarks, in detail, on the bill. The ablest men in the country were ready at his call, with the results of their best inquiries; and no man knew better than Webster how to turn to account the aids thus received."

In his letter of April 19 to Mason, Webster had also said:

My great business of the session remains yet undone, that is, to get through the law for paying the Spanish claims.

These were for damage to American commerce by Spanish cruisers in 1788–89, and Webster represented most of the claimants. Plumer tells us further details:

"I asked him respecting his business before the commissioners on the Spanish claims. He said it had been his principal employment for the last three years; that he was to be paid by a commission of five per cent on the amount received by his clients, and that he thought he might safely calculate upon sixty thousand dollars as his share."

In actual fact, Webster's fees for handling these claims came to more than $70,000. His service in Congress, which enabled him to bring these claims to fruition, may not have been such a financial sacrifice after all.

Congress adjourned May 27, 1824. It was none too soon. What with the tension of the session and the anticipation of the election, its members were in a state of semi-exhaustion. Congressman (later Governor) Lincoln of Maine lapsed into verse:

"What guardian power my country's glory keeps,
When Senates doze, and e'en her Webster sleeps?

Sigh answers sigh, and snore resounds to snore,
Like billows bursting on some dreary shore.
With lazy pace, the long, long hours return,
While worn-out Sibley cries, 'Adjourn, adjourn.'"

Webster sent his family north in early June, accompanying them as far as Philadelphia and then returning to Washington to partici-pate on a committee investigating charges against William H. Craw-ford, Secretary of the Treasury and one of the leading contenders for the presidency. Crawford was unanimously vindicated.

On June 9 and 16 Webster wrote to George Blake and to Mrs. Blake:

[To Mrs. Blake, June 9, 1824]

You will not expect me to say how suddenly and how really all things seemed changed here, when you and your husband departed. No talks, no music, no rides, no little suppers on the light stand, no birthnight balls. And now, since Mrs. Webster and Julia, and that good-for-nothing Ned, are gone, it is lonely enough.

I pray you tell Mr. Blake, that after I get home, if I ever should do so, I expect to find him ready for play the residue of the summer. I am yet not so reduced but that I could walk with a bit of iron on my shoulder.

[To George Blake, June 16, 1824]

I trust I shall get away before the week is out. I am homesick — homesick — homesick. I learn that Mrs. Webster was to embark yesterday from New York for New Haven. I presume she will be in Dorchester by the time you receive this.

We have no news here worth communicating. Pray give my most profound regards to Mrs. Blake. If I live to get home, I shall be glad.

VII

1824–1825

MARSHFIELD — VISIT TO MADISON
AND JEFFERSON — BUNKER HILL ORATION

The family spent August together at Sandwich on Cape Cod, a favorite vacation spot of Webster's. Josiah Quincy described it in 1825 as "a noted resort for sportsmen, with a famous inn whose cook knew how to dress the birds which the guns of the guests never failed to furnish."

It was in the autumn of this year (1824) that they discovered Marshfield, later to become the focal point of Webster's domestic life. Here, he used to say, "he could go out every day of the year and see something new." His friend Peter Harvey described the occasion, as he heard it from Webster, as follows.

"It had been his custom for several years to pass a part of each summer at Sandwich. There, in company with his friend George Blake, he indulged his taste for shooting and fishing. But the establishment of a large glass manufactory, and the arrival of many operatives who, on their holidays, overspread the country with guns and dogs, had thinned out the game to such an extent that the neighborhood ceased to supply good sport. Mr. Webster mentioned this to his friend Isaac P. Davis, who thereupon recommended him to apply to Captain John Thomas of Marshfield, whom Mr. Davis knew well, and who he was confident, would gladly entertain Mr. Webster at his house, and grant him the freedom of his marshes, where he would find a great abundance of sport.

"Mr. Webster resolved to act upon the suggestion. He took his wife and eldest son in a chaise and drove to Marshfield. As they *passed over the brow of Black Mount, in front of Captain Thomas's residence, Mrs. Webster, without knowing that it was the very place they were to visit, called her husband's attention to the beautiful prospect before them, and bade him stop the horse to gaze at the scenery; remarking that, if she ever were to have a retreat in the country, she would prefer the one before her to any she had ever seen. They drove up to the house. Captain Thomas received the party with great cordiality. His wife and sons soon made their appearance and were introduced, and in a short time the unexpected guests were as much at home as they ever were afterwards during their residence at Marshfield.*

"It was this strong preference of his wife that first suggested to Mr. Webster the thought of purchasing the place, which he afterwards did; making large additions to the estate and to the dwelling-house.

"There are some interesting points in the history of Marshfield which give an additional charm to its delightful scenery. It was early settled by the Pilgrims and their followers. It was the residence of Peregrine White, the first white child born in New England; and his remains are buried in the old Winslow grave-yard on the premises of Mr. Webster."

This same autumn Webster was reelected to Congress from Boston in a vote which the newspapers reported as "nearly unanimous." In December he returned to Washington, leaving his wife and family in Boston.

[*Letters to Mrs. Webster: Dec. 4, 1824*]

MY DEAR LOVE — I have made an engagement to take lodgings at a Mr. McIntire's, Pennsylvania Avenue, between Mrs. Peyton's and Brown's on the opposite side. It is a new house, and the people seem to be good people. I have a large room in front to myself, and a very comfortable lodging-room. There are some other persons living in the house, but my establishment is all to myself. Charles is to be my servant; I am to take possession to-morrow, and present prospects are favorable.

[*Dec. 6, 1824*]

MY DEAR LOVE — I am so happy as to have received yours of the 2d instant, and to hear of the health and happiness of you all.

For two days I have been busy in getting into my new lodgings; and by to-morrow's eve hope to have all things in order. I am a good deal like Robinson Crusoe; I have an outer room, and an inner one for retreat, and a man Friday; and beside Friday, am quite alone.

Thus far every thing looks well. The keepers of the house seem to be very obliging, neat, good people; and for convenience of work and business, I have never been better off here. I am sorry to find that my books have suffered much. They look as if they had all been tumbled into the cellar together. However, I hope in a day or two to get the mould off, though the scratches and bruises are likely to remain.

I shall write Julia soon. I hope Edward will not suffer me much longer to languish for a letter from his pen. A single one of his delicate and delightful scrolls would give me pleasure.

Adieu, my dear Grace, give my love "to all the house."

On December 9 Webster left Washington with Mr. and Mrs. George Ticknor of Boston on a visit to Presidents Jefferson and Madison. The trip was described as follows by Mr. Ticknor.

"Early in the autumn of 1824, I was one day dining with Mr. Webster at his own house, and talked about passing some time in Washington the next winter, as I had often done before. I told him that Mr. Jefferson had invited me to meet General Lafayette at Monticello, but that I did not think I should be able to do it. I

thought, however, that, in the event of my going to Washington, I should endeavor, as Mrs. Ticknor would be with me, to take her to Mr. Jefferson's. He said he should like to be of the party. I replied that if he were in earnest, and could afford the time for it, I could easily arrange matters so that it would be agreeable for him to go. He held out his hand and said, 'It is a bargain, if you say so.'

"In consequence of this conversation, I wrote to Mr. Jefferson, intimating that Mr. Webster might visit Virginia with us. He answered immediately, under date of Nov. 8th: 'Whether Mr. Webster comes with you, or alone as suits himself, he will be a welcome guest. His character, his talents and principles, entitle him to favor and respect of all his fellow-citizens, and have long ago possessed him of mine.'

"We left Washington on the 9th day of Dec., and went by steamboat to Fredericksburg Landing. At Fredericksburg, a friend had made all the arrangements necessary for the journey, and we set off the next morning in a carriage and four horses and a gig, all very slovenly, after the Virginia fashion. The roads were very bad. The landlord of the house where we dined dropped his knife and fork with astonishment, as he was carving a very nice turkey, when he understood that he was talking with Mr. Webster of Massachusetts; but he was nothing daunted, and they had a great argument upon the question of internal improvement, the Virginian confessing that if the power were not in the Constitution, he wished it was. We were to pass the night at a tavern kept by Dr. Tyrrel, but the days were short and the roads detestable, and it was long after dark before we reached our destination. Mr. Webster was very amusing, telling stories to keep our spirits up, singing scraps of old songs, and making merry like a boy. Our accommodations for the night were bad enough, but before we went to bed we prepared a note for Mr. Madison, which was to be dispatched the next morning at daylight, and informed him of our intended visit, for which President Monroe had prepared him. At Orange Court-House, five miles from Dr. Tyrrel's, we met our messenger, who brought us a kind welcome

from Mr. Madison, and who was accompanied by Mr. Madison's coachman, whom he had sent to show us the way — a needful provi- dence, where proper roads were none and landmarks very few.

"We were very hospitably received. Mr. Madison and Mr. Web- ster were old acquaintances, and evidently well pleased to see each other again. Mr. Madison talked well, and laid himself out to be agreeable to Mr. Webster. After a long and pleasant dinner, as we were going back to the saloon, Mr. Webster said to me, in an under- tone, 'Stare hic'; for he was afraid I might say something of going away the next day; but I had no such intention. We did not talk that evening very late, for we were tired, and late hours were evi- dently not the habit of the family. The next morning (Sunday), after breakfast, Mr. Webster and I, accompanied by Mr. Todd, took a ride on horseback of eight or ten miles. When we had passed beyond the limits of Mr. Madison's domain, the country looked pretty cheerless. We rode through woods and across fields, Mr. Web- ster making himself merry as he had the day before with wondering where 'Phil Barbour's constituents could be,' for this was Mr. Philip Barbour's district. Before we returned, however, we made a visit to Mrs. Barbour, to whom Mr. Webster gave an account of her hus- band, whom he had left in Washington, which visibly interested her. The dinner that day was as agreeable as the one the day before. Mr. Madison told many stories with much grace and effect. Mr. Webster was much interested in them, especially in those that had a political cast; for, though every thing of a party nature was avoided between persons whose opinions were so opposite, yet both were too much interested in the country and its history not to talk about its affairs. After we returned to Washington, Mr. Webster told me that he had been very much impressed by Mr. Madison's conversation, and that it had fully confirmed him in an opinion he had for some time entertained, that Mr. Madison was the wisest of our Presidents, except Washington.'

"We spent two days at Mr. Madison's, and then went to Mr. Jef- ferson's, which, though only thirty-two miles off, proved a journey of

more than one day. At Charlottesville, before we went up to Monti-
cello, Mr. Webster received a letter which changed his appearance
and manner the moment he had read it. It was from Mrs. Webster,
and gave him bad news of his youngest child, little Charles, who was
thought ill, but not dangerously so. The change was the more ap-
parent from his having previously been so gay. Only the evening
before, at Mrs. Clarke's tavern, he had said, 'that without intending
any compliment to his companions, he would say that he had not
felt so free from care and anxious thought, as he did then, for five
years.'

"We remained at Monticello four or five days, detained one day
beyond our purpose by rains and the consequent swelling of the
streams, which made travelling difficult in a country where bridges
are rare. Mr. Jefferson had regular habits and fixed hours for every
thing; but he was very attentive to Mr. Webster, and plainly liked
to talk with him. Mr. Webster, on his part, was very respectful to
Mr. Jefferson, and led him constantly to converse upon the doings of
the old Congress and the period of the Revolution, on both which
topics Mr. Jefferson was interesting and instructive. Mr. Webster
enjoyed these conversations very much, and spoke of them afterward
with great satisfaction.

"One day, after dinner, Mr. Webster told a story of himself, which
was characteristic of him, and amused Mr. Jefferson very much. Mr.
Jefferson had remarked that 'men not infrequently obtained more
credit for readiness in command of their knowledge, and indeed
for its amount, than they deserved.' He said it had happened to
himself. Mr. Webster replied that he supposed it had happened to
most men, and especially to lawyers. He said that, soon after going
to Portsmouth as a young lawyer, a blacksmith brought him a case
under a will; he was unable to give him a decided answer, and de-
sired him to call again. Having little to do, he went to work upon
the case, and found it a difficult one. He went through all the books
in his own little collection, that could give him any light, and then
borrowed what he could find relating to the point in question, in the

libraries of Mr. Jeremiah Mason, and of Mr. Peyton R. Freeman, a curious black-letter lawyer in Portsmouth. His client called for an opinion, but he was unable to give him one — he had only got far enough into the matter to ascertain that the blacksmith's bequest was either a contingent remainder or an executory devise. He sent to Boston and bought Fearne's Essay on those two subjects, and other books, all together costing him fifty dollars. At last, after a month's hard work, and making out a very elaborate brief, he gave an opinion favorable to his client's claim, argued the case, won it, and received a fee of fifteen dollars; all that the amount in controversy would warrant him to charge.

"Years passed by, and the blacksmith and his case had almost passed away also from his memory. At length, being in New York on his way to Washington, Mr. Aaron Burr sent him a note, saying that he wished to consult him on a matter of some consequence. Mr. Webster gave him an appointment, and, when Mr. Burr began to explain his case to him, he said that he knew in a moment that it was his blacksmith's case over again. He, however, heard Mr. Burr quietly through, and then with the blacksmith's brief full in his mind, began to reply. He cited a series of cases bearing on the point, and going back, if I remember rightly, to a leading one in the time of Charles II. Mr. Burr listened to him for some time, and then interrupted him somewhat suddenly, by asking him whether he had been consulted in the case before. 'He evidently suspected,' said Mr. Webster, 'that I must have been of counsel to the other side. I assured him that I did not know there was such a case or such parties in the world until he explained it to me.' Mr. Webster said that he subsequently gave Mr. Burr a written opinion on his case, and made him pay enough for it to cover all his work for the blacksmith and something moreover for Mr. Burr's suspicion that he had been of counsel for the opposite party. He added, 'Mr. Burr, no doubt, thought me a much more learned lawyer than I was, and, under the circumstances of the case, I did not think it worthwhile to disabuse him of his good opinion of me.'

VISIT TO MADISON AND JEFFERSON

"*Mr. Jefferson, though then eighty-one years old, rode constantly on horseback in fine weather. One day we rode with him to Charlottesville, about four miles, to visit the buildings of his university, which had not yet gone into operation, but was soon to be opened. It was the last great interest of his life, and Mr. Webster took much pleasure in witnessing the beginning of the enterprise. He did not, however, fail to discover some of the defects of the system; he especially suggested to Mr. Jefferson that a project he had introduced into his laws for the university, to train the scholars in military exercises with guns made wholly of wood, because he did not think it safe to trust them with the usual fire-arms, would fail from the ridicule of the young men. It proved so.*

"*Mr. Webster was impatient of our detention by the weather. He was very anxious to get news of his sick child, and could not hope for any letters till he should reach Washington. He wanted also to know what was going on in Congress; but Mr. Jefferson took no newspaper but the* Richmond Enquirer. *With the first fine weather, therefore, we descended the mountain. Several of the young gentlemen of the family accompanied us. On the banks of the Rivanna we found many wagons waiting to be ferried over; the stream was much swollen, and the passage difficult. Many had their turn before us, and, among the rest, a drove of pigs from Kentucky. The ferryman had but one person to assist him — an inefficient slave — they were both much exhausted, having been at work since daybreak. While we were crossing, Mr. Webster, in his usual cheerful manner, began to talk to the ferryman, who found it very difficult to stem the sudden turbulence of the stream. 'You find it hard work enough this morning, I think,' said Mr. Webster. 'Yes, sir,' said the boatman, 'it puts a man up to all he knows, I assure you.' An apt phrase, which amused Mr. Webster very much at the time, which he was constantly using on all occasions through the rest of the journey, and which he often introduced in speaking and writing in after-years. In this way it has become a common phrase in our part of the country, where few persons know its origin.*"

SPEAK FOR YOURSELF, DANIEL

On his return to Washington, just before Christmas, 1824, Webster received word from his brother-in-law, William Paige, that Charles had died on December 18. The following letters are from Mrs. Webster:

[Dec. 28, 1824]

I have a great desire to write to you, my beloved husband, but I doubt if I can write legibly, as I can hold my pen but in my fingers.* I have just received your letter in answer to William, which told you that dear little Charley was no more. I have dreaded the hour that should destroy your hopes, but hope you will not let this event afflict you too much, and that we both shall be able to resign him without a murmur, happy in the reflection that he has returned to his Heavenly Father pure as I received him. It was an inexpressible consolation to me, when I contemplated him in his sickness, that he had not one regret for the past, nor one dread for the future; he was patient as a lamb during all his suffering, and they were at last so great, I was happy when they were ended.

[Jan. 22, 1825]

I was sitting alone in my chamber reflecting on the brief life of our sainted little boy, when your letter came enclosing those lines of yours, which to a "mother's eye" are precious.

Farewell, my beloved husband! I have not time to write more, only to say I regret you have lost the pleasure of Mr. and Mrs. Ticknor's society, which you so much need.

[Excerpt from lines on the death of his son Charles.]

> The staff, on which my years should lean,
> Is broken, ere those years come o'er me;

---

* Mrs. Webster had received an injury on the thumb of the right hand.

My funeral rites thou shoulds't have seen,
But thou art in the tomb before me.

Thou rear'st to me no filial stone,
No parent's grave with tears beholdest;
Thou art my ancestor, my son!
And stand'st in Heaven's account the oldest.

[*On December 29, 1824, Webster had written to Ezekiel:*]

I have not heard from you for a long time, nor had much leisure to write since my return from Virginia. The information which has reached me from home must have reached you sooner. I think of this loss with great grief; but I think also that you lost all your little boys; and I hope to sustain myself with the consciousness that my blessings are still much more numerous than my afflictions. I wish you would sometimes write to my wife, it would give her great pleasure, as I think her affection for you is pretty much her first feeling out of her own family.

On Saturday, January 15, 1825, the Ticknors had left Washington for Baltimore, and Webster wrote:

[*To George Ticknor, Jan. 16, 1825*]

I find that you are really gone; and if I could tell you how sorry I am, I would. I passed the house yesterday, and gave a look to the windows, but saw no inviting faces. To-day I have been at home, except an hour passed with Mr. Tazewell. The general *
has been to see me, and we have had a good long talk. I believe he hopes to catch a sight of your party at Baltimore.

If my constituents accuse me of negligence and inattention this session, I shall lay it all off on Mrs. Ticknor. She had no right, I shall say, to be so agreeable as to draw my attention from the

* General Lafayette.

113

weighty affairs of state while she was here, and to create depression, or a kind of I-am-not-quite-ready-to-go-to-work feeling by her departure. What will State Street say to it, think you, if its affairs should be neglected, although Shakespeare be ever so well read, or all the versions of Sir John Moore's burial revised and corrected?

Please to assure her that I shall put it to her account, if there should happen any dissatisfactions or disaffections hereafter — any mutterings of the "vital commoners," or "petty inland spirits."

[To Mrs. Ticknor, Jan. 17, 1825]

Mr. Wallenstein has given me, my dear Mrs. Ticknor, your very kind note, and I cannot well tell you how much it has gratified my feelings. You have inferred nothing, my dear lady, and can infer nothing, of my regard and affection for yourself and your husband, more than the truth, nor equal to the truth. And I beg you to believe that there are none in the world whose regard and kind feelings I wish more to cultivate and secure.

Our six weeks' acquaintance has been to me a mixture of high enjoyment and severe suffering. The former I owe, mainly, to you and Mr. Ticknor; the last I take, and would wish to bear, as a common visitation of a kind Providence. Yet I have felt it more than might have been expected, and my spirits recover slowly. I am sure that Mrs. Webster and yourself are congenial and assimilated spirits, and that she will cultivate your acquaintance with delight. Let us hope that circumstances may favor an habitual intercourse. At any rate, be assured that the principle of regard and affection will live in my heart.

I write this in the House, while Mr. Clay is speaking on the Cumberland Road. The ladies are all present, inside the House. I have not reviewed them; for I am sure there is none of them that I have lately seen or know, unless it may be Mrs. (A. H.) Everett. I see Wallenstein among them, as becomes a diplomatist. Mr. Clay speaks well. I wish you were here to hear him. The highest enjoyment, almost, which I have in life, is in hearing an able argument or speech. The development of mind, in those modes, is delightful. In books, we see the result of thought and of fancy. In the living speaker, we see the thought itself, as it rises in the speaker's own mind. And his countenance often indicates a perception before it gets upon his tongue. I have been charmed by observing this operation of minds which are truly great and vigorous; so that I sometimes am as much moved, as in reading a part of Milton and Shakespeare, by a striking and able argument, although on the dryest subject.

[*To George Ticknor, Jan. 25, 1825*]

I have been to dine with Mr. Calhoun. He talked to me, among other things, of your good fortune in picking up a companion on the road of life. I did not think that a subject on which I was bound to quarrel with a Secretary of War, whatever I might think of the matter. Mr. Calhoun is a true man.

[*To Mrs. Ticknor, Feb. 4, 1825. From the House of Representatives*]

McDuffie is making a very warm speech, I hardly know why or wherefore; but it relates to the rules of proceeding in electing a President next week, and he, being a pretty ardent Jackson man, seems inclined to make a kind of Jackson speech. I told Mr. Wallenstein to tell you that I should write you during the first long speech — and, depend upon it, the act of *writing* is, in such cases or most of them, less onerous than the act of *listening*. The Hall of Congress is an admirable situation to cultivate the powers of an organ which has been generally too much neglected in its education; I mean the *ear*. Now I have so disciplined this little member that, on being informed that I am not particularly concerned to know what is said, and requested to "bring me no more reports," it very faithfully performs its duty, and leaves me quite at ease to pursue any vocation I may choose. The "enclosed petty spirits" are left entirely undisturbed by what prevails without. This is an admirable improvement on the old maxim, "Hear with both ears." I hear with *neither*.

Times have a good deal changed with me, my dear lady, since your departure. The business of Congress has become more urgent; the event draws near, the session is wearing off. I begin to see *home* at the end of no long prospect, and all these things create a little activity and bustle, which serve, in some poor measure, to fill up such portions of time as I usually passed in your house, while you remained here.

In the latter part of February 1825 John Randolph of Roanoke again challenged Webster to a duel. At the preceding session of Congress they had served together on a committee to investigate charges brought against Secretary of the Treasury Crawford. Randolph had gone abroad in May, before the committee had completed its work, but in an open letter to his constituents had claimed credit for Crawford's exoneration. The other members of the committee, including Webster, publicly denied the accuracy of Randolph's letter, and he had been brooding over it as a reflection on his veracity.

William Plumer, Jr., Congressman from New Hampshire and friend of Webster, tells the story of the challenge:

"Mr. Randolph after brooding in silence for nearly a year, over the castigation given him by Webster, McArthur, and other members of the committee, in consequence of his letter respecting Crawford, sent Webster a challenge to fight a duel with him. I saw it delivered by Col. Benton of the Senate, in the House of Representatives while the House was in session. What notice of it Mr. Webster will take I do not know. Webster was sitting on a sofa back of the members' seats, when Benton came in, and delivered him with some formality a letter, which Webster took and read. He

then very deliberately folded it up; paused a moment, opened and read it again, as if doubtful of its import. Passing his hands slowly over his ample forehead, he resumed at once his usual looks, and turning to Benton gave him an answer, which I was too far off to hear. Benton bowed gravely, and passed on. I do not know that any body else observed what was passing. Webster sat a few moments as if absorbed in thought; and then went to his seat. I turned to Rankin of Mississippi, who sat next to me, and told him what had occurred, and my suspicion that a challenge had been given. He looked a moment at Webster and then said, no, he does not look as if anything unusual had occurred. He is either untouched or very cool.

"An hour or two later while we were at dinner Colonel McKim of Alabama, a friend of Mr. Webster, came in and took out McArthur, who showed by his looks, when he came back, that something unusual had happened. The next morning, while we were sitting alone together in the Committee Room, I asked Mr. Webster what answer he had given to Randolph's challenge. He started and said 'What do you know about it?' I told him what I had seen and what I suspected. He said 'You are right,' and taking two pages out of his hat, said 'I will show you the challenge and the answer I have drawn up, but not yet sent.' The letter of Randolph demanded satisfaction for words uttered by Webster impeaching his veracity. The answer of Webster was that whatever he had said, had been said by him in the House in the discharge of his duties as a Member, for which he could not be made, anywhere else, responsible; but that if convinced he had said what was false he would readily make any reasonable satisfaction. The challenge was I believe afterward withdrawn by Randolph before any answer was given to it.

"Randolph got no credit by his conduct in this affair. It was generally said that he should have challenged McArthur, who had said severer things of him than any body else, and who as a military man it was supposed would fight, and that he should not have

turned round upon Webster, a man of peace, who came from a part of the country where duelling was not justified by public opinion."

On June 17 of this year Webster made another of his great orations, at the laying of the corner stone for the Bunker Hill Monument. It was the fiftieth anniversary of the battle, and General Lafayette was on hand to greet the surviving veterans. One of the Quincy sisters described the occasion in her diary:

"Friday, June 17, 1825. This eventful day was welcomed by the roaring of cannon, which woke us at early dawn. The whole city was soon in motion. Carriages were driving at a tremendous rate; the troops were assembling on the Common; and the streets were thronged by multitudes, hurrying to and fro. Great apprehensions were yesterday entertained with regard to the weather; but every one said, 'It must be a fair day on the 17th,' and I heard that an old man in Andover exclaimed, 'The Lord will not permit it to rain on that day.' The heavens were never more propitious. The showers of yesterday laid the dust and cooled the atmosphere, and it was indeed the perfection of weather.

"The stage for the orator was erected at the foot of the hill, and seats for the ladies extended in a semicircle on each side, forming a kind of amphitheatre. Above us, on the side of the hill, were seats for the soldiers of the Revolution and the multitudes who were to come in the procession. We found ourselves surrounded by an immense number of women, fashionable and unfashionable, high and low, rich and poor, all animated by one interest. The breezes came over the hill perfumed by the new-mown hay — such as was used to form intrenchments on the day of the battle. At length the report of the cannon announced the approach of the procession, and soon the infantry appeared on the brow of the hill.

"Just beside us were the survivors of the battle — a company of venerable old men, covered with badges and attended with the

greatest respect by the young soldiers of the present day, whose brilliant uniforms and youthful appearance formed a most striking contrast with the veterans they were supporting. Opposite were the soldiers of the Revolution, with Lafayette in the midst of them."

The diarist's brother, Josiah Quincy, had been assigned as aide de camp to General Lafayette and tried to usher him into the pavilion set aside for distinguished guests. "No," said the General; "I belong there, among the survivors of the Revolution, and there I must sit." And so he took a seat among the veterans, with no shelter from the rays of a June sun.

"Above the power of any words," said Josiah Quincy, "was the magnificent presence of Daniel Webster. No man, as Sydney Smith said, could be so great as this man looked, and now he looked his very greatest."

The pressure of the crowd was so enormous just as Webster began his oration, some of the seats and barriers gave way. There was a moment of tremendous confusion, amounting almost to panic. "It is impossible to restore order," exclaimed one of the officials. "Nothing is impossible, Sir," said Webster. "Let it be done!" And stepping to the front of the platform he called to the marshals in what Miss Quincy termed a voice of thunder. "Be silent yourselves and the people will obey!" It was as if Zeus had spoken. Almost instantly the commotion ceased.

[*The Bunker Hill oration — brief excerpts*]

This uncounted multitude before me and around me proves the feeling which the occasion has excited. These thousands of human faces, glowing with sympathy and joy, and from the impulses of a common gratitude turned reverently to heaven in this spacious temple of the firmament, proclaim that the day, the place, and the purpose of our assembling have made a deep impression on our hearts.

Human beings are composed, not of reason only, but of imagination also, and sentiment; and that is neither wasted nor misapplied which is appropriated to the purpose of giving right direction to sentiments, and opening proper springs of feeling in the heart. We come, as Americans, to mark a spot which must for ever be dear to us and our posterity. We wish that whosoever, in all coming time, shall turn his eye hither, may behold that the place is not undistinguished where the first great battle of the Revolution was fought. We wish that this structure may proclaim the magnitude and importance of that event to every class and every age.

We live in a most extraordinary age. Events so various and so important that they might crowd and distinguish centuries, are, in our times, compressed within the compass of a single life. When has it happened that history has had so much to record, in the same term of years, as since the 17th of June, 1775? Our own Revolution, which, under other circumstances, might itself have been expected to occasion a war of half a century, has been achieved; twenty-four sovereign and independent States erected; and a general government established over them, so safe, so wise, so free, so practical, that we might well wonder its establishment should have been accomplished so soon, were it not far the greater wonder that it should have been established at all. Two or three millions of people have been augmented to twelve, the great forests of the West prostrated beneath the arm of successful industry, and the dwellers on the banks of the Ohio and the Mississippi become the fellow-citizens and neighbors of those who cultivate the hills of New England. We have a commerce, that leaves no sea unexplored; navies, which take no law from superior force; revenues, adequate to all the exigencies of government, almost without taxation; and peace with all nations, founded on equal rights and mutual respect.

Yet, notwithstanding that this is but a faint abstract of the things which have happened since the day of the battle of Bunker Hill, we are but fifty years removed from it; and we now stand here to enjoy all the blessings of our own condition, and to look abroad on the brightened prospects of the world, while we still have among us some of those who were active agents in the scenes of 1775, and who are now here, from every quarter of New England, to visit once more, and under circumstances so affecting, I had almost said so overwhelming, this renowned theatre of their courage and patriotism.

Venerable men! you have come down to us from a former generation. Heaven has bounteously lengthened out your lives, that you might behold this joyous day. You are now where you stood fifty years ago, this very hour, with your brothers and your neighbors, shoulder to shoulder, in the strife for your country. Behold, how altered! The same heavens are indeed over your heads; the same ocean rolls at your feet; but all else how changed! You hear now no roar of hostile cannon, you see no mixed volumes of smoke and flame rising from burning Charlestown. The ground strowed with the dead and the dying; the impetuous charge; the steady and successful repulse; the loud call to repeated assault; the summoning of all that is manly to repeated resistance; a thousand bosoms freely and fearlessly bared in an instant to whatever of terror there may be in war and death — all these you have witnessed, but you witness them no more. All is peace. The heights of yonder metropolis, its towers and roofs, which you then saw filled with wives and children and countrymen in distress and terror, and looking with unutterable emotions for the issue of the combat, have presented you to-day with the sight of its whole happy population, come out to welcome and greet you with a universal jubilee. Yonder proud ships, by a felicity of position appropriately lying at the foot of this mount, and seeming fondly to cling around it, are not means of annoyance to you, but your country's own means of distinction and defence. All is peace; and God has granted you this sight of your country's happiness, ere you slumber in the grave. He has allowed you to behold and to partake the reward of your patriotic toils; and he has allowed us, your sons and countrymen, to meet you here, and in the name of the present generation, in the name of your country, in the name of liberty, to thank you!

The 17th of June saw the four New England Colonies standing here, side by side, to triumph or to fall together; and there was with them from that moment to the end of the war, what I hope will remain with them for ever, one cause, one country, one heart.

The battle of Bunker Hill was attended with the most important effects beyond its immediate results as a military engagement. It created at once a state of open, public war. There could now be no longer a question of proceeding against individuals, as guilty of treason or rebellion. That fearful crisis was past. The appeal lay to the sword, and the only question was, whether the spirit and the resources of the people would hold out, till the object should be accomplished.

Our history and our condition, all that is gone before us, and all that surrounds us, authorize the belief that popular governments, though subject to occasional variations, in form perhaps not always for the better, may yet, in their general character, be as durable and permanent as other systems. We know, indeed, that in our country any other is impossible. The principle of free governments adheres to the American soil. It is bedded in it, immovable as its mountains.

And let the sacred obligations which have devolved on this generation, and on us, sink deep into our hearts. Let our age be the age of improvement. In a day of peace, let us advance the arts of peace and the works of peace. Let us develop the resources of our land, call forth its powers, build up its institutions, promote all its great interests, and see whether we also, in our day and generation, may not perform something worthy to be remembered. Let us cultivate a true spirit of union and harmony. In pursuing the great objects which our condition points out to us, let us act under a settled conviction, and an habitual feeling, that these twenty-four States are one country. Let our conceptions be enlarged to the circle of our duties. Let us extend our ideas over the whole of the vast field in which we are called to act. Let our object be, *our country, our whole country, and nothing but our country*. And, by the blessing of God, may that country itself become a vast and splendid monument, not of oppression and terror, but of Wisdom, of Peace, and of Liberty, upon which the world may gaze with admiration for ever!

It is said that Webster spoke to an audience of over 20,000, yet even without amplification his voice was audible. George Ticknor Curtis (nephew of George Ticknor) says that as a boy "I was present in the outskirts of that vast audience and well remember that Mr. Webster's clarion voice was distinctly heard at the spot where I stood."

Webster's son Fletcher also had special reason to remember the Bunker Hill oration. He was present during its gestation, which he describes as follows:

"The Mashpee River flows from a large lake, called Wakeby Pond, in Barnstable County, into the ocean on the southeast coast of Massachusetts. It is a short and rapid stream, running in a deep valley, or rather ravine, with high, precipitous sides, covered with a thick growth of small pines and various kinds of brushwoods and shrubs.

"The only method of fishing it is by wading along the middle, and throwing under the banks on either side. It was while middle-deep in this stream that Mr. Webster composed a great portion of his first Bunker Hill address. I followed him along the stream, fishing the holes and bends which he left for me; but, after a while, I began to notice that he was not so attentive to his sport or so earnest as usual.

"He would let his line run carelessly down the stream, or hold his rod still while his hook was not even touching the water, and seemed, indeed, quite abstracted and uninterested in his amusement.

"This, of course, caused me a good deal of wonder, and, after calling his attention once or twice to his hook hanging on a twig, or caught in the long grass of the river, and finding that, after a moment's attention, he relapsed into indifference, I quietly walked up near him and watched. He seemed to be gazing at the overhanging trees, and presently advancing one foot, and extending his right hand, he commenced to speak: 'Venerable men . . .'"

Charles Lanman, Webster's private secretary, adds another anecdote relating to the same period of composition. Webster, off deep-sea fishing, which he loved almost as much as trout fishing, was pondering his welcome to Lafayette when he hooked a cod. "Welcome! All hail! And thrice welcome, citizen of two hemispheres," he declaimed, as he pulled the cod out of the water.

The Bunker Hill celebration did not cease with the public speaking. "There was never a more brilliant and interesting private party given in Boston," says Josiah Quincy, in his first-hand account of the festivities, "than the reception by Mr. and Mrs. Daniel Webster on the evening of the memorable June 17, 1825. Colonel Israel Thorndike, the neighbor of Mr. Webster, had caused a passage to be cut through the brick walls which separated their houses. This doubled the accommodation for guests, by connecting another handsome establishment with that of the host of the evening. Summer Street was as light as day, the houses were brilliantly illuminated, and a fine band was stationed a few yards from Mr. Webster's door. The rooms were filled with strangers from all parts of the country.

"Mr. and Mrs. Webster received the compliments of the hour with great dignity and simplicity. The latter seemed highly to enjoy the success and distinction of her husband, but showed not the slightest symptom of vanity or elation. Indeed, among the most interesting spectacles of the evening was the unassuming serenity of the hosts in the midst of all the honor and congratula-

tions which surrounded them. In alluding to the scene of the morning, Mr. Webster said:

" 'I never desire to behold again the awful spectacle of so many human faces all turned towards me.'

"Colonel Thorndike occupied the somewhat peculiar position of guest in his own house. He was a fine looking person, reputed to be the richest man in New England, and in this capacity was the object of much interest and attention. He was a great shipowner, and everything he touched seemed to succeed.

"Wealth was quite as attractive in those days as it is at present, and it was deemed a happy circumstance that the intellect of the community in one of these adjoining houses should be backed by its purse in the other."

VIII

1825–1827

NIAGARA FALLS — ADAMS–JEFFERSON ORATION — ELECTION TO SENATE

A week after the Bunker Hill Oration, Webster and Justice Story took their wives and Eliza Buckminster on a vacation trip to Niagara Falls, traveling principally by horse-drawn coach. Justice Story described the trip in detail in letters to his brother-in-law, William Fettyplace:

"Our party, consisting of Mr. and Mrs. Webster, Miss Buckminster, Mrs. Story and myself, left Boston on Friday, June 24, at nine o'clock in the morning. The day was delightful, and we enjoyed it in a high degree. We dined at Framingham, and arrived at an early hour at Worcester, where we passed the night. In the evening Mr. Webster and myself called on Governor Lincoln. On the next day we reached Northampton a little after sunset. Here we remained all Sunday. Mr. Gannett, of Boston, preached in the new Unitarian Society, and we went to attend the service both morning and afternoon. After this was over, Mr. Webster and myself went over the river and ascended Mount Holyoke, which is about one thousand feet high; and round its feet the Connecticut flows in silent beauty. The prospect from the height is delightful."

With stops for visits and views the party proceeded westward, attending a dinner with General Lafayette in Albany. "A little further," writes Justice Story, "we took our passage in the canal boat Lady Adams and passed up the Great Western Canal about nine miles, crossing the Mohawk on a fine aqueduct built over the river below us, twenty or thirty feet. After travelling about two hours we stopped for a short time alongside of a small stationary canal boat, which we found was the kitchen where our dinner was cooked. This was a great convenience to us all, as we avoided the heat and smell of the cooking, and we enjoyed a good dinner without any doubtful prognostications.

"At Canajoharie we took the canal boat for Utica. These packet boats are almost thirty-five feet long, with a single deck or story, in which there are two cabins, one for ladies, and the other for gentlemen. They are drawn by three horses attached to the boat by a long rope, and the largest horse is ridden by a driver who regulates the whole, and keeps them on a brisk walk of about four miles an hour. Except when you pass a lock, not the slightest motion is felt in the boat, though the rapidity with which the surrounding objects pass by you is very apt at first to make you a little dizzy.

"On Thursday, July 7, we made an excursion to Trenton Falls, which are about fourteen miles north of Utica, on West Canada Creek. The path up the stream, which you are to pass, is nothing but a narrow projection of the rocky bank, in some places not a foot in width. A single false step and you are precipitated into the gulf below. If you become dizzy you are gone. Here and there chains of iron are fastened into the rock to assist you in holding on, but after all the passage is one that presents difficulties which require some courage to overcome. Mr. Webster at first refused to go up the stream, and it was not until the latter part of the day that he and his wife went down the banks and visited the principal cascade."

Other Story tidbits:

"I find clergymen are travelling in all directions at this season."

"You have no notion how difficult it is to find a Boston newspaper anywhere out of Massachusetts; we are not so important abroad as we imagine ourselves to be."

SPEAK FOR YOURSELF, DANIEL

"What with walking and riding and looking about, I am so fatigued that I can hardly hold a pen."

The party arrived at Niagara Falls on July 13 and spent the next three days marveling. By this time, Webster, who liked to claim that he thoroughly disliked writing, was so stimulated, either by the beauty of the Falls or by Justice Story's journalistic example, that on July 15 he composed a monumental letter to Mrs. George Blake, from which the following are excerpts:

It is one of my most agreeable duties, before leaving this place, to write to you, to tell you how much we have admired the great spectacle here, and how sincerely we have lamented every hour that you were not with us, to partake and increase our pleasure. This is the third day of our being here; the weather has been uniformly fine, and we have seen the Falls under all advantages. You have of course read many accounts of this Fall, to which no account can do justice; and although I am disposed to say something on the subject, I expect no better success than others who have undertaken the description.

From Table Rock, we have what is generally thought the best view of the whole Falls. Fronting us is the American Fall, and the little Cascade; further to the right Goat Island, and the commencement by it of the British Fall; and further to our right is the great circular Fall, or Horseshoe, which will hardly allow the eyes to be withdrawn long enough to look at any thing else. You may stand by the water just where it falls off, and if your head does not swim, you may proceed to the brink of Table Rock, and look over into the gulf beneath. This is all foam, and froth, and spray. As you stand here, it looks as if all the water of the globe was collected round this circle, and pouring down here into the centre of the earth. As we stood to-day at noon, on the projecting point of Table Rock, we looked over into this abyss, and far beneath our feet, arched over this tremendous aggregate of water, foam, and vapor, we saw a perfect and radiant rainbow. This ornament of heaven does not seem out of place, in being half-way up the sheet of the glorious cataract.

We went this afternoon a little lower down the river than the upper staircase, almost indeed down to the ferry, and getting out on a rock, in the edge of the river, we thought the view of the whole Falls the best we had obtained. If, at the bottom of the staircase, instead of descending further, we choose to turn to the right, and go up the stream, keeping close at the foot of the Table Rock, or the perpendicular bank, we soon get to the foot of the Fall, and approach the edge of the falling mass. It is easy to go in behind, for a little distance, between the falling water and the rock over which it is precipitated; this cannot be done, however, without being entirely wet. From within this cavern there issues a wind, occasionally very strong, and bringing with it such showers and torrents of spray, that we are soon as wet as if we had come over the Falls with the water. As near to the Fall in this place as you can well come, is perhaps the spot on which the mind is most deeply impressed with the whole scene. Over our heads hangs a fearful rock, projecting out like an unsupported piazza. Before us is a hurly-burly of waters, too deep to be fathomed, too irregular to be described, shrouded in too much mist to be clearly seen. Water, vapor, foam, and the atmosphere, are all mixed up together, in sublime confusion. By our side, down comes this world of green and white waters, and pours into the invisible abyss. A steady, unvarying, low-toned roar, thunders incessantly upon our ears; as we look up, we think some sudden disaster has opened the seas, and that all their floods are coming down upon us at once; but we soon recollect, that what we see is not a sudden or violent exhibition, but the permanent and uniform character of the object which we contemplate. There, the grand spectacle has stood, for centuries, from the creation even, as far as we know, without change. From the beginning, it has shaken, as it now does, the earth and the air; and its unvarying thunder existed before there were human ears to hear it.

On July 16 he wrote to James William Paige, Mrs. Webster's brother and his own devoted friend:

To-day we have made a ride down the river two or three miles, to a place called the "Whirlpool." It is a fearful eddy; we look upon it from a height, I suppose, of two hundred and fifty feet. No man can approach it; the whole river is in a whirl. It is said that trees and logs, getting in there, will sometimes be carried round for days and weeks before they get out of the eddy. They are tossed about in all directions, sometimes standing up perpendicularly, and going down, and reappearing. I regretted that I had not a glass, that I might better have examined this great boiling caldron. Just below this is another place, called the "Devil's Hole." It is a kind of cut, made into the bank, on this side. In the French war, a party of English were stationed on the bank here to guard the portage round the Falls; they were surprised by a party of French and Indians, all surrounded, and pushed off. Of course they were all killed, except one drummer; he caught by his belt, upon some limb of a tree, running out from the bank, or as some say, fell on his drum. At any rate he survived the fall, and, as I understand, was living in Canada ten years ago.

But enough of Niagara and story-telling. It has taken us so long a time to get here, and must take us so much to get home, that I despair of Canada. I fancy we shall go to Rochester, Utica, Lake George, Burlington, home; but this is only my private opinion. We shall set off East to-morrow, and shall soon determine our course.

P. S. I am going to try to wet a line at the foot of the Falls.

Webster had written Mrs. Blake that "although our eyes are not satisfied with seeing, yet some of us complain of weary limbs, from walking about so much, and going down and climbing up the banks so often."

Justice Story put it somewhat differently in a later letter to his friend J. Evelyn Denison, M. P., in England:

"Mr. Webster and I, with our wives, visited Niagara during this summer. We were absent about six weeks, and returned delighted with our journey. Mr. Webster has a giant's constitution, and can bear every sort of fatigue; but I was a good deal overcome and exhausted, and returned in very indifferent health."

What must the Justice have felt when he received a letter from Webster saying: "My health is good, never better, not having worked off the strength obtained at Niagara and at Sandwich."

Webster's sense of physical well-being also showed itself in other ways. On September 28, 1825, he wrote Henry Clay, then Secretary of State under President John Quincy Adams:

You must allow me to admonish you to take care of your health. Knowing the ardor and intensity with which you may probably apply yourself to the duties of your place, I fear very much you may overwork yourself. Somebody (was it not an Austrian minister?) on being asked how he could get through so much business, replied that he did it by repudiating two false maxims which had obtained currency among men; that for his part he never did any thing to-day which he could put off till to-morrow; nor any thing himself which he could get another to do for him.

[*On Nov. 17, 1825, he wrote Dr. John C. Warren:*]

I am highly pleased with the idea of a gymnasium; it is a subject which has often occupied my thoughts, and in relation to which it has appeared to me that the fashion of the times needs to be changed. Those who have the charge of education seem sometimes to forget that the body is a part of the man. The number of young men who leave our colleges, emulous indeed, and learned, but with pale faces and narrow chests, is truly alarming. The common rustic amusements hung about our literary institutions for a long time; but they at length seem to have been entirely abandoned, and nothing, at least nothing useful, has succeeded them. If it be desirable that there should be cultivated intellect, it is equally so, as far as this world is concerned, that there should be also a sound body to hold it in.

He also took time to bestow some avuncular advice on Charles B. Haddock, the son of his sister Abigail. Haddock graduated from Dartmouth in 1816 with high honors, and for most of his life taught there. Judging from his letters, he took himself very seriously, perhaps too much so. In any event he liked to court the advice of his famous uncle, and thereby afforded Webster one of the great boons of middle age, the opportunity to pontificate. For example:

[Letters to Haddock: Oct. 13, 1825]

We hear much of your Commencement oration. When are we to see it? Print it by all means; especially if it be half so good as report makes it. The tendencies of a college life are doubtless drowsy; and you deserve therefore the more praise for showing signs of life. It is not always that a pulsation manifests itself in those sons of leisure, who, having no absolute engagements for the future, refer to the blank of to-morrow whatever might have made to-day something better than a blank.

[Dec. 23, 1824]

This is an age of free, powerful, and intense thinking, rather than an age of fine writing. The wits of Anne's time were fit to polish the age, perhaps more than to advance it in positive acquirement.

If I have leisure, I will sometime give you my thoughts on this matter at large, but I am so poor a manager of the great treasure, time, that I never have on hand any stock to disburse.

[*Oct. 14, 1826*]

In regard to the moral character generally of our ancestors, the settlers of New England, my opinion is that they possessed all the Christian virtues but charity; and they seem never to have doubted that they possessed that also. And nobody could accuse their system or their practice but of one vice, and that was religious hypocrisy, of which they had an infusion without ever being sensible of it.

It necessarily resulted from that disposition which they cherished, of subjecting men's external conduct, in all particulars, to the influence and government of express rule and precept, either of church or state. That always makes hypocrites and formalists — it leads men to rely on mint and cummin. A man thought it an act of merit, if we may take the blue laws of Connecticut for authority, not to walk within ten feet of his wife in their way to church; as some parents, nowadays, think it a merit to restrain their daughters from a village dance; one is quite as sensible and as much to do with religion as the other. Indeed, it is the universal tendency of strong religious excitement, a tendency of our infirm nature, growing out of our weaknesses and our vices, to run into observances, and make a strong merit of external acts. Our excellent ancestors did not escape the influence of this propensity; but they had so many high and pure virtues, that this spot should not give offence. They were a wonderful people. This very failing, of which I have spoken, leaned so much on the virtues of decision, sense of duty, and the feeling that will bear no compromise with what it thinks wrong, that I forgive it to them.

In the late autumn of 1825 Webster returned to Washington for the 19th Congress, accompanied by Mrs. Webster and their three

133

children, Fletcher, Julia and Edward. From the standpoint of accomplishment it was a dull session; "a talking winter," Webster called it in a later letter to Denison in London. But they found the White House improved by the occupancy of a New Englander, as may be seen from Webster's letters to Ticknor:

[*Jan. 8, 1826*]

The drawing-room is agreed by all to have received great improvement. When I was there it was absolutely warm, within a very few degrees, to the point of comfort. I even saw gentlemen walking in the great hall of entrance, with apparent impunity, without their great-coats on! (This is for Mrs. Ticknor.) We have even dined at the White House — a very good dinner and a very good time. But not liking large dinner-parties at all, I think they are hardly better for having ladies. It is a solemn time, when we are at a dinner-table, where numbers prevent us from being social, and politeness forbids us to be noisy. On the whole, however, the domestic presidential arrangements are approved.

[*Mar. 1, 1826*]

Wallenstein is mourning according to law, and as well and happy as a man can be who belongs to an empire that has so suddenly lost a pretty good head and got another rather doubtful one. I speak, however, of those only in this empire whose honors, or whose bread, depend on this same head of the empire; for, as to the masses, I suppose they care not whose head is lost, so it be not their own. When quite a boy I remember reading some verses of a song, which had some sense though not much poetry. I have looked for them often since in vain. Their moral is as applicable to emperors as others, more striking of course in the case of the great than of the small. I can recall only these few doggerel lines:

ADAMS-JEFFERSON ORATION

When you and I are dead and gone,
This busy world will still jog on,
And laugh and sing, and be as hearty,
As if we still were of the party.

[Letter to Story, May 8, 1826]

My plan is to leave here on the 15th; to send the horses along three or four days earlier, so as to proceed rapidly ourselves to New York. I shall hardly be more than seven or eight days going home; so that I intend to be in your court the second week of its sitting.

From the first day of December, I have not been an inch from my place till Saturday, when I rode a few miles on horseback. I need motion and air more than a court.

Not long after Webster's return to Boston there occurred one of the most astounding coincidences in history. On July 4, 1826, on the fiftieth anniversary of the Declaration of Independence, its two principal proponents, John Adams and Thomas Jefferson, died within a few hours of each other. Such an event called for more than an ordinary memorial, and almost by acclamation Boston turned to Webster for a commemorative address.

This was set for August 2 at Faneuil Hall, leaving little time for preparation. But Webster was at his best under pressure. Moreover, he had the advantage of recent personal contact with both his subjects. He had been a guest of Mr. Jefferson at Monticello in December 1824, and he had been a frequent visitor at Mr. Adams' home, having been in the habit, in passing through Quincy during the later years of Mr. Adams' life, to call upon him to pay his respects.

In June, he told his friend Peter Harvey, he had called upon Mr. Adams late one day. "It was a hot afternoon," he said, and "he found the President lying on the sofa, while some female relative was cooling his brow by fanning him. He went up to the sofa, and said: 'I hope the President is well to-day.' 'No,' replied Mr. Adams. 'I don't know, Mr. Webster; I have lived in this old and frail tenement a great many years; it is very much dilapidated; and, from all that I can learn, my landlord doesn't intend to repair it.' "

George Ticknor gives us a description of the address.

"When Mr. Webster was preparing his discourse in commemoration of Adams and Jefferson, he talked with me much about it. He showed me no part of it while he was writing it, but, when he considered it as finished, he read me the whole. Of course, I had nothing but gratification to express. The very day, however, before he was to deliver it, he sent for me early in the forenoon to come to his house, in Summer Street.

"He was walking up and down his room when I went in, a good deal excited, and at once proceeded somewhat abruptly to repeat the two speeches attributed to an opponent of the Declaration of Independence and to Mr. Adams in reply to him. He said that he had just written them, and that he was quite uncertain whether they were the best or the worst part of the discourse. I had no doubt about the matter. I told him that I did not know whether they were better than the description of eloquence which preceded them or not, but that there was certainly nothing else equal to them in the whole of it.

"The next day, the 2d of August, the weather was fine, and the concourse to hear him immense. It was the first time that Faneuil Hall had been draped in mourning. The scene was very solemn, though the light of day was not excluded. Settees had been placed over the whole area of the hall; the large platform was occupied by many of the most distinguished men in New England, and, as it was intended that every thing should be conducted with as much quietness as possible, the doors were closed when the procession had entered, and every part of the hall and galleries was filled. This

was a mistake in the arrangements; the crowd on the outside, thinking that some space must still be left within, became very uneasy, and finally grew so tumultuous and noisy that the solemnities were interrupted. The police in vain attempted to restore order. It seemed as if confusion would prevail. Mr. Webster perceived that there was but one thing to be done — he advanced to the front of the stage, and said, in a voice easily heard above the noise of tumult without and of alarm within, 'Let those doors be opened.' The power and authority of his manner were irresistible — the doors were opened, though with difficulty, from the pressure of the crowd on the outside; but, after the first rush, every thing was quiet, and the order during the rest of the performance was perfect.

"Mr. Webster spoke in an orator's gown, and wore small-clothes. He was in the perfection of his manly beauty and strength; his form filled out to its finest proportions, and his bearing, as he stood before the vast multitude, that of absolute dignity and power. His manuscript lay on a small table near him, but I think he did not once refer to it. I never heard him when his manner was so grand and appropriate."

[The discourse on Adams and Jefferson — excerpts]

Adams and Jefferson are no more; and we are assembled, fellow-citizens, the aged, the middle-aged, and the young, by the spontaneous impulse of all, to bear our part in those manifestations of respect and gratitude which pervade the whole land. Adams and Jefferson are no more. On our fiftieth anniversary, the great day of national jubilee, in the very hour of public rejoicing, in the midst of echoing and reëchoing voices of thanksgiving, while their own names were on all tongues, they took their flight together to the world of spirits.

Neither of these great men, fellow-citizens, could have died, at any time, without leaving an immense void in our American society. They have been so intimately, and for so long a time, blended with the history of the country, and especially so united, in our thoughts and recollections, with the events of the Revolution, that the death of either would have touched the chords of public sympathy. We should have felt that one great link, connecting us with former times, was broken; that we had lost something more, as it were, of the presence of the Revolution itself, and of the act of independence, and were driven on, by another great remove from the days of our country's early distinction, to meet posterity, and to mix with the future. Like the mariner, whom the currents of the ocean and the winds carry along, till he sees the stars which have directed his course and lighted his pathless way descend, one by one, beneath the rising horizon, we should have felt that the stream of time had borne us onward till another great luminary, whose light had cheered us and whose guidance we had followed, had sunk away from our sight.

But the concurrence of their death on the anniversary of Independence has naturally awakened stronger emotions. Both had been Presidents, both had lived to great age, both were early patriots, and both were distinguished and ever honored by their immediate agency in the act of independence. It cannot but seem striking and extraordinary, that these two should live to see the fiftieth year from the date of that act; that they should complete that year; and that then, on the day which had fast linked for ever their own fame with their country's glory, the heavens should open to receive them both at once. As their lives themselves were the gifts of Providence, who is not willing to recognize in their happy termination, as well as in their long continuance, proofs that our country and its benefactors are objects of His care?

A superior and commanding human intellect, a truly great man, when Heaven vouchsafes so rare a gift, is not a temporary flame, burning brightly for a while, and then giving place to returning darkness. It is rather a spark of fervent heat, as well as radiant light, with power to enkindle the common mass of human mind; so that when it glimmers in its own decay, and finally goes out in death, no night follows, but it leaves the world all light, all on fire,. from the potent contact of its own spirit.

There were many points of similarity in the lives and fortunes. of these great men. They belonged to the same profession, and had pursued its studies and its practice, for unequal lengths of time indeed, but with diligence and effect. Both were learned and able lawyers. They were natives and inhabitants, respectively, of those two of the Colonies which at the Revolution were the largest and most powerful, and which naturally had a lead in the political affairs of the times. When the Colonies became in some degree united, by the assembling of a general Congress, they were brought to act together in its deliberations, not indeed at the same time, but both at early periods.

Each had already manifested his attachment to the cause of the country, as well as his ability to maintain it, by printed addresses, public speeches, extensive correspondence, and whatever other mode could be adopted for the purpose of exposing the encroachments of the British Parliament, and animating the people to a manly resistance. Both were not only decided, but early, friends of Independence. While others yet doubted, they were resolved; where others hesitated, they pressed forward. They were both members of the committee for preparing the Declaration of Independence, and they constituted the sub-committee appointed by the other members to make the draft.

They left their seats in Congress, being called to other public employments, at periods not remote from each other, although one of them returned to it afterwards for a short time. Neither of them was of the assembly of great men which formed the present Constitution, and neither was at any time a member of Congress under its provisions. Both have been public ministers abroad, both Vice-Presidents and both Presidents of the United States. These coincidences are now singularly crowned and completed. They have died together; and they died on the anniversary of liberty.

The Congress of the Revolution, fellow-citizens, sat with closed doors, and no report of its debates was ever made. The discussion, therefore, which accompanied this great measure, has never been preserved, except in memory and by tradition. But it is, I believe, doing no injustice to others to say, that the general opinion was, and uniformly has been, that in debate, on the side of independence, John Adams had no equal.

The eloquence of Mr. Adams resembled his general character, and formed, indeed, a part of it. It was bold, manly, and energetic; and such the crisis required. When public bodies are to be addressed on momentous occasions, when great interests are at stake, and strong passions excited, nothing is valuable in speech farther than as it is connected with high intellectual and moral endowments. Clearness, force, and earnestness are the qualities which produce conviction. True eloquence, indeed, does not consist in speech. It cannot be brought from far. Labor and learning may toil for it, but they will toil in vain. Words and phrases may be marshalled in every way, but they cannot compass it. It must exist in the man, in the subject, and in the occasion. Affected passion, intense expression, the pomp of declamation, all may aspire to it; they cannot reach it. It comes, if it come at all, like the outbreaking of a fountain from the earth, or the bursting forth of volcanic fires, with spontaneous, original, native force.

In July, 1776, the controversy had passed the stage of argument. An appeal had been made to force, and opposing armies were in the field. Congress, then, was to decide whether the tie which had so long bound us to the parent state was to be severed at once, and severed for ever.

Hancock presides over the solemn sitting; and one of those not yet prepared to pronounce for absolute independence is on the floor, and is urging his reasons for dissenting from the declaration.

"Let us pause! This step, once taken, cannot be retraced. This resolution, once passed, will cut off all hope of reconciliation. If success attend the arms of England, we shall then be no longer Colonies, with charters and with privileges; these will all be forfeited by this act; and we shall be in the condition of other conquered people, at the mercy of the conquerors."

It was for Mr. Adams to reply to arguments like these. We know his opinions, and we know his character. He would commence with his accustomed directness and earnestness.

"Sink or swim, live or die, survive or perish, I give my hand and my heart to this vote. It is true, indeed, that in the beginning we aimed not at independence. But there's a Divinity which shapes our ends. The injustice of England has driven us to arms; and, blinded to her own interest for our good, she has obstinately persisted, till independence is now within our grasp. We have but to reach forth to it, and it is ours. Why, then, should we defer the Declaration? Is any man so weak as now to hope for a reconciliation with England, which shall leave either safety to the country and its liberties, or safety to his own life and his own honor? Are not you, Sir, who sit in that chair, is not he, our venerable colleague near you, are you not both already the proscribed and predestined objects of punishment and of vengeance? Cut off from all hope of royal clemency, what are you, what can you be, while the power of England remains, but outlaws?

"Sir, I know the uncertainty of human affairs, but I see, I see clearly, through this day's business. You and I, indeed, may rue it. We may not live to the time when this Declaration shall be made good. We may die; die colonists; die slaves; die, it may be, ignominiously and on the scaffold. Be it so. Be it so. If it be the pleasure of Heaven that my country shall require the poor offering of my life, the victim shall be ready, at the appointed hour of sacrifice, come when that hour may. But while I do live, let me have a country, or at least the hope of a country, and that a free country."

Both Mr. Adams and Mr. Jefferson had the pleasure of knowing that the respect which they so largely received was not paid to their official stations. They were not men made great by office; but great men, on whom the country for its own benefit had conferred office.

SPEAK FOR YOURSELF, DANIEL

There was that in them which office did not give, and which the relinquishment of office did not, and could not, take away. In their retirement, in the midst of their fellow-citizens, themselves private citizens, they enjoyed as high regard and esteem as when filling the most important places of public trust.

There remained to Mr. Jefferson yet one other work of patriotism and beneficence, the establishment of a university in his native State. This last public labor of Mr. Jefferson naturally suggests the expression of the high praise which is due, both to him and to Mr. Adams, for their uniform and zealous attachment to learning, and to the cause of general knowledge.

The cause of knowledge, in a more enlarged sense, the cause of general knowledge and of popular education, had no warmer friends, nor more powerful advocates, than Mr. Adams and Mr. Jefferson. On this foundation they knew the whole republican system rested; and this great and all-important truth they strove to impress, by all the means in their power. Mr. Adams expresses the strong and just sentiment, that the education of the poor is more important, even to the rich themselves, than all their own riches. On this great truth, indeed, is founded that unrivalled, that invaluable political and moral institution, our own blessing and the glory of our fathers, the New England system of free schools.

And now, fellow-citizens, let us not retire from this occasion without a deep and solemn conviction of the duties which have devolved upon us. This lovely land, this glorious liberty, these benign institutions, the dear purchase of our fathers, are ours; ours to enjoy, ours to preserve, ours to transmit. Generations past and generations to come hold us responsible for this sacred trust. Our fathers, from behind, admonish us, with their anxious paternal voices; posterity calls out to us, from the bosom of the future; the world turns hither its solicitous eyes; all, all conjure us to act wisely, and faithfully, in the relation which we sustain. We can never, indeed, pay the debt which is upon us; but by virtue, by morality, by religion, by the cultivation of every good principle and every good habit, we may hope to enjoy the blessing, through our day, and to leave it unimpaired to our children. Let us feel deeply how much of what we are and of what we possess we owe to this liberty, and to these institutions of government. Nature has, indeed, given us a soil which yields bounteously to the hand of industry, the mighty and fruitful ocean is before us, and the skies over our heads shed health and vigor. But what are lands, and seas, and skies, to civilized man, without society, without knowledge, without morals, without religious culture; and how can these be enjoyed, in all their extent and all their excellence, but under the protection of wise institutions and a free government?

Ticknor tells us: "The two speeches attributed to Mr. Adams and his opponent attracted great attention from the first. Soon they were put into school-books, as specimens of English and of eloquence. In time men began to believe they were genuine speeches, made by genuine men who were in the Congress of '76; and at last Mr. Webster received letters asking whether such was the fact or not. The fact is that the speech he wrote for John Adams has such an air of truth and reality about it, that only a genius like Mr. Webster's, perfectly familiar with whatever relates to the Revolution, and imbued with its spirit, could have written it."

To this, Ticknor's nephew, George Ticknor Curtis, adds a further note. In his life of Webster he says, "President Fillmore informs me that he once asked Mr. Webster, in familiar conversation, what authority he had for putting this speech into the mouth of John Adams, the Congress at that period having always sat with closed doors. Mr. Webster replied that he had no authority for the sentiments of the speech excepting Mr. Adams' general character, and a letter he had written to his wife, that had frequently been published. After a short pause, Mr. Webster added, 'I will tell you what is not generally known. I wrote that speech one morning before breakfast, in my library, and when it was finished my paper was wet with my tears.'"

SPEAK FOR YOURSELF, DANIEL

The fall and winter found Webster occupied with Congress, his law practice, and the demands of politics. He furnished the major support in Congress for the administration of President John Quincy Adams, although without the enthusiasm that he had felt for his father, and he continued his friendly overtures to Henry Clay, now Secretary of State, whom Webster considered his party's strongest hope against the rising power of Andrew Jackson. On October 13, 1826, Webster wrote to Clay:

We all rejoice here — I mean all who do not fear that you were born to prevent General J. from being President — in the improvement of your health; and you must allow me to express my most anxious and earnest hope that you will not overwork yourself the ensuing session and winter. What can not be done without the sacrifice of your health must be left undone, at whatever expense or hazard. I have often thought of suggesting to you one practice, if you have not already adopted it, which I have found very useful myself, when my own little affairs have occasionally pressed me; that is, the constant employment of an amanuensis. The difference between writing at the table and dictating to another, is very great. The first is tedious, exhausting, debilitating labor; the last may be done while you are pacing a large room, and enjoying in that way the benefit of an erect posture, and a healthy exercise. If I were you I would not touch a pen, except to write my frank. Make the clerks do all that clerks can do, and for the rest dictate to an amanuensis. I venture to say, that if you once get accustomed to this, you will find your labor greatly lightened.

This advice tells us more about Webster than it does about Clay. But at least Webster followed it himself. Later, when he was Secretary of State, his friend William Plumer visited him at his farm in New Hampshire, where Webster was supposedly enjoying a vacation. Plumer tells us that "while talking to me, Webster was dictating letters on public business to his son and to his secretary,

both of whom he kept busily writing, while he walked the room,
alternately talking to me and dictating to them."
Notwithstanding his efficiency, Webster found himself hard-
pressed for time.

[*Letter to Story, Washington, Dec. 26, 1826*]

Thus far, I have been laboring hard to get the Spanish claims off my hands, so as to be able to attend, without distraction, to my other duties. But these things together, and some new engagements for the court, leave me quite too little time for correspondence. The private affairs with which a member from a large town is necessarily charged, are very numerous. To be a public man, I ought to represent one of the inland counties of my good native State, or else a borough.

You will have seen in a late National Intelligencer, the report of last year, respecting the courts. Something undoubtedly will be done on that subject this session. What shall we do? Shall we increase your bench by two? Shall we relieve your bench from all circuit duties, and establish a uniform system of circuit courts? Shall we provide circuit judges for the western districts?

I must entreat your sentiments fully on these matters. I feel great objection to either of the first two propositions; others have objections to the last. They make a kind of point of honor to have supreme judges in the circuit courts, if other circuits have such.

My plan, if it deserve the name, would be to appoint three or four circuit judges in the West; to provide also, if we could, for the appointment of a circuit judge contingently in the East, to the next vacancy.

My object, in short, would be to provide that all the judges of the supreme court should perform some circuit duty; and as much as they could conveniently; that there should be circuit judges enough to perform the rest; and that such arrangements should be made in this respect, as, when vacancies occur on your bench, giving the opportunity, two supreme judges should be allotted to the West; in other words, that the West should have two judges on the supreme bench.

Is this a right object? If it be, tell me how I shall accomplish it. By the middle of the next month, I must report some plan. Pray sit down, think, and write. We are all well; my wife is very happy. We have good rooms, good fires, good company, and good spirits, *in quomodo sensu, intelligitur.* Mrs. Webster sends her love to Mrs. Story and yourself. I beg to make a large addition to it, as it passes through my hands.

[*Letter to Everett, Dec. 31, 1826*]

It was so cold yesterday that I could not persuade myself to leave my room, or I should have called at your house. As near as I recollect, though my memory is a good deal chilled, it is now about a week since I was warm, out of bed.

[*Letter to Nicholas Biddle, President of the Bank of the United States, Feb. 24, 1827*]

When Mr. Sergeant went away, and I was left in charge of the concerns of the Bank here, he told me that the Bank had, at that time, not lost any cause in the Supreme Court. If he should return, at the next term, I shall have the happiness, I trust, to tell him, that it has lost none since. Dandridge's cause is not yet decided, but I have confidence the judgment below will be reversed; so that that will form no exception to our good fortune.

I shall forward a little statement of my fees & Mr. Wirt's receipt tomorrow. In Dandridge's case, I shall take the liberty of charging somewhat liberally. I never gave more attention, either to the preparation, or the discussion of a cause; & am vain enough to think that my labours were not without some influence on the result.

I have considered myself as having been interested with their cases in consequence of Mr. Sergeant's absence, & that my stewardship will naturally terminate on his return, which probably may be before the next term. But one does not like to part with an old client, any more than an old friend, provided there be no good cause of separation. If therefore it should be your good pleasure to have it understood hereafter, that in suits here, in which Mr. Sargeant may chance to have assistance, he may put my poor services in requisition, unless he sees reason to do otherwise, I should not object to such an understanding, & should not consider myself at liberty to accept retainers against the Bank hereafter.

[*Letter to Story, Apr. 16, 1827*]

Will you have the goodness to give me *one hour* of your valuable life. Let it be devoted to furnishing me with hints & authorities to the following point, viz.

That a right to navigate the upper part of a river (say the St. Lawrence) draws after it a right to go to the ocean.

Whatever you *think* or find on this matter let me know by Wednesday or Thursday.

Yr. troublesome friend.

Meanwhile, Elijah H. Mills, one of the two Senators from Massachusetts, whose term was due to expire in 1827, had become seriously ill.

[*Letter to Joseph E. Sprague, Jan. 10, 1827*]

I cannot persuade myself that the legislature, under present circumstances, will omit to reëlect Mr. Mills. Here, I assure you, we are all of one mind on the subject. We think there is nothing in his health to make it improper, and that every thing else is in favor of it. If the legislature will not agree to that, I hope the election may be postponed. For mercy's sake, do not weaken our power in the Senate. When all the Philistines are against us, do let us have all the strength we can have. If Mr. Mills lives, he is second to no man in the Senate among our friends. Why then should he be now superseded? We shall know more of his health in June; and June is early enough for the election. But, as I will answer for it, that he will not hold the office any longer than he is able to discharge its duties, I should hope he would be now reëlected.

[Letter to Governor Levi Lincoln, May 22, 1827]

I adopt this mode of making a few suggestions to you on a subject of some interest; I mean the approaching election of a Senator in Congress. The present posture of things, in relation to that matter, is so fully known to both of us, that I need not trouble you with much preliminary observation. I take it for granted that Mr. E. H. Mills will be no longer a candidate. The question then will be, who shall succeed him? I need not say to you that you yourself will doubtless be a prominent object of consideration in relation to the vacant place, and the purpose of this communication requires me to acknowledge that I deem it possible also that my name should be mentioned, more or less generally, as one who may be thought of, among others, for the same situation. In anticipation of this state of things, and more especially since I have been awakened by its probably near approach, I have not only given it a proper share of my own reflection, but have also consulted with others in relation to it, in whose judgment and friendship I have confidence. The result is, that there are many strong personal reasons, and, as friends think (and as I think, too), some *public* reasons, why I should decline the offer of a seat in the Senate, if it should be made to me. Without entering, at present, into a detail of these reasons, I will say that the latter class of them grow out of the public station which I at present fill, and out of the necessity of increasing rather than of diminishing, in both branches of the national Legislature, the strength that may be reckoned on as friendly to the present Administration.

To come, therefore, to the main point, I beg to say that I see no way in which the public good can be so well promoted as by *your* consenting to go into the Senate. This is my own clear and decided opinion; it is the opinion, equally clear and decided, of intelligent and patriotic friends here.

[*Letter from Governor Lincoln, May 24, 1827*]

I hasten, on the moment of the receipt of your letter, to a reply, in the hope that it may reach you before you leave the city on your proposed journey. My expressions of personal disinclination to the office of United States Senator were sincere, and openly and repeatedly made, and indeed it became necessary for me to say that I should absolutely decline the place if offered to me. I have since believed and am now confirmed in the opinion (Mr. Mills being out of the question) that the transfer to which you object should be made. To your private interests, it seems to me, it could produce no additional prejudice. The sacrifice of business and of domestic duties and enjoyments is no greater in the one place than the other.

On June 8, 1827, the Massachusetts Legislature elected Webster to the United States Senate for a six-year term, a step which he reported to his friend J. Evelyn Denison in London as follows:

The good people here have seen fit to transfer me from the House of Representatives to the Senate. This was not according to my wishes; but a state of things had arisen, which, in the judgment of friends, rendered the measure expedient, and I yielded to their will. I do not expect to find my situation so agreeable as that which I left.

IX

1827–1829

DEATH OF WIFE AND EZEKIEL — REMARRIAGE

Any gratification which Webster may have felt at his elevation to the Senate was soon marred by the illness of his wife. We first hear of this from his letter to Ezekiel, July 20, 1827:

Mrs. Webster is getting well. At the end of this week I take her to Sandwich; thence I go to Nantucket court, return to Plymouth court, and get home the 10th August.

In November they started for Washington but got no farther than New York, as explained by Webster in a letter of December 1, 1827, to his Senate colleague from Massachusetts, Nathaniel Silsbee:

I am kept here by a concurrence of unfortunate circumstances. Mrs. Webster's health was not entirely good when we left home, but still, such as to allow the hope that we should be able to travel with ordinary speed. Our unfortunate passage from Providence increased her debility, and since she has arrived here, an accidental cause has contributed to make her case worse. From this last, however, she is now fast recovering, and I trust will be able to travel on Monday. To-day I have myself a very painful attack of rheumatism, occasioned, I suppose, by a violent cold I took on the way; and am not now able to leave my room. This will be better, however, I trust soon; so that my present hopes are to set forward on Monday. We shall not make a moment's stop for any purpose not connected with

health. I hope I may not be needed before I can arrive with my
family. But if it were likely that I should be, I would leave them,
at whatever inconvenience, and proceed by the most rapid conveyance, if my own health should be such as to allow of it. You
will receive this on Monday, and I will thank you to write me,
addressed to Philadelphia, saying whether any thing is expected to
occur, in which my vote may be essential. I am fully aware of the
general importance of every member's presence at this moment in
the Senate; and I feel extreme anxiety in consequence of my own
unavoidable absence, even for a single day. Still, I am desirous of
keeping my wife and children with me, if possible; as I should
otherwise be obliged to return for them. Let me hear from you as
above requested. I write this not without great inconvenience. I
can neither walk nor sit upright.

[Letter to Paige, Dec. 5, 1827]

I must now write you more fully upon the afflicting state of Mrs.
Webster's health. Dr. Post, a very eminent physician and surgeon,
has to-day been called into consultation with Dr. Perkins. Their
opinion, I am distressed to say, is far from favorable. I believe they
will recommend her return to Boston as soon as convenient. They
seem to think that it is very uncertain how fast or how slow may
be the progress of the complaint; but they hold out faint hopes of
any cure. I hope I may be able to meet the greatest of all earthly
afflictions with firmness, but I need not say that I am at present
quite overcome. I have not yet communicated to Mrs. Webster
what the physicians think. That dreadful task remains. She will
receive the information, I am sure, as a Christian ought. Under
present circumstances, I should be very glad if you could come here,
although I would not wish you to put yourself to too much inconvenience. If you come on, I think the best way will be to take
the mail stage-coach, with the chance of finding an evening boat at
New Haven. You must let Daniel know, without alarming him too

much, that his mother's health is precarious, and that she will probably return home. I am not yet able to write, as you see, though I think I am getting better.

p. s. 8 o'clock. — I would fain hope that the foregoing is of too alarming a character. I have since seen Mrs. Webster and told her the doctors' opinions. She says she still has courage. If you can come on so as to accompany Mrs. Webster home, it will not be necessary that you should set out the very day you receive this. But I shall not myself go to Washington until I hear from you that you can come to take Mrs. Webster home, if need be.

[*Letter to Story, from Washington, Dec. 18, 1827*]

Yours of the 13th, addressed to New York, has followed me hither. My own health was so far restored, that on Thursday, the 13th, I ventured to set forth, and arrived here Sunday evening, the 16th, without inconvenience, and with far better health than I had when I left New York. I do not now write myself an invalid.

I left Mrs. Webster at New York. Her health was bad, though better than it had been. I know not whether you are acquainted with the nature of her complaint; though Dr. Warren or Mr. Ticknor will readily explain it to you.

Our rooms I found all ready and in order; and notwithstanding Mrs. Webster's illness they will be kept for her, and for you and Mrs. Story. Our good landlady has done all in her power to prepare for us; and if my poor wife had health, I should look forward to a happy session. And as it is I hope for the best. I am sure Mrs. Story will find herself pleasantly situated here.

[*Letter to Paige, from Washington*]

December 25, *Christmas noon*, 1827

Your letter of Sunday has this moment reached me, in which you say Mrs. Webster would be glad if it should be quite convenient for me that I would come to New York to meet Judge Story, and I certainly shall do so. I cannot go for a day or two, because my cold is too severe; but there is nothing to prevent my setting off so soon as I am quite well. Judge Story wrote me that he should probably set out about the 29th, which is next Saturday.

Possibly I may not leave here before Monday, the 31st; but even then I shall be in New York as soon as the judge. On receipt of this, I will thank you to write me, saying whether Mrs. Webster wishes me to bring any of hers or the children's things along with me. Your letter, if written on Friday morning, will be here on Sunday, so that if I happen to stay till Monday, I shall get it. Probably I shall go off before Monday; this will depend a little as well on the weather and the state of the public conveyances as on my getting rid of my cold.

I hope, if it be not too inconvenient, you will stay till I come, and then we can talk about Grace's going to Boston, or Washington. The tone of your letters, for three or four days, has been so much more favorable than before, that I feel encouraged. It will be dull to her, I fear, to be left again by me, after you are gone; but then I must come here, despatch some few things, and return to her again. I shall let no business, public or private, prevent attention to her, as the first duty.

My cold is better to-day, but still I am not quite well. Indeed, so much of rheumatism, and then so severe a cold, have rather reduced this corporeal system of mine to some little degree of weakness. Two or three days of good weather, which I know not when we shall see again, would do me a great deal of good.

P. S. My Christmas dinner is a handful of magnesia, a bowl of gruel.

[Letter to Silsbee, from New York, Jan. 4, 1828]

I arrived here yesterday at eleven o'clock, after a very tolerable journey, and without having added any thing to my cold. Indeed, I think it is better than when I left Washington.

I find Mrs. Webster more comfortable, on the whole, than I expected. She has now enjoyed more rest and repose, and more freedom from pain, for three days together, than in any equal time since we came here, six weeks ago. She has lost flesh since I left her, however, and is now feeble.

As to the original cause of her illness, I do not know exactly what to think of it. Some symptoms are certainly a little more favorable. I cannot help getting a little new hope, on the whole; though I fear I build on a slight foundation.

I find here the Judge and his lady. They are in very good health. He has not looked so well for a long time. It is a great thing to get him out of his study. They set off this afternoon, being anxious to get over the Chesapeake before the boat stops. They will take possession of the rooms at Mrs. McIntyre's, where I hope to join them soon. Mr. Paige went to Boston yesterday. As soon as he shall be able to return, which I think will be in a few days, I shall return to Washington, if Mrs. Webster remains as comfortable as at present.

[Letters to Ezekiel: Jan. 8, 1828]

I cannot say any thing new in regard to Mrs. Webster. Her case is most serious. It is one of rare occurrence; no physician here, but Dr. Perkins, thinking he ever saw one like it. The tumor has not yet broke out, but threatens it, and will, doubtless, soon. Its character will be then better known, and I fear the worst. Dr. Nathan Smith, Dr. Physick, &c. have been written to for opinions and advice; and I have written an urgent letter to Dr. Warren to come here. After all, the case is very much out of the reach of medical application, or surgical aid. The tumor is so large, so situated, embracing so many muscles, nerves, and blood vessels, that an operation is not to be thought of. Internal remedies do not reach it, and external applications have little effect. The result must be left with Providence; but you must be prepared to learn the worst. For three or four days, she has been more free from pain than for some time before; but yesterday she was a good deal distressed again. William Paige went home the day I came. He thinks he can return in a week or ten days, and stay till I make a visit to the court at Washington, if Mrs. Webster should be so as to allow of my leaving her. You will, of course, not alarm your wife and Mrs. Kelly, and Nancy, too much in regard to Grace. There is yet a hope; but I have thought it best to tell you my real opinion.

[*Jan. 17, 1828*]

I cannot give you any favorable news respecting my wife. She is no better, and I fear is daily growing weaker. She is now exceedingly feeble. Dr. Perkins thinks she has altered very much the last three or four days.

The prospect nearly confounds me; but I hope to meet the event with submission to the will of God.

I expect Mr. Paige to-morrow morning. He or I will write you again, soon.

[*Jan. 21, 1828*]

Monday morning, January 21

Mrs. Webster still lives, but is evidently near her end. We did not expect her continuance yesterday, from hour to hour.

Monday, 1/4 past 2 o'clock

Poor Grace has gone to Heaven. She has now just breathed her last breath.

I shall go with her forthwith to Boston, and on receipt of this, I hope you will come there if you can.

I shall stay there some days. May God bless you and yours.

Mr. Ticknor observes in his Reminiscences:

"Mr. Webster came to Mr. George Blake's in Summer Street, where we saw him both before and after the funeral. He seemed

completely broken-hearted. At the funeral, when, with Mr. Paige, I was making some arrangements for the ceremonies, we noticed that Mr. Webster was wearing shoes that were not fit for the wet walking of the day, and I went to him and asked him if he would not go in one of the carriages. 'No,' he said, 'my children and I must follow their mother to the grave on foot. I could swim to Charlestown.' A few minutes afterward, he took Julia and Daniel in either hand, and walked close to the hearse through the streets to the church in whose crypt the interment took place. It was a touching and solemn sight. He was excessively pale."

Josiah Quincy had visited the Websters in Washington in February 1826, and relates in his Figures of the Past *the dinner table anecdote, already quoted, about the Websters bantering each other over the loss of their pipe of wine in the Portsmouth fire. After relating this, Quincy adds:*

"I suppose that there was nothing said at that dinner so little worth preserving as this trifling family jest; yet the sweet and playful manner of Webster has fixed it indelibly upon my memory. That manner I cannot give, and it was everything. It somehow carried one of those aside confessions of the absolute affection and confidence existing between this married pair which were so evident to those admitted beneath their roof. A congenial marriage seems to be essential to the best development of a man of genius, and this blessing rested upon that household. It was like organ music to hear Webster speak to or of the being upon whom his affections reposed, and whom, alas! he was so soon to lose. I am sure that those who knew the man only when this tenderest relation had been terminated by death, never knew him in his perfect symmetry."

[Letter from Story, Jan. 27, 1828]

I do not urge your immediate return here. But yet, having been a like sufferer, I can say, that the great secret of comfort must be

*sought, so far as human aid can go, in employment. It requires ef-
fort and sacrifices, but it is the only specific remedy against unavailing and wasting sorrow; that canker which eats into the heart, and
destroys its vitality. If you will therefore allow me to advise, it would
be that you should return here as soon as you can gather up your
strength, and try professional and public labors. Endeavor to wear
off that spirit of despondency which you cannot but feel, and which
you will scarcely feel any inclination to resist. Saying this, I have
said all that I ought, and I know that you can understand what is
best, better than I can prescribe.*

*Mrs. Story desires her most affectionate regards to you and the
children, and I join in them, being always affectionately.*

*[Letter of Jan. 28, 1828, to Dr. Cyrus W. Perkins, an early friend
of Webster's, in whose New York home Mrs. Webster had died.]*

You have learned by Mr. Paige's letter, that we reached Boston
on Friday evening, and on Saturday committed Mrs. Webster's remains to the tomb. We used the occasion to bring into our own
tomb the coffin containing the remains of our daughter Grace, who
died January 23, 1817. My dear wife now lies with her oldest and
her youngest; and I hope it may please God, when my own appointed hour comes, that I may rest by her side.

All our friends have received us with a sincerity of condolence
and sympathy which we can never forget. The children are well.
Daniel will resume his usual residence and occupation in a day or
two. Mrs. Lee, (Eliza Buckminster,) Mrs. Ticknor, Mrs. Hale, Mrs.
Appleton, and others, have offered, in the most friendly manner, to
take care of Julia and Edward, for the winter. We have not yet decided how we shall dispose of them.

I pray you to give my most affectionate regards to Mrs. Perkins. I
never can express how much I feel indebted to her kindness and
friendship. If Mrs. Webster had been her sister, she could have done
no more.

In a few days, I intend to set out for Washington. If there should come a flight of snow, so as to make sleighing, I shall immediately improve the occasion to get over the hills to New Haven. I am, dear Sir, most truly . . .

[Letter to Ticknor, Feb. 22, 1828]

Washington, February 22, 1828, in Supreme Court

I find myself again in the court, where I have been so many winters, and surrounded by such men and things as I have usually found here. But I feel very little zeal or spirit in regard to the passing affairs. My most strong propensity is to sit down, and sit still; and, if I could have my wish, I think the writing of a letter would be the greatest effort I should put forth for the residue of the winter. I suppose, however, that a sort of necessity will compel me to be here for ten days or a fortnight, and to appear to take an interest in the business of the court. My own health, I think, is a good deal better than when I left home. Indeed, it is very good, and I have nothing to complain of in that respect.

The Judge and Mrs. Story are getting along very well. She has complained a little of *dyspepsia,* but now seems to be well, and enjoys Washington society with reasonable relish. They dine to-day (birthday) at the President's.

I hear that my children are frequent visitors at your house, much to their gratification. I know, my dear sir, with how much kindness you and Mrs. Ticknor treat us all; and feel how greatly we must lean on our friends under our present circumstances.

[Letter to Paige, undated]

I have received to-day your letter of Saturday, which makes me feel a good deal better. I have seldom been five days before without hearing from home; and although I have lost what mainly made home dear to me, there is yet that in it which I love more than all things else in the world. I could not get along without cherishing the feeling that I have a home notwithstanding the shock I have received. You must try to make the children write, when you cannot, so that I may hear from some of you; one every two or three days at least.

The arrangement you suggested some time ago, as to the children's all dining with you on Sunday, and occasionally with our other friends, pleases me very well. I hope they are happy. Edward, I am sure, is as well off as he can be, and since you cannot spare him, I am content he should remain where he is.

In a letter to Mrs. E. B. Lee (Eliza Buckminster), March 15, 1828, Webster refers to his hope to be appointed minister to Great Britain. He had expressed this wish to President John Quincy Adams, but though they were members of the same political party, there was little love lost between them, and Adams had no desire to gratify Webster's wish.

I return you Mr. Parker's letter, which I have read, as you may well suppose, with great pleasure. Nothing is more soothing and balmy to my feelings, than to dwell on the recollection of my dear wife, and to hear others speak of her, who knew her and loved her. My heart holds on by this thread, as if it were by means of it to retain her yet here.

I hear from Mr. Paige, and from Julia, and from Edward, that you are well. Julia has told me all about your party, and how long she sat up. I hear from others, as well as herself, that she is happy as possible under the protection of your care and kindness. You will love her, I know, for her mother's sake, and I hope for her own also; and I trust she will make herself agreeable to your husband. You are kind enough to say, that concern for Julia need not lead me to forbear any purpose which I might otherwise have, of crossing the water. It would be unpleasant, certainly, to leave the children, and especially a little girl of Julia's age, but I should not feel uneasy about her at all, while under your guardianship. There are other considerations, however, which are well to be weighed before I am water-borne. Even if what you allude to were supposed to be at my own option, and however desirable it might be in itself, times and circumstances may nevertheless be such as "give me pause." This is all I can say about it at present; except that I am now too old to do anything in a hurry. I believe this is almost the only time that I have alluded to the subject, to any one; and would not wish to be quoted as having said one word respecting it.

Mrs. Story left us the day before yesterday. The Judge goes in a day or two. I shall be sorry to lose him, though quite willing to have the court break up.

[Letter to Ticknor, Apr. 18, 1828]

I received yours of the 13th this morning, and never executed commission with more alacrity and pleasure than this of looking up rooms for you and Mr. Prescott. It delights me to hear that you are coming, and I shall certainly keep you a fortnight.

The rooms are engaged. They are not strictly in the house I live in, but in the same block, and quite proximate. My landlady has engaged them, and I am to have the pleasure of your company at my table. When you arrive in this far-famed metropolis, please direct the coachman to set down at Mrs. McIntyre's, Pennsylvania Avenue, nearly opposite Gadsby's National Hotel, a little this side, precisely by the side of a pump, at a large wooden platform which supplies the place of a stepping-stone. Inquire for Mr. Webster. If he is out, ask for Charles —, and the rest will follow in regular sequence. I shall see that there is dinner for you at two o'clock on Sunday; and, if that day should not bring you, at four o'clock on Monday.

[Letter to Mrs. Ticknor, May 1828]

I thank you for your letter, enclosing your husband's. He is dressing to go to the President's, and I shall go with him rather than stay to my lonely dinner. He and Mr. Prescott leave me to-morrow. I shall feel their loss very seriously, I assure you, but I cannot persuade them to stay longer. Nothing resists the attraction of wives and children.

You are very kind to tell me about my three little ones. I have the greatest happiness in knowing that they are well, and in feeling how much my friends care for them, and think of them.

In next month I hope to see you all.

It may be wondered whether Ticknor's visit did much to relieve Webster's feeling of loneliness, for Ticknor himself, writing his wife at the end of April, said: "Sunday Morning — A little homesick again, when I think of you going to church, and Nanny standing at the window to see the crowds pass by, my little class of boys, and Mr. Channing's sermon."

[*Letter to Mrs. Lee, May 18, 1828*]

Your very kind letter of the 12th was received to-day. I cannot sufficiently thank you for your goodness and affection towards Julia. Certainly you come nearer to supplying her loss than anybody else. I believe she loves you best of any; and it is my wish, my dear friend, that you should make her as much your own as your feelings prompt you to do. She cannot be better than with you, and I incline to leave it very much to your choice, how much she shall be with you, and when it is best for her to be elsewhere. You have a right to her, if you choose to have, which nobody else will ever divide. You have been among our dearest friends from the day of our marriage, and, as Julia is left motherless, I know not what to do for her so well as to leave her with you, whenever it is agreeable to you to have her with you. If you think her education would not suffer, I should be quite willing she should be with you most of the summer; though I hope to have her with me some of the time.

I thank you, my dear friend, for all your kind remembrance and good wishes. Your regard and friendship are among the objects which make me willing to live longer, and which I shall never cease to value while I do live. You say Mr. Sullivan thought me depressed. It is true. I fear I grow more and more so. I feel a vacuum, an indifference, a want of motive, which I cannot well describe.

I hope my children, and the society of my best friends, may rouse me; but I can never see such days as I have seen. Yet I would not repine; I have enjoyed much, very much; and if I were to die to-night, I should bless God most fervently that I had lived.

Adieu, my dear friend; I hope to be in better spirits when I see you.

By the fall of 1828, fortunately, Webster was cheering up and regaining somewhat of his former interest in outside things. For example:

[*Letter to McGaw, Oct. 11, 1828*]

Boston, Oct. 11, 1828

I thank you for your letter of Sep. 25, detailing the incidents of your tour. It has enabled me to go, pretty accurately, over your track. I have followed you, by the means of it, repeatedly from Boston round by the West, and home to Bangor. I well understand how you should feel excited by visiting such places as Kingsbridge, White Plains, Benn' Heights etc. I never knew a man yet, nor a woman either, with a sound head and a good heart, that was not more or less under the power, which these local associations exercise.

It is true, that *place,* in these things, is originally accidental. Battles might have been fought elsewhere, as well as at Saratoga, or Bennington. Nevertheless here they *were fought;* and nature does not allow us to pass over the scenes of such events with indifference, unless we have a good share of bluntness and stupidity, or unless the scenes themselves have become familiar by frequent visits to them. For my part I love them all, and all such as they. An old drum hangs up in the Senate Chamber of Mass. taken from the Hessians at Bennington, and I do not think I ever went into the room without turning to look at it. And that reminds me to say that I have a pair of silver sleeve buttons the material of which my father picked up on, and brought away from, that same field of Bennington. If I thought either of my boys would not value them, fifty years hence, if he should live so long, I believe I should begin to flog him, now.

The day we parted here was, in truth, very hot. I reached Falmouth, at evening, very much exhausted by heat and fatigue. The next morning we embarked for Nantucket, and had a good passage. There I staid a week, exceedingly busy, all the time, and hurrying through business, in order to shorten our stay. Work and heat (a good deal too much of both) made me sick: and after I returned from the island, it was a month before I felt quite well. Cooler weather and repose have, at length, accomplished my restoration. My health is now good, and I shall have occasion for all of it, for the next month or two, during which professional engagements are usually most pressing.

Julia and Edward are still at Boscawen. At the end of this month they will come home, and both their little cousins with them. Mrs. E. Webster is to come down, and to keep all the children here, for a month or two, while her husband is engaged with the courts, and the legislature. My present purpose is not to be in great haste to depart for Washington, unless some urgent public duty should require it. In the present condition of my household, it is a great object to shorten my absence as far as I well can. I rejoice that you found your little daughter, and your other connexions well; and that the journey proved so favorable to Mrs. McGaw's health. Nothing is better, I think, than a tour of that sort, once in a while, to places not before visited, and to the midst of society a little different from that in our own circle. It is not only gratifying, at the moment, but furnishes many things to think about, and talk over, for a long time. The mind requires occasionally a supply of new ideas, or else it is likely to get out of stock. New books (or books never read before) will sometimes enable the inner man to gratify himself with a change of ideas, which are his diet, and a visit to new scenes and new circles, often does the same thing more effectually. For my part, I journey a good deal, but it is all on the beaten track from Boston to Washington. Once we made an exception, and went, as you know to Niagara. It was a high gratification. I advise you to keep your eye on such a tour, at sometime, hereafter. Why is it not a sort of duty, before we leave this world "thus wondrous fair," to see all the wonders, which it is fairly in our power to see, and, by beholding them to derive a new excitement to our veneration and adoration of the Deity? I confess that natural religion — that conviction of the existence and perfection of the Deity, which the contemplation of natural objects produces — grows daily more and more impressive on my mind. But I must stop or I shall write a sermon — adieu.

I have not written so tediously long a letter, in a twelve-month. Give every good wish of my heart to your wife, and, as we Yorkers say, "the same to yourself."

[Letter to the Rev. John Brazer, Nov. 10, 1828]

I part with Whately, not without regret, as I have not had leisure to go through him regularly, although I have had some good snatches here and there. It is a good book. If it were not for an appearance of self-conceit, I would say that I have found in it twenty things which I have thought of often, and been convinced of long, but never before saw in print. He shows sense, especially in the prominence which he gives to perspicuity and energy, as qualities of style. I like his hatred of adjectives, his love of Saxon words, and his idea of the true use of repetition; this last might be much further explained than it is done by him. There is something which may be called augmentative repetition, that is capable sometimes of producing great effect.

I rejoice to see one Rhetorician who will allow nothing to words but as they are signs of ideas. The rule is a good one, to use no word which does not suggest an idea, or modify some idea already suggested. And this should lead writers to adopt sparingly the use of such words as "vast," "amazing," "astonishing," &c. For, what do they mean? Dr. Watts, who by the way, I do not deem altogether a bad poet, somewhere speaks of the flight of an angel as being with "most amazing speed." But what idea is conveyed by this mode of expression? What is "amazing speed"? It would amaze us, if we saw an oyster moving a mile a day. It would not amaze us to see a greyhound run a mile in a minute.

On the other hand, see with what unequalled skill Milton represents both the distance through which, and the speed with which, Mulciber fell from heaven:

> From morn
> To noon he fell, from noon to dewy eve,
> A summer's day; and with the setting sun,
> Dropt from the zenith, like a falling star.

It is easy to understand Webster's admiration for Archbishop Whately's Rhetoric. Webster himself was a master of style. Few people have had a greater love for simplicity and strength in language, for the avoidance of unnecessary adverbs and adjectives, and for the use of sturdy Anglo-Saxon verbs and nouns.

His literary executor and biographer, George Ticknor Curtis, tells us that he took great pains to edit his formal orations as they were passing through the press. "He would correct them with a severity of taste far more rigorous than any standard that the public was likely to apply to them; and, when he failed to satisfy himself, he would resort to the aid of others. Thomas Kemper Davis, a son of one of his intimate friends, and a good scholar himself, was a student-at-law in Webster's office at the time he delivered his eulogy on Adams and Jefferson. On the morning after its delivery, Webster entered the office and threw down the manuscript before him with the request: 'There, Tom, please to take that discourse and weed out the Latin words.' Such was his love of the Anglo-Saxon element in our language, that he preferred to avoid a word of Latin origin if he could do so without impoverishing his style. At the same time, he was a Latin scholar and a constant reader of the Latin classics."

He was an enthusiastic student of words, their derivation, and their shades of meaning. He strove always for precisely the right word to convey the particular thought. His secretary, Charles Lanman, tells us that his library at Marshfield contained "all the dictionaries that were ever heard of."

The principal political excitement of 1828 was the presidential election, in which Andrew Jackson defeated John Quincy Adams by an electoral vote of 178 to 83. Webster had backed Adams, though without undue enthusiasm, and his attitude may have been reflected in that of his brother Ezekiel who, indulging in a postmortem, said in his letter of February 15, 1829:

"If there had been at the head of affairs a man of popular character like Mr. Clay, or any man whom we were not compelled by our natures, instincts, and fixed fate to dislike, the result would have been different. People cannot have strong affection for the cause, and strong dislike for the man. We cannot disembowel ourselves, like a trussed turkey, of all that is human nature within us."

Webster had already written Ezekiel several letters from Washington:

[*Feb. 5, 1829*]

We are beaten, where we had decisive majorities, by private disagreements and individual partialities.

The City is already full of hungry friends and will overflow before the 3. of March.

Gen. Jackson will be here in a day or two. I am of opinion his health is very feeble, and that there is not much chance of his lasting long.

[*Feb. 23, 1829*]

His friends have no common principle — they are held together by no common tie — and my private opinion is, though I do not wish to be quoted for that, at present, that Genl. J. has not character enough to conduct his measures by his own strength. Somebody must and will lead him.

[*Feb. 26, 1829*]

The elements of dissension will be in the Cabinet itself. Mr. Calhoun (who tho not nominally in the Cabinet, is likely to be *near* the President) and Mr. Van Buren and Mr. McLean will all be looking out for the *succession*.

Webster also wrote a series of letters to Ezekiel's wife, who had come to Boston to look after Webster's children while Ezekiel was campaigning in New Hampshire for Congress, against the Jackson tidal wave, and unsuccessfully:

[*Feb. 19, 1829*]

Senate Chamber, February 19, 1829

MY DEAR SISTER — I must begin with apology; or let me rather say, with confession; for though I am willing to confess great and censurable omissions, I have little to urge by way of apology, and nothing which amounts to justification. Let me pray you, therefore, in the exercise of your clemency, to adopt the rule which Hamlet prescribes for passing judgment on the players. Do not treat me according to my deserts, for if so, "who would escape whipping," but according to your own bounty and dignity; the less I deserve forgiveness, the more will forgiveness exalt your forbearance and mercy.

The children under your good superintendence have written me continually, day by day, very good letters. Mr. Paige also has been kind, as he always is. Your own letters have completed my circle of domestic correspondence, and I must say that it has been very punctual, and highly gratifying. And now what can I tell you worth hearing?

General Jackson has been here about ten days. Of course the city is full of speculation and speculators. "A great multitude," too many to be fed without a miracle, are already in the city, hungry for office.

The fashionable world is and has been full and gay. Crowds have come and are coming to see the inauguration, &c. I have been to three parties, to wit, Mrs. Adams's last, Mrs. Clay's last, and Mrs. Porter's last. Mrs. Porter, wife of the Secretary of War, is a fine woman, whom we visited at Niagara, when there four years ago. With these manifestations of regard for the setting sun and stars, I have satisfied my desire of seeing the social circles. If there should be a ball on the 22d, I shall attend as usual, to commemorate the great and good man born on that day.

Judge Story is well, and in his usual spirits. The court is deeply engaged, and as soon as I get rid of these secret sessions of the Senate, I have enough to do in it.

We are looking to New Hampshire. I shall not engage lodgings for you and your husband next winter, till I see the returns.

[*Mar. 2, 1829*]

I had letters yesterday from Mr. Paige and from Alice, which ought to have been received two days earlier. This, I suppose, is to be placed to the account of your great storm.

With less snow, we have very cold weather here. There has not been a warm day since I came here, although I have often seen the peach-trees in blossom in February. The ground is still covered with snow, the river hard frozen, and the weather steadily cold. It will make bad travelling for those who leave here the 4th.

The court will probably continue its session a fortnight longer, and then I shall set my face northward. I hope your patience will hold out. Consider how cold it must be up at Boscawen, and how busy your husband is now, and how soon he will come to Boston, after the 10th, either for congratulation or condolence. He will need a week in either case, and that will bring March so far along, that I trust you will be able to content yourself till I come.

My health is good, but I find, to confess the truth, that I am growing indolent. I would be glad to have more decisive volitions. I do nothing in Congress or the court, but what is clearly necessary; and in such cases, even, my efforts "come haltingly off." In short, I believe the truth is, that I am growing old, and age you know, or rather you have heard, requires repose.

Adieu, yours, with much affectionate regard . . .

[*Mar. 4, 1829*]

I thank you for yours, received to-day, and thank you both for the letter itself and for your pardon which it contains, and of which I stood in so much need. Your benignity is memorable and praiseworthy. To be serious, however, my dear sister, let me say once for all, that I have a very affectionate regard for you; that I am very glad you are my sister, and the wife of the best of all brothers; and that if, like him, I am not the most punctual of all correspondents, I am like him in sincerity and constancy of esteem. If you find in your connection with my own little broken circle but one half as much pleasure as you bestow, you will have no reason to regret it. Your presence with my children, through the winter, has relieved me from a pressing weight of anxiety.

To-day we have had the inauguration. A monstrous crowd of

people is in the city. I never saw any thing like it before. Persons have come five hundred miles to see General Jackson, and they really seem to think that the country is rescued from some dreadful danger.

The show lasted only half an hour. The Senate assembled at eleven, the judges and foreign ministers came in, the President elect was introduced, and all seated by half-past eleven. The Senate was full of ladies; a pause ensued till twelve. Then the President, followed by the Senate, &c., went through the great rotunda, on to the portico, over the eastern front door; and those went with him who could, but the crowd broke in as we were passing the rotunda, and all became confusion. On the portico, in the open air, the day very warm and pleasant, he read his inaugural, and took the oath. A great shout followed from the multitude, and in fifteen minutes, "silence settled, deep and still." Every body was dispersed. As I walked home, I called in at a bookstore, and saw a volume which I now send you; it may serve to regulate matters of etiquette at Boscawen.

I hope to write Edward to-night. If not, I shall not fail to do so to-morrow.

[Letter to Ezekiel, Mar. 15, 1829]

The Senate will probably adjourn to-morrow, and I hope the court will rise, or at least will dismiss me by Wednesday or Thursday. I shall be immediately off. My books are in trunks. I shall hear from New Hampshire to-morrow, and dispose of them according to circumstances. If no change takes place in my own condition, of which I have not the slightest expectation, and if you are not elected, I shall not return. This, *inter nos,* but my mind is settled. Under present circumstances, public and domestic, it is disagreeable being here, and to me there is no novelty to make compensation. It will be better for me and my children that I should be with them. If I do not come in a public, I shall not in a professional character. I can leave the court now as well as ever, and can earn my bread as well at home as here.

Your company and that of your wife, would make a great difference. I have not much expectation that you will be returned. Our fortune is, as connected with recent and current political events, that if there be opposite chances, the unfavorable one turns up. You had a snow of five feet, which of itself might turn the election against the well-disposed and indifferent, and in favor of the mischievous and the active. I shall not be disappointed if I hear bad news.

I make my point to be home the first day of April, when I trust I shall meet you. We will then settle what is best to do with the children. I shall want Julia and Edward to stay a little while with me. Edward, I think, should then go to Boscawen. I hardly know what I shall think best to do with Julia.

While they were all looking forward to a reunion of the family in Boston, and after Webster had joined Ezekiel's wife there, Ezekiel suffered a sudden heart attack while arguing a case in court. He went over backwards, like a felled tree, without any attempt to turn or to put out an arm to check the violence of his fall. Webster describes the circumstances in a letter to Dr. Perkins, April 17, 1829:

You will have heard of the sudden death of my brother. The event necessarily called me to Boscawen, from which place I returned a day or two ago. It has quite overwhelmed us all. Mrs. Webster and the oldest daughter were here, when it happened. The messenger brought us the news at three o'clock, on Saturday morning, the 11th instant. The death took place the previous afternoon at four o'clock. You will probably have seen some account of it. It seems to me I never heard of a death so instantaneous. He fell in an instant, without any effort to save himself, and without any struggle or sign of consciousness, after he reached the floor.

On receiving the tidings, Mrs. Webster and her daughter, and myself and two sons, set off immediately, and arrived at Boscawen that evening at nine o'clock. The funeral was attended the next day. Mrs. Webster's constitution is feeble, and I knew not how she would get through the dreadful scene; yet she did get through. I left her far better than was to have been expected; and a letter received to-day says she continues so. It was not possible for me to stay long from home, on so sudden a call; but I must return in two or three days to Boscawen, to pay proper attention to the circumstances of the family. My brother has left two daughters, one fourteen and one twelve years old; and a wife, a fine woman, to whom he had been married about four years. He has left a competency to those dependent on him; but it will require care and oversight to preserve it, and make the most of it.

This event, my dear Sir, has affected me very much. Coming so soon after another awful stroke, it seems to fall with double weight. He has been my reliance, through life, and I have derived much of its happiness from his fraternal affection. I am left the sole survivor of my family. Yet I have objects of affection in my children, and I do not intend to repine; though I confess I cannot well describe the effect of this event on my feelings.

[Letter to Mason, Apr. 19, 1829]

I thank you for your kind letter. You do not and cannot overrate the strength of the shock which my brother's death has caused me. I have felt but one such in life; and this follows that so soon that it requires more fortitude than I possess to bear with firmness, such perhaps as I ought. I am aware that the case admits of no remedy, nor any present relief; and endeavor to console myself with reflecting, that I have had much happiness in lost connections; and that they must expect to lose beloved objects in this world, who have beloved objects to lose. My life, I know, has been fortunate and happy beyond the common lot, and it would be now ungrateful, as well as unavailing, to repine at calamities of which, as they are human, I must expect to partake. But I confess the world, at present, has for me an aspect any thing but cheerful. With a multitude of acquaintance, I have few friends; my nearest intimacies are broken, and a sad void is made in the objects of affection. Of what remains dear and valuable, I need not say that a most precious part is the affectionate friendship of yourself and family. I want to see you very much indeed, but know not whether I shall be able soon to visit Portsmouth.

This occurrence is calculated to have effect on the future course of my own life, and to add to the inducements, already felt, to retire from a situation in which I am making daily sacrifices and doing little good to myself or others. Pray give my love to your family.

Yours affectionately and entirely . . .

That autumn Webster spent much time in New York in connection with legal engagements. He was extensively entertained, and also seems to have found means to assuage his loneliness, as we may see from his letter of November 18, 1829, to his old friend Jacob McGaw:

I have a thousand thanks to give you and Mrs. McGaw for your kind invitation to have Julia with you for the winter. I assure you there are no persons living to whom I would more cheerfully give such a pledge of confidence. I know you would both love her for her own sake, as for her father's and mother's also; but Julia is at present so exceedingly well situated and so attached to her present condition, that it seems it would be wrong to change it. She has passed the summer at Brookline with Mrs. Lee (Eliza Buckminster), and had her instruction from Miss Searle, a young lady of our acquaintance of the best character and qualifications, who lives at Brookline with her mother and sisters. Julia has become quite attached to her, and, now that Mrs. Lee has come into town for

SPEAK FOR YOURSELF, DANIEL

the winter, Miss Searle has taken her altogether to herself. In addition to being in an excellent family and having good means of instruction, she is near town, so that her Uncle Paige and other friends can see her frequently in my absence. Under these circumstances, with hearty and repeated thanks for your friendship and kindness, I have concluded to leave her where she is.

And now, my dear sir, I must tell you and Mrs. McGaw (in confidence) a little news — nothing less than my expectation of being again married. The affair is not of long standing, but it looks so much like terminating in a marriage that I may venture to mention it to you — to go no further until you shall hear it from other quarters. The lady is Miss Caroline Le Roy of New York, aged 31 years or thereabouts. She is the daughter of a highly reputable gentleman, now some years retired from the mercantile business. Mrs. McGaw will want to know all about her. What I can say is that she is amiable, discreet, prudent, with enough of personal comeliness to satisfy me, and of the most excellent character and principles. With this account of the lady, your wife must rest content till she has the means of personal acquaintance, which I sincerely hope may happen soon. Tell her she will be sure to like her. Whether this same lady will go to Washington the first of next month, or whether she will be so cruel as to oblige me to go without her and to return for her to New York, about Christmas, are secrets worth knowing, but which are not known to me. I shall endeavor to set forth strongly the inconvenience of a winter journey from W. to N. Y. and back.

I hope to get away on the 27th inst., and intend taking Julia to New York to make a little visit to Mrs. Perkins and for the purpose of giving her an opportunity of seeing the aforesaid lady.

The marriage took place Saturday December 12, 1829, in a small ceremony in New York, in the presence of the bride's immediate family and Julia Webster. On December 14 Webster wrote his son Fletcher:

REMARRIAGE

You have been informed that an important change in my domestic condition was expected to take place. It happened on Saturday. The lady who is now to bear the relation of mother to you, and Julia, and Edward, I am sure will be found worthy of all your affection and regard; and I am equally certain that she will experience from all of you the utmost kindness and attachment. She insists on taking Julia with us to Washington, thinking it will be better for her, and that she will also be good company.

We shall leave New York in about a week. I read your first letter, which gave me pleasure, and hope to have another from you before I leave New York. You will not fail to write me once a week, according to arrangement.

Many of Webster's biographers have sensed a change after his second marriage. He had always been careless in money matters, and this had increased with affluence.

His first wife, Grace, a year his senior, had been the daughter of a country minister. She had learned early to value a dollar, and she and Webster had gone through many hardships together. Consciously or unconsciously, she undoubtedly exercised a restraining influence.

Webster's second wife, Caroline, was seventeen years his junior. She had been born and brought up to wealth. To her, parties and entertaining were a normal part of life, and she reveled in the importance of her husband's position. She stimulated his ambition and dampened such resolves as occasionally overcame him to return to private life in order to rebuild his fortune. Instead of restraining Webster's lavish tendencies, she encouraged them. From the date of their marriage he sank deeper and deeper into debt and became increasingly complacent toward financial favors from his friends.

X

1830

THE DEBATE WITH HAYNE: FIRST SPEECH ON FOOTE'S RESOLUTION

The resumption of his senatorial duties at the end of 1829 found Webster in a happy mood. Marriage had restored his spirit, and the presence in Washington of his new wife and Julia brought contentment. His placidity even extended to that perennial disturber of the peace, the tariff.

[*Letter to Warren Dutton, Jan. 15, 1830*]

The tariff sleepeth. It may be jogged a little during the session, but I think not awakened. Let them go on to spin at Lowell, with the persuasion that if their condition be not made better, it will still not be made worse. I think the duties on tea and coffee will be reduced; and that then reduction will stop. The general face of things appears here, I presume, much as it does with you. Mr. Van Buren has evidently, at this moment, quite the lead in influence and importance. He controls all the pages on the back stairs, and flatters what seems to be at present the Aaron's serpent among the President's desires, a settled purpose of making out the lady, of whom so much has been said, a person of reputation. It is odd enough, but too evident to be doubted, that the consequence of this dispute in the social and fashionable world, is producing great political effects, and may very probably determine who shall be successor to the present chief magistrate.

His relaxed attitude also shows in the easy grace of a letter of condolence to his sister-in-law. For most of us, such letters are the stiffest of all forms of composition.

HAYNE DEBATE

[Letter to Mrs. Ezekiel Webster, Jan. 17, 1830]

MY DEAR SISTER — I have not heard from you since I left Boston, until this day, when I received a letter from C. B. Haddock. He informs me you are at Concord, where your mother is dangerously ill. I grieve for this new calamity. Providence has seen fit to let your sorrows and misfortunes come together. Be assured no one can feel for you more sympathy than myself, who know how much you have suffered for those dear to me. Your mother, however, has arrived at good old age, and her departure from this to a better state, would not and ought not to be so violent a disruption of strong ties as some that you have felt.

I parted with you, I think, the first day of October, not at all foreseeing what was to happen to myself in so short a time. I am now here, settled down for the session, with Mrs. Webster and Julia. When I left home, I did not expect to bring Julia further than New York. She was to have returned with Mr. Paige; but Mrs. Webster chose to have it otherwise, and I believe it is much better as it is. Julia seems exceedingly happy. Her health is better than I ever saw it, and she is much attached to her new mother. With this last personage, I am sure you will be pleased. You will find her amiable, affectionate, prudent, and agreeable; as these are good sober words, you must take them as used for what they ought to mean, and not as the rhapsody of a new husband. It will not be many months, however, I hope, before I shall bring her and yourself face to face, and then you can judge for yourself.

The election of Jackson had placed Webster in the opposition, relieving him of the responsibility of supporting an administration he did not like, and allowing him greater freedom of action. He had more time for cases before the Supreme Court. He even had the leisure to consider editing his speeches for publication.

SPEAK FOR YOURSELF, DANIEL

[Letter to Haddock, Jan. 19, 1830]

MY DEAR NEPHEW — If Messrs. Perkins and Marvin choose to run the risk of such a publication as you mention, I do not know as I can reasonably object to it; though, sure enough, I shall be ashamed to see the likeness of my face in the shop windows, as I go from my house to Court street.

As to any introductory notice, or family memoir, I shall leave that to your own good taste, with the reservation that I must see whatever is prepared before it is published. I hardly know what there is, not already known as mine, which it would be worth while to print. There are, however, some reviews, and an address to the Phi Beta Kappa, in 1806, which for a boy I thought pretty good; but I have not read it since it was delivered. I remember, among other things in it, I urged the necessity of forming agricultural and historical societies, when there were no such things in the State.

But it was the calm before the storm. Unknown to Webster, hostile forces were arraying themselves against him in the Senate, and on January 19 came the thunderclap. On that day Senator Hayne of South Carolina took the floor to make a blistering attack on the policies and people of New England.

To Webster it came as a total surprise. As he later wrote Mason:

The whole matter was quite unexpected. I was busy with the court, and paying no attention to the debate which was going on sluggishly in the Senate, without exciting any interest. Happening to have nothing to do for the moment in court, I went into the Senate, and Mr. Hayne, so it turned out, just then arose. When he sat down, my friends said he must be answered, and I thought so too.

In actual fact the storm had been brewing for some time, triggered by a seemingly innocuous resolution of Senator Foote of Connecticut calling for an inquiry into the expediency of limiting the sale of Public Lands.

This was a subject of acute sensitivity in the West. Government land had been priced by law at a minimum of $1.25 an acre. But even though it had been selling faster than it could be settled, westerners were demanding that it be made cheaper. Senator Benton of Missouri, the most vocal of their leaders, had been pushing legislation to cut the price to twenty-five cents an acre. To him, Foote's resolution was a personal affront.

South Carolina had no direct interest in this controversy, but Vice President Calhoun and his protégé Senator Hayne saw the opportunity of forging a political alliance between the South and West against the North and East. Lurking in the background were the deep antagonisms caused by slavery and the tariff, together with the dispute over the right asserted by South Carolina to nullify federal legislation which it considered contrary to its interests. By fostering western antagonism toward New England, the South Carolinians hoped to gain support in their effort to nullify the federal tariff.

Pursuant to this design, Hayne agreed to support Benton in a deliberate attack upon New England. In carefully coordinated speeches on January 18 and 19 they branded Foote's resolution as a scheme to halt eastern emigration and thereby to stem the drain on New England's supply of industrial labor. Benton opened with a diatribe on January 18 and Hayne followed on the 19th. It was during Hayne's speech that Webster, all unconscious of these moves, returned from the Supreme Court, his law papers tucked under his arm.

Just as Hayne was regarded as the senatorial spokesman for South Carolina, and Benton for the West, so Webster was looked upon as New England's champion, and his friends demanded that he rise up and do battle. He took the floor immediately after Hayne, but it was then late in the afternoon, and Benton, counting on the psychological advantage of closing the day with his position unchal-

lenged, moved for adjournment. Webster, welcoming the additional time, agreed.

Nowhere does Webster's ability to store and marshal facts appear to greater advantage than in his debate with Hayne. He was forced to speak almost extemporaneously, and to parry the carefully prepared thrusts of his opponents. Nevertheless, he more than outmatched them on their own ground and, with consummate skill, maneuvered Hayne into a position for a knock-out blow.

Of the two attacks, Benton's was the more vitriolic. But Webster ignored him and concentrated on Hayne. His design was to shift the field of battle from western land policy to the more fundamental issues of constitutional laws and nullification. He recognized that these were the vital issues to be settled and that Hayne, with the backing of Calhoun, was the one he must defeat. Furthermore, Webster was a born debater. For the sheer joy of it, he must have preferred to face the dash and brilliance of Hayne rather than the humorless verbosity of Benton.

Charles W. March was present at the debate and his Reminiscences paint a vivid picture. "Hayne," he says, "was incontestibly the most formidable of Webster's opponents. Benton discharged all sorts of missiles at the head of an adversary, like a catapulta. Tropes, metaphors, similes, unsavory allusions, vituperative epithets, damnatory personalities, he hurled upon the victim of his temporary anger. But Hayne dashed into debate like the Mameluke cavalry upon a charge. There was a gallant air about him that could not but win admiration. He never provided for retreat; he never imagined it. He had an invincible confidence in himself, which arose partly from constitutional temperament, partly from previous success. Of great fluency and no little force of expression, his speech never halted and seldom fatigued. His oratory was graceful and persuasive. An impassioned manner, somewhat vehement at times, but rarely if ever extravagant; a voice well modulated and clear; these made him a popular and effective speaker."

Webster's notes for what is known as his First Speech on Foote's

Resolution occupy, loosely written, three sheets of ordinary letter paper. The speech itself, as printed, occupies twenty-three pages. Curtis says that the notes were probably prepared on the morning of the 20th, the day the speech was delivered, in which connection he adds this interesting bit as to Webster's work habits:

"Mr. Webster was always an early riser. It was his habit, when he had any important work to do, to rise about four o'clock in the morning, light his own fire, and continue his occupation until the hour of breakfast, or until he chose to go out, as he was very fond of doing, before most people were abroad. In Washington, he could be frequently seen in the market-house, before any other inhabitant of the city, conversing with the tradesmen there, and securing the best choice from their stalls. Every butcher, and fisherman, and country produce-dealer, white or black, man or woman, free or slave, knew him well. Perhaps they did not know to what themes his early morning chats with them were parentheses. It was at such times, however, that his important labor was chiefly performed before people in general had begun the day."

Webster's speech on Wednesday the 20th was relatively short, designed to draw out Hayne rather than to crush him. The following are highlights:

Nothing has been farther from my intention than to take any part in the discussion of this resolution. It proposes only an inquiry on a subject of much importance, and one in regard to which it might strike the mind of the mover and of other gentlemen that inquiry and investigation would be useful. Although I am one of those who do not perceive any particular utility in instituting the inquiry, I have, nevertheless, not seen that harm would be likely to result from adopting the resolution.

But, Sir, although I have felt quite indifferent about the passing of the resolution, yet opinions were expressed yesterday on the general subject of the public lands, and on some other subjects, by the gentleman from South Carolina, so widely different from my own, that I am not willing to let the occasion pass without some reply.

Now it appears, Mr. President, that, in forty years, we have sold no more than about twenty millions of acres of public lands. The annual sales do not now exceed, and never have exceeded, one million of acres. A million a year is, according to our experience, as much as the increase of population can bring into settlement. And it appears, also, that we have, at this moment, surveyed and in the market, ready for sale, two hundred and ten millions of acres, or thereabouts. All this vast mass, at this moment, lies on our hands for mere want of purchasers. Can any man, looking to the real interests of the country and the people, seriously think of inquiring whether we ought not to hasten the public surveys still faster, and to bring, still more and more rapidly, other vast quantities into the market?

The lands cannot be settled but by settlers, nor faster than settlers can be found. A system, if now adopted, of forcing sales, at whatever prices, may have the effect of throwing large quantities into the hands of individuals, who would in this way, in time, become themselves competitors with the government in the sale of land. My own opinion has uniformly been, that the public lands should be offered freely, and at low prices; so as to encourage settlement and cultivation as rapidly as the increasing population of the country is competent to extend settlement and cultivation. Every actual settler should be able to buy good land, at a cheap rate; but, on the other hand, speculation by individuals on a large scale should not be encouraged, nor should the value of all lands, sold and unsold, be reduced to nothing, by throwing new and vast quantities into the market at prices merely nominal.

I now proceed, Sir, to some of the opinions expressed by the gentleman from South Carolina. Two or three topics were touched by him, in regard to which he expressed sentiments in which I do not at all concur.

In the first place, Sir, the honorable gentleman spoke of the whole course and policy of the government towards those who have purchased and settled the public lands, and seemed to think this policy wrong. He held it to have been, from the first, hard and rigorous; he was of opinion, that the United States had acted towards those who had subdued the Western wilderness in the spirit of a step-mother; that the public domain had been improperly regarded as a source of revenue; and that we had rigidly compelled payment for that which ought to have been given away.

Now, Sir, I deny, altogether, that there has been any thing harsh or severe in the policy of the government towards the new States of the West. On the contrary, I maintain that it has uniformly pursued towards those States a liberal and enlightened system, such as its own duty allowed and required, and such as their interest and welfare demanded. The government has been no step-mother to the new States. She has not been careless of their interests, nor deaf to their requests; but from the first moment when the territories which now form those States were ceded to the Union, down to the time in which I am now speaking, it has been the invariable object of the government, to dispose of the soil according to the true spirit of the obligation under which it received it; to hasten its settlement and cultivation, as far and as fast as practicable; and to rear the new communities into new and independent States, at the earliest moment of their being able, by their numbers, to form a regular government.

Let us pause and survey the scene, as it actually existed thirty-five years ago. Let us look back and behold it. Over all that is now Ohio there then stretched one vast wilderness, unbroken except by two small spots of civilized culture, the one at Marietta and the other at Cincinnati. At these little openings, hardly each a pin's point upon the map, the arm of the frontier-man had levelled the forest and let in the sun. These little patches of earth, themselves almost overshadowed by the overhanging boughs of that wilderness which had stood and perpetuated itself, from century to century, ever since the creation, were all that had then been rendered verdant by the hand of man. In an extent of hundreds and thousands of square miles, no other surface of smiling green attested the presence of civilization. The hunter's path crossed mighty rivers, flowing in solitary grandeur, whose sources lay in remote and unknown regions of the wilderness. It struck upon the north on a vast inland sea, over which the wintry tempests raged as on the ocean; all around was bare creation. It was fresh, untouched, unbounded, magnificent wilderness.

And, Sir, what is it now? Is it imagination only, or can it possibly be fact, that presents such a change as surprises and astonishes us when we turn our eyes to what Ohio now is? Is it reality, or a dream, that, in so short a period even as thirty-five years, there has sprung up, on the same surface, an independent State with a million of people? A million of inhabitants! an amount of population greater than that of all the cantons of Switzerland; equal to one third of all the people of the United States when they undertook to accomplish their independence. This new member of the republic has already left far behind her a majority of the old States. She is now by the side of Virginia and Pennsylvania; and in point of numbers will shortly admit no equal but New York herself.

If, Sir, we may judge of measures by their results, what lessons do these facts read us upon the policy of the government? What inferences do they authorize upon the general question of kindness or unkindness? What convictions do they enforce as to the wisdom and ability, on the one hand, or the folly and incapacity, on the other, of our general administration of Western affairs?

Sir, does it not require some portion of self-respect in us to imagine, that, if our light had shone on the path of government, if our wisdom could have been consulted in its measures, a more rapid advance to strength and prosperity would have been experienced? For my own part, while I am struck with wonder at the success, I also look with admiration at the wisdom and foresight which originally arranged and prescribed the system for the settlement of the public domain. Its operation has been, without a moment's interruption, to push the settlement of the Western country to the extent of our utmost means.

But there was another observation of the honorable member, which, I confess, did not a little surprise me. As a reason for wishing to get rid of the public lands as soon as we could, and as we might, the honorable gentleman said he wanted no permanent sources of income. He wished to see the time when the government should not possess a shilling of permanent revenue. If he could speak a magical word, and by that word convert the whole Capitol into gold, the word should not be spoken. The administration of a fixed revenue, he said, only consolidates the government and corrupts the people! Sir, I confess I heard these sentiments uttered on this floor not without deep regret and pain.

Sir, when gentlemen speak of the effects of a common fund, belonging to all the States, as having a tendency to consolidation, what do they mean? Do they mean, or can they mean, any thing more than that the union of the States will be strengthened by whatever continues or furnishes inducements to the people of the States to hold together? If they mean merely this, then, no doubt, the public lands, as well as every thing else in which we have a common interest, tend to consolidation; and to this species of consolidation every true American ought to be attached; it is neither more nor less than strengthening the Union itself. This is the sense in which the framers of the Constitution use the word *consolidation,* and in this sense I adopt and cherish it. They tell us, in the letter submitting the Constitution to the consideration of the country, that, "In all our deliberations on this subject, we kept steadily in our view that which appears to us the greatest interest of every true American, the consolidation of our Union, in which is involved our prosperity, felicity, safety, perhaps our national existence."

I wish to see no new powers drawn to the general government; but I confess I rejoice in whatever tends to strengthen the bond that unites us, and encourages the hope that our Union may be perpetual. And therefore I cannot but feel regret at the expression of such opinions as the gentleman has avowed, because I think their obvious tendency is to weaken the bond of our connection. I know that there are some persons in the part of the country from which the honorable member comes, who habitually speak of the Union in terms of indifference, or even of disparagement. The honorable member himself is not, I trust, and can never be, one of these.

Union, of itself, is considered by the disciples of this school as hardly a good. It is only regarded as a possible means of good; or, on the other hand, as a possible means of evil. They cherish no deep and fixed regard for it, flowing from a thorough conviction of its absolute and vital necessity to our welfare. Sir, I deprecate and deplore this tone of thinking and acting. I deem far otherwise of the union of the States; and so did the framers of the Constitution themselves. What they said, I believe; fully and sincerely believe, that the union of the States is essential to the prosperity and safety of the States.

I come now, Mr. President, to that part of the gentleman's speech which has been the main occasion of my addressing the Senate. The East! the obnoxious, the rebuked, the always reproached East! — we have come in, Sir, on this debate, for even more than a common share of accusation and attack. If the honorable member from South Carolina was not our original accuser, he has yet recited the indictment against us with the air and tone of a public prosecutor. He has summoned us to plead on our arraignment; and he tells us we are charged with the crime of a narrow and selfish policy; of endeavoring to restrain emigration to the West, and, having that object in view, of maintaining a steady opposition to Western measures and Western interests. And the cause of all this narrow and selfish policy, the gentleman finds in the tariff; I think he called it the accursed policy of the tariff. This policy, the gentleman tells us, requires multitudes of dependent laborers, a population of paupers, and that it is to secure these at home that the East opposes whatever may induce to Western emigration.

Sir, I rise to defend the East. I rise to repel, both the charge itself, and the cause assigned for it. I deny that the East has, at any time, shown an illiberal policy towards the West. I deny that, in any part of her history, at any period of the government, or in relation to any leading subject, New England has manifested such hostility as is charged upon her. On the contrary, I maintain that, from the day of the cession of the territories by the States to Congress, no portion of the country has acted either with more liberality or more intelligence, on the subject of the public lands in the new States, than New England.

At the foundation of the constitution of these new Northwestern States lies the celebrated Ordinance of 1787. We are accustomed, Sir, to praise the lawgivers of antiquity; we help to perpetuate the fame of Solon and Lycurgus; but I doubt whether one single law of any lawgiver, ancient or modern, has produced effects of more distinct, marked, and lasting character than the Ordinance of 1787. That instrument was drawn by Nathan Dane, then and now a citizen of Massachusetts. It was adopted, as I think I have understood, without the slightest alteration; and certainly it has happened to few men to be the authors of a political measure of more large and enduring consequence. It fixed for ever the character of the population in the vast regions northwest of the Ohio, by excluding from them involuntary servitude. It impressed on the soil itself, while it was yet a wilderness, an incapacity to sustain any other than freemen. It laid the interdict against personal servitude, in original compact, not only deeper than all local law, but deeper, also, than all local constitutions. Under the circumstances then existing, I look upon this original and seasonable provision as a real good attained. We see its consequences at this moment, and we shall never cease to see them, perhaps, while the Ohio shall flow. It was a great and salutary measure of prevention. Sir, I should fear the rebuke of no intelligent gentleman of Kentucky, were I to ask whether, if such an ordinance could have been applied to his own State, while it yet was a wilderness, and before Boone had passed the gap of the Alleghanies, he does not suppose it would have contributed to the ultimate greatness of that commonwealth?

Sir, I leave the subject. The Senate will bear me witness that I am not accustomed to allude to local opinions, nor to compare or contrast different portions of the country. I have often suffered things to pass without any observation, which I might properly enough have considered as deserving remark. But I have felt it my duty, on this occasion, to vindicate the State I represent from charges and imputations on her public character and conduct, which I know to be undeserved and unfounded. If advanced elsewhere, they might be passed, perhaps, without notice. But whatever is said here is supposed to be entitled to public regard, and to deserve public attention; it derives importance and dignity from the place where it is uttered. As a true representative of the State which has sent me here, it is my duty, and a duty which I shall fulfil, to place her history and her conduct, her honor and her character, in their just and proper light, so often as I think an attack is made upon her, so respectable as to deserve to be repelled.

Hayne thought Webster's speech provocative; probably it was. But Benton was even more provoked, having been ignored, and claimed the right of first reply. He spoke the remainder of the 20th, while Webster irritated him still further by going to the Supreme Court.

On Thursday the 21st, while Benton still had the floor, Senator Chambers of Maryland moved a postponement of the debate so as to permit Webster to argue the important Supreme Court case of Carver's Lessee v. Astor, *involving title to some fifty thousand acres of land in New York. Hayne objected, saying:*

"He saw the gentleman from Massachusetts in his seat, and presumed he could make an arrangement that would enable him to be present here during the discussion to-day. He was unwilling that this subject should be postponed until he had an opportunity of replying to some of the observations which had fallen from the gentleman yesterday. He would not deny that some things had

*fallen from the gentleman which rankled here (touching his breast),
from which he would desire at once to relieve himself. The gentleman had discharged his fire in the face of the Senate. He hoped he
would now afford him the opportunity of returning the shot."*

*Webster arose and said: "I am ready to receive it. Let the dis-
cussion proceed."*

*Hayne followed Benton on the 21st, but at the end of the day
agreed to resume on Monday the 25th so that in the meantime
Webster could attend to his commitments in the Supreme Court.
On the 25th Hayne concluded in a day-long speech which all present
conceded to have been one of the greatest ever delivered in the
Senate. In its course he bitterly arraigned Massachusetts for its
unpatriotic position during the War of 1812, and attacked the
views which Webster had expressed at that time. With much relish
he also held up to scorn Webster's inconsistencies with respect to
the tariff. Then, turning to the broader field into which Webster
had led him, Hayne argued the right of a State to nullify federal
legislation, and the impropriety of permitting the federal government to be the sole judge of its own powers. On this he said:*

*"As to the doctrine that the Federal Government is the exclusive
judge of the extent as well as the limitations of its powers, it seems
to me utterly subversive of the sovereignty and independence of the
States. It makes but little difference, in my estimation, whether
Congress or the Supreme Court are invested with this power."*

*When Hayne finished, Webster rose to speak, but an adjourn-
ment was voted, giving Webster the right to the floor on the next
morning, the 26th.*

XI

1830

THE DEBATE WITH HAYNE:
SECOND SPEECH ON FOOTE'S RESOLUTION

"Gloomy fears oppressed Mr. Webster's friends," said Charles W. March. "The savageness of the attack, its seeming premeditation and powerful support gave them no encouragement of a successful resistance. His friends — even his most intimate — entertained fearful apprehensions."

"I shared a little myself in that fear and apprehension," said Edward Everett. "I was engaged on that day in a committee of which I was chairman, and could not be present in the Senate. But I knew from what I heard concerning General Hayne's speech that it was a very masterful effort, and immediately after the adjournment I hastened to Mr. Webster's house with, I admit, some little trepidation, not knowing how I would find him. But I was quite reassured in a moment after seeing Mr. Webster and observing his entire calmness. He seemed to be as much at his ease and as unmoved as I ever saw him. Indeed, at first, I was a little afraid from this that he was not quite aware of the magnitude of the contest.

" 'Did you take notes, Mr. Webster?' I asked.

"Mr. Webster took from his vest pocket a piece of paper about as big as the palm of his hand, and replied, 'I have it all: that is his speech.' "

On the same evening Justice Story is said to have called on Webster and, after expressing anxiety, offered to aid in looking up materials for his reply.

"Give yourself no uneasiness, Judge Story," said Webster. "I will grind him as fine as a pinch of snuff."

Later, in discussing his speech with Peter Harvey, Webster re-

marked that "no man who was not inspired could make a good speech without preparation; and if there were any of that sort of people, he had never met them." He added that it had often been remarked that he had made no preparation for the Hayne speech.

"That was not quite so," said he. "I was thoroughly conversant with the subject of the debate from having made preparation for wholly different purposes. I had my notes tucked away in a pigeon hole, and if Hayne had tried to make a speech to fit my notes, he could not have hit it any better. No man is inspired with the occasion. I never was."

In actual fact, Webster did have twelve pages of notes, on loose unnumbered sheets, now at the New Hampshire Historical Society, though they do not correspond to the order of the speech and were not all used.

By the morning of Tuesday, January 26, Washington was in a fever of excitement. March tells us that "as early as 9 o'clock crowds poured into the Capitol. At 12 o'clock, the hour of meeting, the Senate Chamber — its galleries, floors and even lobbies — was filled to its utmost capacity. The very stairways were dark with men, who hung on to one another, like bees in a swarm. The floor of the Senate was so densely crowded that persons once in could not get out or change their position. The courtesy of Senators accorded to the fairer sex room on the floor — the most gallant of them, their own seats. The gay bonnets and brilliant dresses threw a varied and picturesque beauty over the scene.

"Mr. Webster never rose to address an audience more self-possessed. There was no tremulousness in his voice or manner; nothing hurried, nothing simulated. The calmness of superior strength was visible in countenance, voice and bearing. A deep-seated conviction of the extraordinary character of the emergency, and of his ability to control it, seemed to possess him wholly."

Mr. President, [he said]: When the mariner has been tossed for many days in thick weather, and on an unknown sea, he naturally avails himself of the first pause in the storm, the earliest glance of the sun, to take his latitude, and ascertain how far the elements have driven him from his true course. Let us imitate this prudence, and, before we float farther on the waves of this debate, refer to the point from which we departed, that we may at least be able to conjecture where we now are. I ask for the reading of the resolution before the Senate.

The Secretary read the resolution, as follows:

"Resolved, *That the Committee on Public Lands be instructed to inquire and report the quantity of public lands remaining unsold within each State and Territory, and whether it be expedient to limit for a certain period the sales of the public lands to such lands only as have heretofore been offered for sale, and are now subject to entry at the minimum price. And, also, whether the office of Surveyor-General, and some of the land offices, may not be abolished without detriment to the public interest; or whether it be expedient to adopt measures to hasten the sales and extend more rapidly the surveys of the public lands."*

We have thus heard, Sir, what the resolution is which is actually before us for consideration; and it will readily occur to every one, that it is almost the only subject about which something has not been said in the speech, running through two days, by which the Senate has been entertained by the gentleman from South Carolina. Every topic in the wide range of our public affairs, whether past or present — every thing, general or local, whether belonging to national politics or party politics — seems to have attracted more or less of the honorable member's attention, save only the resolution before the Senate. He has spoken of every thing but the public lands; they have escaped his notice. To that subject, in all his excursions, he has not paid even the cold respect of a passing glance.

When this debate, Sir, was to be resumed, on Thursday morning, it so happened that it would have been convenient for me to be elsewhere. The honorable member, however, did not incline to put off the discussion to another day. He had a shot, he said, to return, and he wished to discharge it. That shot, Sir, which he thus kindly informed us was coming, that we might stand out of the way, or prepare ourselves to fall by it and die with decency, has now been received. Under all advantages, and with expectation awakened by the tone which preceded it, it has been discharged, and has spent its force. It may become me to say no more of its effect, than that, if nobody is found, after all, either killed or wounded, it is not the first time, in the history of human affairs, that the vigor and success of the war have not quite come up to the lofty and sounding phrase of the manifesto.

I spoke, Sir, of the Ordinance of 1787, which prohibits slavery, in all future times, northwest of the Ohio, as a measure of great wisdom and foresight, and one which had been attended with highly beneficial and permanent consequences. I supposed that, on this point, no two gentlemen in the Senate could entertain different opinions. But the simple expression of this sentiment has led the gentleman, not only into a labored defence of slavery, in the abstract, and on principle, but also into a warm accusation against me, as having attacked the system of domestic slavery now existing in the Southern States.

For all this, there was not the slightest foundation, in any thing said or intimated by me. I did not utter a single word which any ingenuity could torture into an attack on the slavery of the South. I said, only, that it was highly wise and useful, in legislating for the Northwestern country while it was yet a wilderness, to prohibit the introduction of slaves; and I added, that I presumed there was no reflecting and intelligent person, in the neighboring State of Kentucky, who would doubt that, if the same prohibition had been extended, at the same early period, over that commonwealth, her strength and population would, at this day, have been far greater than they are. If these opinions be thought doubtful, they are nevertheless, I trust, neither extraordinary nor disrespectful. They attack nobody and menace nobody. And yet, Sir, the gentleman's optics have discovered, even in the mere expression of this sentiment, what he calls the very spirit of the Missouri question! He represents me as making an onset on the whole South, and manifesting a spirit which would interfere with, and disturb, their domestic , condition!

Sir, this injustice no otherwise surprises me, than as it is committed here, and committed without the slightest pretence of ground for it. I say it only surprises me as being done here; for I know full well, that it is, and has been, the settled policy of some persons in the South, for years, to represent the people of the North as disposed to interfere with them in their own exclusive and peculiar concerns. This is a delicate and sensitive point in Southern feeling; and of late years it has always been touched, and generally with effect, whenever the object has been to unite the whole South against Northern men or Northern measures. This feeling, always carefully kept alive, and maintained at too intense a heat to admit discrimination or reflection, is a lever of great power in our political machine. It moves vast bodies, and gives to them one and the same direction. But it is without adequate cause, and the suspicion which exists is wholly groundless. There is not, and never has been, a disposition in the North to interfere with these interests of the South. Such interference has never been supposed to be within the power of government; nor has it been in any way attempted.

The slavery of the South has always been regarded as a matter of domestic policy, left with the States themselves, and with which the federal government had nothing to do. Certainly, Sir, I am, and ever have been, of that opinion. The gentleman, indeed, argues that slavery, in the abstract, is no evil. Most assuredly I need not say I differ with him, altogether and most widely, on that point. I regard domestic slavery as one of the greatest evils, both moral and political. But whether it be a malady, and whether it be curable, and if so, by what means; or, on the other hand, whether it be the *vulnus immedicabile* of the social system, I leave it to those whose right and duty it is to inquire and to decide.

The domestic slavery of the Southern States I leave where I find it — in the hands of their own governments. It is their affair, not mine. The Union itself is too full of benefit to be hazarded in propositions for changing its original basis. I go for the Constitution as it is, and for the Union as it is.

We approach, at length, Sir, to a more important part of the honorable gentleman's observations. Since it does not accord with my views of justice and policy to give away the public lands altogether, as a mere matter of gratuity, I am asked by the honorable gentleman on what ground it is that I consent to vote them away in particular instances. How, he inquires, do I reconcile with these professed sentiments, my support of measures appropriating portions of the lands to particular roads, particular canals, particular rivers, and particular institutions of education in the West? This leads, Sir, to the real and wide difference in political opinion between the honorable gentleman and myself. On my part, I look upon all these objects as connected with the common good, fairly embraced in its object and its terms; he, on the contrary, deems them all, if good at all, only local good. This is our difference. The interrogatory which he proceeded to put, at once explains this difference. "What interest," asks he, "has South Carolina in a canal in Ohio?" Sir, this very question is full of significance. It develops the gentleman's whole political system; and its answer expounds mine. Here we differ. I look upon a road over the Alleghanies, a canal round the falls of the Ohio, or a canal or railway from the Atlantic to the Western waters, as being an object large and extensive enough to be fairly said to be for the common benefit. The gentleman thinks otherwise, and this is the key to his construction of the powers of the government. He may well ask what interest has South Carolina in a canal in Ohio. On his system, it is true, she has no interest. On that system, Ohio and Carolina are different governments and different countries; connected here, it is true, by some slight and ill-defined bond of union, but in all main respects separate and diverse. On that system, Carolina has no more interest in a canal in Ohio than in Mexico. The gentleman, therefore, only follows out his own principles; he does no more than arrive at the natural conclusions of his own doctrines; he only announces the true results of that creed which he has adopted himself, and would persuade others to adopt, when he thus declares that South Carolina has no interest in a public work in Ohio.

Sir, we narrow-minded people of New England do not reason thus. Our *notion* of things is entirely different. We look upon the States, not as separated, but as united. We love to dwell on that union, and on the mutual happiness which it has so much promoted, and the common renown which it has so greatly contributed to acquire. In our contemplation, Carolina and Ohio are parts of the same country; States, united under the same general government, having interests, common, associated, intermingled. In whatever is within the proper sphere of the constitutional power of this government, we look upon the States as one. We do not impose geographical limits to our patriotic feeling or regard; we do not follow rivers and mountains, and lines of latitude, to find boundaries, beyond which public improvements do not benefit us. We who come here, as agents and representatives of these narrow-minded and selfish men of New England, consider ourselves as bound to regard with an equal eye the good of the whole, in whatever is within our powers of legislation.

These, Sir, are the grounds, succinctly stated, on which my votes for grants of lands for particular objects rest; while I maintain, at the same time, that it is all a common fund, for the common benefit.

There yet remains to be performed, Mr. President, by far the most grave and important duty, which I feel to be devolved on me by this occasion. It is to state, and to defend, what I conceive to be the true principles of the Constitution under which we are here assembled. I might well have desired that so weighty a task should have fallen into other and abler hands. I could have wished that it should have been executed by those whose character and experience give weight and influence to their opinions, such as cannot possibly belong to mine. But, Sir, I have met the occasion, not sought it; and I shall proceed to state my own sentiments, without challenging for them any particular regard, with studied plainness, and as much precision as possible.

I understand the honorable gentleman from South Carolina to maintain, that it is a right of the State legislatures to interfere, whenever, in their judgment, this government transcends its constitutional limits, and to arrest the operation of its laws.

I understand him to maintain this right, as a right existing *under* the Constitution, not as a right to overthrow it on the ground of extreme necessity, such as would justify violent revolution.

I understand him to maintain an authority, on the part of the States, thus to interfere, for the purpose of correcting the exercise of power by the general government, of checking it, and of compelling it to conform to their opinion of the extent of its powers.

I understand him to maintain, that the ultimate power of judging of the constitutional extent of its own authority is not lodged exclusively in the general government, or any branch of it; but that, on the contrary, the States may lawfully decide for themselves, and each State for itself, whether, in a given case, the act of the general government transcends its power.

I understand him to insist, that, if the exigency of the case, in the opinion of any State government, require it, such State government may, by its own sovereign authority, annul an act of the general government which it deems plainly and palpably unconstitutional.

This is the sum of what I understand from him to be the South Carolina doctrine, and the doctrine which he maintains. I propose to consider it, and compare it with the Constitution. Allow me to say, as a preliminary remark, that I call this the South Carolina doctrine only because the gentleman himself has so denominated it. I do not feel at liberty to say that South Carolina, as a State, has ever advanced these sentiments. I hope she has not, and never may. That a great majority of her people are opposed to the tariff laws, is doubtless true. That a majority, somewhat less than that just mentioned, conscientiously believe these laws unconstitutional, may probably also be true. But that any majority holds to the right of direct State interference at State discretion, the right of nullifying acts of Congress by acts of State legislation, is more than I know, and what I shall be slow to believe.

There may be extreme cases, in which the people, in any mode of assembling, may resist usurpation, and relieve themselves from a tyrannical government. No one will deny this. Such resistance is not only acknowledged to be just in America, but in England also. Blackstone admits as much, in the theory, and practice, too, of the English constitution. We, Sir, who oppose the Carolina doctrine, do not deny that the people may, if they choose, throw off any government when it becomes oppressive and intolerable, and erect a better in its stead. We all know that civil institutions are established for the public benefit, and that when they cease to answer the ends of their existence they may be changed. But I do not understand the doctrine now contended for to be that, which, for the sake of distinction, we may call the right of revolution. I understand the gentleman to maintain, that, without revolution, without civil commotion, without rebellion, a remedy for supposed abuse and transgression of the powers of the general government lies in a direct appeal to the interference of the State governments.

Mr. Hayne here rose and said: He did not contend for the mere right of revolution, but for the right of constitutional resistance. What he maintained was, that in case of a plain, palpable violation of the Constitution by the general government, a State may interpose; and that this interposition is constitutional.

Mr. Webster resumed:

So, Sir, I understood the gentleman, and am happy to find that I did not misunderstand him. What he contends for is, that it is constitutional to interrupt the administration of the Constitution itself, in the hands of those who are chosen and sworn to administer it, by the direct interference, in form of law, of the States, in virtue of their sovereign capacity. The inherent right in the people to reform their government I do not deny; and they have another right, and that is, to resist unconstitutional laws, without overturning the government. It is no doctrine of mine that unconstitutional laws bind the people. The great question is, Whose prerogative is it to decide on the constitutionality or unconstitutionality of the laws? On that, the main debate hinges. The proposition, that, in case of a supposed violation of the Constitution by Congress, the States have a constitutional right to interfere and annul the law of Congress, is the proposition of the gentleman. I do not admit it. If the gentleman had intended no more than to assert the right of revolution for justifiable cause, he would have said only what all agree to. But I cannot conceive that there can be a middle course, between submission to the laws, when regularly pronounced constitutional, on the one hand, and open resistance, which is revolution or rebellion, on the other.

This leads us to inquire into the origin of this government and the source of its power. Whose agent is it? Is it the creature of the State legislatures, or the creature of the people? If the government of the United States be the agent of the State governments, then they may control it, provided they can agree in the manner of controlling it; if it be the agent of the people, then the people alone can control it, restrain it, modify, or reform it. It is observable enough, that the doctrine for which the honorable gentleman contends leads him to the necessity of maintaining, not only that this general government is the creature of the States, but that it is the creature of each of the States severally, so that each may assert the power for itself of determining whether it acts within the limits of its authority. It is the servant of four-and-twenty masters, of different wills and different purposes, and yet bound to obey all.

It so happens that, at the very moment when South Carolina resolves that the tariff laws are unconstitutional, Pennsylvania and Kentucky resolve exactly the reverse. *They* hold those laws to be both highly proper and strictly constitutional. And now, Sir, how does the honorable member propose to deal with this case? How does he relieve us from this difficulty, upon any principle of his? His construction gets us into it; how does he propose to get us out?

In Carolina, the tariff is a palpable, deliberate usurpation; Carolina, therefore, may nullify it, and refuse to pay the duties. In Pennsylvania, it is both clearly constitutional and highly expedient; and there the duties are to be paid. And yet we live under a government of uniform laws, and under a Constitution too, which contains an express provision, as it happens, that all duties shall be equal in all the States. Does not this approach absurdity?

If there be no power to settle such questions, independent of either of the States, is not the whole Union a rope of sand? Are we not thrown back again, precisely, upon the old Confederation?

I must now beg to ask, Sir, Whence is this supposed right of the States derived? Where do they find the power to interfere with the laws of the Union? Sir, the opinion which the honorable gentleman maintains is a notion founded in a total misapprehension, in my judgment, of the origin of this government, and of the foundation on which it stands. I hold it to be a popular government, erected by the people; those who administer it, responsible to the people; and itself capable of being amended and modified, just as the people may choose it should be. It is as popular, just as truly emanating from the people, as the State governments. It is created for one purpose; the State governments for another. It has its own powers; they have theirs. There is no more authority with them to arrest the operation of a law of Congress, than with Congress to arrest the operation of their laws. We are here to administer a Constitution emanating immediately from the people, and trusted by them to our administration.

It is not the creature of State legislatures; nay, more, if the whole truth must be told, the people brought it into existence, established it, and have hitherto supported it, for the very purpose, amongst others, of imposing certain salutary restraints on State sovereignties. The States cannot now make war; they cannot contract alliances; they cannot make, each for itself, separate regulations of commerce; they cannot lay imposts; they cannot coin money. If this Constitution, Sir, be the creature of State legislatures, it must be admitted that it has obtained a strange control over the volitions of its creators.

This, Sir, was the first great step. By this the supremacy of the Constitution and laws of the United States is declared. The people so will it. No State law is to be valid which comes in conflict with the Constitution, or any law of the United States passed in pursuance of it. But who shall decide this question of interference? To whom lies the last appeal? This, Sir, the Constitution itself decides also, by declaring, *that the judicial power shall extend to all cases arising under the Constitution and laws of the United States.* These two provisions cover the whole ground. They are, in truth, the keystone of the arch! With these it is a government; without them it is a confederation.

For myself, Sir, I do not admit the competency of South Carolina, or any other State, to prescribe my constitutional duty; or to settle, between me and the people, the validity of laws of Congress, for which I have voted. I decline her umpirage. I have not sworn to support the Constitution according to her construction of its clauses. I have not stipulated, by my oath of office or otherwise, to come under any responsibility, except to the people, and those whom they have appointed to pass upon the question, whether laws, supported by my votes, conform to the Constitution of the country.

And, Sir, if we look to the general nature of the case, could any thing have been more preposterous, than to make a government for the whole Union, and yet leave its powers subject, not to one interpretation, but to thirteen or twenty-four interpretations? Instead of one tribunal, established by all, responsible to all, with power to decide for all, shall constitutional questions be left to four-and-twenty popular bodies, each at liberty to decide for itself, and none bound to respect the decisions of others; and each at liberty, too, to give a new construction on every new election of its own members? Would any thing, with such a principle in it, or rather with such a destitution of all principle, be fit to be called a government? No, Sir. It should not be denominated a Constitution. It should be called, rather, a collection of topics for everlasting controversy; heads of debate for a disputatious people. It would not be a government. It would not be adequate to any practical good, or fit for any country to live under.

And now, Mr. President, let me run the honorable gentleman's doctrine a little into its practical application. Let us look at his probable *modus operandi*. If a thing can be done, an ingenious man can tell how it is to be done, and I wish to be informed how this State interference is to be put in practice, without violence, bloodshed, and rebellion. We will take the existing case of the tariff law. South Carolina is said to have made up her opinion upon it. If we do not repeal it (as we probably shall not), she will then apply to the case the remedy of her doctrine. She will, we must suppose, pass a law of her legislature, declaring the several acts of Congress, usually called the tariff laws, null and void, so far as they respect South Carolina, or the citizens thereof. So far, all is a paper transaction, and easy enough. But the collector at Charleston is collecting the duties imposed by these tariff laws. He, therefore, must be stopped. The collector will seize the goods if the tariff duties are not paid. The State authorities will undertake their rescue, the marshal, with his posse, will come to the collector's aid, and here the contest begins. The militia of the State will be called out to sustain the nullifying act. They will march, Sir, under a very gallant leader; for I believe the honorable member himself commands the militia of that part of the State.

Here would ensue a pause; for they say that a certain stillness precedes the tempest. The trumpeter would hold his breath awhile, and before all this military array should fall on the custom-house, collector, clerks, and all, it is very probable some of those composing it would request of their gallant commander-in-chief to be informed a little upon the point of law; for they have, doubtless, a just respect for his opinions as a lawyer, as well as for his bravery as a soldier. They know he has read Blackstone and the Constitution, as well as Turenne and Vauban. They would ask him, therefore, something concerning their rights in this matter. They would inquire, whether it was not somewhat dangerous to resist a law of the United States. What would be the nature of their offence, they would wish to learn, if they, by military force and array, resisted the execution in Carolina of a law of the United States, and it should turn out, after all, that the law *was constitutional?* He would answer, of course, Treason. No lawyer could give any other answer. John Fries, he would tell them, had learned that, some years ago. How, then, they would ask, do you propose to defend us? We are not afraid of bullets, but treason has a way of taking people off that we do not much relish. How do you propose to defend us? "South Carolina is a sovereign State," he would reply. That is true; but would the judge admit our plea? "These tariff laws," he would repeat, "are unconstitutional, palpably, deliberately, dangerously." That may all be so; but if the tribunal should not happen to be of that opinion, shall we swing for it? We are ready to die for our country, but it is rather an awkward business, this dying without touching the ground! After all, that is a sort of hemp tax worse than any part of the tariff.

Direct collision, therefore, between force and force, is the un-avoidable result of that remedy for the revision of unconstitutional laws which the gentleman contends for. It must happen in the very first case to which it is applied. Is not this the plain result?

I profess, Sir, in my career hitherto, to have kept steadily in view the prosperity and honor of the whole country, and the preservation of our Federal Union. It is to that Union we owe our safety at home, and our consideration and dignity abroad. It is to that Union that we are chiefly indebted for whatever makes us most proud of our country. That Union we reached only by the discipline of our virtues in the severe school of adversity. It had its origin in the necessities of disordered finance, prostrate commerce, and ruined credit. Under its benign influences, these great interests immediately awoke, as from the dead, and sprang forth with newness of life. Every year of its duration has teemed with fresh proofs of its utility and its blessings; and although our territory has stretched out wider and wider, and our population spread farther and farther, they have not outrun its protection or its benefits. It has been to us all a copious fountain of national, social, and personal happiness.

I have not allowed myself, Sir, to look beyond the Union, to see what might lie hidden in the dark recess behind. I have not coolly weighed the chances of preserving liberty when the bonds that unite us together shall be broken asunder. I have not accustomed myself to hang over the precipice of disunion, to see whether, with my short sight, I can fathom the depth of the abyss below; nor could I regard him as a safe counsellor in the affairs of this government, whose thoughts should be mainly bent on considering, not how the Union may be best preserved, but how tolerable might be the condition of the people when it should be broken up and destroyed.

While the Union lasts, we have high, exciting, gratifying prospects spread out before us, for us and our children. Beyond that I seek not to penetrate the veil. God grant that in my day, at least, that curtain may not rise! God grant that on my vision never may be opened what lies behind! When my eyes shall be turned to behold for the last time the sun in heaven, may I not see him shining on the broken and dishonored fragments of a once glorious Union; on States dissevered, discordant, belligerent; on a land rent with civil feuds, or drenched, it may be, in fraternal blood! Let their last feeble and lingering glance rather behold the gorgeous ensign of the republic, now known and honored throughout the earth, still full high advanced, its arms and trophies streaming in their original lustre, not a stripe erased or polluted, nor a single star obscured, bearing for its motto, no such miserable interrogatory as "What is all this worth?" nor those other words of delusion and folly, "Liberty first and Union afterwards"; but everywhere, spread all over in characters of living light, blazing on all its ample folds, as they float over the sea and over the land, and in every wind under the whole heavens, that other sentiment, dear to every true American heart — Liberty *and* Union, now and for ever, one and inseparable!

"The speech was over," writes March, "but the tones of the orator still lingered on the ear, and the audience, unconscious of the close, retained their positions. Everywhere around seemed forgetfulness of all but the orator's presence and words. Silence could almost have heard itself, it was so supernaturally still. The feeling was too over-powering to allow expression by voice or hand. It was as if one was in a trancè, all motion paralyzed.

"The descending hammer of the Chair awoke them, with a start — and with one universal, long-drawn, deep breath, with which the overcharged heart seeks relief — the crowded assembly broke up and departed."

In far-off Marshfield a somewhat different scene was presented, according to Peter Harvey's rendition of a Webster anecdote:

"A great intimacy and friendship had grown up between old Captain Thomas and Webster. The captain, though much his senior, looked up to Webster with respect and admiration, and at the same time entertained for him a sort of paternal affection. He deferred to Webster in all matters, excepting some practical rules of farming, the nicer points of sporting, and the habits of birds, wild fowl, and fish. Their association, always pleasant, grew into mutual affection; and Captain Thomas, who, at Webster's suggestion, subscribed for the semi-weekly Columbian Sentinel, *watched with the most intense interest Webster's course in the Senate as reported in that journal.*

"The good captain read Hayne's first speech. He waited, in confidence, for a triumphant reply. It came, and he was entirely satis-

fied. The faithful Sentinel, *however, soon brought him Hayne's second speech. He read it with extreme and painful interest.*

"It excited in him the gravest apprehensions for the idol of his old age. He was overwhelmed with grief. His hero, his great man, his beloved, almost worshipped friend, was overthrown in debate by his Southern antagonist. The kind old gentleman's pride was humbled; he was in despair — his heart almost broken. Casting away the paper, he rose and retired slowly to his room, directing some one to come and take his boots away, as he should never want them again. His family tried in vain to console him. He refused to be comforted.

"For three days he kept his bed, mourning over the fall of his friend, and refusing all consolation. His eldest son tried to persuade him that Webster was able to defend the cause of New England, and would yet have his triumph. His only reply was: 'It can't be answered, Henry, it can't be answered.'

"The fatal semi-weekly Sentinel *came again in due course. It was evening. The family were gathered around the fire in sad apprehension. The old man's mind seemed almost unhinged — they even feared for his life. The captain still kept his bed, and appeared determined to hold to his vow never to rise from it. All their efforts to rouse him had, thus far, proved ineffectual. On opening the paper, it was found to contain Webster's second reply to Hayne. The family at once resolved that Henry should assume the task of carrying it to his father. Henry entered his father's room with the paper and a candle. The old man groaned, and asked what he wanted. Henry replied;*

" 'Father, I have brought you the Sentinel; *I thought you might like to look at it.'*

" 'No, Henry, I don't want to see it.'

" 'It contains a second speech of Mr. Webster, in reply to Colonel Hayne.'

" 'Oh, Henry!' said the old gentleman, 'it is of no use; it can't be answered; I don't want to see it.'

"*Henry lingered and seemed greatly distressed at his father's re-fusal. At last, Captain Thomas consented to have the paper and candle left, and said that perhaps he would look at it. Henry went downstairs and reported the apparently unsuccessful result of his mission; and the little family drew closely around their winter fire more gloomily than before.*

"*Some time thus elapsed, when they were all suddenly startled by a tremendous shout from their father's room. They all rushed up-stairs together to see what had happened. The Captain was sitting on the side of the bed, with the paper in one hand and the candle in the other. As Henry entered, the captain roared out:*

"*'Bring me my boots, Henry! Bring me my boots!'*"

XII

1830–1834

REPLY TO CALHOUN — THE BANK WAR

Seldom has any speech blended intellect and emotion so success-fully as Webster's reply to Hayne. Nor has any met with a more enthusiastic response. Writing to Mason on February 27, 1830, Webster said:

I may say to you that I never before spoke in the hearing of an audience so excited, so eager and so sympathetic.

In the North and West, and even in parts of the South, Webster was hailed as a hero. The flood of congratulations included a letter from ex-President Madison. It also included a costly silver service from Amos Lawrence, wealthy Massachusetts mill owner, and pro-posals for testimonial dinners and other public honors. Webster's reaction found expression in his correspondence with William Sullivan.

[Letter to Sullivan, May 22, 1830]

Your letter gives me an opportunity of talking freely on a subject which has been suggested to me from various quarters, and about which I have not said much. I am inclined to avail myself of this opportunity to talk right on, and give you the whole of my notions in regard to the matter.

1. I have heard that the good people of Boston would, some of them, like to show me some proof of kindness by a dinner, a ball, or

something else. 2. That the mode or manner is not yet decided, and that all rests, as yet, in intention. Now I shall open my heart to you without reserve.

As to a dinner, there seem to me to be insuperable objections to it. I have received that compliment once, as you know, two years ago; it would, therefore, be nothing new. But what is more important, other persons' feelings might be injured. Our immediate representative has acquitted himself very ably in the House of Representatives, and done great honor to the State; so has Davis, and so has Everett. In truth, our whole delegation in the House of Representatives is uncommonly able, and all true. My colleague, too, though an unpretending man, has been entirely true, and very useful in more cases and ways than one. Now it would be invidious to select me alone, as the object of any particular expression of regard; I should, myself, feel that it would be in some measure unjust; I should think they would have a right to feel hurt.

I am, therefore, my dear Sir, against a dinner, and, indeed, against all ostentation and show, and parade. I believe the interest as well of my constituents as of myself, is likely to be better promoted by abstaining from all such things. I shall see all Boston, and much of the Commonwealth, in the course of the summer, and shall have an opportunity of seeing and shaking hands with most, or many, of those who take an interest in me, or would wish to give me congratulation.

As to a ball, the sun rides too high for that. Let us think of that in October.

And now I will tell you what may be done if you and others see fit. If fifty gentlemen are inclined to make a subscription for a piece of plate, say an urn or some such thing, let them do so. One single article, of size to bear an inscription, would probably be better than more and smaller ones. Yet even this last, which is your suggestion, would be perfectly well.

I have thus spoken to you in confidence, freely and unreservedly. Whatever you and others do, or omit, excepting always a dinner, and any thing else that is ostentatious, will be perfectly satisfactory to me. I know you will, some of you at least, be glad to see me, and that itself is high gratification. I owe my neighbors infinitely more than they can ever owe me; and I am satisfied, and gratified, and more than compensated a thousand times, for any labors or efforts of mine, by the consciousness that I am thought to have done some little good.

God bless you.

Webster's reply to Hayne had scotched the doctrine of nullification but had not killed it. Calhoun and Hayne continued to assert South Carolina's right to disregard federal legislation which it deemed injurious to its interests, and to secede from the Union if its demands were not met. On November 19, 1832, a State Convention at Columbia, South Carolina adopted an Ordinance of Nullification declaring the federal tariff laws of 1829 and 1832 to be of no force or effect in South Carolina. To emphasize the strength and determination of this move, General Hayne was made Governor and Calhoun resigned the vice presidency in order to represent South Carolina on the Senate floor.

President Jackson left no doubt as to his intentions. In this same November he had been triumphantly reelected, and on December 10 he formally proclaimed his determination to enforce the federal laws. On January 21, 1833, in what was known as the "Force Bill," he asked congressional authority to use the army and navy to suppress resistance.

To counter the Force Bill, Calhoun introduced a series of resolutions declaring the Constitution to be a "compact between the States," and asserting that "the general government is not made the final judge of the powers delegated to it; but that, as in all other cases of compact between sovereign parties, each has an equal right to judge for itself as well as of the infraction as of the mode and measure of redress."

Calhoun supported these resolutions in a two-day speech which

REPLY TO CALHOUN

Charles W. March describes as of such "tempestuous eloquence"
that he "tore to pieces the arguments of his opponents as a hurricane
rends the sails." He began by asserting that South Carolina was be-
ing grievously wronged. "Mr. President," he said:

"I know not which is most objectionable, the provisions of this
bill, or the temper in which its adoption has been urged. If the
extraordinary powers with which the bill proposes to clothe the
Executive, to the utter prostration of the Constitution and the rights
of the States, be calculated to impress our minds with alarm at the
rapid progress of despotism in our country, the zeal with which every
circumstance calculated to misrepresent or exaggerate the conduct
of Carolina in the controversy is seized on, with a view to excite hos-
tility against her, but too plainly indicates the deep decay of that
brotherly feeling which once existed between these States, and to
which we are indebted for our beautiful federal system."

According to March, Calhoun then "illustrated his position with
infinite ability and great beauty of language." March adds: "The
crowd was great in the Senate chamber during Mr. Calhoun's speech;
in the galleries more particularly. While he was uttering some of his
brilliant periods, in the very torrent, tempest and whirlwind of his
eloquence, a man in the gallery suddenly confounded the audience
by exclaiming in a shriek-like voice, 'Mr. President!' and before the
presiding officer could take measures to repress the outrage, he con-
tinued, 'Mr. President, something must be done, or I shall be
squeezed to death!' It was some time before order could be restored,
or the dignity of the Senate re-established. The ludicrous nature of
the interruption affected the gravity of almost every person present,
even of grave Senators; of all, perhaps, but the orator, upon whose
countenance there passed not the shade of an emotion. The rigid
muscles showed no relaxation, but every feature remained unmoved
and inflexible. He proceeded as if nought had occurred of singu-

larity, and his deep and earnest tones soon recalled the minds of the
audience to the subject they had for a moment forgotten.

"He spoke parts of two days — concluding at two o'clock of the
second day. As soon as he finished his speech, Mr. Webster took the
floor in reply; universal opinion assuming that he alone was quali-
fied to follow Mr. Calhoun."

Among the feelings which at this moment fill my breast, not the
least is that of regret at the position in which the gentleman has
placed himself. Sir, he does himself no justice. The cause which he
has espoused finds no basis in the Constitution, no succor from
public sympathy, no cheering from a patriotic community. He has
no foothold on which to stand while he might display the powers
of his acknowledged talents. Every thing beneath his feet is hollow
and treacherous. He is like a strong man struggling in a morass:
every effort to extricate himself only sinks him deeper and deeper.
And I fear the resemblance may be carried still farther; I fear that
no friend can safely come to his relief, that no one can approach
near enough to hold out a helping hand, without danger of going
down himself, also, into the bottomless depths of this Serbonian
bog.

The first two resolutions of the honorable member affirm these
propositions, viz.:

1. That the political system under which we live, and under
which Congress is now assembled, is a compact, to which the people
of the several States, as separate and sovereign communities, are
the parties.

2. That these sovereign parties have a right to judge, each for itself, of any alleged violation of the Constitution by Congress; and,
in case of such violation, to choose, each for itself, its own mode and
measure of redress.

It is true, Sir, that the honorable member calls this a "constitutional" compact; but still he affirms it to be a compact between
sovereign States. What precise meaning, then, does he attach to the

term *constitutional?* If he admits our instrument of government to be a *constitution,* then, for that very reason, it is not a compact between sovereigns; a constitution of government and a compact between sovereign powers being things essentially unlike in their very natures, and incapable of ever being the same.

Sir, I must say to the honorable gentleman, that, in our American political grammar, *constitution* is a noun substantive; it imports a distinct and clear idea of itself; and it is not to lose its importance and dignity, it is not to be turned into a poor, ambiguous, senseless, unmeaning adjective for the purpose of accommodating any new set of political notions. Sir, we reject his new rules of syntax altogether. We will not give up our forms of political speech to the grammarians of the school of nullification. By the Constitution, we mean, not a "constitutional compact," but, simply and directly, the Constitution, the fundamental law; and if there be one word in the language which the people of the United States understand, this is that word.

Was it Mirabeau, Mr. President, or some other master of the human passions, who has told us that words are things? They are indeed things, and things of mighty influence, not only in addresses to the passions and high-wrought feelings of mankind, but in the discussion of legal and political questions also; because a just conclusion is often avoided, or a false one reached, by the adroit substitution of one phrase, or one word, for another.

Sir, I intend to hold the gentleman to the written record. In the discussion of a constitutional question, I intend to impose upon him the restraints of constitutional language. The people have ordained a Constitution; can they reject it without revolution? They have established a form of government; can they overthrow it without revolution? These are the true questions.

The necessary import of the resolution, therefore, is, that the United States are connected only by a league; that it is in the good pleasure of every State to decide how long she will choose to remain a member of this league; that any State may determine the extent of her own obligations under it, and accept or reject what shall be decided by the whole; that she may also determine whether her rights have been violated, what is the extent of the injury done her, and what mode and measure of redress her wrongs may make it fit and expedient for her to adopt. The result of the whole is, that any State may secede at pleasure; that any State may resist a law which she herself may choose to say exceeds the power of Congress; and that, as a sovereign power, she may redress her own grievances, by her own arm, at her own discretion.

To allow State resistance to the laws of Congress to be rightful and proper, to admit nullification in some States, and yet not expect to see a dismemberment of the entire government, appears to me the wildest illusion, and the most extravagant folly. The gentleman seems not conscious of the direction or the rapidity of his own course. The current of his opinions sweeps him along, he knows not whither. To begin with nullification, with the avowed intent, nevertheless, not to proceed to secession, dismemberment, and general revolution, is as if one were to take the plunge of Niagara, and cry out that he would stop half way down. In the one case, as in the other, the rash adventurer must go to the bottom of the dark abyss below, were it not that that abyss has no discovered bottom.

Sir, the Constitution of the United States was received as a whole, and for the whole country. If it cannot stand altogether, it cannot stand in parts; and if the laws cannot be executed everywhere, they cannot long be executed anywhere. The gentleman very well knows that all duties and imposts must be uniform throughout the country. He knows that we cannot have one rule or one law for South Carolina, and another for other States. He must see, therefore, and does see, and every man sees, that the only alternative is a repeal of the laws throughout the whole Union, or their execution in Carolina as well as elsewhere. And this repeal is demanded because a single State interposes her veto, and threatens resistance! The result of the gentleman's opinion, or rather the very text of his doctrine, is, that no act of Congress can bind all the States, the constitutionality of which is not admitted by all; or, in other words, that no single State is bound, against its own dissent, by a law of imposts.

This is precisely the evil experienced under the old Confederation, and for remedy of which this Constitution was adopted. The leading object in establishing this government, an object forced on the country by the condition of the times and the absolute necessity of the law, was to give to Congress power to lay and collect imposts *without the consent of particular States.* The Revolutionary debt remained unpaid; the national treasury was bankrupt; the country was destitute of credit; Congress issued its requisitions on the States, and the States neglected them; there was no power of coercion but war, Congress could not lay imposts, or other taxes, by its own authority; the whole general government, therefore, was little more than a name. The Articles of Confederation, as to purposes of revenue and finance, were nearly a dead letter. The country sought to escape from this condition, at once feeble and disgraceful, by constituting a government which should have power, of itself, to lay duties and taxes, and to pay the public debt, and provide for the general welfare; and to lay these duties and taxes in all the States, without asking the consent of the State governments. This was the very power on which the new Constitution was to depend for all its ability to do good; and without it, it can be no government, now or at any time.

And now, Sir, against all these theories and opinions, I maintain —

1. That the Constitution of the United States is not a league, confederacy, or compact between the people of the several States in their sovereign capacities; but a government proper, founded on the adoption of the people, and creating direct relations between itself and individuals.

2. That no State authority has power to dissolve these relations; that nothing can dissolve them but revolution; and that, consequently, there can be no such thing as secession without revolution.

3. That there is a supreme law, consisting of the Constitution of the United States, and acts of Congress passed in pursuance of it, and treaties; and that, in cases not capable of assuming the character of a suit in law or equity, Congress must judge of, and finally interpret, this supreme law so often as it has occasion to pass acts of legislation; and in cases capable of assuming, and actually assuming, the character of a suit, the Supreme Court of the United States is the final interpreter.

4. That an attempt by a State to abrogate, annul, or nullify an act of Congress, or to arrest its operation within her limits, on the ground that, in her opinion, such law is unconstitutional, is a direct usurpation on the just powers of the general government, and on the equal rights of other States; a plain violation of the Constitution, and a proceeding essentially revolutionary in its character and tendency.

Mr. President, if the friends of nullification should be able to propagate their opinions, and give them practical effect, they would, in my judgment, prove themselves the most skilful "architects of ruin," the most effectual extinguishers of high-raised expectation, the greatest blasters of human hopes, that any age has produced. They would stand up to proclaim, in tones which would pierce the ears of half the human race, that the last great experiment of representative government had failed.

But, Sir, if the government do its duty, if it act with firmness and with moderation, these opinions cannot prevail. Be assured, Sir, be assured, that, among the political sentiments of this people, the love of union is still uppermost. They will stand fast by the Constitution, and by those who defend it. I rely on no temporary expedients, on no political combination; but I rely on the true American feeling, the genuine patriotism of the people, and the imperative decision of the public voice.

For myself, Sir, I shun no responsibility justly devolving on me, here or elsewhere, in attempting to maintain the cause. I am bound to it by indissoluble ties of affection and duty, and I shall cheerfully partake in its fortunes and its fate. I am ready to perform my own appropriate part, whenever and wherever the occasion may call on me, and to take my chance among those upon whom blows may fall first and fall thickest. I shall exert every faculty I possess in aiding to prevent the Constitution from being nullified, destroyed, or impaired; and even should I see it fall, I will still, with a voice feeble, perhaps, but earnest as ever issued from human lips, and with fidelity and zeal which nothing shall extinguish, call on the *People* to come to its rescue.

The Ordinance of Nullification and the Force Bill ended in compromise. Under the leadership of Clay, legislation was adopted substantially reducing the tariff, and the antagonists withdrew from their extreme positions.

Webster opposed this compromise, wishing to face down, once and for all, the heresies of nullification. Ultimately, it took the Civil War to settle the issue, but, by 1861, Webster's views, as laid down in his replies to Hayne and Calhoun, had gained complete acceptance in the North and West and united them behind Lincoln in his stand against secession. Indeed, so greatly had opinion shifted that it is now hard to realize that, when originally expressed, Webster's views had run counter to what was probably then the predominant constitutional doctrine.

On the issues of nullification and secession Webster and Jackson saw eye to eye. In fact, Jackson's proclamation had borrowed heavily from Webster's reply to Hayne. But on the other great issue of the day, the Second Bank of the United States, they were poles apart.

For Webster the Bank had long been a comfortable client, and during the absence of its regular counsel, John Sergeant, he had taken full responsibility for its representation before the Supreme Court. He had been on the board of the central bank in Philadelphia, and he had obtained the appointment of his friend Jeremiah Mason as president and counsel of its Portsmouth, New Hampshire branch. He had also received accommodations in the way of loans.

SPEAK FOR YOURSELF, DANIEL

*He saw nothing in his present position that required him to relin-
quish so valuable a client, and, even though the Bank was then
fighting for its life in Congress, he wrote to Nicholas Biddle, its
president, on December 21, 1833:*

Since I have arrived here, I have had an application to be concerned, professionally, against the Bank, which I have declined, of
course, although I believe my retainer has not been renewed, or
refreshed as usual. If it be wished that my relation to the Bank
should be continued, it may be well to send me the usual retainers.

*Webster believed wholeheartedly in the cause of the Bank. He
would undoubtedly have championed its cause even had it not been
a client. Since his legislative views coincided so satisfactorily with
his private interests, he saw no reason why he should lose his fees.*

*Under the extremely able management of Biddle, the Bank had
grown immensely powerful — in Jackson's eyes, too powerful. Although the federal government had furnished one-fifth of its capital
and was entitled by law to appoint one-fifth of its directors, the
Bank was for all practical purposes free of governmental restraint.
Assured of a monopoly on government deposits, it did not merely
serve the Treasury Department, it dominated it.*

*To Biddle, and to businessmen generally, the Bank was an essen-
tial cog in the economy, stabilizing the currency and facilitating the
free flow of funds to meet the demands of business in different parts
of the country and abroad. Jackson, on the other hand, felt that the
Bank wielded power too great to be tolerated in any scheme of democratic government. Unfortunately, there was at the time no feasible
middle ground. Administrative controls of the type with which we
have grown familiar were then unknown. The government could
kill the Bank, by refusing to renew its charter upon its expiration in
1836; but it had developed no technique of regulation. As irascibil-
ity mounted, the gulf widened.*

The presence of two such dominant personalities as Jackson in

218

the White House and Biddle in the Bank made a clash inevitable. And in this situation, not even Clay sought compromise. On the contrary, he and Webster deliberately precipitated the conflict. The Bank's charter would not expire for four years. Nevertheless, they pressured the Bank to apply for a renewal on the eve of the presidential election of 1832, hoping thereby to stem the tide of Jackson's popularity and to confront him with either capitulation or defeat.

[Letter to Biddle, Washington, Dec. 18, 1831]

The state of my health and the severity of the weather have prevented me, since my arrival here, from being much abroad. Nevertheless, I have seen a great number of persons and conversed with them, among other things, respecting the Bank. The result of all these conversations has been a strong confirmation of the opinion which I expressed at Philadelphia that it is expedient for the Bank to apply for the renewal of its Charter without delay. I have thought, My Dear Sir, the best advice I could give you is that you come down here yourself and survey the ground. You will have access to men of all parties and can digest your information, compare opinions, and judge discreetly upon the whole matter. In my judgment this is your true course and ought to be immediately followed.

Instead of surveying the ground in person, Biddle sent his confidential adviser, Thomas Cadwalader, to Washington, who reported on December 25, 1831, that "Webster would be cold, or perhaps hostile, if we bend to the Government influence."

Although Webster was genuinely interested in the welfare of the Bank, he was, like Clay, playing for political advantage. But how widely he misjudged the ultimate outcome appears from his letter of June 28, 1832, to Stephen White:

The Bank subject will now come up shortly in the H. of R. where I expect it will pass, but my opinion is the President will veto it.

This I firmly believe. In the end the Bank will be incorporated. It has an inherent popularity that will and must carry it through, though it will not get there this time.

As forecast, Jackson vetoed, but then, in the presidential election, overwhelmingly defeated Clay on the very issue that the latter had created.

The next battle was over the removal of the Government deposits. On April 8, 1833, Biddle had written Webster that "they will not dare." They not only dared but did, and though Webster made some sixty speeches in support of the Bank, it was to no avail.

Webster was more conciliatory than the other supporters of the Bank, and he urged a compromise that might well have saved it. But Clay's position was one of rule or ruin, and Biddle listened to Clay rather than to Webster. Finally, the Bank became a political liability, and in a Senate speech on February 26, 1835, Webster said:

I wish to say that I consider the question of renewing the Bank charter as entirely settled. It cannot be renewed. Public opinion, very unfortunately, as I think, for the country, has decided against it; and while there is a strong and prevailing sentiment in the minds of the community against a measure, it is quite useless to propose it. For myself, I shall take no part in any attempt to renew the charter of the Bank. The people have decided against its continuance, and it must expire.

In the frustration and anger of defeat Clay drove through the Senate a resolution censuring the President. This brought a sharply worded protest from Jackson which the Senate, including Webster, voted not to receive.

It was difficult to see how the Senate could properly refuse to receive this communication from the President, especially when it had itself thrown the first stone. Clay was happy to administer the slap to show his power and indulge his petulance, but Webster felt it necessary to find some constitutional justification.

BANK WAR

It was wrong, he said, in the President to try to tell the Senate what it must or must not do, and however trivial the occasion, it was important to assert the principle. Webster had to resort to rhetoric to make it appear that the Senate was motivated by principle rather than by pique, but in the process he concocted one of the most artistic and widely quoted of his congressional utterances:

Every encroachment, great or small, is important enough to awaken the attention of those who are intrusted with the preservation of a constitutional government. We are not to wait till great public mischiefs come, till the government is overthrown, or liberty itself put into extreme jeopardy. We should not be worthy sons of our fathers were we so to regard great questions affecting the general freedom. Those fathers accomplished the Revolution on a strict question of principle. The Parliament of Great Britain asserted a right to tax the Colonies in all cases whatsoever; and it was precisely on this question that they made the Revolution turn. The amount of taxation was trifling, but the claim itself was inconsistent with liberty; and that was, in their eyes, enough. It was against the recital of an act of Parliament, rather than against any suffering under its enactments, that they took up arms. On this question of principle, while actual suffering was yet afar off, they raised their flag against a power, to which, for purposes of foreign conquest and subjugation, Rome, in the height of her glory, is not to be compared; a power which has dotted over the surface of the whole globe with her possessions and military posts, whose morning drumbeat, following the sun, and keeping company with the hours, circles the earth with one continuous and unbroken strain of the martial airs of England.

The first object of a free people is the preservation of their liberty; and liberty is only to be preserved by maintaining constitutional restraints and just divisions of political power. Nothing is more deceptive or more dangerous than the pretence of a desire to simplify government. The simplest governments are despotisms, the next simplest, limited monarchies; but all republics, all govern-ments of law, must impose numerous limitations and qualifications of authority, and give many positive and many qualified rights. In other words, they must be subject to rule and regulation. This is the very essence of free political institutions. The spirit of liberty is, indeed, a bold and fearless spirit; but it is also a sharp-sighted spirit; it is a cautious, sagacious, discriminating, far-seeing intelli-gence; it is jealous of encroachment, jealous of power, jealous of man. It demands checks; it seeks for guards; it insists on securities; it intrenches itself behind strong defences, and fortifies itself with all possible care against the assaults of ambition and passion. It does not trust the amiable weaknesses of human nature, and therefore it will not permit power to overstep its prescribed limits, though be-nevolence, good intent, and patriotic purpose come along with it. Every free government is necessarily complicated, because all such governments establish restraints, as well on the power of govern-ment itself as on that of individuals.

Mr. President, the contest, for ages, has been to rescue Liberty from the grasp of executive power. Whoever has engaged in her sacred cause, from the days of the downfall of those great aristocra-cies which had stood between the king and the people to the time of our own independence, has struggled for the accomplishment of that single object.

XIII

1830

THE MURDER OF CAPTAIN JOSEPH WHITE

Along with everything else they did, Webster and Justice Story managed to maintain an active correspondence, as if determined to furnish living proof of the old adage that only the busy have time. From their letters about Story's trip home in the spring of 1830 we get our first glimpse of the White murder case.

[*Letter to Story, Washington, Apr. 10, 1830*]

You do not know what trouble we were in here about having learned that you ran into the storm on the Sound. Now, however, that we learn you got well thro' it, we are vexed with ourselves for having felt anxiety on the subject, since you have not taken the trouble to tell us whether you were dead or alive. How you will settle this omission with a certain person is more than I can tell.

[*Letter from Story to Webster, Cambridge, Mass., Apr. 17, 1830*]

"I was truly comforted by your kind letter, which I received a day or two ago. As soon as I recovered from the severe fatigues of my long and boisterous passage in the Sound (perilous with all) and had escaped from the throng of kind friends that called on me, I was about writing you. But an entire new direction was given to my thoughts by the horrible murder of Old Capt'n White at Salem. You are aware that he died childless and that his principal heirs are Mr. Stephen White and my sister's children. It is altogether the

223

most mysterious and dreadful affair that I ever heard of. Not the slightest trace has yet been found by which to detect the assassins (for I am satisfied there was more than one) and we are yet in a darkness rendered still darker by the utter defeat of every conjecture. I have been obliged to go to Salem several times, and every thing there seems in inextricable confusion.

"Mr. White left a Will. He has given many legacies to his relatives; but the bulk of his fortune goes to Mr. Stephen White, who will get from 150 to 200 thousand dollars. Three of my nieces will receive about 25,000 each."

The murdered man, Captain Joseph White, was an eighty-two-year-old shipowner and sea captain, one of Salem's leading citizens, and the possessor of one of its most beautiful mansions. He was a widower, and his principal heir was his nephew, Stephen White, a State senator, a man of wealth and prominence, and Story's brother-in-law.

This presumably was Webster's first knowledge of the White case, into which he was to be brought as a special prosecutor, and in which he was to give the most famous of his jury speeches. The case held great interest, and we will better understand Webster's participation by considering the details.

At six o'clock on the morning of Wednesday, April 7, 1830, a servant in Captain White's house found a downstairs window open. Ordinarily it was fastened from the inside, but a plank resting against the sill indicated that someone had entered from the back yard. The servant found nothing else disarranged until he entered Captain White's bedroom on the second floor. There lay the Captain, his head bashed in and thirteen stab wounds in his body.

Captain White had gone to bed early the night before, as was his custom, and neither of the two family retainers had heard any commotion. Nor was anything missing, although money, silver, and other valuables were readily accessible.

THE WHITE MURDER

Salem was stunned. A meeting was called at the Town Hall the day after the funeral. More than two thousand citizens empowered a Vigilance Committee of twenty-seven "to search every house and interrogate every individual touching the murder."

Excitement also engulfed the neighboring towns. From Cambridge, Oliver Wendell Holmes, then a student at Harvard, wrote his friend Phineas Barnes:

> Nothing is going on but murder and robbery; we have to look in our closets and under our beds, and strut about with sword-canes and pistols. Poor old Mr. White was stabbed in the dark, and since then the very air has been redolent of assassination.

The community received a further jolt on April 27 from the report that Joseph J. Knapp, Jr., and his younger brother John Francis (known as Frank) had been attacked by three footpads. They had repelled their assailants, and described them in detail. This report gained special significance from the fact that Joseph Knapp was the son-in-law of Captain White's niece and housekeeper, Mrs. Mary Beckford. Joseph's wife, Mary White Beckford, had been a great favorite of the Captain and had married against his wishes. Although he had hired Joseph as the master of one of his ships, the Captain took a dim view of him as a prospective relative. Indeed, he threatened to cut Mary from his will and Joseph from his employment if they married. They did and he did. Nevertheless, a sufficient reconciliation was effected to give Mary and Joseph the run of the White mansion. They lived in Wenham, in a house which Captain White had given to Mrs. Beckford, and had been there on the night of the murder, as had Mrs. Beckford.

At about the time of the report of the Knapp hold-up, word was received from New Bedford that one Joseph S. Hall, in jail for shoplifting, claimed to know something about the murder. He was brought in chains to Salem, where he told the Vigilance Committee that in February he had heard conversation in a gambling establishment about stealing an iron chest from Captain White's bedroom. The chest was supposed to be full of gold. Indeed, Hall himself believed that it was. Three years earlier, while in the Salem jail, he and a cellmate named Joseph Fisher had made plans to steal it. The Vigilance Committee had already learned of this from Fisher, now a resident of the Charlestown prison, but had been unable to locate Hall, who had been incarcerated under a different name.

Fortunately for Hall and Fisher, both had regained the sanctuary of prison bars by the time of the murder. But on the strength of Hall's story, the grand jury indicted four of the gambling room conferees for murder, among whom were two Crowninshield brothers, Richard and George. One of their uncles had been Secretary of the Navy under Presidents Madison and Monroe, and a second uncle had been offered but declined a cabinet post. The talents of Richard and George ran in somewhat different directions. Officially, they operated a machine shop in Danvers, but Richard devoted much of his time to the proprietorship of a gambling room, and George seems to have had a more than casual interest in a house of ill fame. Richard, the older of the two, was much admired by the flashy young men about town, and a few years earlier Frank Knapp, then sixteen, had accompanied him to New York on an expedition which resulted in a conviction for theft.

On May 14, nine days after the indictment, Captain Joseph J. Knapp, Sr., a sea captain and a merchant of Salem, the father of Joseph and Frank, received a mysterious letter from Belfast, Maine, demanding $350 by May 22 on risk of ruin. It was signed "Charles Grant, jun." and said:

It is useless for me to enter into a discussion of facts which must inevitably harrow up your soul — no — I will merely tell you that I am acquainted with your brother Franklin, and also the business that he was transacting for you on the 2d of April last; and that I think you was very very extravagant in giving one thousand dollars to the person that would execute the business for you — but you know best about that, you see that such things will leak out.

THE WHITE MURDER

The letter mystified Captain Knapp; equally so his son Phippen, a recent Harvard graduate and lawyer of impeccable personal standing. Together they drove to Wenham to consult Joseph and Frank. Joseph, the oldest of the three brothers, said that the letter contained "a devilish lot of trash" and advised his father to turn it over to the Vigilance Committee.

When the Committee got the letter, it sent an anonymous reply, enclosing fifty dollars and promising more later. It also dispatched one of its members to watch for Grant, who was taken into custody when he claimed the letter.

Grant turned out to be a twenty-three-year-old ex-convict named Palmer. Brought to Salem, he told the Committee that on April 2, while concealed in the Crowninshield house, he had seen Frank Knapp and a young man named Allen come to the house and walk away with Richard and George Crowninshield. When they returned George said that Frank Knapp had asked them to kill Mr. White, and had promised that Joseph Knapp would pay them one thousand dollars for the job.

Palmer was a man of some versatility. He had served a jail sentence in Maine, and during his recent visit to Massachusetts had kept himself in practice by theft, forgery and counterfeiting. Presumably, these activities were the cause of his hiding out with the Crowninshields. The Vigilance Committee had promised him immunity, but they were now worried about his disappearing and locked him up like the rest.

Palmer's story led to the immediate arrest of Joseph and Frank Knapp. It also galvanized into action the Rev. Henry Colman, minister of the Independent Congregational Church. Stephen White was a member of his congregation. So were Joseph and Mary Knapp. Indeed, Colman had performed their marriage and said that he regarded Mary with "the affection of a father."

Whatever the motivation, whether paternal, ecclesiastical, or inquisitorial, the minister leapt into the fray. He paid three visits to Joseph on the day of his commitment to prison, and promised

227

*him immunity if he would confess. Phippen Knapp came to Jo-
seph's cell during the last of these visits, and accompanied Colman
to Frank's cell to tell him that Joseph was ready to confess in order
to gain immunity but would not do so without Frank's consent.*

*Frank's reply was a matter of later dispute. According to Phippen,
Frank said, "I have nothing to confess; it is a hard case, but if it be
as you say, Joseph may confess if he pleases. I shall stand trial."
Colman testified several times, and not always consistently. The
most damaging of his versions was that "Frank thought it hard, or
not fair, that Joseph should have the advantage of making a confession, since the thing was done for his benefit or advantage."*

*Captain Knapp, the father, had already objected to the minister's
solitary visits to Joseph, and Phippen now exacted a promise that
Colman would not see Joseph again without him. Both Phippen
and Colman then made hurried trips to Boston, the former to
retain counsel for his brothers, the minister to get written authority from the Attorney General to grant immunity for turning
State's evidence. Some time after midnight Colman got the Attorney General to sign a document stating that if either of the
Knapps or George Crowninshield was made a witness, the one
testifying would not be prosecuted for Captain White's murder.*

*Phippen, being unable, or unwilling, to get lawyers out of bed
after midnight, took longer to complete his arrangements. When
he returned to Salem, Colman was not only in Joseph's cell but
refused to let Phippen enter. Colman must have been there for
a considerable time, as he had obtained a detailed written confession. This he delivered to the Vigilance Committee, which refused to let Phippen read it, although furnishing a summary to
the press.*

*Meanwhile, Colman had also taken two members of the Com-
mittee to the Howard Street meeting house in Salem. There, in a
rat hole under the steps, they had found a two foot lead-weighted
bludgeon. Colman later testified that Frank Knapp had told him
of the hiding place. Phippen, who had been present the only time*

that Colman talked to Frank, denied this, and said that it was Joseph who told about the bludgeon. This was borne out by Joseph's confession. It not only described the hiding place, which he had learned from Richard Crowninshield, but stated that Frank had looked for the club and had been unable to find it.

The confession detailed the plans for the murder and gave a report of its execution. Joseph had learned, he said, that Captain White had made a will leaving the bulk of his estate to Stephen White and giving only $16,000 to Mrs. Beckford. Joseph knew (or thought that he knew) that if Captain White were to die without a will, Mrs. Beckford would inherit half the estate, or approximately $100,000.

Captain White was childless, but had had a brother and a sister, both now deceased. Stephen White was one of four living children of the brother; Mrs. Beckford was the only child of the sister. The size of their individual shares, in the event Captain White died without a will, would depend upon whether the distribution was per stirpes or per capita. If the nephews and nieces stood in the shoes of their parents, Mrs. Beckford would receive half; if all were to share equally, she would receive one-fifth.

Massachusetts had adopted the general rule of distribution per stirpes. But the statute made an exception. If all those entitled to share bore the same degree of kindred to the deceased, they were to take equally. This was the situation in the present case.

A little knowledge is a dangerous thing. Joseph had been aware of the general rule but not of the exception. Consequently, he believed that by simultaneously doing away with both Captain White and his will, he could not only increase his family's share from $16,000 to $100,000 but could also assure immediate delivery. He should, of course, have read the fine print.

When he broached the idea to his brother, Frank tried to talk him out of it, but finally agreed to discuss it with the Crowninshields. He did so and promised that Joseph would pay Richard Crowninshield $1,000 if he would take care of Captain White. It *was understood that Joseph would take care of the will. In accordance with this plan, Joseph unfastened a downstairs window in the Captain's house, and at the same time took the will from the iron box. But here he made another mistake. He did not take Captain White's last will, but an earlier one which had been superseded.*

Joseph admitted that the reported hold-up of himself and Frank had been a hoax. What was more important, his confessions showed that Richard Crowninshield had performed the murder alone and that Frank, the only one of the conspirators who lived in Salem, had gone home to bed.

When Richard Crowninshield learned of Palmer's arrest and Joseph's confession, he knew the jig was up. But he was a man of stronger stuff than Joseph. Also he knew when he needed legal advice. He is reported to have consulted Franklin Dexter, one of the defense lawyers whom Phippen Knapp had retained, on the subject of principals and accessories. Dexter apparently told him that under the Massachusetts law an accessory before the fact could not be tried for a felony unless someone had first been convicted as a principal. In an earlier case, involving a burglary, one Thomas Daniel had been indicted as principal and James Phillips as accessory before the fact. Daniels had died, and the Supreme Judicial Court of Massachusetts had held that this barred the prosecution of Phillips. Of the five judges participating in that decision, three were still on the Court. From this Richard reasoned that his brother George could not be tried if he himself were not convicted.

On June 15, Richard's body was found hanging in his cell. He had knotted two silk handkerchiefs together, fastened one end around his neck and, standing on a chair, had tied the other end to a bar at the top of the window. When discovered, his feet were resting on the floor and his knees were only a few inches above it. To accomplish what he did necessarily required extraordinary strength of will.

Richard's suicide posed a serious problem for the prosecution.

Unless someone could be convicted as principal, all the accused would go free. Chief Justice Parker emphasized this in his charge to the grand jury. The rule was an "unwise refinement of ancient times," he said. Nevertheless, the common law was clear that "unless there be a conviction of a principal there can be no trial of the accessory." Ten years earlier, Chief Justice Parker had handed down the decision in the Phillips case; the Legislature had done nothing to change the rule. Therefore, said the Chief Justice, it still stood. Thus goaded, the Legislature rushed to enact a curative statute, but it was too late to affect the present trials.

Chief Justice Parker also explained the distinction between a principal and an accessory before the fact. One who counseled, hired, or otherwise procured a murder was equally subject to punishment by death, but he was not a principal unless he had been present at the commission of the crime. To be "present" in this sense, however, did not require that he actually be at the scene of the murder, or even in sight of it. It was sufficient if he was cooperating in the act, by watching to prevent relief, or to give an alarm, or to assist his confederate to escape.

Thus instructed, the grand jury indicted Frank Knapp as principal and Joseph Knapp and George Crowninshield as accessories.

Under the Massachusetts law as it then stood, offenses punishable by death were required to be tried before the Supreme Judicial Court. For this purpose it sat as a trial court in each of the counties. On July 25, however, while the case was before the Court, Chief Justice Parker died of apoplexy. The trial was adjourned until August 3, at which time it resumed before the three remaining Justices.

This delay led to an important change. Under the Massachusetts law, the official prosecutors were the Attorney General and the Solicitor General. The former was now eighty and the latter almost seventy. Moreover, their talents did not run to this type of work. Joseph Story and his brother-in-law, Stephen White, were seriously concerned. Both had an intense personal interest in the case, and the more they saw of its difficulties the greater became their worry.

Daniel Webster had recently returned from a hard Senate session in Washington. He was tired, a mountain of unfinished work weighed on his conscience, and he longed to enjoy the company of his new wife amid the peace and relaxation of beloved Marshfield. But it was not to be. One could not deny so great and good a friend as Justice Story, and Harriet Martineau tells us that three days before the trial was to recommence, "A citizen of Salem, a friend of mine, was deputed to carry the request. Mr. Webster was at his farm by the seashore. Thither, in tremendous weather, my friend followed him. Mr. Webster was playing checkers with his boy. My friend was first dried and refreshed, and then lost no time in mentioning 'business.' Mr. Webster writhed at the word, saying that he came hither to get out of hearing of it. He next declared that his undertaking anything more was entirely out of the question, and pointed, in evidence, to his swollen bags of briefs lying in a corner. However, upon a little further explanation and meditation, he agreed to the resquest with the same good grace with which he afterward went through with his task. He made himself master of all that my friend could communicate, and before daybreak was off through the woods, in the unabated storm."

The Attorney General and Solicitor General welcomed Webster's help and the Court readily gave its permission. If the defense attorneys were less enthusiastic, they had no opportunity at this time to show it.

Chief defense counsel was Franklin Dexter, brilliant son of Samuel Dexter, earlier leader of the Massachusetts bar and Secretary of the Treasury under President John Adams. He was assisted by William H. Gardiner, also of Boston, and by Robert Rantoul of Salem. There was no dearth of ability for the defense.

In undertaking the prosecution, Webster counted on Story's help. For example, on August 6, early in the trial of the first case, he wrote to Story, who was then in Cambridge:

If we prove F. Knapp a conspirator in the plan of the murder, as one who was deeply concerned in it, if it does not appear that any accessory part was assigned to him, such as to pay, procure weapons, or other like thing, and the murder is found to have been committed by the conspirators, or some of them, but no direct proof who was or who was not present, is not F. Knapp to be deemed a principal, unless he can prove himself so remote from the locus in quo as to show him an accessory only? Suppose two men are overheard to propose to kill a third by poison — they go together to a shop to buy arsenic — the man is found poisoned, and with arsenic, and killed; are not both necessarily to be regarded as principals, unless one can prove that the other actually administered the poison, he being not present.

I pray you collect your thoughts on this point, look to the cases, if convenient, and I will send to you, or more probably see you, on Sunday.

I have not found a letter from you here, tho' I have daily applied at the P. Office. But we have got along on the point suggested to you the other day very well.

The Commonwealth had counted heavily on the testimony of Joseph Knapp. He had obliged the Rev. Mr. Colman with a written confession, and had later supplemented it with a second. But when called to the stand, he refused to testify. The prosecution warned that this would forfeit his immunity, but he remained silent. Perhaps even Joseph's reptilian mind revolted at the prospect of testifying against his brother. Or perhaps he was suffering another of his attacks of smartness. His refusal was not based upon the advice of counsel, as each of the defense attorneys took pains to point out.

Joseph knew that so long as he remained mute, his confessions could not be used against Frank. But if Joseph was trying to be smart again, it was with the usual result. His testimony would probably have freed his brother.

The crucial issue in the case was whether Frank Knapp had been "present" at the commission of the murder. Amid a welter of confusing evidence was testimony indicating that Frank had been in Brown Street, back of Captain White's house, at approximately the time of the murder. If this identification was correct, it must have been because Frank couldn't restrain his impatience and had got up from bed to intercept Richard and find out how the affair had gone. Under the circumstances, however, it was natural to assume that if Frank was there it was to give aid or encouragement to the murderer.

Frank himself could not testify to the contrary. Even had he been willing to take the stand, the law at that time did not permit an accused to be a witness. If Joseph had testified, however, he would have said that Frank had gone home to bed, and that Richard had done the job alone. This was stated in the confessions, and Webster himself came to the conclusion that Frank could not have been convicted if Joseph had testified.

How closely the balance teetered, even without Joseph's evidence, appears from the report of the jury's deliberations in the first case, on August 13:

"The jury came into court after deliberating twenty-four hours, and the Foreman [Solomon Nelson] said that the difficulty was about the presence of Knapp, and the purpose of that presence, in Brown Street. The court said that those were matters of fact and evidence belonging to the jury, and the jury were again instructed that if the defendant was in Brown street at the time of the murder, according to a previous agreement, performing his part in aiding and abetting, he would be implicated and liable under this indictment, as much as if he had been in the chamber of Captain White. If the jury were satisfied that he was there, not for the purpose of aiding and encouraging, but only for the purpose of receiving information that the deed was accomplished, or from curiosity, then the law said he was not present.

"The jury then went out, and after several hours, came in, when the Foreman stated that there was not the least probability of their ever coming to an agreement."

Daniel Webster at 22,
engraving by J. A. J. Wilcox from a miniature

Daniel Webster at 42,
portrait by Joseph Wood

Daniel Webster at 49,
portrait by D. C. Johnston

Daniel Webster at 53,
portrait by Francis Alexander

Daniel Webster at 62,
portrait by T. B. Lawson

Daniel Webster at 63,
portrait by Chester Harding

Daniel Webster in his sixties,
sketch by Joseph Ames

Daniel Webster in his sixties,
engraving by J. C. Buttre

Webster's birthplace, Salisbury, New Hampshire

Sketch of Marshfield Farm

Webster House at Marshfield

Grace Fletcher Webster

Caroline Le Roy Webster

Fletcher Webster

Edward Webster

Washington Feby. 2. 1819

My Dear E.
         all is safe. Judgt was rendered this
morning, reversing the Judgt in N. Hampshire.
Present, Marshall, Washington, Livingston,
Johnson, Duval & Story. — all concurring
but Duval, the giving no reason & otherwise
Contrary — The opinion was delivered by
the Chief Justice — it was very able & very
elaborate. — It goes the whole length — &
leaves not an inch for the University
to stand on ———— Yrs affectionately
                              D Webster
                              in Court

Letter to Ezekiel Webster

A second jury was immediately impanelled. After the earlier test of strength and the elimination of all surprises, the prosecution was able to marshal its evidence with greater effect. In addition, it had an ace up its sleeve in the cooperativeness of the Rev. Mr. Colman. His memory for incriminating detail seemed to improve with each visit to the stand. There was considerable substance in Franklin Dexter's complaint to the jury that "Whatever the Government cannot otherwise prove, Mr. Colman swears the prisoner has confessed and nothing more. Of half an hour's conversation with the prisoner, he cannot remember a word but what turns out to be indispensable to the case of the prosecution. . . ."

Although the first trial had taken ten days, the second was completed in six, and after five hours the jury brought in a verdict of guilty. On the next day, August 21, 1830, Frank Knapp was sentenced to death.

Webster attributed Frank's conviction to Joseph's refusal to testify. The same was not true of Franklin Dexter. He gave the credit to Webster. And so have many others. Henry Cabot Lodge says that Webster's address to the jury "must be placed among the very finest masterpieces of modern oratory. . . ."

Like most orators, Webster was at his best before a crowd. The citizens of Salem and the surrounding country had done their best to oblige. A reporter wrote: "The throng of ladies has been so tremendous that even the poor devils of reporters who have sweated through nearly twenty days of drudgery, confinement, and impure air, have not been allowed to retain their places at this feast of eloquence. If a shoe falls off or a hat drops, it is lost. To stoop is annihilation; bob your head and it is gone."

Webster first addressed himself to the charge that the Vigilance Committee had been over-zealous and had trampled the rights of the innocent, saying:

It is truly said that the law is not established so much to punish the guilty as to protect the innocent. But who are the innocent?

Who are they whom the law is framed to protect? They are the honest, the industrious, the peaceful; the innocent sleepers in their own houses. The law is established that those who live quietly in the fear of God by day, may sleep quietly in his peace by night. The defense can think of none who are innocent but those who are placed at the bar, unconvicted.

You will consider, gentlemen, how much consideration is due to the complaints about the manner in which the perpetrators of this murder have been detected; whether it makes any difference to the guilty by what means his crime is brought to light. The counsel, taking a lofty flight of sentimentality, complain that Palmer has betrayed his bosom friends! They complain that Palmer has been seduced. But why don't they meet the case? Do they mean to deny that Captain White is dead? I thought it would come to that.

This style of complaint has been carried to a great extent against disinterested and respectable witnesses, as if it were as bad to have had a hand in the detection of the murderers as in the perfection of the crime; as if to have known anything of the murderers were an act of the most flagitious and exquisite wickedness. And it would seem that because the crime has been detected by extraordinary exertions, the man accused ought to be mildly and calmly judged. It is not to be endured that honest indignation should be turned from the criminal against those who have detected him. The community are unfit to live under protecting laws if, in a case like this, they would not rise unitedly to see them enforced.

Webster then turned to the crime itself. It should be borne in mind that, in the absence of Joseph's confessions, there was no positive proof that Richard Crowninshield had committed the murder. It was necessary for the jury to so find, however, in order to bring the case within the framework of the conspiracy. Webster addressed himself to this phase of the case in what has become the best-known portion of his argument.

THE WHITE MURDER

Gentlemen, it is a most extraordinary case. This bloody drama exhibited no suddenly excited, ungovernable rage. The actors in it were not surprised by any lion-like temptation springing upon their virtue, and overcoming it, before resistance could begin. Nor did they do the deed to glut savage vengeance, or satiate long-settled and deadly hate. It was a cool, calculating, money-making murder. It was all hire and salary, not revenge. It was the weighing of money against life; the counting out of so many pieces of silver against so many ounces of blood.

An aged man, without an enemy in the world, in his own house, and in his own bed, is made the victim of a butcherly murder, for mere pay. Truly, here is a new lesson for painters and poets. Whoever shall hereafter draw the portrait of murder, let him not give it the grim visage of Moloch, the brow knitted by revenge, the face black with settled hate, and the blood-shot eye emitting livid fires of malice. Let him draw, rather, a decorous, smooth-faced, bloodless demon; a picture in repose, rather than in action; not so much an example of human nature in its depravity, and in its paroxysms of crime, as an infernal being, a fiend, in the ordinary display and development of his character.

The deed was executed with a degree of self-possession and steadiness equal to the wickedness with which it was planned. The circumstances now clearly in evidence spread out the whole scene before us. Deep sleep had fallen on the destined victim, and on all beneath his roof. A healthful old man, to whom sleep was sweet, the first sound slumbers of the night held him in their soft but strong embrace. The assassin enters, through the window already prepared, into an unoccupied apartment. With noiseless foot he paces the lonely hall, half lighted by the moon; he winds up the ascent of the stairs, and reaches the door of the chamber. Of this, he moves the lock, by soft and continued pressure, till it turns on its hinges without noise; and he enters and beholds his victim before him.

The room is uncommonly open to the admission of light. The

face of the innocent sleeper is turned from the murderer, and the beams of the moon, resting on the gray locks of his aged temple, show him where to strike. The fatal blow is given! and the victim passes, without a struggle or a motion, from the repose of sleep to the repose of death! It is the assassin's purpose to make sure work; and he plies the dagger, though it is obvious that life has been destroyed by the blow of the bludgeon. He even raises the aged arm, that he may not fail in his aim at the heart, and replaces it again over the wounds of the poniard! To finish the picture, he explores the wrist for the pulse! He feels for it, and ascertains that it beats no longer! It is accomplished. The deed is done. He retreats, retraces his steps to the window, passes out through it as he came in, and escapes. He has done the murder. No eye has seen him, no ear has heard him. The secret is his own, and it is safe!

Ah! Gentlemen, that was a dreadful mistake. Such a secret can be safe nowhere. The whole creation of God has neither nook nor corner where the guilty can bestow it, and say it is safe. The human heart was not made for the residence of such an inhabitant. It finds itself preyed on by a torment, which it dares not acknowledge to God or man. A vulture is devouring it, and it can ask no sympathy or assistance, either from heaven or earth.

The secret which the murderer possesses soon comes to possess him. He thinks the whole world sees it in his face, reads it in his eyes, and almost hears its workings in the very silence of his thoughts. It has become his master. It betrays his discretion, it breaks down his courage, it conquers his prudence. When suspicions from without begin to embarrass him, and the net of circumstance to entangle him, the fatal secret struggles with still greater violence to burst forth. It must be confessed, it will be confessed; there is no refuge from confession but suicide, and suicide is confession.

On Tuesday, September 28, 1830, Frank Knapp, just turned twenty, was hanged. He met the end with composure, coolly testing the drop of the scaffold with one foot before stepping on it, and then waiting quietly while the noose was adjusted.

THE WHITE MURDER

Joseph's trial commenced November 9, 1830, before the same judges and with the same counsel. On November 10 Webster wrote Story:

J. J. Knapp's trial commenced yesterday morning, and has made little progress. The A.M. yesterday was occupied in impanelling a jury; the P.M. mainly in debating whether the attorney-general had a right to bring in other counsel; on this question, their honors deliberated, and this morning agreed to let me in, I have stated to them that I appeared at the request of the attorney-general, and had not received, and should not receive, any fee in this case; which, of course, was and is true.

Although counsel for the defense had not earlier objected to Webster's participation, probably because they were taken by surprise, they did so now. They pointed out that the Massachusetts statute vested prosecuting responsibility in the law officers of the Government; also, it provided "that no attorney general, solicitor general or county attorney shall receive any fee or reward from or in behalf of any prosecutor, for services in any prosecution, to which it shall be his duty to attend." The law officers were present and able to act; in addition, it was improper, said Dexter, for Webster to be compensated by a private prosecutor.

Webster had received $1,000 from Stephen White, but this was specifically for services in the earlier trials and he stated to the court that he was serving in the present trial "without pecuniary inducement." He could have taken the position, had he chosen to do so, that the statute was not in any event applicable to him, but no doubt it seemed easier to avoid argument by a short answer.

Webster has been severely criticized on the ground that his statement to the court was something less than truthful. Admittedly it was technical, but it is hard to believe that anyone was deceived. Story was a party to the fee arrangement, and it seems likely that the Massachusetts judges were fully aware that Webster was being paid by Stephen White.

SPEAK FOR YOURSELF, DANIEL

Interestingly enough, the receipt for this fee, dated August 14, 1830, is in the Massachusetts Historical Society. Indeed, some of the criticism is based upon a misreading of the document, which is as follows:

> Recd of Hon. S. White One Thousand Dollars, in full of fees for all services rendered or to be rendered, in the prosecutions vs Jn⁰. F. Knapp —
>
> Danl Webster

The authors of Daniel Webster *and the Salem Murder, though otherwise meticulous in their presentation of the facts, have read "Jn⁰. F. Knapp" to mean "Jo. and F. Knapp," which would of course directly contradict Webster's statement to the court. This is clearly improper. "Jn⁰." was a recognized and common way of abbreviating "John." Correctly read, the receipt makes it clear that the fee was specifically limited to Webster's services in the trials of John Francis Knapp.*

With this preliminary skirmish out of the way, there was only one real issue in Joseph's trial. Was his confession admissible in evidence?

Joseph apparently had talked to the Rev. Mr. Colman on the understanding that communications with a clergyman were privileged and could not be used against him. He had made a written confession only after receiving an express promise of immunity from the Attorney General. This was specifically conditioned upon his being a witness at the trial, and he had refused to testify. Was a confession given under such circumstances voluntary?

Ordinarily, a confession induced by a promise of reward is not deemed voluntary, any more than one induced by threats. The law regards both as unreliable, inasmuch as the accused will be prone to say what he knows is required in order to meet the promises or the threats.

Was Joseph's confession of this character? Not at all, argued Webster. Joseph had been promised immunity if he took the stand.

At the time, he intended to do so. Accordingly, he had no objection to writing out the facts for Colman. Later, Joseph changed his mind. He refused to testify and thereby forfeited the promised immunity. But this, said Webster, could not affect the voluntary character of the confession at the time it was made. The State had offered Joseph no inducement to confess, and there was no reason to doubt the reliability of what he said.

The Court agreed and admitted the confession. For all practical purposes, this cooked the goose. But Dexter kept on fighting. He argued that the confession itself showed that Frank had not been "present" at the murder. Accordingly, his conviction as principal had been improper. It was now too late to help Frank, but this did not prevent the point being raised in defense of Joseph. If Frank had not been convicted properly, Joseph as an accessory before the fact could not be tried.

It was a noble attempt. The Court permitted Dexter to question the validity of Frank's conviction for this purpose, but neither the judges nor the jury were much impressed.

The trial took four days, given over mostly to legal arguments, and the jury arrived at its verdict in a few hours. On November 15 Joseph was sentenced, and on Friday, December 31, 1830, he followed his brother.

The next and last of the conspirators, George Crowninshield, was acquitted. Webster did not participate, and some have explained the result by his absence. There was, however, no solid evidence connecting George with the commission of the crime, and the ladies of the house of ill fame could give an alibi for all of his time on the night of the murder. His acquittal was not surprising.

Was justice done? It would seem so. It is especially hard to feel sorry for Joseph, whose mercenary plotting brought death to his brother as well as to Captain White, not to mention Richard Crowninshield and himself. When we think about Joseph the whole affair assumes a monumental irony.

In all likelihood the case would never have arisen if he had not misconstrued the Massachusetts law of inheritance.

Even had he been right in this, he had defeated his own purpose by taking the wrong will.

Worse still, from his standpoint, he had failed to destroy Palmer's incriminating letter when he had the chance. If he had done this and had then silenced Palmer, it seems unlikely that the murder could have been solved.

If there was anything to be admired in Joseph, it was his refusal to testify against his brother in order to gain immunity. Yet even here he outsmarted himself, and in doing so probably cost both their lives.

The writer Artemus Ward was a master of pithy sayings. One would have made the perfect epitaph for Joseph: he was just "too smart to live."

XIV

FRUSTRATIONS AND FRAILTIES

Friends had long been pointing to the flattering prospect of the presidency, and Webster would have been less than human had his mind not turned in that direction.

Webster's ambition required no stimulation. William Plumer tells us that in 1822 "we were walking together one broad moonlight evening in the grounds around the Capitol at Washington when he broke out into the most passionate aspirations after glory. Without it life was he said not worth possessing. Inquiring my age, and finding that I was some seven years his junior, he said 'Oh! that I had those seven years. At thirty, Alexander had conquered the world; and I am forty.' And at forty, said I, Caesar had done nothing. 'Ay,' said he, 'that is better; there is something in that. Caesar at forty had done nothing: we may say then at forty one may still hope to do great things.' Observing that I smiled at his enthusiasm, he smiled too; and said, 'You laugh at me Plumer! Your quiet way of looking at things may be best, after all; but I have sometimes such glorious dreams! And sometimes too, I half believe that they will one day wake into glorious realities.' We walked on, in silence, for some time together — he musing on schemes of ambition, and labors of immortality — I on the duties of a humbler but not unhappy life."

Webster seldom confided his presidential ambitions to paper, and when he did he was apt to ask that the letter be destroyed (a direction which, in the light of human nature, probably operated as a preservative). For example, this one to Mason on January 1, 1835:

Whether it is or will be best for Massachusetts to act at all on the subject of a nomination, is a question which I leave entirely to the judgment of others. I cannot say that I have any personal wishes about it, either one way or the other. A nomination by Massachusetts would certainly be one of the highest proofs of regard which any citizen can receive. As such, I should most undoubtedly esteem it. But, in the present condition of things, and with the prospects which are before us, a nomination is a questionable thing to one who is more desirous of preserving what little reputation he has than anxious to grasp at further distinction.

If a resolution to make a movement in Massachusetts should be adopted, not only should the thing itself be done as soon as practicable, but in the mean time notice of the intention should be given to friends in the neighboring States, and especially in New York, that they may prepare for it. Let us know *here* the moment any thing is determined on.

It looks at present as if Mr. Clay would not do or say any thing. He declares himself in nobody's way; but still it is evident that his particular friends are not prepared to act heartily and efficiently for anybody else.

Be sure to *burn* this letter, and assure yourself also that I write such letters to nobody else.

On January 21, 1835, the Massachusetts legislature adopted resolutions nominating Webster for the presidency, and he assessed the situation in letters to Mason on February 1 and February 6:

[Feb. 1, 1835]

The nomination appears to have been done as well as it could be. I mean, of course, in the manner of it. No fault is found with it by our friends, so far as I know. Measures are in train to produce a correspondent feeling and action, in New York, Vermont, and some other States. The Legislature of Maryland is now in session, and I have seen a letter to-day, which says, that if Mr. Clay were fairly out of the way, that Legislature would immediately second the Massachusetts nomination. Mr. Clay does nothing, and will do nothing, at present. He thinks — or perhaps it is his friends who think — that *something* may yet occur, perhaps a war, which may, in *some* way, cause a general rally round him. Besides, sundry of the members of Congress from Kentucky, in addition to their own merits, rely not a little on Mr. Clay's popularity, to insure their reëlection next August. They have been, therefore, altogether opposed to bringing forward any other man at present.

[Feb. 6, 1835]

It is true that I have looked forward to the events which the approaching election might bring about, as likely to furnish a fit occasion for my retirement from the Senate. I have fixed upon no particular time, nor made, indeed, any such determination as may not be changed by the advice or the wishes of friends. As I am now placed, I shall certainly not leave my place till the time arrives when I may think that its relinquishment will not be unsatisfactory to Massachusetts.

I do not affect, My Dear Sir, to desire to retire from public life, and to resume my profession. My habits, I must confess, and the nature of my pursuits for some years, render it more agreeable to me to attend to political than to professional subjects. But I have not lost all relish for the bar; I can still make something by the practice, and by remaining in the Senate I am making sacrifices which my circumstances do not justify. My residence here, so many months every year, greatly increases my expenses, and greatly reduces my income. You know the charge of living here with a family, and I cannot leave my wife and daughter at home, and come here and go into a "mess," at 10 Dollars a week.

I find it inconvenient to push my practice in the Supreme Court, while a member of the Senate; and am inclined, under any view of the future, to decline engagements, hereafter, in that Court, unless under special circumstances. These are the reasons that have led me to *hope* for a fit occasion of leaving the Senate, and when I can quit with the approbation of friends, I shall eagerly embrace the opportunity. In the meantime, I shall say nothing about it.

I ought, this Spring, to go to the West, as far, at least, as Ken. & Indiana. I am fully persuaded it would be a highly useful thing. My friends urge it upon me, incessantly; and I hold back from promising compliance with their wishes only from an unwillingness to lose six weeks more, after the session closes.

Andrew Jackson, whose political sagacity was unsurpassed, predicted that Webster would never be President. He was, said Jackson, too far east, knew too much, and was too honest.

Added to these disqualifications was the assumption of the Whigs that they could carry Massachusetts as a matter of course, which made them favor candidates whose strength lay elsewhere. Webster also had the misfortune to be junior to Clay, whose thirst for the presidency was even more consuming than his own. Persistent defeat did not dim Clay's hopes, and he regarded Webster as a rival rather than a friend. Without his support Webster never could muster the full backing of the party.

Along with Webster's presidential ambitions, and to some extent associated with them, went his periodic determination to retire from public life. The gap between income and outgo increased with age and prominence. He worked hard and commanded large fees, but he lacked financial restraint. His secretary, Charles Lanman, tells us that Webster "made money with ease and spent it without reflection."

Webster's personal tastes were simple, almost bucolic. He liked to be in bed by nine and up before dawn. While he was Secretary of State he kept chickens, as well as a cow, in his Washington back-

yard, and found relaxation from his official duties by filling up his wife's sewing basket with eggs from his favorite hens. But along with these simple pleasures went other country-bred qualities, a love of dispensing hospitality and a longing for land. The former kept his house and table so continuously overflowing with guests that, like Jefferson, he was virtually eaten into bankruptcy. And his passion for land kept him buying more and more long after it had become obvious that he could not afford what he already had.

By the time of his death in 1852 he had expanded the family farm at Franklin, New Hampshire, beyond 1,000 acres, and had acquired some 1,800 acres at Marshfield, Massachusetts. Fifty of these were bought with borrowed money within a month of his death. In addition, he bought approximately 20,000 acres in Ohio, Indiana, Illinois, Michigan and Wisconsin, pouring into these speculations all the money he could lay his hands on. Over a long enough period his western lands could have yielded a fortune, but Webster overextended himself so greatly that they remained a constant drain on his resources. Some of his borrowings were from the Bank of the United States of Pennsylvania, and a sale of its assets in 1842 furnishes a revealing statistic. Among the items auctioned were two of Webster's promissory notes, in the amounts of $12,750 and $5,000, respectively. Together they sold for $400.

Even worse than Webster's lack of financial restraint was one of its consequences, a growing complacence in accepting money from wealthy friends and backers. In that period, far more than today, the basic political issue was, or seemed to be, between the haves and the have-nots. The French Revolution was still fresh in memory, and words like "leveller" had a spine-chilling effect. Webster's social views were conservative, even if his finances were not, and the business community considered him their strongest champion. They wanted him in Washington and were quite willing to pay his bills to keep him there. They made no attempt to control him, and there was no attempt at subterfuge. Subscription lists were passed around and money paid openly. For example:

SPEAK FOR YOURSELF, DANIEL

[Letter from Harrison Gray Otis, of Boston, to George Harrison, of Philadelphia, Feb. 7, 1845]

The only amusing occurrence of any note is the new subscription for Webster. The project is to raise a fund of 100,000 dollars here & in N York, the income to be settled on him & his wife for life, reversion to ye subscribers. It is confidently said that it will be filled — indeed is nearly so at this moment. I think his good fortune is almost equal to his political preeminence and quite equal to his claims. This is at least the third time that the wind has been raised for him and the most curious fact is that thousands are subscribed by many, who hold his old notes for other thousands, and who have not been backward in their censures of his profusion. I am not a subscriber — not able to be one — though I think it a great point to have him replaced in the Senate — of which the Whig minority will combine great talents, and afford the possibility of preventing or mitigating mischief. This affair of W's reminds me of George Selwyns wit. When a subscription was raised for Charles Fox, somebody adverting to the delicacy of the subject, expressed his wonder how Fox would take it. "Take it" said Selwyn "quarterly to be sure!"

[David Sears to Webster]

Boston, March 21, 1846

I have the honor to inform you that there is now deposited in the Massachusetts Hospital Life Insurance Company, on special contract, the sum of thirty-seven thousand dollars.

Your friends whose names are enclosed have placed this sum there for your benefit, to constitute a fund under the supervision of Messrs. William Amory, Ignatius Sargent and David Sears, Jr. The income will be subject to your order semi-annually, and when not called for will be added to the principal to increase the income appropriated to your use.

This fund has been created freely and cheerfully by your friends in evidence of their grateful sense of the valuable services you have rendered to your whole country. They have done it without your sanction or knowledge, and with some reason to imagine that their purpose might not be entirely acceptable to you.

But they have been moved in this matter by no common feeling.

Government grants nothing beyond the salary of office for services rendered; and the consequence is that our ablest statesmen, on their retirement from the highest positions, are frequently obliged to return to the labors of their early life; and our venerable Judges, even of the Supreme Court of the nation, after years of toil are left in their old age poor and unprovided for. Your friends in Boston, desirous in your particular case to ward off these evils, and furnish you with a supply for your future wants, have determined to show, on their part at least, decided preference for a permanent provision, and offer to you in this way a prop to sustain you hereafter.

They are now numerous and strong; and, with a few exceptions, the same who for five and twenty years rallied around you with minds firm and active, and with hearts warm and grateful. But Time will do its work with all of us, and when increasing age shall have rendered labor irksome to you, and growing infirmities call for repose, where may then be your friends? Most of them probably in their graves, and the few that remain without the influence, and perhaps without the ability to serve you. These considerations have been conclusive with the gentlemen who act with me. All were agreed that it was best to do now what they might not be able to do hereafter.

In their behalf, therefore, I have the honor respectfully to offer you the above annuity of thirty-seven thousand dollars, hoping that, if it be not desirable at present, it may hereafter tend to the comfort of your advancing years, and serve to recall to your mind this last united effort of your friends, whose hearts were with you, and who were anxious, while they had the power, honorably and truly to assist and serve you.

With great respect and consideration, Your obedient servant and friend,   DAVID SEARS

249

[Names referred to in the above letter.]

DAVID SEARS,	EDWARD H. ROBBINS,	DUDLEY S. PICKMAN,
WILLIAM APPLETON,	W. W. STONE,	GEORGE W. LYMAN,
NATHAN APPLETON,	THOMAS B. CURTIS,	C. G. SHADDOCK,
THOMAS H. PERKINS,	THOMAS E. THAYER,	JOHN WELLS,
DAVID S. BROWN,	JOHN C. GREY,	A. BINNEY,
SAMUEL APPLETON,	OSIAS GOODWIN,	C. W. CARTWRIGHT,
ROBERT G. SHAW,	EBEN SMITH,	BENJAMIN LORING,
J. CHICKERING,	FRANCIS C. LOWELL,	EBEN CHADWICK,
W. P. WINCHESTER,	WILLIAM AMORY,	J. W. EDWARDS,
H. GREY,	FRANKLIN DEXTER,	HENRY CABOT,
JOHN D. WILLIAMS,	JOHN A. LOWELL,	JOHN L. GARDINER,
THOMAS LAMB,	JOSIAH QUINCY, JR.,	IGNATIUS SARGENT,
SAMUEL LAWRENCE,	THOMAS B. WALES,	WILLIAM H. PRESCOTT
	BENJAMIN T. REED,	

[Webster to Sears]

Washington, March 26, 1846

I had the honor to receive yesterday your letter of the 21st instant.

The kindness manifested by the transaction, information of which you communicate, is of too important and grave a character to be acknowledged in the forms in which a sense of ordinary obligations are usually expressed. I cannot but feel how entirely unworthy my public services have been of so unusual and munificent a memorial.

It is true I have been in public life many years, to the no small neglect of my profession, and prejudice of my private affairs. I hope that on some occasions I have done good, and that on others, I may have averted evil. But for all I have done, and for much more, if I could have accomplished more, I have found and should have found abundant reward in the evidences of respect, confidence, and kindness already received from political and private friends.

Webster Replying to Hayne,
section of painting by G. P. A. Healy

New England's Choice

HON. DANIEL WEBSTER'S CARRIAGE.

citizens of New York, desiring to offer present Secretary of State some slight onial of their respect and earnest friendor his noble defence of the Constitution, as s to express a full sense of his extraordiaror of usefulness as a statesman, and of aracter as a citizen, presented him lately,

as will be remembered, with a fine carriage and span of horses. Our artist in New York has seized upon the incident as one of interest, and has given a faithful picture of the vehicle and horses, which have formed so appropriate a gift from the generous citizens of New York.

This carriage was manufactured for the pre-

sentors by Wood, Tomlinson & Co., 410 Broadway, N. Y., and is lined with the richest cherrycolored brocatelle, (a very thick figured silk goods), the lace, also of silk, was manufactured for the purpose from silk grown in this country. The mountings were of silver, and the sides wore ornamented with rich silver plate lamps.—

The body of the coach was painted an invisible green,—the whole presenting a plain, substantial and rich appearance. The carved work was elaborate, and when completed, the vehicle was pronounced the most elegant and finished piece of workmanship ever turned out in this country. The whole cost, horses and harness, was $2500.

Christopher Gore

Jeremiah Mason

Joseph Story

George Ticknor

Robert Y. Hayne

John C. Calhoun

William Henry Harrison

John Tyler

Lord Ashburton

Henry Clay

Edward Everett

Millard Fillmore

When I have returned home, after long-continued and exhausting labors, I have forgotten amidst the cordial greetings of those whom I most respect and honor all the inconveniences, toils and losses connected with public life.

The contributions which you now make known to me must be placed entirely to the account of the friendship and the generosity of yourself and the other gentlemen. Expressions of thanks, however warm and sincere, would in a case like this be feeble. I must rest, therefore, in the persuasion that all who have borne a part in this transaction will believe that it has deeply and profoundly impressed me with the sentiments and the emotions justly belonging to the occasion.

I am, dear sir, with the greatest personal regard, your obedient servant . . .

Webster justified these arrangements on practical grounds. As a lawyer, he had developed enormous earning capacity. His service in the Senate and as Secretary of State forced him to forego substantial professional income. Accordingly, if his wealthy constituents desired him to remain in office, it seemed to him proper that they should stand a portion of his loss. There were British precedents for such arrangements, and such matters were then viewed with greater tolerance than they would be today.

In any event, Webster seems not to have suffered from pangs of conscience, and neither his financial troubles nor his presidential disappointments spoiled his delight in simple things.

[Letter to Charles H. Thomas of Marshfield, Feb. 4, 1837]

Even your slightest letters afford me pleasure. Amidst the toil of law and the stunning din of politics, any thing is welcome which calls my thoughts back to Marshfield, though it be only to be told which way the wind blows.

SPEAK FOR YOURSELF, DANIEL

[Letter to Stephen White, from Marshfield, Aug. 12, 1832]

I did not write you, as I promised, on Friday, because, so soon as it ceased raining in the morning, there were certain flocks seen on the meadows, whose visits it was necessary to regard, and Mr. Blake came that evening, and took the field yesterday, so that I was occupied with him. We embarked in Mr. Hatch's boat, at the boat-house, head of South River, and went down to the mouth thereof, through the marshes, and returned same way. We found some birds, though the meadows are not yet sufficiently mown to make them constantly plenty. Immediately after the rain — they were in great numbers, all round us. I have not followed the seas at all, since I saw you last. I reserve the pleasure of renewing that sort of life till you come again, and until The Calypso makes her appearance on this coast. Meantime, Peterson takes care that we do not suffer for want of a fish or two.

The yacht Calypso *was a gift to Webster from Stephen White, whom we have already met in connection with the Salem murder trials. An intimate relationship developed between their families. In 1831, William Paige, younger brother of Webster's first wife, Grace, married one of the three White daughters, Harriette, and in 1836 Webster's son Fletcher married another.*

[Letters to Paige]

Washington, Friday P. M., March 5, 1832.

I give you great joy at the birth of a daughter! There is no event on which I could more sincerely congratulate you. A daughter is one of Heaven's best and sweetest gifts to man. It delights me to hear of her dark hair, dark eyes, and high forehead, although it costs me an involuntary tear, by the recollection of poor little Grace. My dear Sir, I share your feelings and partake your joy. May a thousand blessings hover over the little stranger! I beg to be most particularly remembered to Harriette. What a new world this has become to her by the events of a year! Pray give her my love. I shall write a note forthwith to the Judge,* and send Charles off with it. I met Mr. Appleton between the House and my seat in the Senate, he bringing me the news, I carrying it to him. So you see the young lady makes a stir at Washington already.

Washington, March 10, 1832.

I have been exceedingly glad to hear from you from day to day, with accounts of Harriette and Miss Paige. I rejoice to think, that by the time you receive this, Harriette will be at the head of her own table again; for

> "What is a table, richly spread,
> Without the lady at its head."

Washington, Tuesday morning, April 24, 1832.

I have received yours respecting the lining of the chaise. I do not like a dark lining; such linings look hot in summer, and in winter I go in a sleigh. I reject blue; therefore, the body and carriage being dark, I suppose a light drab would not answer, and dark drab looks dull. On the whole, I am for a brown, or a claret, though if I know what a claret is, it is rather darker than I should like, yet I think it will do very well. Please ask Harriette, whether it shall be a claret or a brown, and decide according to her response, as I hope she will sometimes do my new chaise the honor to take a drive in it.

[*Letter to White, Aug. 17, 1832*]

Green Harbor, August 17, half-past twelve, 1832.

I arrived at sunset yesterday, and found all well. Col. Paige has been busily engaged all day, either shooting or driving out with the ladies. Mrs. Paige seems quite well; and as for the amiable and interesting Miss Paige, she is as gay as a lark and as fat as a plover. The Calypso anchored in the inner roads last evening, before dark,

---

* Judge Story, uncle of Mrs. Paige.

out about seven or eight hours from Boston, and for some time becalmed off the cliffs; all well; spoke nothing. The Commodore speaks of her in the highest manner, as a sea boat. In her build and equipment he holds her unsurpassed. She will proceed on no cruise for halibut, cod, or haddock, until you shall be on board.

The shooting here is now good; the true way is, to hasten down, and enjoy it, but not to proclaim it; don't speak too goldenly of it to Mr. Blake; it is not necessary to bring half the town into the Old Colony, by inflamed account of sports. Remember that this hint is not for yourself, for you have no tongue, except when tongues would be serviceable.

Give my love to the damsels.

Green Harbor was the name given to Webster's home place at Marshfield. The "Commodore" was Seth Peterson, whom George Ticknor Curtis described as "familiar to all Mr. Webster's friends who ever visited Marshfield — a droll, red-faced, old salt, whose occupation, when he was not fishing or shooting with Mr. Webster, was what he called 'lobstering.' His usual dress was a flannel shirt, which might once have been red, but which wind, weather, and salt water had converted into a nameless color; and pantaloons that had been patched until their original fabric and hue were quite undistinguishable. He was a quick-witted, humorous old fellow, smart with his tongue, shrewd, and good-natured. He was a first-rate fisherman and boatman, and was for many years in Mr. Webster's service in those capacities."

[Further letters to White]

Green Harbor, Saturday evening, August 19, 1832.

We can find room for the two sprites somewhere, and if they can undergo Marshfield for a week, we shall be glad to see them. They will be beau-less, it is true; but a short abstraction from the world may cause their light to appear more splendid when they reappear in it.

FRUSTRATIONS AND FRAILTIES

P. S. We look for you on Monday, and the weather being fine we will join the great fishing interest of the country on Tuesday.

Green Harbor, Marshfield, Wednesday afternoon.

We have had a laugh at dinner, though we had to force it a little. We have found out that although we fobbed you off with some thin claret on Sunday, we were really rich, in various good wines, with which your kindness had supplied us. To prevent or alleviate extreme mortification, we have affected to make a joke of it, and tried hard to laugh. The truth is, I found a bottle of brandy, and two bottles of Sherry, in the cooler, neither seeing any more nor hearing of any more; and Mr. Paige having spoken only of a bottle or two, I thought I had seen all; and Henry, who knew all, being absent on Sunday, I was left to remain in my error. I pray you, in accepting thanks for your kindness, to accept also an apology for such a blunder. I assure you, it is not often that good wine is under any roof where I am without my knowing it.

The light-hearted remark that "it is not often that good wine is under any roof where I am without my knowing it," opens up a question which, sooner or later, anyone interested in Webster must resolve for the sake of his own peace of mind. For, of all the slurs cast on Webster's reputation, the most persistent and damaging was the charge of drunkenness.

Unquestionably Webster drank. He took particular pride and pleasure in good wine and good brandy, both for his guests and for himself. On occasion he overindulged. Indeed, one of his speeches gives evidence of it. At a dinner in connection with the Agricultural Fair at Rochester, New York, on September 21, 1843, he was called on to speak not once but several times. Notwithstanding a heavy cold, he responded with ever-increasing enthusiasm. A marathon of toasts and other speeches filled the intervals, and when Webster rose for the last time, to propose a toast to the City of Rochester, he voiced praise for the two hundred and fifty foot waterfall in its great river. A dinner companion, apparently, had mentioned the falls of the Genesee River, where Rochester is located, and it had conjured up a vision of Niagara.

The remarkable thing, perhaps, is not that Webster may have drunk too much on such an occasion, but that he did not do so more often. The accepted practices of the day demanded the drinking of toasts at political dinners, sometimes as many as thirty in an evening, and anyone who did not tilt his glass was regarded as something less than a man. Regardless of such observations, however, the belief that Webster was given to drunkenness has become so widespread that some exploration of the subject is essential if we are to know the whole man and have some rational basis for separating myth from fact.

Needless to say, drinking is something that Webster did not discuss except for occasional remarks in a spirit of banter, as in his letter to White. Accordingly, if we are to consider such matters at all we must depart from our general purpose and speak for him.

During the last two and a half years of his life, for reasons that will later become more plain, accusations of drunkenness were showered so heavily on Webster that some of his biographers obtained formal statements on the subject from his most intimate friends, including his family doctor. Without exception they denied the charge. Some of them said they had never seen Webster intoxicated. Admittedly, such statements were from prejudiced sources, but it would seem surprising that individuals of recognized standing in the community would deliberately lie, even to honor the memory of a friend. Where then did the charges of drunkenness come from?

William Cleaver Wilkinson (1833–1920), a native of Vermont, prominent Baptist theologian, teacher and author, with A.B., A.M. and D.D. degrees from the University of Rochester and an LL. D. from Baylor University, plus several foreign degrees and a three-inch listing in Who's Who, *said in a work published in 1911 that "for more than fifty years one of the eager studies of my life has been to*

learn everything that could be learned about Webster." In Daniel
Webster — A Vindication, *a portion of which was published as
early as 1876 in* Scribner's Monthly, *he tells us that he investigated
the sources of the charges of drunkenness and, where specific instances were cited, interviewed individuals who had been present.
In no instance did the facts, as related by witnesses, bear out the
charges.*

*He made other interesting findings. Although political enemies
had attacked Webster from time to time, it was not until March 7,
1850, that accusations of drunkenness made their appearance. Webster's speech of that date excited the utmost ire on the part of the
abolitionists. They flayed him from press and pulpit. They charged
him with all manner of sins, including immorality with women.
Most of all they concentrated on intemperance. It could not be
denied that Webster drank. Many had seen him do so at public
dinners. Charges of drunkenness were easy to make and hard to dis-
prove.*

*Wilkinson's researches showed beyond the most prudish doubt
that there was no evidence of sexual misconduct. He also made a
strong case for the view that the charges of intemperance represented
a deliberate application of Benjamin Franklin's aphorism, "throw
mud enough and some will stick." In Webster's case the persistence
of the charges and the prominence of their sponsors gave them great
effect. For example, the Rev. Theodore Parker, whose following
was enormous, not only reiterated them from the pulpit but also
wrote them into a formal biography. The charges did indeed stick,
and now appear in many of our standard history books.*

*To Wilkinson's findings may be added a further observation.
During the last years of Webster's life, the period in which he was
claimed to have been so besotted, his personal secretary was a young
man named Charles Lanman, who published a volume of reminiscences. Needless to say, they are eulogistic, but the facts he portrays seem strangely inconsistent with the usual concept of a drunk-
ard.*

"He was always an early riser," wrote Lanman. "If on either of his farms, he literally rose with the lark, and went forth to enjoy the quiet companionship of his cattle; and if in the city, especially in Washington, he was up before the sun, and among the first visitors to the market, where he not only attended to the necessary duty of supplying his table, but also enjoyed the conversation of the various rural characters whom he met there, and with whom it was his pleasure to be on intimate terms. As his habit of early rising and going to market was known, many citizens, who had not otherwise an opportunity of seeing him, embraced these morning occasions of meeting him.

"While his mind was greatly occupied with the affairs of the nation in the spring of 1851, he was even then in the almost daily habit of wetting a line at the Little Falls of the Potomac. His only and constant companion on these occasions was the writer, for whom he was in the habit of calling at the early hour of four in the morning. He was always delighted to capture a few rockfish or bass, but if we happened to catch nothing he was quite contented, for he enjoyed the fresh air and the exercise.

"Mr. Webster admired, above all things, to see the sun rise, especially from his chamber window at Marshfield. On many occasions, at sunrise, both in the spring and autumn, has he stolen into the chamber occupied by the writer, which looked upon the sea, and, with only his dressing-gown on, has stood by his bedside and startled the writer out of a deep sleep, by a loud shout somewhat to this effect:

" 'Awake! sluggard, and look upon this glorious scene, for the sky and the ocean are enveloped in flames!'

"On one occasion the writer was awakened in a similar manner at a very early hour, when, lo! Mr. Webster, who happened to be in a particularly playful mood, was seen going through the graceful motions of an angler, throwing a fly and striking a trout, and then, without speaking a word, disappeared."

XV

1833–1839

TRAVELS AND POLITICAL ASPIRATIONS

Webster's presidential ambitions generated an urge to travel. In April 1833 he wrote General Lewis Cass, earlier a schoolmate and friend at Exeter, later a political enemy:

A journey to the West has long been in contemplation by me, but I have not yet been able to accomplish it. Every other year the session of Congress has been so far protracted as to forbid the undertaking for that season, and professional duties have allowed me no leisure, hitherto, in the intervening years.

This year, accompanied by Stephen White, he made the break, visiting Albany, Utica, Buffalo, Columbus, and Cincinnati. He had planned also to tour Kentucky, home state of Henry Clay, but in Cincinnati received a "welcoming" letter from that gentleman saying, "I shall be mortified and disappointed if you do not visit Kentucky and Lexington; but I regret extremely that you should find us, in so many places, suffering with cholera. Its visit to Lexington has been frightful. Its mortality there has been exceeded in degree at no other point in the United States, New Orleans, perhaps, excepted. . . ."

Webster returned home, making further speeches in Washington, Pennsylvania, and Pittsburgh. From Steubenville, Ohio, he found time for some advice to his son Fletcher, who was a senior at Harvard and had been assigned a part in one of the college exhibitions:

I cross the river this morning, go down to Wheeling, stay there a part of to-morrow, and then go East. My purpose is to get to New York as soon as possible. If it be within the reach of possibility, I will be home before July 15, so as to hear your oration. At present there is no doubt of it, provided I find your mother at New York.

I pray you, spare no pains in regard to that effort. Consider how much depends on it, and how much you owe to those who elected you. Make it long; you will be likely to err on the other extreme. Do not omit a few flowers and flourishes; they become young orators. Let not your taste be too severe. Above all things, be sure to have it perfectly committed, and rehearse and practise it till you feel that you can deliver it perfectly well.

Back in Washington for the 1833–34 session of Congress as a member of the minority party and with few senatorial responsibilities, Webster found congressional life uninspiring, especially as his wife stayed in Boston and did not join him until later.

[Letter to Mrs. Webster, Jan., 1834]

I wish we had a little match-making here, too, or something else to keep one alive, for I confess it has become exceedingly dull.

There is nothing of interest in Congress, and as I do not go out at all, and for a month have asked nobody to my rooms, life has become a little too solitary. I have read every thing in the known world, except Doctor's books; botany, geology, chemistry, novels, travels, children's books, Robinson Crusoe, &c., &c., and at last Dr. Sewall offered me his Medical Dictionary: I hesitate at this for the present.

The same old story is to be told about the weather. It is as cold here to-day as the south part of Greenland.

The Chesapeake and the Delaware are, as yet, all solid ice. Sometime between this and dogdays, I hope they will get a sweat.

I see from your letters that one I. P. Davis is at my house a good deal. Whenever there is a dinner or a supper, whatever other names are sprinkled round by way of garnishment, there his stands always, at the head, or in the middle of the lists. I want to know what Mrs. I. P. has to say to all this.

Neither Fletcher nor Julia has written me for a month. They must be both very busy.

I do not mean to write another word about ice, weather, boats or roads. I take patience, so must you, in large portions.

Dates will show that Dr. Warren was feeling your pulse, and looking solemn, just about the time that Dr. Sewall was bidding me hold out my tongue, and looking at it, from the nearest point to which his nose would let him approach. This I take as a proof that there exists between us, whether together or apart, the proper degree of matrimonial sympathy.

[Letter to Mrs. E. B. Lee, Mar. 12, 1834]

I was very happy to receive your letter, and indeed should have written you long ago, but for the impertinent intrusion of divers secular matters. I have persuaded myself that I have been very busy; a point in which indolence is apt to succeed, when it solicits belief. The success of all argument depends much, in my opinion, on three things, 1st, who speaks; 2d, who is spoken to; 3d, what is asked or contended for. Now, when the speaker is one's self; when, secondly, the party spoken to is also one's self; and when, thirdly, the thing to be proved is, that the speaker and the judge has been too busy to do what would otherwise have been his duty, there is very great chance of success in the argument.

I write this in the Senate. Mr. Brown, of North Carolina, is speaking against a distress memorial.

Mr. Brown is down, and the new senator from Virginia, Mr. Leigh, is speaking. He is an ingenious, fluent, pleasant sort of speaker, a good lawyer, and has very considerable ability of various kinds.

My wife and boys are well. We get along as smoothly as was to have been expected. Mrs. Webster goes a good deal into the gay world, and when I cannot go with her, Daniel is her beau. We hear often from Julia, but I have neglected the poor child dreadfully. I have not written her as I ought.

As to good Dr. Parker's sermons, my dear friend, be sure to put my name down for a half a dozen, or a dozen copies, or just as many as you think so poor a man as I am ought to subscribe for, for the good of so lovely and highly-esteemed friend as Mrs. Parker.

[Letter to Mrs. Paige, Apr. 27, 1834]

My wife and boys ran away last Thursday, and took Mrs. Newbold, her son, and her daughter with them. They are gone up to Harper's Ferry, leaving me "with nobody with me at home but myself."

It is horrid cold here, how is it with you? The ice this morning was as strong as Mrs. Ronckendorf's coffee, that is, it would bear a cat. The wind blows as if old Eolus had just now struck his spear through his bag in twenty places, or his cave, or whatever else he holds all his winds in. We have no rain, and the dust rises as thick as it falls when one pokes a coal fire. Such are our comforts.

I must pray particular regards to Miss Paige. The opportunity afforded by my late visit of cultivating the acquaintance of that lady, has led to the adoption of a decidedly high estimate of her excellent qualities. She is an article, as your husband would say, "steadily improving"; I and other sentimental youths would say of her that "she wins fast, and holds all she wins; that like her mother —— " but I may as well stop. There is no knowing where I might bring myself up.

[Letter to Fletcher, June 5, 1834]

I presume you will be in Boston, by the time this letter shall arrive. So soon as you shall have made a short visit to Marshfield,

I wish you to proceed to Exeter with Edward. It is high time he was at School. You will take him to Mr. Chadwick's, & see him provided for, as to room &c. Ask Mr. Chadwick to be kind enough to take care of him, in all those respects in which a boy needs looking after. He must, among other things, take the trouble of attending to his personal cleanliness, &c. &c. In all these particulars enjoin on Edward the importance of exact & steady habits. As to any clothes, or books, or other articles, if he shall need them Mr. Chadwick will see him supplied, or tell him where to obtain what he wants. You must leave him a little pocket money, & a small monthly allowance can be sent him from home. Go with him to Dr. Abbott, & stay in town a day or two, until he has been at school once or twice, & begins to feel a little at home.

[*Letter to James Brooks, Portland, Me., Aug. 5, 1834*]

I have received your letter of the 3d instant in which you say that the Portland Argus imputes to me the expression of this sentiment, viz., "Let Congress take care of the Rich, and the Rich will take care of the Poor."

The same imputation has appeared in other prints. I know not where it originated, but you are quite correct in supposing it to be an entire and utter falsehood. I never expressed any such sentiment publicly or privately, nor anything like it, nor anything to give the least countenance or color to such an imputation.

I have endeavored to maintain, as great and leading political truths, that Republican Constitutions are established for the benefit of the whole People, and that all measures of government ought to be adopted with strict regard to the greatest good of the greater number; that the Laws should favor the distribution of property to the end that the number of the very rich and the number of the poor may both be diminished as far as practicable consistently with the rights of industry and property; and that all legislation in this country is especially bound to pay particular respect to the earnings of labor; labor being the source of comfort and independence to far the greatest portion of our people.

Webster's thoughts ran more and more to the operation of his farms.

[*Letter to Abraham G. Stevens, at Franklin, N. H., Jan. 1, 1835*]

I wish you to keep some of your young stock (if not the whole) rather better than is usual in the country. I should like to have at least one pair of steers raised every year which might grow to some size. The heifers, calves of the Durham breed, should also be well kept. If you should have a full blooded one, this year, let it run with the cow.

In general, I believe it is better to keep but little stock, and keep it *well.*

[*Letter to Seth Weston, at Marshfield, Mass., Aug. 29, 1835*]

In regard to the sedge flat, you will ascertain where the old river channel was, and mow to that boundary. Captain Asa Hewitt can best tell you where that channel was. The law is, that gradual changes of the bed of a river, by daily washing away from one side, and adding to the other still leave the river the boundary between the proprietors on both sides; but where, by some storm or other sudden cause, a river at once changes its bed or seeks a new mouth, in such cases the old channel remains the boundary.

Mrs. Webster did not accompany him to Washington for the 1835–36 session of Congress. Though this may have been hard on him, it has benefited us with a shower of letters to his wife:

[*Dec. 7, 1835*]

I rec'd your letter yesterday, & all here were **very** glad to hear from you. This leaving home is a pretty hard matter, to those who go, & to those who stay. It may render a reunion more agreeable & more valued.

I went to Church yesterday morning with Mr. Edgar, & for the rest of the day, except a short call at Mr. Curtis', sat over the fire. To day I have calls to make, & business to attend to, besides a dinner to eat with the Sons of St. Nicholas.

I have paid your butter bill, which is enclosed. Also your bonnet bill — $26.25. For both these amounts please give me credit, & charge house-hold expenses. The butter cost 30 cts, here, as you will see. The honor of New England forbids us to send again to N. Y. for butter. Bonnets you may get where you please.

[Dec. 23, 1835]

I am pretty well arranged, now, in my lodgings, & get on well. Dr. Sewall calls often, & always inquires for Mrs. Webster. I have not been out — have invited no company — & occupy myself with common Congress matters, & with some preparation for the Court, — though in the Court, I have not a great deal to do this year, & wish I had less. No Ch. Jus is yet nominated but it is expected Mr Taney will be the man.

[Jan. 1, 1836]

I wish you and the whole house a happy New Year. And as I cannot be present to kiss you all myself, I depute Captain Thomas, if he should be there, or Mr. Blake, or some other friend about my age, to perform the salutations. I went with Commodore Chauncey and daughter to the President's, and have returned. The crowd looked just as usual. A great many faces, whom I did not know, and not many of those I do know. The President was civil, and the Vice-President uncommonly polite. I am going to dine with Dr. Sewall. There were parties last evening at Mr. Cass and Mr. Coxe's; I did not go to either, putting off all my dissipation till you come. As to dinner parties, I have heard of few and been at none. I shall go to the President's, when asked, and be very sparing of my company elsewhere.

[*Jan. 10, 1836*]

I recd. your letter of the 5th yesterday, but today we have no mail north of N. York. Judge Story arrived last Evening, in good health, but bad spirits. He thinks the Supreme Court is *gone*, & I think so, too; and almost everything is gone, or seems rapidly going.

[*Jan. 24, 1836*]

You will see that there is a good deal of heat here. Mr. Benton, & others of the Senate, have attacked the proceedings of last Session. I have felt bound to defend, or help defend, the Senate. This has led Mr. Adams to attack us, in the House, in the most violent manner, & to bestow an especial portion of his wrath & bitterness on me. He has the instinct of those animals, which, when enraged, turn upon their keepers, & mangle those who have showed them most kindness. The members of the Mass. Delegation are exceedingly indignant, & most of them will tell him what they think of him, before the matter is over. He may be alluded to, also, in the Senate, but not by me.

I send you a lot of invitations, that you may see what is going on. I have been to no parties. I like very much the pleasure of staying at home, & sitting by the fire, thro' an evening, & never find it dull, tho' I am alone. Some day this week, I must make a dinner for the Mass. Delegation. They will much miss your Ladyship from the head of the Table.

[*Jan. 29, 1836*]

To day, the Mass. Delegation dine with me, with some exceptions. It is my only effort to raise a dinner of any magnitude, & I doubt how we shall make out.

Mr. Evans made a famous speech yesterday. I did not hear it, but it is universally praised. I understand he told Mr. A. that he had lived to become "the scorn & derision of his enemies, & an object of pity to his friends."

I was in the House this morning. Mr. A. was not there. They said he was probably at home, writing out his speech — or else digesting what he heard yesterday. He has more to hear yet.

[Undated]

Now that you have got your furnace, take care not to keep your house too warm. There is much danger of that with these furnaces.

[Feb. 9, 1836]

It would give me much pleasure, I assure you, to partake of some of those little suppers, which appear so good in your letters. They are articles, of which I have seen no specimen, since I left home. Early in March, I hope to taste a potato, in Summer Street.

I have not been to an Evening party, this winter & only once to dine, viz at Mr Van Buren's, on Saturday. It was a dinner, I presume, mainly intended for the Judges. He lives in much the same manner as when Secretary of State; perhaps not quite so well. I wished to go last Eve' to Mrs Florida Whites last soiree, but I dared not venture out. The President has another great party on Thursday. Mrs Cass, as you will see has her third rout, the 18. They say Mrs Cass must be preparing to make her husband a foreign minister.

[Mar. 6, 1836]

This is a very fine morning, which I hope you are also enjoying. It is warm and summer like, and fills me full of hopes of home. I shall wait only to hear that the Boat has run *once,* intending to go the second trip. My cold has melted off, and I am quite well.

SPEAK FOR YOURSELF, DANIEL

[*Apr. 29, 1836*]

Today we hope to finish the land bill, if Mr. Benton should not wear us all out by an endless speech — which he threatens to do. If we finish the Bill, I think we shall adjourn to Tuesday, to give time for the officer of the Senate to take up the carpet, clean the chamber, etc., for warm weather.

The family letters also included some to his son Fletcher, whom Webster had sent on an expedition to purchase land in what is now the Mid-West:

[*Jan. 15, 1836*]

I am sorry for your disappointment about the aid-ship; but never mind, I believe you are as well without it; if you think not, I will see more about it, when I get home. I believe the military honors of our family terminated with my father. I once tried to be captain, and failed; and I canvassed a whole regiment to make your uncle an adjutant, and failed also. We are predestinated not to be great in the field of battle. We are not the sons of "Bellona's bridegroom"; our battles are forensic; we draw no blood, but the blood of our clients.

If, on a given occasion, a man can, gracefully, and without the air of a pedant, show a little more knowledge than the occasion requires, the world will give him credit for eminent attainments. It is an honest quackery. I have practised it, and sometimes with success.

We find connections and coincidences, helps and succors, where we did not expect them. I have never learned any thing which I wish to forget; except how badly some people have behaved; and I every day find, on almost every subject, that I wish I had more knowledge than I possess, seeing that I could produce it, if not for use, yet for effect.

TRAVELS AND POLITICAL ASPIRATIONS

[Mar. 14, 1836]

It gives me great delight to hear that you have learned how to sit still and read a book. If you have really accomplished that, you have certainly made your fortune.

[June 12, 1836]

I have no letter from you since you left Toledo; but I learn by a letter from Mr. Davis that you left Detroit, on horseback, about the 27th of May, I suppose for Bronson, White Pigeon, & so on to Michigan City & Chicago. At the latter place, you will have found various letters from us.

About coming home — when may we look for you? I think, that there is sometimes fever & ague in the lake country, & as you are not yet well (*acclimated*) if that is the word, you would do well not to stay too long, especially if it should be probable that the affairs which you will have on hand will call you back in the fall. It is expected very important sales will take place in Wisconsin, in October, as you will have learned, & a great many people will be present. There is no doubt, that if you come home in August, having done tolerably well so far, you can take back a good deal of money in the fall. What I would suggest is, that, with the advice of Harding, & other friends in Chicago, or of Mr. Whitney at Green Bay, you employ one or two good men, say two, & send them in different directions to *explore for you,* in Wisconsin in the tracts which are expected to be offered for sale. If you then return some weeks before the sale, you will receive their report, & act accordingly. I understand, that where one has the requisite previous knowledge, a favorable opportunity of entering lands exists, just at the close of the public sales, while others are gone into the woods to examine, &c — all these things, however, you will know more about, than I can tell you.

In all your operations, you should appear to be acting for yourself; or, at least, for yourself & me; and as it is very probable that this business may induce you to make your home in those regions, at least for some time, you should, on all occasions, act as much [as] possible as if you were already a Western man.

[*June 15, 1836*]

I received yesterday your letter from Constantine, and wished, while reading it, I had been with you on the St. Joseph's. I should certainly have made a dash at some of these water powers. It could hardly fail to do well to buy the land embracing a large waterfall, although now in a wilderness, if it be where population must in time reach it.

Two members of the House of Representatives tried to fight a duel yesterday; but they could not hit each other. Six rounds of bullets were discharged in *tenues auras*.

[*June 25, 1836*]

I received last evening your letter from Chicago, of the 13th of June, being your first from that city. I think you did well to buy the 800 acres in the Kalamazoo country, by what I hear of that region.

I hope you will leave some faithful "land-lookers" to explore for you in your absence. You may go back in the fall, with as much capital as you think you can use to advantage.

Later, Webster employed Ray Thomas, of Marshfield, as his western land agent, setting out his instructions in a letter dated March 5, 1838:

You are now about to proceed to Illinois and other Northwestern States as my agent. Your principal duties will be of two kinds.

1st. In the first place you will have the care & disposal of the land lots & parcels of real Estate belonging to me in Ohio, Indiana, Illinois, Michigan & Wisconsin with power to sell excepting the estate or farm called Salisbury near La Salle.

2d. Your other main duty will be to carry on my farm called Salisbury. You will look at the Deeds which are said to be sent to Ottawa — see what land they contain, and see what land they comprise. My wish is to have a very large farm, as large as one active man can well superintend the management of. If this estate be not large enough at present, find out what adjoining lands may be bought and at what prices. Fletcher & his family live in the house, and I presume you will live with them.

My object is to realize an income from this farm. You will therefore manage it with economy and to the best possible advantage. The farm must be well stocked — you will employ your own laborers and will have no master over you in whatsoever respects the farm, but will of course consult freely with Fletcher on all important matters, not only in relation to the farm, but in other concerns of mine.

This arrangement came to an unhappy end. In March 1840, on a visit to Washington to report on his activities, Ray Thomas, whom Webster especially loved and trusted, picked up an infection and died after an agonizing illness, during the last days of which Webster stayed almost continuously at his bedside. Webster was never able to make anything from his western land ventures, or to bail himself out of the indebtedness which they had created.

After the election of Van Buren to the presidency, in 1836, Webster, deeply in debt and faced with another four years of Democratic domination, determined to resign from the Senate.

[*Letter to Everett, Jan. 31, 1837*]

I have this day written to Mr. Kinsman a letter to be shown to friends, intimating my intention to resign my seat, at the end of this session. He will show it to you, no doubt. I place my resignation on the ground of a strong wish for some respite, some leisure, after a continued service of fourteen years.

My purpose is, for the next two years, to travel, in my own country, and by possibility, to make a trip of six months to Europe. My own affairs, too, require looking after, and I should be glad to be able so to arrange them, as to be able to live, without pursuing much longer my profession.

I would as willingly hold on till the fall, as resign now, but have thought it might be better, or be thought better, that the present legislature should have an opportunity of filling the place.

In a similar letter of the same date, to Robert C. Winthrop, he added:

If, two years hence, our friends shall be able and willing to send me back, I will not refuse to come; but I could not well say that in a letter intended to be shown to others.

Will you be kind enough to inform me how long the legislature will probably remain in session. I would prefer to stay out the session here; but if it would be more convenient to have a resignation earlier, I will forward it.

Webster's conservative constituents were appalled at the prospect of losing their champion. Businessmen and politicians joined in making known their anguish, and after a brief interval of soul-searching he bowed to their wishes.

[*Letter to Ketchum, New York, Feb. 20, 1837*]

I write at this moment, merely to say, that my friends in Massachusetts make so much opposition to my resignation at the present moment, that in all probability I must defer the execution of that purpose till the fall.

TRAVELS AND POLITICAL ASPIRATIONS

Although the sad state of his finances hovered over his conscience, Webster undoubtedly was influenced by the brightening prospect of a Whig victory in the next presidential election. The troubles besetting the Van Buren administration were accelerating in both depth and volume. It was no mere coincidence that Webster's political friends in New York picked this moment to arrange a reception for him at a popular political gathering place then known as Niblo's Saloon (subsequently purified by commentators into Niblo's "Garden"). There, on March 15, 1837, he delivered a carefully prepared speech stating his position on the major issues of the day. It covered a great deal of ground, and was remarkable for its forthrightness, but the portion which was to have the greatest future significance was his discussion of the proposed annexation of Texas:

Gentlemen, we all see that, by whomsoever possessed, Texas is likely to be a slave-holding country; and I frankly avow my entire unwillingness to do any thing that shall extend the slavery of the African race on this continent, or add other slave-holding States to the Union. When I say that I regard slavery in itself as a great moral, social, and political evil, I only use language which has been adopted by distinguished men, themselves citizens of slave-holding States. I shall do nothing, therefore, to favor or encourage its further extension. We have slavery already amongst us. The Constitution found it in the Union; it recognized it, and gave it solemn guaranties. To the full extent of these guaranties we are all bound, in honor, in justice, and by the Constitution. All the stipulations contained in the Constitution in favor of the slave-holding States which are already in the Union ought to be fulfilled, and, so far as depends on me, shall be fulfilled, in the fulness of their spirit and to the exactness of their letter. Slavery, as it exists in the States, is beyond the reach of Congress. It is a concern of the States themselves; they have never submitted it to Congress, and Congress has no rightful power over it. I shall concur, therefore, in no act, no measure, no menace, no indication of purpose, which shall interfere or threaten to interfere with the exclusive authority of the several States over the subject of slavery as it exists within their respective limits. All this appears to me to be matter of plain and imperative duty.

But when we come to speak of admitting new States, the subject assumes an entirely different aspect. Our rights and our duties are then both different.

The free States, and all the States, are then at liberty to accept or to reject. When it is proposed to bring new members into this political partnership, the old members have a right to say on what terms such new partners are to come in, and what they are to bring along with them. In my opinion, the people of the United States will not consent to bring into the Union a new, vastly extensive, and slave-holding country, large enough for half a dozen or a dozen States. In my opinion, they ought not to consent to it.

Having staked out his political platform, Webster departed on another tour of the West, this time accompanied by his wife, his daughter Julia, and his godson William Pitt Fessenden. They visited most of the important centers of the Mid-West, including Cincinnati, Louisville, St. Louis, Springfield, Chicago, Toledo, and Detroit, returning by way of Buffalo and Rochester. Webster was received everywhere with enthusiasm; among others, by General William Henry Harrison, Salmon P. Chase, and Abraham Lincoln, then a leading Whig in the Illinois Legislature. Even Clay put on a show, arranging a reception in Lexington, Kentucky, with an array of juleps amply adequate to guard against any lingering vestiges of the earlier cholera epidemic. "The way they drink these things in Kentucky," wrote Fessenden, "is a caution to sinners."

During this trip, the Panic of 1837 struck with chilling force, closing banks, draining specie from circulation, and knocking the bottom out of land prices. Webster suffered the dismaying experience of seeing the value of his western lands melt before his eyes. But discouragement never gripped him for long. He laid the crisis firmly on the doorstep of the Democrats and encouraged his audiences to look to the future, saying at Rochester:

Gentlemen, while I say that no immediate relief is to be expected, I am no preacher of panics. I desire to inspire no distrust or despondency. The country cannot be easily ruined. It is young, great, strong, and full of activity. But my faith is in the people.

The remainder of the Van Buren administration was marked by frustration. The Whigs had focused their hopes too strongly on the 1839 presidential election to be cooperative even in measures for relieving the panic. They counted the troubles of the Democrats among their major blessings. Meanwhile, they justified their intransigence in the belief that the strength and resilience of the country, if left alone, would restore normalcy with more efficiency and less danger than the government.

Early in 1839 the Massachusetts Legislature reelected Webster to the Senate for a further six-year term, the vote in the upper house being unanimous and in the lower house 330 to 65.

XVI

1839

VISIT TO ENGLAND

Webster had long wanted to visit England, which, like many Bostonians, he viewed as a sort of spiritual homeland. During the administration of President John Quincy Adams, Webster had sought appointment as Minister to Great Britain. Rebuffs had not dampened his hopes, and even under the hostile Van Buren he had angled for appointment as a special envoy to negotiate a treaty defining the Maine-Canada boundary. This issue, always sensitive, had grown inflammatory as settlers moved into the disputed area, and by 1838 had brought the countries to the verge of hostilities.

Disappointed in his efforts to head an official mission, Webster now determined to go to England on his own. The immediate and outward justification for the trip was the engagement of his daughter Julia to Samuel Appleton Appleton of Boston, and the latter's desire to be married in England, where he had been born and educated. Greater compulsion came from Webster's hope of relieving his financial distress by selling his western lands to British investors. In January 1839, he wrote to Samuel Jaudon, formerly cashier of the Second Bank of the United States, now living in London:

My main object, My Dear Sir, in writing you at this time is to communicate a plan which I have formed, or wish to form, for the purpose of crossing the water. I have a very great desire to see England once, and if this desire is ever gratified it must be done soon. But my circumstances require that I should connect some business arrangements with the purpose of my voyage; indeed, that I should make such arrangements its leading object.

Tired of the sacrifices which I had been making by remaining in Congress, I endeavored in 1836 to resign my seat with intention of retiring to the law. But I could not resign. My papers were sent back, as friends would not hearken to any suggestion of leaving my place.

Seeing then that I must do something with a view to future means of living, I entered on Western investments, partly in company with Col. Perkins, partly in a company of which Govr Cass was chief, and partly on my own separate account. These investments were made by faithful and careful agents, principally in agricultural lands of excellent quality, in Ohio, Illinois, Michigan, and Wisconsin. Prospects of profit seemed fair at the time and I purchased as far as my means and credit would go.

The events of 1837, although they have not affected the ultimate value of this property, have retarded its sale. It is still all on hand, and the general progress of settlement in these states, and the immense emigration into them, greater the last fall than ever before so far as respects north Illinois and Wisconsin, have no doubt greatly enhanced its value. Now, if I can dispose of this, or a large part, by a trip to England, I should both gratify my curiosity and improve my circumstances.

Now, the question is, can this property be sold in England? If it can I will cross the water. If it cannot, I can hardly afford to lose the time from my profession and to bear the expenses of the trip.

I have not mentioned this subject to my wife, nor to more than two persons living, besides this communication to yourself. In two or three days I shall be in Philadelphia and may perhaps suggest it to Mr. Biddle.

In the course of this letter, which contains details as to proofs of title, etc., Webster described the "large and very elegant tract of land" near La Salle (formerly Peru), Illinois, where he said he hoped to make his home:

La Salle is at the entrance of the Illinois Canal into the Illinois River, at the head of navigation. It is a point of great centrality, many lines of communication meet at it, and it must inevitably become a most important place. I own a good deal of land in the city, and a most splendid tract near it. This is the most beautiful land I ever saw, lying high near the river and interspersed with timber and meadow land most delightfully. It is not at all extravagant or excessive to put this tract at 50 dollars an acre. I think fair and competent judges would estimate my property in and about Peru at 100,000 Dollars.

Jaudon's reply must have added nourishment to Webster's wishful thinking, as did discussions with Nicholas Biddle in Philadelphia. In any event, Webster sailed on the steamship Liverpool *from New York on May 18, 1839, taking with him his wife, his daughter, Julia, and Harriette Paige. They were later joined in England by the bridegroom and by Webster's son Edward.]*

[*Letter to Edward Curtis, from Liverpool, June 3, 1839*]

We have really got over, and are now on this side. Captain Fayrer surrendered his ship to the pilot yesterday morning, Sunday, at five o'clock, being then fourteen days and seven hours from New York. There never was so tame a passage. Peterson could have rowed me over in my boat, at least till we got into the Channel. A great part of the way we had an entire calm, and ran through a smooth, glassy surface.

We came to the Adelphi, one of the two principal hotels. The ladies did not walk with remarkable elegance when they came on shore. They had forgotten to leave their sea feet on board, and the streets were not quite wide enough.

I suppose this is a fair specimen of an English tavern, very plain, but very comfortable and clean, and no show. Rooms rather small, but containing every thing you can want, down to a boot-jack, shoe-rack, and shoe-horn. I find, however, my fates pursuing me, for as I drew aside the window curtains this morning, I looked out on a dark brick wall, distant three feet!

Liverpool is a place of affairs. It is not distinguished for parks, malls, and public walks and squares. The streets are narrow, rather, and not straight. The bricks are dark, which circumstance gives a dull appearance to the city. The blocks of high brick warehouses, connected with the docks, make an appearance of great solidity and wealth. But the docks themselves are the principal and most striking thing, I think, which I have seen. The natural advantages of Liverpool as a port, are small. The Mersey is a little shallow river, and at its mouth the ocean throws in masses of sand, by way of plea in bar. But the tides are very high; and availing themselves of this circumstance, the good people have constructed these docks or basins, into which ships come at high water, and the gates being closed, there they remain, keep their masts erect, and laugh at the disappointed ebb-tide. The ships thus appear to be, not at the wharf, but in the town itself. Indeed, they look like so many strays which had been taken up and put into pound.

What shall I say about the voyage? I believe I have already said all, or nearly all. Conceive of eighty-six passengers, with none too much room, eating and drinking, playing cards, and sleeping; all these operations being contemporaneous; add smoking; put in English, French, German, and Spanish; throw in half a dozen children, uttering quite often the language of nature, and you have the saloon of a steamship; pretty much ditto on deck, bating the cards. The incidents of interest are throwing the log and taking the sun. I studied navigation under the tuition of the first mate, and learned to take an observation, and mark our latitude and longitude tolerably well. By the way, the accuracy by which place is found by the sun and moon, and chronometer, is astonishing. Off the south end of Ireland, Captain Fayrer put a fisherman right, as to his place, of a thick morning, who had only come out the night before to fish, although we had seen no land since we left New York.

Tuesday, 3 o'clock. — We have been to Knowlesly, the seat of the Earl of Derby. The Earl is unwell, having had something like a paralytic stroke near a year ago. But he had heard we were coming, and gave such orders that we were well treated. It is a magnificent place. The house itself is old and not very elegant. But every thing is on a scale of grandeur which strikes one, acquainted only with more moderate habits of life, with astonishment.

I learn the whole estate may contain fifteen or twenty thousand acres. What I saw of it was cultivated like a garden. His annual income is said to be ninety or one hundred thousand pounds sterling. The rural beauty of England, so far as I have seen, quite exceeds my expectation. I confess my conception had not reached it.

[*Letter to Charles H. Thomas, from London, June 9, 1839*]

Two things have struck us very strongly in England: First, the agricultural beauty and richness of the country. For miles together the country appears like a tasteful garden. Even the wheat-sowing and potato-planting are all done so nicely the ground looks as if it had been *stamped* as people stamp butter. And then there are the deep green of the fields, and the beautiful hedges. Of cattle, in driving over so great a part of this little kingdom, I saw many varieties and of different qualities. All around Liverpool the Ayrshire breeds abound, and they far surpass any thing else I have seen. In hundreds of flocks every one looks as if William Sherburne had been feeding and carding it for six months. In parts of Cheshire and some other places, I saw poor cattle.

The other thing which struck us is the ancient ecclesiastical architecture of England. Those old vast cathedral churches, and smaller churches, of all sizes and forms, which have stood for ages and centuries, are such objects as we cannot, of course, see on our side of the ocean. They are, some of them, most magnificent and grand spectacles. We have yet not seen much of London. Many persons have called on us, and we are likely to be busy enough.

For the two days we have been here I have been poking about *incog.*, going into all the courts, and every where else I chose, with the certainty that no one knew me. That is a queer feeling, to be in the midst of so many thousands, and to be sure that no one knows you, and that you know no one. We are apt to feel when we come among great multitudes that, of course, we shall recognize somebody. But a stranger in London is in the most perfect solitude in the world. He can touch everybody, but can speak to nobody. I like much these strolls by myself. This morning we are going to breakfast with Mr. Kenyon, where we are to meet Rogers, the poet, Wordsworth, etc., etc. Yesterday I breakfasted with Sydney Smith, long known as the greatest wit in England. He is a clergyman of much respectability. Among other persons there was Moore, the poet. An English breakfast is the plainest and most informal thing in the world. Indeed, in England, the rule of politeness is to be quiet, act naturally, take no airs, and make no bustle. This perfect politeness has, of course, cost a good deal of drill. Fuss and fidgets can be subdued only by strict discipline. We all go to dinner on Tuesday where we are to meet — who do you think? Boz — the ladies are delighted — they expect he will look just like Mr. Pickwick.

June 12, Wednesday morning. — I have nothing to add, we are all quite well. Boz looks as if he were twenty-five or twenty-six years old, is somewhat older, rather small, light complexion, and a good deal of hair, shows none of his peculiar humor in conversation, and is rather shy and retiring.

[*Letter to John P. Healey, from London, June 9, 1839*]

I went out, quite alone, looked into all the Courts — the whole four were sitting — I saw all their venerable wigs. I stayed long enough to hear several Gentlemen speak. They are vastly better *trained* than we are. They speak short. They get up, begin immediately, & leave off when they have done. Their manner is more like that of a school boy, who gets up to say his lesson, goes right through it, & then sits down, than it is like our more leisurely & elaborate habit. I think Sergeant Wilde, who is esteemed a long speaker, argued an insurance question in 15 minutes, that most of us would have got an hour's speech out of. The rooms are all small, with very inconvenient writing places, & almost nobody present, except the wigged population. I went to the Parliament Houses (Houses not in session). They are very small rooms. Where the Lords sit, I was sure, must be the old painted chamber where the Comees. of conference used to meet. On entering it, I asked the guide, what Comee. room that was. He turned to rebuke my ignorance, & exclaimed, "this is the House of Lords." I was right, however. The H. of C. was burnt, you know, some time ago, & the H. of C. now sit in what was the H. of L., & the Lords sit, temporarily, in the old painted chamber. All these accommodations are small & paltry; & new buildings are in progress for the use of both Houses.

Webster had high hopes for the Whig presidential nomination in 1839, but it became apparent that Clay would again be a contender, and geography, plus his extraordinary personal magnetism, gave him a clear ascendancy over Webster in the party councils. Obviously, Webster had been pondering his own chances, and on June 12, 1839, he wrote to withdraw his candidacy.

[*Letter to Healey, in Boston, June 12, 1839*]

Please cause the enclosed to be published, the same day, in all the Whig newspapers in Boston, & as soon as you receive it.

Yrs   D. WEBSTER

To the People of Massachusetts.
 It is known that my name has been presented to the Public, by a meeting of Members of the Legislature of the State, as a candidate for the office of President of the United States at the ensuing Election. As

it has been expected that a Convention would be holden in the autumn of this year, composed of Delegates from the Several States, I have hitherto thought proper not to anticipate, in any way, the results of that Convention. But I am now out of the country, not to return, probably, much earlier than the period fixed for the meeting of the convention, and do not know what events may occur, in the meantime, which, if I were at home, might demand immediate attention from me. I desire, moreover, to act no part which may tend to prevent a cordial & effective union among those, whose object, I trust, is to maintain, unimpaired, the Constitution of the Country, and to uphold all its great interests, by a wise, prudent, and patriotic administration of the Government. These considerations have induced me to withdraw my name as a Candidate for the office of President at the next Election.

DAN'L WEBSTER

[Letter to Everett, from London, June 12, 1839]

I have only time to say, by the return of The Liverpool, which leaves Liverpool to-morrow, that I send a very short letter for publication in Boston, addressed to the people of Massachusetts. Though shorter, it is to the effect suggested by you. Particular circumstances induced me to keep this back till I reached this side the water.

You will think it strange, but, truly, I have not had time to read a newspaper since I have been in London.

I have so many letters to write by The Liverpool, that you must pardon a very hasty one to yourself, written at an hour when all London is asleep, namely, five o'clock in the morning.

[Letter to Curtis, from London, June 12, 1839]

I find myself kindly remembered by those I have known in America. Sir Charles Bagot, Sir Stratford Canning, Sir Charles Vaughan, Mr. Labouchere, Lord Stanley, and others, have been prompt to find us out, and to tender us all kinds of attention and civility. Denison is in Paris, with his wife's uncle, Lord William

Bentinck, who is there ill. On hearing of my arrival, he sent orders for his coach and horses, coachman and postilion, to come to town, and put themselves at my disposal while I remain in London.

[Letter to Davis, from London, June 24, 1839]

It is the height of what they call "the season"; London is full, and the hospitalities of friends, the gayeties of the metropolis, and the political interests of the moment, keep every body alive. We have made many acquaintances, and have found those persons whom we have known in the United States, quite overflowing in their attentions. I have been to the courts, made the acquaintance of most of the judges, and attended the debates in both Houses of Parliament. London dinners, however, are a great hindrance to attendance on the debates in Parliament.

I have liked some of the speeches very well. They generally show excellent temper, politeness, and mutual respect among the speakers. Lord Stanley made the best speech which I have heard. I was rather disappointed in Macaulay; but so were his admirers, and I have no doubt the speech I heard was below his ordinary efforts.

[Letter to Ketchum, from London, June 24, 1839]

I have not yet seen many sights, having been too much occupied with seeing men, to find much time for looking after things. I have, however, spent a whole morning in Westminster Abbey, and a morning it was worth crossing the Atlantic to enjoy. Nothing strikes me like this ecclesiastical architecture, its antiquity, its grandeur, and often, as in the case of Westminster Abbey, the interesting monuments which it contains. We have also been to the Tower. The ancient armory is well worth seeing, and the rooms, marked with the initials of many well known prisoners of state, of former ages, excite a strong interest. Mrs. Webster is gone this morning to St. Paul's.

VISIT TO ENGLAND

[Letter to Curtis, from London, July 4, 1839]

I have been here now four weeks, and we have seen very many persons; indeed, London hospitalities have nearly overwhelmed us. Breakfasts, dinners, and evening parties belong pretty much to every day of our lives. The breakfast parties are quite pleasant for persons who have entire leisure. The breakfast is about ten, and lasts till twelve. It is not a breakfast with claret, after the French fashion, but a good breakfast, with tea and coffee, &c., and more free from restraint than a dinner table. I do not follow sight-seeing; what comes in the way I look at, but have not time to hunt after pictures, &c. Westminster Abbey and the Tower are two of the best things; they hold such memorials of by-gone times. I will tell you how we pass this day, and let it be an example. It is now eleven o'clock. We breakfasted at home at nine. Mrs. Paige is not yet out of bed, as we came very late last evening from a party at the Countess Dowager of Cork's, a person now ninety-four years old, sister to General Monckton, who was with Wolfe. I was invited to dine with her ladyship yesterday, to meet Lord Holland, but was engaged; but we all went in the evening. Well, to proceed: Mrs. Webster is writing up her journal, she writes as good a journal as Burch; Julia has gone to take a gallop in the Park and Kensington Gardens with Mr. Senior, with whom we dined yesterday. Mrs. Paige will get up by and by, and at two o'clock we are going to see the club-houses, very expensive and noble structures, the resorts of the rich and the idle; having looked at these, the ladies will go to the National Gallery with Mr. Kenyon; I shall come home, go down to the House of Commons or House of Lords, at four o'clock; stay till six; perhaps hear a speech or two, especially in the Lords; come home at six; dress, and go with Mrs. Webster to dine at Kensington with the Duke of Sussex at seven; leave his house about ten; come home, take up Mrs. Paige and Julia, and go to Mrs. Bates's, to a grand concert, where will be a crowd of people, from royal dukes and duchesses down, and all the singers from the Italian Opera.

Here we shall stay, taking in fruit and wine, as well as music, till twelve or one o'clock. To-morrow forenoon I shall shut myself up, to write letters for this conveyance; in the evening we all dine with Mr. Justice Vaughan, and his wife, Lady St. John. There, enough of that. Send over this trashy letter to Ketchum, as I may not find time to write him.

[*Letter to Ketchum, from London, July 23, 1839*]

Some gentlemen here are apparently desirous that I should have an opportunity of saying something publicly in London. Among others, I think Lord Lyndhurst, and Lord Brougham; but it is difficult to find an occasion in which a foreigner can with propriety do more than return thanks, in a very general manner. I do not mean to transgress on propriety, for the sake of talking.

I must say that the good people have treated me with great kindness. Their hospitality is unbounded, and I find nothing cold or stiff in their manners — at least not more than is observed among ourselves. There may be exceptions, but I think I may say this as a general truth. The thing in England most prejudiced against the United States, is the press. Its ignorance of us is shocking, and it is increased by such absurdities as the travellers publish.

[*Letter to John J. Crittenden, from London, July 31, 1839*]

I have attended the debates a good deal, especially on important occasions. Some of their ablest men are far from being fluent speakers. In fact, they hold in no high repute the mere faculty of ready speaking, at least not so high as it is held in other places. They are universally men of business; they have not six-and-twenty other legislative bodies to take part of the law-making of the country off their hands; and where there is so much to be *done*, it is indispensable that less should be *said*. Their debates, therefore, are often little more than conversations across the table, and they usually abide by the good rule of carrying the measure under consideration one step, whenever it is taken up, without adjourning the debate. This rule, of course, gives way on questions of great interest. I see no prospect of any immediate change of administration.

Office here is now no sinecure. Business matters have been in a bad state, and money remains quite scarce; but cotton has risen a little, and some think the worst is over. I expect to hear bad news from the United States. I fear greatly for many of the banks. Nothing can be done with the securities of our States, nor can anything be done with them on the Continent.

[Letter to Davis, from London, July 31, 1839]

Six days ago, an English gentleman read my speech of last year, in which I gave some account of the productive industry of Massachusetts. Two days afterwards, he sold out some other stocks, and invested £40,000 in Massachusetts 5 per. cents, at 103; stocks of other States, bearing the same interest, might have been had at 88. The Bay State forever!

[Letter to Ticknor, from Lowther Castle, Aug. 21, 1839]

You will be glad to hear that we have found time to get a snatch at the scenery of the Lakes, with which you are so well acquainted, and which Mrs. Ticknor and yourself have so lately visited. We thought of you often, as we had "Scarboro' Fell," "Helvellyn," or "Skiddaw" before us. We have not run the beauty of this scenery into the details, with the spirit of professed tourists, but have seen enough to convince us that there is much of beauty and something of sublimity in it. Mountain, dale, and lake, altogether, are interesting and striking in a very high degree. They are striking to us, who have seen higher mountains and broader lakes. Mr. Wordsworth, in his description of the lakes, has said, with very great truth, I think, that sublimity, in these things, does not depend entirely either on form or size, but much, also, on the position and relation of objects, and their capability of being strongly influenced by the changes of light and shade. He might have added, I think, that a certain unexpected disproportion, a sudden starting up of these rough and bold mountains, hanging over the sweet and tranquil lakes below, in the forms and with the frowns of giants, produces a considerable part of the effect.

But although we have enjoyed the scene much, some things have been inauspicious. We did not see Wordsworth, as he was not at home, and although not far off, we did not find it convenient to wait his return. We regretted this the more, as we had the pleasure of making his acquaintance in London, where we met him several times, and were quite delighted with him; so that we were better able to estimate the amount of our loss, in missing him at Ambleside. He had been written to, to meet us here, but had a complaint in his eyes, which prevented him from accepting the invitation.

[Letter to Mrs. Lindsley, from Stirling, Scotland, Sept. 6, 1839]

We have passed rather rapidly through some of the lake scenery in Scotland. Many have seen this, and many have described it. Since Walter Scott's "Lady of the Lake," all have felt a new interest in this part of Scotland, and now since steamboats are on every lake and river, where there is water enough to float them, crowds follow crowds through the whole travelling season, all along the common track. This takes off much of the romance and much of the interest. All travel together, and everybody is in a prodigious hurry. The inns are all crowded, the carriages all crammed, and the decks of the steamboats covered with a mass of men and women, each with a guide-book in his hand learning what to admire! The scenery in itself is truly beautiful, and I have learned enough to know, I think, how one should travel in order to enjoy it. The great majority of travellers only wish to "get on." Their first inquiry is how soon they can get to a place; the next how soon they can get away from it; they incur the expense of the journey, I believe, more for the sake of having the power of saying afterwards that they have seen sights, than from any other motive. If I could go through this lake region at leisure, and with one friend of discernment, taste, and feeling, I should experience, I am sure, the greatest possible delight.

[Postscript from London, Sept. 20, 1839]

We returned from our northern tour yesterday, all well. Julia is to be married on Tuesday, the 24th instant, and will then, I suppose, go to the continent. Edward will go either to St. Omer's or to Geneva.

[Letter to Everett, from London, Oct. 16, 1839]

I have this moment received your letter by The British Queen, for which I thank you. I am on the wing for Paris, where I expect to meet my family. They have been to Switzerland, and have left Edward at Geneva. It is my expectation to embark next month, but by what conveyance, I cannot yet quite say.

I have passed my time very agreeably in England, have run over a good deal of the country; seen a good many people, and enjoyed much. But I now feel a strong wish to get home. I feel that my place is not here; and that I ought not to stay longer than to gratify a reasonable curiosity, and desire to see an interesting part of the world, but not my part. Nevertheless, if I could with propriety, I should like to spend the winter in Europe. Things have not favored that desire. Every thing connected with American affairs here has been bad as possible. I do not suppose any thing American could have been sold.

Adieu, my good friend! I long to see you and to talk with you. I am glad you saw Marshfield even at a distance; poor old, barren, sea-beaten Marshfield. Lowther Castle, or Belvoir or Windsor, neither of these is Marshfield. And so, I am sure, their owners and occupants would think, if they were to see it.

[Letter to Samuel Rogers, London, from Washington, Feb. 10, 1840]

If what Dr. Johnson says be true, I am somewhat advanced in the dignity of a thinking being; as the past and the distant at this moment predominate in my mind, strongly over the present. From amid the labors of law and the strife of politics, I transport myself to London. No sooner am I in London, than I go off to find you, to grasp your hand, to assure myself of your health, and then sit down and hear you talk. I enjoy all this, my dear Sir, most highly, and mean to enjoy it so long as you and myself remain on this little bit of a globe. The pleasure of your acquaintance is not with me the felicity of a few months only. I fund it, and intend to get a very nice annuity out of it; as long as I live I shall be receiving a dividend, whenever I think of you; and if I can persuade myself into the belief that you sometimes remember me and mine, the treasure will be so much the more valuable.

To that end, my dear Sir, as well as for other purposes, for which one writes a friendly letter, I transmit you this. You will learn from it that we are all alive, and safely landed on our side of the ocean. Our passage was of thirty-five days with the alternations of head winds and calms; and our approach to the shore a little dangerous, perhaps, from the season of the year, and the state of the weather. But no accident happened to us. One of the greatest annoyances in such a voyage, at such a time of the year, is the shocking length of the nights. When you come over, look out for short nights and long days.

My wife is at New York, passing a few weeks with her father, an aged gentleman, who has been a good deal out of health. Mrs. Paige is in Boston, entertaining the circles around her with the wonders of London and Paris. Julia is also in Boston, and if she knew I was writing, would be eager to put on my sheet her warm recollections. You have many older admirers, but none more ardent or enthusiastic. If it were proposed to her to visit Europe again, the pleasure of seeing you, I am sure, would be a very powerful inducement. Having visited Boston, I came hither a fortnight ago. Congress is in session and will remain so, not probably quite so late as Parliament will sit, but until June or July. Our affairs are bad enough. The currency is terribly deranged, and the important and delicate questions which always belong to such a subject, are sadly handled, when they become topics for heated and violent parties.

I see, too, that the money crisis is not over in England. Our concerns are indeed much connected, and the same causes affect them all. I am coming to the opinion fast, that new modes of regulation must be adopted in both countries, or else these frequent contractions and expansions of the paper circulation will compel us to give it up, and go back to gold or iron, or the Lord knows what.

XVII

1840–1842

SECRETARY OF STATE UNDER HARRISON AND TYLER — THE WEBSTER–ASHBURTON TREATY

Webster landed in New York December 29, 1839, and a month later took up residence in Washington to attend the Twenty-Sixth Congress.

[Letter to Mrs. Paige, Washington, Feb. 2, 1840]

I have become snugly settled here, in a room as big as a closet, a good wood fire, Charles, my French books, my law books, &. &. Nobody else here, saving Mr. and Mrs. Curtis and Mr. Evans. I am glad to be where I am to remain two months, with a chance of being warm, although I have a good deal of hard work to do.

I have received two letters from your father. He thinks he is going fast in health, and I have urged him strongly to quit that horrid place, Tonawanda, and live on the sea-coast, where alone he will ever enjoy any really good health.

Stephen White (Mrs. Paige's father) said that he had been suffering excessively from the cold at Tonawanda, in the neighborhood of Buffalo, New York; in addition his letter contained this choice morsel of medical interest:

[Letter from White to Webster, Jan. 26, 1840]

My liver having been much affected, the physicians, without the aid of mercury, which my queer constitution will not bear, left for me a phial containing a wash, to be applied to my side, of muriatic acid, aqua fortis, I believe, nitric acid, and sundry other poisonous ingredients. During the accidental absence of my good wife, I took a very considerable dose of it instead of another tonic preparation of iron, left by them at the same time. I was directed to take it in weak brandy and water. I mean the iron mixture. It made wonderfully good punch, and on telling my wife what an agreeable beverage the doctors had prescribed, she was horrified, and sent off express to Buffalo for my physician. Meantime my appetite, of which I had not the slightest experience for six weeks, revisited me, the vomiting which had constantly followed the taking of food, had left me, and here I am waiting the event, and employing myself in my nightgown, writing to you, my dear Sir, perhaps the last scrawl I shall ever indite. It would be queer, and not much to the credit of medical science, if I should have found a specific instead of a poison, by making this awkward blunder.

If it be otherwise, this may be the last epistle from, my dear Sir, your faithful and affectionate friend . . .

Weather and illness had prevented Stephen White from visiting Fletcher and Caroline (another White daughter), who were living on Webster's proposed new farm in Peru, Illinois. But soon news came that cheered the entire family.

[Letter to Fletcher, Mar. 5, 1840]

I am almost afraid to give you joy on the birth of a son, such little things being in their first days so delicate and fragile. I hope, however, that this may reach you finding mother and child well, and the boy a promising little chap. Give my best love to Caroline. So soon as she is well, I suppose she will be writing to some of us. And now for a name. As he has black head and eyes, you may give him mine if you please; or you can name him for his uncle, poor little Charles.

I believe we are all indebted to my father's mother, for a large portion of the little sense and character which belongs to us. Her name was Susannah Bachelder; she was the daughter of a clergyman, and a woman of uncommon strength of understanding. If I had had many boys, I should have called one of them "Bachelder." Your grandfather's name, Ebenezer, and your uncle's name Ezekiel, are not good names; if either of them was, I should like to have it perpetuated. Mothers generally name sons, and I dare say Caroline has a name by this time.

While Webster was on shipboard, en route home from England, the Whigs had renominated General William Henry Harrison for the presidency. Webster did not learn of this until he reached New York, but it did not take him long to conclude that Harrison would be elected. The prospect of a Whig victory, and of the defeat of Van Buren, whom Webster disliked with intensity, restored his political fervor. At the time he left England he had been determined to quit public life, as we know from a letter of his English friend, John Evelyn Denison:

"Webster visited me at Ossington, my country-house in the county of Nottingham, in the course of the autumn. Indeed, his last days in England he passed with me, on his way from London to Liverpool. While he was with me he talked continually of his intention to quit public life, both professional and political, and to withdraw to a property he had purchased in the Western country. He spoke of this as a settled resolve. With these words on his lips, he embarked at Liverpool. While on his passage, General Harrison was nominated for the presidency. You know how he threw himself into the stream — little thought then of waving prairies and oak openings."

Webster not only supported Harrison; he bore a major share of the speechmaking. From the beginning he was optimistic.

SECRETARY OF STATE

[Letter to Everett, Feb. 16, 1840]

We shall choose General Harrison, if no untoward event occurs
between this time and November. But we are to have bad times,
whoever may be in or whoever out. The people have been cajoled
and humbugged. All parties have played off so many poor popular
contrivances against each other, that I am afraid the public mind
has become in a lamentable degree warped from correct principles,
and turned away to the contemplation merely of momentary expedients, not only in regard to men, but to things also.

[Letter to Jaudon, June 23, 1840]

The prospect is now very strong that General Harrison will be
elected. Indeed, we have no doubt of it. If this event shall take
place, it will change my condition, though I cannot say exactly
how. Indeed, some changes, or a change will take place, let the
election go either way. If Mr. Van Buren should be reëlected, I
shall go back to the bar, leaving the Senate, and go to work with all
my might. If General Harrison should be chosen, I shall equally
leave the Senate, and you can judge as well as I, perhaps, whether I
shall thenceforward have any thing to do with the government, or
not. But I have made these remarks, and introduced this subject,
for the purpose of expressing to you a hope, that you will return to
your own country, and connect yourself with its affairs. You have
capacity to be highly useful to the government, in either of various
situations. I have thought it not impossible, looking to the future,
that we might be mutually useful to each other.

[Letter to Curtis, Oct. 10, 1840]

Here I am. I had neither time nor health to go to Raleigh.
Three days' speaking in Richmond, day and night, did me up.
Thursday and Friday I rested and tried to sleep, and left Richmond

this morning. I have been too much excited, as I find I cannot, by night or by day, get speeches &c., out of my head. Dr. Sewall will try to put me to sleep to-night.

[*Letter from General Harrison to Webster, Frankfort, Ky., Dec. 1, 1840*]

Since I was first a candidate for the Presidency, I had determined, if successful, to solicit your able assistance in conducting the administration, and I now ask you to accept the State or Treasury Department. I have myself no preference of either for you, but it may perhaps be more difficult to fill the latter than the former if you should decline it. It was the post designed for you in the supposition that you had given more attention to the subject of the finances than Mr. Clay, to whom I intended to have offered the State Department. This, as well as any other post in the cabinet, I understood before my arrival here, from an intimate friend of that gentleman, he would decline. This he has since done personally to me.

[*Letter to General Harrison, Dec. 11, 1840*]

It becomes me, in the first place, to acknowledge my grateful sense of the confidence evinced by your communication, and to assure you how highly I value this proof of your friendship and regard.

The question of accepting a seat in your cabinet, should it be tendered to me, has naturally been the subject of my reflections and of consultation with friends. The result of these reflections and consultations has been that I should accept the office of Secretary of State, should it be offered to me, under circumstances such as now exist.

You are kind enough to suggest that my acquaintance with the subjects of currency and finance, might render me useful as head of the treasury. On that subject my view has been this: I think all important questions of revenue, finance, and currency properly belonging to the executive, should be cabinet questions; that every member of the cabinet should give them his best consideration; and especially that the results of these deliberations should receive the sanction of the President.

This seems necessary to union and efficiency of action. If to these counsels I may be supposed able to contribute any thing useful, I shall withhold myself from no degree of labor, and no just responsibility.

For the daily details of the treasury, the matters of account, and the supervision of subordinate officers employed in the collection and disbursement of the public moneys, I do not think myself to be particularly well qualified. I take this occasion to say I entirely concur in the opinion which has been expressed by you, that on these subjects of finance and revenue, as on other grave subjects, the duty of originating important measures properly belongs to Congress.

By accepting now the offer of the department of state, however, I do not wish to preclude you from again suggesting the treasury department to me, if you should find it more easy to fill the former than the latter office satisfactorily with another person.

[*Letter to Mrs. Paige, Dec. 13, 1840*]

I give to you the fresh thoughts of the morning, as I write this by candlelight, at six o'clock, A. M. I have already written to Mr. Paige on matters of business, and it is indeed rather a matter of business that I wish to speak to you about in this letter. You must know that Mr. Curtis and myself left our beloved wives in New York, there to remain until we should be able to provide suitable lodgings for them. We have obtained some rooms, and while accommodating our own families, we have got a snug place or two for friends who may happen this way in February or March. At dinner yesterday, Mr. Curtis and I being present, it was voted unanimously that the best of these extra accommodations should be at once tendered to you and Mr. Paige, and I was appointed secretary to make the communication. So you see that really this is a matter of business.

And now, my dear lady, if you will signify to us that we may hope for your company, we will keep a good room for you, and defend it meanwhile against all comers. Be pleased to say you will come, children being well, and nothing happening. It will be your last chance to see me in the Senate, as I mean to resign at the end of the session.

[Letter to Ketchum, Dec. 18, 1840]

I received your letter of the 15th last evening. It had already been intimated to me, that a high judicial office was expected to be tendered to you, in the course of the spring, and I have often reflected upon the subject.

In my opinion, you should decide this matter according to your liking. If you think you should be pleased with the performance of judicial duties, why here is an office, high in dignity, and respectable in emolument, and ought not to be refused. For my own part, I could never be a judge. Somehow I have always shrunk from the idea of judicial employment. There never was a time when I would have taken the office of Chief Justice of the United States, or any other judicial station. But this is matter of taste or feeling. I believe the truth may be, that I have mixed up so much study of politics with my study of the law, that though I may have some respect for myself as advocate, and some estimate of my own knowledge of general principles, yet am not confident of possessing all the accuracy and precision of knowledge which the bench requires. But I am clear that if you like the business, you should not refuse this offer. Such opportunities do not occur every day.

Peter Harvey gives us an account of Webster's first official interviews with President Harrison, and of the inaugural address:

"*General Harrison arrived at Washington, from Cincinnati, about the time Mr. Webster arrived from Massachusetts. Mr. Webster was invited by Mr. Seaton, one of the editors of the 'National Intelligencer,' and a very warm personal friend of his, to come to his house, as he would be more quiet there, and less exposed to intrusion than at a hotel; and to stay until he should get a house and move his family into it. He was constantly occupied with General Harrison on matters connected with the formation of the Cabinet, from early morning until the dinner hour, which was six o'clock. It seems that he had prepared an inaugural message for General Harrison. One day, among other arrangements, he suggested to the new President, in as delicate a way as he could, the fact that he had sketched an inaugural, knowing that General Harrison would be overwhelmed with calls and business after his election, and he himself having leisure to write. The General at once replied that it was not necessary; that he had prepared his own inaugural.*

" '*Oh yes,' said he, 'I have got that all ready.'*

" '*Will you allow me to take it home and read it to-night?' asked Mr. Webster.*

" '*Certainly,' the President replied; 'and please to let me take yours.'*

"*So they exchanged the documents; and the next morning, when they met, General Harrison said to Mr. Webster:*

" '*If I should read your inaugural instead of mine, everybody would know that you wrote it, and that I did not. Now, this is the only official paper which I propose to write, for I do not intend to interfere with my secretaries; but this is a sort of acknowledgment on my part to the American people of the great honor they have conferred upon me in elevating me to this high office; and although, of course, it is not so suitable as yours, still it is mine, and I propose to let the people have it just as I have written it. I must deliver my own instead of yours.'*

"*Mr. Webster told me that he was a good deal annoyed; because the message was, according to his judgment and taste, so inappro-*

priate. It entered largely into Roman history, and had a great deal to say about the States of antiquity and the Roman proconsuls, and various matters of that kind. Indeed, the word 'proconsul' was repeated in it a great many times.

"When he found that the President was bent upon using his own inaugural, Mr. Webster said that his desire was to modify it, and to get in some things that were not there, and get out some things that were there; for, as it then stood, he said, it had no more to do with the affairs of the American government and people than a chapter in the Koran. Mr. Webster suggested to General Harrison that he should like to put in some things, and General Harrison rather reluctantly consented to let him take it. Mr. Webster spent a portion of the next day in modifying the message. Mrs. Seaton remarked to him, when he came home rather late that day, that he looked fatigued and worried; but he replied that he was sorry that she had waited dinner for him.

" 'That is of no consequence at all, Mr. Webster,' said she; 'but I am sorry to see you looking so worried and tired. I hope nothing has gone wrong. I really hope nothing has happened.'

" 'You would think that something had happened,' he replied, 'if you knew what I have done. I have killed seventeen Roman proconsuls as dead as smelts, every one of them!' "

Harrison's presidency lasted only a month. On April 4, 1841, weakened by the ardors of the election and the exposure of the inaugural ceremonies, he succumbed to pneumonia. It was the first time a President had died in office. Led by Webster, the cabinet addressed an official announcement to Vice President John Tyler of Virginia, which was carried to him by Fletcher Webster, now Chief Clerk of the State Department.

Tyler asked the members of the cabinet to continue, and for a time all of them did so. Looking forward to at least four fruitful years in Washington, Webster had already rented, and now purchased and refurbished, the spacious Swann house facing Lafayette

Square on the site now occupied by the United States Chamber of Commerce.

[*Letter to Mrs. Webster, Aug. 8, 1841*]

And now as to the history of things here. First, as to domestics in this house. Fletcher and I get along as usual, except that we are lonely, and wander about almost lost in so many rooms. Our evening calls are few since your departure, and I can generally indulge myself in going to bed as early as possible. Yesterday we had Mr. Winthrop and some other Massachusetts members to dine. We expected the President to drop in, but a number of Virginia friends came in upon him in the evening, and detained him. This morning the weather is cool, and in general it has not been very hot since you went away.

Second, as to the new house. Things go on there very well. The painter has finished the upper stories and is getting down fast. The cellar and kitchen are all in nice order, and the big table, &c. all in place. All outside is done, except repairing the steps and taking up the pavements round about the front door. On the whole all looks well, but Mr. Wilson thinks it better to put on the paper when the paint is on. He is to take care of the house and see that no harm happens to it till we move in. Please speak your mind about the papers.

Third, as to matters personal. I was a good deal unwell the day after I returned from Baltimore, which was Wednesday; but was well again next day. Friday, John undertook to drive me out in a wagon with our coach-horse; the harness broke, and the horse ran away with us. We were in no small danger. He went round three sides of the Capitol Square, at full speed. Finally, the wagon ran against a post, broke the axle-tree, and we were thrown out. I came upon my feet and escaped with only some slight bruises; but I do not wish such another drive. I feel a little stiff yet, but am going out to Mr. Agg's this morning.

Lastly, as to things political. The bank bill passed the House by a majority of thirty-two on Friday, and was yesterday sent to the President.

It did not take long for serious differences to develop between President Tyler and Henry Clay, who regarded himself as the acknowledged leader of the Whig party. The rock on which their relations foundered was the proposal to create a new national bank. Clay, asserting the right to dictate party policy, pushed a bill through Congress which he knew would be unsatisfactory to Tyler.

[*Letter to Mrs. Webster, Aug. 16, 1841*]

A week has run away without my writing to you. It has been an anxious week, on acct of the Bank Bill; but the question is settled, & a Veto will be sent in today. I hardly know what may be the consequences, but the general feeling is not so much irritated as it was a week ago. They may, perhaps, try another Bill, with modifications. Some of Mr. Clay's friends are particularly angry, & this makes it doubtful whether anything will be done. On the whole, we have an anxious & unhappy time, & I am sometimes heart-sick. I hope Congress will get away in a fortnight.

Yesterday morning I rode out to Mr. Agg's as the day was cool & agreeable. I generally ride to the office, in the morning, & sometimes walk home when it is not too hot. My health is good, except that my rheumatic shoulder troubles me a good deal.

I have thought it best to invite the Whig members to a *man* party, tomorrow, in order to keep them in good temper. Charles is to buy some hams, & bread, &c. — no ices, & no fruits — & set them on the table down stairs where people may help themselves.

The house gets along, pretty well. Of course the painting inside is not yet finished, as it takes time for the paint to dry.

I notice what you say about papering the rooms. You may have it arranged as you please. I will write tomorrow, saying what day Mr. Stubbs will be in N. Y. about the carpets. He has been sick, & is now out again.

Fletcher may find it necessary to go to N. Y. on account of Mr. White's death — but he has not yet made up his mind, not having heard from Mr. Paige.

Another bill was promptly passed containing some of the same controversial features.

[*Letter to Ketchum, Aug. 22, 1841*]

I believe the land bill will pass the Senate to-morrow, and the bank bill the House to-morrow or on Tuesday. Beyond that I can foresee little. The President is agitated. Mr. Clay's speech, and Mr. Botts's most extraordinary letter, have much affected him. At the same time, there is no doubt that violent assaults are made upon him from certain quarters, to break with the Whigs, change his cabinet, &c.

Another week will enable us "to see what we shall behold." I try to keep cool, and to keep up courage, as the agony will soon be over. We are on the point of deciding, whether the Whig party and the President shall remain together; and at this critical juncture some of our friends think it very opportune to treat him with satire and disdain. I am tired to death of the folly of friends.

[*Letter to Mrs. Webster, Aug. 28, 1841*]

We have passed three or four more very anxious and excited days. Congress is in a state of great fermentation, and the President appears to be a good deal worried. I know not what it is all to come to. Another bank bill is brought into Congress, and is likely to pass both Houses. If that also should receive the veto, I cannot speculate on the consequences. I am with the President a good deal. He seems quite kind, but is evidently much agitated. I am nearly worn down with labor and care, and shall be most happy when things shall be settled, one way or the other. There is now a breach between the President and Mr. Clay, which it is not probable can ever be healed.

My health continues good. Your shower-bath does wonders. I use it every morning, and think how you used to make the water spatter.

The President vetoed the second bill and Clay's friends resigned from the cabinet.

[*Letter to Ketchum, Sept. 10, 1841*]

Ewing, Bell, Badger, and Crittenden will resign to-morrow. They settled that last evening, at a meeting at which I was not present, and announced it to me to-day. I told them I thought they had acted rashly, and that I should consider of my own course. I shall not act suddenly; it will look too much like a combination between a Whig cabinet and a Whig Senate to bother the President. It will not be expected from me to countenance such a proceeding.

Then, again, I will not throw the great foreign concerns of the country into disorder or danger, by any abrupt party proceeding.

How long I may stay, I know not, but I mean to take time to consider.

From the first, Webster had found his new duties congenial. Or almost from the first. No one could have enjoyed the initial pent-up rush for political jobs, which included, interestingly enough, a request from John T. Stuart, Illinois Whig, for the appointment of his law partner, Abraham Lincoln, as Chargé d'Affaires at Bogotá, Colombia.

One appointment which must have given Webster particular pleasure was that of his friend Edward Everett as Minister to Eng-

land. Years before, Webster had taught Everett briefly in Ezekiel's school in Boston; and Webster's son Edward had been traveling and living with the Everett family in Europe immediately before the appointment. Everett had already been Governor of Massachusetts for four terms; he was later to be President of Harvard, Secretary of State, and United States Senator.

[Letter to Everett, July 24, 1841]

I have the pleasure to inform you that you are nominated to the Senate, as Minister to England; an announcement which you will not doubt it gives me great pleasure to make. I am in hopes the nomination will be confirmed, so as that I may notify it to you by the same conveyance which takes this, but the Senate is much engaged to-day, Saturday, and will probably be so on Monday, so that it may not before Tuesday go into executive session, which would be too late, I fear, for this opportunity. No kind of opposition, however, is expected. So far as I hear, the nomination satisfies everybody but a few violent partisans, like the conductors of The Globe.

If I could have afforded it, I should have put myself in competition with you for this place; but as I wrote to Mr. Brooks the other day, I am too poor even to stay here, and much less am I able to go abroad. You may hear of me soon, for aught I know, at Marshfield, with my friend Peterson.

Webster took office at the lowest point in British-American relations since the War of 1812. So low that Lord Palmerston, the British Foreign Secretary, had formally threatened war and had increased British troop strength in Canada to seventeen regiments.

The immediate occasion for the threat was the trial of a Canadian, Alexander McLeod, in Utica, New York, for murder, stemming from what was known as the "Caroline Affair." Insurgents seeking to overthrow the Canadian Government had used the steamship

Caroline *for transport and supply, and the British had sent a military force to capture it. On December 29, 1837, they had crossed the border, set fire to the* Caroline *in American waters, and drifted it to destruction over Niagara Falls. In the process, Amos Durfee, an American citizen, had been shot and killed.*

Some three years later, while in the state of New York, McLeod had boasted that he had fired the fatal shot. He was arrested and indicted for murder, whereupon the British demanded his release on the ground that he had been acting under military orders for the purpose of suppressing an insurrection. Lord Palmerston went so far as to notify the United States Minister, Andrew Stevenson, that the conviction and execution of McLeod would be considered a cause of war.

The federal government had no constitutional power to interfere with a murder trial by the State of New York. In addition, local feeling was running so high as to create danger that if McLeod were acquitted he might be lynched. Webster was deeply concerned, and in July, 1841, wrote President Tyler:

It becomes us to take all possible care that no personal violence be used on McLeod. If a mob should kill him, war would be inevitable in ten days. Of this there is no doubt.

The evidence showed that, despite his boasts, McLeod had not even been a member of the Caroline *expedition, and he was acquitted. His safe return to Canada averted the crisis, but the fact that such an event could bring the countries to the brink of war was symptomatic of deeper troubles. Of these, the most critical was the long-festering dispute over the Maine-Canada boundary.*

This had been established by the 1783 treaty of peace ending the War of the American Revolution, but the apparent simplicity of the language defining the boundary was deceptive. For example, England insisted that the true St. Croix was one river, the United States that it was another. This particular question was resolved by commissioners appointed under a 1794 treaty, but other differences proved more baffling. Two further sets of commissioners failed to settle anything, and in 1827 the King of the Netherlands was asked to arbitrate. When, after protracted surveys and studies, he came up with a solution, both sides immediately rejected it.

In a later Senate speech giving a blow-by-blow description of developments, Webster said:

Now, Sir, here we are fifty-three years from the date of the treaty of peace, and the boundary not yet settled. General Jackson has tried his hand at the business for five years, and has done nothing. And why not? Do he and his advisers want skill and energy, or are there difficulties in the nature of the case not to be overcome till some wiser course of proceeding shall be adopted?

Well, Sir, Mr. Van Buren then began his administration, under the deepest conviction of the importance of the question. And now, Sir, what did he accomplish? What progress did he make? What step forward did he take, in the whole course of his administration? Sir, not one step in his whole four years. Or rather, if he made any advance at all, it was an advance backward. The subject was entangled in meshes which rendered it far more difficult to proceed with the question than if it had been fresh and unembarrassed.

We all remember the troubles of 1839. Something like a border war had broken out. Maine had raised an armed civil posse; she fortified the line, or points on the line, of territory, to keep off intruders and to defend possession. There was Fort Fairfield, Fort Kent, and I know not what other fortresses, all memorable in history. The legislature of Maine had placed eight hundred thousand dollars at the discretion of the Governor, to be used for the military defence of the State.

Now comes the report of two British commissioners, Messrs. Mudge and Featherstonhaugh, who had made an *ex parte* survey in 1839. And a most extraordinary report it was. These gentlemen had discovered that, up to that time, nobody had been right.

SPEAK FOR YOURSELF, DANIEL

Next, Lord Palmerston proposed that the Kings of Prussia, Sardinia, and Saxony each name a scientific man to explore and to report to his sovereign for the purpose of mediation. To this, said Webster:

It was asked in the House of Commons, not inaptly, What would the people of Maine think, when they should read that they were to be visited by three learned foreigners, one from Prussia, one from Saxony, and one from Sardinia? To be sure, what would they think, when they should see three learned foreign professors, each speaking a different language, and none of them the English or American tongue, among the swamps and morasses of Maine in summer, or wading through its snows in winter — on the Allegash, the Maguadavic, or among the moose deer, on the precipitous and lofty shores of Lake Pohenagamook — and for what? To find where the division was, between Maine and New Brunswick! Instructing themselves by these labors, that they might repair to Frankfort on the Main, and there hold solemn and scientific arbitration on the question of a boundary line, in one of the deepest wildernesses of North America!

Sir, I do not know what might have happened, if this project had gone on. Mr. Fox,* it is said, on reading his despatch, replied, with characteristic promptitude and good sense, "For Heaven's sake, save us from the philosophers!"

I viewed the case as hopeless, without an entire change in the manner of proceeding. I found the parties already "in wandering mazes lost." And having received the President's authority, I did say to Mr. Fox, as has been stated in the British Parliament, that I was willing to attempt to settle the dispute by agreeing on a conventional line, or line by compromise.

In this, fate sided with Webster. In the summer of 1841 the British government under Lord Melbourne gave way to a new one

* The British Minister in Washington.

under Sir Robert Peel, and the belligerent Lord Palmerston was replaced as Foreign Secretary by the more amenable Lord Aberdeen. Webster had already discussed with Edward Everett his hopes for compromise, and Everett found the new ministry agreeable; so much so that Lord Ashburton was sent to the United States to discuss, and if possible settle, all outstanding differences.

It would have been hard to imagine a happier choice than Lord Ashburton. He had headed the powerful British banking firm of Baring Brothers, and was intimately familiar with American affairs. In addition, he had married a Philadelphian, the daughter of Senator Bingham of Pennsylvania. Webster was acquainted with him personally, and on January 29, 1842, wrote to Everett:

Your two despatches and your private letter by The Britannia were duly received. The despatches were read in cabinet council, and I showed your private letter to the President. Every thing done by you thus far, is approved. The special mission was a surprise to us; but the country receives it very well. For my own part, no selection of a minister could be more agreeable to me than that of Lord Ashburton, as I entertain towards him sentiments of great kindness and regard. You are at liberty to signify this, so far as may be proper, to Lord Aberdeen.

I infer on the whole, that the mission will be single. Mr. Fox, doubtless, will be expected to assist, with counsel and advice; but I rather suppose that the authority and official signatures will be sole. It gives me promise of work enough, overwhelmed as I already am, by affairs growing out of the very unhappy state of things among us, and out of the calls and proceedings of Congress. But my health is good — never better — and if I can so far repress anxiety as to be able to sleep, I hope to get through.

Other letters also give evidence of Webster's buoyancy; for example:

SPEAK FOR YOURSELF, DANIEL

[Letters to Weston: Jan. 5, 1842]

Ice, Kelp, Cattle. These are things I wish to hear about, as well as to learn that you are all well. You must write once a week. I suppose you must have some leisure, as the evenings are long, and you have probably done husking.

This is the right time of the moon to put up beef and pork. Give me particulars of the weight of the cattle, and pigs, and the amount put up. I expect that the ox and cow were found to be good beef.

P. S. We are all well. The young Daniel eats so much milk, we have been obliged to buy a cow. Does Mr. Seth Peterson catch any fish? Is the ditching all done? Do the Buck's county chickens prosper? Has John Taylor sent down the cattle? Has he sent the turkeys?

[Feb. 18, 1842]

I am glad you have a good calf from one of the Worcester heifers. That high-horned heifer will make a valuable cow.

As to ice, I fancy you have filled the icehouse before this time.

I hope to see you next month, perhaps before the middle. Keep writing. One letter about farming is worth ten upon politics.

From the beginning, however, Webster recognized the difficulties inherent in a negotiated settlement. There could be no compromise without concessions, and the citizens of Maine had been adamantly opposed to giving up an inch of the disputed territory. In this they were backed by Massachusetts, which still claimed an interest in the area. Without their concurrence no settlement would be politically feasible.

Again fate intervened, this time through the medium of Jared Sparks, Massachusetts historian, later to be President of Harvard. While in Paris examining documents for use in what he termed his "formidable history of the American Revolution," he made a discovery, described in his Journal for Jan. 26, 1841:

"January 26th. — *Completed my researches in the archives, having examined all the papers I want, and prepared them for the copyist. I have found there a letter from Dr. Franklin to Count de Vergennes, dated December 5, 1782, in which he tells him that he returns to him a map in which he had marked with* a strong red line *the boundary of the United States as fixed by the treaty. They will search for this map in the archives, but it is hardly probable that it will be found. It would be an extremely important document at this time, as it would show in the most positive manner the meaning of the commissioners, and put to rest the dispute between England and the United States respecting the northeastern boundary.*"

Sparks did not say anything about this for over a year, but on Feb. 15, 1842, hearing of the proposed negotiations, he wrote Webster:

"*I have deliberated for some time on the propriety of communicating to you the substance of this letter, but at length, believing it important that you should possess a knowledge of all the facts respecting the subject to which it alludes, I have concluded to waive the scruples that have hitherto operated on my mind. While pursuing my researches among the voluminous papers relating to the American Revolution in the Archives des Affaires Étrangères in Paris, I found in one of the bound volumes an original letter from Dr. Franklin to Count de Vergennes, of which the following is an exact transcript:* —

" 'PASSY, *6 December, 1782.*

" 'SIR: *I have the honor of returning herewith the map your Excellency sent me yesterday. I have marked with a strong red line, according to your desire, the limits of the United States as settled in the preliminaries between the British and American plenipotentiaries. With great respect, I am, etc.,*   B. FRANKLIN'

"*This letter was written six days after the preliminaries were signed; and if we could procure the identical map mentioned by Franklin, it would seem to afford conclusive evidence as to the meaning affixed by the commissioners to the language of the treaty on the*

311

subject of the boundaries. You may well suppose that I lost no time in making inquiry for the map, not doubting that it would confirm all my previous opinions respecting the validity of our claim. In the geographical department of the archives are sixty thousand maps and charts, but so well arranged, with catalogues and indexes, that any one of them may easily be found. After a little research in the American division, with the aid of the keeper, I came upon a map of North America by D'Anville, dated 1746, in size about eighteen inches square, on which was drawn a strong red line *throughout the entire boundary of the United States, answering precisely to Franklin's description. The line is bold and distinct in every part, made with red ink, and apparently drawn with a hair pencil, or a pen with a blunt point. There is no other coloring on any part of the map.*

"Imagine my surprise on discovering that this line runs wholly south of the St. John, and between the headwaters of that river and those of the Penobscot and Kennebec. In short, it is exactly the line now contended for by Great Britain, except that it concedes more than is claimed.

"There is no positive proof that this map is actually the one marked by Franklin, yet upon any other supposition it would be difficult to explain the circumstances of its agreeing so perfectly with his description, and of its being preserved in the place where it would naturally be deposited by Count de Vergennes."

Spurred by Sparks's disclosure, Webster combed the government archives and found a copy of Mitchell's map which had belonged to Baron von Steuben. This also contained a bold red mark corresponding in general to the Paris map. These maps set the stage for Webster's masterstroke.

[Letter to Governor Fairfield of Maine, Apr. 11, 1842]

The President proposes that the governments of Maine and Massachusetts should severally appoint a commissioner or commissioners, empowered to confer with the authorities of this government upon a conventional line, or line by agreement, with its terms, conditions, considerations, and equivalents; with an understanding that no such line will be agreed upon without the assent of such commissioners.

The importance of the subject, and a firm conviction in the mind of the President that the interests of both countries, as well as the interests of the two States more immediately concerned, require a prompt effort to bring this dispute to an end, constrain him to express an earnest hope that your Excellency will convene the legislature of Maine, and submit the subject to its grave and candid deliberations.

[Letter to Everett, Apr. 25, 1842]

Lord Ashburton has been received here with much kindness by the government and the public. His personal demeanor makes friends, and we all think he has come with an honest and sincere intent of removing all causes of jealousy, disquietude, or difference between the two countries; and certainly do not suppose a better selection could have been made. On most of the points in difference, I verily believe we could come to a satisfactory adjustment; but I confess my fears stick deep in the boundary business.

The idea of concession and compromise is not very palatable, although considerate men think it is high time the question was settled. But concession and compromise become more difficult from the interference of State claims. There are certain equivalents, connected with boundaries in other parts of the frontier which might be available, but then they do not affect Maine. The object must be to find equivalents in Maine; and this is not easy, unless a liberal spirit pervade the British government.

[Letter to Mrs. Curtis, May 4, 1842]

I must tell you, as one of the secrets of diplomacy, but a secret which all the world I believe already knows, that I am to be your way two or three days hence, on a flying visit to Massachusetts. The "candid public" suppose, doubtless, that I am going to confer with Governor Davis and others on the boundary question; to consult the shipping interest of the North about the right of search, &c., whereas I am really going for the change; to get away from my table for a few days, see a few friends in New York, as many in Boston, and as the great object of all, see Seth Peterson, and catch one trout.

I have a number of things to talk over with Mr. Curtis. I believe he will live a thousand years, and triumph over all his enemies.

My wife is well. The two boys are well. Edward is going to be somebody, if one of the Miss Bayards does not deprive him of intellect. Caroline is well; her babies are well; and Master Dan is another Judge Story. Miss Fletcher is well; the nurse is well; we are all well, down even to my noble collection of cacklers in the poultry yard. But the season advances; summer is coming, according to the almanac, and yet our only warmth is before a good fire. But still, as May is here and June in sight, we all begin to think of flight!! It is merciful in Providence to change the seasons, so that men, and even women too, may find some excuse for change also.

[*Letters to Sparks*]

Boston, May 14, 1842 Saturday Eve'

I arrived in this City today, & have a great desire to see you this evening, for the purpose of engaging you, if so I may do, to proceed to *Augusta,* Maine, on Monday, on a confidential errand. I send out a carriage, to bring you in, & it will take you back. You will find me, if you can make it convenient to come, at Mr. Paige's, Summer Street.

Monday, 1 oclock [May 16, 1842]

I thank you for your letter. Herewith I send a confidential letter to Gov. Fairfield. I have spoken to him of the absolute necessity of secrecy; & you will therefore tell him all you know, relying, as I do, on his discretion & caution. I wish you a pleasant journey.

WEBSTER-ASHBURTON TREATY

[Letter to Everett, June 14, 1842]

I must tell you, in particular confidence, that I hope you will *forbear to press the search after maps in England or elsewhere.* Our strength is on the letter of the treaty.

On his mission to Governor Fairfield of Maine, Sparks took with him a copy of each of the red line maps. The Governor saw the light, and with his backing the legislature authorized four commissioners to commit the state to a boundary settlement. Later, Webster showed them the maps. They also saw the light and acquiesced in the settlement worked out with Lord Ashburton. This was still in the future, but with such a prospect, Webster could write Fletcher on May 21:

Marshfield never looked so well. Peterson and I have talked over politics. He says the fault is in Congress; that Mr. Tyler is not to blame for being President, and that they ought to take right hold, man fashion, and do up the public business.

I am going out this morning to wet a line.

But there were still many anxious moments.

[Letter to Everett, June 28, 1842]

Our movement, for the last ten days, if any has been made, has been rather backward. The boundary business is by no means in a highly promising state, so many obstacles arise, not only between us and England, but between us and the Commissioners, and the Commissioners of the two States themselves; and other questions are still less so. I know nothing of Lord Ashburton's recent instructions, but he appears to me, certainly, to be under restraint, not heretofore apparently felt by him. What increases the embarrassment, and renders a failure more probable, is his great unwillingness to stay longer in the country. The President has desired a personal interview with him, which has been had, and the President has pressed upon him, in the strongest manner, the necessity of staying, till every effort to effect the great object of his mission shall have been exhausted. The President feels, what all must feel, that if the mission should return, *rebus infectis*, the relations of the two countries will be more than ever embarrassed.

And now, added to the other hazards, was the heat of a Washington summer.

[*Letter from Ashburton to Webster, July 1, 1842*]

I must throw myself on your compassion to contrive somehow or other to get me released. I contrive to crawl about in these heats by day and pass my nights in a sleepless fever. In short, I shall positively not outlive this affair, if it is to be much prolonged. I had hoped that these gentlemen from the northeast would be equally averse to this roasting. Could you not press them to come to the point and say whether we can or cannot agree? I do not see why I should be kept waiting while Maine and Massachusetts settle their accounts with the General Government.

Pray save me from these profound politicians, for my nerves will not stand so much cunning wisdom.

Ever, my dear sir, yours sincerely,

A.

It was no more than good sense for Webster to appear officially pessimistic. But we get a somewhat different picture from his letters to Seth Weston, the manager of his farm at Marshfield. Webster had instituted the practice of fertilizing with kelp, which winter storms washed up on the beaches in great quantity, and with menhaden, a fish which could be netted in abundance. He had vast amounts of menhaden plowed into his land, and referred to them as "Marshfield roses," from their effect on the atmosphere.

[Letters to Weston: July 16, 1842]

I wrote you a short letter yesterday, and this morning received yours of the 12th, with your full account of the one thousand one hundred and fifty-three haycocks. Excellent! So much hay, got dry and nice, is of great importance. I hope the good weather will hold out, and that you will all enjoy your health. Keep the hands in good temper. Pay them all promptly, and employ the most deserving and industrious.

You know I always like to give employment to Mr. Seth Peterson, when he needs it, as he has many mouths to feed.

[July 23, 1842]

You are right in getting a new net. We must follow the fish. Look round and see our produce this year, and remember what the same land produced when I went first to Marshfield. It is fish, kelp, and barn manure which has done it.

[Aug. 2, 1842]

Go ahead with the fish. Never mind the ladies.

Finally, the parties agreed to a compromise settlement dividing the disputed territory approximately in half and providing for each side, giving the other what Webster termed "equivalents." With Webster's maps and persuasion, the treaty incorporating these terms was ratified by the Senate by a large majority and is called, officially, the Treaty of Washington. More generally, and popularly, it is known as the Webster–Ashburton Treaty.

[Letter to Jeremiah Mason, Aug. 21, 1842]

I cannot forego the pleasure of saying to an old and constant friend, who, I know, takes a personal as well as a public interest in the matter, that the treaty was ratified last evening by a vote of thirty-nine to nine. I did not look for a majority quite so large. I am truly thankful that the thing is done.

[Letter to Mrs. Paige, Aug. 23, 1842]

I enclose a note of introduction for your husband to Lord Ashburton; please have it sealed, and presented on his arrival. He will be glad to see Mr. Paige and yourself, I am quite sure.

You will hear that the treaty is done! and I am almost done too.

The only question of magnitude about which I did not negotiate with Lord Ashburton, is the question respecting the fisheries. That question I propose to take up with Mr. Seth Peterson, on Tuesday the 6th day of September next, at six o'clock, A. M. In the mean time I may find a leisure hour to drop a line on the same subject at Nahant.

I have to thank you for five beautiful handkerchiefs. Nothing was ever nicer.

[Letter to President Tyler, Aug. 24, 1842]

I shall never speak of this negotiation, my dear Sir, which I believe is destined to make some figure in the history of the country, without doing you justice. Your steady support and confidence, your anxious and intelligent attention to what was in progress, and your exceedingly obliging and pleasant intercourse, both with the British minister and the commissioners of the States, have given every possible facility to my agency in this important transaction. Nor ought I to forget the cordial coöperation of my colleagues in the cabinet, to every one of whom I am indebted for valuable assistance.

As in the case of most such compromises, political enemies on both sides called it a bad bargain. In America, the attack was led by

Senator Benton; in England, by Lord Palmerston, who called it "Lord Ashburton's capitulation."

Lord Palmerston claimed that the treaty had yielded every important point to the United States, but the parliamentary debate brought about an astonishing disclosure. Sir Anthony Panizzi, Director of the British Museum, produced a copy of the so-called Mitchell map used by Oswald, the Bristish negotiator at the 1782–83 Versailles Conference. On this, marked in the handwriting of George III with the words "Boundary as described by Mr. Oswald," was a line which followed not the British but the American claims. Palmerston had known of the map and had hidden it; it had not come to the attention of Lord Aberdeen and Lord Ashburton. This cut the ground from under Lord Palmerston, and the treaty was ratified by Parliament without further difficulty.

Nor was Mr. Oswald's map the last surprise, as we may see from Webster's letter of April 25, 1843 to Everett:

Two or three months ago, Mr. P. A. Jay, of New York, one of the sons, as you know, of John Jay, died. About the end of last month, it was made known that among his papers was found a copy of Mitchell's map, with evident marks upon it of having belonged to his father, and of having been used in Paris in 1782. The map was carried to Mr. Gallatin, who still keeps up great interest for whatever relates to the Boundary question, and Mr. Gallatin thought it of considerable importance, and it was agreed that he should take an occasion to read a lecture to the N. Y. Historical Society, of which he is President, on the Boundary subject, in which he should explain the bearing of whatever evidence this new found map might furnish. I happened to be in New York the 6th or 7th of April, and visited Mr. Gallatin and saw the map. His lecture was then fixed for Saturday, the 15th, and I promised to attend. I did attend, heard the lecture, and made a short speech myself. Some account of these things you will see in the papers. Mr. Gallatin's lecture, which is interesting, will be printed by the Society, and my little speech, corrected from the newspapers, appended. I have some hopes that the publication will be completed, so that some copies may go to you by this conveyance. If that should happen, please give one to Lord Ashburton, Lord Aberdeen, Sir Robert Peel, &c.

I had hardly reached my post here, from New York, before I learned, by your letters as well as by the published debates in the House of Commons, that Mr. Oswald's copy of Mitchell's map was at last found. I have read your account of that matter with interest, and have also perused all the debates, down to what I think Lord Ashburton might fairly call Lord Palmerston's "capitulation."

You will see that Mr. Jay's map and Mr. Oswald's map are alike. What one proves, the other proves. Neither of them is absolutely conclusive, because neither proves the line found upon it to have been drawn, in any part, after the Treaty was agreed to, and for the purpose of setting forth the Boundary *as* agreed to. On the contrary, it is clear that the greater part of the line, called Mr. Oswald's line, never was agreed to. I concur, therefore, entirely, in the opinion expressed by Sir Robert Peel, that no map, nor all the maps, settle the question; because they bear no marked lines which may not have been lines of proposal, merely. In other words, none of them shows a line clearly purporting to be a line drawn for the purpose of showing on the map a boundary which had been agreed on.

Regardless of which map, if any, was right, Webster had played his hand to perfection. He was even able to crow a little in a letter to Sparks on March 11, 1843:

As to the Boundary subject, you understand it well. What is likely to be overlooked by superficial thinkers, is the value of Rouse's Point. England will never visit us with an army from Canada for the purpose of conquest; but if she had retained Rouse's Point, she would at all times have access to Lake Champlain, & might in two days place a force within two days' march of the City of Albany. The defence of the Country, therefore, would require a large military force in that neighborhood.

As to the *conduct* of the negotiation, there is one point on which I wish to speak to you very freely, even at the hazard of a well founded imputation of some vanity. The grand stroke was to get the *previous* consent of Maine & Massachusetts. Nobody else had attempted this; it had occurred to nobody else; it was a movement of great delicacy, & of very doubtful result. But it was made, with how much skill & judgment in the manner you must judge; & it succeeded, & to this success the fortunate result of the whole negotiation is to be attributed.

XVIII

1842–1845

RETURN TO PRIVATE LIFE

By the time of the Treaty of Washington, feeling between the Whigs and the President had risen to such a pitch that Webster's political friends were urging him to withdraw from the cabinet.

[*Letter from Mason, Aug. 28, 1842*]

"*When the late cabinet so hastily resigned their places, under the supposed influence of Mr. Clay, I certainly thought you acted rightly in not going out at his dictation. The eminent services you have since performed will satisfy all whose opinions are of any value that you judged rightly in remaining in office to enable you to do what you have done. This important affair is now brought to a happy conclusion, and your best friends here think that there is an insuperable difficulty in your continuing any longer in President Tyler's Cabinet. Having no knowledge of your standing, or personal relations with him, or of your views, I do not feel authorized to volunteer any opinion or advice. I suppose you are aware of the estimation in which the President is held in this region. By the Whigs he is almost universally detested. This detestation is as deep and thorough as their contempt for his weakness and folly will permit it to be. I use strong language but not stronger than the truth justifies. Your friends doubt whether you can, with safety to your own character and honor, act under, or with such a man.*

"*Lord Ashburton has been received here in a manner, I presume, quite satisfactory to himself. He lauded you publicly, and also in private conversation, in terms as strong as your best friends could desire."*

Not all of Webster's supporters were so mild in their comments, or had his interests so genuinely at heart. Clay's followers were bitter and proposed to read Webster out of the party if he did not break with Tyler. At a meeting in Faneuil Hall on September 14, 1842, the Massachusetts Whigs affirmed their loyalty to Clay and adopted resolutions calling for "a full and final separation from the President of the United States." In effect they warned Webster that they no longer recognized his leadership and would cast him out of the party if he did not conform.

Webster's answer was to have some of his friends arrange a reception at Faneuil Hall on September 30, at which he would discuss his relations with Tyler. Long before the appointed hour the Hall was packed, and at eleven o'clock Webster was ushered to the platform to face the cold chill of a predominantly hostile audience. Fresh and tanned from a vacation at Marshfield, he gave not an inch, and such was the power of his presence and his eloquence that when the meeting adjourned he had faced them down and was once more master of the Massachusetts Whigs.

I know not how it is, Mr. Mayor, but there is something in the echoes of these walls, or in this sea of upturned faces which I behold before me, or in the genius that always hovers over this place, fanning ardent and patriotic feeling by every motion of its wings — I know not how it is, but there is something that excites me strangely, deeply, before I even begin to speak.

The Mayor was kind enough to say, that having, in his judgment, performed the duties of my own department to the satisfaction of my country, it might be left to me to take care of my own honor and reputation. I suppose that he meant to say, that in the present distracted state of the Whig party, and among the contrariety of opinions that prevail (if there be a contrariety of opinion) as to the course proper for *me* to pursue, the decision of that question might be left to myself. I am exactly of his opinion. I am quite of opinion that on a question touching my own honor and character, as I am to bear the consequences of the decision, I had a great deal better be trusted to make it. No man feels more highly the advantage of the advice of friends than I do; but on a question so delicate and important as that, I like to choose myself the friends who are to give me advice; and upon this subject, Gentlemen, I shall leave you as enlightened as I found you.

I give no pledges, I make no intimations, one way or the other; and I will be as free, when this day closes, to act as duty calls, as I was when the dawn of this day.

There were many persons in September, 1841, who found great fault with my remaining in the President's Cabinet. You know, Gentlemen, that twenty years of honest, and not altogether undistinguished service in the Whig cause, did not save me from an outpouring of wrath, which seldom proceeds from Whig pens and Whig tongues against any body. I am, Gentlemen, a little hard to coax, but as to being driven, that is out of the question. I chose to trust my own judgment, and thinking I was at a post where I was in the service of the country, and could do it good, I staid there.

Gentlemen, and Mr. Mayor, a most respectable convention of Whig delegates met in this place a few days since, and passed very important resolutions. There is no set of gentlemen in the Commonwealth, so far as I know them, who have more of my respect and regard. They are Whigs, but they are no better Whigs than I am. They have served the country in the Whig ranks; so have I, quite as long as most of them, though perhaps with less ability and success.

I notice among others, a declaration made, in behalf of all the Whigs of this Commonwealth, of "a full and final separation from the President of the United States." If those gentlemen saw fit to express their own sentiments to that extent, there was no objection. Whigs speak their sentiments everywhere; but whether they may assume a privilege to speak for others on a point on which those others have not given them authority, is another question. I am a Whig, I always have been a Whig, and I always will be one; and if there are any who would turn me out of the pale of that communion, let them see who will get out first. I am a Massachusetts Whig, a Faneuil Hall Whig, having breathed this air for five-and-twenty years, and meaning to breathe it, as long as my life is spared. I am ready to submit to all decisions of Whig conventions on subjects on which they are authorized to make decisions; I know that great party good and great public good can only be so obtained. But it is quite another question whether a set of gentlemen, however respectable they may be as individuals, shall have the power to bind me on matters which I have not agreed to submit to their decision at all.

Generally, when a divorce takes place, the parties divide their children. I am anxious to know where, in the case of this divorce, I shall fall. This declaration announces a full and final separation between the Whigs of Massachusetts and the President. If I choose to remain in the President's councils, do these gentlemen mean to say that I cease to be a Massachusetts Whig? I am quite ready to put that question to the people of Massachusetts.

[*Letter to Fletcher, Oct. 4, 1842*]

I returned yesterday from Boston. The meeting went off quite as well as I expected. It will cause some ripples upon the waters, but not strong enough to upset any of us.

I had an opportunity to do the President justice, which I endeavored to improve. The feeling of the people, after all, is undoubtedly kind towards the President, many of them thinking he has been most unjustly treated, and all Whigs remembering that he came into power by their own choice, and their own votes.

[*Letter to Curtis, Oct. 4, 1842*]

I arrived here yesterday, at three o'clock, notwithstanding the

storm; found Mrs. Webster and Edward well, and Marshfield looking as well as usual, what little there is left of it. My great elm has
furnished wood for the winter, and the garden fences are gone over
to Duxbury. We have had a non-such of a blow, for thirty-six hours.
Two vessels are ashore close by us. One, a lumberman, came on the
beach Sunday night, lost two men; Edward and the neighbors saved
the rest. The other got ashore last night, a large schooner. I see her
across the meadows this morning, but she seems high and dry, and I
hope no lives are lost. Edward has gone to see. I believe there is not
an apple or pear on any tree, this side Boston, but then there are
plenty on the ground, which are so much handier. The storm is
breaking, we shall have fine weather, and shall be all ready for you
Saturday, according to contract.

You will see that the Whig committee of Massachusetts are on the
right tack. Seth Peterson goes for the President, notwithstanding
the vetoes. He says, there is sometimes an odd fish that won't take
clams; you must try him with another bait.

Remember Saturday, three o'clock. Mrs. Curtis may expect a
salute. Mrs. Webster is delighted you are coming, and is already
meditating murderous deeds in the poultry yard. Don't let any of
the party fail.

*The Edward Curtises lived in New York and were among Web-
ster's most intimate and congenial friends, but this was Mrs. Curtis's
first visit to Marshfield. On May 26, 1842, Webster had written:*

You are one of those unfortunate persons who have not seen
Marshfield. It would be cruel to speak of its beauties, if your fate,
in this respect, were irreversible. But as you may, and I trust do,
cherish the hope of one day beholding it, I must prepare you for
something like an ecstasy. And yet a single sight would hardly produce that effect. Superficial observers see nothing at Marshfield but
rocks, and sands, and desolation; as one uninitiated runs his eye
over the pictures of an old master, and wonders what folks can see

that is pleasing in such a grim and melancholy looking thing. Marshfield is to be studied. Do not come, therefore, without weeks before you. Some may tell you that its excellence is like transcendentalism, so refined and invisible as to hang on the very verge of nonsense or nonentity. But these are malignant persons, and not to be believed.

And now, from generalities to facts. An old-fashioned two-story house, with a piazza all round it, stands on a gentle rising, facing due south, and distant fifty rods from the road, which runs in front. Beyond the road is a ridge of hilly land, not very high, covered with oak wood, running in the same direction as the road, and leaving a little depression, or break, exactly opposite the house, through which the southern breezes fan us, of an afternoon. I feel them now coming, not over beds of violets, but over Plymouth bay, fresh, if not fragrant. A carriage way leads from the road to the house, not bold and impudent, right up straight to the front door, like the march of a column of soldiers, but winding over the lower parts of the ground, sheltering itself among trees and hedges, and getting possession at last, more by grace than force, as other achievements are best made. Two other houses are in sight, one a farm-house, cottage built, at the end of the avenue, so covered up in an orchard as to be hardly visible; the other a little further off in the same direction, that is to the left on the road, very neat and pretty, with a beautiful field of grass by its side. Opposite the east window of the east front room, stands a noble spreading elm, the admiration of all beholders. Beyond that is the garden, sloping to the east, and running down till the tide washes its lower wall. Back of the house are such vulgar things as barns; and on the other side, that is to the north and northwest, is a fresh water pond of some extent, with green grass growing down to its margin, and a good walk all round it one side, the walk passing through a thick belt of trees, planted by the same hand that now indites this eloquent description. This pond is separated on the east by a causeway, from the marshes and the salt water; and over this causeway is the common passage to the northern parts of the farm. I say nothing of orchards, and copses, and clumps, interspersed over the lawn, because such things may be seen in vulgar places. But now comes the climax. From the doors, from the windows, and still better from twenty little elevations, all of which are close by, you see the ocean, a mile off, reposing in calm, or terrific in storm, as the case may be. There, you have now Marshfield.

Back in Washington, Webster wrote to Everett on November 28, 1842:

My family is yet at the North, but I look for Mrs. Webster to join me this week. I had a glorious month of leisure on the seacoast, where Seth Peterson and I settled many a knotty point. I went also to my native hills for ten days, and frolicked with other young fellows of that region. My health is quite good, and I mean to take political events with a good deal of philosophy.

[*Letter to Mrs. Paige, Nov. 28, 1842*]

I think the love of family grows upon us, as we get along in life. 'Tis certain that I find myself more frequently than formerly thinking over my remote kindred, and dwelling on the connections created by the ties of blood. We are thinking of getting up a little Thanksgiving in this District. Many people desire it, and I have recommended to the President to issue a short proclamation or recommendation. It will seem to bring us more into the circle of Christian communities.

Mr. Curtis came on with me and stayed a week. Since his departure I have been quite alone, and not having once dined out since I came here, I, of course, sit down daily to a table with one plate. This is not cheerful, certainly, but then it encourages the virtue of temperance. No two-legged thing can eat much, if he eat alone.

RETURN TO PRIVATE LIFE

[Letters to Weston, Marshfield: Dec. 8, 1842]

Keep the ox and cow, intended for our beef, upon meal and hay, till after New Year's day. Then slaughter them, the first day of proper weather; and put up the meat in the very best manner. Perhaps it need not all go into our cellar; but put up enough, and more than enough. I shall run away from Marshfield next summer, if the provisions are not better than they were last. Put me up three hundred pounds of clear pork, first quality, in the same nice way.

Sometime about the middle of February, or 1st of March, put up a small hog, say one hundred and eighty or two hundred pounds to be pork for boiling. The ribs of this not to be taken out of the middling, as in clear pork, but to be cut through. Salt the shoulders and hams, and give them a good deal of brown sugar, and have them smoked.

I trust the late storm left a good winrow of kelp on the beach. Make the oxen, steers, and horses pay for their keeping, by hauling it up.

I send you a number of copies of "Captain Tyler's" message. Write once a week.

[Jan. 27, 1843]

We must have a good flock of turkeys. We ought to know by this time how to make them live, and I think we can do it. I am glad to hear the great establishment of the hen house is completed.

If the frost does not come back, keep the ploughs going. If kelp comes, don't let it have any rest on the shore.

[Mar. 6, 1843]

Go ahead with the cherry window-sashes. My only doubt is about the size. I doubt whether eleven by fourteen is quite large

enough, as well as I can judge by the windows where I am writing.
I think you had better go twelve by fifteen, if that be a good proportion, if not twelve by sixteen. I like rather a long-looking pane.

It is useless for me to think of going North till the weather
changes. For four or five weeks we have had a very unusual degree
of cold, which still continues.

In all probability we shall want a large supply of firewood, next
fall; and perhaps you may as well get it out this winter. If your
steers should not get to be obedient by the time I get home, I can
lend a hand in driving them.

[*Mar. 12, 1843*]

I like the suggestions in your last letter about fields for oats,
except the proposition to plough up another part of the Baker
pasture. That I am opposed to. An old pasture is the thing, if you
will only cherish it by proper top-dressing. I dislike much to see a
new pasture, with only here and there a spear of grass starting up.
The fine, sweet grass, the soft velvet of an old pasture, cannot be
produced in a hurry.

As to other matters, you appear to understand them. Go ahead.
Proverbs: xxvii. Chap. 23rd Verse.*

*A new political complication had by now come to a head. Presi-
dent Tyler was anxious to bring about the annexation of Texas.
Webster was adamantly opposed. Rather than let the matter grow
into a personal crisis, Webster decided that the time had come to
resign.*

[*To John Tyler, May 8, 1843*]

MY DEAR SIR — I have caused a formal resignation of my office
as Secretary of State to be filed in the Department.

* "Be thou diligent to know the state of thy flocks, and look well to thy herds."

RETURN TO PRIVATE LIFE

In ceasing to hold any connection with the Government, I remember with pleasure the friendly feelings and personal kindness which have subsisted between yourself and me, during the time that I have borne a part in your counsels. And I must be permitted to add that while entertaining the best wishes for your personal welfare, there is, at the same time, no one who more sincerely or ardently desires the prosperity, success, and honor of your administration. Yours very truly, DANL. WEBSTER

[*The President to Mr. Webster, May 8, 1843*]

MY DEAR SIR — *I have received your note of this day, informing me of your formal resignation of the office of Secretary of State.*

It only remains for me to reciprocate, as I truly do, the warm sentiments of regard which you have expressed towards me, and to return you my thanks for the zeal and ability with which you have discharged the various and complicated duties which have devolved upon you. I do not mean to flatter you in saying that in conducting the most delicate and important negotiations, you have manifested powers of intellect of the highest order, and in all things a true American heart.

Take with you, my dear sir, into your retirement, my best wishes for your health, happiness, and long life. JOHN TYLER

[*Letter to Mrs. Curtis, Washington, May 10, 1843*]

I "signed off" two days ago. My wife has turned up all the carpets, and packed away most of the things, so that our house is as empty as a deserted castle; its echoes are horrible. But Miss Priscilla is here, and we three sit before the fire on a rug, I in the middle, which is a comfortable berth. There is not a book in my room, except one stray volume of Shakespeare. The President has gone to Virginia for a month. We wait only for Fletcher and for the next steamer, and hope to get away Monday, the 13th.

The envelop in which this is enclosed bears another name than mine. This seems strange. For twenty years and more, without interruption, I have written my name at the upper corner, at the right-hand side of all my letters. But alas! "beggar that I am, I am even poor in franks."

[Letter to Mrs. Paige, New York, Sept. 18, 1843]

I am obliged to you for remembering me, and sending me Lockhart's sixth volume of Sir Walter's Life. I have been reading it at intervals, and find much that is interesting. The truth is, that although I looked into some of these volumes formerly, I never read them through. It is pleasant to meet in this volume with names of persons whom we have known, and thereby recall the recollection of our acquaintance. In some parts of Sir Walter's journal there is much to amuse; while in others are evidences of profound, sober, and just thinking on the most important subjects. I admire the resolution with which he set himself to work to repair his shattered fortunes. I know his love of Abbottsford, and hope it may remain in his name, and in his family, forever.

The weather is exceedingly hot. My head and eyes are not in the best condition. I am unwilling to go South, 'till some change comes, and have little to do here. Do not wonder if you hear of me making a sudden expedition to western New York, to be gone four days. There are to be cattle and sheep at Rochester!

[Letter to Weston, Washington, Nov. 1, 1843]

In the first place, put the barns, sheds, &c., all in order, to put up the cattle. Winter will be upon us soon. The stanchels, or some of them, must be moved a little, in Peleg's barn, so as to bring the calves nearer together. They must all be put up now, and well kept. Give them turnips and a few oats. Let Peleg take especial care of the fatting sheep. They must have plenty of turnips and oats, or small corn, with some salt hay, every day, as well as grass, or English hay. I am to exhibit some of this mutton, both in Boston and New York, and I shall be shamed, if any thing beats.

[*Letter to Paige, Boston, Nov. 1843*]

It has been suggested to me, that you would perhaps like to go to Marshfield this week. Of all things, this would suit me, you are just the man I want, and I think it will be such a jaunt as will do you good.

I go in the stage-coach, Monday eleven o'clock; arrive at dinner at half-past four o'clock — roast turkey and cranberry; a game of whist, that evening, Mrs. Thomas and Henry.

Wednesday morning, bright and early, four hogs to kill; two oxen ditto; three or four sheep ditto. Wednesday's dinner, pair canvass-backs, which Mr. Tucker gives me, unless Marshfield has something better.

Thursday, putting up the beef and pork. Friday morning, home.

Meanwhile, Fletcher had gone to China as Secretary of the Mission headed by Caleb Cushing, leaving his wife and children at home in Boston; and, in December, Webster invited himself to dinner.

DEAR CAROLINE, DAUGHTER CAROLINE, NOT WIFE CAROLINE — I had made up my mind to enjoy the luxury of a dish of baked beans to-day; but I am willing to dine with you, and shall do so with great pleasure, if you will let me bring my beans with me. Therefore, look out for me and the beans, already cooked, at two o'clock.   D. W.

Monday, three o'clock, 1844

DEAR CAROLINE — Mr. Blatchford and I will dine with you to-morrow, at half-past two o'clock. I will look out for the marketing, and also for a drop of something.   Yours,   D. W.

Efforts were now made to induce Webster to return to the Senate. His friend Rufus Choate, who had succeeded him when he became Secretary of State, was willing to resign, and the appointment was within the control of the Whigs. All that was needed was Webster's cooperation, and this was sought in a letter from David Sears. On February 5, 1844, Webster replied:

Your letter of the 27th of January, has been some days before me, and I have reflected on its contents. Indeed, similar suggestions had been made to me from other quarters.

I suppose it is true that Mr. Choate intends to leave the Senate, sometime in March, or perhaps not till April. The term for which Mr. Choate was elected will expire in March, 1845. There will therefore remain only the remnant of this session, and the short session of next winter. I doubt whether any thing important will be done, or seriously attempted this session, except on the subject of the tariff, and I hope that may not be successfully assailed.

Before next session, a new president will be chosen, and the greater part of a new Congress, so that an expiring Congress, with an expiring administration, would hardly be likely to venture on great public measures, especially as one House seems an effectual check on the other.

Under these circumstances, my dear Sir, I do not see, even supposing me capable of performing an important part in public affairs, that I could be in any considerable degree useful in the Senate, for this session or the next. And there are weighty private reasons, which render it desirable that I should not for some time be charged with responsible public duties.

I will not affect to deny, that if all other things favored, I should prefer suitable public employment, to returning to the bar at my age. I have seen enough of courts of law, to desire to be in and among them no more. But my affairs require attention, and the means of living, you know, must be had.

In 1836, by the aid of friends and my own exertions, I settled up my concerns, and owed no man any thing. I was then desirous of leaving Congress, and resuming professional labor vigorously. But friends opposed it, and my papers of resignation were sent back to me. It was a day of buoyancy and great hope, in matters of business, and what money I had or could get, I laid out in the West, principally in well-selected government lands. But times soon changed, and I have since had nothing but a struggle. If in the Senate, I should have time to attend to affairs private and personal, but not to affairs professional.

I may say to you in confidence, that I am now earning and receiving fifteen thousand dollars a year, from my profession, which must be almost entirely sacrificed by a return to the Senate. I am sanguine enough to hope for better times and a better state of things, in which I may turn some considerable remnants of property to good account. And if after this Congress it should seem to friends desirable that I should be in the Senate, and I should be able to see that I could possibly afford it, I should probably feel it right to put myself at their disposition. But for the remnant of this year, and until March of the next, I cannot but think it more important to me, that I should remain where I am than it can be to the country that I should return to the Senate.

I have said more, my dear Sir, than was perhaps necessary; but your letter manifests much kindness and good feeling on your part. I value your friendship highly, and have thought it right therefore to give you my thoughts frankly and in full.

To his old friend Mason, Webster put it in a slighlty different light, in a letter of February 6, 1844:

I am now a little engaged in the law, and need strongly enough what fees I may be able to pick up. To be sure, I should be very glad to be done with the courts; but their atmosphere, if not altogether pleasant, is yet usefully *bracing,* to those whose purses are slender, however it may be with their constitutions. On all accounts, therefore, I think it better that I should, for the present, remain where I am. Let us see what the ensuing election may bring forth. I dare say there is no *very strong* desire that I should return to the Senate. The body of the Whigs may wish it, but there are other candidates who may like the chance, and there are also some prominent men who have not yet digested the spleen generated by past events. As to these last, let them indulge themselves, I shall bide my time.

While leaving others to digest their spleen, Webster proceeded with a light heart.

[*Letter to a young lady who had left her bonnet*]

Monday Morning, March 4, 1844

MY DEAR JOSEPHINE — I fear you got a wetting last evening, as it rained fast soon after you left our door; and I avail myself of the return of your bonnet to express the wish that you are well this morning, and without cold.

I have demanded parlance with your bonnet; have asked it how many tender looks it has noticed to be directed under it; what soft words it has heard, close to its side; in what instances an air of triumph has caused it to be tossed; and whether, ever, and when, it has quivered from trembling emotions proceeding from below. But it has proved itself a faithful keeper of secrets, and would answer none of my questions. It only remained for me to attempt to surprise it into confession, by pronouncing sundry names one after another. It seemed quite unmoved by most of these, but at the apparently unexpected mention of one, I thought its ribbands decidedly fluttered! I gave it my parting good wishes, hoping that it might never cover an aching head, and that the eyes which it protects from the rays of the sun, may know no tears but of joy and affection.

Yours, dear Josephine, with affectionate regard,

336

RETURN TO PRIVATE LIFE

[Letter to Mrs. Paige]

New York, Wednesday Morning, March 26, 1844

On our arrival here yesterday, I found your letter. It always gives me pleasure to open a letter of yours; I am sure to find in it every thing that is friendly, kind, and hospitable.

Toward the end of this week I hope to go to Boston; and although Julia may expect me, yet, in the present state of her health, I think she will not need a great deal of my company. So I shall be most happy to come to an anchor in Summer street, and to ride at those moorings while I stay in port. William and I are very good mess-companions, he having as little to do with my eggs as I have with his hominy. A good Boston breakfast! Only think of it.

While Webster was in Boston, death struck again. This time it was Fletcher's daughter Grace. Webster wrote to him in China, on April 1, 1844.

Although you hear often from us, by communications from your wife and various friends, yet it seems due to affection, that I should sometimes write you a parental line. Nothing since the death of your mother and my brother, has affected me so deeply as the loss of dear little Grace. There were causes, beside her sweetness and loveliness, which tied her very close to my heart.

Caroline seems now very well; Dan. is growing and is in perfect health, and little Harriette Paige, who was christened yesterday, is as pretty a baby as ever was. The health of Mr. and Mrs. Paige is improving; Julia and her three children are well; and our family circle here is resuming an appearance of cheerfulness and happiness. I stay at Mrs. Paige's, and attend to some little business in court. Mrs. Webster is in New York, waiting for the dissolving of the snows, and the building of a new kitchen at Marshfield. We broke up at Washington about the middle of March. Mr. Pakenham took our house on a lease, and bought some of the furniture;

a part of the rest was sold, and the final residue sent to Marshfield.

According to what we hear at home, the Chinese mission, so far as heard from, is doing well. The country takes an interest in it. Mr. Cushing's letters from Suez, &c. have been read with interest.

I must ask you to make my most cordial regards to him, and I intend to send by the next ship a parcel of pamphlets, books, &c. for you and him.

Adieu! my dear son, and may a gracious Providence ever have you in His holy keeping.

[Letter to Mr. and Mrs. Paige]

November, Sunday evening, 1844

DEAR WILLIAM — I send you some venison. It was killed on Thursday. If Harriette should order a part of it cooked for to-morrow, I may probably be present at your holding forth, say about half-past two to three o'clock.

DEAR HARRIETTE — How lovely the weather; yesterday I was on the sea, it was as mild as summer, and the atmosphere over it absolutely delicious. To-day is a warm day. I wish you and yours were all here. The bright sun on our green lawn, and the skies absolutely cloudless, and a picture of youth, hope, and happiness, brilliant, though fleeting, but to be enjoyed while it lasts.   D. W.

More and more, Webster's thoughts turned to Marshfield; and more and more, Marshfield cost money.

[Letters to Weston:]

New York, Jan. 27, 1845

My money in Boston did not hold out quite so well as I expected. I thought there was something of it, for me — but a keg is soon emptied, if it be tapped at both ends, & then turned over, & the bung knocked out.

I enclose herein a check for $500 on the *New York* Merchant's Bank. Mr. Haven, at the *Boston* Merchant's Bank will readily give Boston money.

Remember that you must put your name on this check.

Write me, to Washington, & tell me among other things, how the *ice* comes on. To hear from Marshfield is almost the only pleasure I expect to enjoy at Washington.

Philadelphia, Tuesday evening, January 28, 1845

I enclose one hundred dollars for the wood-lot, and like what you propose. Go ahead. Get out the timber at once, for the barn, wagon-house, and addition to the small barn. As to this last, make it large enough for a stable for three farm horses, and a stall for the bull. While you are about it, a few feet, more or less, are of no importance.

Washington, February 5, 1845

As I did not furnish you with as much money, by two hundred dollars, as I intended, I now make up the deficiency, and add one hundred dollars more; you have here a draft for three hundred dollars. If I can get it in any honest way, I intend sending you more soon.

New York, February 20, 1845

I came to this city last week, and shall return to Washington on the 24th or 25th. Your letter came to hand just as I was leaving. You said things would go about as smooth as oil, if I could catch another five hundred dollar check. So, I baited and threw over, and here it is. I had hopes of double game, but one got off, before I could get him out of the water.

New York, February 24, 1845

I have seen here some Leicester sheep, from the State of Delaware. They are much admired, but do not appear to me to come up to ours. I want you to weigh our large wether, now fatting, as he now stands, and send me an account of his weight. I have concluded to remain here till near the end of this week. So on receipt of this, you may weigh the gentleman, and send me the account by return of mail. Direct, Astor House, New York. You and I seem to be carrying on rather a brisk correspondence.

Washington, March 12, 1845

This money is for Daniel Wright. I have sent so much to Marshfield already, that I am squeezed as dry as an orange peel. You must none of you say "money" to me again, till after the 4th of July.

XIX

1845–1848

WAR WITH MEXICO — TRIP TO THE SOUTH

In the presidential campaign of 1844 Webster campaigned hard for Clay, who lost to James K. Polk, the Democratic candidate, by a narrow margin. The result hinged upon New York, and the votes which the Whigs lost to the "Liberty," or anti-slavery party, cost them the election.

Had Clay been elected, Webster could probably have had any office he wanted, including Secretary of State or Minister to England. As it was, he yielded to the urgings of his political friends and returned to the Senate. To accommodate this, his friend Rufus Choate announced on January 8, 1845, that he would not be a candidate for reelection, and a week later the Massachusetts Legislature elected Webster for the term commencing March 4.

[*Letter to Everett, New York, Feb. 26, 1845*]

I left Washington ten days ago, where I had passed a fortnight, on professional business, and I return this week, say March 1, to take my seat in the Senate. I dare say you think this resumption of a seat in that body, a foolish business, and I certainly think so myself. I do not think I can do much good, and the personal sacrifice is considerable.

The Texas question is likely to be settled to-day or to-morrow. The great probability is, that, in some form, Texas is to be admitted. Southern senators have not been able, some of them, to resist the popular feeling which has been excited upon the subject.

Mr. Polk talks fair about liberal administration, disregard of party, &c. &c. But this can mean nothing. He may not be abrupt or violent, but this administration, I am sure, must and will be a strictly party administration. If his own volitions were the other way, he could not follow them, any more than a dray-horse can jump out of the fills. In both cases nothing is allowed, but to go ahead and draw hard.

The most critical question facing the new administration was the possibility of war with Mexico. Regarding the election as a popular mandate, President Tyler had effected the annexation of Texas by joint resolution of Congress shortly before the end of his term. Webster had opposed this while he was in the cabinet, but it was done after he left, and by the time he resumed his seat in the Senate it was an accomplished fact.

[*Letters to Fletcher, Washington: Mar. 11, 1845*]

The Secretary of State yesterday wrote a mild and conciliatory letter to General Almonté, in answer to his "protest." The substance of it is, that the annexation of Texas is a thing done; that it is too late for a formal protest to have any effect; that Mexico has no right to complain of such a transaction between independent States; that the government of the United States respects all the just rights of Mexico, and hopes to bring all questions pending with her to a fair and friendly settlement, &c.

That Mr. Polk and his cabinet will desire to keep the peace, there is no doubt. The responsibility of having provoked war, by their scheme of annexation, is what they would greatly dread.

Nor do I believe that the principal nations of Europe, or any of them, will instigate Mexico to war. The policy of England is undoubtedly pacific. She cannot want Texas herself; and though her desire would be to see that country independent, yet it is not a point she would seek to carry by disturbing the peace of the world. But she will, doubtless, now, take care that Mexico shall not cede California, or any part thereof, to us. You know my opinion to have been, and it now is, that the port of San Francisco would be twenty times as valuable to us as all Texas.

[*Mar. 13, 1845*]

Mr. Polk will nominate no Whig, and, in due time, will remove what few Whigs remain from the scythe of Mr. Tyler. I must do him the justice to say, however, that he appears to me to make rather good selections from among his own friends.

As a member of the minority party, Webster's legislative duties were light. He used the opportunity to expand his law practice, returning, as he said, "to the everlasting company of plaintiff and defendant." But mostly his thoughts gravitated to Marshfield.

[*Letters to Weston: May 13, 1845*]

You were right. The grass is Luzerne, or French clover. The Luzerne is often raised for feeding green to cattle, which you know is called soiling. It comes along rather late, and is excellent for milch cows, in the drought of August. It requires a light, loamy soil, and does best when sown in drills, so as to be kept free from weeds, till it has got good root. It does not spring up soon or strong, at first; hence it is subject to be choked by weeds, and many crops entirely fail for that reason. Its roots are large, and run deep; and when it gets well set, it does not go out, like our clover, in one or two seasons, but, as you see, lasts several years. If the ground be entirely free of weeds, it may be sown broad-cast; but much the safest and best way is to sow it in drills. For sowing in drills, say eighteen or twenty inches apart, ten pounds to the acre will answer. For broad-cast, twenty pounds will be requisite; now, as this is a year of experiments, we must try an acre of Luzerne, with guano.

Let an acre, therefore, be immediately ploughed, and ploughed rather deep. Put on guano, in the common quantity, and a good dressing of ashes with it, and sow the seed, just as soon as the weather favors. Sow in drills, north and south. Turner will lend a hand for this part of the operation. You will receive by the stage-coach to-day, twenty pounds of seed, fresh from France. Therefore, let the Luzerne go ahead, and "no mistake."

Did you ever see a tailor's pattern card, on which he puts his samples, of various colors, for waistcoats? Our Cushman field, if we have a good season, will look like that. There will be first, sapling clover and oats; then Luzerne; then buckwheat; then beans; then potatoes. Now, let us see if we cannot show a handsomer "pattern card" than any tailor in the county.

[*May 15, 1845*]

There is one thing of importance in farming business, to be more strictly attended to hereafter. That is, to employ men more exclusively who have families. Whenever we can, we must avoid employing labor to be paid altogether in money. We must try to find somebody to live in one part of the Carswell house, and somebody else to take part of the John Taylor house. We must pay a great part of our labor in beef and pork, and productions of the farm, the use of cows, rent, firewood, &c. Hereafter we may stick to this rule more closely. Be on the look-out for some good men with families.

Summer at the seacoast renewed his strength, and brought a visit from the painter George P. A. Healy, commissioned to paint portraits of Webster for two highly placed admirers abroad. But it did nothing to alleviate the annual catarrh.

[*Letter to Curtis, Oct. 3, 1845*]

Since the 17th day of August, I have been more or less under the influence of my miserable catarrh. Some days I have felt quite discouraged. Now it seems a little better. Its paroxysms are not so frequent, though two days ago, I had a very bad forenoon. It came on in a moment, and went off, when it did go, just as quick.

Healy is here, and is trying to fit me up for Louis Philippe, and for Lord Ashburton. Mrs. Paige and Ellen Fletcher are with us. We shall linger hereabouts till the middle of the month, and then go to Boston. Marshfield never looked better. Every thing is green as June, except what ought to show maturity, at this season.

Pray, my dear Sir, give me one scrape of your pen; address me "Boston."

Webster had a passion for hunting and fishing. He was not only an expert angler but seemed to know the daily whereabouts of the fish. A crack shot, he expressed disdain for the British practice of raising and freeing birds for shooting in preserves. It was, he said, "like going out and murdering the barn-door fowl." He was not above murderous practices of his own, however, although national pride made him prefer the American to the British style of slaughter.

[Letter to Paige, undated]

We send you a black duck or two; but I must tell you how we got them. Yesterday morning Edward and I went to a pond out in the woods, four or five miles off. At this time of the year the black duck, at certain times of tide, visits these fresh waters. They are shot after this manner: The gunner makes a little stand, or booth of bushes, close on the shore, behind which he stands. He then sends out a tame duck, with a string tied to her leg, to keep her from swimming away; and generally anchors her by a small stone, so that she cannot swim back to the shore. It is her duty to invite other ducks, which may light in the pond to join her, and if they do so, they come within the reach of shot. Other tame ducks are in the basket, to be thrown out into the pond, if occasion require. Well, yesterday morning Edward and I went forth, he to sit one side of the pond, with a hand to put out the decoy ducks, and I with another to the other side. None came near us; but a flock of fourteen came near Edward's stand, and seemed to take notice of his anchored duck. At that moment his man threw off another duck from behind his screen, which flew thirty or forty yards into the pond and there lighted, and all the wild ducks came down with her. Thereupon Edward and his man let fly at the same moment, and killed ten out of the fourteen. This is murderous and hardly fair sport, but it shows how things are done down here at Marshfield.

The year 1846 opened so uneventfully that Webster found time to deliver an occasional lecture to his son.

[*Letter to Fletcher, Washington, Jan. 11, 1846*]

If you will write me a letter every other day, I will keep you well advised of every thing here; but you have a foolish notion that one should not write unless he has something to say. That is nonsense. If he has nothing to say, let him say so, and that is something.

One other rule — never put a private matter in a general letter. Don't you know that others always want to read general letters? Let every private matter have its own letter; and, if convenient, in another handwriting from the address. Remember this. All the women in Washington want to see a letter if the superscription be by you.

And to write long, descriptive letters to his friends.

[*Letter to Blatchford, Franklin, N. H., May 3, 1846*]

Where I now write was once the east end of the town of Salisbury, which town was four miles wide, along the west bank of the Merrimac River, and ran west seventeen degrees south, nine miles, nearly to the top of a very conspicuous mountain, in these parts called Kearsarge. From where I sit is two miles and a half to the head of the Merrimac River, which river is then formed by the confluence of two beautiful streams, but rejoicing in harsh Indian names, namely, 1. Pemigewasset, which rises in the White Hills, pours down their southern slopes and declivities, dashing over many cascades, and collecting the tributes of various smaller rivers and brooks in its course. It is the beau ideal of a mountain stream; cold noisy, winding, and with banks of much picturesque beauty.

2. The Winnepiseogee. This river issues from the great lake of that name, which lies about northeast from this spot. It is a lake near thirty miles long, with various arms and bays like a sea. Its shores are mountainous and strikingly beautiful; especially on the north and east.

The water of this river is several degrees warmer generally, than that of the Pemigewasset; the difference being that between a mountain stream and a stream issuing from large and deep lakes. It is a curious fact, that when the River Merrimac was full of fish, on their arrival at the confluence of these two streams, the salmon and shad shook hands and parted, the shad all going into the lakes, and the salmon all keeping up the mountain torrent, which they continued to ascend, as used to be said, till their back fins were out of the water.

I have said, these two streams unite two miles and a half above where I now am. The place was formerly called Webster's Falls, but is now the site of a flourishing manufacturing village called "Franklin," or more specifically, "Franklin Upper Village."

From Concord, the railroad follows the river through Boscawen, where I began to plead law, passes through this beautiful bottom land, where I now am (here called Interval) goes much nearer to my house than I could wish, and keeps on up to Franklin Upper Village. There it leaves the Merrimac exactly at his head, and turning still further to the west than the line or valley of the Pemigewasset, it follows up a little stream called Hancock Brook, to a beautiful lake in the midst of the woods called "Como." Adjoining this classical sheet of water, I have a large real estate, forty acres of pine land costing one dollar and fifty cents per acre, and on a distinguished point along the shore, quite conspicuous for a great distance, a white-washed boat-house, nine feet by eighteen. The railroad having approached the lake, and done homage to this edifice, inclines still further to the southwest, and twists and turns, and wriggles and climbs, till it finally struggles over the height of land, near Cardigan Mountain, and then glides down like a rippling brook through Shaker Pond, and the Mascoma, its outlet, to Connecticut River! There, I have done till evening.

At first, Webster discounted the possibility of war with Mexico.

[*Letter to Fletcher, Washington, Jan. 14, 1846*]

Mr. Polk said to a friend of mine last night, *that he had not the slightest apprehension of War.* The administration must either have some assurances of the *absolute* disposition of England to keep the peace, under all circumstances, (which I do not believe) or else it must have a curious notion of the tendency of its own measures, & the declarations & speeches of its own friends.

Still, I do not believe there will be war.

But clashes took place, and on May 13, 1846, war was declared. Webster was in New England for the installation of his friend Edward Everett as President of Harvard, and did not vote against the declaration of war, but he was opposed to it and was inclined to treat the situation lightly. He wrote Fletcher from Washington:

[*June 13, 1846*]

As to **Mexico**, the idea here is that the war will not last long.

[*Aug. 6, 1846*]

There is no doubt that the President is desirous of putting an end to this Mexican War; but how to do it is the question. We hear nothing at all from Mexico — not one word: & when she will speak, no one knows. The President I have no doubt is anxious to hear from her, but she is silent. Mexico is an ugly enemy. She will not fight — and will not treat.

[*Letter to Weston, Aug. 10, 1846*]

Washington, Monday morning, August 10, 1846, not quite late enough to write without a candle

We hope to bring our evil doings to a close at twelve o'clock to-day, and I hope to leave Washington this P. M., and shall proceed to Marshfield without much delay.

I do not know that I should be up so early, if it was not too hot to sleep. I never more ardently longed to see Blue Fish Rock, and smell the sea.

Later in the year the war was brought closer home when his son Edward organized a company of volunteers in Massachusetts. Early in 1847 the regiment of which they formed a part left for service in Mexico. Edward, as a captain, was entitled to a body-servant and took with him Henry Pleasants, a former slave and longtime family retainer whose freedom Webster had purchased for $500.

[*Letter to Edward, Washington, Feb. 5, 1847*]

I write you this, in the hope you will get it before sailing; & I trust I shall hear from you every day till you sail, & also on your first touching land, anywhere; & after that as often as you shall know of conveyances.

I feel interest, of course, My Dear Son, in your success, in your new calling. I am afraid of no unbecoming conduct, no fear, on one side, & no foolish recklessness on the other. But I know the accidents of War; & what I fear most of all, is the *climate.* Pray study to guard agt the effects of climate, in every possible form.

Take good care of Henry. There is no one else he wd have gone with. I shall write you constantly.

At first the Massachusetts regiment was assigned to General Taylor in northern Mexico. Webster, still thinking that hostilities would soon end, was less concerned about Edward's status during the war than afterwards.

[*Letter to Edward, Washington, Apr. 11, 1847*]

It gave us great pleasure to hear from you, on your arrival at the Brazos de San Jago, and to learn your health. Our latest intelligence through the newspapers, leaves you at Matamoras, stationed in the Plaza, but whether from this to infer that you are to remain there, we do not know. We hope you are to keep on towards General Taylor's headquarters. The newspapers compliment the appearance of your company, and it was remarkable that not a man was on the sick list.

[*Letter to Fletcher, Apr. 25, 1847*]

I shall go to-morrow and have a full conversation with the Secretary of War about the Massachusetts regiment; but I suppose nothing can be done. One day or another we shall have peace; and what is Edward then to do? He must think for himself, and you must think for him. When these new regiments and volunteer corps are all disbanded, there will be a rush of military men into civil life; especially if a military man be at the head of government. If we can keep colonels off the bench, and captains out of the pulpit, we shall do well. It is time, quite time, for Edward to enter upon something for life.

The probability now is, that General Taylor will come in President with a general rush. He would, certainly, were the election now to come on. It is in the nature of mankind to carry their favor towards military achievement. No people yet have ever been found to resist that tendency.

Later the regiment was sent to join General Scott in his expedition against Mexico City, and, although the capital fell before Edward's arrival, Webster's worries grew.

[*Letter to Edward, Boston, Sept. 27, 1847*]

If through sickness, or other causes, you should find yourself in want of funds for your expenses, you may draw on me for any necessary amount, from any place, and you may show this as your authority.

Meanwhile, Webster's court appearances became more frequent. Among the most important were the series of arguments in the Passenger Cases, involving the imposition of state taxes on ships bringing immigrants into the country. Typically lawyer-like, he wrote his son Fletcher on December 7, 1847:

In these cases, I have no doubt whatever that the law is with us, but where the Court may be I know not.

Earlier, on February 7, 1847, he had written Fletcher:

The Massachusetts law laying a tax on passengers, is now under discussion in the Supreme Court. It is strange to me how any Legislature of Massachusetts could pass such a law. In the days of Marshall & Story it could not have stood one moment. The present Judges, I fear, are quite too much inclined to find apologies for irregular & dangerous acts of State Legislation; but whether the law of Massachusetts can stand, even with the advantages of all these predispositions, is doubtful. There is just about an even chance, I think, that it will be pronounced unconstitutional. Mr. Choate examined the subject, on Friday, in an argument of great strength & clearness. Mr. Davis is on the other side, & I shall reply.

Choate and Webster were often paired in court, sometimes on the same side, sometimes opposed. They were the leading advocates of their day and the quality of their relationship, as well as of their scholarship, is revealed by a sidelight during the embezzlement trial of William Wyman, President of the Phoenix Bank of Charlestown, Massachusetts. The defense had a large array, including Webster and Choate, and the feeling of every attorney that he must earn his fee dragged out the proceedings interminably.

During a particularly humdrum period a wave of excitement swept the courtroom as spectators craned their necks to watch Webster and Choate, those titans of the bar, exchanging notes at the trial table and summoning a messenger to fetch a reference book.

It seems that Webster had solemnly passed Choate a slip of paper on which he had written a couplet from Alexander Pope's Dunciad:

> Lo, where Maeotis sleeps, and softly flows
> The freezing Tanais through a waste of snows.

Choate, after intense concentration, wrote the word "Wrong," and amended the couplet to read:

> Lo, where Maeotis sleeps, and *hardly* flows
> The freezing Tanais through a waste of snows.

Webster changed it back and offered a bet. Choate called a messenger and in due course passed over to Webster a volume of Pope's poems, triumphantly marking the passage which confirmed his memory. "Spurious edition!" wrote Webster, returning it.

Webster never lost his love for travel and had long wanted to visit the South. With the hopes that he nurtured for the forthcoming presidential election, 1847 seemed especially propitious for this purpose. On April 28, 1847, he set out, planning originally to go all the way to New Orleans, and to return by way of Nashville,

Cincinnati, Columbus, and Cleveland. Writing to Mrs. Paige from Richmond he said:

Richmond, April 29, five o'clock, A. M., 1847

Whether it be a favor or an annoyance, you owe this letter to my habit of early rising. From the hour marked at the top of the page, you will naturally conclude that my companions are not now engaging my attention, as we have not calculated on being early travellers today.

This city has a "pleasant seat." It is high — the James River runs below it, and when I went out an hour ago, nothing was heard but the roar of the falls. The air is tranquil, and its temperature mild.

It is morning — and a morning sweet and fresh, and delightful. Every body knows the morning, in its metaphorical sense, applied to so many objects, and on so many occasions. The health, strength, and beauty of early years, lead us to call that period the "morning of life." Of a lovely young woman, we say, she is "bright as the morning," and no one doubts why Lucifer is called "son of the morning." But the morning itself, few people, inhabitants of cities, know any thing about. Among all our good people of Boston, not one in a thousand sees the sun rise once a year. They know nothing of the morning. Their idea of it is, that it is that part of the day which comes along after a cup of coffee and a beefsteak, or a piece of toast. With them, morning is not a new issuing of light; a new bursting forth of the sun; a new waking up of all that has life, from a sort of temporary death, to behold again the works of God, the heavens and the earth; it is only a part of the domestic day, belonging to breakfast, to reading the newspapers, answering notes, sending the children to school, and giving orders for dinner. The first faint streak of light, the earliest purpling of the east, which the lark springs up to greet, and the deeper and deeper coloring into orange and red, till at length the "glorious sun is seen, regent of day," this they never enjoy, for this they never see.

I know the morning; I am acquainted with it, and I love it, fresh

353

and sweet as it is, a daily new creation, breaking forth, and calling all that have life, and breath, and being, to new adoration, new enjoyments, and new gratitude.

We left Washington yesterday, at nine o'clock, Mrs. Webster, Miss Seaton, and myself; Mr. Seaton coming with us, and Mary Scott and Mr. Shroeder as far as the boat comes; and just as the boat was leaving the wharf, who should jump aboard but Mr. Edward Curtis! We had not looked for him, and great was our joy. We kept him on board, and brought him and Mary Scott here. They go back to Washington at eight o'clock. We stay here to-day. Mrs. Webster has some headache. To-morrow we leave for Raleigh, at an hour which the world calls "morning." The air is fine, quite cool enough, and dry. What struck me last evening, was the dryness of the night air. Of all the cities of the Atlantic South, this is probably the finest for elevation, situation, handsome houses, and public buildings, and prospects of growth.

[*Letter to Fletcher, May 5, 1847*]

Goldsboro', N. C., on the Wilmington railroad, eighty miles
north of Wilmington, Wednesday, May 5, six A. M., 1847

We spent a day or two pleasantly at Raleigh, and came thence to this place yesterday, through the pine country.

The pines are the long-leaved pines. In one of these, a foot from the bottom, a notch is cut, and its capacity enlarged, and its shape fashioned a little, so as to hold the liquid, by chiselling, and then it is called the "box." Above the box the bark is cut off, for a foot or so, and the turpentine oozes out of the tree on to this smooth surface, and then runs slowly into the box. The box holds about a quart. In a good large tree, it will fill five times a season. Sometimes there are two boxes in one tree, so that some trees will yield ten quarts a year. But the greatest yield is the first year; after that it gradually is diminished, and in seven or eight years the tree dies, or will yield no more turpentine. Tar is made by bringing together wood, full of turpentine, either trees or knots, and pieces picked up in the woods, and burning it in a pit, just as charcoal is made, then running off into a hole prepared for it, in the ground. At the present prices of the article, this is said to be the best business now doing in the State. I am told good, fresh, well-timbered pine lands can be bought for $1.25 to $1.50 per acre.

We leave this morning; hope to be at Wilmington at one o'clock, and at Charleston to-morrow forenoon. All well.

[Letter to Mrs. Paige, May 9, 1847]

Charleston, May 9, Sunday morning, six o'clock, 1847

Charleston lies on the sea, between the two little rivers, Ashley on the south or west, and Cooper, on the north or east; the mouths of these two rivers running into the sea about a mile apart, and one of them, the Ashley, winding up round the city, pretty much as Charles River and bay runs round the back part of Boston. The city is flat, as is all the adjacent country. I suppose its elevation is hardly more than ten feet above the tide. It is, as you know, an old city, and is regularly built in squares. It may contain now about forty thousand people. The houses are quite large, and many of them palace-looking, most having piazzas on one or more sides. The houses are principally of brick, many of them painted, and the sea air or other cause, has given them a dingy appearance. The city looks very much like some parts of London, much more so than any other city in the United States. The hue of the old houses is very much that of St. Paul's.

Before the Revolution, Charleston contained, doubtless, the most fashionable and highest bred society in the United States. It was the residence of very many distinguished and opulent families, who held large estates in the neighborhood or the interior. Sumpters, Marions, Pinkneys, Hugers, &c., lived here in great hospitality and great splendor.

As a commercial city, its importance, as you know, has comparatively dwindled, and as it has no manufactures, it is not now a city of great activity. But there is another cause, always over looked, which has essentially altered the fabric of Southern society and that of Charleston in particular. It is the abolition of the righ of primogeniture. The estates were originally large, in extent o acres, and with country-houses fit for princes. While these estate were transmitted entire, from oldest son to oldest son, they retained their importance and magnificence. But they are evidently thing which do not bear division and subdivision, and the doing awa of the right of primogeniture, therefore, has essentially broken in upon the whole old fashioned aristocratic system of Southern life I do not say it has made things worse; I only say it has made a great change, which must continue to go on.

Slave labor, and rice and cotton cultivation, work in badly with democratic subdivisions of property, such as suit us in New Eng land.

[*Letter to Fletcher, May 10, 1847*]

Charleston, May 10, 1847. Monday, seven A. M.

We arrived here from Wilmington on Friday morning, the 7th and have therefore already been here three days. The people are all kind and civil, and I get along with the Nullifiers, withou making any sharp points.

To-day there is a bar dinner, to-morrow a little excursion in a steamboat to see a rice plantation, and a ball for the ladies in the evening. The next day, Wednesday, the 12th, we go to Columbia My present purpose is to go from Columbia to Augusta, thence b railroad to Savannah, for two days, thence west, on the same and other railroads four hundred miles, thence by stage-coach to Nash ville, and thence north. But whether all this will be accomplished I know not. I quite give up New Orleans.

Yesterday morning I received your letter of the 5th. I feel a good deal concerned about Edward, especially in regard to hi health. We must make a strong point of putting him in some regu lar business, as soon as this war is over.

TRIP TO THE SOUTH

At the Charleston bar dinner Webster drew the utmost enthusiasm from his fellow members of the bar when he said:

I love our common profession. I regard it as the great ornament, and one of the chief defences and securities, of free institutions. It is indispensable to and conservative of public liberty. I honor it from the bottom of my heart. If I am anything, it is the law that has made me what I am.

The atmosphere of Charleston, and of South Carolina, could easily have become one of hostility. But Webster was especially adept with the soft answer that turneth away wrath. On one occasion, when a speaker sought to revive some of the animosities of the Webster-Hayne debate, Webster suavely rose and proposed a toast to the memory of General Hayne. On another occasion he said:

Gentlemen, allow me to tell you of an incident. At Raleigh, a gentleman purposing to call on me, asked his son, a little lad, if he did not wish to go and see Mr. Webster. The boy answered, "Is it that Mr. Webster who made the spelling-book, and sets me so many hard lessons; if so, I never want to see him as long as I live."

Now, gentlemen, I am that Mr. Webster who holds sentiments on some subjects not altogether acceptable, I am sorry to say, to some portions of the South. But I set no lessons. I make no spelling-books.

[*Letter to Weston, May 10, 1847*]

Charleston, South Carolina, May 10, 1847.
Monday, half-past two o'clock, P. M.

The great object of agriculture in this quarter is rice. It is a beautiful crop; but it causes an unhealthy climate. It must grow, for half the time, under water. We have seen some plantations, and are going up one of the rivers to-morrow in a steamboat, to view a famous one. The rice is now six or eight inches high, of a beautiful soft, light green, like the color of a gosling's wing, and the vast fields are all laid off in squares, as regularly as the beds in Mr. Morrison's garden.

The day after to-morrow we move west, into the interior of the State, and the heart of the cotton country; though not of the sea island, or long staple cotton. The cotton is now up, three or four inches, and in common seasons would have been much higher The fields are pretty, but are said to be exceedingly beautiful when the plant is in blossom. The word "cotton" originally mean a thin, light cloth, made in England out of wool and linen; and when the uses of this plant were found out, and people learned to make a similar light cloth out of it, they called its product "cotton wool." There! I do not believe there is a man in all Marshfield but you and me, who knows why this plant is called "cotton."

We saw yesterday twenty miles of rice fields, one after another along the river. In some fields one hundred hands hoeing.

Alligators were to be seen along the banks, and on the flats. I saw three lying together, each as heavy as two of our cows. I had a little gun on board, with two buck shot in the barrel. The boat was running quite near the shore, and I put these two shot in the neck of one of the fellows. They made him jump well, and lash the water with his tail, till it foamed, like the track of a boat.

This country is full of hogs, and they sometimes swim a stream and then the alligators catch them. They sometimes also kill a calf, or cow, if feeding near the water. They strike with their tail The negroes often kill small ones.

[*Letters to Mrs. Paige: May 13, 1847*]

Columbia, S. C., May 13, 1847, Thursday
morning, six o'clock, at Mr. Preston's
Columbia is on one of the large sand hills, flattened on the top

and hence called a "Plateau." It rises, I should think, a hundred feet or more above the river, and much of the hill is still covered with original pitch pines. The soil is pretty good, having, like others of these "plateaus," clay mixed with the sand; and the situation and the town are very handsome.

The college was established forty or fifty years ago, and is flourishing, and here is the seat of government, and here sit the principal courts. Great care was taken early to plant ornamental trees in the squares and along the streets, so that the town is now one of the handsomest looking and "nicest" of our little inland cities. It contains, I suppose, five or six thousand people.

We arrived last evening by railroad, at six o'clock, and were received with all kinds and degrees of hospitality. The college buildings were illuminated in the evening, and the boys made a torchlight procession through the college campus, or square. Mrs. Preston had a little party. The governor and all the judges, and the people of the town, and the professors, &c., all present.

To-day we all go to dine at Colonel Hampton's, he not being at home, but his daughters doing the honors of the house. He has a great and profitable cotton plantation. We mean to go over it, and examine it, and see exactly what a cotton plantation is.

[May 15, 1847]

Columbia, May 15, 1847, Saturday morning, half-past six

The cotton culture was commenced in this State about the year 1795. Before that time, people lived by raising corn, tobacco, and indigo. These last articles are now scarcely raised. There is some tobacco and a little indigo down in the southeast corner of the State, but through all this region the crops are corn and cotton. Cotton is a tender plant in its early stages, and must be cultivated cleanly and carefully. When out of the ground two or three inches, the plants look very much like beans, as well in the shape as the color of their leaves. The seed is sown in rows or drills, three feet apart, in common light lands, and four or four and a half in land of richer quality. On light lands it grows about two feet, or two and a half high, on the bottoms four and a half or five. The yield is of course greater on the bottom lands, but the cotton itself not quite so white and valuable. It is said to be very beautiful when in blossom. Each petal or flower leaf comes out white, then turns to scarlet, and then falls. The flowers come out not all at once, but in long succession, like those of buckwheat. But the owners think the cotton looks best in the autumn, when the pod or ball opens and the wool comes out full. They say the whole field looks as if it was covered with snow, and it looks too as if the planters might pay some of their debts.

In general, the proportion of labor to land, is one hand to six or seven acres, and one mule to three hands. The hoeing being light work, is mostly done by the women. Every morning the day's work is staked out into "tasks," and a task assigned to each hand. On the plantations I have seen, the people do not appear to be overworked. They usually get through their tasks by twelve or one o'clock, and have the rest of the day to themselves.

The "settlement" or "negro quarter," or huts in which the negroes live, are better or worse according to the ability or pleasure of the proprietor. Sometimes they are miserable straggling log hovels. On the larger and better conducted estates, they are tolerably decent boarded houses, standing along in a row. These are near the plantations, but not always near the mansion of the owner. Provisions are distributed by weight and measure to each family once a week. They consist in this region of bacon, cornmeal, and molasses. Most of the slaves have gardens, or little patches of land, in which they raise sweet potatoes and cabbages, &c., and they also keep poultry and catch fish. They usually assemble on Sundays, and have somebody to preach to them.

In Columbia, Webster became ill, and in Augusta, Georgia, he took to bed. Some have attributed this to over-exposure to southern hospitality, but until illness caught up with him he had regularly been writing long letters at six or seven each morning.

[*Letters to Fletcher: May 23, 1847*]

Augusta, Ga., May 23, 1847, Sunday morning, eight o'clock

I am pretty well over with my ill turn, and shall leave this place to-morrow. My attack was bilious and feverish, not unlike one I experienced about ten years ago, in the same season of the year; a little inflamed, perhaps, by climate. I feel now a great deal better than when I left Washington. I wish I had another month, so that I could see New Orleans; but the chance is lost, and I know not when I shall have another. Most of the rest of the West I have seen already, and care less about visiting it now; but I grieve at losing the opportunity for New Orleans.

We go home in The Southerner, if nothing prevents, and it will be a good thing to get home.

For once Marshfield left something (or perhaps several things) to be desired.

[*Letters to Fletcher: June 11, 1847*]

State of things in the gun-room. Fish baskets all gone, great and small. Every landing net gone or broken to pieces, so that I cannot take a minnow. Book of flies and hooks, belonging to the Edgar rod, gone. Cap of leather case of do., do. All the tops of the beautiful red rod, which Mr. Edgar gave me, gone; so that the rod is entirely good for nothing. Mr. Edgar gave twenty dollars for it. One, two — unless Edward took his — rods entirely gone. There is not one rod whole, with its equipments.

Ask Mr. Bradford to send down a fish basket, and a landing-net and handle, by to-morrow Friday's stage.

SPEAK FOR YOURSELF, DANIEL

[June 12, 1847]

I received yours last night, with the fishing gear. It is quite possible that my losses and damages occurred last year, except the baskets, which I am sure I left here. I shall not need yours or Edward's rods, but shall let them remain here till you come down. I am glad of the basket. I have fixed my old John Trout rod, and it does very well. "Venerable men."

But now I have something new to say. I found in the gun-room an unopened box. Nobody knew whence it came, nor exactly when. It was found to contain the most splendid angling apparatus you can imagine. There are three complete rods, all silver mounted, with my name engraved; beautiful reels, and books of flies and hooks, and quantities of other equipments. The maker's card was in the box containing the books, &c. He is Mr. Welch, of New York.

That is all my information. You will be glad to examine the articles, and I hope will hereafter use them. They are enough for two lives.

Nor were his only troubles in Marshfield. Franklin too had its problems, though also its compensations. Earlier he had written to Edward Curtis:

They have laid out a railroad at Franklin right through our wood-house, and fourteen feet from the corner of the house itself. John Taylor is in a fright, and I must go up. I suppose the house must be moved. This railroad will bring wood and lumber into Boston, from the Franklin property, the first year enough to pay one half the estimated value, beside expense. Cord wood, such as mine, is seven and a half dollars in Boston. I imagine we have two or three thousand cords very handy.

On August 28, 1847, when this section of the railroad was placed in service, Webster was asked to participate in the opening cere-

monies. As a business lawyer and a leading proponent of American expansion, he could hardly be expected to oppose railroads, but his extemporaneous speech on this occasion included some remarkably modern comments on the price of progress:

Sometimes, it is true, these railroads interrupt or annoy individuals in the enjoyment of their property. I have myself had a little taste of this inconvenience. When the directors of the road resolved to lay it out upon the river (as I must say they were very wise in doing), they showed themselves a little too loving to me, coming so near my farm-house, that the thunder of their engines and the screams of their steam-whistles, to say nothing of other inconveniences, not a little disturbed the peace and the repose of its occupants. There is, beside, an awkward and ugly embankment thrown up across my meadows. It injures the looks of the fields. But I have observed, fellow-citizens, that railroad directors and railroad projectors are no enthusiastic lovers of landscape beauty; a handsome field or lawn, beautiful copses, and all the gorgeousness of forest scenery, pass for little in their eyes. Their business is to cut and to slash, to level or deface a finely rounded field, and fill up beautifully winding valleys. They look upon a well-constructed embankment as an agreeable work of art; they behold with delight a long, deep cut through hard pan and rock, such as we have just passed; and if they can find a fair reason to run a tunnel under a deep mountain, they are half in raptures.

By the end of the year he was once more at peace with the world; so much so that he could write his friend Blatchford from Marshfield on December 7, 1847:

It is a beautiful, clear, cold, still morning. I rose at four o'clock, and have looked forth. The firmament is glorious. Jupiter and Venus are magnificent, "and stars unnumbered, gild the glowing pole." I wish I could once see the constellations of the South, though I do not think they can excel the heavens which are over our heads. An hour or two hence we shall have a fine sunrise. The long twilights of this season of the year, make the sun's rising a slow and beautiful progress. About an hour hence, these lesser lights will begin to "pale their ineffectual fires." Meantime Mr. Baker and his men are already milking and feeding the cows, and his wife has a warm breakfast for them, all ready, before a bright fire. Such is country life, and such is the price paid for manly strength, and female health, and red cheeks.

I hear the sea, very strong and loud at the north, which is not unusual after violent atmospheric agitations, and when the wind has lulled. They call this the rote or rut, of the sea. Either expression is correct. The Latin *rota* is the root of both words. The ruts in the road are the results of rolling, or the repeated and successive pressure or blows of the wheel. Rotation means repetition as well as succession. To learn a thing by rote, is to possess the mind of it, by repeated readings or hearings. The rote, or rut of the sea, therefore, means only the noise produced by the action of the surf, the successive breaking of wave after wave on the shore; and the beach means precisely the smooth shore, beaten by this eternal restlessness of the ocean. There is another expression for the same thing, sometimes used instead of rut or rote; I hear our people speak of the "cry of the sea," not an unapt phrase to signify the deep, hollow-sounding, half groaning, or loud wailing voice of the ocean, uttered as if in resentment of its violent disturbance by the winds. As an indication of wind and weather, the rote of the sea is generally understood to signify either that the wind has recently left the quarter whence the rote is heard, or else is soon to spring up in that quarter. The moon changes to-day, the tides are high, and at eleven o'clock, the sea will cover all the meadows, and reach the wall of our garden.

Our harvest accounts are good. We think we have a thousand bushels of corn, three thousand of turnips, and seven or eight hundred of beets. The barns are full of hay. Six or eight oxen are eating turnips by way of preparation for the Brighton market, in March. We are in snug winter quarters, with only men enough to take care of the cattle, get the wood, and look out for kelp. To-day I shall try to look over accounts, count the cattle and sheep, see to the curing of the pork and hams, &c., and to-morrow try to get back to Boston.

P. S. I went down to the mouth of the river at high water. The marshes are all covered, there was not a breath of wind, but the sea looked cold and blue. Our port was deserted, and the lobster-houses all vacated. Half a dozen great wild geese were in the river, just below the boat-house, who seemed very happy as they had the whole scene to themselves. It is winter. I have taken my last look of Marshfield, out of doors, for the season, and not without re-luctance give it all up, for toilsome law, and wrangling politics. I am thankful for the past. Adieu!

1848–1849

DEATH OF EDWARD AND JULIA —
TRIP TO MARTHA'S VINEYARD

The year 1848 was to be one of family sorrow and political frustration. On December 7, 1847, Webster had written Fletcher:

Is it not time to hear from Edward? I get quite uneasy about him.

But his concerns for Edward were now eclipsed by far worse fears for Julia. Of all Webster's children, she was the most congenial. She had designed his library at Marshfield and seemed always to have time and thought to devote to her father's concerns, notwithstanding the care and rearing of five children of her own. But like so many others in those days she became prey to tuberculosis, then an ever-present scourge which seemed to creep up unawares and not to manifest itself until too late for cure.

[*Letters to Fletcher, from Washington: Jan. 31, 1848*]

We have been long concerned about Julia, and at length have become alarmed. Your letter was received this morning. Mrs. Webster will leave to-morrow, and proceed to Boston as fast as weather will permit.

[*Feb. 4, 1848*]

We got two mails this morning, from Boston, and I have your letters of the 1st and 2d. I am infinitely concerned about Julia;

and unless I hear better tidings soon, shall leave every thing, and go to Boston.

[*Feb. 10, 1848*]

I have your letters of the 7th and 8th. There is nothing for me to do, but to remain here and prepare myself, as well as I can, for events.

Send this to your mother, as I am going to court. I may not be able to write her to-day.

[*Letter to Julia (Mrs. S. A. Appleton), Feb. 14, 1848*]

MY DEAR DAUGHTER — Your mother writes me daily, about all Boston things, the state of your health among the rest; but I hope her face will be turned this way by the time you receive this.

I have not been out of my house for some two or three days, having given myself up for that time to Dr. Lindsley, to see if he cannot melt out of my bones and muscles some lingering rheumatism.

Your mother says you are indignant about "Vice-Presidents," and "such things," as Mr. Biddle used to say. On all such subjects, my dear child, my notion is this. I am allowed to be the first farmer in Marshfield, South Parish, and I am content with this, unless I should be called to be first, elsewhere, where I can do more good.

Give my best love to your husband, and to Miss Caroline Le Roy Appleton, Master Samuel Appleton, Miss Julia W. Appleton, Master Daniel Webster Appleton, Miss Constance Mary Appleton.

The reference to "Vice-Presidents" related to a proposal that the Whigs nominate General Taylor for President and Webster for Vice President. Webster and his friends spurned the idea, although, as events fell, it would have made him President.

Even while Webster was doing his best to keep up his daughter's spirits, while at the same time tensing for the inevitable, another blow fell like a lightning-stroke in the form of a communication from Mexico.

[*Letter to Fletcher, Feb. 23, 1848*]

MY DEAR AND ONLY SON — I have just received this; when shown to Julia and the rest of the family, send it back safely to me.

My own health is pretty good, but I hardly know how I shall bear up under this blow. I have always regarded it as a great misfortune to outlive my children; but I feel now, but more intensely, as when Grace and Charles died.

But the will of Heaven be done in all things!

Julia died April 28, 1848. Peter Harvey gives this picture of Webster awaiting the event.

"*A few years before his death, Mr. Webster had a double and terrible affliction. At the same time that his daughter, Mrs. Julia Webster Appleton, lay dying of consumption, the remains of his son Edward were being brought back from Mexico, where he had lost his life fighting the battles of his country. Mr. Webster was in Boston, awaiting the arrival of the remains of the son and the last hour of the beloved daughter. He was very much bowed down and broken with grief. He had been retained by the Lowell Railroad to go before a committee of the Legislature which was then in session, to procure some grant, or to resist some measure directed against their charter. The hearing was held in the hall of the House of Representatives; because, when it was known that Mr. Webster would appear as counsel, there was always a crowd anxious to see and hear him. He appeared before the committee, with other counsel, to argue his client's cause. When the committee adjourned, and he came out, he took my arm and we walked down the steps of the State House, toward Mr. Paige's house in Summer Street, where he was stopping with Mrs. Webster. As we came into Winter Street (Mr. Appleton's house was in this street) he stopped at his daughter's door. I saw that he was very much affected.*

" 'Come in a moment,' said he, 'and see poor Julia; I cannot pass the house without stopping, although I have been in four times to-day already.'

"So I entered the hall.

" 'Go up,' he whispered.

"It was a raw day, I remember, although the sun shone brightly; it was one of those deceitful days peculiar to our climate. The door which led to Mrs. Appleton's room was thrown open; she was seated in front of an open grate, surrounded by her nurses. The glass over the mantle revealed her face to me, although I was behind her; it was more corpse-like than any living face I had ever seen. She had her father's eyes, those great black lustrous eyes; and the contrast with this deathly expression was very startling. Mrs. Appleton had recognized the voice of her father, who had remained downstairs. I was announced, and stepped forward and took her hand. She merely grasped my hand in return, and immediately spoke of her father.

" 'Did he wear an overcoat to-day?' said she.

"I told her that he did not.

" 'Father, oh, how can you expose yourself so? Do, for my sake, put on an overcoat! It is very imprudent in you to be out in such weather without an overcoat.'

"She seemed absorbed in his welfare. He did not come into the room; and when I shook her hand and passed out, he was waiting by the foot of the stairs; he was in tears, but restrained any audible expression of grief.

"As soon as we had passed out he took my arm, and we started down the street to Mr. Paige's house. His whole expression was that of the deepest grief. He seemed to be absorbed in a terrible struggle until we got to the door of Mr. Paige's house. We passed in, and Mr. Webster threw himself upon the sofa in the parlor. No

*one was there, and he burst into a paroxysm of grief, such as I do
not think I ever before witnessed. He wept and wept, as if his
heart would break.*

*" 'That poor child,' said he, 'there she is suffering and dying,
and, just like her mother, thinking of everybody but herself. That is
what affects me so — to see the poor child dying, and not thinking
of herself, but of everybody else first. She is the best woman that
ever lived except her mother! What shall I do? What shall I do?'*

*"Mr. Webster was completely overcome by his grief. He dropped
asleep after a while, and I left him."*

*From the time of the General's spectacular victories in the Mexi-
can War, Webster had been predicting Taylor's nomination for
President, expressing doubt only as to which party would be able
to claim him. But Webster still hoped for the nomination himself,
and was disheartened when at the June 1848 convention the Whigs
went for Taylor.*

[*Letters to Fletcher, from Washington: June 10, 1848*]

As to the future, *keep entirely quiet till I see you.* I suppose
there will be an *emeute;* but it may be quite a question, whether
you & I, & our particular circle of friends, had not better stand
quite aloof. That is my opinion, at present; and until we see into
things farther than we can at present.

[*June 16, 1848*]

I shall endeavor to steer my Boat with discretion, but it is evident,
that I must say something, or else it will be said for me, by others
— and I can see no way, but acquiescence in Taylor's nomination;
not enthusiastic support, nor zealous approbation; but acquiescence,
or forbearance from opposition.

THE TAYLOR ADMINISTRATION

I see no way but to *fall in,* & acquiesce. The run is all that way. We can do no good by holding out. We shall only isolate ourselves. Northern opposition is too small & narrow to rely on.

I must say *something, somewhere,* soon. My purpose is, to enlarge on the necessity of a change of Administration, to say something of the North, & its expectations, &, on the whole, to express a hope for Taylor. I must either do this, or go right into opposition.

Taylor's ownership of a large plantation and several hundred slaves in Louisiana necessarily injected the issue of slavery into the campaign, and Van Buren, essaying a come-back, broke ranks with the Democrats to accept nomination by the Free Soil party. Webster was asked by a friend to support the Free Soil, or anti-slavery, ticket as a matter of principle. He replied:

[Letter to E. Rockwood Hoar, Marshfield, Aug. 23, 1848]

You are not one of them my dear sir, but there are those who will not believe that I am an anti slavery man unless I repeat the declaration once a week. I expect they will soon require a periodical affidavit.

It is utterly impossible for me to support the Buffalo nomination; I have no confidence in Mr. Van Buren, not the slightest. I would much rather trust Genl. Taylor than Mr. Van Buren even on this very question of slavery, for I believe that Genl. Taylor is an honest man and I am sure he is not so much committed on the wrong side as I know Mr. Van Buren to have been for fifteen years.

Webster dulled his disappointment in the nomination by absorption in other matters.

SPEAK FOR YOURSELF, DANIEL

[Letter to Blatchford, Boston, July 12, 1848]

I have no news here except the French news. France must be governed, and can only be governed, in one of two ways; either a fierce democracy, in the shape of a directory, or some such thing, or by some individual holding imperial power. As to a government of regulated, restrained, constitutional liberty, it cannot exist in France, in my opinion, for any length of time. Look at their constitution. It undertakes to guarantee to all Frenchmen, not only liberty and security, but also, "employment and property." How can any government fulfil such a promise?

[Letter to Mrs. Paige, Marshfield, Thanksgiving, 1848]

Here are a wild black duck and a summer duck, or wood duck, which have been fed in our poultry yard. I send them with their feathers on, that you may see what beautiful productions of nature the voluptuous human biped devours every day, with no other thought than whether they "taste good."

[Letter to Everett, Boston, Nov. 28, 1848]

I am tired of Congress. The long sessions wear me down, with their tediousness, as much as with their toil. In the mean time, life is running off, while I make no progress towards accomplishing an object which has engaged my contemplations for many years, "A History of the Constitution of the United States, and President Washington's Administration." This project has long had existence as an idea; and as an idea I fear it is likely to die. My remarks before the young merchants, were heads of what I have thought might fill a chapter or two. If my time were not all frittered or wasted between a little attention to politics and a little attention to professional and personal duties, I might possibly yet achieve part of my purpose.

But, as usual, it was Marshfield and the love of making things grow that revived his spirits.

[*Letter to Porter Wright, Dec. 14, 1848*]

Washington, December 14, 1848

I arrived here last evening, in good health, except a slight cold, taken in the cars. On the way I fell in with Governor Hill, and had another talk with him about potatoes. He says he has raised two thousand bushels this year; and sold one thousand in Boston, at over three dollars per barrel. He says his potato crop has paid all the labor on his whole farm. His land is pine land, sandy, and with a thin soil. He ploughed it, and subsoil ploughed it. He thinks subsoil ploughing excellent for all lands; that it doubles the crop. His principal kind of potatoes is the York red, sometimes called the Pennsylvania red; it is not much like our long reds. He uses compost for manure altogether, ploughing or harrowing it in, and puts none in the hole. He plants as early as he can. He says he has twenty acres now under way for next year. There is also a Mr. Kimball, living on Long Island, on land much like ours, who says his potato crop this year has given him one hundred dollars per acre.

These statements have half led me to think of one more trial, on a large scale; that is, the whole field opposite your house. The only difficulty in making the trial, will be the manure. Can we make compost enough? That is the question. With mud and manure from the ox barn, with a hundred bushels of bone dust, together with some lime, and some ashes, can we make three hundred loads of compost manure? I am afraid it would be difficult; but I wish you to consider it. We have strength of team enough to do the work. If we could be getting the mud and the barn manure, and hog manure together in a pile, in January and February, we might, toward the 1st of March, pitch it over, and mix with it the bone dust, ashes, and lime, and put all in a heap, and by April it would be heated, dissolved, and fit for use. Think of all this. I do not wish to break up a small field. If we make trial, it must be on a large scale, and exactly according to the approved course in such husbandry. The main mass must be mud. If you have resolution to undertake the job, I will get the lime and bones when I go home, and the ashes when we can. I repeat, the great ingredient must be mud, heated and dissolved by barn manure, bone dust, lime, etc.

I believe there is no doubt I shall return about Christmas.

That he did not get home for Christmas we know from his letters to George Ticknor and to Fletcher.

[Letter to Ticknor, Dec. 21, 1848]

Washington, Louisiana Avenue, next the Unitarian Church. December 21, 1843, Thursday Evening, alone, over a small wood-fire

I thank you for yours, which I received this morning. I remember that next Monday is Christmas; and I have an idea, not indistinct, of Park Street, four o'clock — certain ladies — a certain gentleman, and a good dinner. But pity me; here I am. A case is before the court, of some importance.

Mr. Ashmun spoke yesterday, all day, "from morn till noon, from noon till dewy eve," and dropped, etc., "with the setting sun."

Mr. John Davis has occupied this whole day, and he has either not finished, or else, like the angel to whom enraptured Adam listened, though he has finished, he "seems still speaking."

Meanwhile, I am, with affection for you and yours,

RUSTICUS EXPECTANS

[Letter to Fletcher, Dec. 26, 1848]

My rheumatism seems going off, & I hope to get away, either

this afternoon or tomorrow. I have written Mr. Geo. T. Curtis not to let the Patent cause wait for me.

Saving & excepting a stiff back, I am quite well. I suppose I took cold, in the Court room, on Friday. When I finished, the heat was suffocating, the thermometer being at 90. The Court immediately adjourned — all the doors & windows were opened, & the damp air rushed in. I did all I could to protect myself. It was just such an exposure which caused Mr. Pinkney's death. He had been arguing, against me, the cause arising on Gov. Dudley's Will, the first case, I think in 10 or 11 Wheaton. He came into Court next morning, pale as a Ghost; spoke to me, went to his lodgings at Browns, & never again went out alive.

I argued my cause well enough, & if I were not always unlucky, now a days, in such cases, I should think I saw a glimmering of success. But tho' we shall get 4 Judges, I fear we may not a 5th.

I am reading Lord Campbell's lives of the Lord Chancellors. If you have credit enough, run in debt for the Book, & read it the first thing you do. Do this, careful & thoroughly, & you will imbibe a new love for legal studies.

Another letter written shortly thereafter gives us a further indication of Webster's mood, reflecting his discouragement and the longing to lighten the load of his practice. In another three days he would be sixty-seven.

[*Letter to Gen. S. P. Lyman, Boston, Jan. 15, 1849*]

I am afraid my luck is always bad, and I fear is always to be so. It will be said, or may be said hereafter, Mr. Webster was a laborious man in his profession and other pursuits; he never tasted of the bread of idleness; his profession yielded him, at some times, large amounts of income: but he seems never to have aimed at accumulation, and perhaps was not justly sensible of the importance and duty of preservation. Riches were never before his eyes as a leading object of regard. When young and poor, he was more earnest in struggling for eminence than in efforts for making money; and, in after life, reputation, public regard, and usefulness in high pursuits mainly engrossed his attention. He always said, also, that he was never destined to be rich; that no such star presided over his birth; that he never obtained any thing by any attempts or efforts out of the line of his profession; that his friends, on several occasions, induced him to take an interest in business operations; that as often as he did so loss resulted, till he used to say, when spoken to on such subjects, "Gentlemen, if you have any projects for money-making, I pray you keep me out of them; my singular destiny mars every thing of that sort, and would be sure to overwhelm your own better fortunes."

Many thought that Webster would or should be included in Taylor's cabinet. Webster revealed his own thoughts on the subject in letters to his friend Blatchford:

[*Boston, Dec. 5, 1848*]

My dear friend! I am old, and poor, and proud. All these things beckon me to retirement, to take care of myself — and, as I cannot act the first part, to act none. That is exactly my feeling; without being pressed to say what I would or would not do, in case of the arising of an exigency, in which these who have been friendly, and are entitled to best regards from me, might think I could be of *essential* service.

[*Washington, Jan. 1, 1849*]

A beautiful bright morning. The long twilight of such a morning is charming — the sun shining along beneath the horizon, showing his light a great while before he shows himself. As all is open before my southern and eastern windows, I gazed on his "bright track" an hour this morning. The evening twilight of winter would be equally beautiful in fine weather, and more often seen, but the air is usually not clear enough toward evening.

My dear sir, I hardly think a "certain event" so probable as Mr. Hall seems to regard it. In the first place, there will be "cliques" opposed to it, formed by those who wish the principal control themselves. In the next place, allowing much good sense and magnanimity to the President-elect, he still knows that, if my opinion had prevailed, he would not have been nominated.

Pray think of something else, and if something better cannot be done. I am willing to stay in the Senate, if that should be thought desirable, though I should prefer to leave it. What I sincerely wish, and all that I wish respecting myself, is to see Fletcher placed in a position to support his family, and myself left to my profession, my studies, or my ease.

[*Jan. 16, 1849*]

My dear sir, if possible, without sacrificing objects dear and important to friends, let me be left out of all cabinets but that of Porter Wright, Seth Weston, and Seth Peterson.

[*Feb. 25, 1849*]

I passed half an hour last evening with Genl Taylor. He was pleasant and conversable enough, and by no means of such a harsh and stern countenance as the pictures represent him. Our conversation was general. He said nothing to me, nor I to him, of Cabinet appointments.

All comes back to the original points. General Taylor means well, but he knows little of public affairs, and less of public men. He feels that he must rely on somebody; that he must have counsel, even in the appointment of his counsellors, and, regarding Mr.

Crittenden as a fast personal friend, he feels safest in his hands. This I think is the present state of things.

You had better burn this letter.

Webster was too buoyant by nature to retain a somber mood for long. By February his spirits had revived, as we may see from his correspondence.

[*Letter to Blatchford, Feb. 1, 1849*]

In the Senate, a quarter past twelve, Thursday morning, February 1, 1849

A cold and raw morning, the pavements all ice, no sunshine, and dark and lowering. But Mr. Edward Curtis was up at five this morning, out walking as soon as it was daylight; was in the market before the candles were out; brought over for Paul a grand turkey; then walked round the Capitol Square, touched the toes of Washington's statue, found he had cold feet, and came back as far as our house, in time to read the newspapers before breakfast. I heard him calling up Paul, to take the turkey, as I was kindling my fire.

[*Letter to March, Washington, Feb. 5, 1849*]

At that poor place called Marshfield, which you have never thought it worth your while to visit, and I am afraid never will, there are a few bottles, though but a few, of good old Madeira wine, introduced in the country through your agency, and some of it the fruit of your bounty. But here, in this great city, I have not a single drop of such wine as I have now mentioned. Not having fallen into the Sherry heresy, I like a glass of Madeira sometimes myself. But that is not important. There comes our new President, however, and I should like to be able to offer to him and his attendants a glass of what you and I regard as fit to drink.

Therefore, I will be obliged to you to send me a dozen or two of such a quality of wine as you think likely to make a favorable impression on the taste of the chief magistrate elect, and I will cheerfully defray cost and charges.

Mr. Edward Curtis is now with us, with health marvellously improved.

Washington, February 10, 1849.

In the Senate, two o'clock, Monday

[Mr. Hale making a speech on the "flogging of sailors," and Mr. Atherton raising a question of order. A gloomy day, — snowing out doors.]

I write to you to-day from habit, and from pleasure of thinking of you, and speaking a word or two without having any thing to say. If I meet a friend in the morning, I say, "How are you," and offer him my hand, and say five words about the weather, the ladies, &c., without having any thing of importance to communicate or expecting to hear any news.

If writing and sending were as ready and easy as talking and shaking hands, these morning salutations of friends would be equally pleasant on paper. Perhaps electricity will help us to the means of all this yet; so that when you are giving advice or receiving fees, in your office in Hanover street, I may speak to you from on board my boat, at "Sunk Rock," and tell you when I have a bite.

Mr. Badger is making a very able speech in reply to Mr. Hale.

[*Feb. 15, 1849*]

Our mornings here have been fine, cold, and bright, and the middle of the day warm. It is what we farmers call sugar weather, and if it shall last a month or six weeks, the productions of the year will be great. When the nights are cold, the days warm, and the wind west, the sugar maple or rock maple yields its sap freely. If the wind shifts, and brings warmer nights and cloudy days, the flow of the sap stops. And now, learned reader, "mark a distinction," as Lord Coke says. Good sugar weather is bad wheat weather. Wheat, sown last fall, shows itself, you know, as soon as the snow is off. If then there be cold nights and warm days, the young plant suffers. Under the warmth and heat of the sun, it vegetates, expands, and becomes full of sap and tender. And then the cold of the nights chills it, and often kills it, though it may spring again from the root. This is winter killing. It is indeed the same process of things as that which injures the peach-trees when their vernation is too early. Now, my dear Sir, you know many things; but I doubt whether you knew before that when you buy a maple orchard in Western New York, and a wheat farm by the side of it, the weather in March and April, which shall be favorable to your sugar crop, will be unfavorable to your wheat crop; so, you see, you grow daily wiser by my elaborate correspondence.

Mr. Edward Curtis left us last evening. We feel his loss heavily. He is one of the sensible and the agreeable members of the human race.

As always, there was the comfort of his farms.

[*Letters from Washington to John Taylor at Franklin, N.H.: Feb. 16, 1849*]

Be prepared to put in the plough. How large a piece of potatoes do you think you can manage? The ground must be ploughed, you know, with two ploughs.

It will be a very good thing to get some timber to the mill. We shall want boards. But I do not wish to cut any timber for sale. What I sell, I shall sell standing.

[*Mar. 9, 1849*]

I am sorry about the steer, but why do you not tell me how his leg got broken? You must know. I am afraid there was some carelessness, something left out of place. Was there not a cart, or a harrow, or something else in the yard or in the shed, which ought not to have been there? A steer does not break his leg in play or in fighting with other cattle. Why did you not tell me in your first letter what caused the accident? Let me know the whole truth immediately.

[*Mar. 17, 1849*]

I have received your letter about the steer. It is all well. I am satisfied there was no carelessness, and that is all I wished to know. But it was a strange accident.

You must now keep the cattle well. All the steers should have a little cob meal, to get them in good heart, before they go to pasture. The old oxen, especially, should be well fed.

Remember, that to plant ten acres of potatoes, is no small job, and that they must be planted very early. Porter Wright will do his best to beat you. But you have the best land.

[*Letters to Blatchford, from Washington: Mar. 11, 1849*]

I have yours of Friday. There are but two objections to my spending a month in New York, 1. It would cost me more than I can afford to pay for a month's subsistence and forage. 2. In and amidst the hospitality of the city, I should do no work.

My present purpose is to stay here till you come. Then stay a week longer. Then go to New York, stay there a few days; thence go to Boston, visit Marshfield, and then go to New Hampshire for a good month. You may think this odd, as New Hampshire mountains are cold in the spring. But Franklin is behind the first ridge from the sea, so that the damp and dreadful east winds do not reach us. The house has been fitted up a little since you were there, and is more comfortable, and there is plenty of dry oak chips. At that season there will be no out door attractions, and in one unbroken month I can do some useful things. It is easier to slip down to Boston and back, than it is to slip up from Marshfield.

[*June 15, 1849*]

I have been so engaged here, for eight or ten days, that I have hardly been able to raise my eyes from the table. I will write you again tomorrow, and tell you when I think I can get to N. York — and take you to Marshfield. And then, let the halibut and blue fish tremble!

A quirk in Webster's character was brought to light by the request of his old friend Eliza Buckminster (now Mrs. Lee) for permission to use a portion of his autobiography in a memoir she was writing about her father and brother.

[*Letter from Mrs. Lee to Webster, Mar. 16, 1849*]

In the memoir of my father and brother, which is just completed, I have made a short extract, of half a page perhaps, from the autobiography, which you were so kind as to give me many years ago. It is the passage relating to your receiving instruction from my brother at Exeter Academy, and the difficulty which you found in taking part in the declamations of your class. The anecdote is equally honorable to you and to him, and I mention it to you only, because I did not wish to take from that biography one word, or use any liberty with it, unless favored with your permission.

Will you be so kind as to let me know, before it is too late, if a shadow of objection should occur to you.

[*Letters to Mrs. Lee: May 25, 1849*]

I was quite willing to trust your discretion in publishing any thing said or written by me, respecting your father and brother.

But the extract which you have published from the "manuscript" says quite too much about myself, while it says little of your brother; and I regret that it should be known, publicly, that any such thing as my "autobiography" should exist anywhere. Under the permission which I gave you, I do not see but you are entirely justified in publishing what you have published; yet I fear it will set people to talking on things in relation to which I wish nothing to be said in my lifetime. I trust, therefore, to your tried and ever faithful friendship to resist all importunity to make any other portion of the manuscript public, or to suffer any person whomsoever to peruse it or any part of it, or become acquainted in any way with its contents.

I do not know but my feelings are peculiar; but, truly, I am distressed whenever I see any thing in print about myself, which does not regard my public acts, conduct, and character.

With the truest attachment, always your friend . . .

[*May 29, 1849*]

I have received yours of the 26th. All that you say is perfectly reasonable and just, and entirely satisfactory to me. Give yourself not another thought on the subject. I am anxious to read the book, which I have a good account of from a common friend.

Yours, with true and affectionate regard . . .

Another quirk of character was Webster's feeling of fellowship for animals. He had three of his favorite horses buried with what he called "the honors of war," standing upright with their shoes and halters on, as a mark of respect. For his horse "Steamboat" he erected a monument with the Latin inscription:

> Obiit Nov. 3, 1838
> Siste, Viator!
> Viator te major hic sistit.

(Stop traveler! A greater traveler than you stops here.)

Even more than his horses he loved his oxen. One day as he was in the barn feeding ears of corn to his favorites, he said to Fletcher, "I had rather be here than in the Senate. I think it better company."

With little to hold him in Washington, Webster left early in the spring of 1849 and indulged his penchant for traveling.

[*Letters to Mrs. Paige: Apr. 21, 1849*]

> Steamboat *"Curtis Peck,"* James
> River, forty miles below Richmond,
> April 21, 1849. Nine o'clock, A. M.

We left Washington yesterday morning for home, commencing our journey by a little trip through the lower part of Virginia. But we have constantly regretted that we had not postponed our departure till spring. We find winter travelling in these parts very disagreeable. The sun is clear and bright to-day, but the weather quite cold, and all the stoves removed from the saloon of the boat because it ought to be warm weather. Mr. Seaton and Mr. William A. Bradley accompany us, and Mary Scott came as far as Richmond.

James River is a fine stream for steamboats; I have never been on it before. It is crooked, like all other rivers which creep through meadows and level countries, and the alluvial lands on its banks, are rich. Further down, they grow thinner and poorer. Here were the ancient aristocratic families planted, from which comes the saying, still in use, and now always laughed at, "First Families in Virginia," or "F. F. V." These great estates were broken up by the abolition of the right of primogeniture, which took place soon after the Revolution. The great houses remain, many of them, but half deserted and desolate, the estates divided or sold; horse-racing and fox-hunting done away with, or fallen into vulgar hands, and the ancient and affluent hospitality of Virginia, known no more.

In the mean time the perverse practice of tobacco planting has worn out and impoverished the lands, and they are only now recovering under the better husbandry of wheat-growing.

384

[Apr. 23, 1849]

Norfolk, April 23, 1849. Monday morning, six o'clock

I am rather apt to look at maps with attention, and to form tolerably accurate ideas respecting the situation of places, but confess my notions of the localities, at and near the outlet, or inlet, of the Chesapeake, were not precisely just. The entrance into the bay, between the Capes, is twenty miles wide; the great breadth of the bay then stretches away to the north and east, but opposite to the entrance, and nearest to its southern side, is the mouth of James River, coming down from the west, and here about eight or ten miles wide, and running into the bay between Old Point Comfort on the north, and Willoughby Point on the south. Above these points, the river widens considerably; and here is the celebrated riding-place, or anchorage-ground, Hampton Roads.

A century hence, when negro labor shall have been done away with, and white men become willing to work; when clearing the swamps, draining the marshes, and a better general husbandry shall have not only improved the soil, but expelled, as they would do, a great portion of the causes which produce autumnal fevers, this will be a most agreeable region.

Back in Marshfield, Webster wrote to Fletcher on May 2, 1849.

To-day I asked Commodore Peterson to go out with Mr. Hatch, at high water, seven o'clock, and go to "Ned's Ground," and there to fish, patiently, till after low water. I told him by so doing, he would get a halibut, or some large cod. The commodore obeyed instructions, and came in to-night with a noble halibut, and a fare of the largest cod ever remembered to have been brought into the river.

The secrets were two; first, he went to the right place for the season; second, I brought down seven fresh mackerel for bait; and as the schools of mackerel have not yet got into our bay, but have been daily expected, the halibut seemed ready to taste the first bit.

I grow stronger every hour. The giants grew strong again by touching the earth; the same effect is produced on me by touching the salt seashore.

[Letter to Blatchford, May 6, 1849]

The work of the farm has gone on well. The spring, though very cold, has been dry, and the weather therefore favorable to field labor. Porter Wright has planted twelve or fifteen acres of potatoes in one field. They are "Mercers," "Pink eyes," and "Peach blossoms," and are intended for early market in Boston. Another piece of as many acres is receiving corn. By the ancient rules of husbandry in New England, corn should be planted by the 1st day of May, old style, which is the 11th by the new style. But this was arbitrary, and had no reference to the actual advancement of the warm weather. The Indians' rule was a better one; namely, "to plant corn when the new leaf of the white oak has got to be as big as a mouse's ear." The field where the beets and turnips were last year, twenty acres, is laid down in clover. You remember it, on the left hand as you go down to the gate. The ploughed land inside the gate, on the right hand, is to rejoice in a crop of millet, and be put down to grass. Opposite, in the old orchard, two acres of pumpkins are to show what land we live in. I believe you were here in the early part of last autumn, when our hands were putting kelp on part of Fletcher's enclosure. Beets are to have the enjoyment of six acres of that, and a large kind of field pease, sowed in drills, of the remainder.

Cherry Hill, near the garden, will make a show of an acre or two of beans; and if all human purposes shall be accomplished, the north side of Black Mount, facing the house, which you know has had the appearance of a dry and arid pasture, will be planted with turnips by the 1st day of July.

The cattle have been well taken care of, and look well; the sheep especially. We have lambs, both South Downs and Cheviot, as fine as I have ever seen. In regard to the piggery, I omit particulars; the general state of things in that department is satisfactory. The progenitor of all the porkers, now eighteen years old, if not nineteen, still bristles up if you come near his habitation.

With the aging of his friends and the losses in his own family, Marshfield was less a center of life than it had been, and the urge to see other places was still strong. In the summer of 1849 Webster gives us another travelogue.

[*Letters to Blatchford: Boston, Aug. 5, 1849*]

If to-morrow should be fair, we think of going to New Bedford, and perhaps to Nasahwn, Martha's Vineyard, or Nantucket. Our objects are not yet exactly defined.

Like you, I am disposed to ramble. I have no urgent professional business on hand, and am disposed to play. But in three weeks I must be looking out for the return of my annual affliction. What can I do with it? If they tell me it has not been known in Martha's Vineyard and Nantucket, I shall stay there. Perhaps I am as likely to be benefited there as I should be at Halifax. I will write you "from the first port." I have been talking about blue fish and bass in the Vineyard Sound, and parts adjacent; but shall say nothing to you, until I shall have had some personal experience.

Edgartown, sometimes called Old Town,
Martha's Vineyard. August 7, 1849.

[Half-past five in the morning, and not another soul up in the house. A little rain last night, but a pretty fair and cool morning.]

We left Boston yesterday at eight, arrived at New Bedford, originally named "Bedford," by a Mr. Russell, in honor of the ducal family, then however only an earldom, of that title, at half-past ten. Waited some time for the boat, which the ladies occupied in driving round the city. Left New Bedford a quarter before two in the steamboat, dined on board, stopped to land passengers at Nasahwn; came through Wood's Hole, where the tide runs like Hellgate; stopped here also for passengers; this place is eighteen miles from New Bedford; then crossed the Vineyard Sound, seven miles to Holmes Hole, then landed, took seats in a public stage wagon, crossed over a level sandy country covered with shrub oaks, and arrived here at six exactly. Ten hours from Boston.

I thought I knew nobody here, but the hotel was soon full of friends, some of whom I well recollected, all tendering boats, men, tackle, &c., for fishing; guns and company for the plover plains; and carriages, with attendants, for the ladies. All sorts of expeditions were planned before we parted at ten o'clock. Among others these, namely; to-day blue fish; to-morrow, shooting on the plains; next day sword fish; the next a party to Gay Head, and so on. The ladies are delighted. I am looking round and meditating about locality, climate, ocean scenery, &c., that is, I have meditated in bed, and am now looking round by daylight.

It is a singular and charming spot. But of this more hereafter.

Ibid. Wednesday morning. August 8

Yesterday morning I went forth for blue fish. The boatman steered direct for the Sound, five miles north, then doubled the eastern chop of the harbor, Cape Poge, called Pogue, where the light is, and ran along close to the shore on the eastern side of the island. The wind was unsteady and baffling, and much thwarted and perplexed the boatman, who intended to make a great day of it. At half-past nine o'clock we found fish, and practised our vocation at intervals, as the breeze would allow, till half-past one. We took forty-three fish, I think my takings were twenty-five. The boatman took a few, and a gentleman with us the rest.

In point of size, the fish are not much different from those we found in Duxbury Bay, perhaps a little larger, but this may be owing to the advance of the season. I thought them remarkably fat and plump, and they pulled like horses. Once or twice we saw schools of them above water, leaping and frollicking. I thought as good fishing as any we had was when we lay at anchor, and threw the hook, at the end of a long line, into the foaming and roaring surf. One thing was new to me. You have seen on the surface of the sea, those smooth places, which fishermen and sailors call "slicks." We met with them yesterday, and our boatman made for them, whenever discovered. He said they were caused by the blue fish chopping up their prey. That is to say, these voracious fellows get into a school of menhaden, which are too large to swallow whole, and they bite them into pieces, to suit their tastes. And the oil from this butchery, rising to the surface, makes the slick. Whatever the cause may be, we invariably found fish plenty whenever we came to a "slick."

Ubi Supra. Wednesday evening, nine o'clock

I have made a poor hand to-day, among the plovers, though I have had a good deal of pleasant driving over the plains. The mode of shooting is from a wagon, after the manner of Hampstead. My eye is hardly quick enough to see the birds in the grass, and I am a little too much out of play to be sure of them when they rise. I remember once at Sandwich, having Fletcher in the chaise, and Julia in my lap, and holding them both, and also the reins in one hand, and shooting a plover on the wing, holding the gun in the other, the bird being so directly over head as to fall within two rods of the chaise.

Ibid., August 10, ten A. M.

We went to Gay Head yesterday, a distance of twenty miles, and returned, tired and covered with dust, in the evening. The eastern end of the island is a sandy plain, the western a region of high, rocky hills. In both the roads are bad. But Gay Head is a place worth seeing. It is a remarkable promontory, at the western extremity of the island, one hundred and fifty feet high, with a naked face, or escarpment, toward the sea. The cliff is not perpendicular, though nearly so, nor is it smooth or unbroken. It presents alternate ridges and depressions, or ravines, not always running in straight lines. The great peculiarity is the geological structure, which is exposed to view. The whole hill, generally speaking, seems to be clay, but this clay is of various colors, black, white, red, green, &c. Some of these colors are exceedingly bright, so that they present a very gay aspect; hence the name. In the afternoon sun, and especially when recently washed by rain, the appearance is splendid and gorgeous. Fossil remains are found, from the water up to the surface, in several of the clay strata. We picked up, or rather picked out, sharks' teeth, and the vertebræ of some large fish, besides numerous shell-fish. Whales' teeth have been found very near the surface. Iron is also found, and pieces of charred wood, apparently limbs of trees, being exactly like charcoal. I do not know, or remember, what the geologists say of it, but I think it a great curiosity. It must have had, I imagine, a volcanic origin.

A light-house stands upon the height. When originally built it was found too high. It raised the lantern so far above the horizon, that mariners mistook it for a star. It became necessary, therefore, to lower the building. If this place were more accessible, it would be much visited.

We propose to leave this place to-morrow morning, at seven o'clock, take the boat at Holmes Hole at half-past eight, and be at Wood's Hole (Falmouth, on Cape Cod,) by nine.

Wood's Hole, August 12, seven A. M.

This place, sometimes called "Woodville," is the southern point of Falmouth, in the county of Barnstable, and is exactly opposite to the eastern end of Nasahwn Island. There is a passage or strait between the two, through which vessels bound from New Bedford to the East, or *vice versa,* usually pass. The current is rapid at the flow of the tide, the water not very deep and full of rocks. It has long been distinguished as a place for trailing for bass. It is a high promontory of some extent, and uneven surface, with a snug little harbor, which causes it to be called a hole. It has a fine view of Buzzard's Bay and New Bedford, Martha's Vineyard, the Sound, and Nasahwn. In point of position, and in regard to prospect, it is the handsomest place in these regions. Mr. Ticknor has passed several summers here. He says it is most remarkable for the uniform temperature of its atmosphere, hardly varying a few degrees for weeks, and even months, in the summer. It is almost an island.

From the room in which I write this, I overlook the Vineyard Sound, and see the land of the Vineyard, of course, quite plain; it being but five miles off. The number of vessels which pass up and down this Sound is prodigious. A hundred of them sometimes put into Holmes Hole in a day, if a head wind arise. Nearly all the coasting trade between the East and South, goes through this passage, as do often ships from South America, the West Indies, and India. I was told that in the height of the late Mr. Gray's business in navigation, five ships of his from China and Canton, were in Holmes Hole at the same time. Ships come this way to avoid the south shoals of Nantucket, which stretch off fifty miles to the southeast from the visible part of that vast and extensive sand-bank. Of late years, however, since improved chronometers make shipmasters more sure of their longitude in thick weather, it has become more usual to keep to the eastward, and make no land till they see Cape Cod.

You will be glad that I have arrived at length to the bottom of the last page.

Webster left Martha's Vineyard before he could test its effect on his annual affliction, and instead went to his farm in Franklin, New Hampshire. Here he had gained relief in prior years, and here again he found peace.

[Letter to Blatchford, Aug. 30, 1849]

I arrived here with General Lyman, Monday, half-past three P. M., from Marshfield, that morning.

My cold was severe coming up in the cars, but since Monday evening, I have hardly felt it. My eyes are weak, and I am obliged to avoid the sun; but, so far, I have suffered nothing in comparison with former years.

This place looks charmingly. It is the delight of my eyes to behold. Some of the crops were short, but the rains have revived every thing, and this beautiful meadow before me seems the sweetest spot on earth, verdant and smiling as it is, and surrounded by high hills. It was the view of some such spot which Dr. Watts spiritualized —

> A little spot, enclosed by Grace
> From out the world's wide wilderness.

The weather is warm, but the mornings and evenings are delicious. Salted meats are plenty, the chickens are tender and good, and the water so exquisite, as strongly to induce to teetotalism.

XXI

1850

THE SEVENTH OF MARCH SPEECH

Webster returned to his Senate duties in excellent spirits. For proof we need only read his letter of January 25, 1850, to Edward Curtis. They had sometimes shared quarters in Washington, but on this occasion were living a block or two apart and it was necessary to turn corners to get from one house to the other. Planning an evening together, Webster wrote:

Mrs. Webster and myself are fully resolved on essaying a visit to McLellan House this evening. Your directions as to the route are so precise, we have full confidence in being able to find our way. It is true the night is likely to be dark, and we shall be favored by no guidance from the stars. But I have always near me, for such occasions, a pocket compass.

> If dark and boisterous prove some nights
> Philosophy puts forth her lights;
>
> Though pleased to see the dolphins play,
> I mind my compass and my way.

Be pleased, therefore, to be ready to receive us, weary and way-worn, about half-past seven o'clock.   D. W.

It was as well that Webster was in a buoyant mood, for the session was to hold the maximum bitterness of all those he attended.

He had predicted that the annexation of Texas and the acquisition of additional territory from Mexico would fan sectional differences into a new crisis. He was right.

Northerners, adamant against any further extension of slavery, tried to bar it from any territory acquired from Mexico. The Wilmot Proviso, introduced in Congress for this purpose, became their battle cry. Southerners, equally determined to maintain a balance between slave and non-slave states, threatened secession if the Wilmot Proviso became law.

This was the third major sectional crisis. The first had been allayed by the Missouri Compromise in 1820, admitting Missouri as a slave state and Maine as a free state, and banning slavery from the remainder of the Louisiana Territory above the line 36° 30'.

The second had been brought to a head in 1833 by South Carolina's Ordinance of Nullification and also had been quieted by compromise.

Webster had publicly opposed both compromises. But now, once more, extremists were fanning the fires of sectionalism. In the South, Calhoun was saying "Disunion is the only alternative left us." In the North, William Lloyd Garrison and Wendell Phillips were preaching disunion in order to purify themselves from the taint of slavery.

Before 1850 the northern extremists had been relatively ineffective. But the mood was changing. The abolitionists were gaining in both numbers and power, and were exerting a profound effect upon public sentiment, both North and South. Early in 1850, Alexander H. Stephens, later to become Vice President of the Confederacy but at that time still a strong supporter for Union, wrote his brother Linton:

"On the 25th of December I looked to a preservation of the Union. But I have lately been taking a farther and broader view of the future. When I look at the causes of the present discontent, I am persuaded there will never again be harmony between the two great

sections of the Union. . . . We have ultimately to submit or fight. . . ."

More and more Southerners were swinging to this view. With them it seemed a matter of principle. Many conservative Southerners, especially in the upper tier of slave states, deplored the existence of slavery and sought means for its curtailment by schemes for gradual emancipation, colonization in Africa, etc. But they felt that the slave states must solve the problem for themselves, and they resented northern interference.

Worst of all, feelings on both sides were rubbed raw by the problem of fugitive slaves. In economic effect this had little significance. Fugitives represented only an infinitesimal part of the total slave population. But nothing so inflamed the mind, both North and South. Today, we tend to think only of the effect on northern sentiment, forgetting that the situation was equally inflammatory in the South. Southerners viewed the personal liberty laws of the North, and the active assistance given slaves to escape, as a form of theft and a flagrant breach of the rights expressly guaranteed by the Constitution. If the North was not willing to observe the constitutional requirement for the return of fugitives, Southerners felt that they had legal justification for terminating the Union. Indeed, Webster himself expressed this view, saying in a speech at Capon Springs, Virginia (now W. Va.):

If the Northern States refuse, wilfully and deliberately, to carry into effect that part of the Constitution which respects the restoration of fugitive slaves, and Congress provides no remedy, the South would no longer be bound to observe the compact. A bargain cannot be broken on one side and still bind the other side.

In 1850 these controversies erupted with explosive force. At a meeting of southern leaders in Mississippi, a convention of southern states was summoned to meet at Nashville, Tennessee, on June 3.

SPEAK FOR YOURSELF, DANIEL

Horace Greeley did no more than state the general understanding when he said in a New York Tribune *editorial on February 25, "We have no doubt the Nashville Convention will be held and that the leading purpose of its authors is the separation of the slave states." Webster's attitude toward slavery was clear and unequivocal. On February 15, 1850, he wrote the Rev. Mr. Furness:*

From my earliest youth, I have regarded slavery as a great moral and political evil. I think it unjust, repugnant to the natural equality of mankind, founded only in superior power; a standing and permanent conquest by the stronger over the weaker. All pretence of defending it on the ground of different races, I have ever contemned. I have even said that if the black race is weaker, that is a reason against, not for, its subjection and oppression. In a religious point of view, I have ever regarded it, and ever spoken of it, not as subject to any express denunciation, either in the Old Testament or the New, but as opposed to the whole spirit of the Gospel and to the teaching of Jesus Christ.

But the Constitution recognized the right of the states to determine this question for themselves. Indeed, without this fundamental concession there could have been no Union. Webster continued, quoting St. Paul for the benefit of his ecclesiastical correspondent:

But now, my dear Sir, what can be done by me, who act only a part in political life, and who have no power over the subject of slavery, as it exists in the States of the Union? I do what I can to restrain it; to prevent its spread and diffusion. But I cannot disregard the oracles which instruct me not to do evil that good may come. I cannot coöperate in breaking up social and political systems, on the warmth, rather than the strength, of a hope that, in such convulsions, the cause of emancipation may be promoted.

It was California that brought the issue of disunion to a head. In October 1849 a convention at Monterey adopted a constitution prohibiting slavery, and on November 13 this was ratified by the vote of the people, with substantial backing from Southerners as well as Northerners. President Taylor immediately urged the admission of California as a state, his message being read to Congress on January 21, 1850.

The President hoped that California could be admitted without arousing, as he put it, "those exciting topics of a sectional character which have hitherto produced painful apprehensions in the public mind." Webster, Clay, and others of longer memory and experience knew otherwise.

What Webster was to call an "Act of Providence" had brought Henry Clay back to the Senate after an absence of almost eight years. Although seventy-three and physically infirm, he still retained his genius for compromise. He himself expressed his philosophy as follows:

"I go for honorable compromise whenever it can be made. Life itself is but a compromise between death and life, the struggle continuing through our whole existence until the Great Destroyer finally triumphs. All legislation, all government, all society, is formed upon the principle of mutual concession, politeness, comity, courtesy; upon these everything is based."

Clay had worked out an elaborate plan, embodied in eight separate proposals designed to satisfy the essential interests of North and South, and, so far as possible, to remove the irritants to disunity. Spurred into action by President Taylor's message on California, Clay sought Webster's help. The occasion is described in an anonymous memorandum quoted by George Ticknor Curtis:

"Monday Evening, Jan. 21, 1850
"At seven o'clock this evening, Mr. Clay came to Mr. Webster's house, and held a long interview with him concerning the best mode of action to settle the difficulties growing out of slavery, and the newly-acquired Territories. I heard part of the conversation. Mr. Clay retired after an interview of about an hour. Mr. Webster

397

called me to his side, and spoke to me of Mr. Clay in words of great kindness. He said he agreed in substance with Mr. Clay; that he thought Mr. Clay's objects were great and highly patriotic; that Mr. Clay seemed to be very feeble, had a very bad cough, and became quite exhausted during the interview; that he had no doubt it was Mr. Clay's anxious desire to accomplish something for the good of the country during the little time he had left on earth. That perhaps Providence had designed the return of Mr. Clay to the Senate, to afford the means and the way of averting a great evil from our country.

"Mr. Webster said, further, that he regarded Mr. Clay's plan as one that ought to be satisfactory to the North, and to the reasonable men of the South; that he had not reflected enough upon any part of it, but his first impression was that he could adopt the whole of it; and, if, upon further consideration, he should hold his present opinion, he would devote himself to this cause in the Senate, no matter what might befall himself at the North; that as to the Wilmot Proviso, that was no shibboleth for him; that from Niblo's Garden, in 1837, to this day, he had declared his purpose not to assist in giving slavery a new home in any Territory of the United States. But, he added, if New Mexico be let alone, she will no more have slavery than California; that it is useless, and more than useless to be interdicting slavery where it could not exist, and with the sole effect of needlessly irritating the South."

Clay introduced his resolutions on January 29, and on February 5 supported them in a speech of great power. He pleaded for peace and understanding, and, with reference to the state legislatures, for a dampening down of the "Twenty-odd furnaces in full blast, emitting heat, passion, and intemperance."

At first, Webster was not inclined to share Clay's sense of crisis.

[*Letter to Haven, Washington, Jan. 13, 1850*]

I fear the prospect of a useful session is not encouraging. There is so much excitement and inflammation on the subjects of Slavery, Dissolution, etc., as that it overwhelms, or threatens to overwhelm, all really important measures. All this agitation, I think, will subside without serious result, but still it is mischievous, and creates heart burnings. But the Union is not in danger.

[*Letter to Harvey, Washington, Feb. 13, 1850*]

Things will cool off. California will come in. New Mexico will be postponed. No bones will be broken — and in a month all this will be more apparent.

[*Letter to Harvey, Washington, Feb. 14, 1850*]

I do not partake in any degree in those apprehensions, which you say some of our friends entertain of the dissolution of the Union, or the breaking up of the Government. I am mortified, it is true, at the violent tone assumed here by many persons, because such violence in debate only leads to irritation, and is, moreover, discreditable to the Government and the Country. But there is no serious danger, be assured; and so assure our friends.

But as tempers tautened and voices grew shrill, it became increasingly clear that the spirit of sectionalism was infecting even the moderates, upon whom the Union must depend. The Boston Daily Advertiser *reported that on February 23 "several Southern members of Congress had a long and interesting interview with Mr. Webster," and on February 24 he wrote Fletcher:*

I am nearly broken down with labor and anxiety. I know not how to meet the present emergency, or with what weapons to beat down the Northern and Southern follies, now raging in equal extremes.

SPEAK FOR YOURSELF, DANIEL

A week later, on March 1, he wrote Charles Henry Warren, in Boston:

I shall get the floor, if I can, on Wednesday, but fear it will be later. I mean to make an honest, truth-telling speech, and a Union speech; but I have no hope of acquitting myself with more than merely tolerable ability. Whether the speech be good or bad, nobody will care a fig about it a month hence, if any thing occurs, meantime, to give quiet to the country.

He also advised his Boston friend Peter Harvey of his intentions. Harvey came to Washington and later took particular pride in Webster's instructions to the Sergeant-at-Arms of the Senate:

However crowded the Senate chamber is, I want you to be sure to save two good seats; one for Mrs. Webster, and the other for my old friend Harvey here, who has come all the way from Boston to hear my speech.

Webster did not obtain the floor until the 7th of March. His plan to make a speech on that day became known in advance, and the setting is described in an article written the next day for the New York Daily Times *by General S. P. Lyman:*

"The day itself was glorious. At an early hour crowds of ladies and gentlemen moved along the avenue and besieged every door of the Senate chamber.

"On the opening of the galleries they were immediately filled by the most fortunate, but the crowd without was not sensibly diminished. At 10 o'clock, two hours before the Senate was to convene, privileged persons and other gentlemen and ladies with permits from Senators, began to pour into the Senate chamber itself. Soon all the seats, except the chairs of the Senators, were occupied by ladies whose smiles had won the privilege to enter, while the lobbies

400

were crowded with members of the other house, and other eminent gentlemen, standing. Soon the Senators themselves made their appearance with more ladies — their wives, daughters and friends — and then extra chairs and sofas, and temporary seats made with public documents piled one upon another, were called into use. The steps which surround the Vice President's chair were occupied by ladies, while between every two Senators was sandwiched at least one pretty woman. In many instances gallantry so far overcame convenience that the Senators gave up their own seats to ladies, standing themselves in the crowd. There was not unoccupied a spot in that chamber, above or below, or in any avenue leading to it, where the sound of Mr. Webster's voice could be heard.

"At 12 o'clock the Vice President took the chair, and a rap on the table with the ivory mallet before him called the Senate to order; then a prayer was made by the Rev. Mr. Butler, and the minutes of the previous day were read by the Secretary. The Vice President said that Mr. Walker, of Wisconsin, not having finished his speech the day before, was entitled to the floor. Thereupon Mr. Walker rose and said —

" 'Mr. President, this vast audience has not assembled to hear me; and there is but one man, in my opinion, who can assemble such an audience. They expect to hear him, and I feel it to be my duty, as well as my pleasure, to give the floor therefore to the Senator from Massachusetts.' "

Webster spoke three hours, and General Lyman says, "he never looked at his notes, except to take from them extracts which he asked Mr. Greene of Rhode Island, whose seat is near his own, to read for him. He never transposed a sentence, or attempted to change the phraseology of an idea he had put forth; but the speech came on, as the Mississippi rolls from its fountains, increasing in depth and width till it terminates in the ocean."

Mr. President [he said], I wish to speak to-day, not as a Massachusetts man, nor as a Northern man, but as an American, and a member of the Senate of the United States.

It is not to be denied that we live in the midst of strong agitations, and are surrounded by very considerable dangers to our institutions and government. The imprisoned winds are let loose. The East, the North, and the stormy South combine to throw the whole sea into commotion, to toss its billows to the skies, and disclose its profoundest depths. I speak to-day for the preservation of the Union. "Hear me for my cause." I speak to-day, out of a solicitous and anxious heart, for the restoration to the country of that quiet and that harmony which make the blessings of this Union so rich, and so dear to us all. These are the topics that I propose to myself to discuss; these are the motives, and the sole motives, that influence me in the wish to communicate my opinions to the Senate and the country; and if I can do any thing, however little, for the promotion of these ends, I shall have accomplished all that I expect.

Mr. President, it may not be amiss to recur very briefly to the events which, equally sudden and extraordinary, have brought the country into its present political condition. In May, 1846, the United States declared war against Mexico. Our armies, then on the frontiers, entered the provinces of that republic, met and defeated all her troops, penetrated her mountain passes, and occupied her capital. The marine force of the United States took possession of her forts and her towns, on the Atlantic and on the Pacific. In less than two years a treaty was negotiated, by which Mexico ceded to the United States a vast territory, extending seven or eight hundred miles along the shores of the Pacific, and reaching back over the mountains, and across the desert, until it joins the frontier of the State of Texas. It so happened, in the distracted and feeble condition of the Mexican government, that, before the declaration of war by the United States against Mexico had become known in California, the people of California, under the lead of American officers, overthrew the existing Mexican provincial government, and raised an independent flag. When the news arrived at San Francisco that war had been declared by the United States against Mexico, this independent flag was pulled down, and the stars and stripes of this Union hoisted in its stead. So, Sir, before the war was over, the forces of the United States, military and naval, had possession of San Francisco and Upper California, and a great rush of emigrants from various parts of the world took place into California in 1846 and 1847. But now behold another wonder.

In January of 1848, a party of Mormons made a discovery of an extraordinarily rich mine of gold, or rather of a great quantity of gold, hardly proper to be called a mine, for it was spread near the surface, on the lower part of the south, or American, branch of the Sacramento. They attempted to conceal their discovery for some time; but soon another discovery of gold, perhaps of greater importance, was made, on another part of the American branch of the Sacramento, and near Sutter's Fort, as it is called. The fame of these discoveries spread far and wide. They inflamed more and more the spirit of emigration towards California, which had already been excited; and adventurers crowded into the country by hundreds, and flocked towards the Bay of San Francisco. This, as I have said, took place in the winter and spring of 1848. The digging commenced in the spring of that year, and from that time to this the work of searching for gold has been prosecuted with a success not heretofore known in the history of this globe. You recollect, Sir, how incredulous at first the American public was at the accounts which reached us of these discoveries; but we all know, now, that these accounts received, and continue to receive, daily confirmation, and down to the present moment I suppose the assurance is as strong, after the experience of these several months, of the existence of deposits of gold apparently inexhaustible in the regions near San Francisco, in California, as it was at any period of the earlier dates of the accounts.

It so happened, Sir, that although, after the return of peace, it became a very important subject for legislative consideration and legislative decision to provide a proper territorial government for

California, yet differences of opinion between the two houses of Congress prevented the establishment of any such territorial government at the last session. Under this state of things, the inhabitants of California, already amounting to a considerable number, thought it to be their duty, in the summer of last year, to establish a local government. Under the proclamation of General Riley, the people chose delegates to a convention, and that convention met at Monterey. It formed a constitution for the State of California, which, being referred to the people, was adopted by them in their primary assemblages. Desirous of immediate connection with the United States, its Senators were appointed and representatives chosen, who have come hither, bringing with them the authentic constitution of the State of California; and they now present themselves, asking, in behalf of their constituents, that it may be admitted into this Union as one of the United States. This constitution, Sir, contains an express prohibition of slavery, or involuntary servitude, in the State of California. It is said, and I suppose truly, that, of the members who composed that convention, some sixteen were natives of, and had been residents in, the slave-holding States, about twenty-two were from the non-slave-holding States, and the remaining ten members were either native Californians or old settlers in that country. This prohibition of slavery, it is said, was inserted with entire unanimity.

It is this circumstance, Sir, the prohibition of slavery, which has contributed to raise, I do not say it has wholly raised, the dispute as to the propriety of the admission of California into the Union under this constitution.

We must view things as they are. Slavery does exist in the United States. It did exist in the States before the adoption of this Constitution, and at that time. Let us, therefore, consider for a moment what was the state of sentiment, North and South, in regard to slavery, at the time this Constitution was adopted.

Mr. President, three things are quite clear as historical truths. One is, that there was an expectation that, on the ceasing of the importation of slaves from Africa, slavery would begin to run out here. That was hoped and expected. Another is, that, as far as there was any power in Congress to prevent the spread of slavery in the United States, that power was executed in the most absolute manner, and to the fullest extent.

The vote of every State in the Union was unanimous in favor of the Ordinance of 1787, with the exception of a single individual vote, and that individual vote was given by a Northern man. This Ordinance prohibiting slavery for ever northwest of the Ohio has the hand and seal of every Southern member in Congress. It was therefore no aggression of the North on the South. The other and third clear historical truth is that the Convention meant to leave slavery in the States as they found it, entirely under the authority and control of the States themselves.

Now, as to California and New Mexico, I hold slavery to be excluded from those territories by a law even superior to that which admits and sanctions it in Texas. I mean the law of nature, of physical geography, the law of the formation of the earth. That law settles for ever, with a strength beyond all terms of human enactment, that slavery cannot exist in California or New Mexico.

If a resolution or a bill were now before us, to provide a territorial government for New Mexico, I would not vote to put any prohibition into it whatever. Such a prohibition would be idle, as it respects any effect it would have upon the territory; and I would not take pains uselessly to reaffirm an ordinance of nature, nor to reënact the will of God. I would put in no Wilmot Proviso for the mere purpose of a taunt or a reproach. I would put into it no evidence of the votes of superior power, exercised for no purpose but to wound the pride, whether a just and a rational pride, or an irrational pride, of the citizens of the Southern States.

Sir, wherever there is a substantive good to be done, wherever there is a foot of land to be prevented from becoming slave territory, I am ready to assert the principle of the exclusion of slavery. I am pledged to it from the year 1837; I have been pledged to it again and again; and I will perform those pledges; but I will not do a thing unnecessarily that wounds the feelings of others, or that does discredit to my own understanding.

Mr. President, in the excited times in which we live, there is found to exist a state of crimination and recrimination between the North and South. There are lists of grievances produced by each; and those grievances, real or supposed, alienate the minds of one portion of the country from the other, exasperate the feelings, and subdue the sense of fraternal affection, patriotic love, and mutual regard. I shall bestow a little attention, Sir, upon these various grievances existing on the one side and on the other. I begin with complaints of the South, especially to one which has in my opinion just foundation; and that is, that there has been found at the North, among individuals and among legislators, a disinclination to perform fully their constitutional duties in regard to the return of persons bound to service who have escaped into the free States. In that respect, the South, in my judgment, is right, and the North is wrong. Every member of every Northern legislature is bound by oath, like every other officer in the country, to support the Constitution of the United States; and the article of the Constitution which says to these States that they shall deliver up fugitives from service is as binding in honor and conscience as any other article.

As it now stands, the business of seeing that these fugitives are delivered up resides in the power of Congress and the national judicature, and my friend at the head of the Judiciary Committee has a bill on the subject now before the Senate, which, with some amendments to it, I propose to support, with all its provisions, to the fullest extent. And I desire to call the attention of all sober-minded men at the North, of all conscientious men, of all men who are not carried away by some fanatical idea or some false impression, to their constitutional obligations.

I repeat, therefore, Sir, that here is a well-founded ground of complaint against the North, which ought to be removed, which it is now in the power of the different departments of this government to remove; which calls for the enactment of proper laws authorizing the judicature of this government, in the several States, to do all that is necessary for the recapture of fugitive slaves and for their restoration to those who claim them. Wherever I go, and whenever I speak on the subject, and when I speak here I desire to speak to the whole North, I say that the South has been injured in this respect, and has a right to complain; and the North has been too careless of what I think the Constitution peremptorily and emphatically enjoins upon her as a duty.

Then, Sir, there are the Abolition societies, of which I am unwilling to speak, but in regard to which I have very clear notions and opinions. I do not think them useful. I think their operations for the last twenty years have produced nothing good or valuable. At the same time, I believe thousands of their members to be honest and good men, perfectly well-meaning men. They have excited feelings; they think they must do something for the cause of liberty; and, in their sphere of action, they do not see what else they can do than to contribute to an Abolition press, or an Abolition society, or to pay an Abolition lecturer. I do not mean to impute gross motives even to the leaders of these societies, but I am not blind to the consequences of their proceedings. I cannot but see what mischiefs their interference with the South has produced. Public opinion, which in Virginia had begun to be exhibited against slavery, and was opening out for the discussion of the question, drew back and shut itself up in its castle. I wish to know whether any body in Virginia can now talk openly as Mr. Randolph, Governor McDowell, and others talked in 1832, and sent their remarks to the press? We all know the fact, and we all know the cause; and every thing that these agitating people have done has been, not to enlarge, but to restrain, not to set free, but to bind faster, the slave population of the South.

Mr. President, I should much prefer to have heard from every member on this floor declarations of opinion that this Union could never be dissolved, than the declaration of opinion by any body, that, in any case, under the pressure of any circumstances, such a dissolution was possible. I hear with distress and anguish the word "secession," especially when it falls from the lips of those who are patriotic, and known to the country, and known all over the world, for their political services. Secession! Peaceable secession! Sir, your eyes and mine are never destined to see that miracle. The dismemberment of this vast country without convulsion! The breaking up of the fountains of the great deep without ruffling the surface! Who is so foolish, I beg every body's pardon, as to expect to see any such thing? There can be no such thing as a peaceable secession. Peaceable secession is an utter impossibility. Is the great Constitution under which we live, covering this whole country, is it to be thawed and melted away by secession, as the snows on the mountain melt under the influence of a vernal sun, disappear almost unobserved, and run off? No, Sir! No, Sir! I will not state what might produce the disruption of the Union; but, Sir, I see as plainly as I see the sun in heaven what that disruption itself must produce; I see that it must produce war.

Sir, I hear there is to be a convention held at Nashville. I am bound to believe that, if worthy gentlemen meet at Nashville in convention, their object will be to adopt conciliatory counsels; to advise the South to forbearance and moderation, and to advise the North to forbearance and moderation; and to inculcate principles of brotherly love and affection, and attachment to the Constitution of the country as it now is. I believe, if the convention meet at all, it will be for this purpose; for certainly, if they meet for any purpose hostile to the Union, they have been singularly inappropriate in their selection of a place. I remember, Sir, that, when the treaty of Amiens was concluded between France and England, a sturdy Englishman and a distinguished orator, who regarded the conditions of the peace as ignominious to England, said in the House of Commons, that, if King William could know the terms of that treaty, he would turn in his coffin! Let me commend this saying of Mr. Windham, in all its emphasis and in all its force, to any persons who shall meet at Nashville for the purpose of concerting measures for the overthrow of this Union over the bones of Andrew Jackson!

And now, Mr. President, instead of speaking of the possibility or utility of secession, instead of dwelling in those caverns of darkness, instead of groping with those ideas so full of all that is horrid and horrible, let us come out into the light of day; let us enjoy the fresh air of Liberty and Union; let us cherish those hopes which belong to us; let us devote ourselves to those great objects that are fit for our consideration and our action; let us raise our conceptions to the magnitude and the importance of the duties that devolve upon us; let our comprehension be as broad as the country for which we act, our aspirations as high as its certain destiny; let us not be pigmies in a case that calls for men.

XXII

1850

SEVENTH OF MARCH SPEECH —
THE AFTERMATH

[Letter to Ticknor, Mar. 17, 1850]

My poor speech is launched forth, and is a good deal tossed upon the waves. I am happy that Mrs. Ticknor's good wishes attend it. There is one comfort, and that is, that if its fate should be to go to the bottom, it has no cargo of value, and only one passenger to be drowned.

Webster had addressed his appeal to the moderates. He expected opposition from the extremists, but if the middle-of-the-roaders, North and South, would pull together, the Union could be saved. On March 13 he wrote Franklin Haven in Boston:

I thank you for your letter, rec'd this morning. We shall have a fight with the abolitionists, under the lead I fear of Mr. Seward; and a fight, too, with the violent party of the South under the lead of Mr. Calhoun. But I shall stand on the principles of my speech to the end; & we shall beat them, & the Union party will triumph. Tell Peter Harvey not to despond. If necessary, I will take the stump in every village in New England. We will put the disorganizers down, if we can.

The conservative reaction was enthusiastic. Letters poured in, and with them some remarkably tangible evidences of approval. William W. Corcoran, Washington banker, went to his safe and canceled two notes of Webster's for upwards of $5,000, and for-

warded them to him, together with a personal check for $1,000. On March 9 Webster replied:

In all sincerity I am proud of your approbation of my speech, as I feel you are a competent judge, and one who can have no wish but for the preservation of the Government and the safety and security of private rights.

For what else I received with your note I pray you to receive my thanks. If there be a man in the country who either doubts your liberality or envies your prosperity, be assured I am not that man.

From New York came a letter bearing fourteen signatures, saying: "In behalf of our fellow-citizen, Mr. Geo. W. Egleston, now in California, we transmit to you a golden chain, manufactured under his direction, from the mineral products of that portion of our country, and which he desires to present to you, as a fitting symbol of that glorious Union, of which you stand preeminently the ablest defender."

Webster's friend Edward Curtis, writing to Peter Harvey on April 12 from Washington, said:

"The Gold Watch & Chain are here — the latter about as big as your leg, above the knee."

Meanwhile Webster had prepared the speech for distribution in pamphlet form.

[*Letter to Fletcher, Mar. 21, 1850*]

The clamor for Speeches, So. & West, is incredible. Two hundred thousand will not supply the demand.

[*Letter to Harvey, Mar. 22, 1850*]

Letters come in thick; & all one way. As soon as we can get a decent edition out, I mean to send a copy to the members of the Mass.

Legislature & every Judge, Lawyer, Justice of the peace, Doctor, & Clergyman in the Commonwealth.

[*Letter to Harvey, Apr. 4, 1850*]

I do not care what a portion of the Press may say, if we can only get the Speech into the hands of the People. It is impossible to meet the demands here, under some time.

At this point fate intervened to lend the cause a helping hand. Webster's great protagonist, John C. Calhoun, had been suffering from consumption. On March 7, looking like a wraith, he had come to the Senate to hear Webster's speech. It was his last appearance there. On March 30, still murmuring concern for the future of the South, he died. Calhoun had long been the intellectual stalwart of secession and his death left the movement disorganized.

[*Letter to Fletcher, Mar. 31, 1850*]

Mr. Calhoun died this morning at seven o'clock. It is remarkable, that his body servant, who has waited upon him for thirty years, died also last night.

Mr. Calhoun was just about my own age, born in the same year. I found him a prominent member of the House of Representatives when I first took a seat in that body, in May, 1813, the year of your birth.

The Secretary of the Senate has come to signify Mr. Benton's wish that I should say something in the Senate to-morrow, which I shall try to do.

[*Letter to J. P. Healey, Apr. 2, 1850*]

We have a beautiful spring day. It is the day of Mr. Calhoun's funeral. It brings to my mind the saying of that sensual and heartless wretch, Louis the 15. One of his mistresses, Madame Pompadour, to whom he had been very much attached, but whom he forsook, for some other, died. On the morning of her funeral, looking out of his window, as he rose, he said, "Madame Pompadour will have a fine day of it."

Mr. Calhoun's death has certainly produced a strong impression. He has been in public life so long, that a vast majority of the people have no recollection of any Congress without him. South Carolina can hardly supply his place.

But the issue of union or disunion was still touch and go.

[*Letter to Samuel Lawrence, June 10, 1850*]

It is certain — quite certain — that if Massachusetts members would cooperate, the Compromise Bill *would pass,* and I fully believe, that with their concurrence, wd put down abolitionism effectually. Thus far I have not one concurring vote from Massachusetts. I regret this much, but hope I may be able to stand, though I stand alone. At any rate, I shall stand till I fall. I shall not sit down.

[*Letter to Franklin Haven, July 4, 1850*]

We labor under two great disadvantages. The first is, that many members do not wish to vote against the President's Plan. He seems to have more feeling on the subject than I can well account for, and I believe some members of his Administration take a good deal of pains to defeat the compromise.

In the next place, Mr. Clay with all his talents, is not a good leader, for want of temper. He is irritable, impatient, and occasionally overbearing; and drives people off.

On the day of Webster's letter to Haven, President Taylor was stricken ill and on July 9 he died. Again it seemed as if fate had taken a part, for the effect was to shift the power of the administration from opposition to support of the compromise measures.

[*Letter to Haven, July 11, 1850*]

It is not easy to say what will be the extent of the changes in consequence of General Taylor's death, and Mr. Fillmore's accession. It is at this moment supposed that there will be an entirely new Cabinet. Certainly not more than one or two can remain. Who will succeed to the vacant places, I have no means of saying with any certainty. One thing I feel sure of, and that is that they will be sound men. The President is a sensible man, and a conservative Whig, and is not likely to be in favor of any "isms," such as have votaries at the present day.

I believe Mr. Fillmore favors the Compromise, and there is no doubt that recent events have increased the probability of the passage of that measure. Nothing will be done in congress this week. The funeral ceremonies will take all that remains of it.

[*Letter to Haven, Sept. 12, 1850*]

I use the confidential hand of another to write you a short letter, my eyes holding out only to perform a small part of the duty expected from them every day. I am in the midst of my periodical catarrh, or "hay fever," or whatever you please to call it, but which you know all about. I read nothing, and hardly write any thing but signatures. The disease is depressing and discouraging. I know that there is no remedy for it, and that it must have its course. It produces loss of appetite and great prostration of strength, but since the event of last week terminated, I have some little time for rest, and shutting myself up very much, I keep as quiet as I can.

General Taylor was an honest and truly patriotic man; but he had quite enough of that quality, which, when a man is right, we call firmness, and when he is wrong, we denominate obstinacy.

General Taylor told me, in the last conversation I had with him, that he preferred that California should not come in at all, rather than that she should come in bringing the territories on her back. And if he had lived, it might have been doubtful whether any general settlement would have been made. Yet long before his death, and in the face of that observation which he made to me, as already stated, I made up my mind to risk myself on a proposition for a general pacification. I resolved to push my skiff from the shore alone, considering that, in that case, if she foundered, there would be but one life lost.

To Henry W. Hilliard, Webster expressed himself even more strongly, saying, according to that gentleman: "Mr. Hilliard, if General Taylor had lived we should have had civil war."

President Taylor's death undermined the power of the anti-slavery wing of the Whig party. As its leader, Senator Seward of New York had achieved a position of dominance in the Taylor administration. In the process he had clashed over patronage with Vice President Fillmore, leader of the New York conservatives, and the latter's accession to the presidency reversed the balance. And now Fillmore, long an admirer of Webster, turned to him for leadership.

[Letter to Haven, July 12, 1850]

You will hear various rumors respecting appointments to the Cabinet, but none of them will deserve credit any further than they rest on general probability. Nothing is decided as yet. The present Cabinet have all tendered their resignations, but they will not be answered till after the funeral.

The three important departments are State, Treasury, and Interior. I have no doubt some man known to be thoroughly sound in revenue matters, will be appointed to the Treasury. As to the State Department, I have no idea who will have it, although, if the power were with me, I think I could find a man without going out of Massachusetts, who has talent enough, and knowledge enough; but whether he is at this moment so fresh in the minds of the people that his appointment would strike the public mind favorably, may be a doubt. Nobody can well be Secretary of State who has not fortune, unless he be a bachelor.

Webster's reference to a potential Secretary of State was to his friend Edward Everett, but with the conservative Whigs back in power, Webster himself was the logical selection. His chief problem was financial, and his friends were again asked to subscribe to a subsidy.

[Letter to Haven, July 21, 1850]

In the morning, I received your letter, and one from Mr. Mills, and one from Mr. Harvey; and I thought it better to decide, at once, as affairs are pressing, and as the President, who had agreed that I might have time to go home, before deciding whether I would take the office or not, felt some anxiety, nevertheless, about the delay, and was desirous that, if possible, I should accept at once. He behaved in the most handsome manner, in all respects; and when the proper time came, sent me word, by a member of the Senate, offering me the Dep't of State, and desiring me to come to his house at once and confer on other appointments. I am quite satisfied with the Cabinet, in all respects. Mr. Fillmore is exceedingly cautious, and takes time for consideration; but he is not wanting in firmness, I think, and is a thorough conservative Whig.

I never did anything more reluctantly than taking the office which I have taken. From the time of General Taylor's death, I supposed it might be offered, and pressed hard upon me, by members of Congress. The fear rendered my nights sleepless. And the truth is, I was so much urged, on all hands, that resistance was out of the case, except upon the grounds which the letter received yesterday removed.

With money worries temporarily solved, Webster settled happily into the State Department duties which he had already grown to love.

THE AFTERMATH

[Letter to Fletcher, July 23, 1850]

I gave directions yesterday to have my old rooms arranged for me. This morning, at ten o'clock, I was sworn in, and I write this at my old high table in my little room. The rooms are all clean, and very nice. Mr. Zantzinger is appointed agent and superintendent of the building, and Charles Brown* is put again on "Continental Establishment."

[Letter to Ticknor, Aug. 15, 1850]

The President is a good tempered, cautious, intelligent man, with whom it is pleasant to transact business. He is very diligent, and what he does not know he quickly learns. More than all, he has read the Scriptures, and knows upon what authority it is said, "Be not puffed up."

Mrs. Webster has gone to her sister's, near New York. Mr. Curtis and myself are chums in this, the "vine cottage." We propose to remain here. Neither Mrs. Webster nor myself inclines to take the trouble of a large establishment. Our landlord says he will put up a little adjunct one-story building, after the Washington fashion, for a dining-room, and, with that superadded elegance, we shall have, as far as a house is concerned, all that little which man wants here below. Nor shall we want that little long.

His last speech in the Senate, on July 17, 1850, was a plea for the Compromise, ending:

It is natural, in times of irritation, for one part of the country to say, If you do that, I will do this, and so get up a feeling of hostility and defiance. Then comes belligerent legislation, and then an appeal to arms. The question is, whether we have the true patriotism, the Americanism, necessary to carry us through such a trial. The whole

* A Negro who had been with Webster for many years.

world is looking towards us with extreme anxiety. For myself, I propose, Sir, to abide by the principles and the purposes which I have avowed. I shall stand by the Union, and by all who stand by it. I shall do justice to the whole country, according to the best of my ability, in all I say, and act for the good of the whole country in all I do. I mean to stand upon the Constitution. I need no other platform. I shall know but one country. The ends I aim at shall be my country's, my God's, and Truth's. I was born an American; I will live an American; I shall die an American; and I intend to perform the duties incumbent upon me in that character to the end of my career. I mean to do this, with absolute disregard of personal consequences. What are personal consequences? What is the individual man, with all the good or evil that may betide him, in comparison with the good or evil which may befall a great country in a crisis like this, and in the midst of great transactions which concern that country's fate? Let the consequences be what they will, I am careless. No man can suffer too much, and no man can fall too soon, if he suffer or if he fall in defense of the liberties and Constitution of his country.

As Secretary of State, Webster continued to press the Compromise measures, marshaling all the influence he could bring to bear upon individual Senators and Representatives, and preparing an eloquent plea for the President's signature.

[*Letter to Haven, Aug. 1850*]

We shall get thro'. The weather is excessively hot, but my courage holds out, and so does my strength.

[*Letter to Haven, Sept. 5, 1850*]

We are all doing what we can with propriety. I consider it a fearful crisis. Northern abolitionists, & free soilers, & Southern disunionists, are the most reckless men, I think, I ever met with in public life.

Webster's driving force, coupled with the influence of the administration, swung the balance and by the middle of September all the Compromise measures had passed both Senate and House.

[Letter to Harvey, Sept. 10, 1850]

You have heard how all things have gone, so far. I confess I feel relieved. Since the 7th of March, there has not been an hour in which I have not felt a "crushing" weight of anxiety and responsibility. I have gone to sleep at night, and waked in the morning with the same feeling of eating care. And I have set down to no breakfast or dinner to which I have brought an unconcerned and easy mind. It is over. My part is acted, and I am satisfied. The rest I leave to stronger bodies and fresher minds. My annual cold is now heavy upon me, weakening my body, and depressing my spirits. It has yet a fortnight to run; and perhaps will sink me lower than it did, when strong excitement enabled me to withstand it. I have lost a good deal of flesh, and you will think me thin and haggard. I have had little sleep, not four hours a night, on an average for the whole six months. Now I mean to grow stupid and lazy, and, if I can get rid of my catarrh, to eat and drink like an Alderman.

Webster had won his cause. But success came at a prodigious personal cost. His New England background made him the prime target of the abolitionists. Their animosities boiled over and spilled into the histories of the period.

It is difficult today to comprehend the fury generated by Webster's 7th of March speech. But of its actuality there can be no doubt. Emerson, the philosopher, lost all sense of detachment in the bitterness of his denunciation. Whittier, in white heat, composed a poem of hatred likening Webster to Satan. Theodore Parker, the most powerful preacher of his day, was so consumed with passion that it became an obsession. Two and a half years later, the Sunday after Webster's death, when others were paying their respects, he burst forth in a sermon of violence and vitriol, damning the memory of the deceased.

Nor were they alone. Most of the great literary figures of Boston, then the "Athens of America," were zealous abolitionists; for example, Garrison, Longfellow, Lowell, Phillips, Sumner, and Thoreau. They rivaled each other in the fervor of their execration, and they set the tone of history for succeeding generations. Jefferson Davis, when President of the Confederacy, warned his compatriots that if they lost the war, their history would be written by Northerners. His prediction proved correct, but in these histories it was Webster who suffered most.

Perhaps the most rational explanation of the outburst was that of Webster himself. In discussing and deploring the separation of the Methodist Episcopal Church into hostile factions, North and South, he referred in his 7th of March speech to the disposition of northern intellectuals to think of slavery wholly as a question of morality and to dismiss as immoral the constitutional guaranties of the rights of slaveholders.

Sir, [he said,] When a question of this kind seizes on the religious sentiments of mankind, and comes to be discussed in religious assemblies of the clergy and laity, there is always to be expected, or always to be feared, a great degree of excitement.

It is in the nature of man, manifested by his whole history, that religious disputes are apt to become warm in proportion to the strength of the convictions which men entertain of the magnitude of the questions at issue. In all such disputes, there will sometimes be found men with whom every thing is absolute; absolutely wrong, or absolutely right. They see the right clearly; they think others ought so to see it, and they are disposed to establish a broad line of distinction between what is right and what is wrong. They are not seldom willing to establish that line upon their own convictions of truth and justice; and are ready to mark and guard it by placing along it a series of dogmas, as lines of boundary on the earth's surface are marked by posts and stones.

There are men who, with clear perceptions, as they think, of their own duty, do not see how too eager a pursuit of one duty may involve them in the violation of others, or how too warm an embracement of one truth may lead to a disregard of other truths equally important. As I heard it stated strongly, not many days ago, these persons are disposed to mount upon some particular duty, as upon a war-horse, and to drive furiously on and upon and over all other duties that may stand in the way. There are men who, in reference to disputes of that sort, are of opinion that human duties may be ascertained with the exactness of mathematics. They deal with morals as with mathematics; and they think what is right may be distinguished from what is wrong with the precision of an algebraic equation. They have, therefore, none too much charity towards others who differ from them.

Not all the abolitionists followed William Lloyd Garrison in calling the Constitution a "covenant with death and an agreement with hell," but almost to a man they felt that slavery presented a moral issue with which there could be no compromise, regardless of the law.

To the abolitionists, the Wilmot Proviso, barring slavery from the territories, was an article of faith. Until the 1850 Compromise, Webster had supported it. When on the 7th of March he spoke against it, Sumner called it "apostasy," and Parker said, "I know no deed in American history done by a son of New England to which I can compare this but the act of Benedict Arnold."

The moderates, for whose minds Webster was striving, thought he was right. Almost a thousand prominent Massachusetts citizens signed a public testimonial backing his stand. But the abolitionists did not relent. They never forgave Webster, and in their bitterness they gave credence and endorsement to even the most specious charges against him.

In time some of them came to claim that there had been no crisis. "Tush! Tush!" said Parker, "fear boys with bugs," adding as alleged proof that "the funds of the United States did not go down one mill." But with Parker facts come second to emotion. The reality of the crisis could not be denied; and, as Wilkinson was later to point out, there had been a sharp drop in the price of United States securities before Webster's speech and a gradual recovery thereafter.

For half a century after Webster's death the major histories of the period were dominated by abolitionist thinking. More recently, the tide has turned and historians now give a more balanced appraisal of the motives and effect of the 7th of March speech. For example, in Ordeal of the Union, *Allan Nevins has said: "No speech more patriotic or evincing a higher degree of moral courage has ever been made in Congress. For once Webster rose to the highest level of statesmanship. In the fierce light of history written by events during the next generation, hardly a line of his address failed to meet the test of truth and wisdom."*

Webster hoped that the Compromise would not only avert the immediate threat of secession but would also gain a cooling period during which some of the critical differences between North and South could be composed. The Missouri Compromise of 1820 had brought peace for thirty years. If this could be stretched for another thirty, it was not too much to hope that in the growth of the country new developments might swallow up the old dissensions.

This was not to be. But if the Compromise of 1850 did no more than to defer the Civil War for ten years, it was of immense significance. During that period the North multiplied its population and its industrial strength, whereas the South stood comparatively still. Even in the sixties it took the North four long bloody years to overpower the South. Had the war been fought ten years earlier, it is hard not to believe that the result would have been different.

XXIII

1850–1852

THE HÜLSEMANN LETTER —
BID FOR THE PRESIDENCY

*The immediate crisis over, Webster's thoughts turned northward.
In reality, Marshfield and Franklin had been in his mind all along,
providing a cushion for his Washington frustrations. In the midst of
the turmoil he had written letters to his farm managers from which
one would have assumed that he had no problems more serious than
theirs.*

[*Letters to Porter Wright: May 13, 1850*]

Mr. Frothingham prefers the young cow; so, when she calves, you
may take away the calf, and have the cow taken up, carefully, to
"Samuel Frothingham, Jun., Milton Hill." I suppose he would be
glad of her, as soon as he can get her.

I have heard so much of guano, for grass land, since I left home,
that I have determined to try it on the Cushman field, from the road
down as far as hay seed has been sown.

I wish, therefore, that you would obtain two tons of the best
Peruvian guano. It will cost, I suppose, about forty-five or fifty dollars a ton. Perhaps you had better go up yourself, and see Mr.
Breck, and consult him as to the best place of getting it. As the
season is advancing, no time is to be lost.

It is to be applied at the rate of four hundred pounds to the acre.
Two tons, therefore, would be enough for ten acres. I believe there
are about ten acres in the piece. At any rate, put on four hundred

pounds to the acre, and stop there, or keep the residue, if it should overrun.

The guano must be pulverized, and sowed like grain or grass seed, on the grass. If there are lumps among it, they must be broken and pounded.

Take care to sow it in wet weather, or just before a rain. It will be necessary to wet it a very little, to keep it from blowing into the eyes of the sower.

Now see how soon you can accomplish it.

[*June 19, 1850*]

Make the turnip-field wherever you think best; but be sure to make a good and large one. Have you sent some turnip-seed to John Taylor?

We shall not need Mr. Ames's geese.

Ask Henry Thomas to write me a long letter, all about the farm. It may be long before I see it.

But the strain was telling. No longer could he, like Antaeus, regain his strength from the touch of mother earth.

[*Letters to Blatchford: Oct. 19, 1850*]

You are exceedingly kind to write to me so frequently, while I am so unable to make you any suitable return. My health has been miserable ever since I arrived in Boston. I have been at Marshfield, and hardly able to drive round the farm more than twice. My eyes are well, and my head pretty clear; but a sort of asthma remains, with spells of coughing, and I am weak and reduced. I stay here to-day and to-morrow, and intend to go to New Hampshire on Monday morning, alone, to try the air of the mountains; and there to remain till I am better, or worse.

THE FILLMORE ADMINISTRATION

[*Oct. 21, 1850*]

Elms Farm, Franklin, N. H.

I am here, in two hours and three-quarters from Boston, ninety-two miles, without fatigue, and feeling pretty strong. The weather cold — a little cloudy — heavy frost yesterday morning. The foliage *indescribably beautiful*. John Taylor straight up. Henry and I his only guests, and three glorious chip-fires already burning. Can you resist that?

[*Oct. 22, 1850*]

This castle has a pleasant seat; the air
Kindly and sweetly recommends itself
Unto our gentle senses —

Throw physic to the dogs; I'll none of it;
Nor rhubarb, senna, nor a purgative drug.

But Dunsinane was a poor, foggy, sickly spot, compared with Elms Farm; nor did Scotland ever see such a *forest* prospect as the sun at this moment begins to shine upon. The row of maples, by the side of my field, for half a mile, shows like a broad line of burnished gold; and the side-hill, west of the house, displays every possible variety of tint, from the deepest and darkest evergreen to the brightest orange.

Nor could he escape from politics and visitors, even in Franklin.

[*Letter to Curtis, Oct. 24, 1850*]

I like much the spirit of your advice, about keeping people away. In the forenoon, I do pretty well, when the weather is good, as I leave home at seven o'clock; nobody knowing where I am going, and often not knowing myself, and I do not return till two or three o'clock. But in the afternoon, they are often pressing. The day before yesterday, I lay down on the sofa after dinner, and told John Taylor to take the great kitchen tongs, stand at the door and defend the castle. When I rose, he reported that he had knocked down seventeen, some of whom he thought would be crippled for life.

[Letters to President Fillmore: Oct. 24, 1850]

Franklin, N. H. Oct. 24, 1850

To the President, My dear Sir — I have been here five days, with evident improvement; but am concerned to say, I am not yet strong, nor has my cough entirely ceased. In dry weather I feel nothing of it; but it returns with rain and damp. I shall leave to go straight to Washington, as soon as I feel any way able.

The politics of Massachusetts are in a state of utter confusion. Many Whigs are *afraid* to act a manly part, lest they should lose the State government. They act a most mean part in their courtship of abolitionism.

Seven imported Unitarian Priests are now candidates for public office — viz. members of Congress; besides a host of others who offer for the legislature. These are all free soil, or abolition men. The Postmaster at Lowell is represented to be a brawling abolitionist — preaching daily, the duty of resistance to the fugitive slave law. I shall inquire into this, when I return to Boston.

I have been able to make a draft of a reply to Mr. Hülsemann, which I hope you will approve.

[Nov. 13, 1850]

Boston, November 13, 1850

My dear Sir — My only good news respects the state of my health. I have no longer catarrh, or cough, though not yet as strong as a lion, several pounds avoirdupois of flesh having dissolved into thin air, since the 23d of August.

Our election is all bad. The coalition forces have carried the Government of Massachusetts by storm. The Whigs will differ and perhaps quarrel about the causes which have led to this overthrow. I ascribe it entirely to the conduct of the members of Congress from this State, and some of the leading papers, in opposing and denouncing the peace measures of the last session.

I took leave of Marshfield yesterday, not without regret. The trees were leafless, but the fields were green, and the sea was calm as summer.

Among the things which detained me, was the seeing to the completion of a vault or tomb, for the deposit of me and mine.

I have lost one wife and three children. Their remains are now under a church in this city, which the progress of change is very likely ere long to remove.

At Marshfield, by my own land, on the margin of the upland, is a spot on which a party of pilgrims from Plymouth, erected a church, in the very earliest period of the colony; and here is the ancient burial-ground. It is quiet, and secure against change, and not far from my house.

To this spot I shall be taken not many years hence, and those loved ones, whose spirits have gone before me to another world, will be gathered around me.

I dwell on these things without pain. I love to see a cheerful old age; but there is nothing I should dread more than a thoughtless, careless, obtuse mind, near the end of life. Of course, it makes no difference in our future state, on which spot we mingle again with our parent earth; but it sobers the mind, I think, and leads us to salutary reflections, to contemplate our last resting-place.

While at Franklin, Webster put the finishing touches on what has come to be known as the Hülsemann letter, reasserting in the guise of diplomacy what had always been one of Webster's favorite topics, the superiority of republican institutions over the old-fashioned absolutism of European monarchies. This had been the basic theme of his speech on the Greek Revolution, and it had reemerged on occasion when extolling the accomplishments of the American Revolution.

In 1848 the Hungarians, under the leadership of Louis Kossuth, revolted against the rule of the Hapsburgs. For a time they seemed destined to succeed, and President Taylor dispatched A. Dudley Mann to observe developments and to recommend whether and when the United States should recognize Hungarian independence. The revolt was crushed through the intervention of Czarist Russia, and the Austrian Government took vehement exception to Mr. Mann and his mission. It called him a spy, and addressed an arrogant protest to the United States Government. This was delivered to Webster by Chevalier J. G. Hülsemann, Austrian Chargé d'Affaires in Washington.

Webster rose to the challenge. He asked his friend Edward Everett, as well as William Hunter of the State Department, to draft a reply. Then, into their circumspect diplomatic language, he inserted a bold, almost bumptious, statement of the manifest superiority of our principles of government over the absolutism of the Hapsburgs, saying:

The power of this republic, at the present moment, is spread over a region one of the richest and most fertile on the globe, and of an extent in comparison with which the possessions of the house of Hapsburg are but as a patch on the earth's surface. Its population, already twenty-five millions, will exceed that of the Austrian empire within the period during which it may be hoped that Mr. Hülsemann may yet remain in the honorable discharge of his duties to his government. Its navigation and commerce are hardly exceeded by the oldest and most commercial nations; its maritime means and its maritime power may be seen by Austria herself, in all seas where she has ports, as well as they may be seen, also, in all other quarters of the globe. Life, liberty, property, and all personal rights, are amply secured to all citizens, and protected by just and stable laws; and credit, public and private, is as well established as in any government of Continental Europe; and the country, in all its interests and concerns, partakes most largely in all the improvements and progress which distinguish the age. Certainly, the United States may be pardoned, even by those who profess adherence to the principles of absolute government, if they entertain an ardent affection for those popular forms of political organization which have so rapidly advanced their own prosperity and happiness, and enabled them, in so short a period, to bring their country, and the hemisphere to which it belongs, to the notice and respectful regard, not to say the admiration, of the civilized world.

It would be idle now to discuss with Mr. Hülsemann those acts of retaliation which he imagines may possibly take place at some indefinite time hereafter. Those questions will be discussed when they arise; and Mr. Hülsemann and the Cabinet at Vienna may rest assured, that, in the mean time, while performing with strict and exact fidelity all their neutral duties, nothing will deter either the government or the people of the United States from exercising, at their own discretion, the rights belonging to them as an independent nation, and of forming and expressing their own opinions, freely and at all times, upon the great political events which may transpire among the civilized nations of the earth.

Needless to say, the letter did nothing to mollify either the Chevalier Hülsemann or his royal master, but it quickly became one of the most popular of all American state papers. This was, of course, just what Webster had hoped.

[Letter of Jan. 16, 1851, to Ticknor]

If you say that my Hülsemann letter is boastful and rough, I shall own the soft impeachment. My excuse is twofold: 1. I thought it well enough to speak out, and tell the people of Europe who and what we are, and awaken them to a just sense of the unparalleled growth of this country. 2. I wished to write a paper which should touch the national pride, and make a man feel *sheepish* and look *silly* who should speak of disunion.

The Hungarian affair was to have further repercussions for Webster. In December 1851 Kossuth staged a triumphal tour of the United States and received such an enthusiastic welcome that it greatly embarrassed the administration, and Webster as Secretary of State. In addition, the affair inspired the gift by Webster's friend Roswell L. Colt of some prize Hungarian cattle.

[*Letters to John Taylor: Mar. 25, 1852*]

Trenton, N. J., March 25, 1852

I am here, attending a court, and shall return to Washington about next Monday. Mr. Colt, of this State, an old friend of mine, has made me a present of three imported Hungarian cattle — one bull, one cow, and one yearling heifer. He will start them to-morrow for Boston, where they will be by the time you receive this letter; and I wish you to go immediately down and take them to Franklin in the cars. Mr. Colt does not like Kossuth, and requests that the bull shall not be called by that name. You may call him "Saint Stephen." I do not propose to keep these Hungarian cattle on your farm, to mix with your stock. We will find room for them in due time on the Sawyer place, or elsewhere. I enclose you a check for thirty dollars. When you have seen the cattle, write me and tell me how you like them.

[*Apr. 21, 1852*]

I am glad you are so careful with the Hungarian cattle. I would not have a fatal injury happen to either of them for five hundred dollars. As to St. Stephen, now undoubtedly the best bull in the

United States, I would be glad to keep him at Franklin, if I could afford it. But it is worth more than a hundred dollars a year to keep such an animal, as he is not only to be fed, but must have somebody to look after him, both summer and winter; and I suppose it cost one thousand dollars to buy him and bring him where he is, and I fear our farmers in the neighborhood will not be willing to contribute what is reasonable towards his cost and expense of keeping. I wish you would consult and inquire, and let me know what can be done. If cows are sent to him, some of them will come from a distance, and must be pastured. It will be a man's business to take care of him. Now, how many cows would be likely to be sent, and what price would the farmers be willing to pay? Those are the questions.

I do not wish to make any money out of such a concern, and wish to benefit all the neighbors; but I am not rich enough to bear the whole expense. He is wanted in western New York, but, if I could, I should prefer to keep him where he is. How old is he? and how old the cow and heifer?

In due course, St. Stephen tossed and gored John Taylor, who was saved only by his enormous strength. Prostrate on the ground, he managed to grasp the bull's nose ring and, by twisting it, kept him from further mayhem until help could arrive. On July 16, 1852, Webster wrote to Edward Curtis:

John Taylor has recovered from the bull; and a painter has come all the way from Boston to paint an animal that could throw John Taylor over his head. John Taylor entertains a very bad opinion of that bull, and says he is no more fit to run at large than Kossuth himself.

This has, however, gotten us ahead of current events. The winter of 1851 was a busy one and on March 28, 1851, Webster wrote to Blatchford from Washington:

I have nothing from you to-day and am besides a little out of sorts. I am a little overworked. Yesterday over my table from nine to four, and then four hours in the evening in my study, upon an embarrassing Mexican correspondence. The day is fine, I mean to mount Morgan, in ten minutes, and take the air. Business seems to press quite as hard as when Congress was here; but I will break off and go North, next Tuesday, if I am well. I want to see the sea; I want to see Mr. Blatchford pull in a great cod; I want to see Mr. Baker's Alderney cows.

I have directed a boat to be made ready. We will hope that the skies may be propitious in the first ten or twelve days in April, so that we two, and Durf Hatch, and Dwelly Baker, may be on Ned's Ground, some warm, still, smoky day.

That summer found Webster again at Marshfield, soaking up health and in such good spirits that he could not resist sermonizing on the joys of country life. He did this with such easy grace that he could write the same vein both to his farmers and to the President, and could convey a like sense of warmth and companionship to each.

[Letter to President Fillmore, July 23, 1851]

Having despatched Mr. Benjamin late last evening, I rose quite early this morning and went out upon the sea. The day has been delicious, and the sea air seems to give me new life and strength. I ate more dinner on board the boat (cold salted beef and bread) than I have eaten any day since I left Capon Springs. Fishing for cod, haddock, and halibut is a common and coarse amusement, which the connoisseurs in angling reject. I like it, however, as it gives me occupation while we are out for the benefit of the air and the ocean. I caught thirty codfish to-day, weighing from eight to twelve pounds each, and as the boatmen were also fortunate we brought home a fare which astonished our neighbors. They represented fish as very scarce at this season, as they retire in hot weather into deep water. I told them that I thought I should know where to look for fish.

I never saw Marshfield look so well as it does now; the crops are heavy, the lawns and pastures perfectly green, and the trees remarkably bright and glossy. There are several hundred thousands of trees here, which I have raised myself from the seeds; they are all arranged in avenues, copses, groves, long rows by the roads and fences, and some of them make beautiful and impenetrable thickets on hills which were mere sand hills when I came here. The herds and flocks are in fine order. Llamas from Peru feed in the pastures with the sheep. We have a little fresh-water lake, which is frequented not only by the ordinary ducks and geese, but by beautiful Canada geese or wild geese, which breed in retired places, but will always join their kindred in their emigrations, spring and fall, unless their wings are kept cropped. We have also China geese, India geese, and in short, the same birds from almost every quarter of the world. As to the poultry yard, there is no end to the varieties which my man has collected. I do not keep the run of half the names and breeds.

The situation of this place is rather peculiar. Back of us, inland, rises a large forest, in which one may hide himself, and find as odorous an atmosphere as among the pines of Maine. In front of us, a mile distant, is the sea, every mast visible over the beach bank, and all vessels visible, hulls as well as masts, from the chambers of the house. A drive of one mile and a half, almost entirely over my own farm, brings us to what is called Duxbury beach, a breadth of clean, white, hard sand, seven miles long, which forms at low water a favorite ride or drive in hot weather.

These, my dear Sir, are all trifles, and of course without much interest to any one but myself; but, I confess, that to me Marshfield is a charming place; perhaps one reason is that so many things about it which now appear handsome, are the result of my own attention. I sometimes try to read here, but can never get on, from a desire to be out of doors.

SPEAK FOR YOURSELF, DANIEL

[Letter to John Taylor, Marshfield, July 29, 1851]

You will know this handwriting to be that of one R. M. Blatchford. You have seen the name. You have made up many a good fire of chips for him, and your wife has furnished him with many a good meal of mutton and turkeys. He and I are sitting over a fire here to-day in a severe easterly storm, and have been talking about your last letters. We hope before a long time to be both at Franklin together, and to have Mrs. Webster with us, and to see your crops and cattle, about which you write so favorably. We went a fishing yesterday, and brought in a good fare; but we did not catch a halibut, nor did we see or hear of a single haddock; there are a few mackerel in the bay, of an uncommonly large size, and we have just had one for our breakfast. Porter Wright's English haying is nearly done; he got in ten tons yesterday, well dried, from that old English meadow below Fletcher's house, where I have seen you swing that long scythe of yours without getting more than five hundred pounds to the acre. I suppose this year it yielded about two tons to the acre. Our barns will all be full. The potatoes on Blackmount are first rate. Our corn is rather behindhand; the ground was injured by the overflow of the sea in April; besides which, the season, you know, has been backward. We have eight or ten acres of the best-looking wheat we have ever raised here; the spring rye is not more than middling. Our turnips have come up very well, and the high hill where the flagstaff is, is all as white as a sheet with the blossoms of the buckwheat. Buckwheat means beech-wheat, because its kernel so much resembles the beech-nut. For instance, Buckingham County in England means the Beech County. Buckwheat is very good for poultry; it will grow on light land, and you ought to have a small field every year. It makes the best honey of any known flower.

Mrs. Webster is making us a nice chowder for our dinner to-day out of a codfish, very large and grey, which Mr. Blatchford took yesterday at a quarter past two o'clock, the Cliffs being just outside of the Gurnet Bank, and the topsail schooner Pine a little south of the south end of the Hummock. We then went north, and found cod and mackerel in abundance; the Gurnet light being in a line with the first falling off of Monumet, and the point of Brant Rock in a line with my Island barn.

It is likely that after this dish of chowder, we shall be so fortunate as to have some nice baked beans with a little slice of pork. If you were here we should invite you to partake of all these good things.

Webster was constantly pressing his farm managers for letters and reports. Like most outdoor workers, they despised paper work, and one can easily see from the correspondence that it was a troublesome burden. In addition, Webster kept them so pinched for funds that it is difficult to understand how their dispositions survived the persistence of his demands. Yet they worshiped him, and though they could not match his grammar, something of their spirit occasionally shines through their words. For example:

[Letter from John Taylor, Dec. 31, 1851]

Yesterday, I received a great present from Mr. Webster, from Washington; a large basket of canvasback ducks and a large turkey. Please accept my greatest thanks for all your great favors, and I hope I shall live to pay you for a part of them. I am sure that I never shall, nor ever can, pay you for them all.

Part of the secret was that Webster treated them as friends and men of intelligence equal to his own. Sometimes he even quoted Virgil for their edification.

[Letter to John Taylor, Mar. 13, 1852]

I sometimes read books on farming, and I remember that a very sensible old author advises farmers "to plough naked, and to sow naked." By this, he means that there is no use in beginning spring's work, till the weather is warm, that a farmer may throw aside his winter clothes, and roll up his sleeves. Yet he says we ought to begin as early in the year as possible. He wrote some very pretty verses on this subject, which, as far as I remember, run thus:

> While yet the spring is young, while earth unbinds
> Her frozen bosom to the western winds;
> While mountain snows dissolve against the sun,
> And streams, yet new, from precipices run;
> E'en in this early dawning of the year,
> Produce the plough, and yoke the sturdy steer;
> And goad him, till he smoke beneath his toil,
> And the bright share is buried in the soil.

John Taylor, when you read these lines, do you not see the snow melting, and the little streams beginning to run down the southern slopes of your Punch Brook pasture, and the new grass starting and growing in the trickling water, all green and bright and beautiful? And do you not see your Durham oxen, smoking from heat and perspiration, as they draw along your great breaking up plough, cutting and turning over the tough sward in your meadow, in the great field?

The name of this sensible author is Virgil, and he gives farmers much other advice, some of which you have been following all this winter, without ever knowing that he had given it.

This was typical of Webster's wide-ranging intellectual interests. And he liked nothing better than to share any items that intrigued his curiosity. For example:

[*Letter to J. Prescott Hall, Washington, Feb. 22, 1852*]

It is now settled that the turkey is an American bird, and was not known in Europe until after the conquest of Mexico, in 1521. Between that year and 1532, they became known in England, France, Spain, and Italy. Oviedo, a Spaniard, who wrote about the year 1525, describes them with great accuracy. He has no name for them, but calls them a kind of peacock. They appear to have been called in England indifferently, Turkey fowl, Indian fowl, or Guinea cocks. In France, they were called Poulets d' Inde; hence the present French name Dindon. In Italy and Spain also they were called by the same name. A pretty full account of them is in Beckmann's History of Inventions, London edition, of 1846, Vol. I, p. 147. But why were they called Turkey fowl? For no other reason, probably, than that, from the time of Henry VIII, the remote foreign trade of England was principally with Turkey, or through the Levant to the East Indies. But they had also trade on the coast of Africa as far south as Guinea. The vulgar notion was of some that this fowl was brought from Turkey, of others that they came from Guinea; hence they were called Turkey fowl or Guinea cocks. It is strange that so late as 1781, Mr. Daines Barrington, a man of very considerable learning, maintained that Guinea was their native country.

But the most interesting personal relationship during Webster's final years was that with the President. Eighteen years the junior, Millard Fillmore had been catapulted into the presidency by the accident of General Taylor's death. A solid, substantial citizen, greatly respected in his home community of Buffalo, Fillmore was almost unknown outside of New York and had none of Webster's brilliance. Webster was so clearly the dominant member of the new cabinet that a man of lesser stature might have taken it upon himself to command rather than merely to advise. But he treated the President with all the deference due his office, seeking and accepting his views and approaching their mutual problems in a spirit of whole-hearted cooperation. As a result, the relationship ripened into a friendship that was to survive even their competing ambitions for the next presidency.

SPEAK FOR YOURSELF, DANIEL

At seventy, it was obvious that the 1852 election would be Webster's last chance. For a time his prospects seemed excellent. His great rival, Henry Clay, was no longer in the running, and there was no one else who could match Webster in national stature. He came almost to think of the presidency as his due, and Fillmore gave him reason to believe that he would stand aside. Later, Fillmore changed his mind and became a contender, and in the split General Winfield Scott was nominated by the Whigs. The circumstances made it appear that either Webster or Fillmore might have won without the rivalry of the other, and the potential irritation was made the more serious by the fact that Webster had continued in office as Secretary of State. But notwithstanding the strains, their mutual respect continued, not merely superficially but with every appearance of genuine reality.

Webster's letters portray the rise and fall of his hopes.

[Letter to Fillmore, Jan. 1851]

I was informed by a member of Congress yesterday, "that Mr. Webster had been with the President at least one hour every day for the last ten days, that their interviews had no witness, & that it was well understood that it related to the next Presidential Election, & the candidates, &c." I replied that all this was news to me, that I did not recollect that a word about *Candidates* at the next election ever passed between the President & myself, & certainly never a word upon the point of *our* being candidates. My "informant" was Mr. Gentry. He had picked the matter up in the Hotel.   Yrs always   D. W.

[Letter to Haven, Washington, June 11, 1851]

You are as much, my Dear Sir, in the centre of my political friends, in & about Boston, as any other person, & rather more so. You see many of them, daily. And I have thought that I would, this morning, give you a little statement, of my present idea & purposes; not because any thing is definitely fixed, in my own mind, but for your consideration, & that of other friends, as you may happen to meet them, incidentally.

First, then, I am inclined to do little or no more hard work, this year. There is nothing urgent, or highly important, in the Department, if I stay in it: & I mean to cease labor, in great measure, & look after my health. But then, how long can I stay? If this movement in Massachusetts should make a strong impression on the Country, & especially if it should appear to receive responses from other States, will it not be proper for me to resign, & go home? I have no doubt Mr. Fillmore's friends urge him constantly to be a candidate; and altho' he has often said to me, & others, that he should not, I think he has been inclined, lately, to change his purpose. I infer this, partly from some appointments, which he has made, & partly from other occurrences. I do not know, however, how far *his* opinion or decision, may be influenced, by what he has recently seen, in N. Y.

Supposing Mr. Fillmore to be a candidate, or to intend to become one, I could not, after that should [be] ascertained remain in the Cabinet, with propriety.

[Letter to Fillmore, Franklin, N. H., Aug. 23, 1851]

I live in fear and trembling. This is the day for the catarrh; and it is now 2 o'clock and as yet no sign of its approach; but it comes like a thief in the night. My general health is so much improved that I think I can make a pretty stout resistance when it does come. I have passed this week in the neighborhood of the White Mountains. The weather has been delightful, and the air invigorating. If my disease should come on, in force, I suppose it will be best to go to the sea shore; otherwise I shall stay here some time longer. In the meantime I keep close, avoid all heats and colds, and damps and fatigues.

I have received today two letters from you, from the White
Sulphur, one dated the 14th, and one the 17th; and am happy
that you meet so cordial a reception from the Virginians, and enjoy
yourself so well. There is hope of Virginia, at least, that a strong
Union party can be mustered among her population; of South
Carolina, there is none. The only difference between her sets of
politicians seems to be, that one party wishes to secede, at once,
the other proposes to wait for company. Both, and all deprecate
and anathematize the union; and both attempt to rival, the one the
other, in giving it opprobrious names, and ascribing to it a hateful
character. I have no more respect for one of these divisions than
the other. Of true Union men, with half a dozen exceptions, there
seem to be none in the State.

*Although Fillmore had increased his political travels, he still ex-
pressed a determination not to succeed himself as President. There
was as yet no sense of rivalry between him and Webster, and their
relations remained cordial, even intimate.*

[Letter to Fillmore, from Boston, Sept. 10, 1851]

A very important vacancy is created by Judge Woodbury's death.
The general, perhaps, I may say the almost universal sentiment
here is, that the place should be filled by the appointment of Mr.
B. R. Curtis. Mr. Choate is perhaps Mr. Curtis' leader & is more
extensively known, as he has been quite distinguished in public life.
But it is supposed he would not accept the place. He must be
conferred with; & I should have seen him to-day, but he is out of
town. I shall see him as soon as possible. Everything being put at
rest in that quarter, as I presume it will be the moment I can see
Mr. Choate, I recommend the immediate appointment of Mr.
Curtis.

I came down from Franklin on the 8th with rather bad luck. To
avoid the heat, I took the evening train, which met with an accident

that delayed us, & kept me out till late at night. I took cold and was not well yesterday, but am pretty well to-day, & am going to Marshfield by the Hingham boat, & a carriage. I avoid the cars as much as I can.

The "accident" was a train wreck. Charles Lanman, who was with Webster, tells us that all the cars were thrown off the track except the one they were in. This was perched at a forty-five-degree angle, and the locomotive could be seen in the middle of a neighboring field. According to Lanman, Webster inquired of the conductor, "Can you inform me to what part of the world we are travelling? I have paid my fare to Boston and I will thank the locomotive to proceed to its original destination."

Webster realized that Fillmore would be under great pressure from his political friends and followers to seek the nomination. But as late as December 1851 the indications were that he would not yield.

[Letter to Haven, Washington, Dec. 14, 1851]

Mr. Ashmun leaves for home this afternoon. He *has seen many persons, & conversed with them, from the lowest to the Highest; & he thinks the coast will be clear, & known to be clear, in due time.* His visit has evidently done good, & helped much to bring things to a point.

P. S. I must pray you not to give a single hint to any living person, of what is contained in the lines which I have underscored.

Notwithstanding the assurances from "the Highest" that the coast would be clear, Fillmore was in the end persuaded to run. Clay came out strongly for him in what was almost a deathbed appeal, while at the other extreme Seward's followers in New York opened up such a bitter personal attack that it became embarrassing for Fillmore not to be a candidate.

On the first ballot at the Whig convention which opened in Baltimore on June 16, 1852, Fillmore led with 133 votes, Scott was second with 131, and Webster was a poor third with 29. Fillmore's main strength came from the South, Webster's from New England. For forty-six ballots the deadlock continued.

Fillmore had early asked his managers to transfer his votes to Webster, but there were too many whose second choice was Scott. Finally, it was arranged that if Webster could swing enough votes from Scott to boost his total to 40, Fillmore's managers could and would transfer a sufficient number to assure Webster victory. But the 40 could not be corralled, the critical stumbling block being the delegates from Maine who still smarted from the loss of territory brought about by the Webster–Ashburton Treaty.

On June 21 Webster sent the following note to Fillmore:

I have sent a communication to Baltimore this morning to have an end put to the pending controversy. I think it most probable you will be nominated before one o'clock.

Fillmore's reply was more accurate.

"I had intimated to my friends who left last evening a strong desire to have my name withdrawn. Your communication, I apprehend, may be too late to effect anything."

Scott was nominated but was defeated in the general election by the Democratic candidate, General Franklin Pierce of New Hampshire.

On July 4, 1852, Webster wrote to Fletcher:

I confess I grow inclined to cross the seas. I meet, here, so many causes of vexation, and humiliation, growing out of the events connected with the convention, that I am pretty much decided and determined, to leave the Department early in August, and either go abroad, or go into obscurity.

XXIV

1852

THE END

From the struggle for the presidency, Webster turned to a struggle for life itself. On May 8, 1852, he had suffered painful — and as it turned out, permanent — injuries in a carriage accident which he described in letters to President Fillmore.

Marshfield, Sunday morning, May 9, 1852

You will have heard of my accident yesterday morning, in falling from a carriage. The day was very fine, and I set out to make a visit to Plymouth, ten or twelve miles distant, with Mr. Lanman, my clerk. We were in a large buggy, or more properly, an old-fashioned phaeton, of course open in front, and with two horses. About nine miles from home, the king-bolt or transom-bolt, as I believe they call it (which from the fore part of the carriage goes down through the perch into the forward axle-tree, and so connects the fore wheels with the hind wheels) broke, and the body of the carriage, of course, fell to the ground and threw us both out, headlong, with some violence. Fortunately, however, we were ascending a hill, and going slowly; had it been otherwise, we could hardly have escaped with our lives. In falling, I threw my hands forward to protect my head from the ground, and this brought the whole weight of the body upon the hands and arms, turning back the hands, and very much spraining the wrists. The shock of the whole system was very great. My head hit the ground, though very lightly, and with no injury except a little scratching of the forehead upon the gravel. Nor was there any internal injury.

443

It was thought, at first, that no bone was injured in any degree, but I think now that one of the bones of the wrist on the left hand, was slightly fractured, but not so as to be dislocated, or be put out of place. It may probably make the wrist stiff for some time. We got another carriage, and came home as soon as I felt well enough, foreseeing that my bruised limbs would be more swollen and painful to-day, than they then were. In point of fact, the pain, though very severe last night, has abated this morning, but the swelling has not. I cannot use my hands at all, and am quite afraid it will be several days before I shall be able to leave my room.

A similar accident happened to me more than twenty years ago, and from that time I have generally been quite careful to avoid the like occurrence by the use of a chain, or some other contrivance, to supply the place of the bolt, temporarily, in case the bolt should break. With the exception of that used yesterday, there is not a carriage on our premises, great or small, double or single, which has not this security, but the unlucky carriage of yesterday was not built originally for my use, and I had omitted to see to this important particular. It is quite a mercy that the consequences of the fall were not more serious.

Marshfield, May 12, 1852

I received yours of the 9th at ten o'clock last evening, and thank you for your kind solicitude about my health. I had a great escape, and the more I think of it, the more I marvel that I am among the living. The carriage was old-fashioned, and very high from the ground. A fur robe had been thrown over the front board or dasher for use in case of rain. This incumbered my feet, so that when the carriage fell, I could not escape a direct headlong plunge to the earth. My arms saved me, but it is a wonder they were not broken all to pieces. It is not true, as some of the papers have reported, that I lost my senses, even for an instant; but it is true, that after I had walked to the house, a chill came on, which made

my teeth chatter, and caused a shivering of the whole body, which
I am told is not uncommon in such cases, and then for a moment
my eyes swam, and I felt dizzy. We were three miles north of Plymouth, on a high ground, which commanded a beautiful view of the
bay. I was pointing out to Mr. Lanman where The Mayflower came
to anchor, and showing him the island, still called Captain's Island,
which was the possession of Miles Standish, and where his descendants now reside. All doors were opened, and every aid rendered,
as all the villagers know me, at least by sight. I was particularly
struck by the attention paid to me by an intelligent person of more
than eighty years af age. He kept his eye on mine for half an hour,
hearing my conversation with others, but not saying a word. He
was a very old political friend. At length, I perceived his face began
to color. He put his handkerchief to his eyes, and said with emotion: "Your mind is clear, and your life is safe."

*His injuries were more severe than they at first appeared, and on
May 19 he wrote the President from Boston:*

Yesterday being a fair day, for a wonder, I came up from Marshfield in the cars, but am sorry to say that I suffered more from the
jarring of the cars than I anticipated. My shoulders and arms were
full of pain, and to be sure of right treatment, I immediately sent
for Dr. Warren, and Dr. Jeffries, who held a consultation. They
thought that in my anxiety to get well enough to travel soon, I
had made too much application of ice water, liniments, poultices,
&c.; they recommended an abstinence from every thing of that kind,
and to be content with the simple use of the sling, and as much
rest in the limbs as I could obtain. I can walk with ease and
strength, but I cannot put on or take off my hat, nor without difficulty raise a cup of tea to my mouth. I can sign my name, though
not without effort.

He was back in Washington before the end of May, however, and

445

*on June 13 he wrote Porter Wright: "Have a good long scythe
ready for me the first day of July."*

*Still sore from both his carriage accident and the convention, he
tried to regain his strength and spirits by visits to his farms and to
friends. On July 13 he wrote a long chatty letter to the President
from Franklin.*

I came up from Boston yesterday with Mr. Lanman; and Mrs.
Webster went to Marshfield, where she has affairs of painting, &c.
to attend to. Yesterday was a very hot day, but the cars were not
crowded, and they have an ingenious contrivance to keep out the
dust, without excluding the air.

This place is a spot of absolute quiet. It is a valley, lying in the
bend of the river. Railroad cars run across it three or four times a
day, and that is all the motion which is seen or heard. There is no
manufacturing; no coach, wagon, or cart going along the highway,
except very infrequently. The fields are quite green, shaded with
beautiful elms and maples, with high ranges of hills on both sides
of the river. There are seven houses in the village, of which two
are mine, one for our own use, and one for my tenants. Under my
eyes, at this moment, is the site of one of the last forts built on the
frontiers to protect the inhabitants of this and the neighboring
towns against the Indians. The Indians made constant attacks,
often so suddenly that they could not be resisted. A Mrs. Call was
killed by them on this spot, about the year 1755. The cellar of her
cabin is close by my house. She was an elderly woman; and her
husband and her son were at work in a field not half a mile off.
Her daughter-in-law, with her child in her arms, seeing the Indians coming, jumped in behind the chimney, hushed her baby,
and so avoided discovery, and escaped death. This baby, whose
name was John Call, I knew very well when I was a boy. My
father bought this place of that family. This is one of the very
many border stories, to which I have listened of winter evenings,
in the early part of my life. You will perceive, my dear Sir, that I

am old enough to begin to become garrulous; for it is certain that Mrs. Call's murder by the Indians, a hundred years ago, has little to do with the legislation or diplomacy of the present time. But amid these scenes of memory, I am apt to talk, when there is anybody present to talk to, and to write when alone.

From there he went to Boston and to the Paiges' in Nahant (north of Boston), as we know from the following to a fishing companion.

[*Letter to B. C. Clark, Jr., July 23, 1852*]

Mr. Paige's, Nahant, Friday Morning, July 23rd., 1852

MY YOUNG FRIEND — I propose joining you this morning, to pay our respects to the Tautog, but fear we shall hardly be able to tempt them from their lurking-holes, under this bright sun. They are naturally shy of light. "Tautog" means simply the "black fishes," "og" being a common termination of plural nouns in the language of our Eastern Indians. I believe the fish is not known in Europe. Its principal *habitat* originally seems to have been Long Island Sound, Buzzard's Bay, and the Elizabeth Islands. Seventy years ago the Hon'ble Stephen Gorham, father of the Hon'ble Benjamin Gorham, now of Boston, brought some of these fish alive from New Bedford and put them into the sea at Boston. They are now found as far East as the mouth of the Merrimac. They abound, as you know, on the south side, as well as on the north side of our Bay. Indeed, it is thought that by their own progress north they doubled Cape Cod, not long after Mr. Gorham's deposit, at Boston.

Thirty years ago, Mrs. Perkins, the wife of the late Samuel G. Perkins, a lady whose health led her to pass her summers on the sea-coast and who had a true love for fishing, caught a Tautog, with a hand-line, off these rocks, which weighed 20 lbs.

Still uncertain of his strength and future plans, he wrote the President from Marshfield on July 26.

I feel obliged to regard it as a settled thing, that I ought not to think of passing the ensuing hot months at the table of a department in Washington. You know how very ill I was when I left Washington last summer, and how severe, though rather a short, attack of catarrh I afterwards suffered. I should feel in imminent peril if I were to undertake to work through August and September, as I have heretofore done.

This being settled, the question is, what is it best to do thereupon? and when I say what is best, I mean best for you, and the success and honorable winding up of your administration. Now, acting from purely personal motives, regarding my health, and independent of all other considerations, it would suit me as well as any way, to resign at once, without going back to Washington at all, although I confess I should be willing, on divers accounts, to be in Washington from the commencement of cool weather till the 3d of March.

I wish, my dear Sir, that you would consider these matters, and signify frankly your own opinion and your own wishes. Or if you should be of opinion that it would be convenient to defer a final decision, then, as I have said, I will go to Washington to see you some ten days hence, if I feel strong enough, and the weather should not be too intolerable.

Early in August he was back in Washington. With the return of his hay fever he fled northward to Marshfield.

[*Letter to Fillmore, Sept. 12, 1852*]

I suppose that by this time you must have returned from Berkley, and hope you have had a pleasant and refreshing visit.

THE END

My march hitherto was rapid from Washington, using the boat when I could, and, when in the cars, travelling by night, to save my eyes from the glare of the sun. I was quite sick nearly all day in New York, and unable to sit up; but feeling better towards evening, took the Fall River boat, arrived at Boston the next morning, Monday, at seven o'clock, and came immediately home in a coach. I have thus been here a week; and the state of my health is pretty much this:

The catarrh is upon me in its various forms, alternating as usual, but as yet not so severe and heavy as on former occasions. My general health is not so much prostrated. If the weather be wet or damp, I must stay in the house, and have a little fire, to prevent fits of sneezing and noseblowing; when the sun is very bright, I am obliged to avoid going out, on account of my eyes, except indeed when the sea is calm, and I am protected by an awning. The bracing air of the ocean, I find very beneficial.

Mr. Abbot from the Department, joined us night before last, and Mr. Blatchford, who is fond of the sea and of boats, and content with fishing on a small scale. We talk of every thing but law and politics, and one advantage of my condition is, that it excuses me from looking into any newspapers.

But this time he did not bounce back to health. On September 16 he gave a gloomy report to the President.

I have not eaten an ounce of flesh, or fruit, or vegetables since I arrived, nor do I use tea or coffee at all. My diet is milk with half lime-water, water gruel, and sometimes a little thin soup.

I give up medicine very much, and try to get well by the strictest regimen. My physician says I shall succeed, but that it will require time.

And still gloomier ones on October 4 and 15.

449

SPEAK FOR YOURSELF, DANIEL

[Letters to Fillmore: Oct. 4, 1852]

I thank you for your kind and sympathizing letters respecting my health. The doctors have agreed to have another conference, before they make any statement. The reason is, that although all who know Dr. Jeffries and Dr. Porter have entire confidence in them, yet friends in Boston insist that they shall be permitted to send down a medical man of high national reputation, in his profession; and they have proposed either Dr. Warren, senior, or Dr. Jackson; of course, I could not object to this, and in a day or two I shall see them here. The great object, at present, is to check the tendency to inflammation and distension in the stomach and bowels. To this end some leeches have been applied liberally, and it is thought with good effect. I feel to-day as if I might regard myself as rather on the mending hand; but how long this may last I know not.

[Oct. 15, 1852]

I thank you from the bottom of my heart, for your kind letter. Your letters are always kind. I have been in great danger. I am attended, nearly every day, by two physicians; and yet, strange as it may seem, when I have got through the night, I can sit an hour at the table, and write a letter, and sign others. I don't foresee the result. I am in the hands of God, and may He preserve and bless you and yours evermore.

As the reality came home that he might not survive, Webster's thoughts turned to others than himself.

[Letters to Fillmore: Oct. 17, 1852]

It has been so kind in Mr. Conrad to trouble himself with the concerns of my Department, in my absence, that I should be glad to show him some mark of grateful respect.

THE END

It is a feather in the life of a public man to sign a treaty, and I should be glad that he should have the opportunity of signing one before my return. If you have concluded to submit the copyright treaty to the Senate, I propose that you suggest to him, as from yourself, but with my hearty concurrence, that he should sign it. I do not think of any other treaty we have now on hand.

[*Monday, Oct. 18, 1852*]

By the blessing of Providence, I have had another comparatively good night, the afternoon attack coming later, and not lasting so long, and then an excellent sleep. At this hour (ten o'clock,) I feel easy and strong, and as if I could go into the Senate and make a speech! At one, I shall sink all away, be obliged to go to bed at three, and go through the evening spasms. What all this is to come to, God only knows. My dear Sir, — I should love to pass the last moments of your administration with you, and around your council board. But let not this embarrass you. Consider my resignation as always before you, to be accepted any moment you please. I hope God, in His mercy, may preserve me; but His will be done!

Our remaining letters are from the pen of George J. Abbot of the State Department, who had come to Marshfield to be with Webster.

[*Letters from Abbot to Fillmore: Oct. 21, 1852*]

You will be deeply pained to learn that within the last few hours the disease under which the Secretary of State is laboring, has taken an unfavorable turn, and that no hopes are entertained for his recovery.

[*Oct. 25, 1852*]

It was my mournful duty, in connection with one of my colleagues in the Department, to transmit to you yesterday, the sad intelligence of the death of Mr. Webster, the Secretary of State, at his mansion-house, on the early morning of the Sabbath. I have now to enclose to you, as I do, herewith, the result of the autopsy, made this day by Drs. Jeffries, Porter, Jackson, Parker, Warren, and Wyman.

Mr. Webster died as he wished, in the secluded and beautiful spot where he had fixed his abode, and which he had done so much to improve and embellish; in sight and within sound of the ocean, which he loved so well; beneath overshadowing trees, planted by his own hand; surrounded by kind-hearted neighbors and loving friends; in the midst of domestic affections and domestic happiness; in the full possession and exercise, till the last moment, of every power of his mind, and every affection of his heart; and in the arms of his son and only surviving child. He died in the consciousness of duty performed; in the assured belief of the truth of Christianity and "the divine reality of the mission of Jesus Christ."

His remains will be interred by the side of those of his family whose gentle spirits had preceded his own to their destined rest.

It may be a mournful satisfaction to you, Mr. President, to be assured that the last letter, written with his own hand, was to yourself only the Monday preceding his death.

But the truly final words were those of Webster's will, prepared with clear-minded precision shortly before his death:

I wish to be buried without the least show or ostentation, but in a manner respectful to my neighbors, whose kindness has contributed so much to the happiness of me and mine, and for whose prosperity I offer sincere prayers to God.

Biographical Notes
on Principal Correspondents

Notes and Sources

Index

BIOGRAPHICAL NOTES
ON PRINCIPAL CORRESPONDENTS

Bingham, James Hervey
(Apr. 11, 1781 — Mar. 31, 1859)

Born Lempster, N. H.; attended Exeter Academy with Webster, and in his class at Dartmouth; practiced law in Lempster and served in both houses of the N. H. Legislature; in 1849, through Webster's good offices, he obtained an Interior Department clerkship in Washington, where he lived thereafter.

Blake, George
(1769 — Oct. 6, 1841)

Born Hardwick, Mass.; admitted to the Boston bar, 1792; a member, with Webster, of the Massachusetts Constitutional Convention of 1820, and for many years U. S. District Attorney for Massachusetts. He possessed independent means and was better known for his charm than for his diligence. In the 1820's a fire destroyed his papers and Webster tells us that ever afterward, when Mr. Blake wished to delay the trial of a case, whatever the date of its inception, he invariably began a dilatory motion with the words, "May it please your Honors, the disastrous fire in Court Street which consumed every one of my papers makes it necessary for me to throw myself upon the indulgence of the Court."

Blatchford, Richard Milford
(Apr. 23, 1798 — Sept. 4, 1875)

Born Stratford, Conn., the ninth of seventeen children of a non-conformist minister who had emigrated from England in 1795; graduated

Union College, Schenectady, N. Y., 1815; taught school and studied law; admitted to N. Y. bar, 1820, and became prominent in his profession, as well as in political and public life; among other things, he served as counsel and financial agent for the Bank of England, Bank Commissioner for the State of N. Y., U. S. Minister to the Vatican, and Com'r. of Parks, N. Y. City.

He was one of the original members of the Hone Club, a group of twelve convivial and distinguished New Yorkers who met periodically for dinner at each other's houses. Blatchford's was located on the East River at Hell Gate, then some distance from the City, and Philip Hone's diary for Oct. 9, 1844, describes the prospect from it as follows: "When I arose in the morning at Mr. Blatchford's, I contemplated the delightful scene: the clumps of fine old trees clothed in the gorgeous foliage of autumn, the lawn still bright and green, the mild, refreshing breeze, the rapid waters of Hell-Gate covered with sailing vessels and steamboats, all combined to present a picture of consummate beauty."

Webster was a frequent guest of the Hone Club and was elected an honorary member on Oct. 26, 1843. Its members included some of his most congenial friends, and the following are referred to in the present book: Edward Curtis, J. Prescott Hall, Roswell L. Colt, and Samuel Jaudon. Blatchford did much to assist Webster in his financial difficulties, became one of his intimates, and was named executor of his will. His son Samuel was a federal judge in New York and in 1882 was appointed to the U. S. Supreme Court.

Curtis, Edward
(Oct. 25, 1801 — Aug. 2, 1856)

Born Windsor, Vt.; graduated Union College, Schenectady, N. Y., 1821; admitted to N. Y. bar 1824 and practiced there and in Washington; Member of Congress 1837–41; Collector of the Port of New York 1841–44. Thurlow Weed, in his *Autobiography,* says of Curtis: "I was intimately associated with him politically, personally, and socially, from 1835 until he died, and can truthfully say that I have never known a man possessing a greater, if an equal, degree of political common sense, tact, and efficiency. These qualities, to which zeal and fidelity were added, commended Mr. Curtis at an early day to the regard and confidence of Mr. Webster. All the poetic ideas of friendship were realized in the endearing relations which grew up between those two men."

BIOGRAPHICAL NOTES

Davis, Isaac P.
(Oct. 7, 1771 — Jan. 13, 1855)

Born Plymouth, Mass.; in business in Boston as a rope maker but met financial reverses and was never wealthy; for many years represented Boston in the Massachusetts Legislature; active in the Mass. Historical Society, and a trustee of the Boston Athenaeum. Robert C. Winthrop called him "a man of cheerful yesterdays and confident tomorrows" and said, "it would be difficult to name a man who had been happier in his social relations." Webster dedicated the second volume of his *Works* (1851 Edition) to him as follows: "My Dear Sir: A warm friendship has subsisted between us for half our lives, interrupted by no untoward occurrence, and never for a moment cooling into indifference. Of this friendship, the source of so much happiness to me, I wish to leave, if not an enduring memorial, at least an affectionate and grateful acknowledgment."

Denison, John Evelyn
(Jan. 27, 1800 — Mar. 7, 1873)

Born Ossington, Nottinghamshire, England; graduated Oxford, 1823; met Webster during a tour of Canada and the U. S.; Member of Parliament for many years, and Speaker of the House of Commons, 1857–72; created Viscount Ossington in 1872 and took seat in House of Lords; President of Royal Agricultural Society in 1857.

Everett, Edward
(Apr. 11, 1794 — Jan. 15, 1865)

Born Dorchester, Mass.; graduated Harvard, 1811, with highest honors although youngest in his class; entered ministry, taught Greek literature at Harvard, and edited the *North American Review;* elected to Congress for five terms; Gov'r. of Mass. for four terms, 1836–39; Minister to England, 1841–45; President of Harvard, 1846–49; Secretary of State, 1852–53; U. S. Senate, 1853; popular orator, delivered oration at Gettysburg immediately preceding Lincoln's address, Nov. 19, 1863; donated lecture fees of $69,064 to preservation of Mt. Vernon as a national monument; wrote *Memoir of the Public Life of Daniel Webster* (I, 1–175), and edited the 1851 edition of his *Works*.

BIOGRAPHICAL NOTES

Fillmore, Millard
(Jan. 7, 1800 — Mar. 8, 1874)

Born in wilderness cabin, Locke township, Cayuga County, N. Y., to which his parents had migrated two years before from Bennington, Vt. After scanty schooling he was apprenticed at fourteen to a cloth-dresser and later worked in a fulling mill. From his earnings he purchased a dictionary and set himself to learn all the words. He later taught school at Sempronius, N. Y., and studied law in the office of Judge Wood. He was admitted to the bar in 1823 and practiced law in East Aurora and Buffalo. Becoming associated politically with Thurlow Weed, Whig boss of N. Y., he was elected to the N. Y. Legislature in 1828 and to Congress in 1832, serving as Chairman of the House Ways and Means Committee in 1840. After defeat in race for the governorship of N. Y. he was elected State Comptroller, and in 1848 was nominated and elected Vice President of the U. S., becoming President in 1850 upon the death of General Zachary Taylor. He had broken with Weed and Seward over patronage, and in 1852 they backed General Scott for the Whig presidential nomination.

Later, on the wave of anti-Catholicism then sweeping the country, Fillmore joined the American or "Know Nothing" party and was its candidate for the presidency in 1856. At the time of his nomination he was traveling abroad, and not long before had been granted an audience with the Pope. After his acceptance of the invitation Fillmore was informed, to his consternation, that he would be expected to kiss the prelate's foot. In actual fact, however, the Pope received him sitting and did not offer either hand or foot for salutation.

Fillmore continued his activity in civic and public affairs, being the first Chancellor of the University of Buffalo, and the first President of the Buffalo Historical Society.

Gore, Christopher
(Sept. 21, 1758 — Mar. 1, 1827)

Born Boston, Mass.; Harvard, 1776; member of both houses of the Mass. Legislature; U. S. District Attorney, Mass., 1789–96; Commissioner to England, 1796–1803; Gov'r. of Mass., 1809; U. S. Senate, 1813–16; Fellow of the Harvard Corporation; left his estate to Harvard, which named Gore Hall for him.

BIOGRAPHICAL NOTES

Harvey, Peter
(July 10, 1810 — June 27, 1877)

Born Barnet, Vt., son of Alexander Harvey of Glasgow, Scotland; apprenticed at 15 to mercantile firm in Plymouth, N. Y.; later went to Boston and became a member of several business firms, as well as treasurer of the Rutland Railroad and president of the Kilby Bank; a member of both houses of the Mass. Legislature. Certain of Webster's biographers, with a professional, looking-down-their-noses air, say that Harvey aspired to be Webster's Boswell. Be that as it may, his *Reminiscences and Anecdotes of Daniel Webster,* although sometimes unreliable as to details, is the warmest and most intimate of all the biographies. Harvey also assembled an extensive collection of letters and documents relating to Webster, which he gave to the N. H. Historical Society.

Haven, Franklin
(May 30, 1804 — Oct. 31, 1893)

Born Cambridge, Mass. and attended public schools in Boston; starting at 20 as a bank teller, in 1836 he became president of the Merchants Bank, in Boston, a position which he held for 46 years. He was prominent in Civil War finance, was first president of the Boston Clearing House, and was one of the original directors of the Illinois Central Railroad. A man of literary, as well as professional, tastes, he became one of Webster's most trusted advisors in both political and financial matters, and bore some of the brunt of Webster's perennial inability to make ends meet. Webster named him as testamentary trustee of his estate, along with Edward Curtis and James William Paige.

Hopkinson, Joseph
(Nov. 12, 1770 — Jan. 15, 1842)

Born Philadelphia, Pa., a son of Francis Hopkinson, signer of the Declaration of Independence; graduated Univ. of Pa. 1786; admitted to the bar 1791 and became a prominent lawyer in Philadelphia, as well as active in literary affairs. Member of Congress 1814-20. Author of the song "Hail Columbia."

459

BIOGRAPHICAL NOTES

Ketchum, Hiram

A leader of the conservative wing of the N. Y. Whigs and a close political friend and advisor of Webster. In 1840 Governor Seward nominated him to the N. Y. Court of Appeals, but while this was awaiting legislative confirmation Ketchum appeared before the Legislature on behalf of the Public School Society of New York and opposed Seward's school recommendations, whereupon the Governor withdrew the nomination.

Lanman, Charles
(June 14, 1819 — Mar. 4, 1895)

Born Monroe, Mich.; attended school Norwich, Conn., where he lived with grandfather, James Lanman, U. S. Senator 1819–25; after ten years in mercantile business in New York, devoted himself to exploring, sketching, and writing; on editorial staff N. Y. *Express* 1847–48; librarian War Department, Washington, 1849; private secretary to Webster 1850–52; thereafter librarian of various branches of the government in Washington, and American Secretary of the Japanese Legation; author of many works on natural history, travel, Congress, biography, and the Japanese. Said to have been a handsome man of genial presence, popular in society, and an excellent raconteur.

Lee, Eliza Buckminster
(c. 1788 — June 22, 1864)

Born Portsmouth, N. H., daughter of the Rev. Joseph Buckminster; married 1827 to Thomas Lee, wealthy resident of Brookline, Mass.; engaged extensively in literary pursuits, being author of several books and many translations.

March, Charles

Born near Portsmouth, N. H., son of Clement March of Greenland, N. H.; friend and contemporary of Webster; became merchant in New York. References sometimes confuse him with Charles W. March (1815–

BIOGRAPHICAL NOTES

1864), who was of the next generation and wrote *Reminiscences of Congress,* later published under the title *Daniel Webster and His Contemporaries.*

Mason, Jeremiah
(Apr. 27, 1768 — Oct. 14, 1848)

Born Lebanon, Conn.; graduated Yale 1788; studied law and after practice in smaller towns, settled in Portsmouth, N. H., where he and Webster became close friends and professional rivals. Webster considered him the best lawyer he had ever known, and, years later, claimed that his bones still ached from the pounding he had received from Mason during their Portsmouth days. Mason served in the U. S. Senate 1813–17, and in the N. H. Legislature 1820–24; he declined appointment as Chief Justice of New Hampshire. It has been said that no other lawyer ever tried so many cases and lost so few in proportion to the number that he tried.

McGaw, Jacob
(Sept. 8, 1778 — May 12, 1867)

Born Merrimack, N. H.; graduated from Dartmouth 1797 and studied law in the office of Thomas W. Thompson in Salisbury, N. H., where he got to know Webster. He was practicing law at Fryeburg, Maine, while Webster was teaching school there, and they roomed together, reading aloud, alternately, all of Pope's poetry, the *Tatler,* the *Spectator,* and other works. He later moved to Bangor, Maine, where he practiced law until his death.

Merrill, Thomas A.
(Jan. 18, 1780 — April 1855)

Born Deering, N. H.; first scholar of Webster's class at Dartmouth; went into the ministry and was a clergyman at Middlebury, Vt., for approximately fifty years.

461

BIOGRAPHICAL NOTES

Paige, James William
(1792 — May 19, 1868)

Born Hopkinton, N. H., half-brother of Webster's first wife, Grace Fletcher. He became one of the closest friends of Webster, who called him "William," and was one of the three trustees named in his will. He prospered as a merchant in Boston, and in 1831 married Harriette Story White, daughter of Stephen White and niece of Justice Joseph Story. Webster regarded Mrs. Paige with almost fatherly affection and she was one of his favorite correspondents.

Story, Joseph
(Sept. 18, 1779 — Sept. 10, 1845)

Born Marblehead, Mass.; graduated Harvard 1798; admitted to the bar 1801 and practiced in Salem. Mass. Legislature 1805–08, 1811; U. S. House of Representatives 1808–09. In early life was a Jeffersonian Republican and was appointed to the U. S. Supreme Court by President Madison in 1811; under the influence of Chief Justice Marshall, with whom he developed an affectionate congeniality, he became a staunch Federalist. In 1829 he was appointed head of the Harvard Law School, which he combined with his court duties, writing a large number of texts which were classics in the law. He had a round cherubic face, wore steel-rimmed spectacles, and in his later years had a foxy grandpa look. He had a keen sense of humor and claimed that every man should laugh at least an hour a day. In 1845 he made arrangements to resign from the Supreme Court so that he could devote his entire time to the Law School, but in his conscientious effort to clear up his circuit court dockets, he drove himself so hard that he died of a heart attack.

Taylor, John

Born Marshfield, Mass.; employed by Webster, who later placed him in charge of his farm at Franklin (Salisbury), N. H. A man of giant stature, his size was equalled only by his devotion to Webster.

BIOGRAPHICAL NOTES

Thompson, Thomas W.
(Mar. 15, 1766 — Oct. 1, 1821)

Born Boston, Mass.; graduated Harvard 1786; admitted to the bar 1791; practiced at Salisbury, N. H. until 1810 and thereafter at Concord. Trustee of Dartmouth College; N. H. Legislature 1807–14, and for the last two years Speaker of the House; served in Congress as both a Representative and a Senator.

Ticknor, George
(Aug. 1, 1791 — Jan. 26, 1871)

Born Boston; entered Dartmouth as a junior at fourteen and graduated in 1807; studied in Germany, joined the Harvard faculty, and was largely responsible for a fundamental reorganization of its teaching methods. He was one of the leading intellectual and social figures of his day and entertained a constant stream of distinguished guests at his beautiful home at the corner of Beacon and Park streets, Boston. Josiah Quincy tells us that "There seemed to be a cosmopolitan spaciousness about his very vestibule."

Webster, Mrs. Caroline Le Roy
(1797 — Feb. 26, 1882)

Daughter of Herman Le Roy, prosperous merchant of N. Y. and one-time Dutch Consul there. She and Webster were married on Dec. 12, 1829, at which time she was thirty-three and he was seventeen years older. She is described as slender and graceful, with a resemblance to Elizabeth Barrett Browning, curls and all. Vivacious and temperamental, she was accustomed to balls and formal dinners and encouraged her husband's fondness for entertaining and high living. They had no children.

Webster's will expressly gave her the right to live at Marshfield, but she preferred N. Y., where for many years she kept house on 33rd Street. Later she lived with a niece, Mrs. Robert W. Edgar, in New Rochelle, N. Y., in whose home she died at age eighty-five.

Her personal papers were placed in the attic of Mrs. Emmet Hall of Ashfield, Mass., a great-great grandniece. One day while home on vacation from college and rummaging about, Mrs. Hall's daughter Helena

463

came upon an old manuscript diary in a trunk and found it interesting reading. She showed it to her mother and to Ives Washburn, a publisher, who happened to be visiting them. It was Mrs. Webster's personal account of their trip to England and the Continent in 1839. Mr. Washburn published it in 1942 under the title *Mr. W. & I*, with an introduction by Claude M. Fuess.

Webster, Ezekiel
(March 11, 1780 — Apr. 10, 1829)

Born Salisbury, N. H., and spent his first nineteen years working on the family farm; then, upon Daniel's urging and their parents' decision to stake the family future on his and Daniel's education, he attended Salisbury Academy for two terms and tutored in the classics with the Rev. Samuel Wood of Boscawen. He entered Dartmouth in 1801 and became the leading scholar of his class, but left before graduation to take over the school of Cyrus W. Perkins in Short Street, Boston. He kept up with his college work sufficiently to obtain his diploma in August 1804, and then studied law with James Sullivan of Boston and Parker Noyes of Salisbury, being admitted to the N. H. bar in September 1807. He practiced law at Boscawen, attaining high standing and financial success.

He was tall, strong, and of commanding presence, but of a complexion the exact opposite of Daniel's, not having inherited the black hair and swarthy skin of the Bachelders. He married twice and had two daughters: Alice, who married Prof. Jarvis Gregg of the Boscawen Academy and, after his death, the Rev. George Whipple of Oberlin, Ohio; and Mary Ann, who married Prof. Edwin D. Sanborn of Dartmouth.

He was made a trustee of Dartmouth in 1819, and ran unsuccessfully for Congress as a Federalist in 1829, going down to defeat in the Jacksonian democratic landslide. Shortly thereafter he suffered a fatal stroke while arguing a case in court, his death being described by his son-in-law, Prof. Sanborn (XVII, 42):

"Mr. Webster was speaking, standing erect, on a plain floor, the house full, and the court and jurors and auditors intently listening to his words, with all their eyes fastened upon him. Speaking with full force and perfect utterance, he arrived at the end of one branch of his argument. He closed that branch, uttered the last sentence and the last word of that sentence, with perfect tone and emphasis, and then, in an instant, erect, and with arms depending by his side, he fell backward, without bending a joint, and, so far as appeared, was dead before his head reached the floor."

BIOGRAPHICAL NOTES

Webster, Fletcher

(July 23, 1813 — Aug. 30, 1862)

Born Portsmouth, N. H., he was christened "Daniel Fletcher Webster" but later dropped the first name and was known during most of his life as "Fletcher Webster." He attended Boston Latin School and entered Harvard in 1829, graduating with the Class of 1833, which elected him class orator. He studied law with Samuel B. Walcott of Hopkinton, Mass., and with his father, and was admitted to the Suffolk County bar.

In 1836 he married Caroline Story White and moved to Detroit, Mich., to practice law; then, in 1837, to La Salle, Ill. He found the practice of law uncongenial, it being said by George S. Hillard that "He had the quick perception, the ready tact, and the easy elocution which are so important in the trial of causes, but he disliked the drudgery of preparation and was not patient in the investigation of legal questions."

When his father became Secretary of State under President Harrison, Fletcher came to Washington as Chief Clerk of the State Department, in which capacity he was called upon to deliver to John Tyler at his home in Virginia the official notification of his accession to the presidency. It was the first time that a president of the United States had died in office and a more formal protocol was worked out than has since been customary. Fletcher acted as personal secretary to his father, who is quoted as saying that "no one could prepare a paper in conformity with verbal instructions more to his satisfaction."

In 1843 he accompanied Caleb Cushing on a mission to China, as secretary of the legation, returning in 1845. In 1850 he was appointed Surveyor of the Port of Boston, a post which he held until 1861, when displaced by an appointee of President Lincoln.

On April 20, 1861, he ran a notice in the Boston papers asking for volunteers to raise a new regiment for the Union army. The response was so great that the unit was filled within three days, Fletcher being named Colonel. The regiment was assigned to guard duty in western Virginia, but saw action in the Second Battle of Bull Run, during which Fletcher was shot through the body and killed. In addition to his widow, he left three children, all of whom died childless.

A memoir by George S. Hillard in *Harvard Memorial Biographies* says of Fletcher:

"His tastes were strongly social, and his powers of social entertainment were such as few men possess. He had an unerring sense of the ludicrous, his wit was ready and responsive, and no man could relate an amusing incident or tell a humorous story with more dramatic power. Nor was he without faculties of a high order. His perceptions were quick and accurate, he was an able and forceful speaker, and he wrote with the clearness and strength which belonged to him by right of inheritance."

Webster, Mrs. Grace Fletcher
(Jan. 16, 1781 — Jan. 21, 1828)

Daughter of the Rev. Elijah Fletcher, minister of Hopkinton, N. H., who died Apr. 8, 1786, leaving a widow and four small children, of whom Grace was the youngest. The widow then married the Rev. Christopher Paige, also of Hopkinton, by whom she had three sons and a daughter, the third son being James William Paige.

Grace graduated from the Atkinson Academy in 1800 and taught school, first in Boscawen and later in Salisbury, where she lived with her sister Rebecca, who had married Judge Israel W. Kelley. On Sunday, May 29, 1808, she and Webster were married in Judge Kelley's house, the ceremony being performed by the Rev. Thomas Worcester. They had five children, two of whom died in childhood. In 1827, while accompanying Webster to Washington, Grace was taken ill and after a brief illness died at the N. Y. home of Webster's friend, Dr. Cyrus W. Perkins. She was buried in Boston, and her remains were later removed to Marshfield.

An obituary written by Justice Story in the *National Intelligencer*, Jan. 26, 1828, said, among other things: "The death of this excellent woman has spread a general gloom among her numerous friends. Few persons have been more deservedly or more universally beloved." Peter Harvey tells us that Webster could never speak of his first wife without visible emotion (Harvey, 318–19).

Weston, Seth

Selectman of Marshfield, whose truthfulness and exactness were so well recognized that his neighbors commonly said: "If Mr. Weston says so, it must be so." He was a skillful carpenter, and was much employed by Webster both in that capacity and to manage his farm. His status in the family is indicated by the fact that he was one of those present at Webster's death.

BIOGRAPHICAL NOTES

White, Stephen
(July 10, 1787 — Aug. 10, 1841)

Nephew and residuary legatee of the murdered Captain Joseph White of Salem; served in both houses of the Mass. Legislature; married Harriet Story, sister of Justice Joseph Story, and had three daughters, one of whom (Harriette) married Webster's brother-in-law, James William Paige, and another (Caroline) married Webster's son Fletcher. Out of friendship, and perhaps gratitude for Webster's handling of the trial of the Knapp brothers for the murder of Captain White, Stephen White presented Webster with the beautiful small yacht *Calypso*.

Wright, Charles Porter

A native of Marshfield employed from youth on Webster's farm, and for the last eight years as manager. He is said to have been grave, quiet, clear-headed, with a quick eye, a ready hand, and few words.

NOTES AND SOURCES

Webster's letters are given in the form in which they appear in the National Edition (1903) of *The Writings and Speeches of Daniel Webster,* which is not consistent in its treatment of them. The first extensive compilation was in two volumes published in 1856 under the title "Private Correspondence of Daniel Webster." These were edited by or under the direction of his son Fletcher, who revised the punctuation, eliminated abbreviations, corrected spelling (including the quaintnesses of the farm managers), etc. This compilation became Volumes XVII and XVIII of the National Edition. Correspondence collected subsequently was placed in Volume XVI, but in this instance was printed as written, with the original punctuation or lack of punctuation, ampersands, abbreviations, etc.

References are made to the books listed below. Those to the National Edition of Writings and Speeches (1903) are by volume and page only (e.g., XVII, 56); other books are identified in the notes by the author's last name.

Books Noted

Herbert Baxter Adams, *The Life and Writings of Jared Sparks* (Boston, Houghton, Mifflin & Co., 1893)

American State Trials, John D. Lawson, Editor (St. Louis, F. H. Thomas Law Book Co., 1917)

Maurice G. Baxter, *Daniel Webster and the Supreme Court* (Amherst, University of Massachusetts Press, 1966)

Stephen Vincent Benét, *The Devil and Daniel Webster* (New York, Rinehart & Co., 1937)

Josiah H. Benton, *A Notable Libel Case* (Boston, C. E. Goodspeed, 1904)

The Correspondence of Nicholas Biddle dealing with National Affairs,

1807–1844, Reginald C. McGrane, Editor (Boston, Houghton Mifflin Co., 1919)

Howard A. Bradley and James A. Winans, *Daniel Webster and the Salem Murder* (Columbia, Mo., Artcraft Press, 1956)

Ralph C. H. Catterall, *The Second Bank of the United States* (Chicago, Univ. of Chicago Press, 1902)

Richard N. Current, *Daniel Webster and the Rise of National Conservatism* (Boston, Little, Brown & Co., 1955)

George Ticknor Curtis, *Life of Daniel Webster* (N. Y., D. Appleton & Co., 1869)

Sydney George Fisher, *The True Daniel Webster* (Philadelphia, J. B. Lippincott Co., 1911)

Claude Moore Fuess, *Rufus Choate, The Wizard of the Law* (N. Y., Minton, Balch & Co., 1928)

Claude Moore Fuess, *Daniel Webster* (Boston, Little, Brown & Co., 1930); references merely to "Fuess" are to this.

Thomas Hamilton, *Men and Manners in America* (Edinburgh, William Blackwood, 1834)

A Sketch of Chester Harding, Artist, Drawn by His Own Hand, Edited by his Daughter, Margaret E. White (Boston, Houghton Mifflin Co., 1929)

Harvard Memorial Biographies (Cambridge, Sever & Francis, 1867)

Peter Harvey, *Reminiscences and Anecdotes of Daniel Webster* (Boston, Little, Brown & Co., 1877)

Henry W. Hilliard, *Politics and Pen Pictures at Home and Abroad* (N. Y., G. P. Putnam's Sons, 1892)

The Diary of Philip Hone, 1828–1851 (N. Y., Dodd, Mead & Co., 1889)

Richard M. Johnston and William H. Browne, *Life of Alexander H. Stephens* (Phila., J. B. Lippincott & Co., 1878)

Charles Lanman, *The Private Life of Daniel Webster* (N. Y., Harper & Bros., 1852)

Walker Lewis, *Without Fear or Favor, A Biography of Chief Justice Taney* (Boston, Houghton Mifflin Co., 1965)

Henry Cabot Lodge, *Daniel Webster* (Boston, Houghton, Mifflin & Co., 1897)

S. P. Lyman, *Life and Memorials of Daniel Webster* (N. Y., D. Appleton & Co., 1853)

Charles W. March, *Reminiscences of Congress* (N. Y., Baker & Scribner, 1850)

Harriet Martineau, *Retrospect of Western Travel* (London, Saunders & Otley, 1838)

NOTES AND SOURCES

A Memorial of Daniel Webster from the City of Boston (Boston, Little, Brown & Co., 1853)

Charles Moore, *Washington Past and Present* (N. Y., Century Co., 1929)

Samuel Eliot Morison, *Harrison Gray Otis 1765–1848: The Urbane Federalist* (Boston, Houghton Mifflin Co., 1969)

John T. Morse, Jr., *Life and Letters of Oliver Wendell Holmes* (Boston, Houghton, Mifflin & Co., 1896)

Allan Nevins, *Ordeal of the Union* (N. Y., Charles Scribner's Sons, 1947)

Harriette Story Paige, *Daniel Webster in England — Journal of Harriette Story Paige,* Edward Gray, Editor (Boston, Houghton Mifflin Co., 1917)

Theodore Parker, *A Discourse Occasioned by the Death of Daniel Webster, Preached at the Melodeon on Sunday, October 31, 1852;* reprinted in *Historic Americans* (Boston, American Unitarian Association, 1908)

Josiah Quincy, *Figures of the Past, from the Leaves of Old Journals* (Boston, Roberts Bros., 1883); quotations are from 1926 edition of Little, Brown & Co., with introduction and notes by M. A. De Wolfe Howe

The Quincy sisters, *The Articulate Sisters, Passages from the Journals and Letters of the Daughters of President Josiah Quincy of Harvard University,* M. A. De Wolfe Howe, Editor (Cambridge, Harvard University Press, 1946)

Robert J. Rayback, *Millard Fillmore* (Buffalo, Buffalo Hist. Soc., 1959)

James Ford Rhodes, *History of the U. S. from the Compromise of 1850* (New York, Harper & Bros., 1896)

Josephine Seaton, *William Winston Seaton of the "National Intelligencer"* (Boston, James R. Osgood & Co., 1871)

Life and Letters of Joseph Story, William W. Story, Editor (Boston, Charles C. Little & James Brown, 1851)

Life, Letters, and Journals of George Ticknor (Boston, James R. Osgood & Co., 1876)

Caroline Le Roy Webster, *Mr. W. & I* (N. Y., Ives Washburn, 1942)

The Letters of Daniel Webster, Claude H. Van Tyne, Editor (N. Y., McClure, Phillips & Co., 1902)

The Writings and Speeches of Daniel Webster (Boston, Little, Brown & Co., 1903)

Autobiography and Memoir of Thurlow Weed (Boston, Houghton, Mifflin & Co., 1884)

Edwin Percy Whipple, *American Literature and Other Papers* (Boston, Ticknor & Co., 1887); includes chapter on "Daniel Webster as a Master of English Style."

NOTES AND SOURCES

William Cleaver Wilkinson, *Daniel Webster: A Vindication* (N. Y., Funk & Wagnalls Co., 1911)

For those who wish to know more about Webster, or to view him more objectively, the best book (in my opinion) is the Fuess biography (two volumes, 1930). For an excellent, though now somewhat outdated, bibliography on Webster by Mark Van Doren, see *The Cambridge History of American Literature* (N. Y., G. P. Putnam's Sons, 1918), II, 480–88.

Notes on Illustrations

Page

xi In 1883, General James Dana listed, without descriptive data, more than sixty portraits and ten statues or busts of Webster. *Mass. Hist. Soc. Procs.*, Second Series, II, 262–65. In May 1897, *McClure's Magazine* published an article on "Life Portraits of Daniel Webster," with introduction and notes by Charles Henry Hart, from which the data on the Alexander, Lawson, and Harding portraits is taken. The story about Webster and the *Princeton* disaster has also been attributed to a sitting for Harding, but the Lawson version was accepted by Charles Henry Hart.

xii For Lanman's comments on the Billings drawing of Webster's birthplace, see Lanman, 65.

Introduction

xvi Bingham's description, XVII, 55.
xvi McGaw's, XVII, 50.
xvii Mrs. Lee's, XVII, 438–39.
xvii Hamilton, II, 151–54.
xviii Martineau, I, 143, 165.
xviii Hilliard, 2.
xix Carlyle letter of June 24, 1839, to Emerson: Curtis, II, 21.

I. Family — Childhood — Dartmouth

1 The primary source for this Chapter is Webster's Autobiography (XVII, 1–27). It was written in 1829 for his friend, Mrs. Eliza Buckminster Lee, but extends only to 1817.

471

NOTES AND SOURCES

2 The reference to Ezekiel is from Webster's letter of May 3, 1846, to Richard M. Blatchford, XVIII, 225, at 228.

4 The marksmanship anecdote is undoubtedly apocryphal, but gives interesting evidence of the sense of fun which Webster shared with his father. It is from Harvey, 411–12.

6 The description of William Hoyt and the "Constitution handkerchief" is from XVIII, 398.

8 The scythe story is substantially as it appears in Lanman, 20.

8 The anecdote about Abiel Foster is from XVIII, 228.

11 Webster's failure to take an official part in the commencement exercises of his class has kicked up a spate of scandalous speculations. So generally has it been attributed to either the bottle or the ladies, that one of his biographers found great significance in the loyalty of his classmates, not one of whom was ever willing to point an accusing, or even an explanatory, finger at his supposed fall from grace. The truth of the matter is less glamorously but more reliably stated by Fuess, who points out that the Latin Salutatory went as a matter of course to the top scholar of the class, Thomas A. Merrill, and that the English Valedictory had usually been awarded by a vote of the class. A feud between the two literary societies — the Social Friends and the United Friends (whose candidate was Webster) — prevented a choice. The faculty thereupon appointed Caleb Tenney, afterwards a minister at Wethersfield, Connecticut. Webster was offered as consolation either a poem or an oration in English, but, disgruntled at not receiving the English Valedictory, he requested to be excused from appearing on the Commencement platform. "The story that in a fit of petulance he tore up his diploma . . . is entirely mythical." Fuess, I, 51.

11 Webster's remarks on the quality of his scholarship are quoted from a letter of Nov. 16, 1852, from Jacob McGaw to Prof. E. D. Sanborn, XVII, 51.

II. Preparation for the Law

Page

14 The letters to Bingham are in XVII, 92 and 95.

16 Webster owed his teaching position to a college friend, Samuel A. Bradley (1774–1844) who had graduated from Dartmouth in 1799 and had settled in Fryeburg to practice law.

17 The May 18, 1802 letter to Bingham is in XVII, 107.

472

20 The June 7, 1802 letter to Merrill is in XVII, 116.

21 The Dec. 21, 1802 letter to Bingham is in XVII, 127.

22 The letters to Merrill were dated Jan. 4 and Dec. [no day given], 1803, and are in XVII, 128 and 152.

24 The Dec. 23, 1803 and April 3, 1804 letters to Bingham are in XVII, 153 and 162.

28–29 The letters to and from Ezekiel are in XVII, 122–24.

30 The "young man" who undertook to introduce Webster to Mr. Gore was Samuel A. Bradley, the same friend who had been responsible for his teaching job at Fryeburg. *Fuess*, I, 66, 77.

31 The Nov. 30, 1804 letter to Merrill is in XVII, 194.

32 The Jan. 2, 1805 letter to Bingham is in XVII, 198.

32 The Albany trip was arranged by a Mr. Taylor Baldwin, a wealthy and eccentric gentleman who had met Webster at Mrs. Whitwell's boarding house in Court Street and took him along for company. Fuess, I, 79.

33 The Mar. 10, 1805 and Oct. 17, 1804 letters to Fuller are in XVII, 199 and 191.

III. Early Practice

Page

38 Letters to Bingham, May 4, 1805 and Jan. 19, 1806: XVII, 206 & 220.

40 Letter to McGaw, Jan. 12, 1807: XVII, 223.

40–41 Letters to Bingham, Feb. 27 and May 5, 1808: XVII, 227 & 231.

41 Mrs. Lee's description of Mrs. Grace Webster is in XVII, 440.

42 Webster's statement as to Mason's effect on his style is from Curtis, I, 90.

43 The Rockingham Memorial is in XV, 599–610.

46 Letters to Ezekiel and Cutts, May 24 and 26, 1813: XVI, 14 & 15.

46 Letter to March, May 31, 1813: XVI, 17.

46 Letter to Bingham, June 4, 1813: XVII, 233.

47 Letter to March, June 24, 1813: XVI, 22.

48 Letter to Ezekiel, Dec. 29, 1813: XVII, 237.

48 The pipe of wine anecdote is from Quincy, 212–13.

49 Speech on Repeal of Embargo: XIV, 35.

50–51 Letters to Ezekiel, Oct. 20 & Nov. 29, 1814: XVI, 30 & 31.

51 Letters to Ezekiel, Oct. 30 & Dec. 22, 1814: XVII, 245 & 248.

51–52 Letters to Kent, Dec. 22, 1814 and Jan. 14, 1815: XVI, 32 & 33.

52 Undated letter to Hiram Ketchum: XVIII, 184. Although ground-

less, the charge kept recurring that Webster had participated in the Hartford Convention and had advocated disunion. In the 1828 presidential election, the *Jackson Republican,* a Boston semi-weekly newspaper organized to support Jackson against John Quincy Adams, in order to split the latter's following, reported that Adams had called Webster a traitor and had stated that he and other leading Federalists had plotted "to dissolve the Union and to re-annex New England to Great Britain." Webster thereupon instigated a prosecution for criminal libel against the publisher, Theodore Lyman, Jr., in the Supreme Judicial Court of Massachusetts. Being a criminal, rather than a civil, proceeding the critical issue was one of intent. It was obvious that Lyman's attack had been directed at Adams. Had he been guilty of a criminal intent to defame Webster? On this issue the jury disagreed, and the prosecution was dropped. It was reported in the press that ten jurors were in favor of conviction and two opposed. For details of the case, see Benton.

53 Letter to Ezekiel, Mar. 26, 1816: XVII, 256.

53 Undated letter to John Randolph: XVII, 258. John Randolph was described by a contemporary as having an "Ishmaelitish nature which delighted in provoking every man's hand against his own." Seaton, 150.

54 Letter to Mason, Oct. 29, 1816: XVI, 35.

55 Letter to Story, Dec. 9, 1816: XVI, 36.

55 Letter to Sullivan, Jan. 2, 1817: XVII, 254.

56–57 Letters to Ezekiel, Jan. 19 & 26, 1817: XVII, 263.

IV. The Dartmouth College Case

Page

58 Letter to Dunham, Aug. 25, 1815: XVII, 251.

60 Letter to Mason, Sept. 4, 1817: XVII, 265.

60 Letter to Mason, Nov. 27, 1817: XVII, 266.

61 Letter to Jeremiah Smith, Dec. 8, 1817: XVII, 267.

61 Letter to Mason, Jan. 1818: XVII, 270.

62 Letter to Mason, Feb. 22, 1818: XVII, 271.

62 Letter to Sullivan, Feb. 27, 1818: XVII, 273.

62–65 Opening legal argument: X, 195–233.

65–67 Account of Peroration: XV, 9–13.

68 Letter to Mason, Mar. 13, 1818: XVII, 275.

68 Letter to Smith, Mar. 14, 1818: XVII, 276.

69 Letter to Mason, Apr. 23, 1818: XVII, 280.

69 Letter to Story, Sept. 9, 1818: XVII, 287.

69 Letter from Hopkinson to Webster, Nov. 17, 1818: XVII, 288.

70 Letter to Mason, Feb. 4, 1819: XVI, 43.

70 Letter to Ezekiel, Feb. 2, 1819: XVII, 300. A facsimile of this letter is included in the illustrations.

70 The U. S. Supreme Court opinions in the Dartmouth College Case are reported in 4 Wheat. 518 (1819).

70 Letter from Hopkinson to Brown, Feb. 2, 1819: XVII, 301.

71 Letter to Hopkinson, Mar. 22, 1819: XVI, 47.

71 Letter from Hopkinson to Webster, Apr. 19, 1819: XVII, 305.

72 Letter to Mason, Apr. 10, 1819: XVI, 48.

V. Supreme Court Practice — Plymouth Oration

Page

73 *McCulloch v. Maryland,* 4 Wheat. 316 (1819). For Webster's Supreme Court practice generally, *see* Baxter.

73 *Gibbons v. Ogden,* 9 Wheat. 1 (1824).

73 Harvey, 140–43. Fuess cautions that details in Harvey's account are inaccurate, as, for instance, the statement that Webster followed Wirt.

75 The excerpts are from XI, 9, 11.

76 Letter to Mason, Feb. 23, 1819: XVI, 52.

76 Letter to Mason, Aug. 10, 1819: XVII, 308.

77 Excerpt from Memorial to Congress: XV, 72.

77 Excerpt from Faneuil Hall speech, Oct. 2, 1820: XIII, 8.

78 Story letter to Mason, Jan. 21, 1821: Story, I, 395–96.

78 Excerpt from Dec. 4, 1820 speech in Constitutional Convention on requirement of religious qualification: V, 6–7.

79 George Ticknor description of Plymouth oration: Curtis, I, 192–93.

81 Plymouth oration: I, 181–226.

VI. Congressman from Massachusetts
Speech on the Greek Revolution

Page

87 Letter to Story, Jan. 3, 1821: XVII, 313.

88 Letter to Story, Dec. 18, 1822: XVI, 72.

88 For Webster's later statement as to his service in the Massachusetts House of Representatives, see XIII, 422.

88 Letter of Oct. 18, 1822 notifying of nomination for Congress: XVII, 321.

89 Letter to Story, April 5, 1822: XVI, 68.

89 Letter to Story, May 12, 1823: XVII, 325.

89 Letter with postscript to Mrs. Webster, Feb. 6, 1823: XVI, 73.

90 Letter to Mason, Nov. 30, 1823: XVII, 329.

90 Letter to Ezekiel, Dec. 4, 1823: XVII, 330.

90 Letter to Everett, Nov. 16, 1823: XVII, 328. The article to which he refers was in the *North American Review* for October, 1823.

91 Letter to Everett, Dec. 5, 1823: XVII, 331.

91–92 Letters to the Blakes, Dec. 20, 1823: XVII, 333, 334.

93 Letter to Everett, Dec. 21, 1823: XVII, 335.

93 Letter from Davis, Jan. 6, 1824: XVII, 340.

94 Webster's speech of Jan. 19, 1824 in support of his Greek resolution is in V, 61–93.

98 For Webster's comment on his Jan. 19, 1824 speech, see Curtis, I, 205.

98 Letters from Hopkinson, Jan. 23 and Feb. 1, 1824; XVII, 341, 343.

99 Letter to Mason, Feb. 15, 1824: XVI, 80.

99 Letter to Ezekiel, Feb. 22, 1824: XVII, 346.

100 Letter to Mason, May 9, 1824: XVI, 85.

100 Letter to Everett, Feb. 13, 1824: XVII, 345.

100–01 Letter to Ezekiel, Mar. 14, 1824: XVII, 347.

101 Letter to Mason, April 19, 1824: XVI, 84.

101 The Plumer quote is from XVII, 549–50.

102 Plumer's reference to the Spanish claims is at XVII, 552.

102–03 Congressman Lincoln's verse on adjournment is in XVII, 337.

103 Letter to Mrs. Blake, June 9, 1824: XVII, 352.

103 Letter to George Blake, June 16, 1824: XVII, 352–53.

VII. Marshfield — Visit to Madison and Jefferson — Bunker Hill Oration

104 Quincy, 149.

104 Marshfield is located on the Atlantic coast a few miles north of

Plymouth Bay. This general area was the scene of Longfellow's poem "The Courtship of Miles Standish," in which that grizzled but bashful warrior sent his young friend John Alden to plead his cause with the fair Priscilla and to ask her hand in marriage, to whose embassy she replied, "Why don't you speak for yourself, John?"

104 Harvey, 264–65.

105–06 Letters to Mrs. Webster, Dec. 4 and 6, 1824: XVII, 355–56.

106 The Ticknor quote is from Curtis, I, 222–26.

112 Letter from Mrs. Webster, Dec. 28, 1824: XVII, 359.

112 Letter from Mrs. Webster, Jan. 22, 1825, and the lines composed by Webster: XVII, 375–76.

113 Letter to Ezekiel, Dec. 29, 1824: XVII, 362.

113–14 Letters to the Ticknors, Jan. 16 and 17, 1825: XVI, 93, 95. In the Nat. Ed. the first of these erroneously bears a December date.

115 Letter to Ticknor, Jan. 25, 1825: XVI, 96.

115 Letter to Mrs. Ticknor, Feb. 4, 1825: XVI, 97.

116 Plumer account of Randolph challenge: XVII, 553–55; see also XVI, 102–07.

118 Miss Quincy's diary is quoted in Quincy, 113–15.

119 The portrayal of Webster is from Quincy, 112.

119 Bunker Hill oration: I, 235–54.

123 The George Ticknor Curtis quote is from Curtis, I, 249, n. 1.

123 The Fletcher Webster anecdote is in Curtis, I, 250–51.

124 The welcome to Lafayette anecdote is in Lanman, 99.

124 The quotations are from Quincy, 117–18.

VIII. Niagara Falls — Adams-Jefferson Oration — Election to the Senate

Page

126 Story's letters describing the Niagara Falls trip are in Story, I, 450–62.

128 Letter to Mrs. Blake, July 15, 1825: XVII, 385.

130 Letter to Paige, July 16, 1825: XVII, 394.

131 Story letter to Denison, Jan. 20, 1826: Story, I, 487.

131 Webster letter to Story, Dec. 31, 1825: XVII, 400.

131 Letter to Clay, Sept. 28, 1825: XVI, 116.

131 Letter to Dr. Warren, Nov. 17, 1825: XVII, 397.

132 Letter to Haddock, Oct. 13, 1825: XVII, 396.

132 Letter to Haddock, Dec. 23, 1824: XVII, 357.

133 Letter to Haddock, Oct. 14, 1826: XVII, 410.

134 Letter to Denison, May 3, 1826: XVI, 128.

134 Letters to Ticknor, Jan. 8, Mar. 1, 1826: XVI, 118, 119. The reference is to the death of Czar Alexander I of Russia and his succession by Nicholas I.

135 Letter to Story, May 8, 1826: XVII, 405.

135 The John Adams anecdote, as told by Webster to Peter Harvey, is in Harvey, 210. There is a slightly different version in March, 62.

136 Ticknor's description is from Curtis, I, 274–75.

137 Discourse on Adams and Jefferson, I, 289–324.

143 Ticknor's and Curtis's comments are in Curtis, I, 275–76.

144 Letter to Clay, Oct. 13, 1826: XVI, 138.

144 Plumer anecdote: XVII, 565.

145 Letter to Story, Dec. 26, 1826: XVII, 412.

146 Letter to Everett, Dec. 21, 1826: XVII, 413

146 Letter to Biddle, Feb. 24, 1827: XVI, 141.

147 Letter to Story, Apr. 16, 1827: XVI, 160.

147 Letter to Sprague, Jan. 10, 1827: XVII, 414.

148 Letter to Lincoln, May 22, 1827: XVI, 161.

149 Letter from Lincoln, May 24, 1827: Curtis, I, 294.

149 Letter to Denison, July 28, 1827: XVI, 167.

IX. Death of Wife and Ezekiel — Remarriage

150 Letter to Ezekiel, July 20, 1827: XVII, 421.

150 Letter to Senator Silsbee, Dec. 1, 1827: XVII, 422.

151 Letter to Paige, Dec. 5, 1827: XVII, 424. The reference to "Daniel" is to Webster's oldest son, Daniel Fletcher, then called by his first name but later, and generally, known as "Fletcher."

152 Letter to Story, Dec. 18, 1827: XVII, 426.

152 Letter to Paige, Dec. 25, 1827: XVII, 429.

153 Letter to Silsbee, Jan. 4, 1828: XVII, 431.

154 Letter to Ezekiel, Jan. 8, 1828: XVII, 432.

155 Letter to Ezekiel, Jan. 17, 1828: XVII, 435.

155 Letters to Ezekiel, Jan. 21, 1828: XVII, 435, 436.

155 Ticknor Reminiscence: Curtis, I, 314.

156 Quincy, 213–14. Mrs. Webster was a great favorite with Webster's friends. In a family letter dated Jan. 8, 1827, Mrs. William W. Seaton, one of the acknowledged social and intellectual elite of

Washington, wrote: "Mrs. Everett and many members' wives have
been to see me, but Mrs. Webster is not here, I regret to say as she
is one of the strangers whose society I most enjoy." Seaton, 192–93.

156 Letter from Story, Jan. 27, 1828: XVII, 445.

157 Letter to Dr. Cyrus W. Perkins, Jan. 28, 1828: XVII, 446.

158 Letter to Ticknor, Feb. 22, 1828: XVI, 172.

158 Letter to Paige, undated: XVII, 451.

159 Letter to Mrs. Lee, Mar. 15, 1828: XVII, 452.

160 Letter to Ticknor, Apr. 18, 1828: XVI, 174.

160 Letter to Mrs. Ticknor, May 1828: XVI, 174.

161 Ticknor letter to Mrs. Ticknor, April 27, 1828: Ticknor, I, 382.
"Nanny" was Ticknor's oldest daughter, Anna Eliot, then five.

161 Letter to Mrs. Lee, May 18, 1828: XVII, 457.

162 Letter to McGaw, Oct. 11, 1828: XVI, 184.

164 Letter to Brazer, Nov. 10, 1828: XVII, 463. The reference was to
the book on *Rhetoric* by Richard Whately, one of the great intel-
lects of his day, shortly to be appointed Archbishop of Dublin.

165 Curtis, I, 252–53. For critiques of Webster's style, see: Whipple,
139–233; and Henry Cabot Lodge in *Cambridge History of American Literature*, II, Ch. XVI.

166 Lanman, 75.

166 Letter from Ezekiel, Feb. 15, 1829: XVII, 469.

166 Letter to Ezekiel, Feb. 5, 1829: XVI, 186.

167 Letter to Ezekiel, Feb. 23, 1829: XVI, 188.

167 Letter to Ezekiel, Feb. 26, 1829: XVI, 188.

167 Letter to Mrs. Ezekiel Webster, Feb. 19, 1829: XVII, 470.

168 Letter to Mrs. Ezekiel Webster, Mar. 2, 1829: XVII, 472.

169 Letter to Mrs. Ezekiel Webster, Mar. 4, 1829: XVII, 473.

170 Letter to Ezekiel, Mar. 15, 1829: XVII, 474.

171 Letter to Dr. Perkins, Apr. 17, 1829: XVII, 475.

172 Letter to Mason, Apr. 19, 1829: XVII, 477.

173 Letter to McGaw, Nov. 18, 1829: XVI, 190.

174–75 Letter to Fletcher, Dec. 14, 1829: XVII, 482.

X. The Debate with Hayne:
First Speech on Foote's Resolution

176 Letter to Dutton, Jan. 15, 1830: XVII, 483. The contretemps to
which Webster refers involved Peggy Eaton, a lady of questionable
background, now the wife of the Secretary of War. She was publicly

ostracized by the wives of Calhoun's friends in the Cabinet, where-upon Jackson indignantly championed her virtue and Van Buren used the controversy as a means of bringing about the resignation of the entire Cabinet. By this deft maneuver, Van Buren elimi-nated Calhoun's friends from the administration and set the stage for his own elevation, first to the vice presidency and ultimately to the presidency. For details of this episode, see Lewis, 114–19.

177 Letter to Mrs. Ezekiel Webster, Jan. 17, 1830: XVII, 484.
178 Letter to Haddock, Jan. 19, 1830: XVII, 485.
178 Letter to Mason, Feb. 27, 1830: XVII, 488.
178 In many accounts of the Webster-Hayne Debate, Senator Foote's name appears without an *e,* but in the *Biographical Dictionary of the American Congress* he is listed as Samuel Augustus Foote (1780–1846).
180 March, 97, 100, 101.
181 Curtis, I, 356, n. 2.
181 First Speech on Foote's Resolution, V, 248–69.

XI. The Debate with Hayne
Second Speech on Foote's Resolution

190 March, 125.
190 The Everett quote is from Harvey, 150–51.
190 The Story anecdote is from Harvey, 156.
191 The twelve pages of notes to which reference is made are included in the National Edition, VI, 289–92, as to which see Fuess, I, 373. Curtis also refers to Webster's notes for his Second Speech on Foote's Resolution, but somewhat differently, saying: "These notes are also now before me. Like those which he prepared for the First Speech on Foote's Resolution, they are written with great brevity on common letter-paper, and extend through five sheets." Curtis, I, 358. It is possible that there were two sets of notes, and that the ones to which Curtis refers were destroyed in a warehouse fire which consumed many of the documents which had been as-sembled by Curtis as one of Webster's literary executors.
191 The descriptions are from March, 132, 135.
191 The Second Speech on Foote's Resolution: VI, 3–75.
205 The description of the audience at the end of the speech is from March, 148–49.
205 The Captain Thomas anecdote is from Harvey, 269–71. Captain

Thomas was not the only one to believe at the end of Hayne's speech that Webster had been overborne. Everyone but Webster himself seems to have shared this feeling. Chester Harding, the artist, was in Washington at the time, working on a portrait of Calhoun, and heard the major speeches. He wrote:

"Mr. Hayne was most eloquent, and exceedingly bitter in his remarks upon Mr. Webster's [first] speech; and so scathing in his denunciations of New England and her policy, that I felt his sarcasms were unanswerable. I think all the friends of Mr. Webster thought so too . . . At night I went to see the fallen great man, as I considered him. My daughter was visiting Mr. Webster's daughter at the time. To my surprise, I found him cheerful, even playful. He had the two girls upon his knees . . .

"Mr. Calhoun gave me another sitting the next morning. He seemed to think the great champion of the North was annihilated . . . Later, I asked Mr. Calhoun what he thought of Webster's reply. He said simply, but with great emphasis, 'Mr. Webster is a *strong man,* sir, a *very strong man.*'" Harding, 148–49.

XII. Reply to Calhoun — The Bank War

208 Letter to Mason, Feb. 27, 1830: XVII, 488.

208 Madison's letter, dated Montpelier Mar. 15, 1830, is in XVII, 496.

208 Letter to Sullivan, May 22, 1830: XVII, 502.

211 The description of Calhoun's speech is from March, 234–35.

212 Webster's reply to Calhoun is in VI, 181–238. This is a long, closely reasoned speech; excerpts cannot possibly convey an adequate impression.

217 As to Webster's membership on the board of the central bank, see Catterall, 117–18.

218 Letter to Biddle, Dec. 21, 1833: Biddle, 218.

219 Letter to Biddle, Dec. 18, 1831: Biddle, 145.

219 Letter from Cadwalader to Biddle, Dec. 25, 1831: Biddle, 158.

219 Letter to White, June 28, 1832: XVII, 519.

220 Webster's speech of Feb. 26, 1835: VII, 200.

221 Webster's speech on the presidential protest, May 7, 1834: VII, 103–47.

NOTES AND SOURCES

XIII. The Murder of Captain Joseph White

Page

223 Letter to Story, Apr. 10, 1830: XVI, 199.

223 Letter from Story to Webster, Apr. 17, 1830: Van Tyne, 153.

223 The White murder case is the subject of a full-length book by Bradley and Winans. The legal proceedings are set out in Vol. 7 of *American State Trials*.

224 Captain White's house at 128 Essex Street, Salem, is now known as the Pingree House, for a later owner.

225 Letter from Holmes to Barnes, May 8, 1830: Morse, I, 69. Holmes, the father of the justice, was attending Harvard Law School, prior to his switch to medicine.

226 The "Charles Grant" letter is in *American State Trials*, VII, 438.

230 *Commonwealth v. Phillips*, 16 Tyng (Mass.) 423 (1820).

231 The three remaining Justices were Samuel Putnam, Samuel S. Wilde, and Marcus Morton. Lemuel Shaw was appointed Chief Justice, to succeed Parker, but he had represented one of the individuals included in the first indictment, and disqualified himself. The official prosecutors were Perez Morton, Attorney General, and Daniel Davis, Solicitor General.

232 Martineau, I, 167–68.

232–33 Letter to Story, Aug. 6, 1830: XVI, 205.

234 The quote is from *Amer. State Trials*, VII, 422; see also *Commonwealth v. J. F. Knapp*, 9 Pickering 496 (1830).

235 For Dexter's statement, see *Amer. State Trials*, VII, 503.

235 Lodge, 198–99.

235 The first quote from Webster's argument to the jury is from the contemporary report in the Boston *Evening Transcript* (Bradley & Winans, 145–46); it does not appear in this form in *Writings and Speeches*.

237 The second Webster quote is from XI, 52–54. Richard's testing of his victim's pulse was narrated in Joseph's confession. Although this demonstrated Richard's professional spirit and his commendable recognition that a $1,000 customer was entitled to the best of service, the only way it could have been known to Webster was from the confession; as this was not in evidence, it was improper for him to refer to it.

239 Letter to Story, Nov. 10, 1830: XVII, 506, where it is erroneously dated Aug. 11, 1830.

240 A facsimile of the receipt is set out in Bradley & Winans, 222.

241 *Commonwealth v. J. J. Knapp*, 10 Pickering 477 (1830).

241 *Commonwealth v. George Crowninshield*, 10 Pickering 497 (1830).

XIV. Frustrations and Frailties

Page

243 The quote from Plumer's Reminiscences of Webster is from XVII, 560.

243–44 Letter to Mason, Jan. 1, 1835: XVI, 245.

244–45 Letters to Mason, Feb. 1 and Feb. 6, 1835: XVI, 250, 252.

246 The quote is from Lanman, 90.

247 The anecdote about gathering eggs is from Harvey, 278.

247 As to Webster's land holdings, see: Fuess, II, 324, 337; also, Current, 93.

247 As to the sale of Webster's notes, see Fuess, II, 129 n 1.

248 Letter from Otis to Harrison, Feb. 7, 1845: Morison, 507.

248 Letter Sears to Webster, Mar. 21, 1846: XVI, 445.

250 Letter to Sears, Mar. 26, 1846: XVI, 446.

251 Letter to Thomas, Feb. 4, 1837: XVI, 283.

252 Letter to White, Aug. 12, 1832: XVII, 520.

252–53 Letters to Paige, Mar. 5 and 10, and Apr. 24: XVII, 514, 518.

253 Letter to White, Aug. 17, 1832: XVII, 523.

254 The description of Commodore Peterson is from Curtis, II, 663.

254–55 Letters to White: XVII, 524.

256 Wilkinson, 96.

258 Lanman, 85–86, 99–100, 89–90.

XV. Travels and Political Aspirations

Page

259 Letter to Cass: XVII, 536.

259 Letter from Henry Clay, June 17, 1833: Curtis I, 462.

259–60 Letter to Fletcher, July 1, 1833: XVII, 538.

260 Letter to Mrs. Webster, Jan. 1834: XVIII, 3.

261 Letter to Mrs. Lee, Mar. 12, 1834: XVIII, 4.

262 Letter to Mrs. Paige, Apr. 27, 1834: XVIII, 7.

262 Letter to Fletcher, June 5, 1834: XVI, 236.

263 Letter to James Brooks, Aug. 5, 1834: XVI, 241.
264 Letter to Stevens, Jan. 1, 1835: XVI, 246.
264 Letter to Weston, Aug. 29, 1835: XVIII, 11.
264-68 Letters to Mrs. Webster:
 Dec. 7, 1835: XVI, 261.
 Dec. 23, 1835: XVI, 262.
 Jan. 1, 1836: XVIII, 14.
 Jan. 10, 1836: XVI, 264.
 Jan. 24, 1836: XVI, 264.
 Jan. 29, 1836: XVI, 266.
 Undated: XVIII, 18.
 Feb. 9, 1836: XVI, 268.
 Mar. 6, 1836: XVI, 270.
 Apr. 29, 1836: XVI, 275.
268-70 Letters to Fletcher:
 Jan. 15, 1836: XVIII, 16.
 Mar. 14, 1836: XVI, 271.
 June 12, 1836: XVI, 278.
 June 15, 1836: XVIII, 20.
 June 25, 1836: XVIII, 20.
270 Letter to Ray Thomas, Mar. 5, 1838: XVI, 295.
271 Letter to Everett, Jan. 31, 1837: XVIII, 24.
272 Letter to Winthrop, Jan. 31, 1837: XVIII, 26.
272 Letter to Ketchum, Feb. 20, 1837: XVIII, 27.
273 Address in Niblo's Saloon, Mar. 15, 1837: II, 205–06.
275 Speech at Rochester, N. Y., July 20, 1837: XIII, 88.

XVI. Visit to England

Page
276 Letter to Jaudon, Jan. 1839: Van Tyne, 723.
278 Letter to Curtis, June 3, 1839: XVIII, 46.
280 Letter to Charles H. Thomas, June 9, 1839: XVI, 307.
281 Letter to Healey, June 9, 1839: XVI, 309.
282 Letter to Healey, June 12, 1839: XVI, 311.
283 Letter to Everett, June 12, 1839: XVIII, 50.
283 Letter to Curtis, June 12, 1839: XVIII, 48.
284 Letter to Davis, June 24, 1839: XVIII, 50.
284 Letter to Ketchum, June 24, 1839: XVIII, 53.

NOTES AND SOURCES

285 Letter to Curtis, July 4, 1839: XVIII, 55.

286 Letter to Ketchum, July 23, 1839: XVIII, 58.

286 Letter to Crittenden, July 31, 1839: XVI, 313.

287 Letter to Davis, July 31, 1839: XVIII, 61.

287 Letter to Ticknor, Aug. 21, 1839: XVIII, 63.

288 Letter to Mrs. Lindsley, Sept. 6, 1839: XVIII, 67.

289 Letter to Everett, Oct. 16, 1839: XVIII, 71.

290 Letter to Rogers, Feb. 10, 1840: XVIII, 74.

291 In addition to Webster's letters, two accounts of the family trip to England have been published: *Daniel Webster in England*, from the journal of Harriette Story Paige; and *"Mr. W. & I.,"* from the diary of Mrs. Caroline Le Roy Webster. Some of the contrasts are illuminating; for example, the descriptions of Lowther Castle, where they were the guests of Lord Londsale, wealthy British mine owner. Webster, writing to Ticknor, says, "You know all about Lowther Castle. One may safely say of it what Mr. Mason said of his house in Portsmouth, that it is a comfortable shelter against the weather!" Mrs. Webster, on the other hand, became almost ecstatic over its luxurious efficiency, with 46 domestic servants, separate larders and kitchens for different types of meat, silver plates for luncheon, gold for dinner, etc. Her description accentuates the ironic humor of Webster's letter of Oct. 16 to Everett, comparing "poor old, barren, sea-beaten Marshfield" to Lowther Castle, Belvoir, and Windsor, and saying, "neither of these is Marshfield. And so, I am sure, their owners and occupants would think if they were to see it." Webster's daughter, Julia, also kept an account of this trip in her diary, now in the possession of her grandson, Mr. Lewis Addison Armistead of Cambridge, Mass.

XVII. Secretary of State under Harrison and Tyler — The Webster-Ashburton Treaty

Page

292 Letter to Mrs. Paige, Feb. 2, 1840: XVIII, 73.

292 Letter from White to Webster, Jan. 26, 1840: XVIII, 72.

293 Letter to Fletcher, Mar. 5, 1840: XVIII, 76.

294 Undated letter from Denison to G. T. Curtis: Curtis, II, 27.

295 Letter to Everett, Feb. 16, 1840: XVIII, 75.

295 Letter to Jaudon, June 23, 1840: XVIII, 87.

295 Letter to Edward Curtis, Oct. 10, 1840: XVIII, 89.

296 Letter from Harrison to Webster, Dec. 1, 1840: XVIII, 90.
296 Letter to Harrison, Dec. 11, 1840: XVIII, 93.
297 Letter to Mrs. Paige, Dec. 13, 1840: XVIII, 94.
298 Letter to Ketchum, Dec. 18, 1840: XVIII, 95.
298 Harvey, 160–63.
301 Letter to Mrs. Webster, Aug. 8, 1841: XVIII, 107.
302 Letter to Mrs. Webster, Aug. 16, 1841: XVI, 353.
303 Letter to Ketchum, Aug. 22, 1841: XVIII, 109.
303 Letter to Mrs. Webster, Aug. 28, 1841: XVIII, 109.
304 Letter to Ketchum, Sept. 10, 1841: XVIII, 110.
304 As to Stuart letter requesting appointment for Lincoln, see Fuess, II, 94.
305 Letter to Everett, July 24, 1841: XVIII, 105.
306 Letter to Tyler, July, 1841: XVI, 344.
307 Treaty of Washington speech: IX, 78, at 86–97.
309 Letter to Everett, Jan. 29, 1842: XVIII, 113.
310 Letter to Weston, Jan. 5, 1842: XVIII, 111.
310 Letter to Weston, Feb. 18, 1842: XVIII, 115.
310–11 Adams, II, 392.
311 Letter from Sparks to Webster, Feb. 15, 1842: Adams, II, 394.
312 Letter to Fairfield, Apr. 11, 1842: XI, 272.
313 Letter to Everett, Apr. 25, 1842: XVIII, 120.
313 Letter to Mrs. Curtis, May 4, 1842: XVIII, 125.
314 Letters to Sparks, May 14 and 16, 1842: XVI, 371.
315 Letter to Everett, June 14, 1842: XVI, 374.
315 Letter to Fletcher, May 21, 1842: XVIII, 128.
315 Letter to Everett, June 28, 1842: XVI, 375.
316 Letter from Ashburton to Webster, July 1, 1842: Curtis, II, 113.
317 Letter to Weston, July 16, 1842: XVIII, 139.
317 Letter to Weston, July 23, 1842: XVIII, 139.
317 Letter to Weston, Aug. 2, 1842: XVIII, 142.
317 Letter to Mason, Aug. 21, 1842: XVIII, 146.
318 Letter to Mrs. Paige, Aug. 23, 1842: XVIII, 146.
318 Letter to Tyler, Aug. 24, 1842: XVIII, 146.
319 Letter to Everett, Apr. 25, 1843: XVI, 402.
320 Letter to Sparks, Mar. 11, 1843: XVI, 397.

XVIII. Return to Private Life

322 Letter from Mason to Webster, Aug. 28, 1842: XVIII, 148.

323 Speech at Faneuil Hall, Sept. 30, 1842: III, 117–40.

325 Letter to Fletcher, Oct. 4, 1842: XVIII, 150 (date misstated).

325 Letter to Edward Curtis, Oct. 4, 1842: XVIII, 151 (date misstated).

326 Letter to Mrs. Curtis, May 26, 1842: XVIII, 129. Unhappily, modern Marshfield retains none of the charm that Webster depicts. "Progress" has obliterated the outlines of the estate, as well as all semblance of farm and wilderness. Almost the only thing that remains to remind one of Webster is the family lot in the graveyard.

328 Letter to Everett, Nov. 28, 1842: XVIII, 153.

328 Letter to Mrs. Paige, Nov. 28, 1842: XVIII, 156.

329 Letter to Weston, Dec. 8, 1842: XVIII, 158.

329 Letter to Weston, Jan. 27, 1843: XVIII, 164.

329 Letter to Weston, Mar. 6, 1843: XVIII, 168.

330 Letter to Weston, Mar. 12, 1843: XVIII, 169.

330 Letter to President Tyler, May 8, 1843: XVI, 404.

331 Letter from Tyler to Webster, May 8, 1843: XVI, 404.

331 Letter to Mrs. Curtis, May 10, 1843: XVIII, 172.

332 Letter to Mrs. Paige, Sept. 18, 1843: XVIII, 174.

332 Letter to Weston, Nov. 1, 1843: XVIII, 175.

333 Letter to Paige, Nov. 1843: XVIII, 176.

333 Letters to Mrs. Fletcher Webster, Dec. 1843: XVIII, 177 and 179.

334 Letter to David Sears, Feb. 5, 1844: XVIII, 182.

335 Letter to Mason, Feb. 6, 1844: XVI, 424.

336 Letter to Josephine, Mar. 4, 1844: XVI, 425. Although I have no positive proof, I am satisfied that "Josephine" was the daughter of Webster's intimate friend, William W. Seaton, Editor of the *National Intelligencer* and Mayor of Washington. Webster and Seaton were shooting companions, and on at least one occasion Webster had stayed in the Seaton home in Washington (see page 299). Josephine Seaton was 21 at the time of the letter (Webster being 62). Three years later, in 1847, she accompanied Mr. and Mrs. Webster on their trip through the South. Still later, in a biography of her father, she had this to say about Webster:

"The world knew Mr. Webster in the majesty of his intellectual greatness, but little comprehended the sprightly humor, the playful grace, the tender sweetness which rendered him so captivating in an intimate circle . . . As is known, Mr. Webster was an unconscionably early riser . . . He had a habit of scribbling notes to Mr. Seaton at this matutinal hour, not infrequently sending impromptu doggerel lines indited while at breakfast on an empty egg shell." Seaton, 299–302.

Josephine Seaton appears to have been singularly self-effacing. Although her biography of her father is full of family letters and data, she excluded all mention of herself. Her name appears only once in the book, on the title page. In a 1906 genealogical work about the Seaton family, the author, Oren Andrew Seaton, says: "Josephine was born at Washington, D. C., on Sept. 7, 1822. From that time until the day of her death we find no mention of her name, except that she was the author of the Biographical Sketch of William W. Seaton, her father."

337 Letter to Mrs. Paige, Mar. 26, 1844: XVIII, 186.

337 Letter to Fletcher, Apr. 1, 1844: XVIII, 187.

338 Letter to Mr. and Mrs. Paige, Nov. 1844: XVIII, 194–95.

338 Letter to Weston, Jan. 27, 1845: XVI, 429.

339 Letter to Weston, Jan. 28, 1845: XVIII, 197.

339 Letter to Weston, Feb. 5, 1845: XVIII, 197.

339 Letter to Weston, Feb. 20, 1845: XVIII, 199.

339 Letter to Weston, Feb. 24, 1845: XVIII, 201.

340 Letter to Weston, Mar. 12, 1845: XVIII, 205.

XIX. War with Mexico — Trip to the South

341 Letter to Everett, Feb. 26, 1845: XVIII, 201.

342 Letter to Fletcher, Mar. 11, 1845: XVIII, 203.

343 Letter to Fletcher, Mar. 13, 1845: XVIII, 205.

343 For Webster's characterization of his law practice, see Curtis, II, 216.

343 Letter to Weston, May 13, 1845: XVIII, 206.

344 Letter to Weston, May 15, 1845: XVIII, 207.

344 Letter to Curtis, Oct. 3, 1845: XVIII, 211; George P. A. Healy (misspelled "Healey" in the letter) was a popular portrait painter of the period; among his better known works is the painting of Webster debating Hayne, which is in Faneuil Hall, Boston.

345 For Webster's comment about British shooting, see Curtis, II, 222.

345 Letter to Paige, undated, 1845: XVIII, 209.

346 Letter to Fletcher, Jan. 11, 1846: XVIII, 213.

346 Letter to Blatchford, May 3, 1846: XVIII, 225.

348 Letter to Fletcher, Jan. 14, 1846: XVI, 440.

348 Letter to Fletcher, June 13, 1846: XVI, 455.

348 Letter to Fletcher, Aug. 6, 1846: XVI, 465.

349 Letter to Weston, Aug. 10, 1846: XVIII, 233.

349 Letter to Edward, Feb. 5, 1847: XVI, 468.

350 Letter to Edward, Apr. 11, 1847: XVIII, 237.

350 Letter to Fletcher, Apr. 25, 1847: XVIII, 238.

351 Letter to Edward, Sept. 27, 1847: XVIII, 260.

351 Letter to Fletcher, Dec. 1847: XVI, 487.

351 Letter to Fletcher, Feb. 7, 1847: XVI, 469; as to the Passenger Cases, 7 Howard 283 (1849), see also Webster's letter to J. Prescott Hall, XVI, 511.

352 For the anecdote about the couplet from Pope's *Dunciad,* see especially Fuess, *Rufus Choate,* 236.

353 Letter to Mrs. Paige, Apr. 29, 1847: XVIII, 240.

354 Letter to Fletcher, May 5, 1847: XVIII, 242.

355 Letter to Mrs. Paige, May 9, 1847: XVIII, 244.

356 Letter to Fletcher, May 10, 1847: XVIII, 245.

357 Webster's address to the Charleston, S. C., bar on May 10, 1847, is in IV, 87.

357 The spelling-book anecdote is from Lanman, 144.

357 Letter to Weston, May 10, 1847: XVIII, 246.

358 Letter to Mrs. Paige, May 13, 1847: XVIII, 249.

359 Letter to Mrs. Paige, May 15, 1847: XVIII, 252.

361 Letter to Fletcher, May 23, 1847: XVIII, 254.

361 Letter to Fletcher, June 11, 1847: XVIII, 256.

362 Letter to Fletcher, June 12, 1847: XVIII, 257.

362 Letter to Curtis, Oct. 27 (year not given): XVIII, 261.

363 Excerpt from speech at Grafton, N. H., Aug. 28, 1847: IV, 107, at 110.

363 Letter to Blatchford, Dec. 7, 1847: XVIII, 262.

XX. Death of Edward and Julia — Trip to Martha's Vineyard

366 Letter to Fletcher, Dec. 7, 1847: XVI, 487.

366 Letter to Fletcher, Jan. 31, 1848: XVIII, 268.

366 Letter to Fletcher, Feb. 4, 1848: XVIII, 268.

367 Letter to Fletcher, Feb. 10, 1848: XVIII, 269.

367 Letter to Julia, Feb. 14, 1848: XVIII, 269; unfortunately, Julia

destroyed almost all letters from her father, feeling, apparently, that they were too personal to come to the eyes of others.

368 Letter to Fletcher, Feb. 23, 1848: XVIII, 271.
368 The anecdote about Webster and Julia is from Harvey, 329–32.
370 Letter to Fletcher, June 10, 1848: XVI, 495.
370 Letter to Fletcher, June 16, 1848: XVI, 495.
371 Letter to Fletcher, June 29, 1848: XVI, 497.
371 Letter to Hoar, Aug. 23, 1848: XVI, 498.
372 Letter to Blatchford, July 12, 1848: XVIII, 280.
372 Letter to Mrs. Paige, Thanksgiving, 1848: XVIII, 289.
372 Letter to Everett, Nov. 28, 1848: XVIII, 289.
373 Letter to Porter Wright, Dec. 14, 1848: XVIII, 290.
374 Letter to Ticknor, Dec. 21, 1848: XVI, 508.
374 Letter to Fletcher, Dec. 26, 1848: XVI, 509.
375 Letter to Lyman, Jan. 15, 1849: XVI, 510.
376 Letter to Blatchford, Dec. 5, 1848: XVI, 501.
376 Letter to Blatchford, Jan. 1, 1849: XVI, 503.
377 Letter to Blatchford, Jan. 16, 1849: XVI, 504.
377 Letter to Blatchford, Feb. 25, 1849: XVI, 507.
378 Letter to Blatchford, Feb. 1, 1849: XVIII, 294.
378 Letter to March, Feb. 5, 1849: XVIII, 297.
379 Letter to Blatchford, Feb. 10, 1849: XVIII, 297.
379 Letter to Blatchford, Feb. 15, 1849: XVIII, 299.
380 Letter to John Taylor, Feb. 16, 1849: XVIII, 301.
380 Letter to John Taylor, Mar. 9, 1849: XVIII, 305.
381 Letter to John Taylor, Mar. 17, 1849: XVIII, 307.
381 Letter to Blatchford, Mar. 11, 1849: XVIII, 305.
382 Letter to Blatchford, June 15, 1849: XVI, 524.
382 Letter from Mrs. Lee, Mar. 16, 1849: XVIII, 306.
382 Letter to Mrs. Lee, May 25, 1849: XVIII, 326.
383 Letter to Mrs. Lee, May 29, 1849: XVIII, 326.
383 As to Webster's mortuary arrangements for his horses, see Harvey, 282, and Lyman, II, 129.
384 Letter to Mrs. Paige, Apr. 21, 1849: XVIII, 315.
385 Letter to Mrs. Paige, Apr. 23, 1849: XVIII, 318.
385 Letter to Fletcher, May 2, 1849: XVIII, 321.
386 Letter to Blatchford, May 6, 1849: XVIII, 322.
387 Letter to Blatchford, Aug. 5, 1849: XVIII, 330.
387 Letter to Blatchford, Aug. 7, 1849: XVIII, 331.
388 Letter to Blatchford, Aug. 8, 1849: XVIII, 332.

NOTES AND SOURCES

389 Letter to Blatchford, Aug. 8, 1849: XVIII, 334.
389 Letter to Blatchford, Aug. 10, 1849: XVIII, 334.
390 Letter to Blatchford, Aug. 12, 1849: XVIII, 337.
391 Letter to Blatchford, Aug. 30, 1849: XVIII, 341.

XXI. The Seventh of March Speech

393 Letter to Curtis, Jan. 25, 1850: XVIII, 351.
394 Letter from Alexander H. Stephens, Jan., 1850, to his brother, Linton: Johnston and Browne, 244.
395 Speech at Capon Springs, Va., June 28, 1851: XIII, 429.
396 Letter to Furness, Feb. 15, 1850: XVIII, 353.
397 Excerpt from reply of Clay to Senator Benton: Congr. Globe, XXII, Part 1, 1st Sess., 31st Cong, 1849–50, 660.
397 Curtis, II, 397; also in XIII, 562.
398 Letter to Haven, Jan. 13, 1850: XVI, 529.
399 Letter to Harvey, Feb. 13, 1850: XVI, 532.
399 Letter to Harvey, Feb. 14, 1850: XVI, 533.
399 Letter to Fletcher, Feb. 24, 1850: XVI, 533.
400 Letter to Warren, Mar. 1, 1850: XVI, 534.
400 Harvey, 220.
400 Lyman, II, 154.
401 Seventh of March speech: X, 57–98.

XXII. Seventh of March Speech — The Aftermath

410 Letter to Ticknor, Mar. 17, 1850: XVIII, 358.
410 Letter to Haven, Mar. 13, 1850: XVI, 537.
410–11 For Corcoran's gift and Webster's acknowledgment, see Moore, 209–10.
411 Gift letter, dated Mar. 28, 1850: XVIII, 361.
411 Letter from Curtis to Harvey, Apr. 12, 1850: Van Tyne, 408.
411 Letter to Fletcher, Mar. 21, 1850: XVI, 535.
411 Letter to Harvey, Mar. 22, 1850: XVI, 535.
412 Letter to Harvey, Apr. 4, 1850: XVI, 536.
412 Letter to Fletcher, Mar. 31, 1850: XVIII, 363.

412 Letter to Healey, Apr. 2, 1850: XVI, 537.

413 Letter to Samuel Lawrence, June 10, 1850: XVI, 548.

413 Letter to Haven, July 4, 1850: XVI, 549.

414 Letter to Haven, July 11, 1850: XVIII, 376.

414 Letter to Haven, Sept. 12, 1850: XVIII, 386.

415 Hilliard, 231.

415 Letter to Haven, July 12, 1850: XVIII, 376.

416 Letter to Haven, July 21, 1850: XVI, 552.

417 Letter to Fletcher, July 23, 1850: XVIII, 379.

417 Letter to Ticknor, Aug. 15, 1850: XVI, 561.

417 Speech of July 17, 1850: X, 144, at 169–70.

418 Letter to Haven, Aug. 1850: XVI, 556.

418 Letter to Haven, Sept. 5, 1850: XVI, 561.

419 Letter to Harvey, Sept. 10, 1850: XVIII, 385.

420 Not all the literary figures were on the other side. George S. Hillard, one-time law partner of Charles Sumner, and a writer of considerable renown in his own right, described the situation this way: "It was natural that men, whose fervid sympathies are wedded to a single idea, should have felt aggrieved by the stand Webster then took; and if decency and decorum had governed their expressions, neither he nor his friends could have had any right to complain. But in many cases the attacks were so foul and ferocious that they lost all claim to be treated as moral judgments, and sunk to the level of the lowest and coarsest effusions of malice and hatred." Memorial of D. W. from Boston, 254.

420 Excerpt from Mar. 7, 1850 speech: X, 63–64.

422 Parker, 338. See Rhodes, I, 288–90, in which that eminent historian, who was not himself always kind to Webster, has this to say about Parker's sermon on Oct. 31, 1852, the Sunday following Webster's death: "Even had the discourse been true, it was, considering the occasion, indecent. But in it there was much of error . . . Yet we may not utterly condemn Parker. He was sincere, and meant to be truthful; but he had the mental constitution which could see only his side of any question . . . His sermon on Webster moulded many opinions. Of all the indictments it is the most severe . . . and it is gratifying that fewer men now believe the charges than when the sermon was delivered; that instead . . . it is regarded as the raving of an honest fanatic."

422 Nevins, I, 290–91.

XXIII. The Hülsemann Letter —
Bid for the Presidency

423 Letter to Porter Wright, May 13, 1850: XVIII, 368.

424 Letter to Porter Wright, June 19, 1850: XVIII, 375.

424 Letter to Blatchford, Oct. 19, 1850: XVI, 572.

425 Letter to Blatchford, Oct. 21, 1850: XVI, 572.

425 Letter to Blatchford, Oct. 22, 1850: XVI, 574.

425 Letter to Curtis, Oct. 24, 1850: XVIII, 397.

426 Letter to Fillmore, Oct. 24, 1850: XVI, 573.

426 Letter to Fillmore, Nov. 13, 1850: XVI, 575; XVIII, 402.

428 Letter to Hülsemann, Dec. 21, 1850: XII, 165 at 170 & 178; see also Curtis, II, 534–36.

429 Letter to Ticknor, Jan. 16, 1851: XVI, 586.

430 Letter to John Taylor, Mar. 25, 1852: XVI, 648.

430 Letter to John Taylor, Apr. 21, 1852: XVIII, 524.

431 Letter to Curtis, July 16, 1852: XVIII, 538.

431–32 Letter to Blatchford, Mar. 28, 1851: XVIII, 426.

432 Letter to Fillmore, July 23, 1851: XVIII, 452.

434 Letter to John Taylor, July, 29, 1851: XVIII, 455.

435 Letter from John Taylor, Dec. 31, 1851: XVIII, 502.

435 Letter to John Taylor, Mar. 13, 1852: XVIII, 513.

436 Letter to Hall, Feb. 22, 1852: XVIII, 508.

438 Letter to Fillmore, Jan. 1851: XVI, 583.

438 Letter to Haven, June 11, 1851: XVI, 617.

439 Letter to Fillmore, Aug. 23, 1851: XVI, 624.

440 Letter to Fillmore, Sept. 10, 1851: XVI, 625; Lanman, 133.

441 Letter to Haven, Dec. 14, 1851: XVI, 630.

442 Letter to Fillmore, June 21, 1852: XVI, 647.

442 Letter from Fillmore, June 21, 1852: Rayback, 361.

442 Letter to Fletcher, July 4, 1852: XVI, 658.

XXIV. The End

443 Letter to Fillmore, May 9, 1852: XVIII, 528.

444 Letter to Fillmore, May 12, 1852: XVIII, 529.

445 Letter to Fillmore, May 19, 1852: XVIII, 531.

446 Letter to Porter Wright, June 13, 1852: XVIII, 534.

446 Letter to Fillmore, July 13, 1852: XVIII, 535.

NOTES AND SOURCES

447 Letter to B. C. Clark, Jr., July 23, 1852: XVI, 660.
448 Letter to Fillmore, July 26, 1852: XVIII, 544.
448 Letter to Fillmore, Sept. 12, 1852: XVIII, 552.
449 Letter to Fillmore, Sept. 16, 1852: XVIII, 553.
450 Letter to Fillmore, Oct. 4, 1852: XVIII, 556.
450 Letter to Fillmore, Oct. 15, 1852: XVIII, 558.
450 Letter to Fillmore, Oct. 17, 1852: XVIII, 559.
451 Letter to Fillmore, Oct. 18, 1852: XVIII, 560.
451 Letter from Abbot to Fillmore, Oct. 21, 1852: XVIII, 560.
451 Letter from Abbot to Fillmore, Oct. 25, 1852: XVIII, 561.
452 Quote from Will: Curtis, II, 703.

INDEX

Abbot, George J., 449, 451–52
Abbott, Benjamin, Principal of Phillips Exeter Academy, 9, 38, 263
Aberdeen, Lord, British Foreign Secretary, 309, 319, 320
Abolitionists, 257, 394, 407, 410, 413, 419–22
Adams, John, 2nd President of the U. S.: death, 135; anecdote of, 135–36; oration on, 136–43, 165–66
Adams, John Quincy, 6th President of the U. S.: election, 1824, 99–100; defeat, 1828, 166; hostility, 52n, 144, 159; attack on Webster in House, 1836, 266, 267; mentioned, 131, 276
Adams-Jefferson Oration, 136–43, 165–66
Alden, John, 104n
Amory, William, 250
Annexation of Texas, 273, 342
Appleton, Mrs. Julia Webster, wife of Samuel A. Appleton: birth, 41; with Mrs. E. B. Lee, 157, 159, 161, 173–74; in West with Webster, 274; on English trip, 276, 278, 285, 290, 291n; marriage, 289; illness and death, 366–70; mentioned, 91, 103, 106, 134, 156, 163, 171, 176, 177, 261, 262, 337, 368, 368n, 389; letter to, 367
Appleton, Nathan, 250, 253
Appleton, Samuel, 250
Appleton, Samuel Appleton, marriage to Julia Webster, 1839, 276, 289
Appleton, William, 250
Apthorp, J. W. T., 88

Armistead, Lewis Addison, grandson of Julia Webster, 291n
Ashburton, Lord (Alexander Baring): negotiates Treaty of Washington, 309, 313, 315–21; Healy portrait, 345; letter from, 316
Ashmun, George, Mass. Congressman, 374, 441
Augusta, Georgia, 360

Bachelder, Reverend Stephen, 1
Bachelder, Susannah, grandmother of Webster, 2, 294
Bagot, Sir Charles, 283
Baldwin, Taylor, 33n
Ballard, Achasa, see Webster, Mrs. Achasa Ballard
Bank of the United States: as a client, 146, 217–18; Webster supports, against Jackson, 217–20
Barbour, Philip Pendleton, 90, 108
Baring, Alexander, see Ashburton, Lord
Batchelder, see Bachelder
Beckford, Mrs. Mary, 225, 229
Benét, Stephen Vincent, xv
Benton, Thomas Hart, Missouri Senator: delivers Randolph challenge, 116–17; in Webster-Hayne debate, 179–80, 188–89; attacks Webster-Ashburton Treaty, 319; mentioned, 266, 268, 412
Biddle, Nicholas, President Second Bank of the U. S.: Bank War with Jackson, 217–20; encourages Webster to sell land in England, 277–78; mentioned, 367; letters to, 146, 218, 219

INDEX

Bingham, James Hervey: 455; description of Webster, xvi; mentioned, 10; letters to, 14, 15, 17, 21, 24, 32, 38, 40, 46

Binney, A., 250

Blake, George, Boston lawyer: 455; shares cask of wine, 88; hunting companion, 103, 104, 252; mentioned, 93, 155, 254, 265; letters to, 91, 103

Blake, Mrs. Sarah Murdock: 130; letters to, 92, 103, 128

Blatchford, Richard Milford, N. Y. lawyer: 455–56; member of Hone Club, 456; executor under Webster's will, 456; mentioned, 333, 434, 449; letters to, 346, 363, 372, 376, 377, 378, 379, 381, 382, 386, 387, 388, 389, 390, 391, 424, 425, 431

Boscawen, N. H.: practice of law in, 37, 38, 40

Bracket, J. W., 10

Bradley, Samuel A.: arranges Fryeburg teaching position, 16; introduces Webster to Gore, 30

Brazer, Reverend John: letter to, 164

Brooks, James: letter to, 263

Brougham, Henry Peter, Lord Chancellor, 286

Brown, Charles, 106, 160, 253, 292, 302, 417

Brown, David S., 250

Buckminster, Eliza, see Lee, Mrs. E. B.

Buckminster, Joseph Stevens, 9, 382

Bunker Hill, cornerstone celebration, 118–25

Burr, Aaron, 110

Cabot, Henry, 250

Cadwalader, Thomas, 219

Calhoun, John C.: Secy. of War, 115; presidential candidate, 99; Vice Pres., 100, 167, 176n, 179; comments on Webster-Hayne debate, 207n; Senator, 210; nullification, 210–12; Webster's reply to, 212–17; advocates disunion, 394, 412; death, 412–13

Calhoun-Webster debate, 210–17

Call, Sarah, 446–47

Calypso, The, 252, 253, 467

Canadian boundary dispute, 306–21

Canal boat travel, 126–27

Canning, Sir Stratford, 283

Capon Springs, 395

Carlyle, Thomas: description of Webster, xix

Caroline Affair, The, 305–06

Cartwright, C. W., 250

Cass, Lewis: at Exeter, 10; Western land speculation, 277; mentioned, 265; letter to, 259

Catarrh, annual afflictions of, 344–45, 387, 392, 414, 419, 424, 439, 449

Caucuses, Webster's views on, 90

Chadwick, Eben, 250

Charleston, S. C.: visit to, 355–57

Chase, Salmon Portland, 274

Chickering, J., 250

Choate, Rufus: at White murder trial, 235n; retires from Senate, 334, 341; anecdote re Wyman trial, 352; considered for Supreme Court, 440; eulogy on Webster, 65

Clark, B. C., Jr.: letter to, 447

Clay, Henry: Speaker of the House, 90; presidential candidate, 100; favors protective tariff, 100; Webster opposes, 101–02; supports U. S. Bank against Jackson, 219–20; frustrates Webster's hopes for presidential nomination, 244, 245, 246, 259, 282, 441; reception for Webster in Kentucky, 274; break with Pres. Tyler, 302–04, 322–23; proposes plan for 1850 Compromise, 397–98; Webster's characterization of, 413; mentioned, 114, 166, 168, 296; letters to, 131, 144; letter from, 259

Colman, Reverend Henry: Salem murder trials, 227–29, 233, 235, 240, 241

Colt, Roswell L.: member of Hone Club, 456; gift of prize cattle, 430

Columbia, S. C.: visit to, 358–60

Compromise of 1850, 397–422

Concord, N. H.: 4th of July oration, 1806, 43

Conrad, Charles M., Secretary of War, 450

Corcoran, William W.: 410; letter to, 411

INDEX

Crawford, William H., Secretary of Treasury, 99, 100, 103, 116

Crittenden, John J.: 304, 378; letter to, 286

Crowninshield, George, 226–41

Crowninshield, Richard, 226–41

Curtis, Benjamin Robbins, Associate Justice, U. S. Supreme Court, 440

Curtis, Edward: 456; member of Hone Club, 456; in Washington, 292, 297, 328, 378, 379, 380, 417; accompanies Webster to Richmond, 354; characterized by Webster, 380; describes gold watch and chain, 411; trustee under Webster's will, 459; mentioned, 314; letters to, 278, 283, 285, 295, 325, 344, 362, 393, 425, 431

Curtis, Mrs. Edward: 326; letters to, 313, 326, 331

Curtis, George Ticknor, literary executor and biographer of Webster: at Bunker Hill oration, 123; description of Seth Peterson, 254; on speech attributed to Adams, 143; on Webster's style, 165; on Webster's work habits, 181; on Webster's notes for reply to Hayne, 191n; on 1850 conference between Webster and Clay, 397–98; mentioned, 375

Curtis, Thomas B., 250

Cushing, Caleb, 333, 338, 465

Cutts, Edward, Jr.: letter to, 46

Dana, General James, xin

Dane, Nathan, draftsman of 1787 Ordinance, 187

Dartmouth College: Webster as freshman, 10; graduation, 11, 11n, 14; charter, 58–60

Dartmouth College case, 4 Wheat. 518 (1819), 58–72

Davis, Isaac P.: 457; tells Webster of Marshfield, 104; at Plymouth oration, 79; shares cask of wine, 88; mentioned, 260; letters to, 284, 287; letter from, 93

Davis, Jefferson, 420

Davis, John, 209, 314, 374

Denison, John Evelyn: 457; correspondent of Story, 131; furnishes coach to Webster in England, 283–84; Webster tells of intention to quit public life, 294; letters to, 134, 149

Dexter, Franklin: in Salem murder trials, 230, 232, 235, 239, 241; subscribes to Webster annuity, 250

Dickens, Charles, 281

Drunkenness, charges of, 255–58, 422

Duels, Randolph challenges to, 53, 116–18

Dunham, Josiah: letter to, 58

Durfee, Amos, killed in *Caroline* Affair, 306

Dutton, Warren: letter to, 176

Eastman, Abigail, see Webster, Mrs. Abigail Eastman

Eaton, Peggy, 176, 176n

Edgar, Mrs. Robert W., 463

Edwards, J. W., 250

Egg shells, use by Webster for doggerel lines to his friends, 336n

Egleston, George W., 411

Elms, The, Webster family place at Franklin, N. H., descriptions of, 346–48, 425, 446–47

Emerson, Ralph Waldo: characterization of Webster, xv; letter from Carlyle, xix; denounces 1850 Compromise, 419

Everett, Edward: 457; on Greek Revolution, 90–93; in Congress, 190, 209; Minister to England, 304–05; Canadian boundary dispute, 309, 313; Pres. of Harvard, 348; Hülsemann letter, 428; mentioned, 79, 416; letters to, 90, 91, 93, 100, 146, 271, 283, 295, 305, 309, 313, 315, 319, 328, 341

Exeter, N. H., 9–10, 263

Fairfield, John, Governor of Maine: 312–15; letter to, 312

Fessenden, William Pitt, 274

Fillmore, Millard, 13th President of the U. S.: 458; presides over Senate at Seventh of March speech, 401; accession to presidency, 415; appoints Webster Secy. of State, 415–16; Webster's characterization of, 416, 417; personal relations with Webster, 437–

Fillmore, Millard, (contd.)
38; rivalry for Whig nomination, 438, 441–42; mentioned, 143; letters to, 426, 432, 438, 439, 440, 442, 443, 444, 445, 446, 448, 449, 450, 451; letter from, 442
Fletcher, Grace, see Webster, Mrs. Grace Fletcher
Foote, Samuel Augustus, Senator: resolution on sale of public lands, 178, 178n, 179
"Force" Bill, 210, 217
Foster, Abiel, 8
Fox, Henry James, British Minister to U. S., 308, 309
Franklin, Benjamin, 311, 312
Franklin, N. H., descriptions of, 346–48, 425, 446–47
Freeman, Peyton R., 110
Fryeburg, Maine: Webster teaches school, 16–17, 21; and copies deeds, 16–17; 4th of July oration, 1802, 43
Fuess, Claude Moore, biographer of Webster, 11n, 464, 472
Fugitive slave issue, 395, 406–07
Fuller, Habijah Weld, Dartmouth classmate: letter to, 33
Furness, The Reverend Mr.: letter to, 396

Gallatin, Albert, 319
Gardiner, John L., 250
Gardiner, William H., 87, 232
Garland, William, 10
Garrison, William Lloyd: advocates disunion, 394; denounces 1850 Compromise, 420; denounces U. S. Constitution, 421
Gibbons v. Ogden, 9 Wheat. 1 (1834), 73–76
Goodrich, Professor Chauncey A.: account of Webster argument in Dartmouth College case, 65–68
Goodwin, Osias, 250
Gore, Christopher: 458; employs Webster as clerk, 30–33; advises against accepting court clerkship, 34–35; sponsors Webster's admission to bar, 37
Gray, Francis Calley, 79

Greek Revolution, speech on, 94–99
Greeley, Horace, 396
Green Harbor, Webster's home at Marshfield, see Marshfield
Greene, Albert C., 401
Grey, H., 250
Grey, John C., 250

Haddock, Charles Brickett, nephew of Webster: 132, 177; letters to, 132, 133, 178
Hall, Mrs. Emmet, 463
Hall, J. Prescott, N. Y. lawyer: member of the Hone Club, 456; letter to, 436
Hamilton, Thomas: description of Webster, xvii
Hampton, General Wade: visit to plantation of, 359
Handkerchief copy of Constitution, 6
Harding, Chester, xin, 205n
Harrison, George, 248
Harrison, William Henry, 9th President of U. S.: Webster meets on western trip, 1837, 274; Webster supports for presidency, 1840, 294–96; offers Webster Secy. of State or Secy. of Treasury, 296; anecdote re inaugural address, 298–300; death of, 300; letter to, 296; letter from, 296
Hart, Charles Henry, xin
Hartford Convention, 52–53
Harvey, Peter: 459; anecdotes on: Steamboat case, 73–75, Marshfield, 104–05, John Adams, 135–36, Webster-Hayne debate, 190–91, 205–07, Harrison's inaugural address, 298–300, Julia's illness, 368–70; present at 7th of March speech, 400; mentioned, 73n, 410, 411, 416, 466; letters to, 399, 411
Haven, Franklin: 339, 459; letters to, 398, 410, 413, 414, 415, 416, 418, 438, 441
Hay Fever, 344–45, 387, 392, 414, 419, 424, 439, 449
Hayne, Robert Young: in Webster-Hayne debate, 178–80, 188–93, 198, 205, 205n, 206; Governor of S. C., 210; Webster toast to, 357

INDEX

Hayne-Webster debate, 178–207
Healey, John P., law associate of Webster in Boston: letters to, 281, 282, 412
Healy, George P. A., portrait painter, 344, 344n
Hillard, George Stillman, 420n, 465
Hilliard, Henry W.: 415; description of Webster, xviii
Hoar, Ebenezer Rockwood: letter to, 371
Holmes, Dr. Oliver Wendell, 225
Hone, Philip, 456
Hone Club, 456
Hopkinson, Joseph, Philadelphia lawyer: 459; in Dartmouth College case, 61, 68; letter to, 71; letters from, 69, 70, 71, 98–99
Hoyt, William, school teacher, 5–6
Hülsemann letter, 426–30
Hunter, William, 428

"Ichabod," Whittier poem attacking Webster, 419

Jackson, Andrew, 7th President of the U. S.: presidential candidate, 99, 100, 144; election, 1828, 166, 167, 168, 170; opposes Nullification, 210, 217; Bank War with Biddle, 218–20; protest at Senate censure, 220; Webster speech on, 221–22; view of Webster as presidential candidate, 246; mentioned, 176, 176n, 177, 265, 409
Jackson, Dr. James: at Webster's deathbed, 450, 452
Jaudon, Samuel, cashier of Second Bank of U. S.: member of Hone Club, 456; encourages Webster trip to England, 276, 278; letters to, 276, 295
Jay, John, 319, 320
Jefferson, Thomas, 3rd President of the U. S.: Webster visits, 106–11; death of, 135; Adams-Jefferson oration, 136–43, 165–66; mentioned, 247
Jeffries, Dr. John: at Webster's last illness, 445, 450, 452
Josephine: letter to, 336, 336n

Kelley, Mrs. Israel W. (Rebecca Fletcher), xi, 155, 466
Kelp, use as fertilizer, 310, 316, 365
Kent, Moody: letters to, 51, 52
Kenyon, British poet and philanthropist, 281, 285
Ketchum, Hiram: 286, 460; letters to, 52, 272, 284, 286, 298, 303, 304
Kinsman, Henry W., law associate of Webster in Boston, 271
Knapp, John Francis, 225–42, 467
Knapp, Joseph J., Jr., 225–42, 467
Kossuth, Louis, Hungarian revolutionary leader, 428, 430, 431

Labouchere, Henry (Lord Taunton), 283
Lafayette, Marquis de: in Washington, 113; at Bunker Hill celebration, 118–19; Lanman anecdote, 124; in Albany, 126; mentioned, 106
Lamb, Thomas, 250
Landholdings, 247, 268–71, 276–78
Lanman, Charles: 460; Lafayette anecdote, 124; Webster's lack of financial restraint, 246; Webster's habit of early rising, 258; train wreck, 441; carriage accident, 443, 445; mentioned, xiin, 166, 446
La Salle, Illinois: description of Webster property, 278
Lawrence, Amos, 208
Lawrence, Samuel: 250; letter to, 413
Lawson, Thomas Bayley, xi, xin
Lee, Mrs. E. Buckminster: 460; description of Webster, xvii; Webster's autobiography written for, 1n; description of Grace Fletcher, 41; on trip to Niagara Falls, 126; helps care for Webster children, 157, 173–74; mentioned, 57; letters to, 159, 161, 261, 382, 383; letter from, 382
Le Roy, Caroline, see Webster, Mrs. Caroline Le Roy
Le Roy, Herman, 463
Lincoln, Abraham: Webster meets on western trip, 1837, 274; request for diplomatic appointment, 1841, 304; mentioned, 457

Lincoln, Levi, Governor of Mass.: 126; letter to, 148; letter from, 149
Lindsley, Mrs.: letter to, 288
Lodge, Henry Cabot, 166n, 235
Longfellow, Henry Wadsworth, 104n, 420
Lonsdale, Lord, William Lowther, 291n
Loring, Benjamin, 250
Louis Phillippe, King of France, 345
Lowell, Francis Cabot, 250
Lowell, James Russell, 94, 420
Lowell, John A., 250
Lowther Castle, 291n
Lyman, George W., 250
Lyman, General S. P.: with Webster at Franklin, 391; description of 7th of March speech, 400–01; letter to, 375
Lyman, Theodore, Jr., 52n
Lyndhurst, Lord, John Singleton Copley, 286

Macaulay, Thomas Babington, 284
Madison, James, 4th President of the U. S.: Webster attacks administration, 1812, 43; needles him in Congress, 1813, 46–48; visits him in Virginia, 1824, 106–08; concludes he was the wisest President except Washington, 108; and in 1830 receives Madison's congratulations on reply to Hayne, 208
Maine boundary dispute, 306–21
Mann, A. Dudley, 428
Maps, battle of the, in boundary dispute, 311–20
March, Charles, N. Y. merchant, 460; letters to, 46, 47, 378
March, Charles W., author: describes Webster-Hayne debate, 180, 190–91, 205; describes Webster-Calhoun debate, 211–12
Marshall, John, Chief Justice of the U. S.: Dartmouth College case, 62, 66, 67, 68, 70; McCulloch v. Maryland, 73; Gibbons v. Ogden, 74–75; mentioned, 351, 462
Marshfield, Webster's home during later life: acquisition of, 104–05; location, 104n; descriptions of, 326–

28, 328n, 433; mentioned, 232, 251, 254, 290, 315, 326, 337
Marshfield "Roses," 316
Martha's Vineyard, trip to, 387–91
Martineau, Harriet: description of Webster, xviii; White murder case, 232
Mason, Jeremiah, lawyer, Portsmouth and Boston: 461; Webster's characterization of, 42; hospitality to the Websters, 48; U. S. Senator from N. H., 54; Dartmouth College case, 60, 69, 72; friend of Story, 78; officer of Bank of U. S., 217; mentioned, 54, 110; letters to, 54, 60, 61, 62, 68, 69, 70, 72, 76, 90, 99, 100, 101, 102, 172, 178, 208, 243, 244, 245, 317; letter from, 322
Mason, Miss Mary, 79
Massachusetts Constitutional Convention, 78–79
McCulloch v. Maryland, 4 Wheat. 316 (1819), 73
McGaw, Jacob, 461; description of Webster, xvi; letters to, 40, 162, 173
McLean, John, 167
McLeod, Alexander, 305–06
Menhaden, use as fertilizer, 316, 317
Merrill, Thomas A., Dartmouth classmate: 461; mentioned, 11n; letters to, 20, 22, 31
Mexican War, 342, 348–51, 370
Mills, Elijah Hunt, U. S. Senator from Mass., 147–49
Missouri Compromise, 77, 394, 422
Moore, Thomas, Irish poet, 281

Nashville Convention, 396, 408–09
National Bank, causes rupture between Henry Clay and President Tyler, 302–04. See also Bank of United States
Nevins, Allan, 422
Niagara Falls: trip to, 126–30; Webster's description, 128–30
Niblo's Garden speech, 273–74, 398
Northeastern boundary dispute, 306–21
Nullification, 210–17

INDEX

Ordinance of 1787, 187–88, 193, 405
Ordinance of Nullification, 210, 217
Osgood, James, 16–17
Oswald, Richard, 319, 320
Otis, Harrison Gray, 248

Paige, Mrs. Harriette Story, wife of James William Paige: marriage, 252; birth of daughter, 252–53; with Webster on trip to England, 278, 285, 290, 291n; mentioned, 224, 253, 337, 345, 462, 467; letters to, 262, 292, 297, 318, 328, 332, 337, 338, 353, 355, 358, 359, 372, 384, 385

Paige, James William, brother of Webster's first wife: 462; notifies Webster of death of Charles, 112; at illness and death of Grace Fletcher Webster, 151, 153–57; marries Harriette White, 252; trustee under Webster's will, 459; mentioned, 159, 168, 174, 177, 253, 255, 297, 303, 314, 318, 337, 368, 369, 447, 466, 467; letters to, 130, 151, 152, 158, 252, 253, 333, 338, 345

Palmerston, Lord, British Foreign Secretary, 305, 308, 309, 319, 320

Panizzi, Sir Anthony, Director of the British Museum, 319

Parker, Isaac, Chief Justice of Mass., 231

Parker, Reverend Theodore: denounces 1850 Compromise, 419–20, 421; attacks on Webster, 257, 419–20, 421, 422, 422n; mentioned, 262

Passenger Cases, The, 7 Howard 283 (1849), 351

Peel, Sir Robert, British Prime Minister, 309, 320

Perkins, Cyrus W.: turns over Boston school to Ezekiel, 29, 464; death of Grace Fletcher Webster in his N. Y. home, 151–55, 466; mentioned, 30; letters to, 157, 171

Perkins, Thomas H., 79, 88, 250

Peterson, "Commodore" Seth: description, 254; droll sayings, 315, 326; mentioned, 252, 305, 310, 314, 317, 318, 328, 377

Phillips, Wendell: advocates disunion, 394; denounces 1850 Compromise, 420

Phillips Exeter Academy, 9–10, 263, 455

Pickman, Dudley S., 250

Pierce, Franklin, 14th President of the U. S., 442

Pilgrim Society, The, 79

Pinkney, William, Baltimore lawyer: Dartmouth College case, 69–70; death, 375; mentioned, 73

Pleasants, Henry, 349

Plumer, William, Jr., on: Webster's tariff speech, 101–02; Webster's Spanish claims, 102; Randolph's second challenge, 116–18; Webster at work, 144–45; Webster's ambition, 243

Plymouth Oration, 81–86

Polk, James K., 11th President of the U. S., 341, 342, 343, 348

Porter, Dr., Webster's Marshfield physician, 450, 452

Portsmouth, N. H., and Webster: practice of law in, 25, 38, 40–42, 54; 4th of July oration, 1812, 43; elected to Congress from, 1812, 46; fire destroys his house, 48–49

Prescott, William Hickling, author, 160, 161, 250

Princeton, U.S.S., disaster aboard, xi, xin

Priscilla, 104n

Quincy, Josiah: Portsmouth fire anecdote, 48–49; Sandwich, Mass., 104; Bunker Hill celebration, 119, 124–25; Webster and first wife, 156; hospitality of Ticknor, 463; subscribes to Webster annuity, 250

Randolph, John, of Roanoke: challenges Webster to duels, 53, 116–18

Rantoul, Robert, 232

Red-line maps, Canadian boundary dispute, 311–20

Reed, Benjamin T., 250

Rhodes, James Ford: on Parker's charges against Webster, 422n

Richmond, Va.: Webster's visits to, 295, 353–54

INDEX

Robbins, Edward H., 250
Rochester, N. Y.: Webster's toast at agricultural fair dinner, 255–56
Rockingham Memorial, 43–45, 49
Rogers, Samuel, British poet, 281; letter to, 290
Roger's Rangers, xx, 2
Rouse's Point, N. Y.: strategic importance of, 320
Russell, Benjamin, 88

St. Stephen, prize Hungarian bull, 430–31
Salisbury, N. H.: originally Stevenstown, 3; later, part becomes Franklin, 346; Webster's father a town officer, 26–27; birthplace of Webster, 4; Webster studies law there, 14, 21; 4th of July oration, 1805, 43; descriptions, 346–48, 425, 446–47
Saltonstall, Leverett, 10
Sandwich, Mass., 104
Sargent, Ignatius, 250
Scott, Sir Walter, 288, 332
Scott, General Winfield, 351, 438, 442, 458
Sears, David: 250; letters to, 250, 334; letter from, 248
Seaton, Josephine, 336n, 354; letter to, 336
Seaton, William W., editor of the National Intelligencer, 299, 336n, 354
Seaton, Mrs. William W., 156n
Senior, Nassau William, 285
Sergeant, John, Philadelphia lawyer, 146, 147, 217
Seventh of March speech, 401–09
Sewall, Dr. Thomas, Webster's Washington physician, 261, 265, 296
Seward, William H., 410, 415, 458, 460
Shaddock, C. G., 250
Shaw, Lemuel, Chief Justice of Mass., 231n
Shaw, Robert G., 250
Silsbee, Nathaniel, U. S. Senator from Mass.: letters to, 150, 153
Slavery, Webster's views on, 77, 85, 187–88, 193–95, 273–74, 371, 396

Smith, Eben, 250
Smith, Jeremiah, N. H. lawyer and former Chief Justice: Dartmouth College case, 60, 61, 69, 72; letters to, 61, 68
Smith, Mehitable, see Webster, Mrs. Mehitable Smith
Smith, The Very Reverend, Canon of St. Paul's, London: comments on Webster, xv, 119; Webster breakfasts with, 281
Spanish claims, 91, 102, 145
Sparks, Jared, historian, President of Harvard: Canadian boundary dispute, 311–12, 314, 315; letters to, 314, 320; letter from, 311
Sprague, Joseph E.: letter to, 147
Stanley, Lord (later, Earl of Derby), 283, 284
"Steamboat," favorite horse, 383
Stephens, Alexander H., 394
Steuben, Baron von, 312
Stevens, Abraham G.: letter to, 264
Stone, W. W., 250
Story, Joseph, Associate Justice of U. S. Supreme Court: 462; Dartmouth College case, 66, 69, 72; Mass. Constitutional Convention, 78; shares cask of wine, 88; on trip to Niagara Falls, 126–31; offers help on reply to Hayne, 190; Salem murder trials, 223–24, 231–32, 239; mentioned, 77, 89, 153, 154, 158, 160, 168, 253, 266, 351, 462, 467; letters to, 55, 69, 87, 88, 89, 131, 135, 145, 147, 152, 223; letters from, 156, 223
Sturgis, William, 88
Style, Webster's views on: in speaking, 42; in writing, 164–66
Sullivan, William, Boston lawyer: 88, 162; letters to, 55, 62, 208
Sumner, Charles, 420, 421

Taney, Roger Brooke, Chief Justice of the U. S., 265
Tariff, Webster's views on: opposes tariff in 1814, 49–50, in 1819, 77–78, and in 1824, 100–02; later seeks protection for Massachusetts manufacturers, 176, 186–87

Tautog fishing, 447

Taylor, John, Webster's overseer at Franklin, N. H.: 462; protects Webster from visitors, 426; gored by St. Stephen, 431; Webster quotes Virgil to, 435–36; mentioned, 310, 362, 424, 425; letters to, 380, 381, 430, 434, 435; letter from, 435

Taylor, General Zachary, 12th President of the U. S.: candidate for the presidency, 350–51, 367, 370, 371; President, 376, 377, 397, 428; opposition to 1850 Compromise, 413–15; death, 413, 458

Tenney, Caleb, Dartmouth classmate, 11n

Thayer, Thomas E., 250

Thomas, Charles Henry: 206–07, 424, 425; letter to, 280

Thomas, Captain John, owner of Marshfield: 104, 105, 205–07, 265; letter to, 251

Thomas, Nathaniel Ray, of Marshfield: letter to, 270

Thompson, Thomas W., N. H. lawyer: 463; Webster studies law under, 14, 15, 20, 21, 25; Trustee of Dartmouth, 16; mentioned, 6, 58, 461

Thoreau, Henry David, 420

Thorndike, Israel, 124–25

Ticknor, Mrs. Anna Eliot: visit to Madison and Jefferson, 106–11; mentioned, 157, 287; letters to, 114, 115, 160

Ticknor, George, author, Harvard professor: 463; at Plymouth oration, 79–81; visit to Madison and Jefferson, 106–11; at Adams-Jefferson oration, 136–37, 143; at funeral of Grace Fletcher Webster, 155–56; mentioned, 123, 152, 160, 161; letters to, 113, 115, 134, 158, 160, 287, 410, 417, 429

Treaty of Washington, 317–18, 322, 442

Trenton Falls, N. Y., 127

Tyler, John, 10th President of the U. S.: succeeds Harrison, 300; conflict with Clay, 302–04, 322–25; mentioned, 316, 329, 331, 342, 343, 465; letters to, 306, 318, 330; letter from, 331

Van Buren, Martin, 8th President of the U. S.: rivalry with Calhoun, 167, 176, 176n; presidency, 271, 275; in election of 1840, 294, 295; Webster's views on candidacy in 1848, 371; mentioned, 265, 267, 273

Van Doren, Mark, 472

Vaughan, Sir Charles Richard, Minister to U. S., 1825–35, 283, 286

Vergennes, Count de, French Foreign Minister, 311, 312

Virgil, on farming, 435–36

Wales, Thomas B., 250

Walker, Isaac P., Senator from Wis.: yields floor to Webster for 7th of March speech, 401

Wallenstein, Julius von, Russian attaché, 114, 115, 134

Warren, Charles Henry, 400

Warren, Dr. John C., Webster family physician: at death of Webster, 445, 450, 452; mentioned, 152, 154, 261; letter to, 131

Washburn, Ives, 464

Washington, Bushrod, Associate Justice U. S. Supreme Court, 67, 68, 70

Webster, Mrs. Abigail Eastman, mother of Daniel, xx, 4, 5, 37

Webster, Mrs. Achasa Ballard, 2nd wife of Ezekiel: 171, 172; letters to, 167, 168, 169, 177

Webster, Mrs. Caroline Le Roy, 2nd wife of Daniel: 463; description of, 174, 175; marriage, 174; with Webster in Washington, 176, 177, 328, 366; and on trips: to West, 274, to England, 278, 284, 285, 291n, to South, 354; mentioned, 290, 326, 337, 417, 434, 446; letters to, 260, 264, 265, 266, 267, 268, 301, 302, 303

Webster, Mrs. Caroline White, wife of Fletcher: 224, 252, 293, 294, 314, 337, 465, 467; letters to, 333

Webster, Charles, son of Daniel: birth, 41, 89; illness and death, 109, 111, 112–13; mentioned, 91

Webster, Daniel: birth, 4; early schooling, 5–10; frailty as a child, 8; Phillips Academy, Exeter, 9–10; early

INDEX

Webster, Daniel (*contd.*)
stage fright, 9; Dartmouth College, 10–11; use of tobacco, 14–15; studies law, Salisbury, N. H., 14–15, 20–23, 25; teaches, Fryeburg, Me., 16–21; moves to Boston, 29; in office of Christopher Gore, 30–37; refuses court clerkship, 34–37; admitted to bar, 37; practices law: Boscawen, N. H., 38; Portsmouth, N. H., 40–43; marries Grace Fletcher, 41; children, 41; Rockingham Memorial, 43–45; Congress, from N. H., 46, 50; moves to Boston, 53, 54; John Randolph challenges, 53–54, 116–17; Dartmouth College case, 58–72; *McCulloch v. Md.*, 73; *Gibbons v. Ogden*, 73–75; Mass. Constitutional Convention, 78–79; Plymouth oration, 81–86; Congress, from Mass., 89, 105; on Greek Revolution, 94–98; discovers Marshfield, 104–05; visits Madison and Jefferson, 106–11; Bunker Hill oration, 119–23; trip to Niagara Falls, 126–30; Adams-Jefferson oration, 137–43, 165–66; U. S. Senate, 149; death of wife, Grace, 155–56; remarriage, to Caroline Le Roy, 174; Hayne debate, 176–207; Calhoun debate, 210–17; U. S. Bank, 217–20; presidential protest, 220–22; Salem murder trials, 223–42; Niblo's Garden, 273–74; visit to England, 276–91; Secy. of State: under Harrison, 296–97, under Tyler, 300; the *Caroline* Affair, 305–06; Canadian boundary dispute, 306–21; Webster-Ashburton Treaty, 317–18; anti-Tyler Whigs, 322–25; resigns as Secy. of State, 330–31; reelection to Senate, 341; trip to South, 352–61; death of Edward and Julia, 366–68; trip to Martha's Vineyard, 387–91; 7th of March speech, 401–09; Secy. of State under Fillmore, 416; Hülsemann letter, 427; defeat for Whig nomination, 438–42; death, 452
Acceptance of financial help, 247–51, 416; alleged drunkenness, 255–58, 419–22; early rising, 181, 258, 353–54;
love of animals, 246–47, 383–84; landholdings, 247, 268–71, 276–78; mastery of English style, 42, 164–66; unreceptiveness to judicial appointment, 298; views on: eloquence, 140; religious hypocrisy, 133; slavery, 77, 85, 187–88, 193–95, 273–74, 371, 396; tariff, 49–50, 77–78, 100–02, 176, 186–87
Webster, Daniel Fletcher, *see* Webster, Fletcher
Webster, Ebenezer, father of Daniel: xx, 1–13, 26–27, 28, 34–37; death, 37; Webster's comment on name, 294
Webster, Edward, son of Daniel: birth, 41; trip to England, 278, 289; War with Mexico, 349; death, 368; mentioned, 91, 103, 106, 134, 157, 159, 163, 170, 171, 263, 305, 314, 326, 346, 350, 356, 361, 366; letters to, 349, 350, 351
Webster, Ezekiel, brother of Daniel: 464; description of, 2, 11–12; education, 12–13, 17, 21, 29; school in Boston, 29, 305; moves to Boscawen, 40–41; scholastic ability, 7, 26; defeated for Congress, 167, 171; death, 171–72; Webster's comment on name, 294; letters to, 28, 46, 48, 50, 51, 53, 56, 57, 70, 90, 99, 100, 101, 113, 150, 154, 155, 166, 167, 170; letters from, 28, 166
Webster, Fletcher, son of Daniel: 465; birth, 41; "Venerable Men," 123–24; marries Caroline Story White, 252; Chief Clerk State Dept., 300; mission to China, 333, 337; mentioned, 54, 91, 104, 134, 144, 151, 156, 157, 261, 262, 271, 303, 331, 377, 389, 434, 467; letters to, 175, 260, 262, 268, 269, 270, 293, 315, 325, 337, 342, 343, 346, 348, 350, 351, 354, 356, 361, 362, 366, 367, 368, 370, 371, 374, 385, 399, 411, 412, 417, 442
Webster, Miss Grace Fletcher, daughter of Daniel: birth, 41; illness and death, 55–57; mentioned, 54, 157, 252
Webster, Mrs. Grace Fletcher, first wife of Daniel: 466; description of, 41; marriage, 41; children: 41; death of

INDEX

Grace, 56–57; death of Charles, 112; trip to Niagara Falls, 126–30; illness and death, 150–57; congeniality with Webster, 156; mentioned, 79, 91, 92, 103, 104, 133, 157, 175, 252, 462; letters to, 89, 105, 106; letters from, 112

Webster, Julia, *see* Appleton, Mrs. Julia Webster

Webster, Mrs. Mehitable Smith, first wife of Daniel's father, xx, 4

Webster, Mrs. Susannah Bachelder, grandmother of Daniel, 2, 294

Webster, Thomas, earliest American ancestor of Daniel, 1

Webster-Ashburton Treaty, 317–18, 322, 442

Webster-Calhoun debate, 210–17

Webster-Hayne debate, 176–207, 357

Weed, Thurlow, 456, 458

Wells, John, 250

Weston, Seth, Marshfield carpenter and farm manager: 377, 466; letters to, 264, 310, 317, 329, 330, 332, 338, 339, 340, 343, 344, 349, 357

Whately's *Rhetoric*, 164–65

Wheelock, Eleazar, founder of Dartmouth College, 58, 62, 71

Wheelock, John, 2nd President of Dartmouth College, 31, 58–60, 68

Whipple, Edwin Percy, 166n

White, Caroline Story, *see* Webster, Mrs. Caroline White

White, Harriette Story, *see* Paige, Mrs. Harriette Story

White, Captain Joseph, murder of, 223–42, 467

White, Peregrine, 105

White, Stephen; 467; Salem murder trials, 224, 231, 240; trip to West with Webster, 259; death, 303; mentioned, 252, 292; letters to, 219, 252, 253, 254, 255; letter from, 292

Whittier, John Greenleaf, 419

Wilkinson, William Cleaver, theologian and author, 256–57, 422

Williams, John D., 250

Wilmot Proviso, 394, 398, 405, 421

Winchester, W. P., 250

Winslow grave-yard, at Marshfield, 105

Winthrop, Robert C.: 301, 457; letter to, 272

Wirt, William, lawyer of Va. and Md., Attorney General under three Presidents: Dartmouth College case, 68, 70; *Gibbons v. Ogden*, 74–75; mentioned, 146

Wise, Robert, 27–28

Wood, Reverend Samuel, prepares Daniel and Ezekiel for Dartmouth, 10, 13, 464

Woodbury, Levi, 440

Wood's Hole, Mass., description of, 388, 390–91

Woodward, William H., Secretary-Treasurer of Dartmouth College, 60

Wordsworth, William, 281, 287, 288

Wright, Charles Porter, Marshfield farm manager: 377, 381, 386, 434, 467; letters to, 373, 423, 424, 446

Wyman, William, trial of, 352

Zantzinger, William C., 417

505